The **Rough Guide** to

Paris

written and researched by

Ruth Blackmore and James McConnachie

with additional contributions by

Amy Jordan

NEW YORK • LONDON • DELHI

www.roughguides.com

Contents

Paris architecture - the shock of the new colour section following p.144

From wine bars to three stars colour section following p.336

Colour maps following p.512

◄◄ Pont Alexandre ◄ Place de la Concorde

Introduction to Paris

Long considered the paragon of style, Paris is the most glamorous city in Europe. It is at once deeply traditional – a village-like metropolis whose inhabitants continue to be notorious for their hauteur – and famously cosmopolitan. While such contradictions and contrasts may be the reality of any city, they are the makings of Paris: consider the tiny lanes and alleyways of the Quartier Latin or Montmartre against the monumental vistas from the Louvre to La Défense; the multiplicity of street markets and old-fashioned pedestrian arcades against the giant underground commercial complexes of Montparnasse and Les Halles; or the aristocratic wealth of the grand quarters against the vibrant chaos of the poorer districts.

At times, Paris can feel inhumanly magnificent, the arrogance of its monuments encompassing the chilly pomp of the Panthéon, the industrial chic of the Eiffel Tower and the almost spiritual glasswork of the Louvre pyramid. Yet it also operates on a very human scale, with exquisite, secretive little nooks tucked away from the Grands Boulevards and very definite little communities revolving around games of boules and the local boulangerie and café. And even as Paris's culture is transformed by its large immigrant and gay populations, even as extravagant new buildings are commissioned and erected, many of the city's streets, cafés and restaurants remain remarkably, defiantly unchanged.

In the great local tradition of the *flâneur*, or thoughtful boulevard-stroller, Paris is a wonderful city for aimless wandering. Relaxed quarters such as the vibrant Marais, elegant St-Germain and romantic Montmartre are ideal for street-browsing, shopping and café-sitting, and the city's lack of open space is redeemed by beautiful formal gardens, by the pathways and pavements that run beside the River Seine, and by endless hidden or unexpected havens.

▲ Eiffel Tower

And everywhere you go, historic landmark buildings and contemporary architectural wonders remind you of the city's pride and grandeur – and stop you getting lost.

There are nearly 150 **art galleries** and **museums** in the city – few of them duds – and an uncounted number of **cafés**, **brasseries** and **restaurants** lining every street and boulevard. The variety of style and décor is hard to beat, ranging from ultra-modern fashion temples to traditional, mirrored palaces, and from tiny *bistrots* where the emphasis is all on the cooking to bustling Vietnamese diners. After dark, the city's theatres and concert halls host inventive and world-leading productions of **theatre** and **dance**, while many classical **concerts** take place in fine architectural settings, particularly chapels and churches. Above all, Paris is a real **cinema** capital, and the city's vibrant cultural mix puts it at the forefront of the **world music** scene.

What to see

Paris has a remarkably coherent and intelligible structure. The city lies in a basin surrounded by hills. It is very nearly circular, confined within the limits of the **boulevard périphérique,** which follows the line of the nineteenth-century city boundary. At its widest point, Paris is only about 12km across, which, at a brisk pace, is not much more than two hours' **walk** – by far the best way to discover the life of the

The métro

Physically, the métro just isn't like other subways, starting with the rubber wheels that make central journeys so smooth and quiet. Then there's the way that stations are sometimes so close that you can see people waiting at the next platform down the line, the anti-social spacing of the platform seating, and the mania for double- or treble-barrelled station names like "Maubert-Mutualité" or "Maisons-Alfort-les-Juillottes". The best stations have distinct characters: check out the funky multicoloured lamps at Bonnes Nouvelles station, or the cabinets of treasures in Palais Royal-Musée du Louvre.

The métro even has its own style and courtesy culture. You're just supposed to know instinctively when it gets too crowded to remain seated in the wonderfully named *strapontins*, the folding seats by the doors. It takes a little longer to learn the effortlessly Parisian flick of the wrist that lifts that little steel lever and opens the doors.

Travelling by métro puts you into closer contact with Parisians than you're likely to get anywhere else. As soon as you set foot below ground, greater Paris's true ethnic and social mix is instantly apparent – the old working-class men, the women in West African dress and the kids from the *banlieue*, so conspicuously absent from the posh boulevards. And every new immigrant group fleeing the latest conflict zone sends a wave of buskers down the tunnels. For tourists, the best things about the métro are its reliability – most of the four and a half million journeys a day pass without event, except when there's a strike – and its cost: roughly two-thirds of the ticket price is subsidized by the French taxpayer.

city. Through its middle, the **River Seine** flows east to west in a satisfying arc. At the hub of the circle, in the middle of the river, is the island from which all the rest grew: the **Ile de la Cité** (Chapter 1) . Here, the city's oldest religious and secular institutions – the cathedral and the royal palace – overlook the river, which was itself both the capital's raison d'être and its lifeline.

The city is divided into twenty **arrondissements**, whose spiral arrangement provides a fairly accurate guide to its historical growth. Centred on the Louvre, they wind outwards in a clockwise direction. Paris's inner hub comprises arrondissements 1er to 6e, and it's here that most of the major sights and museums are to be found. The royal palace and museum of the **Louvre** (Chapter 2) lies on the north or **Right Bank** (*rive droite*) of the Seine, which is the more bustling and urban of the city's two sides. To the west of the Louvre runs the longest and grandest vista of the city – **La Voie**

Triomphale (covered in Chapter 3) – comprising the Tuileries gardens, the **Champs-Elysées**, the Arc de Triomphe and the Grande Arche de la Défense, each an expression of royal or state power across the centuries. North of the Louvre is the commercial and financial quarter, where you can shop in the department stores on the broad **Grands Boulevards** (Chapter 4), in the little boutiques of the glass-roofed **passages**, or in the giant, underground mall of **Les Halles** (Chapter 5). To the east of the Louvre, the **Marais** (Chapter 6) was the prestige address in the seventeenth century; along with the **Bastille** next door (Chapter 12), it's now one of the most exciting areas of the city, alive with trendy shops, cafés and nightlife. Further east, the **Canal Saint-Martin** and **Ménilmontant** (both Chapter 13) are the places to go for cutting-edge bars and nightlife.

The south bank of the river, or **Left Bank**, has a quite different feel, quieter and more village-like. The **Quartier Latin** (Chapter 7) is the traditional domain of the intelligentsia – of academics, writers, artists and the liberal professions – along with **St-Germain** (Chapter 8), which becomes progressively snootier as you travel west towards the ministries, embassies and museums that surround the **Eiffel Tower** (Chapter 9). Once you move towards glitzy **Montparnasse** and the southern swathe of the Left Bank (Chapter 10), high-rise flats alternate with charming bourgeois neighbourhoods.

Back on the Right Bank, many of the outer or higher-number arrondissements were once outlying villages, and were gradually absorbed by the expanding city in the nineteenth century – some, such as **Montmartre** (Chapter 11), **Belleville** (Chapter 13) and **Passy** (Chapter 14), have succeeded in retaining something of their separate village identity. The areas to

▲ Brasserie Flo

The Seine

Referred to by some as Paris's main avenue or the city's 21st arrondissement – and by others as a murky, polluted waterway – the Seine is integral to Paris, sashaying through its centre in a broad arc, taking in the capital's grandest monuments on its way. It even makes its way into the city's coat of arms, which depicts a ship sailing on choppy waters accompanied by the words *fluctuat nec mergitur* – "it is tossed about but does not sink", a singularly apt motto for a city that has weathered events as turbulent as the French Revolution and the Commune.

The Seine brought the city into being and was for centuries its lifeblood, a major conduit of trade and commerce. Floods, however, have always been a regular hazard, sometimes sweeping away bridges, houses and lives. One of the worst recorded was in 1176, when the city was almost completely engulfed. The construction of the *quais* in the nineteenth century helped to alleviate the problem and these tree-lined walkways have today become one of Paris's major assets – attractive and leafy havens from the city's bustle. Traffic is banned from a large section of the Right Bank *quai* on Sundays, making way for cyclists, rollerbladers and strollers, and each summer since 2002 tonnes of sand have been imported to create a kind of Paris-sur-Mer on the *quais*, complete with palm trees and deckchairs.

the east were traditionally poor and working-class, while those to the west held the aristocracy and the newly rich – divisions which to some extent hold true today. One thing Paris is not particularly well endowed with is **parks**. The best are on the fringes of the city, notably the **Bois de Vincennes** (Chapter 12) and the **Bois de Boulogne** (Chapter 14), at the eastern and western edges, respectively.

▲ Passage des Panoramas

The region surrounding the capital, the **Ile-de-France**, is dotted with cathedrals and châteaux. Suburban sights such as the Gothic cathedral at **St-Denis** and the royal palace at **Versailles** are covered in Chapter 15, while day-trip destinations a little further afield, including the cathedral town of **Chartres** and Monet's garden at **Giverny**, are described in Chapter 16.

▲ Ile St Louis

An equally accessible outing from the capital is that most un-French of attractions, **Disneyland Paris** (Chapter 17).

When to go

Paris's **climate** is fairly stable, with longish stretches of sun (or rain) year round. Summers are generally hot and quite humid, winters cold and windy, and spring and autumn mild. It can rain at any time of year, however: summer sees fewer heavier showers, while at other times of year there's a tendency to drizzle. Spring is deservedly the classic time to visit, with bright days balanced by rain showers. Autumn and winter can be very rewarding, but on overcast days – all

◀ Bar du Marché

▲ Jardin du Luxembourg

too common – the city can feel very melancholy. Winter sun, on the other hand, is the city's most flattering light, and hotels and restaurants are relatively uncrowded in this season. By contrast, Paris in high summer can be choking, both with fellow visitors and with the fumes of congested traffic. Between mid-July and the end of August, the balance of Parisian and tourist life can become distorted as large numbers of Parisians desert the city for the coast or mountains. There is, too, the **commercial calendar** to consider – fashion shows, trade fairs and the like. Paris hoteliers warn against September and October, and **finding a room** even at the best of times can be problematic. Early spring, autumn if you book ahead, or the midwinter months will be most rewarding.

Paris climate

	Jan	Feb	Mar	Apr	May	Jun	Jul	Aug	Sep	Oct	Nov	Dec
Average daily temperature												
Max(°F)	43	45	54	61	68	72	77	75	70	61	50	45
(°C)	6	7	12	16	20	23	25	24	21	16	10	7
Min(°F)	34	34	40	43	50	55	59	57	54	46	41	36
(°C)	1	1	4	6	10	13	15	14	12	8	5	2
Average rainfall												
inches	2.2	1.8	1.4	1.7	2.2	2.1	2.3	2.5	2.2	2.0	2.0	2.0
mm	56	46	35	42	57	54	59	64	55	50	51	50

things not to miss

It's not possible to see everything Paris has to offer on a short trip – and we don't suggest you try. What follows is a subjective selection of the city highlights, in no particular order, ranging from art-house cinemas to the Sainte Chapelle, all arranged in colour-coded categories to help you find the very best things to see, do and experience. All entries have a page reference to take you straight into the guide, where you can find out more.

01 The Eiffel Tower Page **155** • The closer you get to its radical structure, the more exhilarating and less familiar the Eiffel Tower feels.

02 Hammam at the Paris mosque Page **416** • Steam-baths, or hammams, are among the city's better-kept secrets. At the Paris mosque, you can bathe, have a massage, then drink mint tea in the tiled courtyard.

03 Pompidou Centre Page **100** • The Pompidou's radical "inside-out" architecture still draws the crowds, but don't miss its fine modern art museum inside, with significant holdings of works by Matisse, Kandinsky and Picasso.

04 Notre-Dame Page **52** • The mighty Gothic cathedral of Notre-Dame, with its exquisite rose windows and soaring nave, is an awe-inspiring sight.

05 Left Bank cafés Page **334** & **339** • The cafés of St-Germain and Montparnasse may have swapped writers, artists and existentialists for fashionistas and glitterati, but they remain gloriously Parisian institutions.

06 Musée du Quai Branly Page **159** • The newest and flashiest museum in town is worth seeing just for its cutting-edge architecture, never mind the eye-popping collection of folk art objects inside.

07 Sainte Chapelle Page **49** • The glorious interior of the Sainte Chapelle, with its almost entirely stained-glass walls, ranks among the finest achievements of French High Gothic.

08 The Louvre Page **58** • If the brilliance of the Louvre's art collection doesn't bring you to your knees, the sheer scale of the place will.

09 Sundays in the Marais Page **109** • The twin attractions of "le brunch" and the chance to do some designer shopping make a relaxed Sunday visit to the Marais a must in every trendy Parisian's week.

10 Place des Vosges Page **111** • A superb architectural ensemble, the elegant Place des Vosges is lined with arcaded seventeenth-century buildings and has an attractive and popular garden at its centre.

11 Musée Jacquemart-André Page **82** • This sumptuous Second Empire residence, built for the art-loving Jacquemart-André couple, is preserved more or less intact, complete with its fabulous collection of Italian, Dutch and French masters.

12 Art-house cinemas Page **367** • With screenings ranging from old Hollywood classics to avant-garde international cinema, Paris is one of the world's best cities to watch the big screen.

13 Père-Lachaise Page **238** • Pay homage to Chopin, Oscar Wilde or Jim Morrison – just some of the countless notables buried in what is arguably the world's most famous cemetery.

14 Site de Création Contemporaine Page **168** • If you're tired of galleries that feel like mausoleums for the dead art of the past, make for this chic, bohemian gallery, which showcases the exciting work of contemporary artists.

15 Jardin du Luxembourg Page **145** • The oasis of the Left Bank: students hang out on the lawns, old men play chess under the trees and children sail toy yachts around the pond.

16 Chartres Page **274** • Chartres has the world's loveliest Gothic cathedral, period. And it's only an hour from Paris.

17 Musée Rodin Page **164** • Elegance matched with passion: Rodin's powerful works are shown off to their best advantage in the sculptor's beautiful eighteenth-century mansion.

18 Brasseries Page **316** • Exquisite *Belle époque* interiors, enormous platters of seafood, perfect steaks and bustling white-aproned waiters: the city's traditional brasseries offer an authentic slice of Parisian life.

19 Passages Page **95** • Paris's nineteenth-century arcades are gradually being restored to their former glory and are a fertile hunting ground for curios and one-off buys.

20 Puces de St-Ouen Page **208** • It's easy to lose track of an entire weekend morning browsing the acres of fine antiques, covetable curios and general bric-a-brac at St-Ouen, the mother of Paris's flea markets.

Basics

Basics

Getting there

Paris has direct connections with airports all over the world. If you're travelling from England consider the Eurostar rail link, which makes the journey from London to Paris in just two hours fifteen minutes.

Air fares usually depend on the season, with the highest being around early June to the end of August; the lowest prices are available from November to March (excluding Christmas and New Year).

By Eurostar from the UK and Ireland

The most enjoyable way to reach Paris from Britain is probably the **Eurostar** train (Ⓣ0870/518 6186, Ⓦwww.eurostar.com). It's competitively priced, relatively environmentally friendly and can be as quick as the plane if you live in the southeast: flying time from London is around one hour ten minutes, but you have to add on travel to and from airports, extended check-in times and ever-more frequent delays. The Eurostar takes two hours fifteen minutes from London St Pancras to **Paris Gare du Nord**. (Note that the UK terminus shifted from Waterloo to St Pancras in 2007.) A number of services stop at Ashford International and Ebbsfleet International stations, in Kent.

Prices of Eurostar tickets depend on how far in advance you book, and how much flexibility you need. The lowest fares are almost always for early-morning trains, especially those departing mid-week. You'll usually pay more if you don't stay over a Saturday night. It's possible to find tickets for as little as £59, but you'll often pay double that. A number of **discounted seats** are set aside on each train for young people aged 12–25 and for the over-60s; the longer you book in advance the better your chances are of securing one of these. Fares for children aged 4–11 typically start at around £20.

Eurostar tickets can be bought from travel agents or by phone or online directly from Eurostar. If you're coming from outside London, it usually pays to buy a through ticket – available from any main-line station.

Flights from the UK and Ireland

The most competitive air fares from the UK and Ireland tend to be with **no-frills airlines** such as **bmibaby**, **EasyJet**, **Ryanair** and a number of other operators on regional routes – **bmi**, for instance, currently flies from East Midlands and Leeds Bradford, while **flyBE** serves Paris from Exeter and Norwich. Tickets are best purchased by phone or online. Once you've added airport tax, real **fares** typically work out at around £70–100 return, though you can sometimes pick up tickets for less if you book well in advance and travel at off-peak times. The national carriers, **British Airways**, **Air France** and **Aer Lingus**, are usually only slightly more expensive than the low-cost airlines. Be aware, however, that they do often have special offers, and the airports they serve may be more convenient. **Charles de Gaulle** (CDG) and **Orly** (ORY) are roughly equally handy airports at which to arrive; Paris **Beauvais** (BVA), however, which is served by Ryanair, stands a good 65km northwest of the city.

Students and those under 26 should enquire about discounts on scheduled flights or contact STA Travel or USIT (see p.23).

By car, coach and sea from the UK and Ireland

The most convenient way of taking a **car** across to France is to drive down to the Channel Tunnel, load it on **Eurotunnel**'s frequent train shuttle service, and be whisked under the Channel in 35 minutes to Sangatte on the French side, just outside Calais. The tunnel entrance is off the M20 at junction 11A, just outside Folkestone. You can just buy a ticket at one of the booths and drive straight on, as there are departures roughly every fifteen minutes (but only every hour

Fly less – stay longer! Travel and climate change

Climate change is the single biggest issue facing our planet. It is caused by a build-up in the atmosphere of carbon dioxide and other greenhouse gases, which are emitted by many sources – including planes. Already, flights account for around 3–4% of human-induced global warming: that figure may sound small, but it is rising year on year and threatens to counteract the progress made by reducing greenhouse emissions in other areas.

Rough Guides regard travel, overall, as a global benefit, and feel strongly that the advantages to developing economies are important, as are the opportunities for greater contact and awareness among peoples. But we all have a responsibility to limit our personal "carbon footprint". That means giving thought to how often we fly and what we can do to redress the harm that our trips create.

Flying and climate change

Pretty much every form of motorized travel generates CO_2, but planes are particularly bad offenders, releasing large volumes of greenhouse gases at altitudes where their impact is far more harmful. Flying also allows us to travel much further than we would contemplate doing by road or rail, so the emissions attributable to each passenger are greater. For example, one person taking a return flight between Europe and California produces the equivalent impact of 2.5 tonnes of CO_2 – similar to the yearly output of the average UK car.

Less harmful planes may evolve but it will be decades before they replace the current fleet – which could be too late for avoiding climate chaos. In the meantime, there are limited options for concerned travellers: to reduce the amount we travel by air (take fewer trips, stay longer!), to avoid night flights (when plane contrails trap heat from Earth but can't reflect sunlight back to space), and to make the trips we do take "climate neutral" via a carbon offset scheme.

Carbon offset schemes

Offset schemes run by **climatecare.org, carbonneutral.com** and others allow you to "neutralize" the greenhouse gases that you are responsible for releasing. Their websites have simple calculators that let you work out the impact of any flight. Once that's done, you can pay to fund projects that will reduce future carbon emissions by an equivalent amount (such the distribution of low-energy lightbulbs and cooking stoves in developing countries). Please take the time to visit our website and make your trip climate neutral.

ⓦwww.roughguides.com/climatechange

from midnight to 6am), but it's cheaper to book in advance. Expect to pay in the region of £50–150 per car, each way, depending on the time of year and how far ahead you book. In summer and around Easter you should definitely book ahead to avoid queues and higher tariffs – don't worry if you miss your departure, as you can usually just roll onto the next available train. Once on the French side, it's little more than three hours' drive to Paris on the fast autoroutes A26 and A1 (tolls payable).

The car **ferries** from Dover to Calais or Boulogne are slower (1hr 30min) but less expensive than Eurotunnel. P&O and SeaFrance run regular services on both routes. **Fares** vary according to season, with school and bank holidays being the most expensive, but expect to pay around £50–150 on a ferry, depending on when you travel and, on certain routes, how many passengers there are. Lower fares are usually available if you can avoid travelling out on Fridays and Saturdays. The P&O services from Hull to Rotterdam and Zeebrugge can cut driving time if you're travelling from the north.

Eurolines runs regular **bus-and-ferry** services from Victoria coach station in London to Paris. Off-peak return fares can be as low as £26, but it's usually more like

£40, and the journey takes a tedious eight to ten hours. Tickets are available from the company direct (see below), from National Express agents and most high-street travel agents. As for the classic **ferry–train** route, sadly the few remaining services usually work out more expensive than the Eurostar, and the journey takes roughly nine hours from London Victoria to Paris. For those intent on making the trip, excellent and detailed advice can be found at ⓦwww.seat61.com.

Ferry, Eurotunnel and rail contacts

Eurodrive UK ⓣ0870/990 8492, ⓦwww.eurodrive.co.uk. Discount agent for ferry and Eurotunnel tickets.
Eurolines UK ⓣ0870/580 8080, ⓦwww.eurolines.co.uk. International coach company.
Eurotunnel UK ⓣ0870/535 3535, ⓦwww.eurotunnel.com. Folkestone to Calais car-loading train service through the Channel Tunnel.
Ferrysavers UK ⓣ0870/990 8492, ⓦwww.ferrysavers.com. Discount agent for the major ferry companies.
Norfolkline UK ⓣ0870/870 1020, ⓦwww.norfolkline-ferries.co.uk. Dover to Dunkerque ferries.
P&O Ferries UK ⓣ0870/520 2020, ⓦwww.poferries.com. Dover to Calais; Hull to Rotterdam and Zeebrugge.
Rail Europe UK ⓣ0870/837 1371, ⓦwww.raileurope.co.uk. The main UK agent for European trains.
Sea France UK ⓣ0870/571 1711, ⓦwww.seafrance.com. Ferries from Dover to Calais.
SNCF France ⓣ08.36.35.35.35, ⓦwww.sncf.fr. The French national rail company.

Flights from the US and Canada

The widest choice of **flights** to Paris is offered by **Air France**, with regular nonstop scheduled services to Paris CDG from across **the US**. From New York, there are up to eight departures a day. **American Airlines**, **Continental** and **Delta** are usually a little cheaper, but you may have to stop off en route from smaller cities. The least expensive deals of all may be found with non-French European carriers, but you'll probably have to change flights once you've crossed the Atlantic. **Virgin Atlantic**, for instance, has frequent flights to London – and offers the unique selling point that the business is committed to putting all profits towards developing renewable energy technologies. Typical midweek **fares** from New York or Washington DC range from around US$600 in low season to US$900 in high season; expect to add US$50–200 to the price the further west you go.

Air France and Air Canada both fly non-stop to Paris from all the major cities in **Canada**. There's little to choose between them in terms of fares: count on CDN$1000/1600 (low/high season) from Montréal, Québec and Toronto, and CDN$1400/1900 from Vancouver. Air Transat offers good-value charter flights from a number of bases.

Flights from Australia, New Zealand and South Africa

There are scheduled **flights** to Paris from Auckland, Brisbane, Cairns, Melbourne, Perth and Sydney, but you can find a wider range of options by flying to another European capital – usually **London** – and making a connection from there. The best deals from Australia or New Zealand to Europe are routed **via Asia**, often with a transfer or overnight stop in the airline's home city. Flights **via the US** are usually slightly more expensive. **From Australia**, you should be able to find scheduled **fares** to Paris for around AUS$1600 in low season (roughly Oct–Feb, excluding Christmas and New Year), but you'll pay more like AUS$2500 in high season. From **New Zealand** you might pay from NZ$2000 right up to NZ$3000 in peak season. Flight times vary considerably depending on the route, but it's roughly thirty hours from Sydney or Auckland to Paris.

From South Africa, Johannesburg is the best place to start, with Air France flying direct to Paris from around R6140 return; from Cape Town, they fly via Amsterdam and are more expensive at around R7600. BA, flying via London, are pricier still, with fares at around R10,000 from Cape Town and R8600 from Johannesburg. Flight times are around ten hours from Johannesburg to Paris, and fourteen hours from Cape Town including a stopover in Amsterdam.

Airlines, agents and operators

Full contact details for the main **airlines** serving Paris are given below. Almost all airlines now allow you to book your tickets directly online, but it's worth shopping around to see if you can get a better deal from an online agent.

Even if you're not interested in a package tour, it's worth considering booking a **hotel and flight package** ahead, as these can save you considerable sums, especially if you're aiming to stay in three- or four-star hotels. The drawback is that the hotels on offer tend to be larger or less characterful, and of course you're more restricted in your choice than if you book independently. You can book packages through airlines, travel agents or specialist tour operators – some of the best or most interesting of which are listed below. The Maison de la France, the government tourist office for countries outside France (ⓦ www.franceguide.com), can provide a longer list of package operators.

Online booking

ⓦ **www.expedia.co.uk** (in UK)
ⓦ **www.expedia.com** (in US)
ⓦ **www.expedia.ca** (in Canada)
ⓦ **www.lastminute.com** (in UK)
ⓦ **www.lastminute.com.au** (in Australia)
ⓦ **www.opodo.co.uk** (in UK)
ⓦ **www.orbitz.com** (in US)
ⓦ **www.travelocity.co.uk** (in UK)
ⓦ **www.travelocity.com** (in US)
ⓦ **www.travelocity.ca** (in Canada)
ⓦ **www.zuji.com.au** (in Australia)
ⓦ **www.zuji.co.nz** (in New Zealand)

Airline contacts

Aer Lingus Ireland ⓣ 0818/365 000, France ⓣ 08.21.23.02.67, ⓦ www.aerlingus.com.
Air Canada US and Canada ⓣ 1-888/247-2262, France ⓣ 08.25.88.08.81, ⓦ www.aircanada.com.
Air France UK ⓣ 0870/142 43443, Ireland ⓣ 01/605 0383, US ⓣ 1-800/237-2747, Canada ⓣ 1-800/667-2747, Australia ⓣ 1300/390 190, France ⓣ 08.20.82.08.20, ⓦ www.airfrance.com.
Air India Australia ⓣ 02/9283 4020, New Zealand ⓣ 09/303 1301, ⓦ www.airindia.com.
Air Transat Canada ⓣ 1-877-872-6728, ⓦ www.airtransat.com.
American Airlines US ⓣ 1-800/433-7300, ⓦ www.aa.com.
bmi UK ⓣ 0870/607 0555, France ⓣ 01.41.91.87.04, ⓦ www.flybmi.co.uk.
Bmibaby UK ⓣ 0871/224 0224, France ⓣ 08.90.71.00.81, ⓦ www.bmibaby.co.uk.
British Airways UK ⓣ 0870/850 9850, Australia ⓣ 1300/767 177, New Zealand ⓣ 09/966 9777, France ⓣ 08.25.82.54.00, ⓦ www.ba.com.
Cathay Pacific Australia ⓣ 13 17 47, New Zealand ⓣ 09/379 0861, ⓦ www.cathaypacific.com.
Continental US Airlines ⓣ 1-800/523-3273, ⓦ www.continental.com.
Delta US ⓣ 1-800/221-1212, France ⓣ 08.00.35.40.80, ⓦ www.delta.com.
easyJet UK ⓣ 0870/600 0000, France ⓣ 08.25.08.25.08, ⓦ www.easyjet.co.uk.
Emirates Australia ⓣ 02/9290 9700, New Zealand ⓣ 09/968 2200, South Africa ⓣ 0861/364 728, ⓦ www.emirates.com.
flyBE UK ⓣ 0870 889 0908, Republic of Ireland ⓣ 1890/925 532, ⓦ www.flybe.com.
Garuda Indonesia Australia ⓣ 1300/365 330, New Zealand ⓣ 09/366 1862, ⓦ www.garuda-indonesia.com.
Japan Airlines (JAL) Australia ⓣ 02/9272 1111, New Zealand ⓣ 09/379 9906, ⓦ www.jal.com.
KLM Australia ⓣ 1300/303 747, New Zealand ⓣ 09/921 6040, ⓦ www.klm.com.
Lufthansa Australia ⓣ 1300/655 727, ⓦ www.lufthansa.com.
Malaysia Airlines Australia ⓣ 13 26 27, New Zealand ⓣ 0800/777 747, ⓦ www.malaysia-airlines.com.
Northwest Airlines US ⓣ 1-800/225-2525, ⓦ www.nwa.com.
Qantas Australia ⓣ 13 13 13, New Zealand ⓣ 0800/808 767, France ⓣ 08.20.82.05.00, ⓦ www.qantas.com.
Ryanair UK ⓣ 0871/246 0000, Ireland ⓣ 0818/303 030, France ⓣ 08.92.55.56.66, ⓦ www.ryanair.com.
Singapore Airlines Australia ⓣ 13 10 11, New Zealand ⓣ 0800 808 909, ⓦ www.singaporeair.com.
South African Airways South Africa ⓣ 0861 359 722, ⓦ www.flysaa.com.
Thai Airways Australia ⓣ 1300/651 960, New Zealand ⓣ 09/377 3886, ⓦ www.thaiair.com.
United Airlines US ⓣ 1-800/UNITED-1, Australia ⓣ 13 17 77, ⓦ www.united.com.
Virgin Atlantic ⓣ 1-800/821-5438, ⓦ www.virgin-atlantic.com.

Agents and operators

Abercrombie & Kent US ⓣ 1-800/554-7016 or 630/954 2944, ⓦ www.abercrombiekent.com. An upmarket travel agency, which runs a variety of guided tours to France, many including a number of days in Paris. A eleven-day tour of Northern France, taking in Tours and Dijon, for example, starts at $8000.

Co-op Travel Care UK ⓣ 0870/112 0085, ⓦ www.travelcareonline.com. Flights and holidays around the world, including flight/accommodation packages in Paris.

Cresta Holidays UK ⓣ 0871/664 7963, ⓦ www.crestaholidays.co.uk. Short, inexpensive hotel/flight packages covering Paris and Disneyland.

Discover France US ⓣ 1-800-960-2221, ⓦ www.discoverfrance.com. Offers "self-guided" bicycle, walking and getaway tours to destinations all over France, with a dedicated offshoot putting together flights, hotel reservations and tickets and passes for Paris itself, ⓦ www.gotoparis.net. Prices are moderate. Went "carbon neutral" in 2007.

Europe Through the Back Door US ⓣ 425/771-8303, ⓦ www.ricksteves.com. Off-the-beaten-track, small-group guided tours to Europe, especially France. Seven days in Paris starts from $1495, excluding air fares.

Eurostar.com UK ⓣ 0870/518 6186, from France ⓣ +44 1233/617 575 ⓦ www.eurostar.com. The website puts together rail and hotel packages which can represent significant savings on doing it separately yourself – though of course the choice of hotels is relatively limited.

The French Experience US ⓣ 1-800/283-7262 or 212/986 3800, ⓦ www.frenchexperience.com. Self-drive tours, apartment rentals, air fare arrangements. A three-night city break starts from $500, excluding air fares but including accommodation, travel passes, transfers, etc.

French Travel Connection Australia ⓣ 02/9966 1177, ⓦ www.frenchtravel.com.au. Award-winning specialists in French travel, offering everything from cooking classes and barge holidays to Paris accommodation and museum passes.

Kirker Europe UK ⓣ 0870/112 3333, ⓦ www.kirkerholidays.com. Specialists in quality short breaks in characterful, relatively classy hotels within walking distance of major sights. Departures from most regional airports, with arrival transfers included.

Martin Randall Travel UK ⓣ 020/8742 3355, ⓦ www.martinrandall.com. Runs high-quality, small-group cultural and wine/gastronomic tours, led by serious experts in their field. Tours occasionally take in Paris; in a given year you might find "French Gothic" or "Opera in Paris" listed – these include tickets, hotels, travel and the attentions of an architectural historian and a musicologist respectively.

North South Travel UK ⓣ 01245/608 291, ⓦ www.northsouthtravel.co.uk. Friendly, competitive travel agency, offering discounted fares worldwide – profits are used to support projects in the developing world, especially the promotion of sustainable tourism.

Rail Europe UK ⓣ 0870/837 1371, ⓦ www.raileurope.co.uk; US ⓣ 1-877/257-2887, Canada ⓣ 1-800/361-RAIL, ⓦ www.raileurope.com. Rail, air, hotel and car reservations.

ShortBreaks Ltd UK ⓣ 0870/027 6002, ⓦ www.short-breaks.com. Well-established specialists in European city breaks. Offers some inexpensive Eurostar/hotel package deals, and can help book exhibition and show tickets.

STA Travel UK ⓣ 0870/1600 599, ⓦ www.statravel.co.uk; US ⓣ 1-800/781-4040, ⓦ www.sta-travel.com; Australia ⓣ 1300/733 035, ⓦ www.statravel.com.au; New Zealand ⓣ 0508/782 872, ⓦ www.statravel.co.nz; South Africa ⓣ 0861/781 781, ⓦ www.statravel.co.za. Worldwide specialists in low-cost flights and tours for students and under-26s, though other customers welcome.

Thomas Cook UK ⓣ 0870/750 5711, ⓦ www.thomascook.co.uk. Long-established 24-hour travel agency for package holidays or scheduled flights. Does short breaks to Paris by air or Eurostar (and Orient Express packages for £550). TwoRail packages for two nights in a two-star hotel by Eurostar start at £145, by air £155. Costs are slightly higher for packages including flights from any number of regional airports.

Trailfinders UK ⓣ 020/7628 7628, ⓦ www.trailfinders.co.uk; Republic of Ireland ⓣ 01/677 7888, ⓦ www.trailfinders.ie. One of the best-informed and most efficient agents for independent travellers.

USIT Republic of Ireland ⓣ 01/602 1904, Northern Ireland ⓣ 028/9032 7111, ⓦ www.usit.ie. Student and youth specialists for flights and trains.

VFB Holidays UK ⓣ 01452/716 833, ⓦ www.vfbholidays.co.uk. This award-winning operator specializes in cottages and villas in France, but also offers flights from Irish and regional airports as well as London (and Eurostar) as part of travel/hotel packages. The hotels are mostly good three- and four-stars, and packages include city travel and museum passes.

Arrival

Many British travellers to Paris arrive by Eurostar at the central Gare du Nord train station, while more far-flung visitors are likely to land at one of Paris's two main airports: Charles de Gaulle and Orly. Trains from other parts of France or continental Europe draw in at one of the six central main-line stations. For details of arrival at Disneyland Paris, see p.260.

By air

The two main Paris **airports** that deal with international flights are Roissy-Charles de Gaulle and Orly, both well connected to the centre. Detailed information on both can be found on Ⓦwww.adp.fr. A third airport, Beauvais, is used by some low-cost airlines.

Roissy-Charles de Gaulle Airport

Roissy-Charles de Gaulle Airport (24hr information in English ⓣ01.48.62.22.80), usually referred to as **Charles de Gaulle** and abbreviated to CDG or Paris CDG, is 23km northeast of the city. The airport has three terminals: CDG 1, CDG 2, and CDG T3. A TGV station links the airport (CDG 2) with Bordeaux, Brussels, Lille, Lyon, Nantes, Marseille and Rennes.

The cheapest and probably the quickest way to get to the centre of Paris is the **Roissyrail** train link which runs on RER line B (every 15min from 5am until midnight; 30min; €8.10 one-way). You can pick it up direct from T3 and most parts of CDG 2, but from CDG 1 and CDG 2A and 2B you have to get a shuttle bus (*navette*) to the RER station. The train stops at Gare du Nord, Châtelet-Les Halles, St-Michel and Denfert-Rochereau, all of which have métro stations for onward travel. On the way back to the airport, if you're picking up the RER from the Gare du Nord, note that all but the first train of the day depart from platform 43, where there's an English-speaking information desk indicated by a large question mark (daily 8am–8pm); confirm here which of the two RER stations you should get off at by checking the airline code on your ticket against the information board, or ask the staff to help you. A number of regular **RER stopping trains** also serve the airports; these only take about five minutes more than the Roissyrail to get to the centre, though they aren't designed to accommodate luggage.

Various bus companies provide services from the airport direct to a number of city-centre locations, but they're slightly more expensive than Roissyrail and may take longer. The **Roissybus**, for instance, connects CDG 1 and CDG 2 with the Opéra-Garnier (corner of rues Auber and Scribe; M° Opéra/RER Auber); it runs every fifteen minutes from 5.45am to 11pm, costs €8.50 one-way and takes around 45 minutes. There are also two **Air France buses**: the green-coded line 2 stops outside Charles-de-Gaulle-Etoile RER/métro while the yellow-coded line 4 stops at the Gare de Lyon before terminating near the Gare Montparnasse. The timings are similar to the Roissybus, but tickets are more expensive at €20–22 return; for detailed information on routes and prices see Ⓦwww.cars-airfrance.com.

Taxis (metered) into central Paris from CDG cost around €40–50, including a small luggage supplement (€1 per piece of luggage), and should take between fifty minutes and one hour. Slightly less expensive is the **minibus door-to-door service**, Paris Blue, which costs from €34 for two people, with no extra charge for luggage. It operates round-the-clock but bookings must be made at least 24 hours in advance on ⓣ01.30.11.13.00 or via their website Ⓦwww.paris-blue-airport-shuttle.fr. Note that if your flight gets in after midnight your only means of transport is a taxi or the minibus.

Orly Airport

Orly Airport (information in English daily 6am–11.30pm ⓣ01.49.75.15.15), 14km south of Paris, has two terminals, Orly Sud (south, for international flights) and Orly Ouest (west, for domestic flights), linked by shuttle bus but easily walkable. One of the easiest ways into the centre is the fast **Orlyval train shuttle** link to RER line B station Antony, followed by métro connection stops at Denfert-Rochereau, St-Michel and Châtelet-Les Halles; it runs every four to seven minutes every day from 6am to 11pm (€9.10 one-way; 35min to Châtelet). Alternatively, you can take an **ADP shuttle bus** (*navette*) to RER line C station Pont de Rungis, from where trains leave every fifteen minutes from 5am to 11.30pm for the Gare d'Austerlitz and other métro connection stops on the Left Bank (€5.15 one-way; train 25min, total journey around 45min). Leaving Paris, the trains run from Gare d'Austerlitz from 5.40am to 10.40pm.

Two bus services are also worth considering: the **Orlybus**, which runs to Denfert-Rochereau RER/métro station in the 14ᵉ (every 15–20min, 6am–11.30pm; €6 one-way; around 30min); and **bus 285**, which runs to métro Villejuif-Louis-Aragon (métro line 7) every ten to twenty minutes (every 30min on Sun) between 5.05am and 1am (€5.20; 15min). Finally, the red-coded **Air France bus** on line 2 (ⓦwww.cars-airfrance.com) runs to the Invalides Air France Terminal on rue Esnault Peletrie, close to Les Invalides itself, via Montparnasse (stopping at Porte d'Orléans and Duroc if requested in advance) every fifteen minutes from 6am to 11.30pm (€14 return; about 35min). Leaving Paris, the bus can be caught from the Invalides Air France Terminal at 2 rue Robert Esnault Pelterie, and from Montparnasse on rue du Commandant Mouchotte in front of the *Méridien Hotel*.

Taxis take about 35 minutes to reach the centre of Paris and cost at least €30.

Beauvais Airport

Beauvais airport (ⓣ08.92.68.20.66, ⓦwww.aeroportbeauvais.com), 65km northwest of Paris, is served by Ryanair from Dublin, Shannon and Glasgow. It's sometimes called Paris Beauvais-Tillé airport. **Coaches** (€13 each way) shuttle between the airport and Porte Maillot in the 17ᵉ arrondissement, where you can pick up métro line 1 to the centre. The journey takes about an hour in all. The coach leaves between fifteen and thirty minutes after the flight has arrived and three hours and fifteen minutes before the flight departs on the way back. Tickets can be bought at Arrivals or from the Beauvais shop at 1 boulevard Pershing, near the Porte Maillot terminal.

Lost baggage

Orly ⓣ01.49.75.04.53; Charles de Gaulle ⓣ01.48.62.10.86.

By train

Paris has six main-line train stations. **Eurostar** (ⓣ08.92.35.35.39, ⓦwww.eurostar.com) terminates at the **Gare du Nord**, rue Dunkerque, in the northeast of the city – a bustling convergence of international, long-distance and suburban trains, the métro, RER and several bus routes. Coming off the train, turn left for the métro and the RER, right for taxis (a sample price would be €10 to a hotel in the 4ᵉ) and the secure left luggage (daily 6.15am–11.15pm; around €7 for 24 hours, depending on the locker size), both down the escalators opposite the Avis car rental desk. You can get a shower (€7 for 20min) in the public toilets (daily 6am–midnight; small charge payable) at the bottom of the métro escalators, and change money at two bureaux de change at the station (daily 7.30am–11.40pm). The Gare du Nord is also the arrival point for trains from Calais and other north European countries. Watch out for scammers offering to "help" with tickets or taxis.

Nearby, the **Gare de l'Est** (place du 11-Novembre-1918, 10ᵉ) serves eastern France and central and eastern Europe. The **Gare St-Lazare** (place du Havre, 8ᵉ), serving the Normandy coast and Dieppe, is the most central, close to the Madeleine and the Opéra-Garnier. Still on the Right Bank but towards the southeast corner is the **Gare de Lyon** (place Louis Armand, 12ᵉ), serving

Left luggage

Left luggage offices are located at Gare Saint Lazare, Gare de l'Est, Gare du Nord, Gare de Lyon, Gare d'Austerlitz and Montparnasse.

trains from Italy and Switzerland and TGV lines from southeast France. South of the river, the **Gare Montparnasse** on boulevard de Vaugirard, 15e, is the terminus for Chartres, Brittany, the Atlantic coast and TGV lines from southwest France. **Gare d'Austerlitz**, on boulevard de l'Hôpital, 13e, serves the Loire Valley and the Dordogne. The motorail station, **Gare de Paris-Bercy**, is down the tracks from the Gare de Lyon on boulevard de Bercy, 12e.

All the stations are equipped with cafés, restaurants, *tabacs*, ATMs and bureaux de change (long waits in season), and all are connected with the métro system; the tourist office at Gare de Lyon can also book same-day accommodation (see p.46). Left-luggage facilities are available at all train stations under heavy security, but are limited in number.

For **information** on national train services and reservations phone ⓣ36.35 (within France only), ⓣ01.40.18.20.00 or consult the website ⓦwww.sncf.fr. For information on suburban lines call ⓣ08.91.36.20.20.

By bus and car

Almost all the **buses** coming into Paris – whether international or domestic – arrive at the main **gare routière** at 28 avenue du Général-de-Gaulle, Bagnolet, at the eastern edge of the city; métro Gallieni (line 3) links it to the centre. If you're **driving** into Paris yourself, don't try to go straight across the city to your destination unless you know what you're doing. Use the ring road – the **boulevard périphérique** – to get around to the nearest "porte"; except at rush hour, it's very quick – sometimes frighteningly so – and relatively easy to navigate.

City transport

While walking is undoubtedly the best way to discover Paris, the city's integrated public transport system of bus, métro and RER trains – the RATP (Régie Autonome des Transports Parisiens; ⓣ08.92.68.77.14 6am–9pm premium rate, or ⓣ08.92.68.41.14 in English, premium rate, ⓦwww.ratp.fr) – is cheap, fast and meticulously signposted. For details on tickets and the various passes available see p.28.

The métro and RER

The **métro**, combined with the **RER** (Réseau Express Régional) suburban express lines, is the simplest way of moving around the city and also one of the cheapest – €1.40 for a single journey anywhere in the centre. Many of the métro lines follow the streets above; line 1 for example shadows the Champs Elysées and rue de Rivoli. The métro runs from 5.30am to around 12.30am (1.30am on Saturdays), RER trains from 5am to 1am.

Stations (abbreviated: Mº Concorde, RER Luxembourg, etc) are evenly spaced and you'll rarely find yourself more than 500m from one in the centre, though the interchanges at big stations can involve a lot of legwork. You'll find a métro map in the colour section at the back of this book; alternatively, free **maps** of varying sizes and detail are available at most stations: the largest and most useful is the *Grand Plan de Paris numéro 2*, which overlays the métro, RER and bus routes on a map of the city so you can see exactly how transport lines and streets match up. If you just want a handy pocket-sized métro/bus map ask for the *Petit Plan de Paris* or the smaller *Paris Plan de Poche*. Métro lines are colour-coded and designated by numbers for the métro and by letters for the RER. You also need to know the **direction of travel** – signposted using the names of the terminus: for example, travelling from Montparnasse to Châtelet, you follow the sign "Direction Porte-de-Clignancourt"; from Gare d'Austerlitz to Grenelle on line 10 you follow "Direction Boulogne–Pont-de-St-Cloud". The numerous interchanges (*correspondances*) make it possible to cover most of the city in a more or less straight line. For RER journeys beyond the city, make sure that the station you want is illuminated on the platform display board. For more on métro life and etiquette see the box, p.7.

Buses

Buses are often rather neglected in favour of the métro, but can be very useful where the métro journey doesn't quite work. They aren't difficult to use and naturally you see much more, plus journeys are getting quicker with the introduction of bus lanes. Free **route maps** are available at métro stations, bus terminals and the tourist office; the best, showing the métro and RER as well, is the *Grand Plan de Paris*. Every bus stop displays the numbers of the buses that stop there, a map showing all the stops on the route, and the times of the first and last buses. Generally speaking, buses run from 7am to 8.30pm with some services continuing to 1.30am. Around half the lines don't operate on Sundays and holidays – the *Grand Plan de Paris* lists those that do. You can buy a single **ticket** (€1.40) from the driver, or use a pre-purchased *carnet* ticket or pass (see p.28). Press the red button to request a stop. Most bus lines are now easily accessible for wheelchairs and prams; these are indicated on the *Grand Plan de Paris* and on the ⓦ www.ratp.fr website.

From mid-April to mid-September, a special orange and white **Balabus** service (not to be confused with Batobus, see p.29) passes all the major tourist sights between the Grande Arche de la Défense and the Gare de Lyon. They run on Sundays and holidays every fifteen to twenty minutes from noon to 9pm. Bus stops are marked "Balabus", and you'll need one to three bus tickets, depending on the length of your journey: check the information at the bus stop or ask the driver. The Paris Visite, Mobilis and Carte Orange passes (see p.28) are all valid too. **Night buses** (*Noctilien*) run on 42 routes every hour (with extra services

Touring Paris by public transport

A good way to take in the city sights is to hop on a bus. Bus #20 (wheelchair accessible) from the Gare de Lyon follows the Grands Boulevards and does a loop through the 1er and 2e arrondissements. Bus #24 (also wheelchair accessible) between Porte de Bercy and Gare St-Lazare follows the left bank of the Seine. Bus #29 is one of the best routes for taking in the city: it ventures from the Gare St-Lazare past the Opéra Garnier, the Bourse and the Centre Pompidou, through the heart of the Marais and past the Bastille to the Gare de Lyon. For La Voie Triomphale, take a trip on bus #73 between La Défense and the Musée d'Orsay, while bus #63 drives a scenic route along the Seine on the Rive Gauche, then crosses the river and heads up to Trocadéro, where there are some wonderful views of the Eiffel Tower. Many more bus journeys – outside rush hours – are worthwhile trips in themselves: you can get hold of the *Grand Plan de Paris* from a métro station and check out the routes of buses #38, #48, #64, #67, #68, #69, #82, #87 and #95.

The métro, surprisingly, can also provide some scenery: the overground line on the southern route between Charles-de-Gaulle/Etoile and Nation (line 6) gives you views of the Eiffel Tower, the Ile des Cygnes, the Invalides, the new Bibliothèque Nationale and the Finance Ministry.

on weekends) from 1am to 5.30am between place du Châtelet, west of the Hôtel de Ville, and the suburbs. Details of the routes are available on the *Grand Plan de Paris*.

Tickets and passes

For a short stay in the city, it's worth buying **carnets** of ten tickets, available from any station or *tabac* (€10.90, as opposed to €1.40 for an individual ticket). Greater Paris's integrated transport system is divided into five **zones**; the métro system more or less fits into zones 1 and 2. The same **tickets** are valid for bus, métro and, within the city limits and immediate suburbs (zones 1 and 2), the RER express rail lines, which also extend far out into the Ile de France. Only one ticket is ever needed on the métro system, and within zones 1 and 2 for any RER or bus journey, but you can't switch between buses or between bus and métro/RER on the same ticket. For **RER journeys** beyond zones 1 and 2 you must buy an RER ticket; visitors often get caught out, for instance, when they take the RER to La Défense instead of the métro. **Children** under 4 travel free and from ages 4 to 10 at half price. Don't buy from the touts who hang around the main stations – you'll pay well over the odds, quite often for a used ticket – and be sure to keep your ticket until the end of the journey as you'll be fined on the spot if you can't produce one. If you're doing a number of journeys in one day, it might be worth getting a **Mobilis day pass** (from €5.50 for the city to €18.70 to include the outer suburbs, though not the airports), which offers unlimited access to the métro, buses and, depending on which zones you choose, the RER.

If you've arrived early in the week and are staying more than three days, it's more economical to buy a **Carte Orange weekly ticket** (*coupon hebdomadaire*). It costs €16 for zones 1 and 2, is valid for an unlimited number of journeys from Monday morning to Sunday evening. You can only buy a ticket for the current week until Wednesday; from Thursday you can buy a ticket to begin the following Monday. There's also a monthly ticket (*coupon mensuel*) for €52.50 for zones 1 and 2. The **Carte Orange** consists either of an identity card (for which you'll need a passport photo) and accompanying ticket (*coupon*), on which you have to write your Carte Orange number, or an all-in-one Navigo swipe card, which you simply touch against the reader on the ticket barriers, and which you can recharge at automatic machines.

Paris Visites, one-, two-, three- and five-day visitors' passes, are not as good value as the Carte Orange and Mobilis passes, but they do give reductions on certain tourist attractions. If you're going to Paris by Eurostar, you could save yourself time by buying the passes at Waterloo International – either from the information point or the souvenir shop underneath the escalator that heads up to platform entrances 21A/22A. You can get the Carte Musées et Monuments (see p.31) and Disneyland tickets here, too.

Both the Carte Orange and the Paris Visites entitle you to unlimited travel (in the zones you have chosen) on bus, métro, RER, SNCF and the Montmartre funicular. On the métro you put the Carte Orange coupon through the turnstile slot (make sure you retrieve it afterwards); on a bus you show the whole carte to the driver as you board – don't put it into the punching machine.

The RATP also runs numerous **excursions**, some to quite far-flung places, which are far less expensive than those offered by commercial operators. Details are available online or at the RATP's Agence Commerciale (51 rue Chausée d'Antin, 9e; M° Chausée d'Antin). For 24-hour **recorded information** in English on all RATP services call ⓣ08.92.68.41.14 (premium rate) or visit online at ⓦwww.ratp.fr.

Taxis

The best place to get a **taxi** is at a taxi rank (*arrêt taxi* – there are around 470 of them) – usually more effective than hailing from the street. The large white light signals the taxi is free; the orange light means it's in use. You can also call a taxi out: **phone numbers** are shown at the taxi ranks, or try Taxis Bleus (ⓣ08.91.70.10.10, ⓦwww.taxis-bleus.com), Alpha Taxis (ⓣ01.45.85.85.85) or Taxis G7 (ⓣ01.47.39.47.39). That said, finding a taxi at lunchtime and any time after 7pm can be almost impossible: the powerfully unionized and heavily regulated system is stacked against the user, and there simply aren't enough cabs, or drivers willing to work the graveyard shifts.

Taxis are metered and **charges** are fairly reasonable: between €6 and €12 for a central daytime journey, though considerably more if you call one out. Before you get into the taxi, you can tell which of the three rates is operating from the three small indicator lights on its roof: "A" (passenger side; white) indicates the daytime rate (7am–7pm) for Paris within the boulevard périphérique (around €0.80 per km); "B" (orange) is the rate for Paris at night, on Sunday and on public holidays, and for the suburbs during the day (€1.10 per km); "C" (blue) is the night rate for the suburbs (€1.30 per km). In addition there's a minimum charge of €5, a time charge of around €25 an hour for when the car is stationary, an extra charge of €0.70 if you're picked up from a main-line train station, and a €0.90 charge for each piece of luggage carried. Taxi drivers do not have to take more than three passengers (they don't like people sitting in the front); if a fourth passenger is accepted, an extra charge of €2.60 will be added. A **tip** of 10 percent, while optional, is generally expected.

Boats

There remains one final mode of public transport, **Batobus** (ⓦwww.batobus.com), which now operates all year round, stopping at eight points along the Seine between Port de la Bourdonnais (M° Eiffel Tower/ Trocadéro) and Port des Champs-Elysées (M° Champs-Elysées). Boats run every fifteen to thirty minutes from 10am to 9.30pm from June to September, from 10am to 7pm in March, April, May, September and October, and from 10.30am–4.30pm in November, December and February. The total journey time is around thirty minutes, and tickets (€8) are valid for one journey for a maximum of four stops. There is also a €12 day pass.

Driving and parking

Travelling around **by car** – in the daytime at least – is hardly worth it because of the difficulty of finding parking spaces. You're better off finding a motel-style place on the edge of the city and using public transport. But if you're determined to use the pay and display parking system you must first buy a **Paris Carte** (like a phonecard) from a *tabac*, then look for the blue "P" signs alongside grey parking meters. Introduce the card into the meter and it automatically deducts from the value on the card – it costs €2 an hour, for a maximum of two hours. Alternatively, make for one of the many underground **car parks**, which cost up to €2.40 per hour, or around €25 for 24 hours. Whatever you do, don't park in a bus lane or the Axe Rouge express routes (marked with a red square). Should you be towed away, you'll find your car in the pound (*fourrière*) belonging to that particular arrondissement – check with the local *mairie* for the address. If you'll be using your car for a while, you might want to pick up *Parkings de Paris*, a guide to locating over two hundred public car parks in the city. It's available in most large bookstores and you can even pre-book your parking space on their website (ⓦwww.parkingsdeparis.com).

The French **drive on the right**, and, if your car is right-hand drive, you must have your headlight dip adjusted to the right before you go – it's a legal requirement – and as a courtesy, change or paint them to yellow or stick on black glare deflectors. Remember also that you have to be 18 years of age to drive in France, regardless of whether you hold a licence in your own country.

In the event of a **breakdown**, call Dan Dépann (ⓣ08.00.25.10.00) or Action Auto Assistance (ⓣ08.00.00.80.00) for round-the-clock assistance. Alternatively, ask the police for advice. For **traffic conditions** in Paris tune in to 105.1 FM (FIP), for the boulevard périphérique and main routes in and out of the city, ring ⓣ08.26.02.20.22, or log onto ⓦwww.securiteroutiere.gouv.fr.

Car rental

The big international **car rental** companies have offices at the airports and at several locations in the city. **Avis** (ⓣ08.20.61.16.24, ⓦwww.avis.com), located at the Gare du Nord, does good weekend rates: their "Parisien weekend" car rental extends from

Pedestrians

French drivers pay no heed to **pedestrian/zebra crossings**, marked with horizontal white stripes on the road. It's very dangerous to step out onto one and assume drivers will stop as is usually the case at home. Take just as great care as you would crossing at any other point, even at traffic lights.

noon on Thursday to noon on Tuesday, with two days working out at around €50 per day, to five days at about €45 per day. Other big names are listed below.

North Americans and Australians in particular should be forewarned that it's difficult to rent a car with automatic transmission in France; if you can't drive a manual/stickshift, try and book an automatic (*voiture à transmission automatique*) well in advance, and be prepared to pay a much higher price for it.

Car rental firms

Some national firms to try include:
Budget ⓣ08.00.10.00.01, ⓦwww.budgetrentacar.com.
Europcar ⓣ08.25.35.23.52, ⓦwww.europcar.com.
Hertz ⓣ01.55.31.93.21, ⓦwww.hertz.com.
Good local firms include:
Buchard 99 bd Auguste-Blanqui, 13e ⓣ01.45.80.15.15; M° Place-d'Italie.
Locabest 3 rue Abel, 12e ⓣ01.43.46.05.05; M° Gare-de-Lyon; also at 104 bd Magenta, 10e (ⓣ01.44.72.08.05; M° Gare-du-Nord); ⓦwww.locabest.fr.

Look up "location d'automobiles" in the yellow pages for others.

Cycling

Since 1996, the Mairie de Paris has made great efforts to introduce dedicated **cycle lanes** in Paris. You can pick up a free leaflet, *Paris à Vélo*, outlining the routes, from town halls, the tourist office or bike rental outlets. For details of bike rental and guided cycling tours, see pp.419–420 of "Activities and sports ".

Costs

Paris has the potential to be very expensive, certainly more so than the rest of France, but it compares favourably to other North European capitals because of the relatively low cost of accommodation and public transport. If you are one of two people sharing a comfortable central hotel room, you can get by happily on €100 per person per day (around £70/US$135). At the bottom line, by watching the pennies, staying at a hostel and visiting monuments and museums on free entry days (see opposite), you could survive on as little as €45 (around £30/US$60) a day, including a cheap restaurant meal.

In **hotels**, perfectly adequate but simple doubles can be had from €35, but for reasonable comfort, prices start at more like €65. Single-rated and -sized rooms are often available, starting at around €30 in a cheap hotel. Breakfast at most hotels is an extra €4.50–8. You can spend as much or as little as you like on eating out. There are large numbers of reasonable, if not very exciting, **restaurants** with three-course *menus* for between €15 and €25; the lunchtime *menu* is nearly always cheaper and you can get a filling midday *plat du jour* (dish of the day) of hot food for under €10. **Picnic fare**, obviously, is much less costly, especially when you buy in the markets and cheap supermarket chains. The mark-up on wine in restaurants is high, though the house wine, served by the carafe in less fancy establishments, is often good value. **Drinks in cafés and bars** are what really make a hole in your pocket; remember that it's cheaper to be at the bar than at a table in cafés and most expensive to sit outside on the terrace. A black espresso coffee (*un café*) is the cheapest drink (around €1.20 if drunk at the bar). A *café crème* ranges from around €2 at the bar to anything up to €6 on the terrace. Wine and draught lager are similarly priced. Mixed drinks or cocktails cost €6.50–11. Glasses of tap water are free.

Transport within the city is inexpensive. A carnet of ten tickets, valid on buses and métro/RER in central Paris, for example, costs €10.90.

Reductions

The cost of entry to museums and monuments can really add up, though some state-run museums are free (see below) or have free admission on Sundays. For **children and teenagers**, the range of reductions can be quite bewildering, as each institution has its own policy. In many museums under-18s are free; all monuments are free for under-12s. Universally, however, under-4s are usually free, less often under-8s. Half-price or reduced admission is normally available for 5- to 18-year-olds. Some more commercial attractions, however, begin to charge adult rates at age 12.

If you are a full-time **student**, it's worthwhile carrying the **ISIC Card** (International Student Identity Card; ⓦwww.isiccard.com) to gain entrance reductions (usually about a third off). The card is universally accepted as ID, while the student card from your home institution is not. You have to be 26 or younger to qualify for the **International Youth Travel Card**. For those over 60 or 65 (depending on the institution), reductions are only patchily available. You will need to carry your passport around with you as proof of age.

Whatever your age, if you are going to do a lot of museum duty, it's worth considering buying the **Carte Musées et Monuments** (€30 two-day, €45 three-day, €60 five-day; ⓦwww.parismuseumpass.com). Available from the tourist office and museums, as well as the Eurostar terminal at London St Pancras, they're valid for seventy museums and monuments, including all the main ones (though not special exhibitions) in and around Paris, and allow you to bypass ticket queues (though not the security checkpoints).

Paris for free

The permanent collections at all **municipal museums** are **free** all year round. These museums are: Musée d'Art Moderne de la Ville de Paris; Maison de Balzac; Musée Carnavalet; Musée Cognac Jay; Musée de la Vie Romantique; Musée Zadkine; Maison de Victor Hugo; and Musée Jean Moulin. All **national museums** are free the first Sunday of the month, including the Louvre, Pompidou Centre, and the Picasso and Rodin museums; see ⓦwww.rmn.fr for a full list. Additionally, hundreds of museums across the country grant free admissions for one day in the **spring** (ⓦwww.printempsdesmusees.culture.fr for specific dates and museums).

Churches, **cemeteries** and, of course, **markets** are free (except for some specialist annual antique and book markets). Most **parks** are free but some gardens within have small entry charges, usually around €1.50. **Libraries** and the cultural centres of different countries put on films, shows and exhibitions for next to nothing (details in the listings mags, see p.36); most libraries themselves are free, but some have entry charges – in such cases a day pass might cost around €4. Other **free cultural offerings** appear regularly, from bands in the streets to firework shows, courtesy of the Mairie de Paris (publicized on the electronic billboards around Paris).

Money

France's currency is the euro. The euro (€) is split into 100 cents. There are seven euro notes – in denominations of 500, 200, 100, 50, 20, 10 and 5 euros (though many vendors are reluctant to accept the 500 and 200 euro notes) – and eight different coin denominations, from 2 euros down to 1 cent. Euro coins feature a common EU design on one face, but different country-specific designs on the other. No matter what the design, all euro coins and notes can be used in any of the EU member states.

At the time of writing, the **exchange rate** hovered around €1.47 to the pound, €0.73 to the US dollar, €0.65 to the Canadian dollar, €0.60 to the Australian dollar, and €0.55 to the New Zealand dollar. For the most up-to-date exchange rates, consult the Currency Converter website ⓦwww.oanda.com.

The easiest way to access your funds while away is with a **debit or credit card** – just check with your bank first that they can be used in ATMs abroad and make sure you know your PIN. It's not necessarily the cheapest option, however, with many UK banks levying charges totalling around 5 percent on foreign withdrawals. Most foreign bank cards will work in a French ATM/cash machine (called a *distributeur* or *point argent*). Note that there is often a minimum charge, so it may be worth getting out a sizeable sum each time you use the machine.

You might also want to bring some **travellers' cheques** as a backup, and it's always a good idea to have some euros on you when you arrive. An inexpensive way to buy euros is by ordering them in advance online at ⓦwww.travelex.co.uk, then picking up the cash at the airport. Alternatively, the Post Office often offers decent exchange rates. You can also use credit cards for **cash advances** at banks (with a passport as ID) and ATMs. To cancel lost or stolen cards, call the following 24hr numbers: American Express ⓣ01.47.77.72.00; Diners' Club ⓣ08.10.31.41.59; MasterCard ⓣ0800.90.13.87; Visa ⓣ0800.90.11.79.

Credit cards are widely accepted and one of the most convenient ways of paying for things. They also tend to offer the most competitive exchange and commission rates. Visa – often referred to as Carte Bleue in France – is almost universally recognized. Access, MasterCard – sometimes called EuroCard – and American Express rank a bit lower. It's always worth checking first, however, that restaurants and hotels will accept your card; some smaller ones won't, despite the sign. And note that some machines don't recognize foreign cards – transport vending machines and automatic petrol pumps are particularly problematic. French cards use the **chip-and-pin system**.

Changing money and banking hours

Exchange rates and **commission fees** charged by banks and bureaux de change vary considerably. On the whole, the best exchange rates are offered by **banks**, though there's always a commission charge on top (1–2 percent commission on travellers' cheques, and a 2–4 percent commission on cash). It pays to be very wary of **bureaux de change** as they can really overcharge you. Check their rates very carefully – the "buy" not the "sell" rate is the one that counts – and shop around. The exchange bureaux on the Champs-Elysées, near McDonald's, are usually pretty reputable, even if the rates aren't exactly loaded in your favour.

Standard **banking hours** are Monday to Friday from 9am to 4 or 5pm. Some banks close at midday (noon/12.30pm–2/2.30pm); some are open on Saturday 9am to noon. All are closed on Sunday and public holidays. They will have a notice on the door if they do currency exchange. Money-exchange bureaux stay open longer (until 6 or 7pm), tend not to close for lunch and may even open on Sundays in the more touristy areas.

There are **automatic exchange machines** at the airports and train stations and outside many money-exchange bureaux. They accept £10 and £20 notes as well as dollars, but offer a very poor rate of exchange.

Banks and exchange

Some of the more conveniently located bureaux de change are at Charles-de-Gaulle airport (daily 7am–10pm), Orly airport (daily 6.30am–11pm) and Beauvais airport (daily 10am–7pm); at Gare d'Austerlitz (Mon–Fri 7am–9pm), Gare de l'Est (7.30am–9.30pm), Gare de Lyon (Mon–Sat 8am–8pm), Gare du Nord (8am–11pm), Gare St-Lazare (9.30am–7pm). Try also the following for exchange:

American Express 11 rue Scribe, 9e ⓣ01.47.14.50.00; M° Opéra. Bureau de change open Mon–Fri 9am–6pm, Sat 9am–5pm, Sun 10am–4pm, public hols 9am–5pm.

Barclays 6 Rond-Point-des-Champs-Elysées, 8e ⓣ01.44.95.13.80; M° Franklin-D. Roosevelt; Mon–Fri 9.15am–4.30pm. Many other branches throughout the city (info on ⓣ01.42.92.39.08 or at ⓦwww.barclays.fr).

Chequepoint 150 av des Champs-Elysées, 8e ⓣ01.42.56.48.63; M° Charles-de-Gaulle-Etoile. Charges high rates of exchange but is open daily 24hr.

Travelex 125 av des Champs-Elysées, 8e ⓣ01.47.20.25.14; M° Charles de Gaulle-Etoile; daily 10am–9.30pm; 4 bd St Michel, 6e ⓣ01.42.34.70.00; M° St Michel; daily 10am–7.30pm, Sun 10am–7pm; and many other branches throughout the city (see ⓦwww.travelex.fr). Issues travellers' cheques and does exchange.

Wiring money

If you really find yourself strapped for cash, having **money wired** from home works well as a last resort: Western Union allows you to send money directly from a credit card to any one of several hundred branches across the city – including all post offices. Once the money has been sent, it is available immediately: you simply show up at the designated location, present a form of identification and they hand you the cash. Use with discretion, though, as the commissions tend to hover around fifteen percent (ⓦwww.westernunion.com).

Health

Citizens of all EU countries are entitled to take advantage of French health services under the same terms as residents, if they have the correct documentation. For British citizens, this means the new European Health Insurance Card. As with the old E111, this can be applied for, free of charge, at UK post offices or online at ⓦwww.dh.gov.uk/travellers. Non-EU citizens have to pay for most medical attention and are strongly advised to take out some form of travel insurance (see p.42).

Under the French Social Security system, every hospital visit, doctor's consultation and prescribed medicine incurs a charge, which you have to pay upfront. Although all EU citizens with the correct documents are entitled to a refund of 70–75 percent of the standard fee for medical and dental expenses, providing the doctor is government-registered (a *médecin conventionné*), this can still leave a hefty shortfall, especially after a stay in hospital.

Doctors and pharmacies

To find a **doctor**, ask at any *pharmacie*, local police station, tourist office or your hotel. Alternatively, look under "Médecins" in the

Yellow Pages of the phone directory. An average consultation fee should be between €20 and €25. You will be given a *Feuille de Soins* (statement of treatment) for later insurance claims. Prescriptions should be taken to a *pharmacie* and must be paid for; the medicines will have little stickers (*vignettes*) attached to them, which you should remove and stick to your *Feuille de Soins*, together with the prescription itself.

In serious emergencies you will always be admitted to the nearest hospital (*hôpital*), either under your own power or by ambulance, which even French citizens must pay for. Many people call the fire brigade (*pompiers*) instead; they are equipped to deal with medical emergencies and are the fastest and most reliable emergency service.

Pharmacies, signalled by an illuminated green cross, can give advice on minor complaints and prescribe appropriate medicines. They're also equipped to provide first-aid help on request (for a fee). They keep normal shop hours (roughly 9am–7pm), and some stay open all night: details of the nearest one open are posted in all pharmacies. You can find a good English-speaking chemist at Swann, 6 rue Castiglione, 1er (☎01.42.60.72.96). Pharmacies open at night include Dérhy/Pharmacie des Champs-Elysées, 84 avenue des Champs-Elysées, 8e (☎01.45.62.02.41; 24hr; M° George-V); Pharmacie Européenne, 6 place de Clichy, 9e (☎01.48.74.65.18; 24hr; M° Place-de-Clichy); Pharmacie des Halles, 10 boulevard Sébastopol, 4e (☎01.42.72.03.23; Mon–Sat 9am–midnight, Sun 9am–10pm; M° Châtelet); Pharmacie Internationale de Paris, 5 place Pigalle, 9e (☎01.48.78.38.12; Mon–Fri 8.30am–midnight, Sat & Sun 8.30am–1am; M° Pigalle); Grande Pharmacie de la Nation, 13 place de la Nation, 11e (☎01.43.73.24.03; daily 8am–11pm; M° Nation).

Safer sex

Paris has the highest incidence of **AIDS** of any city in Europe; people who are HIV positive are just as likely to be heterosexual as homosexual. Condoms (*préservatifs*) are readily available in supermarkets, and from dispensers in clubs, on the street – often outside pharmacies – and in the métro. From pharmacies you can also get spermicidal cream and jelly (*dose contraceptive*), suppositories (*ovules*, *suppositoires*) and (with a prescription) the pill (*la pilule*), a diaphragm or IUD (*le stérilet*). Pregnancy test kits (*tests de grossesse*) are sold at pharmacies; emergency contraceptive or the "morning-after" pill (*la pilule du lendemain*) is available from pharmacies without prescription.

Medical emergency numbers and helplines

Fire brigade/paramedics ☎18
Medical emergencies/ambulance ☎15
SIDA info service ☎08.00.84.08.00 (toll-free, 24 hours), English-speaking on Mon, Wed & Fri 2–7pm. An AIDs information and counselling service.
SOS Médecins ☎08.20.33.24.24. Doctor call-out.
SOS Dentaire ☎01.43.37.51.00. Emergency dental care.

English-speaking private hospitals

American Hospital in Paris 63 bd Victor-Hugo, Neuilly-sur-Seine, M° Porte-Maillot, then bus #82 to terminus; ☎01.46.41.25.25, ⓦwww.american-hospital.org.
Hertford British Hospital 3 rue Barbès, Levallois-Perret, M° Anatole-France; ☎01.46.39.22.22, ⓦwww.british-hospital.org.

Travellers with special needs

While the situation is certainly improving, Paris has never had any special reputation for providing ease of access or facilities for disabled travellers. The way cars park on pavements makes wheelchair travel a nightmare, and the métro system has endless flights of steps. Museums, however, are getting much better; the Cité des Sciences has won European awards for its accessibility to those with sight, hearing and mobility disabilities. The Louvre has similarly good access. In a number of theatres the text is displayed for the deaf and hard-of-hearing during some performances. Note that admission to museums is free for blue badge holders, and one companion.

Up-to-date **information** is best obtained from organizations at home before you leave, as well as from the French tourist board (ⓦwww.franceguide.com) or from the French disability organizations (see p.36). One of the best sources of information for disabled travelling in France (with a large section on Paris) is *Handitourisme*, published in 2004 in France by Petit Futé (ⓦwww.petitfute.fr; €15). Written in French, the book lists hundreds of sites, museums, hotels and restaurants with full accessibility to handicapped travellers. Another useful resource, in English, is *Access in Paris* by Gordon Couch and Ben Roberts, published in Britain by Quiller Press, a thorough guide to accommodation, monuments, museums, restaurants and travel to the city. The current publication dates from 1997, so some of the information will be out of date. Holiday Care (ⓣ0845/124 9972, ⓦwww.holidaycare.org.uk) also has an information sheet on accessible accommodation in France. In the US, try the Society for the Advancement of Travel for the Handicapped (ⓣ212/447-7284, ⓦwww.sath.org)

Eurostar offers an excellent deal for wheelchair-users. There are two spaces in the first-class carriages for wheelchairs, each with an accompanying seat for a companion. Fares are a flat rate of £59 return for both passengers from Paris and London (with semi-flexible conditions), and though it's not absolutely guaranteed, you will normally get the first-class meal as well. No advance bookings are necessary, though the limited spaces make it wise to reserve ahead and arrange the special assistance which Eurostar offers at either end.

The French Government Tourist Office in London distributes a booklet on hotels, called *Paris, Ile de France: Hôtels et Residences de Tourisme* which details those with disabled access. For more information contact the organizations listed below.

Getting around

If you are physically handicapped, **taxis** are obliged by law to carry you and to help you into the vehicle, also to carry your guide dog if you are blind. The suburban agency **GiHP** (Mon–Fri 6.30am–6.30pm; ⓣ01.60.77.20.20, ⓦwww.gihpidf.asso.fr) has taxicabs and minibuses fully adapted to wheelchairs; at least 24-hour advance notice is needed. **Aihrop** (Mon–Fri 10.15am–3pm, ⓣ01.41.29.01.29, ⓦwww.aihrop.com) arranges transport to and from the airports and within the city, though be sure to call ahead.

For **travel on the buses, métro or RER**, the RATP offers accompanied journeys for disabled people not in wheelchairs – *Les compagnons du voyage* – which costs €14 an hour and is available daily 6.30am–8pm. You have to book on ⓣ08.92.68.77.14 (Mon–Fri 6am–7pm, Sat & Sun 9am–6pm) at least a day in advance. As long as they are registered with the organization, **blind passengers** can request a free companion from the volunteer organization Auxiliaires des Aveugles (ⓣ01.43.06.39.68).

For **wheelchair-users**, around twenty RER stations are accessible, though only a very few, like Vincennes and Marne-la-Vallée (for Disneyland), can be used autonomously, while others, including Châtelet-les-Halles, Denfert-Rochereau, Gare de Lyon and Grande Arche de la Défense, require an official to work the lift for you. The new Météor métro line (14) and the RER line E are designed to be easily accessible by all, though there are no plans to improve accessibility to other métro lines. Most **bus lines** now have mechanical platforms for getting on and off and a designated wheelchair space in the bus; you can find a full list on the Paris transport site ⓦwww.ratp.fr – click on the wheelchair sign. You can also download a transport map of Paris showing exactly which RER stops are wheelchair accessible. Another useful source of information on getting around Paris (in French only) is ⓦwww.infomobi.com. A **Braille métro map** and a separate bus map are obtainable from L'Association Valentin Haûy (AVH), 5 rue Duroc, 7e (ⓣ01.44.49.27.27, ⓦwww.avh.asso.fr). **Cars with hand controls** (category O) can be rented from Hertz, usually with 48 hours' advance notice (in France call ⓣ01.39.38.38.38).

Paris contacts

APF (Association des Paralysés de France) 17 bd Auguste-Blanqui, 13e ⓣ01.40.78.69.00, ⓦwww.apf.asso.fr. A national organization providing useful information including guides on Paris (in French only) for disabled visitors. Their guide, *Paris comme sur des roulettes* (Paris on Wheels), detailing how to get about on wheels (not cars) in Paris, is available at FNAC, Virgin Megastore, Gilbert Jeune and other large bookstores, or can be downloaded from ⓦwww.coliac.cnt.fr, the site for the Comité de liaison pour l'accessibilité, which promotes the rights of the disabled in France. To download the guide look up *dans votre région* and click on Ile de France/Paris.

ⓦwww.jaccede.com A handy website (in French only) giving a list of museums, monuments and other public places in Paris that are accessible with a wheelchair.

The media

The French press is currently in something of a financial crisis – circulation is low, prices high and print costs some of the highest in Europe. Things are slightly healthier in TV, where the choice of stations has widened recently, though the quality of programmes isn't very high on the whole, with lots of light entertainment and dubbed foreign soaps. Some serious programmes, such as political and philosophical debates do exist, though, and make no attempt to dumb down for their audience.

Newspapers and magazines

British **newspapers**, the *Washington Post*, *New York Times* and the *International Herald Tribune* are widely on sale in the city on the day of publication. The free monthly *Paris Voice* magazine (ⓦwww.parisvoice.com), produced by the American Church at 65 quai d'Orsay, 7e, has good listings, ads for flats and courses, and interesting articles on current events. It's available from the church and from English-language bookshops (see p.395). *FUSAC* (France USA Contacts; ⓦwww.fusac.fr), a free American fortnightly available in various cafés, restaurants, shops and colleges, is also useful for flats, jobs, travel, alternative medicine, therapy and the like.

Of the quality **French daily papers**, the centre-left *Le Monde* is the most intellectual;

it is widely respected, though somewhat austere. Left-wing *Libération*, founded by Jean-Paul Sartre in the 1960s, is slightly more colloquial and choosy in its coverage, but its survival is currently in question as circulation dwindles. *Le Figaro* is the most respected right-wing national. The best-selling tabloid is *Le Parisien* (known as *Aujourd'hui* outside Paris), good on local news and events.

Weeklies of the *Newsweek/Time* model include the wide-ranging and socialist-inclined *Le Nouvel Observateur*, the centrist *L'Express* and staunchly Republican *Marianne*. The best investigative journalism is to be found in the weekly satirical paper *Le Canard Enchaîné*. *Charlie Hebdo* is a sort of *Private Eye* or *Spy Magazine* equivalent.

TV and radio

With the launch of TNT (télévision numérique terrestre), or digital terrestrial **TV**, in 2005, French viewers can now access fourteen free French TV channels, providing they have a decoder or are hooked up to satellite or cable. The main public channels are **France 2** (ⓦwww.france2.fr), which puts out variety acts, chat shows and crime series, and slightly more highbrow **France 3** (ⓦwww.france3.fr), which serves up drama, debates and arts programmes; **Arte/France 5** (ⓦwww.arte-tv.com) is a Franco-German cultural channel, with lots of documentaries and subtitled films. The two main commercial channels are distinctly lowbrow **TF1** (ⓦwww.tf1.fr), with dubbed soaps and reality shows, and **M6** (ⓦwww.m6.fr), which does mostly low-budget shows such as cookery and home improvement programmes, and kids' TV. The main French **news broadcasts** are at 8pm on F2 and TF1. The main subscription channel is **Canal Plus**, good for films and sports. In addition, there are numerous cable networks. At the end of 2006, France launched its own rolling news station, **France 24** (ⓦwww.france24.fr), in a bid to rival CNN and BBC World and put across a French outlook on world affairs. It broadcasts in both English and French, and has just launched an Arabic service. As well as politics, it covers arts and culture.

With a **radio**, you can tune into various English-language broadcasts. BBC (ⓦwww.bbc.co.uk/worldservice), Radio Canada (ⓦwww.rcinet.ca) and Voice of America (ⓦwww.voa.gov) list all the world service frequencies around the globe. You can also listen to the news in English on Radio France International (RFI; ⓦwww.rfi.fr) at 7am, 2.30pm and 4.30pm on 738kHz AM. For radio news in French, there's the state-run France Inter (87.8FM), Europe 1 (104.7FM), or round-the-clock news on France Info (105.5FM).

Crime and personal safety

Petty theft is as common in the crowded hang-outs of the capital as in most major cities; the métro, train stations and Les Halles are notorious pickpocket grounds. It makes sense to take the normal precautions. But the best security is having a good insurance policy, keeping a separate record of cheque numbers, credit card numbers and the phone numbers for cancelling them, and the relevant details of all your valuables.

If you need to **report a theft**, go along to the commissariat de police of the arrondissement in which the theft took place, where they will fill out a *constat de vol*. The first thing they'll ask for is your passport, and vehicle documents if relevant. Although the police are not always as cooperative as they might be, it is their duty to assist you if you've lost your passport or all your money. If you've lost something less grave, you could try the **lost-and-found office** at 36 rue des Morillons, 7e ☎01.55.76.20.20.

Should you be **arrested** on any charge, you have the right to contact your consulate (see below). **Drug use** is as risky, as severely punished and as common in France as anywhere else in Europe. If you're discreet, you're probably not likely to get caught, but if you do get caught don't expect the authorities – or your consulate – to be sympathetic just because you're on holiday.

Free legal advice over the phone (in French) is available from SOS Avocats (☎08.03.39.33.00; Mon–Fri 7–11.30pm; closed July & Aug).

Foreign embassies and consulates in Paris

Australia 4 rue Jean-Rey, 15e; Mº Bir-Hakeim ☎01.40.59.33.00, ⓦwww.france.embassy.gov.au.
Canada 35 av Montaigne, 8e; Mº Franklin-D-Roosevelt ☎01.44.43.29.00, ⓦwww.amb-canada.fr.
Ireland 4 rue Rude, 16e; Mº Charles-de-Gaulle-Etoile ☎01.44.17.67.00.
New Zealand 7 rue Léonard-de-Vinci, 16e; Mº Victor-Hugo ☎01.45.00.24.11, ⓦwww.ambafrance-nz.org.
South Africa 59 quai d'Orsay, 7e; Mº Invalides ☎01.53.59.23.23, ⓦwww.afriquesud.net.
UK 35 rue du Faubourg-St-Honoré, 8e; Mº Concorde ☎01.44.51.31.00, ⓦwww.amb-grandebretagne.fr.
US 2 av Gabriel, 1er; Mº Concorde ☎01.43.12.22.22, ⓦwww.amb-usa.fr.

The police

French **police** (in popular slang, *les flics*) are barely polite at the best of times, and can be extremely unpleasant if you get on the wrong side of them. You can be stopped at any time and asked to **produce ID**. If that does happen to you, it's highly inadvisable to be difficult or facetious.

Emergency numbers

Police ☎17 (or ☎112 from a mobile)
Medical emergencies/ambulance ☎15
Fire brigade/paramedics ☎18
Rape crisis (SOS Viol) ☎08.00.05.95.95
SOS Help (crisis line/any problem: 3–11pm) in English ☎01.46.21.46.46, ⓦwww.soshelpline.org.

The two main types of police – the Police Nationale and the Gendarmerie Nationale – are for all practical purposes indistinguishable. The CRS (Compagnies Républicaines de Sécurité), on the other hand, are an entirely different proposition. They are a mobile force of paramilitary heavies, used to guard sensitive embassies, "control" demonstrations, and generally intimidate the populace on those occasions when the public authorities judge that it is stepping out of line.

Racism and harassment

France has a bad reputation for **racist attitudes** and behaviour. There are occasional reports of unpleasant incidents such as hotels or restaurants claiming to be fully booked, and travellers of north African or Arab appearance may be unlucky enough to encounter outright hostility or excessive police interest. That said, Paris is an urbane and deeply cosmopolitan city, and most non-white travellers won't have any problems. Carrying your passport at all times is a good idea (everyone is legally required to have some identification on them in any case).

☎114 is a free national helpline for victims of **discrimination**. The police are unlikely to be sympathetic – your consulate may be more helpful. Full-on **sexual harassment** is extremely unusual, though female travellers from Anglophone countries may find ordinary male behaviour chauvinistic.

Living in Paris

Work

EU nationals can legally **work in France**, while most North Americans and Australasians (specialists aside) who manage to work and live in Paris do so on luck, brazenness and willingness to live in pretty grotty conditions. The days when Hemingway could live for months on his wife's dollars are definitely over. Unless you've got a serious trust fund, an exhausting combination of bar and club work, freelance translating, data processing, typing, busking, providing novel services like home-delivery fish'n'chips, teaching English or computer programming, dancing or modelling are some of the ways you'll need to get by. Great if you're into self-promotion and living hand-to-mouth, but, if you're not, it might be wise to think twice – and remember that unemployment in France is high.

Anyone staying in France for more than three months must have a **Carte de Séjour**, or residency permit – citizens of the EU are entitled to one automatically. You must apply for your *carte* within three months of your arrival in France at the préfecture in the arrondissement you are resident of. For other, non-EU citizens, it is more complicated and generally involves applying for a long-stay visa before leaving your home country; contact the French embassy in your country for your specific situation. France has a **minimum wage** (the SMIC – *Salaire Minimum Interprofessionnel de Croissance*); indexed to the cost of living, it's currently around €8.30 an hour (for a maximum 152-hour month). By law, all EU nationals are entitled to exactly the same pay, conditions and trade union rights as French nationals. Employers, however, are likely to pay lower wages to temporary foreign workers who don't have easy legal resources, and make them work longer hours. It's also worth noting that if you're a full-time non-EU student in France (see p.41), you can get a **non-EU work permit** for the following summer as long as your visa is still valid.

If you're looking for secure employment, it's important to begin planning before you leave home. A few **books** that might be worth consulting are *Work Your Way Around the World* by Susan Griffith, *Live and Work in France* by Victoria Pybus and *Summer Jobs Abroad*, all published by Vacation Work (Ⓦwww.vacationwork.co.uk). Another, slightly more irreverent, treatise is *Vagabonding* written by Rolf Potts and published by Villard.

Finding a job in a **French language school** is best done in advance. In Britain, jobs are often advertised in the *Guardian*'s "Education" section (every Tues) and in the weekly *Times Educational Supplement*. Late summer is usually the best time. You don't need fluent French to get a post, but a degree and a TEFL (Teaching English as a Foreign Language) qualification are usually required. A useful resource is *Teaching English Abroad* published by Vacation Work (see above), while the British Council's website, Ⓦwww.britishcouncil.org/jobs, has a list of English-teaching vacancies. If you apply for jobs from home, most schools will fix up the necessary papers for you. EU nationals don't need a work permit, but getting a *Carte de Séjour* and social security can still be tricky should employers refuse to help. It's quite feasible to find a teaching job once you're already in France, but you may have to accept semi-official status and no job security. For addresses of schools, look under "cours de langues" in the phone book (Ⓦwww.pagesjaunes.fr). Offering **private lessons** (via university noticeboards or classified ads), you'll have lots of competition.

For **temporary work** check the ads in *Paris Voice* and *FUSAC* (see p.36) and keep an eye on the noticeboards at the Anglophone churches: the American Church in Paris (65 quai d'Orsay, 7[e]; M° Invalides); St George's English Church (7 rue Auguste-Vacquerie, 16[e]; M° Charles-de-Gaulle/Etoile); St Michael's Anglican Church (5 rue d'Aguesseau, 8e; M° Madeleine); and the American Cathedral (23 av George V, 8e; M° Alma-Marceau). You could also try the noticeboards located in the offices of CIDJ at 101 quai Branly, 15e (Mon–Sat 10am–6pm; M° Bir-Hakeim), and CROUS, 39 av Georges Bernanos, 5e (RER Port-Royal), both youth information agencies which advertise a number of temporary jobs for foreigners.

The **national employment agency**, **ANPE** (Agence Nationale pour l'Emploi; Ⓦwww.anpe.fr), advertises temporary jobs in all fields and, in theory, offers a whole range of services to job-seekers; though it's open to all EU citizens, it is not renowned for its helpfulness to foreigners. If your French is up to par, France 5 (Ⓦhttp://france5.keljob.com) hosts an informative site that can help with your CV, interview questions and other job-seeking issues.

Other possible sources include the "Offres d'Emploi" (Job Offers) in *Le Monde*, *Le Figaro* and the *International Herald Tribune*, and noticeboards at English bookshops. Some people have found jobs **selling magazines** on the street and **leafleting** just by asking people already doing it for the agency address. The American/Irish/British **bars and restaurants** sometimes have vacancies. You'll need to speak French, look smart and be prepared to work very long hours. Obviously, the better your French, the better your chances are of finding work.

Although **working as an au pair** is easily set up through any number of agencies (lists are available from French embassies or consulates, and there are lots of ads in *The Lady* in the UK), this sort of work can be total misery if you end up with an unpleasant employer. If you're determined to try – and it can be a very good way of learning the language – it's better to apply once in France, where you can at least meet the family first and check things out. If you want to arrange it first through an agency try Avalon Au Pairs, in Britain (Ⓣ0800/298 8807, Ⓦwww.aupairsbyavalon.com), in the US the American Institute for Foreign Study (Ⓣ866 906 2437, Ⓦwww.aifs.com), or in Paris itself Accueil Familial des Jeunes Etrangers (Ⓣ01.42.22.50.34, Ⓦwww.afje-paris.org). These have positions for female au pairs only and will fill you in on the general terms and conditions (never very generous); you shouldn't get paid less than €280 a month (on top of board and lodging and some sort of travel pass). Working hours are officially capped at thirty hours a week, plus two or three evenings' baby-sitting.

Claiming benefit in Paris

Any EU citizen who has been signing on for **unemployment benefit** for a minimum period of four to six weeks at home, and intends to continue doing so in Paris, needs a letter of introduction from their own social security office, plus an E303 certificate of authorization (be sure to give them plenty of warning to prepare this). You must register within seven days with the Agence Nationale pour l'Emploi (ANPE), whose offices are listed under Administration du Travail et de l'Emploi in the Yellow Pages or ANPE in the White Pages.

French bureaucracy: a warning

French officialdom and bureaucracy can damage your health. That Gallic shrug and "*C'est pas possible*" is not the result of training programmes in making life difficult for foreigners: they drive most French citizens mad as well. Sorting out social security, long-stay visas, job contracts, bank accounts, tenancy agreements, university enrolment or any other financial, legal or state matter requires serious commitment. Your reserves of patience, diligence, energy (both physical and mental) and equanimity in the face of bloody-mindedness and Catch 22s will be tested to the full. Expect to spend days repeatedly visiting the same office and considerable sums on official translations of every imaginable document. Before you throw yourself into the Seine in despair, remember that others are going through it, too, and sharing the frustration may well help: the American Church (see p.39) is the place for such contacts.

It's possible to claim benefit for up to three months while you look for work, but it can often take that amount of time for the paperwork to be processed (also see box opposite). Pensioners can arrange for their **pensions** to be paid in France, but cannot receive French state pensions.

Study

It's relatively easy to be a **student** in Paris. Foreigners pay no more than French nationals to enrol on a course, and the only problem then is to support yourself. Your *Carte de Séjour* and – for EU nationals – social security will be assured, and you'll be eligible for subsidized accommodation, meals and all the student reductions. Few people want to do undergraduate degrees abroad, but for higher degrees or other diplomas, the range of options is enormous. Strict entry requirements, including an exam in French, apply only for undergraduate degrees.

Generally, French universities are much less formal than British ones, and many people perfect their fluency in the language while studying. For full details and prospectuses, go to the Cultural Service of any French embassy or consulate (see p.38 for the addresses).

Embassies and consulates can also give details of **language courses**, which often combine with lectures on French "civilization" and are usually very costly. In Britain, the **French Institute**, 17 Queensbury Place, London SW7 2DT (Ⓣ020/7073 1350, Ⓦwww.institut-francais.org.uk), can provide a list of language courses in France. Courses at the non-profit-making **Alliance Française** (101 bd Raspail, 6e; Ⓣ01.42.84.90.00, Ⓦwww.alliancefr.org; M° St-Placide) are fairly reasonably priced (€150 per week for three hours of class every day) and well regarded, while the **Sorbonne** (47 rue des Ecoles, 5e; Ⓣ01.40.46.22.11, Ⓦwww.ccfs-sorbonne.fr) has special short courses aimed at foreigners. Saying you studied French at the latter may impress your friends, but there are no entry requirements and the courses are very old-fashioned and grammar-based. US students could also get in touch with the **CIEE** (Council on International Educational Exchange; Ⓦwww.ciee.org), which can arrange gap-year and study programmes in Paris.

Student/youth organizations in Paris

Student information (CROUS) 39 av Georges-Bernanos, 5e Ⓣ01.40.51.36.00, Ⓦwww.crous.fr; RER Port-Royal. The University of Paris student organization, providing help with student accommodation and other services.

Youth information (CIDJ) (Centre d'Information et de Documentation de la Jeunesse), 101 quai Branly, 15e (Mon–Fri 10am–6pm & Sat 9.30am–1pm; Ⓣ01.43.06.15.38, Ⓦwww.cidj.com; M° Bir-Hakeim). Provides all sorts of information for young people and students, for example on studying in France, finding somewhere to live, etc.

Travel essentials

Electricity

220V out of double, round-pin wall sockets. If you haven't bought the appropriate adaptor (*adapteur*) or transformer (*transformateur* – for US appliances) before leaving home, try the electrical section of a large department store like BHV (see p.386).

Entry requirements

Citizens of EU (European Union) countries, and 31 other countries, including Canada, the United States, Australia, New Zealand and Norway, do not need any sort of visa to enter France, and can stay for up to ninety days. Citizens of all other countries must obtain a visa before arrival. A complete list of all French government websites, including embassies and consulates, can be found at Ⓦwww.gksoft.com/govt/en/fr.html.

Three types of tourist **visa** are currently issued: a transit visa (*visa de circulation*), valid for multiple stays of up to ninety days in a three-year period; a short-stay (*court séjour*) visa, valid for multiple stays of up to ninety days in a six-month period; and a long-stay (*long séjour*) visa, which allows for multiple stays of more than ninety days over three years, but which is issued only after an examination of an individual's circumstances. Note that it's very hard to get a long-stay visa if you've already arrived in France on a short-stay visa.

EU citizens and non-visa citizens who stay longer than ninety days are officially supposed to apply for a **Carte de Séjour**, for which you'll have to show a passport, birth certificate, proof of residence (eg an electricity bill or copy of a lease), details of a French bank account, evidence of health insurance (if you're not an EU citizen), and proof of adequate funds to support a long stay in France; you'll also need two stamped SAEs and three passport-size photos. Make your application at the Préfecture de Police, 9 boulevard du Palais, on the île de la Cité (Ⓦwww.prefecture-police-paris.interieur.gouv.fr), where there's a special counter. However, EU passports are rarely stamped, so there may be no evidence of how long you've been in the country. For further information on visa regulations consult the Ministry of Foreign Affairs website Ⓦwww.diplomatie.gouv.fr.

Insurance

Even though EU health-care privileges apply in France, you'd do well to take out an **insurance policy** before travelling to cover against theft, loss and illness or injury. Before paying for a new policy, however, it's worth checking whether you are already covered: some all-risks home insurance policies may cover your possessions when overseas, and many medical schemes include cover when abroad.

After exhausting the possibilities above, you might want to contact a specialist travel insurance company, or consider the travel insurance deal we offer (see box below). Many policies can be chopped and changed to exclude coverage you don't need – for example, sickness and accident benefits can often be excluded or included at will. If you do take medical coverage, ascertain whether benefits will be paid as treatment proceeds or only after you return home, and whether there is a 24-hour medical emergency number. When securing baggage cover, make sure that the per-article limit – typically under £500 – will cover your most valuable possession. If you need to make a claim, you should keep receipts for medicines and medical treatment (see "Health", p.33), and in the event you have anything stolen you must obtain an official statement from the police (called a *constat de vol*).

Internet

Many hotels now have **Internet terminals** in their foyer, which guests can use for free or for a small fee, and commercial Internet points have blossomed all over Paris. Most

Rough Guides travel insurance

Rough Guides has teamed up with Columbus Direct to offer you travel insurance that can be tailored to suit your needs. Products include a low-cost backpacker option for long stays; a short-break option for city getaways; a typical holiday package option; and others. There are also annual multi-trip policies for those who travel regularly. Different sports and activities (trekking, skiing, etc) can be usually be covered if required.

See our website (Ⓦwww.roughguidesinsurance.com) for eligibility and purchasing options. Alternatively, UK residents should call Ⓣ0870/033 9988; Australians should call Ⓣ1300/669 999 and New Zealanders should call Ⓣ0800/55 9911. All other nationalities should call Ⓣ+44 870/890 2843.

are open long hours and charge similar rates for access (usually €5 per hour with a one-hour minimum). Post offices also have terminals. You can get **free Wi-Fi** access in the Pompidou Centre, and by the end of 2007 the city authorities claim there will be 400 Wi-Fi hotspots throughout the city, including all 200 Paris gardens.

Laundry

You shouldn't have any trouble finding a **laundry** in Paris. If you can't immediately spot one near your hotel, look in the phone book under "Laveries Automatiques". They're often unattended, so come pre-armed with small change. Generally, self-service laundry facilities open at 7am and close between 7pm and 10pm. The alternative *blanchisserie*, or pressing services, are likely to be expensive, and hotels in particular charge very high rates. If you're doing your own washing in hotels, keep quantities small, as most forbid doing any laundry in your room.

Lost property

The **lost property office** (Bureau des Objets Trouvés) is located at the Préfecture de Police, 36 rue des Morillons, 15e; ⓣ08.21.00.25.25 (Mon & Wed 8.30am–5pm, Thurs 8.30am–8pm, Fri 8.30am–5.30pm; M° Convention). For property lost on public transport, phone the RATP on ⓣ01.40.30.52.00. If you lose your passport, report it to a police station and then your embassy.

Mail

French **post offices** (*bureaux de poste* or *PTTs*) – look for bright yellow-and-blue La Poste signs – are generally open from 8am to 7pm Monday to Friday, and 8am to noon on Saturday. However, **Paris's main office,** at 52 rue du Louvre, 1er (M° Etienne-Marcel), is open 24 hours (for all postal services, but not banking and money changing).

Standard letters (20g or less) and postcards within France and to European Union countries cost €0.60 and to North America, Australia and New Zealand €0.85. For sending letters, remember that you can also buy stamps from **tabacs**. For further information on postal rates, among other things, log on to the post office website ⓦwww.laposte.fr.

You can send **faxes** from post offices: the official French word is *télécopie*, but "fax" is commonplace. You can also use the Internet at post offices, change money, and make photocopies and phone calls. To post your letter on the street, look for the bright-yellow **post boxes**.

Parisian addresses

The **postcode** in Parisian addresses consists of the generic 750 plus the number of the arrondissement: so, for example, the 14e becomes 75014 Paris. *Bis* and *ter* (as in 4bis rue de la Fontaine) are the equivalent of "a" and "b".

Maps

The **maps** in this guide and the free *Paris Map* available from the tourist office (see p.46) should be adequate for a short sight-seeing stay, but for a more detailed map your best bet is the pocket-sized *L'indispensable Plan de Paris* 1:15,000, published by Atlas Indispensable; it comes in a robust plastic cover, and gives full A-Z street listings. Also very detailed, but rather more unwieldy, is the large fold-out Michelin no. 10, the 1:10,000 *Plan de Paris*. More conveniently sized are the *Rough Guide Map: Paris,* produced on waterproof, crease-resistant paper, and the *Falkplan*, which folds out only as you need it.

Opening hours and public holidays

Most shops, businesses, information services, museums and banks in Paris stay open all day. The exceptions are the smaller shops and enterprises, which may close for lunch sometime between 12.30pm and 2pm. Basic **hours of business** are from 8 or 9am to 6.30 or 7.30pm Monday to Saturday for the big shops and Tuesday to Saturday for smaller shops (some of the smaller shops may open on Monday afternoon). You can always find boulangeries and food shops that stay open on days when others close – on Sunday normally until noon. See above for standard banking hours.

Restaurants, **bars** and **cafés** often close on Sunday or Monday, and quite a few restaurants also close on Saturdays, especially at midday. It's common for bars and cafés to stay open to 2am, and even extend hours on a Friday and Saturday night, closing earlier on Sunday. Restaurants won't usually serve after 10pm, though some brasseries cater for night owls and serve meals till the early hours. Many restaurants and shops take a **holiday** between the middle of July and the end of August, and over Easter and Christmas.

Museums open between 9 and 10am and close between 5 and 6pm. Summer times may differ from winter times; if they do, both are indicated in the listings of the Guide. Summer hours usually extend from mid-May or early June to mid-September, but sometimes they apply only during July and August, occasionally even from Palm Sunday to All Saints' Day. Don't be caught out by museum **closing days** – usually Monday or Tuesday and sometimes both. **Churches** and **cathedrals** are almost always open all day, with charges only for the crypt, treasuries or cloister.

Public holidays

France celebrates eleven **national holidays** (*jours fériés* or j.f.) – not counting the two that fall on a Sunday anyway. Throughout the Guide, opening hours given for Sundays also apply to public holidays. With three and sometimes four holidays, **May** is a particularly festive month. It makes a peaceful time to visit, as people clear out of town over several weekends, but many businesses will have erratic opening hours. Just about everything, including museums, is closed on May 1. July 14 heralds the beginning of the French holiday season and people leave town en masse between then and the end of August.

Note that if a public holiday falls on a Tuesday or a Thursday, many people *faire le pont* ("bridge it") by taking an unofficial day off on the adjacent Monday or Friday.

National holiday dates

January 1 le Jour de l'an
Easter Sunday Pâques
Easter Monday Lundi de Pâques
May 1 la Fête du travail/May Day
May 8 la Fête de la Victoire 1945/VE Day
Ascension Day (40 days after Easter: mid-May to early June) l'Ascension
Whitsun (7th Sunday after Easter: mid-May to early June) la Pentecôte
Whit Monday (7th Monday after Easter: mid-May to early June) Lundi de Pentecôte
July 14 la Fête nationale/Bastille Day
August 15 l'Assomption/Feast of the Assumption
November 1 la Toussaint/All Saints' Day
November 11 l'Armistice 1918/Armistice Day
December 25 Noël

Phones

You can make international **phone calls** from any **telephone box** (*cabine*) and receive calls where there's a blue logo of a ringing bell. You'll need to buy a **phone card** (*télécarte*), as coin boxes have been phased out. **Credit cards** can be used in many call boxes.

If you're making a lot of calls it's worth buying a **card with a PIN** (*une carte à code*), available in various denominations from *tabacs* or newsagents, which can be used with a public or private telephone; just dial the toll-free number provided, followed by your PIN (given on the card) and then the number you want to reach. One of the best-value cards for calling abroad to Europe and the US is the Kosmos France/Monde card (ⓦwww.ksurf.net). Dozens of other companies sell similar cards, though beware of hidden connection fees and higher peak rates. Also, remember that ringing a mobile uses up credits much more quickly.

For **calls within France** – local or long-distance – dial all ten digits of the number. Paris and Ile-de-France numbers start with ⓣ01. Numbers beginning with ⓣ08.00 are free numbers; ⓣ08.10 is charged at local rates, no matter where you're calling from; all other ⓣ08 numbers are premium rate (from €0.34 per minute) and can't be accessed from outside France. Numbers beginning with ⓣ06 are **mobile** and therefore expensive to call (usually €0.40 per minute). Local calls are timed in France.

Off-peak charges (30 percent less than the peak rate, for local, long-distance and international calls) apply on weekdays between 7pm and 8am, and all day Saturday and Sunday, as well as holidays. Hotel phones usually carry a significant mark-up.

For French **directory enquiries** or **operator** assistance, dial ⓣ12.

International calls

To **phone abroad from Paris** (or from anywhere in France), dial ⓣ00 plus the country code, then the area code, minus the initial zero, followed by the local number you want to reach. International off-peak hours are the same as for domestic phone calls (see above). At peak rates, €1 gets you about five minutes to the EU countries and the US, or two minutes to Australia and New Zealand. For **international directory enquiries** dial ⓣ32.12, followed by your country code (€3 per call). You can, of course, make a reverse charge or **collect call** – known in French as *téléphoner en PCV*. To get through to the UK, dial the Home Direct number ⓣ0800.99.00.44 and ask for a "reverse charge call"; to get an English-speaking operator for North America, dial ⓣ0800.99.00.11. For other countries, use the standard PCV number ⓣ30.06.

To **call France from abroad**, use the IDD code for your country (00 or 011 in most cases) followed by the French country code (33), then the local number minus the initial "0". So to call Paris from the UK, Ireland, New Zealand and Netherlands dial ⓣ00 33 1 then the eight-digit number, or from the US, Canada and Australia, dial ⓣ011 33 1.

Mobile phones

The easiest – if most expensive – option for Europeans, Australians and New Zealanders wishing to make phone calls is to use a **mobile phone**. If you haven't used your mobile abroad before you'll probably need to contact your provider to get it activated for foreign use. Remember that you'll pay for people to call you while you're abroad. Note that France operates on the European GSM standard, so US cellphones won't work in France unless you've got a tri-band phone.

If you're making a lot of calls, consider buying a whole new phone on a pre-pay (*mobicarte*) package once in Paris. There are always cheap deals on offer. You could also use Call'Phone, a mobile phone **rental service** that charges you only for the calls you make. You can pick up and drop off the phone at the airport or have it delivered for free to your hotel (ⓣ01.48.62.37.53, ⓦwww.callphone.com; €0.70 per minute).

Sales tax

VAT (Value Added Tax) is referred to as TVA in France (*taxe sur la valeur ajoutée*). The standard rate in France is 20.6 percent; it's higher for luxury items and lower for essentials, but there are no exemptions. However, non-EU residents who have been in the country for less than six months are entitled to a refund (*détaxe*) of some or all of this amount (but usually around fourteen percent) if you spend at least €175 in a single trip to one shop. Not all stores participate in this scheme, though, so you'll need to ask first. The procedure is rather complicated: present your passport to the shop when you pay and ask for the three-page *bordereau de vente à l'exportation* form. They should help you fill it in and provide you with a self-addressed envelope. When you leave the EU, get customs to stamp the filled-in form (look for the *douane de détaxe* counter); you will then need to send two of the pages back to the shop in the envelope within six months; the shop will then transfer the refund through your credit card or bank. Some shops deduct the VAT there and then, but you still have to go through the procedure described above. The Centre de Renseignements des Douanes (ⓣ08.25.30.82.63, ⓦwww.douane.gouv.fr) can answer any customs-related questions.

Smoking

In February 2007 the first phase of a **ban on smoking** in public places in France, including transport, schools, shops and offices, was introduced, followed by a full ban in January 2008. Restaurants, bars and cafés and nightclubs are still allowed to have smoking rooms, but these now have to be strictly supervised and staff are not obliged to enter or serve them.

Time

Paris, and all of France, is in the **Central European Time Zone** (GMT+1): one hour ahead of the UK, six hours ahead of Eastern Standard Time and nine hours ahead of Pacific Standard Time. France is eight hours behind all of eastern Australia and ten hours behind New Zealand from March to October (but ten hours behind southeastern Australia and twelve hours behind New Zealand from October to March). In France, and all of the EU, **Daylight Saving Time** (+1hr) lasts from the last Sunday of March through to the last Sunday of October, so for one week in late March and/or early April North American clocks lag an extra hour behind.

Toilets

Ask for *les toilettes* or look for signs for the WC (pronounced "vay say"); when reading the details of facilities outside hotels, don't confuse *lavabo*, which means washbasin, with lavatory. French toilets in bars are still sometimes of the hole-in-the-ground squatting variety, and tend to lack toilet paper. Standards of cleanliness aren't always high. Toilets in railway stations and department stores are commonly staffed by attendants who will expect a bit of spare change. The tardis-like automatic public toilets on the streets, known as "sanisettes", are now free.

Tourist information

The main **Paris tourist office** is at 25 rue des Pyramides, 1er (June–Oct daily 9am–7pm, Sun 11am–7pm; Nov–May Mon–Sat 10am–7pm, Sun 11am–7pm; ⓣ08.92.68.31.12, ⓦwww.paris-info.com; M° Pyramides/RER Auber). There are **branch offices** at the Gare du Nord (daily 8am–6pm); at the Gare de Lyon (Mon–Sat 8am–6pm) by the Grandes Lignes arrivals; on the corner of the Champs-Elysées and avenue de Marigny (April to mid-Sept daily 9am–7pm; M° Champs-Elysées-Clémenceau); opposite 72 bd Rochechouart (daily 10am–6pm; M° Anvers); and 21 place du Tertre, 18e (daily 10am–7pm; M° Abbesses). The tourist offices give out information on Paris and the suburbs, and all but the place du Tertre branch can book hotel accommodation and also sell the Carte Musées et Monuments (see p.31) and Paris Visite travel passes (see p.28). You might also consider shelling out the €5 for their *Paris City Passport*, a guidebook of listings and attractions that's filled with nearly fifty coupons for discounts on various activities.

While you're there, pick up the free *Paris Map* – this might be behind the counter, so you'll need to ask. Within the Carrousel du Louvre, underground, below the triumphal arch at the east end of the Tuileries, is the **Espace du Tourisme d'Ile de France** (daily 10am–6pm; ⓣ08.92.68.30.00, ⓦwww.pidf.com), which has stylishly presented information on attractions and activities in Paris and the surrounding area.

Alternative sources of information are the **Hôtel de Ville information office** – Bureau d'Accueil – at 29 rue de Rivoli, 4^{e} (Mon–Sat 9.30am–6pm; ⓣ01.42.76.43.43, ⓦwww.paris.fr; M° Hôtel-de-Ville). For detailed **what's-on information** you'll need to buy one of Paris's **listings magazines**, *Pariscope* (€0.40) or *L'Officiel des Spectacles* (€0.35), available from all newsagents and kiosks. *Pariscope*, in particular, has a huge and comprehensive section on films and a small English section with weekly entertainment highlights, restaurant reviews and a special-interest page put together by *Time Out*. On a Wednesday, both *Le Monde* and *Le Figaro* bring out free listings supplements, offering a more discerning selection of events for the week. *Nova* magazine is good for nightlife listings. You could also keep a lookout for the free weekly listings newspaper, *A nous Paris*, which comes out every Monday and is available from métro stations. In addition, a number of small, pocket-sized independent nightlife guides (*Lylo* is a good one) can be picked up in many stores and cafés all over the city for free.

Weather

For the weather forecast for Paris and Ile-de-France ring ⓣ08.36.68.02.75, for the rest of France ⓣ01.36.68.01.01. Or go online at ⓦwww.meteofrance.com or ⓦwww.weather.com.

The City

The City

1

The Islands

There's nowhere better to start a tour of Paris than with the two river islands at the centre, the **Ile de la Cité** and the **Ile St-Louis**. The former is the core from which the rest of Paris grew and harbours the capital's most treasured monuments – the Gothic cathedral of Notre-Dame and the stunning Sainte-Chapelle – while the smaller Ile St-Louis, linked to the Ile de la Cité by a footbridge, has no heavyweight sights to speak of, but possesses a charm all of its own, with its handsome ensemble of seventeenth-century houses, villagey streets and tree-lined *quais*.

Ile de la Cité

The **Ile de la Cité** is where Paris began. It was settled in around 300 BC by a Celtic tribe, the Parisii, and the town that grew up was known as Lutetia Parisiorum. In 52 BC it was overrun by Julius Caesar's troops. A natural defensive site commanding a major east–west river trade route, it was an obvious candidate for a bright future – the Romans garrisoned it and laid out one of their standard military town plans. While they never attached any great political importance to the town, they endowed it with an administrative centre, constructing a palace-fortress that became the stronghold of the Merovingian kings in 508, then of the counts of Paris, who in 987 became kings of France.

The Frankish kings set about transforming the old Gallo-Roman fortress into a splendid palace, of which the **Sainte-Chapelle** and the **Conciergerie** prison survive today. At the other end of the island, they erected the great cathedral of **Notre-Dame**. By the twelfth century the small Ile de la Cité teemed with life, somehow managing to accommodate twelve parishes, not to mention numerous chapels and monasteries. It was all too much for the monks at one of the monasteries, the Saint-Magloire: finding the island too noisy, they moved out in 1138 to quieter premises on the right bank.

It takes some stretch of the imagination today to picture what this medieval city must have looked like, for nearly all of it was erased in the nineteenth century by Baron Haussmann, Napoléon III's Préfet de la Seine (a post equivalent to mayor of Paris), displacing some 25,000 people and destroying ninety streets (which had, it has to be said, become squalid and notoriously dangerous at night). In their place were raised four vast Neoclassical edifices, largely given over to housing the law and police. The few corners of the island that remain untouched by Haussmann include the **square du Vert-Galant** and **place Dauphine**, delightful havens of tranquillity.

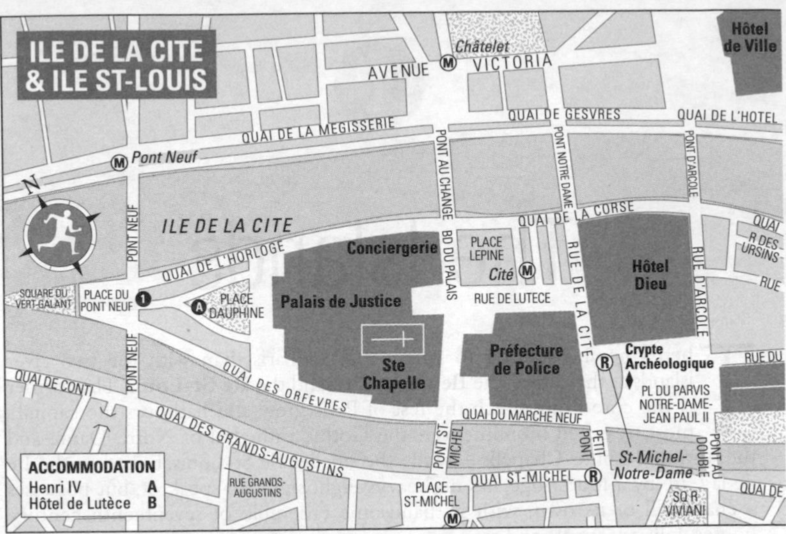

The cathedral, Conciergerie and Sainte-Chapelle inevitably attract large **crowds** and it's not unusual to have to queue for entry. Things are generally a bit quieter if you visit early in the morning or late afternoon.

Pont-Neuf and the square du Vert-Galant

A popular approach to the Ile de la Cité is via the graceful, twelve-arched **Pont-Neuf**, which, despite its name, is Paris's oldest surviving bridge, built by Henri IV. In 2007 it emerged from a lengthy period of cleaning and renovation, just in time for its four hundredth anniversary. Made of stone rather than wood and free of the usual medieval complement of houses, it was a radical departure from previous structures, hence its name "New Bridge". Henri IV, one of the capital's first great town planners, took much interest in the Pont Neuf's progress and would sometimes come by to inspect it, delighting the workmen on one occasion by taking a flying leap over an incomplete arch (some of his less agile companions ended up in the Seine).

So impressive was the bridge in scale and length that it soon became the symbol of the city itself and drew large crowds: pedlars, secondhand booksellers, flower sellers, dog-barbers and toothpullers set up stalls in the bridge's bays (now occupied by stone seats), while acrobats and actors entertained passers-by.

Henri IV is commemorated with an equestrian statue halfway across the bridge and also lends his nickname to the **square du Vert-Galant**, enclosed within the triangular stern of the island, reached via steps leading down behind the statue. "Vert-Galant", meaning a "green" or "lusty" gentleman, is a reference to the king's legendary amorous exploits, and he would no doubt have approved of this tranquil, tree-lined garden, a popular haunt of lovers – the prime spot to occupy is the knoll dotted with trees at the extreme point of the island. If being this close to the river gives you the urge to get out onto it, you could hop onto one of the river boats, the Bateaux-Vedettes du Pont-Neuf, that dock here on the north side of the *square* (for details of these and other river boats see p.29).

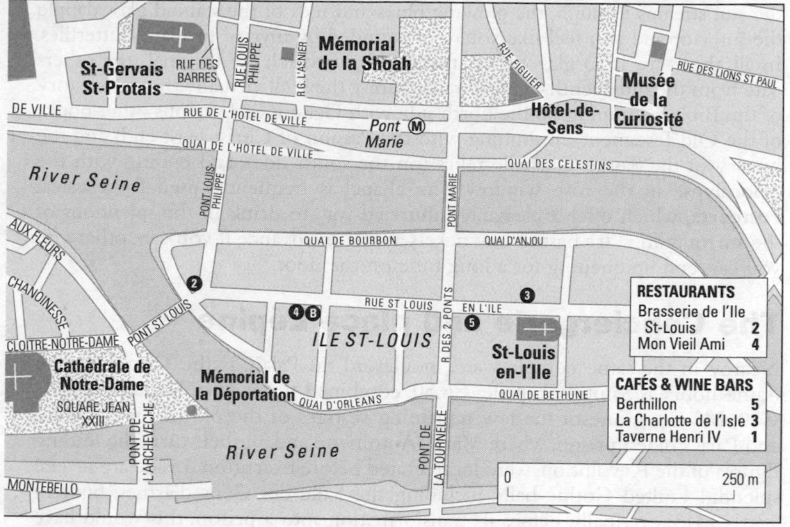

Place Dauphine and the Sainte-Chapelle

On the eastern side of the bridge, across the street from the statue of Henri IV, red-brick seventeenth-century houses flank the entrance to **place Dauphine**, one of the city's most secluded and attractive squares. The noise of traffic recedes and is likely to be replaced by nothing more intrusive than the gentle tap of boules being played in the shade of the chestnuts. The far end is blocked by the hulking facade of the **Palais de Justice**, which swallowed up the palace that was home to the French kings until Etienne Marcel's bloody revolt in 1358 frightened them off to the greater security of the Louvre.

The only part of the old palace that remains in its entirety is the **Sainte-Chapelle** (daily: March–Oct 9.30am–6pm; Nov–Feb 9am–5pm; €7.50, combined admission to the Conciergerie €10; M° Cité), its fragile-looking spire soaring above the Palais buildings and its excessive height in relation to its length giving it the appearance of a lopped-off cathedral choir. Though damaged in the Revolution, during which it was used as a flour warehouse, it was sensitively restored in the mid-nineteenth century, and remains one of the finest achievements of French High Gothic, renowned for its exquisite stained-glass windows. It was built by Louis IX in 1242–48 to house a collection of holy relics he had bought at an extortionate price – far more than it cost to build the Sainte-Chapelle – from the bankrupt empire of Byzantium. The relics – supposedly Christ's crown of thorns and fragments of the True Cross – are now kept in Notre-Dame's treasury and displayed only on certain days, including Good Friday.

The Sainte-Chapelle actually consists of two chapels: the simple **lower chapel** was intended for the servants, while the upper chapel, reached via a spiral staircase, was reserved for the court. The **upper chapel** is a truly dazzling sight, its walls made almost entirely of magnificent stained glass held up by powerful supports, which the medieval builders cleverly crafted to appear delicate and fragile by dividing them into clusters of pencil-thin columns. When the sun streams through, the glowing blues and reds of the stained glass dapple the interior and you feel like you're surrounded by myriad brilliant butterflies. In all, there are 1113 glass panels, two-thirds of which are original (the others date from the nineteenth-century restoration); they tell virtually the entire story of the Bible, beginning on the north side with Genesis and various other books of the Old Testament, continuing with the Passion of Christ (east end) and the history of the Sainte-Chapelle relics (on the south side), and ending with the Apocalypse in the rose window. The chapel is frequently used for classical **concerts**, which offer a pleasant, unhurried way to drink in the splendour of the surroundings. It's best to buy tickets a little in advance if you can, otherwise you can end up queuing for a long time on the door.

The Conciergerie and place Lépine

Nearby in the same complex, at 2 boulevard du Palais, is the **Conciergerie** (same hours as Sainte-Chapelle; €6.50, combined ticket with Sainte-Chapelle €10; M° Cité), one of the few remaining vestiges of the old medieval palace and Paris's oldest prison, where Marie-Antoinette and, in their turn, the leading figures of the Revolution, were incarcerated before execution. Inside are several splendid vaulted Gothic halls, including the Salle des Gens d'armes, built in 1301–1315; originally, before its transformation into a prison, this would have been the canteen and recreation room of the royal household staff. The far end is separated off by an iron grille; during the Revolution this area was reserved for the *pailleux*, prisoners who couldn't afford to bribe a guard for their own cell and had to sleep on straw (*paille*).

Beyond is a corridor where prisoners were allowed to wander freely – there's a number of reconstructed rooms here, such as the innocent-sounding "salle de toilette", where the condemned had their hair cropped and shirt collars ripped in preparation for the guillotine. On the upper storey is a mock-up of **Marie-Antoinette's cell** in which the condemned queen's crucifix hangs forlornly against peeling fleur-de-lys wallpaper.

Outside the Conciergerie stands the **Tour de l'Horloge**, a square tower built around 1350, and so called because it displayed Paris's first public clock. The ornate clock face, set against a background of fleurs de lys, is flanked with statues representing Law and Justice, added in 1585. The clocktower's bell, which would once have rung out to mark special royal occasions and would have sounded during the St Bartholomew's Day massacre (see p.447), was melted down during the Commune.

East from here is **place Lépine**, named after the police boss who gave Paris's coppers their white truncheons and whistles. The police headquarters in fact stands on one side of the square, better known as the Quai des Orfèvres to readers of Georges Simenon's Maigret novels, though rumour has it that the police will be moving out soon to new modern offices Livening up the square on the other side is an exuberant **flower market**, held daily and augmented by a chirruping bird market on Sundays.

Cathédrale de Notre-Dame

One of the masterpieces of the Gothic age, the **Cathédrale de Notre-Dame** (daily 7.45am–6.45pm; free; Ⓦ www.cathedraledeparis.com; M° St-Michel/Cité) rears up from the Ile de la Cité like a great ship moored by huge flying buttresses. Built on the site of the Merovingian cathedral of Saint-Etienne, itself sited on the old Roman temple to Jupiter, Notre-Dame was begun in 1160 under the auspices of Bishop de Sully and completed around 1345. The cathedral's seminaries became an ecclesiastical powerhouse, churning out six popes in the course of the thirteenth and fourteenth centuries, though it subsequently lost some of its pre-eminence to other sees, such as Rheims and St-Denis. The building fell into decline over the centuries, suffering its worst depredations during the Revolution when the frieze of Old Testament kings on the facade was damaged by enthusiasts who mistook them for the kings of France. Napoleon restored some of the cathedral's prestige by crowning himself emperor here in 1804, though the walls were so dilapidated they had to be covered with drapes to provide a sufficiently grand backdrop.

It was only in the 1820s that the cathedral was at last given a much-needed **restoration** – largely thanks to a petition drawn up by Victor Hugo, who had also stirred public interest through his novel *Notre-Dame de Paris*, in which he lamented the sorry state of the cathedral (Gothic architecture was particularly favoured by Romantic novelists like Hugo, who deemed the soaring naves of the great cathedrals singularly suited to sheltering "tormented souls"). The task of restoration was entrusted to architect-restorer Viollet-le-Duc, who carried out an extensive and thorough renovation – some would say too thorough – remaking much of the statuary on the facade (the originals can be seen in the Musée National du Moyen-Age, see p.130) and adding the steeple and baleful-looking gargoyles, which you can see close up if you brave the ascent of the **towers** (daily: April–June & Sept 10am–6.30pm; July & Aug Mon–Fri 10am–6.30pm, Sat & Sun 10am–11pm; Oct–March 10am–5.30pm; last entry 45mins before closing time; €7.50). Viollet-le-Duc's parting contribution was a statue of himself among the angels lining the roof: it's the only one looking heavenwards.

The **facade** is one of the cathedral's most impressive exterior features; the Romanesque influence is still visible, not least in its solid H-shape, but the overriding impression is one of lightness and grace, created in part by the filigree work of the central rose window and the gallery above. Of the magnificent **carvings over the portals** perhaps the most arresting is the scene over the central portal, showing the Day of Judgement: the lower frieze is a whirl of movement as the dead rise up from their graves, while above Christ presides, sending those on his right to heaven and those on his left to grisly torments in hell – the condemned include a fair number of what look like bishops and kings, suggesting that the craftsmen of the day were not without freedom to criticize the authorities. They weren't lacking in a sense of humour, either: all around this arch peer out alert and mischievous-looking angels, said to be modelled on the cathedral choirboys of the time. The left portal shows Mary being crowned by Christ, with scenes of her life in the lower friezes, while the right portal depicts the Virgin enthroned and, below, episodes from the life of St Anne (Mary's mother) and the life of Christ. These are masterfully put together, using visual devices and symbols to communicate more than just the bare bones story – in the nativity scene, for example, the infant Christ is placed above Mary to show his elevated status and lies on an altar rather than in a crib, symbolizing his future sacrifice.

Inside, you're struck immediately by the dramatic contrast between the darkness of the nave and the light falling on the first great clustered pillars of the choir, emphasizing the sacred nature of the sanctuary. It is the end walls of the transepts that admit all this light, nearly two-thirds glass, including two magnificent rose windows coloured in imperial purple. These, the vaulting and the soaring shafts reaching to the springs of the vaults, are all definite Gothic elements, while there remains a strong sense of Romanesque in the stout round pillars of the nave and the general sense of four-squareness. The **trésor**

Peter Abélard

On rue Chanoinesse, the cathedral school of Notre-Dame, forerunner of the Sorbonne, once flourished. Around the year 1200, one of the teachers was **Peter Abélard**. A philosophical whiz kid and cocker of snooks at the establishment intellectuals of his time, he was very popular with his students and not at all with the authorities, who thought they caught a distinct whiff of heresy. Forced to leave the cathedral school, he set up shop on the Left Bank with his disciples and, in effect, founded the University of Paris. Less successful, though much better known, is the story of his love life. While living near the rue Chanoinesse, behind the cathedral, he fell passionately in love with his landlord's niece, Héloïse, and she with him. She had a baby, her uncle had him castrated, and the story ended in convents, lifelong separation and lengthy correspondence. They were reunited in death and lie side by side in Père-Lachaise cemetery (see p.238).

(Mon–Sat 9.30am–6pm, Sun 1.30–5.30pm; €2.50) is unlikely to appeal unless ornate nineteenth-century monstrances and chalices are your thing.

Free guided **tours** (1hr–1hr 30min) take place in English (Wed & Thurs 2pm, Sat 2.30pm) and in French (Mon–Fri, though not 1st Fri of the month, 2pm & 3pm, Sat & Sun 2.30pm); gather at the welcome desk near the entrance. A leisurely way to take in the interior is at the free **organ recitals**, held every Sunday at around 4 or 5pm. The instrument, crafted by the great nineteenth-century organ-maker Aristide Cavaillé-Coll, is one of France's finest, with over six thousand pipes.

Before you leave, walk round to the public garden at the east end for a view of the **flying buttresses** supporting the choir, and then along the riverside under the south transept, where you can sit – in springtime with the cherry blossom drifting down. On the other side of the cathedral, to the north, lie **rues Chanoinesse**, **des Ursins** and **de la Colombe**, three of the few streets on the island to have survived Haussmann's attentions. There's nothing particularly special about them, but the old houses here give some flavour of the more atmospheric pre-Haussmann Ile de la Cité.

The kilomètre zéro, parvis and crypte archéologique

Notre-Dame isn't only at the heart of Paris, it's also the symbolic heart of the country – outside on the pavement by the west door is a spot, marked by a bronze star, known as **kilomètre zéro**, from which all main-road distances in France are calculated.

The large windswept square, built by Haussmann in the 1860s, in front of the cathedral is known as the Parvis (from "paradise") Notre-Dame – or at least it was until 2006, when it was renamed by the City of Paris as the **Parvis Notre-Dame/place Jean Paul II**, amid protests from green, gay, AIDS and pro-choice groups, unhappy about honouring a pope known for his uncompromising stance on contraception and abortion (although it's hard to see how their alternative proposal – "Esplanade des Religions et de la Conscience Universelle" – could have caught on).

For an idea of what the square might have looked like before Haussmann came along, it's worth descending the steps at the far end into the atmospherically lit **crypte archéologique** (Tues–Sun 10am–6pm; €3.30). This large excavated area under the *parvis* reveals remains of the original cathedral, Saint Etienne, as well as vestiges of the streets and houses that once clustered around Notre-Dame; most are medieval, but some date as far back as Gallo-Roman times and include parts of a Roman hypocaust (heating system).

Le Mémorial de la Déportation

At the eastern tip of the island is the stark and moving symbolic tomb of the 200,000 French who died in Nazi concentration camps during World War II

△ Lle St-louis

– Resistance fighters, Jews and forced labourers among them. The **Mémorial de la Déportation** (daily 10am–noon & 2–7pm, closes 5pm in winter; free) is scarcely visible above ground; stairs hardly shoulder-wide descend into a space like a prison yard and off here is a stifling crypt where thousands of quartz pebbles represent the dead; floor and ceiling are black, and it ends in a black, raw hole, with a single naked bulb hanging in the middle. On either side are empty barred cells. Above the exit are the words "Pardonne. N'oublie pas" ("Forgive. Do not forget"). In contrast, the little green park surrounding the memorial is more of a celebration of life and a popular hang-out on a fine evening.

The Ile St-Louis

The **Ile St-Louis** is arguably the most romantic part of Paris and prime strolling territory. Unlike its larger neighbour, the Ile de la Cité, it has no monuments or sights as such, save for a small **museum** at 6 quai d'Orléans devoted to the Romantic Polish poet Adam Mickiewicz (Thurs 2.15–4.30pm, Sat 9am–noon or by appointment on ⓣ01.43.54.35.61; €5). Instead, you'll find tall, austerely beautiful houses on single-lane streets, tree-lined *quais*, a school, a church, assorted restaurants and cafés, and interesting shops. The island feels somewhat removed from the rest of Paris, with its own distinct charm, an oasis little touched by the city's turbulent years of revolution and upheaval. Inhabitants of the island even have their own name – "Louisiens".

For centuries the Ile St-Louis was nothing but swampy pastureland, a haunt of lovers, duellists and miscreants on the run, until in the seventeenth century the real-estate developer, Christophe Marie, had the bright idea of filling it with elegant mansions, so that by 1660 the island was quite transformed. In the 1840s the Ile gained popularity as a Bohemian hang-out, much like the Ile de Louviers (see p.124) a decade earlier. The Haschischins club met every month on the ground floor of the **Hôtel Lauzun**, 17 quai d'Anjou. As the club's name suggests, hashish was handed round – apparently in the form of a green jelly – at these gatherings, attended by Manet, Balzac, Nerval and Baudelaire, among others. Baudelaire in fact lived in the building for a while in a small apartment on the second floor, where he wrote much of *Les Fleurs du mal* and ran up large debts furnishing his rooms with antiques. The *hôtel*, built in 1657 by Versailles architect Le Vau, has an intact interior, complete with splendid trompe l'oeil decorations; it's often used for government receptions, and is sometimes open for guided tours to the public – details are given in the "Visites conferences" section in *Pariscope* (see p.46).

Le Vau also built the splendid **Hôtel Lambert** at the tip of the island, 1 quai d'Anjou. Decorated by two of seventeenth-century France's greatest painters, Charles Le Brun, who painted Versailles' Galerie des Glaces, and Eustache Le Sueur, it's widely thought to be the most beautiful residence in Paris. Past inhabitants include Voltaire, who lived here with his mistress the Marquise du Châtelet, and the exiled Polish prince Adam Czartorisky, famed for his lavish parties attended by Chopin, George Sand, Delacroix and other luminaries. At the time of writing the current owner, Baron Guy de Rothschild, had put the house up for sale amid speculation that it could fetch up to a staggering 150 million euros.

A visit to the island wouldn't be complete without a stop at *M. Berthillon*, 31 rue St-Louis-en-l'Ile (see p.318); buying one of their exquisite sorbets or ice creams and then wandering down rue St-Louis-en-l'Ile, ice cream in hand, is something of a tradition. For absolute seclusion, head for the **southern quais**, or climb over the low gate on the right of the garden across boulevard Henri-IV to reach the best sunbathing spot in Paris. The island is particularly atmospheric in the evening, and an arm-in-arm wander along the *quais* is a must in any lovers' itinerary.

2

The Louvre

The **Louvre** – catch-all term for the palace and the museum it houses – cuts a grand Classical swathe right through the centre of the city, its stately ranks of carved pilasters, arches and pediments stretching west along the right bank of the Seine from the Ile de la Cité towards the Voie Triomphale. When François Mitterrand added a futuristic steel-and-glass pyramid bang in the middle of its courtyard in the late 1980s, he was making a statement: the Louvre was to be transformed from a dusty dinosaur into a modern, inspiring and accessible wonder of the world.

A cultural edifice as monumental and venerable as the Louvre no doubt needed a big broom to sweep away the cobwebs, but in opening up new wings to the public the state was only continuing a tradition started two hundred years earlier, when the French Revolution threw open the doors of the royal palace to the citizens of the new republic. And as architectural patron, Mitterrand was simply following in the footsteps of François I, Catherine de Médicis, Louis XIV, Napoleon, and all the other French rulers who have knocked down, rebuilt, extended or altered the palace. Even if you don't venture inside, the sheer bravado of the architectural ensemble is thrilling.

The palace is now almost entirely given over to the **Musée du Louvre**, one of the world's great museums, covering the finest European painting, sculpture and objets d'art from the Middle Ages to the beginnings of Impressionism, plus an unrivalled collection of antiquities from Egypt, the Middle East, Greece and Rome. Giant in scale and stature, the French collection is nothing less than the gold standard of the nation's artistic tradition.

Quite separate from the Louvre proper, but still within the palace, are three design museums under the aegis of **Les Arts Décoratifs**, dedicated to fashion and textiles, decorative arts and advertising.

The palace

The original **Palais du Louvre** was little more than a feudal fortress, begun by Philippe-Auguste in the 1190s to store his scrolls, jewels and swords, while he himself lived on the Ile de la Cité. Charles V was the first French king to make the castle his residence, in the 1360s – the ground plan of his new palace can be seen traced on the pavement of the Cour Carré – but it wasn't until 1546, the year before the death of François I, that the first stones of the Louvre we see today were laid by the architect Pierre Lescot. Henri II continued François I's plans, building the two wings that now form the southwestern corner of the **Cour Carré** (to the left of the clock tower). It's still possible to imagine how extraordinary and how graceful the building would have looked, a gleaming example of the new Renaissance style surrounded by the late Gothic of Charles V's day.

When Henri IV took charge in 1594, he began a project of typical ambition: to link the Louvre with Catherine de Médicis' Palais des Tuileries (see box, p.60), to the west. He got as far as building the long wing along the Seine that now forms the Grande Galerie (see p.67). The architects working under Louis XIII and Louis XIV were less bold, contenting themselves with completing the Cour Carré by largely copying Lescot's original facade. Altogether different in design, but no more architecturally innovative, is Claude Perrault's academically Classical colonnade facing rue de l'Admiral de Coligny, which somehow beat Bernini's stunning Baroque design for the same contract. Napoléon III's main contributions – the courtyard facades of the nineteenth-century Richelieu and Denon wings, designed by Visconti and Hector Lefuel – conservatively repeat the basic theme of the Cour Carré.

For all its many additions and alterations, the palace long remained a surprisingly harmonious building with a grandeur, symmetry and Frenchness entirely suited to this most historic of Parisian landmarks. That is, until 1989, when, following a century of stagnation, I.M. Pei's controversial **Pyramide** erupted from the centre of the Cour Napoléon like a visitor from another architectural planet. (Just for the record, the pyramid has 673 panes of glass, not *The Da Vinci Code*'s 666 – close, but then a miss is as good as a mile with numerology.) As part of Mitterrand's same "**Grand Louvre**" makeover, the basement Carrousel du Louvre shopping complex was created, its central chamber lit by the downward-pointing **Pyramide Inversée**. Used primarily for fashion shows and other glitzy, high-rent events, this space acquired brief

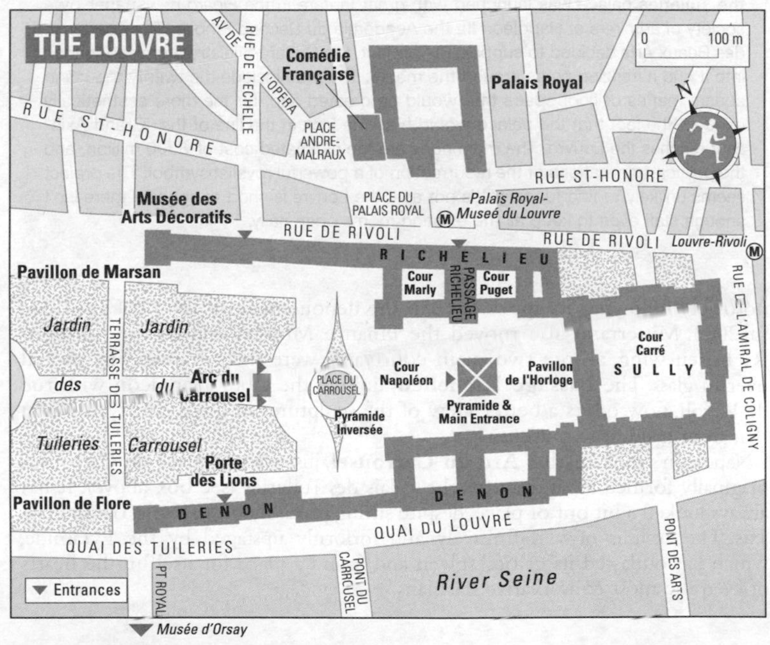

The lost Palais des Tuileries

For much of its life, the Louvre stood facing a twin sister some 500m to the west, the **Palais des Tuileries**. Built in 1559 for **Catherine de Médicis** shortly after the accidental death of her husband, Henri II, it was a place where she could maintain her political independence while wielding power on behalf of her sickly son, François II. It was apparently Catherine herself who conceived the idea of linking the two palaces by a *grande galerie* running along the right bank of the Seine, but in 1572 she abandoned the entire project. Tradition has it that she was warned by a soothsayer to "beware of St-Germain" if she wanted to live into old age – the Tuileries lay in the parish of St-Germain l'Auxerrois. It's more likely that the palace's situation just outside the protection of the city walls was the problem, as 1572 was a dangerous year: on August 24, the bells of St-Germain l'Auxerrois rang out according to a pre-arranged signal, whereupon radical Catholics set about the murder of some three thousand Parisian Protestants, possibly under the secret orders of Catherine herself.

It wasn't until forty years after the St Bartholomew's Day Massacre that the two palaces were finally linked, in the reign of Henri IV. Louis XIV moved across from the Louvre in 1667, but the court soon departed for Versailles, and the Tuileries remained largely empty until the Revolution, when Louis XVI was kept under virtual house arrest there by the revolutionary mob until the *sans-culottes* finally lost patience on June 20, 1792, breaking in and forcing the king to don the revolutionary red bonnet. The Tuileries was revived under Napoleon, who built the Arc du Carrousel facing its central pavilion, and its status grew still greater under his nephew, Napoléon III, who finally enclosed both royal palaces around a single gigantic courtyard, the whole complex being dubbed the Cité Impériale. This glorious perfection didn't last long: the Tuileries was set alight by the revolutionary Communards as they lost control of the city in May 1871 (see box, p.455).

Other buildings destroyed by the Communards, like the Hôtel de Ville, were swiftly rebuilt, but the ruins of the Tuileries were simply cleared away for the gardens that now bear the illustrious name (see p.84). But in February 2004 a campaign to **rebuild the Tuileries** palace was launched with great fanfare in the *Figaro* newspaper by a society of admirers of Napoléon III, the Académie du Second Empire. The Académie des Beaux Arts decided to support the project, the Culture Ministry promised to look into it and a frenzied press argued the merits. The pros include the twenty thousand square metres of floor space that would be created and, for the more aesthetically minded, the fact that the palace would hide the kink in the line of the "Grand Axis" as it reaches the Louvre. The main cons are the estimated cost of €300 million, and the political implications of the resurrection of a powerful royalist symbol. The project seems unlikely to find funding. It's not as if the Louvre is short of space – there isn't enough staff even to keep all the existing rooms open daily.

notoriety following its appearance in the denouement of *The Da Vinci Code*, in 2003. Mitterrand also moved the Finance Ministry out of the northern Richelieu wing, whose two main courtyards were then dramatically roofed over in glass. The **Passage Richelieu**, linking the Cour Napoléon with rue de Rivoli, now offers a better view of the sculptures in these courtyards than that from inside the museum.

Napoleon's pink marble **Arc du Carrousel**, just west of place du Carrousel, originally formed a gateway for the Palais des Tuileries (see box above). It has always looked a bit out of place, despite sitting precisely on the Voie Triomphale axis. The arch is now definitively and forlornly upstaged by the Pyramide, which has outlasted its critics' spleen and found a place for itself in the hearts of even the most conservative Parisians.

The museum

The origins of the **Musée du Louvre** lie in the personal art collection of François I, who in 1516 summoned Leonardo da Vinci from Milan to add some prestige to the French Renaissance. Leonardo brought his greatest works with him across the Alps, including the *Mona Lisa*, which remains the museum's most famous possession and the *idée fixe* of an unhealthy number of visitors. Later kings set up "cabinets" of artworks and antiquities in the Louvre, but these were very much private collections. Although artists and academics – as well as prostitutes – lived in the palace under Louis XIV, and the Académie royale de peinture et de sculpture mounted exhibitions here, known as *salons*, as early as 1725, the Louvre was only opened as an art gallery in 1793, the year of Louis XVI's execution. Turning the palace into a museum wasn't quite the revolutionary gesture it seems, however, as the original plan had been conceived in the 1740s, under Louis XV, and purchases began in 1779. The Revolution, if anything, delayed the creation of the museum. Within a decade of opening, however, Napoleon's wagonloads of war booty – not all of which has been returned – transformed the Louvre's art collection into the world's largest. The only major changes since then have been President Mitterrand's grand makeover in the 1980s, and the decision, in 2007, to license a "Louvre Abu Dhabi" annexe. The controversial annexe, which is due to open in 2012, will borrow pictures from the home collection, and help to subsidize the enormous running costs of what might now be called "Louvre France".

Though there are too many masterpieces to highlight here, few visitors will be able to resist the allure of the **Mona Lisa** (see box, pp.70–71), if only to see what the fuss is all about. If you're planning on a short visit, you might consider confining yourself to this, the **Denon section** of the museum, which also houses the rest of the Italian paintings and the great French nineteenth-century canvases, as well as **Italian** and **Classical sculptures**. A relatively peaceful alternative would be to focus on the grand chronologies of French painting and sculpture.

Orientation

At first overwhelming, the supremely rational **layout** of the museum can actually be quite fun to master. Core to the plan are the **three wings**, each accessible from under the great pyramid: Denon (south), Richelieu (north) and Sully (east, around the giant quadrangle of the Cour Carré). Within these wings, each floor falls into one of seven sections: Antiquities (Oriental, Egyptian and Classical); Sculpture; Painting; the Medieval Louvre; and Objets d'art. Some sections spread across two wings, or two floors of the same wing.

From the Hall Napoléon, under the Pyramide, stairs lead south into the **Denon wing**, by far the most popular area of the museum, with the must-see Italian masterpieces of the Grande Galerie, the famous nineteenth-century French large-format paintings and the *Mona Lisa*, all on the first floor. Denon also houses Classical and Italian sculpture on its two lower floors.

Serious lovers of French art will head north to the **Richelieu wing** for the French sculpture collection, the grand chronology of French painting, which begins on the second floor, and the superb objets d'art collection on the first floor, which includes everything French that's not painting or sculpture – furniture, tapestries, crystal, jewels. Richelieu also houses Middle Eastern antiquities and Islamic art (ground and lower ground floors), and northern

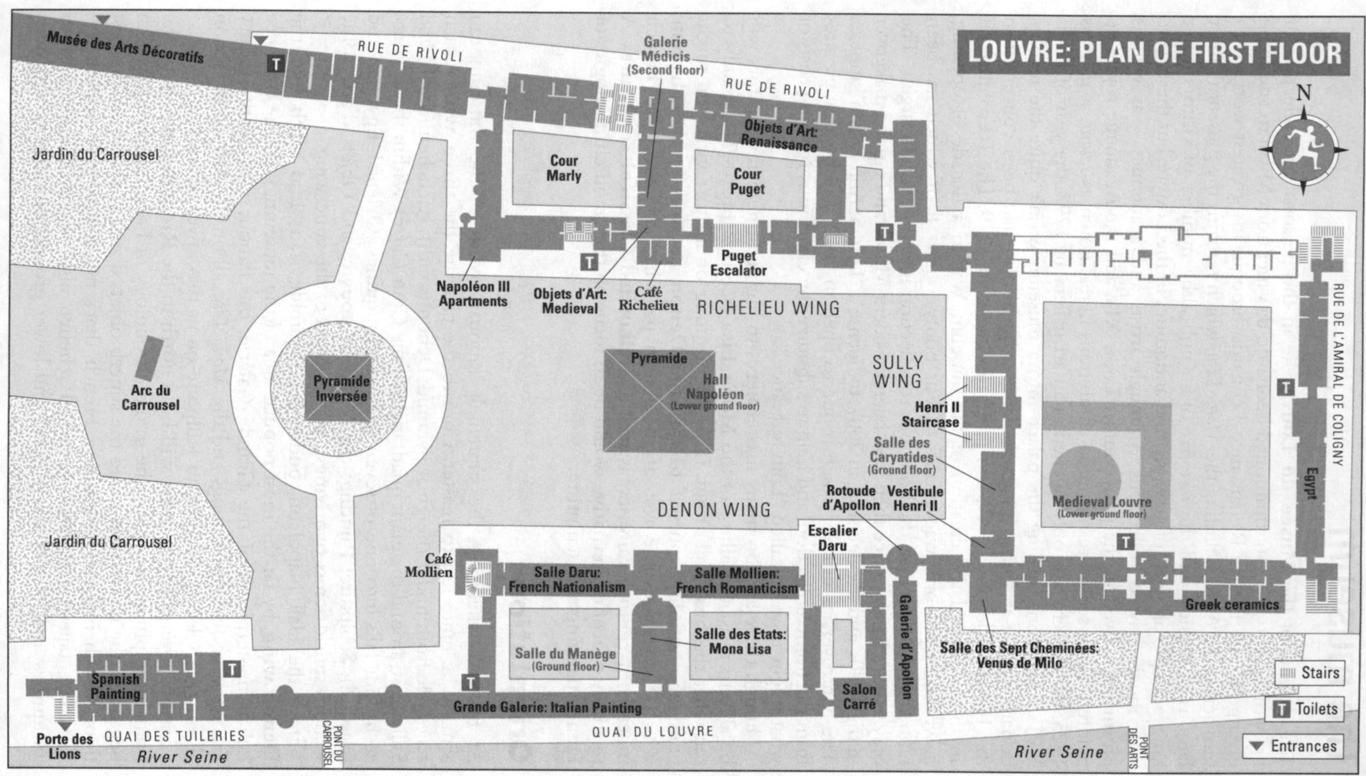
LOUVRE: PLAN OF FIRST FLOOR
N
Musée des Arts Décoratifs
RUE DE RIVOLI
Galerie Médicis (Second floor)
RUE DE RIVOLI
Objets d'Art: Renaissance
Jardin du Carrousel
Cour Marly
Cour Puget
Puget Escalator
Napoléon III Apartments
Objets d'Art: Medieval
Café Richelieu
RICHELIEU WING
Pyramide
Hall Napoléon (Lower ground floor)
SULLY WING
Henri II Staircase
Salle des Caryatides (Ground floor)
Arc du Carrousel
Pyramide Inversée
DENON WING
Rotoude d'Apollon
Vestibule Henri II
Medieval Louvre (Lower ground floor)
Egypt
RUE DE L'AMIRAL DE COLIGNY
Jardin du Carrousel
Escalier Daru
Café Mollien
Salle Daru: French Nationalism
Salle Mollien: French Romanticism
Galerie d'Apollon
Greek ceramics
Salle des Etats: Mona Lisa
Salle du Manège (Ground floor)
Salle des Sept Cheminées: Venus de Milo
Spanish Painting
Grande Galerie: Italian Painting
Salon Carré
Porte des Lions
QUAI DES TUILERIES
PONT DU CARROUSEL
QUAI DU LOUVRE
River Seine
River Seine
PONT DES ARTS
Stairs
Toilets
Entrances

European painting (second floor). It's here, too, that you'll find the most dramatic architecture, with the glazed-over courtyards and the Utopian escalators rising alongside the Cour Puget.

Rather fewer visitors begin with the **Sully wing**, although it's here that the story begins, with the foundations of Philippe-Auguste's twelfth-century fortress on the lower ground floor, and some fine rooms from the original palace above (see box, p.60). The floors above mostly continue chronologies begun in other wings, with antiquities from Greece and the Levant (ground floor), and the seventeenth- and eighteenth-century periods from the Objets d'art (first floor) and French painting (second floor) sections. The complete Pharaonic Egypt collection is here, too.

The Porte des Lions, on the Quai des Tuileries, provides one of the quickest ways into the museum, via the **Pavillon des Sessions**, whose half-dozen

Louvre practicalities and survival

Tales of queues outside the Pyramide, miles of energy-sapping corridors and paparazzi-style jostles in front of the *Mona Lisa* can leave you feeling somewhat intimidated by the Louvre before you've even set foot in the place. The following practical information and survival tips should help to make the most of a visit.

On fine days, queueing for the **main entrance** at the Pyramide at least gives you time to appreciate the geometric pyramids and fountains of the Cour Napoléon. If it's raining or the queues look too long it's worth making for the **alternative entrances**: via the Porte des Lions, just east of the Pont Royal (closes at 5pm), or directly under the Arc du Carrousel; the latter can also be accessed from 99 rue de Rivoli and from the line #1 platform of the Palais Royal-Musée du Louvre métro stop. If you've already got a ticket or a museum pass (see p.31) you can also enter from the Passage Richelieu. **Disabled access** is via the futuristic rising and sinking column in the middle of the Pyramide; visitors with limited mobility can also apply to visit on a Tuesday (call ⓣ01.40.20.59.90) – in which case you'll have the Louvre almost to yourself.

Opening hours for the permanent collection are 9am to 6pm every day except Tuesday (and January 1, May 1 and May 8), when the entire museum is closed. On Wednesdays and Fridays the museum stays open till 9.45pm. Almost a quarter of the museum's rooms are closed one day a week on a rotating basis, so if you're interested in a particular section it's worth checking the schedule on the museum noticeboards or online at ⓦwww.louvre.fr, though the most popular rooms are always open.

The **entry fee** is €9. Under-18s get in free at all times, and on the first Sunday of each month admission is free for everyone. **Tickets** can be bought in advance from branches of FNAC (see p.396), Virgin Megastore (conveniently, there's one right outside the entrance under the Arc du Carrousel) and the big Parisian department stores: Le Bon Marché, Printemps, Galeries Lafayette and BHV. You can also buy tickets by calling ⓣ08.92.68.46.94 or online via ⓦwww.louvre.fr, but as you have to go to a FNAC to pick them up anyway it's hardly worth it.

Your ticket allows you to step outside for a break, though the museum itself has three beautiful and only moderately overpriced **cafés**. The elegantly modern and relatively quiet *Café Richelieu* (first floor, Richelieu) has a wonderful summer-only terrace with a view of the Pyramide. *Café Denon* (lower ground floor, Denon) is small and cosy. *Café Mollien* (first floor, Denon) is much the busiest but also has a summer terrace. The various cafés and restaurants under the Pyramide itself are mostly noisy and unpleasant.

Don't attempt to see too much – even if you spent the entire day here you'd only see a fraction of the collection. If you want to explore the Louvre **in peace**, stay away from the Denon wing or, best of all, time your visit to coincide with the evening openings on Wednesdays and Fridays.

rooms currently house statuary from **Africa**, **Asia**, **Oceania** and **the Americas**. From the *pavillon*, a staircase leads up into Spanish and Italian paintings, just a few steps from the Grande Galerie.

It's well worth picking up a **floor plan** from the information booth in the Hall Napoléon, or at one of the alternative gates. This makes sense of it all by colour-coding the various sections, as well as highlighting a few of the best-known masterpieces. The only drawback is that it doesn't spotlight the magnificently decorated suites and rooms that give such a strong identity to certain sections of the palace (see box, p.60).

Painting

The largest section by far is **Painting**, divided into two areas on opposite sides of the museum, one devoted to French and Northern European painting, the other to Italian, Spanish and large-scale nineteenth-century French works. Interspersed throughout are rooms dedicated to the Louvre's impressive collection of **Prints and Drawings**, including prized sketches and preliminary drawings by Ingres and Rubens and some attributed to Leonardo da Vinci. Because of their susceptibility to the light, the drawings are exhibited in rotation.

French painting

The main chronological circuit of **French painting** begins on the second floor of the Richelieu wing, and continues right round the Cour Carré in the Sully wing. It traces the extraordinary development of French painting from its edgy pre-Renaissance beginnings through Classical bombast and on to ardent Romanticism, ending with Corot, whose airy landscapes anticipate the Impressionists. Surprisingly few works predate the Renaissance, and the preliminary Richelieu section is chiefly of interest for the portraits of French kings, from the Sienese-style *Portrait of John the Good* to Jean Fouquet's pinched-looking *Charles VII* and Jean Clouet's noble *François I*, who attracted numerous Italian artists to his court. Look out too for the strange atmosphere of the two **Schools of Fontainebleau** (rooms 9 and 10), which were heavily influenced by Italian Mannerist painting. Two portraits of royal mistresses are provocatively erotic: from the First School of Fontainebleau (1530s), Henri II's mistress, Diane de Poitiers, is depicted semi-nude as the huntress Diana, while in a Second School piece from the 1590s, Gabrielle d'Estrées, the favourite of Henri IV, is shown sharing a bath with her sister, pinching her nipple as if plucking a cherry.

It's not until the seventeenth century, when Poussin breaks onto the scene (room 13), that a definitively French style emerges. As the undisputed master of **French classicism**, his profound themes, taken from antiquity, the Bible and mythology, were to influence generations of artists to come. *The Arcadian Shepherds*, showing four shepherds interpreting the inscription "et in arcadia ego" (I, too, in Arcadia), has been taken to mean that death exists even in pastoral paradise. You'll need a healthy appetite for Classicism in the next suite of rooms, but there are some arresting portraits by Hyacinthe Rigaud, whose *Louis XIV* shows all the terrifying power of the king, and Philippe de Champaigne, whose portrait of his patron Cardinal Richelieu is even more imposing. The paintings of Georges de la Tour are more idiosyncratic. *Card Sharp* is compelling for its uneasy poise and strange lack of depth, though his *Christ with Joseph in the Carpenter's Shop* is a more typical work, mystically lit by a single candle.

Moving into the rather less severe **eighteenth century**, the more intimate paintings of Watteau come as a relief, as do Chardin's intense still lifes – notably *The Skate* – and the inspired rococo sketches by Fragonard known as the *Figures*

△ The Galerie and Apollon

of Fantasy, traditionally thought to have been completed in just one hour. From the southern wing of Sully to the end of this section, the chilly wind of **Neoclassicism** blows through the post-Revolution paintings of Gros, Gérard, Prud'hon, David and Ingres, contrasting with the more sentimental style that begins with Greuze, and continues into the **Romanticism** of Géricault and Delacroix, which largely supplanted the Neoclassical style from the 1820s onwards. Ingres' exquisite portraits were understandably much in demand in his day, but his true predilection was for historical subject matter and the female form, the latter appearing throughout the whole of his career, in his bathers from 1808 and 1828 and in his *Turkish Bath*, at once sensuous and abstracted. The final set of rooms takes in Millet, Corot and the **Barbizon school** of painting, the precursor of Impressionism. For anything later than 1848 you'll have to head over to the Musée d'Orsay.

Northern European painting

The western end of Richelieu's second floor is given over to a relatively selective collection of **German**, **Flemish** and **Dutch** paintings, though the seventeenth-century Dutch suite is strong, with no fewer than twelve paintings by Rembrandt – look out for *Bathsheba* and *The Supper at Emmaus* in room 31 – and two serene canvases from Vermeer, *The Astronomer* and *The Lacemaker*, in room 37. An awesome set of two-dozen works by Rubens can be found in the **Galerie Médicis** (room 18), a stripped-down modern replica of what was originally a giant room in the Palais du Luxembourg (see p.145). The entire cycle is dedicated to the glory of Queen Marie de Médicis, as commissioned by herself. Rubens painted the entire 300 square metres of canvas himself, and his swirling colours and swathes of flapping cloth were to influence French painters from Fragonard to Delacroix.

Italian and Spanish painting

Over in the Denon wing, on the first floor, the second area of the Louvre devoted to painting is dominated by the staggering **Italian collection**. The first two rooms house frescoes including two exquisite Botticelli allegories painted for the Villa Lemmi near Florence. Next, the high-ceilinged **Salon Carré** (room 3), used to exhibit paintings since the first exhibition or "salon" of the Académie royale in 1725, displays the so-called Primitives, with thirteenth- to fifteenth-century works from Italian painters such as Giotto, Cimabue and Fra

Inside the palace

From the Hall Napoléon, under the glass pyramid, it's easy to be lured straight into the Denon wing and its super-celebrity collection of Italian paintings. But if you take the entrance marked "Sully" instead, you can reach the same section of the museum while passing through some of the **finest rooms** remaining from the days when the Louvre was a palace rather than a museum.

On the lowest level of the Sully wing you can continue through to the Louvre's medieval foundations (see p.72), or take the Henri II staircase up to the Renaissance Salle des Caryatides (room 17; see p.72), on the ground floor. Up again, on the first floor, there's a succession of finely decorated rooms: the Vestibule Henri II, where the gilded sixteenth-century ceiling is graced with George Braque's *The Birds* (room 33; see p.72); the Salle des Sept Cheminées, once the royal bedroom (room 74); and the Rotonde d'Apollon (off room 34), built for Louis XIV by Le Vau, the architect of Versailles. Most stunning of all is the golden Galerie d'Apollon (room 66), its utterly splendid decor conceived by Charles Le Brun in 1661. It represents Louis XIV (the Sun King) as Apollo (the sun god), Eugène Delacroix adding his *Apollo Slaying the Serpent Python* to the central medallion of the ceiling in 1851. Set in a glass case amid the splendour are the crown jewels of France, including the mammoth Regent diamond sported by Louis XV, Louis XVI, Charles X and Napoleon I. It's particularly atmospheric at night. From here you can skirt the grand Escalier Daru (see p.72) to enter the Italian painting section, passing through the lofty Salon Carré (room 3) on your way to the Grande Galerie (rooms 5–12).

For architectural gems from the grand Third Empire remodelling, seek out the Salle du Manège on the ground floor of Denon (room A; see p.72), and the Appartements Napoléon III on the first floor of Richelieu (see p.60). Apart from the Hall Napoléon, under the main pyramid, the highlights of the Louvre's most recent transformation, under I.M. Pei, are the Pyramide Inversée in the Carrousel du Louvre shopping complex (see p.59), the two glazed-over courtyards of the Richelieu wing (see p.60), and the magnificent escalator climbing alongside the Cour Puget.

Angelico, as well as one of Uccello's bizarrely theoretical panels of the Battle of San Romano.

To the west of the Salon, the famous **Grande Galerie**, originally built to link the Louvre and Tuileries palaces, stretches into the distance on a ribbon of pale, perfect parquet. On its walls, it parades all the great names of the Italian Renaissance, kicking off with Mantegna's opulent *Madonna of Victory* and his meticulous miniature of the Crucifixion, and continuing through Giovanni Bellini, Filippo Lippi, Raphael, Coreggio and Titian, in the first part of the gallery alone. Leonardo da Vinci's *Virgin of the Rocks*, *St John the Baptist* and *Virgin and Child with St Anne* are on display just after the first set of pillars, untroubled by crowds. Roughly halfway along the Grande Galerie, the Mannerists make their entrance with a wonderfully weird *St Anne with Four Saints* by Il Pontormo and a Rosso Fiorentino *Pietà*. The later part of the Galerie dwindles in quality and breadth as it moves towards the eighteenth century.

The relatively small **Spanish collection** is relegated to the far end of Denon but has a few gems, notably Murillo's tender *Beggar Boy*, and the *Marquise de Santa Cruz* amongst the Goya portraits. From room 32, stairs lead down to the ground floor and the temporary section on the art of Africa, Asia, Oceania and the Americas.

French Nationalism and Romanticism

Running parallel to the Grande Galerie are two giant rooms dedicated to post-Revolution **French Nationalism** and early to mid-nineteenth-century Romanticism. The plan labels this section "large-format French paintings", and it features some of the best-known French works. The Salle Mollien (room 75) boasts David's epic *Coronation of Napoleon I*, in which Napoleon is shown crowning himself with a rather crestfallen clergy in the background; almost unbelievably, David conceived this work as part of a much larger composition. Nearby are some fine portraits of women, including Prud'hon's Leonardo-like *Josephine in the Park at Malmaison*, some compellingly perfect canvases by Ingres and a self-portrait (with her daughter) by Elisabeth-Louise Vigée Lebrun, the court artist to Marie-Antoinette.

In the Salle Daru (room 77), **Romanticism** is heralded by Géricault's dramatic *Raft of the Medusa*, based on a notorious incident off the coast of Senegal in 1816. The survivors are seen despairing as a ship disappears over the horizon – as a survivor described it, "from the delirium of joy we fell into profound despondency and grief". The fifteen shown here were the last of 150 shipwrecked sailors who had escaped on the raft – thirst, murder and cannibalism having carried off the rest. The dead figure lying face down with his arm extended was modelled by Delacroix, whose *Liberty Leading the People* also hangs in this room; Delacroix's work is a famous icon of revolution, though you can tell by the hats that it depicts the 1830 revolution, which brought in the "bourgeois king" Louis-Philippe, rather than that of 1789. On seeing the painting, Louis-Philippe promptly ordered it kept out of sight so as not to give anyone dangerous ideas.

The Salle des Etats and Mona Lisa

After five years of restoration, the **Salle des Etats** (room 6) is once again the proud setting for Leonardo da Vinci's **Mona Lisa** (see box, pp.70–71). You normally have to enter via the room between the Salles Daru and Mollien (see above). If you want to meet *la Joconde* – as she's known to the French – without the usual swarm for company, be the first to arrive or the last to leave. Better still, come for one of the evening opening sessions on Wednesdays and Fridays; 8pm to 9.45pm is the best time. At busy periods, you may find yourself jostling for a glimpse for a few hectic moments before being unceremoniously hussled out into the relative hush of the Grande Galerie by the *gardiens*.

Elsewhere in the same room, you can't miss Paolo Veronese's huge *Marriage at Cana*, which once hung in the refectory of Venice's island monastery of San Giorgio Maggiore. Sadly, there's little chance to enjoy the other Venetian works nearby in peace.

Sculpture

The museum's extensive collection of **French Sculpture** is arranged on the lowest two levels of the Richelieu wing, with the more monumental pieces housed in two grand, glass-roofed courtyards. Many sculptures removed from the park at Marly-le-Roi grace the Cour Marly, notably the four triumphal equestrian statues known as the *Marly Horses*, two by Coysevox for Louis XIV, at the top of the stairs, and two by Costou for Louis XV, on the tall plinths to the side of the courtyard. Cour Puget has Pierre Puget's dynamic *Milon de Crotone* as its centrepiece, the lion's claws tearing into Milon's apparently soft flesh and the entire piece writhing around its skilfully diffused axis.

The surrounding rooms trace the development of sculpture in France from painful Romanesque Crucifixions through to the nineteenth century and the lofty public works of David d'Angers. Among the startlingly realistic Gothic pieces, you can't miss the Burgundian *Tomb of Philippe Pot*, borne by hooded mourners known as *pleurants*. The Italian influence is strongly felt in Michel Colombe's relief of *St George Slaying the Dragon*, but there is something distinctively French in the strangely liquid bas-reliefs sculpted by Jean Goujon in the 1540s, at around the same time as he was working on Lescot's facade for the Cour Carré. Towards the end of the course you may find yourself crying out for an end to all the gracefully perfect nudes and grandiose busts of noblemen. The charming vignette of François Rude's *Neapolitan Fisherboy* provides some respite, but the only real antidote is Rodin and you'll have to leave the Louvre to see any of his works, as he postdates the 1848 watershed.

Alternatively, make for the smaller, more intense **Italian sculpture** section in the long Galerie Mollien (room 4), on the ground and basement floors of Denon. Here you'll find such bold masterpieces as two of Michelangelo's writhing *Slaves*, the anonymous *Veiled Woman* and Canova's irresistible *Cupid and Psyche*. At the gallery's western end, the grand Escalier Mollien leads up towards the main painting section (see p.64) while, immediately below, in the old stables on the lower ground floor (room 1), you'll find early Italian sculpture, notably Duccio's virtuoso *Virgin and Child Surrounded by Angels*, and the **Tactile Gallery**, where you can run your hands over copies of some of the most important sculptures from the collection. In the small, adjacent rooms A–C you can seek out some severe but impressive **Gothic Virgins** from Flanders and Germany.

Objets d'art

The vast **Objets d'art** section, on the first floor of the Richelieu wing, presents the finest tapestries, ceramics, jewellery and furniture commissioned by France's most wealthy and influential patrons, beginning with an exquisite little equestrian sculpture of Charlemagne (or possibly it's Charles the Bald) and continuing through 81 relentlessly superb rooms to a salon decorated in the style of Louis-Philippe, the last king of France. Walking through the entire chronology is an enlightening experience, giving a powerful sense of the evolution of aesthetic taste at its most refined and opulent. The exception is the Middle Ages section, of a more pious nature, which includes carved ivories, Limoges enamels, and three precious vases commissioned by Abbot Suger, the mastermind of the Gothic basilica at St-Denis.

Numerous rooms have been partially re-created in the style of a particular epoch, and in these surroundings it's not hard to imagine yourself strutting through a Renaissance chamber or gracing an eighteenth-century salon, especially as whole suites are often devoid of other visitors. The apotheosis of the whole experience comes towards the end, as the circuit passes through the breathtaking **apartments** of Napoléon III's Minister of State (room 87), full of plush upholstery, immense chandeliers, gilded putti and dramatic ceiling frescoes, in true Second Empire style.

An even more astonishing outpost of the Objets d'art collection lies on the far side of the museum, in the splendidly gilded **Galerie d'Apollon** (see p.66).

Antiquities

The enormous **Antiquities** collection practically forms a parallel museum of its own, taking up most of the Sully wing, other than the top floor, and creeping into Denon and Richelieu on the lower levels. The embarrassment of riches, a perennial problem for visitors to the Louvre, is at its most intractable here. The superb Egyptian collection reflects the long-standing French fascination with Egyptology, while the outstanding Greek and Roman collections date back to the eager acquisitions of François I, Richelieu and Mazarin. The so-called Oriental section, which presents a major collection of artefacts from the Near and Middle East, is relatively manageable in size.

Oriental Antiquities

Oriental Antiquities (Richelieu wing, ground floor) covers the sculptures, stone-carved writings, pottery and other relics of the ancient Middle and Near East, including the Mesopotamian, Sumerian, Babylonian, Assyrian and Phoenician civilizations, plus the art of ancient Persia. The highlight of this section is the boldly sculpted stonework, much of it in relief. Watch out for the statues and busts depicting the young Sumerian prince Gudea, and the black, two-metre-high Code of Hammurabi, which dates from around 1800 BC, during the Mesopotamian civilization. Standing erect like a warning finger, a series of royal precepts (the "code") is crowned with a stern depiction of the king meeting the sun god Shamash, dispenser of justice. The Cour Khorsabad, adjacent, is dominated by two giant Assyrian winged bulls (one is a reproduction) that once acted as guardians to the palace of Sargon II, from which many treasures were brought to the Louvre. The utterly refined **Arts of Islam** collection lies below, on the lower ground floor. Bizarrely, the so-called *Baptistery of St Louis*, an exquisite fourteenth-century Syrian brass bowl, was used for numerous royal christenings in the nineteenth century.

Egyptian Antiquities

Jean-François Champollion, who translated the hieroglyphics of the Rosetta Stone, was the first curator of the collection of **Egyptian Antiquities** – now the biggest and most important in the world after the Egyptian Museum in

The Mona Lisa

The **Mona Lisa** receives some six million visitors a year. Reason enough to smile, maybe, but how did a small, rather dark sixteenth-century portrait acquire such unparalleled celebrity? It can't be Leonardo's sheer excellence, as other virtuoso works of his hang nearby, largely ignored. Nor the painting's famously seductive air – even if Napoleon was so captivated that he had the picture hung in his bedroom in the Tuileries, there are other, far sexier portraits in the Louvre. (Sadly, the nude version Leonardo apparently painted has been lost for centuries, and is known only from early copies.) Instead, the answer to the mystery of the Mona Lisa's fame lies in its own story.

"Mona Lisa" is, in fact, an English corruption of Monna Lisa – the sixteenth-century historian Giorgio Vasari's polite way of referring to *madonna* (my lady) Lisa Gherardini, the wife of one Francesco del Giocondo. It's from his surname that the Italians get their name for the painting, *la Gioconda*, and the French their *la Joconde*, and it may even explain the Mona Lisa's "smile", as *giocondo* means "light-hearted" in Italian. Vasari, however, claimed Lisa smiled because Leonardo employed singers and jesters to keep her happy, while some modern critics have interpreted her half-and-half expression as symbolizing pleasure or Christian joy or firmness – in contrast with the opposing qualities represented by the darker, unsmiling half of her face.

In fact, it's not even certain that the *Mona Lisa* depicts Monna Lisa. The portrait Vasari described (though he'd never actually seen it himself), had eyebrows where the hair "grows thickly in one place" (the *Mona Lisa* has none) and "parting lips" (she smiles, but her mouth is closed). What is at least certain is that the *Mona Lisa* turned up in the bathroom of Fontainebleau, which Henri IV decided to restore in the 1590s. It remained neglected by public and art historians alike until, after it had been hanging in the Louvre for almost seventy years, the poet and novelist Théophile Gautier turned his hand to a guidebook to the museum. He singled out the "adorable Joconde" for praise: "She is always there smiling with sensuality, mocking her numerous lovers. She has the serene countenance of a woman sure that she will remain beautiful forever." A few years later, Gautier's erotic obsession had deepened, and the myth of the smile was given its finest articulation: "the sinuous, serpentine mouth, turned up at the corners in a violet penumbra, mocks the viewer with such sweetness, grace and superiority that we feel timid, like schoolboys in the presence of a duchess."

In England, the painting was made famous by the prose stylist, Walter Pater, in 1869. According to him: "The presence that rose thus so strangely beside the waters, is expressive of what in the ways of a thousand years men had come to desire… She is older than the rocks among which she sits; like the vampire, she has been dead many times, and learned the secrets of the grave; and has been a diver in deep seas,

Cairo. Starting on the ground floor of the Sully wing, the thematic circuit leads up from the atmospheric crypt of the Sphinx (room 1) to the Nile, source of all life in Egypt, and takes the visitor through the everyday life of pharaonic Egypt by way of cooking utensils, jewellery, the principles of hieroglyphics, musical instruments, sarcophagi, a host of mummified cats and dozens of examples of the delicate naturalism of Egyptian decorative techniques, such as the wall tiles depicting a piebald calf galloping through fields of papyrus, and a duck taking off from a marsh.

Upstairs, on the first floor, the chronological circuit keeps the masterpieces on the right-hand side, while numerous pots and statuettes of more specialist interest are displayed to the left. Among the major exhibits are the *Great Sphinx*, carved from a single block of pink granite; the polychrome statue *Seated Scribe*;

and keeps their fallen day about her; and trafficked for strange webs with Eastern merchants; and, as Leda, was the mother of Helen of Troy, and, as Saint Anne, the mother of Mary; and all this has been to her but as the sound of lyres and flutes, and lives only in the delicacy with which it has moulded the changing lineaments, and tinged the eyelids and hands."

But the *Mona Lisa* only really hit the big time when she was stolen by an Italian security guard in August 1911. By the time she was recovered, in December 1913, her face had graced the pages of endless books and newspapers. Then, in 1919, the Dadaist Marcel Duchamp bought a cheap postcard reproduction, coloured in a goatee beard and scrawled underneath "L.H.O.O.Q", which spoken aloud in French comes out as "*elle a chaud au cul*" – which loosely translates as "she's got a hot ass". Since then, celebrity has fed on itself, despite the complaints of art critics. Bernard Berenson, for example, decided she was "distastefully unlike the women I had hitherto known or dreamt of, a foreigner with a look I could not fathom, watchful, sly, secure, with a smile of anticipated satisfaction and a pervading air of hostile superiority"; Roberto Longhi claimed to prefer Renoir's women to this "wan fusspot". Still, she now faces more flashguns every day than a well-dressed starlet on Oscar night.

La Gioconde's fame has only swelled as a result of her bit-part appearance in Dan Brown's conspiracy thriller, *The Da Vinci Code*. For the record, "Mona Lisa" is not a coded reference to "Amon L'Isa" – a supposed combination of the names of the ancient Egyptian fertility deities Amun and Isis – and she is not, therefore, a representation of the male–female "feminine divine". After all, "Mona Lisa" is an English-language nickname for the painting that didn't exist in Leonardo's day. There may be more truth in the thriller's assertion that the *Mona Lisa* is a Leonardo self-portrait in drag. Or rather, the artist was known for painting androgynous-looking figures, and one art historian has suggested similarities in the facial proportions to a self-portrait sketch by Leonardo.

Visitors today are sometimes as unimpressed as Roberto Longhi, or Dan Brown's heroine Sophie Neveu, who finds the painting "too little" and "foggy". The painting is indeed surprisingly small – 53x76cm (21x30"), to be exact – and very dark. Basically, it's filthy, and while most reproductions routinely "improve" the colours of the original, no art restorer has yet dared to propose actually working on the picture. Eventually, time may force the museum's hand, as the thin poplar panel that the image is painted on is reported to be slowly warping. A new, air-conditioned glass frame – designed, appropriately, by a Milanese firm – may help. Meanwhile, if you can struggle past the crowds, the patina of fame, the dirt of centuries and your own familiarity with the image, you might just discover a strange and beautiful painting.

the striking, life-size wooden statue of Chancellor Nakhti; a bust of Amenophis IV; and a low-relief sculpture of Sethi I and the goddess Hathor. Post-pharaonic Egypt is exhibited on the lower ground-floor level of the Denon wing. The legacy of the pharaohs is easily discernible in the funerary trappings of Roman Egypt, though a new and startling naturalism stares out of the faces of the mummy portraits.

Greek and Roman Antiquities

The collection of **Greek and Roman Antiquities**, mostly statues, is one of the finest in the world. To begin at the beginning, make for the lower ground floor of Denon and the **Pre-Classical Greece** section, where you'll be confronted by the extraordinary, stylized Cycladic *Woman's Head* of around

2700–2300 BC, followed by the *Dame d'Auxerre*, from seventh-century BC Crete, in the very centre of the room. Immediately above, on the ground floor, the plain stone vaults of the **Galerie Daru** make a good setting for some of the Louvre's finer Roman marbles, including the famous *Gladiator*. You may be able to glimpse building works in the adjacent Cour Visconti (Denon's mirror image of the Cour Puget), which is supposed one day to become a courtyard for displaying works of late antiquity.

On the ground-floor level, the first room off the main pyramid hall is the handsomely vaulted **Salle du Manège** (room A), built as a riding school for the short-lived son of Napoléon III – a use symbolized by the grotesque animal sculptures carved atop its snowy columns. It houses Italian Renaissance copies and restorations of antique sculptures. On either side of the adjoining vestibule, long, stone-vaulted galleries recede into the distance. To the west, the Galerie Mollien (room 4; see p.67) begins the Italian sculpture section, while the **Galerie Daru** (room B) kicks off the main Antiquities section with the poised energy of Lysippos's *Borghese Gladiator*.

At the eastern end of the gallery, Lefuel's imperial **Escalier Daru** rises triumphantly under the billowing, famous feathers of the *Winged Victory of Samothrace* towards the Italian painting section and the Grande Galerie. Skirt the staircase to continue into the **Etruscan and Roman** collections, which incorporate some beautiful mosaics from Asia Minor and stunning, naturalistic frescoes from Pompeii and Herculaneum. Beyond, in the Sully wing, you enter Pierre Lescot's original sixteenth-century palace. In the **Salle des Caryatides** (room 17), which houses Roman copies of Greek works, the musicians' balcony is supported by four giant caryatids, sculpted in 1550 by Jean Goujon. Just beyond, the **Henri II staircase** is carved with the initials H and D for Henri and his mistress Diane de Poitiers, along with symbols of the hunt recalling the Roman goddess Diana. Greek Antiquities continue in the main Sully wing. You'll find the graceful marble head known as the *Tête Kaufmann* here (room 16) and the delightful *Venus of Arles* – both early copies of the work of the great sculptor Praxiteles.

Up on the first floor are smaller groupings by medium – primarily the daunting terracotta and ceramics collections. The section on Greek and Roman **bronze**, **glass** and **precious objects** is more manageable, however, and room 33 is well worth visiting for its heart-stirring ceiling decoration of blue and white birds, painted by **Georges Braque** in 1953.

The Medieval Louvre

For a complete change of scene, you can always descend to the strange **Medieval Louvre** section, on the lower ground floor of Sully. The dramatic stump of Philippe-Auguste's keep soars up towards the enormous concrete ceiling like a pillar holding up the entire modern edifice, while vestiges of Charles V's medieval palace walls buttress the edges of the vast chamber. A similar but more intimate effect can be felt in the adjacent Salle St-Louis, with its carved pillars and vaults cut short by the modern roof.

To see how Charles V's Louvre used to look, check out the postcards (on sale everywhere) of the October scene from *Les Très Riches Heures du Duc de Berry*, a mid-fifteenth-century prayer book that depicted some of the great châteaux of the realm. Seen rising behind the high city walls that run along the Seine, the Louvre seems impossibly remote, a strange blend of fairy-tale castle and imposing fortress. In the foreground, peasants are shown ploughing and sowing in the green fields of St-Germain-des-Prés.

Les Arts Décoratifs

The westernmost wing of the Palais du Louvre, on the north side, houses a second, entirely separate museum called, simply, **Les Arts Décoratifs**, which could be translated as "the art of design" or, more prosaically, as "applied arts". The entrance is at 107 rue de Rivoli (Tues–Fri 11am–6pm, Sat & Sun 10am–6pm; €8; Ⓦwww.lesartsdecoratifs.fr). The core of the collection is found in the newly revamped **Musée des Arts Décoratifs**, which occupies the western half of the building, to the right of the main entrance. The rather grand "nave" on the first floor – an original feature of the building, which dates from the 1870s – is used for temporary exhibitions. The smaller eastern side of the museum showcases fashion and advertising in the **Musée de la Mode et du Textile** and **Musée de la Publicité.**

Musée des Arts Décoratifs

To visit the collections in chronological order, start on the third floor, with the rooms dedicated to the **Middle Ages** and **Renaissance**. You'll find some wonderful tapestries here, including a pair of vivid, rustically themed Belgian works, *Le Berger* and *Les Bûcherons aux Armes*. There are also some paintings attributed to the celebrated French portraitist François Clouet, but most of the objects on display are furnishings. The highlight is a room entirely reconstructed as a late fifteenth-century bedchamber, complete with original wall panelling, canopied bed, chairs and benches – even the door, fireplace and windows date from the period.

The collections continue with a sequence of rooms running alongside the nave on the third and fourth floors, covering the **seventeenth**, **eighteenth** and **nineteenth centuries**. While these may be the glory years of French furniture design, the endless gilt cabinets, commodes and consoles can be a little wearisome for the non-enthusiast. Again, the highlights are the complete, reconstructed rooms. One shows off panelling installed in the Hôtel de Verrûe in the 1720s, when the fashion for *singeries*, or frescoes themed around monkeys dressed in human clothing, was in full swing. Another, found on the terrace level overlooking the nave, is a reconstruction of the splendid panelling from the aptly named "golden study" of the Hôtel de Rochegude, at Avignon.

More satisfying are the **Art Nouveau** and **Art Déco** rooms, grouped at the far end of the nave on the first, third and fourth floors. In the first decades of the twentieth century, French designers once again shaped the tastes of the world, and looking at the furnishings displayed here it's easy to see why. A number of rooms have been preserved lock, stock and barrel, including a complete 1903 bedroom by Hector Guimard – the designer behind the original Paris métro stations – for the wedding of an industrialist's daughter. Representing the Art Deco era, there's a 1925 study by Pierre Chareau, and an entire apartment created in the early 1920s by Armand-Albert Rateau for the *couturière* Jeanne Lanvin. Down on the first floor, don't miss the **Salon des Boiseries**, which shows off the best in French wood-panelling, and the **Salon du Bois**, a huge drawing room made for the 1900 Universal Exhibition by Georges Hoentschel.

The final part of the chronology takes you through a suite of interlinked rooms stacked inside the lofty **Pavillon Marsan**. There are stunning views of the rue de Rivoli and Jardin des Tuileries. You begin on the ninth floor with the 1940s, and end many, many designer chairs later on the fifth floor, with the contemporary collections. The most interesting section is probably the one devoted to the 1980s and 1990s, on the sixth floor, where you'll find the original carriage design for the TGV high-speed train, and various podiums devoted to individual designers. **Philippe Starck**, for instance, is represented by five hyper-cool chairs, a stool, a mirror and a lampshade.

The second floor of the museum is occupied by a quartet of themed galleries. One houses a progression of **toys** from wooden soldiers and china dolls to Star Wars figures and (playable) computer games. Another gallery is devoted to over a thousand pieces of **jewellery**; there are a number of older pieces but the focus is on twentieth-century designs, and you'll find most of the great names represented here, notably the Art Nouveau jeweller René Lalique. A third gallery contains paintings by **Jean Dubuffet** (1901–1985), while the **Galerie d'Etudes** houses themed exhibitions. These change every year, but the inaugural show studied the various ways – some distinctly unusual – in which designers have accommodated the human need to sit down.

Musées de la Mode et de la Publicité

The eastern half of the museum, to the left of the main entrance, puts on exhibitions dedicated to fashion and advertising. These can be among the city's most innovative, as most shows are curated by industry professionals rather than state museum administrators. On the first and second floors, the **Musée de la Mode et du Textile** holds high-quality temporary exhibitions drawn from the large permanent collection aimed at demonstrating the most brilliant and cutting-edge of Paris fashions from all eras. Recent exhibitions have included retrospectives of Jean-Paul Gaultier's designs for the ballet choreographer Régine Chopinot, and a personal "history of fashion" curated by Christian Lacroix. On the third floor, directly above the fashion museum, the **Musée de la Publicité** shows off its collection of advertising posters and video through cleverly themed, temporary exhibitions. The space is appropriately trendy – half-exposed brickwork and steel panelling, and half-crumbling Louvre finery – and you can access the archive at a dozen computers.

3

The Champs-Elysées and around

Synonymous with glitz and glamour, the **Champs-Elysées** sweeps through one of the city's most exclusive districts, studded with luxury hotels and top fashion boutiques. The avenue in turn forms part of a grand, nine-kilometre axis that extends from the Louvre at the heart of the city to the Défense business district in the west. Offering impressive vistas along its length, this grand axis, often referred to as the **Voie Triomphale**, or Triumphal Way, incorporates some of the city's most famous landmarks – the **place de la Concorde**, **Tuileries gardens** and the **Arc de Triomphe**. The whole ensemble is so regular and geometrical it looks as though it might have been laid out by a single town planner rather than successive kings, emperors and presidents, all keen to add their stamp and promote French power and prestige. Last to join the list was President Mitterrand (whose *grands projets* for the city outdid even Napoleon's) – his glass pyramid entrance to the Louvre (see Chapter 2) and immense marble-clad cubic arch at La Défense (see Chapter 15) effectively marking each end of the historic axis. The two great constructions echo each other in scale and geometry, with both aligned at the same slight angle away from the axis – a detail that, given the distance involved, has to be appreciated conceptually rather than visually.

The Arc de Triomphe

The best view of the Champs-Elysées and Voie Triomphale is from the top of the **Arc de Triomphe** (daily: April–Sept 10am–11pm; Oct–March 10am–10.30pm; €8; M° Charles-de-Gaulle-Etoile), towering up in the middle of place Charles-de-Gaulle, better known as place de l'Etoile and once dubbed "place de la Traffic" for reasons that become clear as you approach what's essentially a giant roundabout. The arch is modelled on the ancient Roman triumphal arches and is impressive in scale, memorably likened in Guy de Maupassant's novel *Bel Ami* to "a shapeless giant on two monstrously large legs, that looks as if it's about to stride off down the Champs Elysées". The arch was begun by Napoleon in 1806 in homage to his Grande Armée, but it wasn't actually finished until 1836 by Louis-Philippe, who dedicated it to the French army in general. Later, victorious

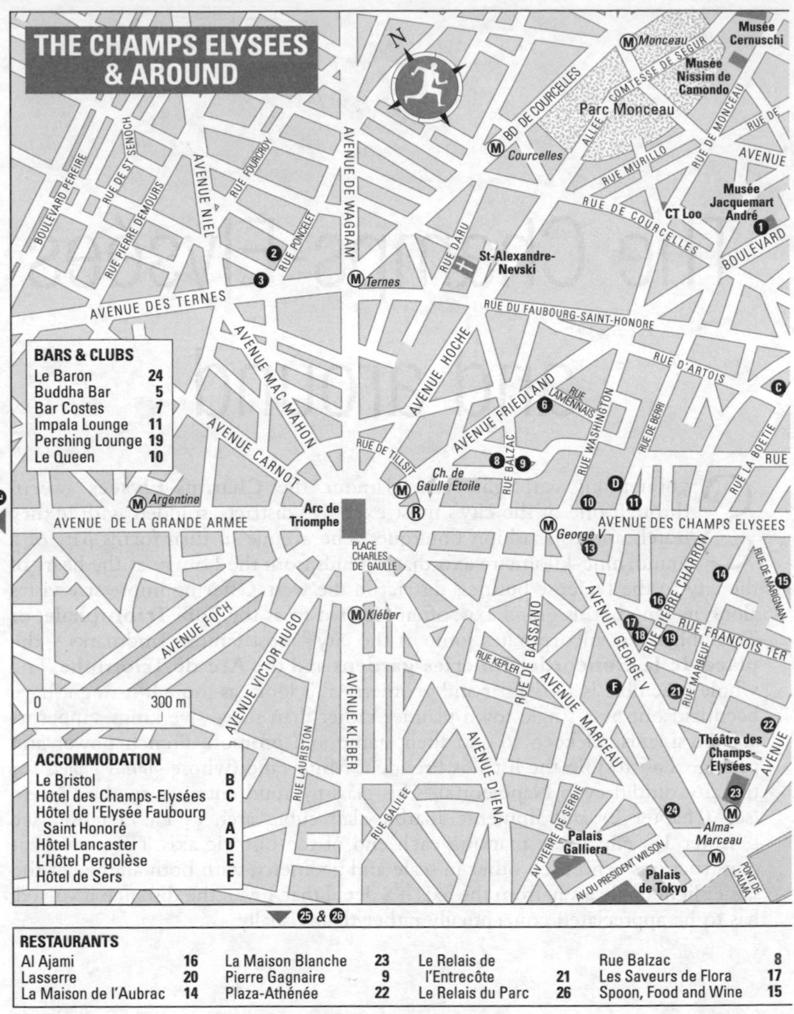

German armies would make a point of marching through the arch to compound the humiliation of the French. After the Prussians' triumphal march in 1871, Parisians lit bonfires beneath the arch and down the Champs-Elysées to eradicate the "stain" of German boots. Still a potent symbol of the country's military might, the arch is the starting point for the annual Bastille Day procession, a bombastic march-past of tanks, guns and flags. A more poignant ceremony is conducted every evening at 6.30pm at the foot of the monument, when war veterans stoke up the flame at the **tomb of an unknown soldier**, killed in the Great War. Not even the Nazi occupation of Paris on June 14, 1942, could interrupt this sacred act of remembrance. At 6.30pm that day German troops gathering around the Arc de Triomphe were astonished to see two elderly

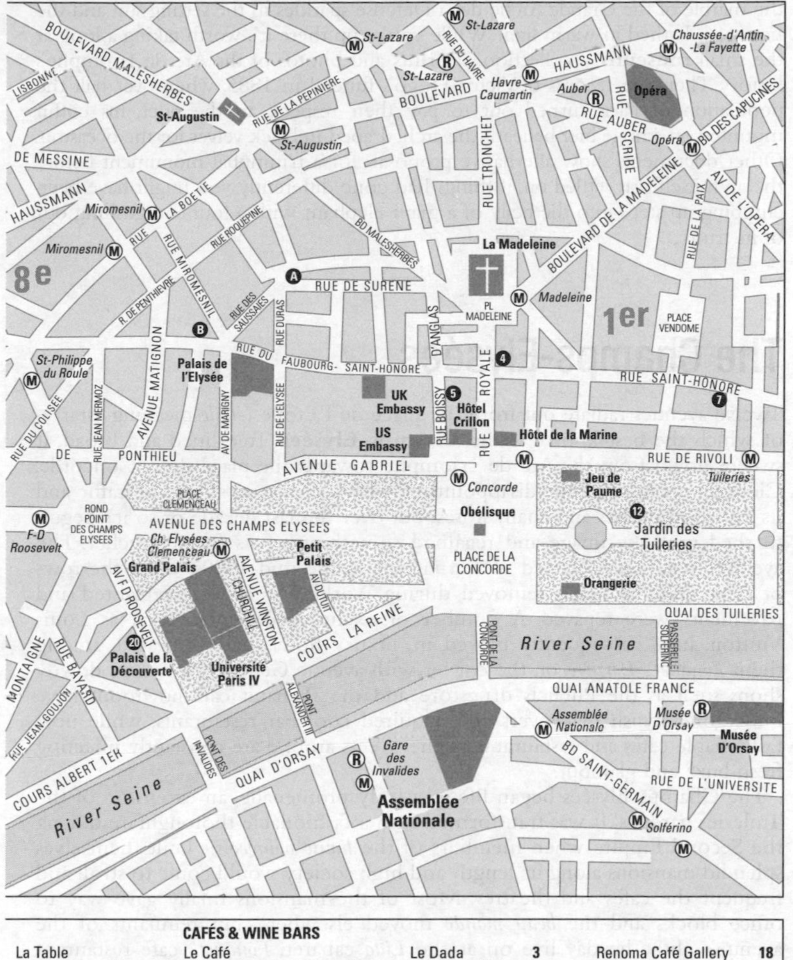

CAFÉS & WINE BARS

La Table Lauriston	25	Le Café Jacquemart-André	1	Le Dada	3	Renoma Café Gallery	18
Taillevent	6	Café Véry	12	Le Fouquet's	13	Le Stübli	2
				Ladurée	4		

French soldiers marching towards them in full dress uniform. The Germans instinctively stood to attention while Edmond Ferrand, the guardian of the Eternal Flame, and André Gaudin, a member of the flame's committee, solemnly saluted it; the Germans, somewhat disconcerted, apparently followed suit.

Access to the arch is via underground stairs on the north corner of the Champs-Elysées. The names of 660 generals and numerous French battles are engraved on its inside, while reliefs adorn the exterior; the best is François Rude's extraordinarily dramatic *Marseillaise*, in which an Amazon-type figure personifying the Revolution charges forward with a sword, her face contorted in a fierce rallying cry. If you're up for climbing the 280 steps to the top, you'll be amply rewarded with panoramic views, at their best towards dusk on a sunny day when the marble of the Grande Arche de la Défense sparkles in the setting sun and the Louvre is bathed in warm light. While you're up there it's worth taking a look at the small **museum**, a collection of prints and photos of the Arc de Triomphe's history. There are records of Victor Hugo's funeral in 1885, when over half the population of Paris turned out to pay their respects to the poet, his coffin mounted on a huge bier beneath the arch, draped in black velvet for the occasion. Other documents show alternative proposals for a triumphal monument before the arch itself was settled on; if things had gone differently you might have been climbing up steps into the belly of a giant elephant with a fountain gushing out of its trunk.

The Champs-Elysées

Twelve avenues radiate out from the place de l'Etoile (*étoile* meaning "star"), of which the best-known is the **Champs-Elysées**. Tree-lined and broad, it sweeps down from the Arc de Triomphe towards the place de la Concorde. Close up it can be a little disappointing, with its constant stream of traffic and its fast-food outlets and chain stores, but over the last decade or so it's begun to shed its tacky image and regained something of its former cachet. The avenue's renaissance started with a facelift in the mid-1990s, when the rows of trees that the Nazis removed during World War II were replanted and pavements were repaved. A number of exclusive designers, such as Louis Vuitton, have subsequently moved in, luxury hotels have appeared, among them *Fouquet's Barrière*, on the corner with avenue George V, formerly dowdy shops such as the Publicis drugstore and the Renault car showroom have undergone stylish makeovers and acquired cool bar/restaurants, while new, fashionable cafés and restaurants in the streets around are constantly injecting fresh buzz and glamour.

The Champs-Elysées began life as a leafy promenade, an extension of the Tuileries gardens. It was transformed into a fashionable thoroughfare during the Second Empire when members of the *haute bourgeoisie* built themselves splendid mansions along its length and high society would come to stroll and frequent the cafés and theatres. Most of the mansions finally gave way to office blocks and the *beau monde* moved elsewhere, but remnants of the avenue's glitzy heyday live on at the *Lido* cabaret, *Fouquet's* café-restaurant (see p.320), the perfumier Guerlain's shop, occupying an exquisite 1913 building, and the former *Claridges* hotel, now a swanky shopping arcade. One of the most opulent of the mid-nineteenth-century mansions also survives, the Travellers Club at no. 25, once the residence of the famous courtesan, La Païva, whose bathroom alone, it is said, was worthy of a Sultana in the Arabian Nights.

The Champs-Elysées occupies an important place in the national psyche and is a popular rallying point at times of crisis as well as celebration; crowds thronged here to greet Général de Gaulle as he walked down the avenue just after the Liberation in May 1944 and many turned out to support him again in 1968 in the wake of the student riots, while thousands congregated in 1998 to party all night after France won the World Cup. It's also the scene of annual processions on November 11 and Bastille Day, and the Tour de France ends here in July with a final flourish.

The Triangle d'Or and Théâtre des Champs-Elysées

The area bounded by the Champs-Elysées and, to the south, **avenue Montaigne** and **rue Francois 1er** is nicknamed the **Triangle d'Or** (Golden Triangle) on account of its exclusive character: this is the domain of flagship designer stores, including Dior, Prada, Chanel and Givenchy, as well as luxury hotels, such as the *Plaza Athénée* and *George V*.

Right at the bottom of avenue Montaigne is the **Théâtre des Champs-Elysées**, one of the city's premier concert halls. Erected in 1913, it was among the first buildings in Paris to be made of reinforced concrete, its exterior softened with marble reliefs by the sculptor Bourdelle, who studied under Rodin. The architect, Auguste Perret, went on to rebuild much of Le Havre in the aftermath of World War II. The theatre has seen a number of notable premieres and debuts, including that of Josephine Baker in 1925, who created a sensation with her sensual, abandoned dancing. It's perhaps best known, though, for being the scene of great uproar on May 29, 1913, on the occasion of the world premiere of Stravinsky's *Rite of Spring*. The music's unprecedented rhythmic and harmonic ferocity provoked violent reactions among the audience. The whole performance was punctuated with catcalls so loud the dancers could barely hear the orchestra, objects were thrown at the conductor and fist fights broke out in the stalls.

Beyond the Rond-Point des Champs-Elysées

The lower stretch of the Champs-Elysées between the **Rond-Point des Champs-Elysées**, whose Lalique glass fountains disappeared during the German occupation, and place de la Concorde is bordered by chestnut trees and municipal flowerbeds, the pleasantest part of the avenue for a stroll. The gigantic building with grandiose Neoclassical exteriors, glass roofs and exuberant flying statuary rising above the greenery to the south is the **Grand Palais**, created with its neighbour, the **Petit Palais**, for the 1900 **Exposition Universelle**. Both have recently emerged from extensive restoration projects and look more splendid than ever. The Petit Palais contains a fine arts museum, while the Grand Palais hosts major exhibitions and special events and also contains a science museum. Between the two palaces lies the **place Clemenceau**, presided over by statues of Georges Clemenceau, French prime minister at the end of World War I, and a recently added bronze of Général de Gaulle in mid-stride. From here the **avenue Winston-Churchill** leads down towards the Seine, culminating with a statue of the man himself. To the north of Place Clemenceau, combat police guard the high walls round the presidential **Palais de l'Elysée** and the line of ministries and embassies ending with the US in prime position on the corner of place de la Concorde. On Thursdays and at weekends you can see a different manifestation of the self-images of states in the **postage-stamp market** at the corner of avenues Gabriel and Marigny.

The Grand Palais

The 45-metre-high glass cupola of the **Grand Palais** (Ⓦ www.grandpalais.fr; M° Champs-Elysées-Clemenceau) can be seen from most of the city's viewpoints and forms the centrepiece of the *nef* (nave), a huge, impressive exhibition space, whose glass and steel ceiling allows light to flood the interior. The nave has just emerged from a lengthy restoration project – it was hastily closed in 1993 when a metal rivet fell 35m from the ceiling. The glass of the dome – covering some 15,000 square metres – has been entirely replaced and the steel supports given a fresh coat of sea-green paint. Renovation work on the exterior is ongoing, but the *palais* has now all but resumed its role as the city's premier special events venue, hosting music festivals and art exhibitions, as well as trade fairs and fashion shows.

In the west wing of the building is the **Galeries Nationales** (Mon & Wed–Sun 10am–8pm, till 10pm on Wed; €10; ⓦwww.rmn.fr/galeries nationalesdugrandpalais), one of the city's major exhibition spaces and well known for its blockbuster shows, such as the Courbet retrospective in 2007.

The Grand Palais's eastern wing houses the **Palais de la Découverte** (Tues–Sat 9.30am–6pm, Sun & hols 10am–7pm; €7, combined ticket with planetarium €10.50; ⓦwww.palais-decouverte.fr), Paris's original science museum, which was opened in the late 1930s. Although it can't really compete, it's been brightened up considerably since the Cité des Sciences (see p.231) came on the scene and has plenty of interactive exhibits, some engaging temporary exhibitions on subjects such as climate change and the Brazilian rainforest, as well as an excellent **planetarium**.

The Petit Palais

The **Petit Palais** (Tues–Sun 10am–6pm; free; ⓦwww.petitpalais.paris.fr; M° Champs-Elysées-Clemenceau), facing the Grand Palais on avenue Winston Churchill, holds the **Musée des Beaux Arts de la Ville de Paris**. It's hardly "petit", but it's certainly palatial, with its highly decorated Neoclassical exterior, interior garden with Tuscan colonnade, beautiful spiral wrought-iron staircases and a grand gallery on the lines of Versailles' Hall of Mirrors. A major renovation, completed in 2005, has returned the building to its original splendour, allowing more natural light to enter and illuminate the restored stained-glass windows and ceiling frescoes. The revamp has freed up more space for the museum's extensive holdings of paintings, sculpture and decorative artworks, displayed on two floors and ranging from the ancient Greek and Roman period up to the early twentieth century. At first sight it looks like it's mopped up the leftovers after the city's other galleries have taken their pick, but there are some real gems here, such as Monet's *Soleil couchant sur la Seine à Lavacourt*, Courbet's provocative *Demoiselles des bord de la Seine* and Pissarro's delicate *Le Pont royal et le Pavillon de Flore*, painted a few months before he died. Decorative arts feature strongly, especially eighteenth-century furniture and porcelain, including a whimsical clock decorated with an orchestra of monkeys in Meissen china. There's also fantasy jewellery of the Art Nouveau period, an elegant dining room in pear wood designed by Hector Guimard (who designed the original Paris métro stations), Russian icons, and a fine collection of seventeenth-century Dutch landscape painting. Changing exhibitions, such as a recent one on Sargent and Sorolla, allow the museum to display works from its vast reserves. If your own reserves are running low you could head for the smart new café, which opens out onto the restored interior garden.

North of the Arc de Triomphe and Champs-Elysées

North of the Arc de Triomphe, the **16e** and **17e** arrondissements are for the most part cold and soulless, their huge fortified apartments empty much of the time while their owners – royal, exiled royal, ex-royal or just extremely rich – jet between their other residences dotted about the globe. The **8e** arrondissement, north of the Champs-Elysées, however, has more to offer commercially and culturally, with some of the *hôtels particuliers* (mansions) housing select museums – the **Musée Cernuschi** with its collection of Asian art, the **Musée Nissim de Camondo**, a treasury of eighteenth-century decorative art, and, most magnificent of all, the **Musée Jacquemart-André**, boasting a choice collection of Italian Renaissance paintings.

The best avenue to start wandering down from place de l'Etoile – apart from the Champs-Elysées – is the northerly **avenue de Wagram**. Devotees of Art Nouveau can stop in front of no. 34 and contemplate Jules Lavirotte's facade of 1904, which shocked the Académie des Beaux Arts on account of its swirly lines and brightly painted ceramics (sadly rather faded now). A little further on you come to the flower market and cafés of **place des Ternes**, the first big junction on avenue de Wagram. From here you could make a short detour down avenue des Ternes to savour the sights and aromas of the little **rue Poncelet street market**, the first turning on the right. Alongside the butchers, grocers and fishmongers' stalls are some very fine food shops, such as Alléosse (13 rue Poncelet), arguably the best cheesemonger in Paris, with an impressive selection of goats' cheeses, and nearby Le Stübli, catering for sweet cravings with *echt* Austrian pastries.

Back at place des Ternes, you can head southeast down the rue du Faubourg-St-Honoré and take the second left (rue Daru) to admire the five gold onion domes of the Russian Orthodox **Cathédrale Alexandre-Nevski** (open to visitors Tues, Fri & Sun 3–5pm), witness to Picasso's marriage to Olga Khoklova in 1918 (they lived for a while at 29 rue de la Boétie, a few blocks southeast). Continuing down Faubourg-St-Honoré, at no. 252 you'll come to the prestigious **Salle Pleyel** concert hall (see p.377), up and running again after a four-year refit. The most exotic building in the area can be seen by continuing on one block and turning left into rue de Monceau – the red **Chinese pagoda**, built for the Shanghai-born antiques dealer C. T. Loo in 1926 and now a commercial art gallery, selling fine oriental antiques (Tues–Sat 2–6pm).

Heading north up rue de Courcelles brings you to the enormous gilded gates of the avenue Hoche entrance to **Parc Monceau** (M° Monceau), an informal English-style garden with undulating lawns, rock gardens, moss-grown mock-Classical columns and statues of brooding romantic French poets. Most likely half the people who command the heights of the French economy spent their infancy in this park, promenaded in prams by their nannies.

The Musée Cernuschi

On avenue Velásquez, by the east gate of Parc de Monceau, at no. 7, the **Musée Cernuschi** (Tues–Sun 10am–5.40pm; free; M° Monceau/Villiers) houses a small collection of Far-Eastern art, mainly ancient Chinese, bequeathed to the state by the banker Cernuschi, who nearly lost his life for giving money to the insurrectionary Commune of 1871. Cernuschi's elegant mansion is the setting for the museum. A grand staircase takes you from the ground-floor temporary exhibitions up to the first floor, which displays the permanent collection. There are some exquisite pieces here, including a selection of ceremonial jade objects dating from 3000 BC, highly worked bronzes from the Shang era (1550–1005 BC), and some unique ceramics detailing everyday life in ancient China. On the mezzanine floor among a collection of Buddhas and other statuary a beautiful, sinuous figure playing a lute, dating from the Wei dynasty, stands out.

The Musée Nissim de Camondo

Right beside the Cernuschi, with its entrance at no. 63 rue de Monceau, is the **Musée Nissim de Camondo** (Wed–Sun 10am–5.30pm; €6; M° Monceau/Villiers), an impressive collection of eighteenth-century decorative art and painting, built up by Count Moïse de Camondo, son of a wealthy Sephardic Jewish banker who had emigrated from Istanbul to Paris in the late nineteenth century. In order to provide a fitting showcase for his treasures, the count commissioned a mansion in authentic eighteenth-century style, modelled on the Petit Trianon at Versailles. The ground-floor rooms, decorated in original eighteenth-century panelling, overflow with Gobelin tapestries, paintings of pastoral scenes by Huet and Vigée-Lebrun, gilded furniture and delicate Sèvres porcelain; an excellent free audioguide, available in English, helps you get the most out of the exhibits. The upper-floor rooms, where the family spent most of their time, are homelier and less museum-like; here and there some of the anachronistic mod-cons of an early twentieth-century aristocratic home surface, such as the count's well-appointed bathroom. These rooms take on a progressively melancholy air, however, as you learn more about the Camondo family and its fate: after a few years of marriage Moïse's wife left him for the head groom; his beloved son, Nissim, after whom the museum is named, died on a flying mission in World War I, while his remaining child, Béatrice, perished together with her children in the camps in World War II.

Musée Jacquemart-André

Just a few blocks to the south of the Parc de Monceau, at 158 boulevard Haussmann, stands the lavishly ornamented palace of the nineteenth-century banker and art-lover Edouard André and his wife, former society portraitist Nélie Jacquemart. Built in 1870 to grace Baron Haussmann's grand new boulevard, the Hôtel André is now the **Musée Jacquemart-André** (daily 10am–6pm; €9.50; Ⓦ www.musee-jacquemart-andre.com; M° Miromesnil/St-Philippe-du-Roule), housing the couple's impressive art collection and a fabulous *salon de thé* (see p.219) – the meeting place of the elegant and discreet. Bequeathed to the Institut de France by Edouard's widow, the Hôtel André deploys the couple's collection exactly as they ordained. Nélie painted Edouard's portrait in 1872 – on display in what were their private apartments on the ground floor – and nine years later they were married, after which Nélie gave up her painting career and the pair devoted their spare time to collecting art, travelling around Europe for six months of the year searching for pieces. Their preference for **Italian art** is evident in the stunning collection of fifteenth- and sixteenth-century genius, including the works of Tiepolo, Botticelli, Donatello, Mantegna and Uccello, which forms the core of the collection. Almost as compelling as the splendid interior and art collection is the insight gleaned into an extraordinary marriage and grand nineteenth-century lifestyle, brought to life by the fascinating narration on the free audioguide (available in English).

In Room 1, mostly eighteenth-century French paintings are displayed, including several portraits by **Boucher**, in addition to two lively paintings of Venice by Canaletto. Room 2, the reception area, has specially constructed folding doors which, when opened, transformed the space into a ballroom large enough to contain a thousand guests. Room 3 contains three huge tapestries depicting Russian scenes that capture the fashion for Slav exoticism of the mid-eighteenth century. Room 6, formerly the library, focuses on Dutch and

Flemish paintings, including three by **Van Dyck** and two by **Rembrandt** – *The Portrait of Dr A. Tholinx* and an early work, *The Pilgrims of Emmaus*, showing remarkable use of chiaroscuro. Room 7 is the Salon de Musique (and the other half of the ballroom), whose dramatic high ceiling is decorated with a mural by Pierre Victor Galant; the musicians would play from the gallery, and you're treated to a mini-concert on the audioguide as you gaze at the ceiling. In Room 8, a huge, animated fresco by **Tiepolo**, depicting the French king Henri III being received by Frederigo Contarini in Venice, graces the extraordinary marble, bronze and wrought-iron double spiral staircase that leads from an interior garden of palm trees up to the musician's gallery. Room 9, once the smoking room, where the men would retreat after dinner, is hung with the work of eighteenth-century English portraitists, among them a painting by **Joshua Reynolds**.

Leading off the music gallery are the rooms in which the couple displayed their **early Renaissance Italian collection**. The first was intended as Nélie's studio, but she instead decorated it as a sculpture gallery – including three bronzes by **Donatello** – its walls covered in low-relief sculpture. The dimly lit Florentine room next door includes a wonderful, brightly coloured *Saint George Slaying the Dragon* (1440) by **Paolo Uccello**, a **Botticelli** *Virgin and Child* (1470) depicted with touching beauty and fragility, and an exquisite sixteenth-century inlaid choir stall. Adjacent is the Venetian room, with paintings by **Bellini** and **Mantegna** among others.

Place de la Concorde

At the eastern end of the Champs-Elysées lies the grand, pleasingly harmonious **place de la Concorde**, marred only by its constant stream of traffic. Its centrepiece is a gold-tipped obelisk from the temple of Ramses at Luxor, given by Mohammed Ali to Louis-Philippe in 1831, and flanked by two ornate bronze fountains, modelled on those in St Peter's Square, Rome. The square's history is much less harmonious than its name "Concorde" suggests. The equestrian statue of Louis XV that formerly stood at the centre of the square was toppled in 1792, and between 1793 and 1795 some 1300 people died here beneath the Revolutionary guillotine, Louis XVI, Marie-Antoinette, Danton and Robespierre among them. On one occasion there was so much blood on the square from the guillotines that cows being driven to slaughter at Les Halles refused to pass across it. When deciding later what to put in place of Louis XV's statue, Louis-Philippe thought the obelisk would be ideal – having no political message, it wasn't likely ever to be demolished or become the focus of popular discontent. It was erected with much pomp in October 1836 in the presence of 200,000 spectators, while an orchestra played tunes from Bellini's *I Puritani*.

From the centre of the square there are magnificent views of the Champs-Elysées and Tuileries, and you can admire the alignment and symmetry of the Assemblée Nationale, on the far side of the Seine, with the church of the Madeleine at the end of rue Royale, to the north. The Neoclassical *Hôtel Crillon* – the ultimate luxury address for visitors to Paris – and its twin, the Hôtel de la Marine, housing the Ministry of the Navy, flank the entrance to rue Royale, which, needless to say, meets the Voie Triomphale at a precise right angle.

The Tuileries gardens

Extending for around 1km from the Place de la Concorde to the Louvre, the **Jardin des Tuileries** is the formal French garden *par excellence*. The grand central alley is lined with shady, clipped chestnuts and manicured lawns, and framed at each end by ornamental ponds. Surrounding these is an impressive gallery of statues (by the likes of Rodin, Coustou and Coysevox), many brought here from Versailles and Marly (Louis XIV's retreat from Versailles, no longer in

△ The Tuileries gardens

existence), though a number are copies, the originals having been transferred to the Louvre. The much sought-after chairs strewn around the ponds are a good spot from which to admire the statues, watch children chase boats around the pond and observe promenading Parisians. There are also a number of cafés nestling among the trees, ideal retreats on sunny days when the glare of the sun on the gravel of the central alley can be quite dazzling.

The garden originated in the 1570s when Catherine de Médicis had the site cleared of the medieval warren of tilemakers (*tuileries*) that stood here to make way for a palace and grounds (see box, p.60). The Palais des Tuileries, as it became known, was surrounded by formal vegetable gardens, a labyrinth and a chequerboard of flowerbeds. The present layout, however, is largely the work of the landscape architect Le Nôtre, who was commissioned by Louis XIV a hundred years later to redesign the gardens on a grander scale. Employing techniques he later perfected at Versailles, Le Nôtre took the opportunity to indulge his passion for symmetry, straight avenues, formal flowerbeds and splendid vistas. During the eighteenth century, the gardens were where chic Parisians came to preen and party, and in 1783 the Montgolfier brothers, Joseph and Etienne, launched the first successful hot-air balloon here. The first serious replanting was carried out after the Revolution, and in the nineteenth century rare species were added to the garden, by this time dominated by chestnut trees. Sadly, some of the oldest specimens were lost in the December 1999 storms; the centennial chestnuts around the two central oval ponds are now the most senior.

At the eastern end of the gardens in front of the Louvre is the **Jardin du Carrousel**, a raised terrace where the Palais des Tuileries, burnt down by the Communards in 1871, was sited. It's now planted with trim yew hedges, between which stand oddly static bronzes of buxom female nudes by Maillol.

The two buildings flanking the garden at the western, Concorde end, are the Orangerie, by the river, and the **Jeu de Paume**, by the rue de Rivoli (Tues noon–9pm, Wed–Fri noon–7pm, Sat & Sun 10am–7pm; €6; Ⓦwww.jeudepaume.org; M° Concorde), once a royal tennis court and the place where French Impressionist paintings were displayed before being transferred to the Musée d'Orsay. Since 2004 it's been a major exhibition space (not as well lit as you might expect from the lovely light-filled foyer) dedicated to photography and video art; one of 2007's highlights was an exhibition of Edward Steichen's work. It has a sister site at the Hôtel de Sully (see p.112).

Opposite the Jeu de Paume is the **Orangerie** (Wed–Sat & Sun 12.30–7pm, till 9pm Fri; groups only 9am–12.30pm; €6.50; Ⓦwww.musee-orangerie.fr), a quietly elegant stone Neoclassical-style building, originally designed to protect the Tuileries' orange trees, and now housing a private art collection including eight of Monet's giant waterlily paintings. It reopened in 2006 after six years of renovations designed to bring Monet's masterpieces "back into the light". In the 1960s a concrete ceiling had been added to accommodate a new storey; this has now been removed and once again the natural light illumines the waterlilies – exactly how Monet wished them to be seen. These vast, mesmerizing canvases were executed in the last years of the artist's life, a period when he almost obsessively painted the pond in his garden at Giverny, attempting to capture the fleeting light and changing colours.

On the lower floor of the museum is an excellent collection of paintings by Monet's contemporaries. Highlights include some Cézanne still lifes, portraits and landscapes, among them *Le Rocher Rouge*, one of the artist's finest mature works, where the intense colours seem to vibrate and shimmer, rendering the heat of a Provençal summer almost palpable. Renoir is represented by some sensuous nudes and touching studies of children, such as *Jeunes filles au piano*, the two girls' rapt concentration on the music wonderfully conveyed. There are some fine works by Picasso and Matisse; the latter's *Les Trois Soeurs* stands out for its striking portrayal of three women, the simplicity of line and colour reminiscent of a Japanese print. Much space is devoted to works by Derain, including some iridescent nudes and vibrant landscapes, and a room is given over to the more expressionistic canvases of Soutine.

4

The Grands Boulevards and passages

Built on the site of the city's old ramparts, the **Grands Boulevards** extend in a long arc from the **Eglise de la Madeleine** in the west to the Bastille in the east. Once highly fashionable thoroughfares where *le tout Paris* would come to promenade and seek entertainment, they're still a vibrant and colourful part of the city, with their brasseries, theatres and cinemas.

The streets off the Grands Boulevards constitute the city's main **commercial and financial district**. Right at the heart of the area stand the solid institutions of the Banque de France and the **Bourse**, while just to the north, beyond the glittering **Opéra Garnier**, are the large department stores **Galeries Lafayette** and **Printemps**. Rather more well-heeled shopping is concentrated on the rue St-Honoré in the west and the streets around elegant **place Vendôme**, lined with top couturiers, jewellers and art dealers. Scattered around the whole of the area are the delightful **passages** – nineteenth-century arcades with glass roofs and tiled floors that hark back to shopping from a different era.

In the south, the **Palais Royal** arcades and gardens provide a perfect retreat from the traffic and make a handy shortcut through to the **Bibliothèque Nationale**. Further east, the **Sentier** district is the centre of the rag trade, while nearby **rue St-Denis** sees trade of a seedier kind.

The Grands Boulevards

The **Grands Boulevards** is the collective name given to the eight streets that form one continuous, broad thoroughfare running from the Madeleine to République, then down to the Bastille. Lined with classic nineteenth-century apartment blocks, imposing banks, cinemas, theatres, brasseries and neon-lit fast-food outlets, the Grands Boulevards are busy and vibrant, if not the most

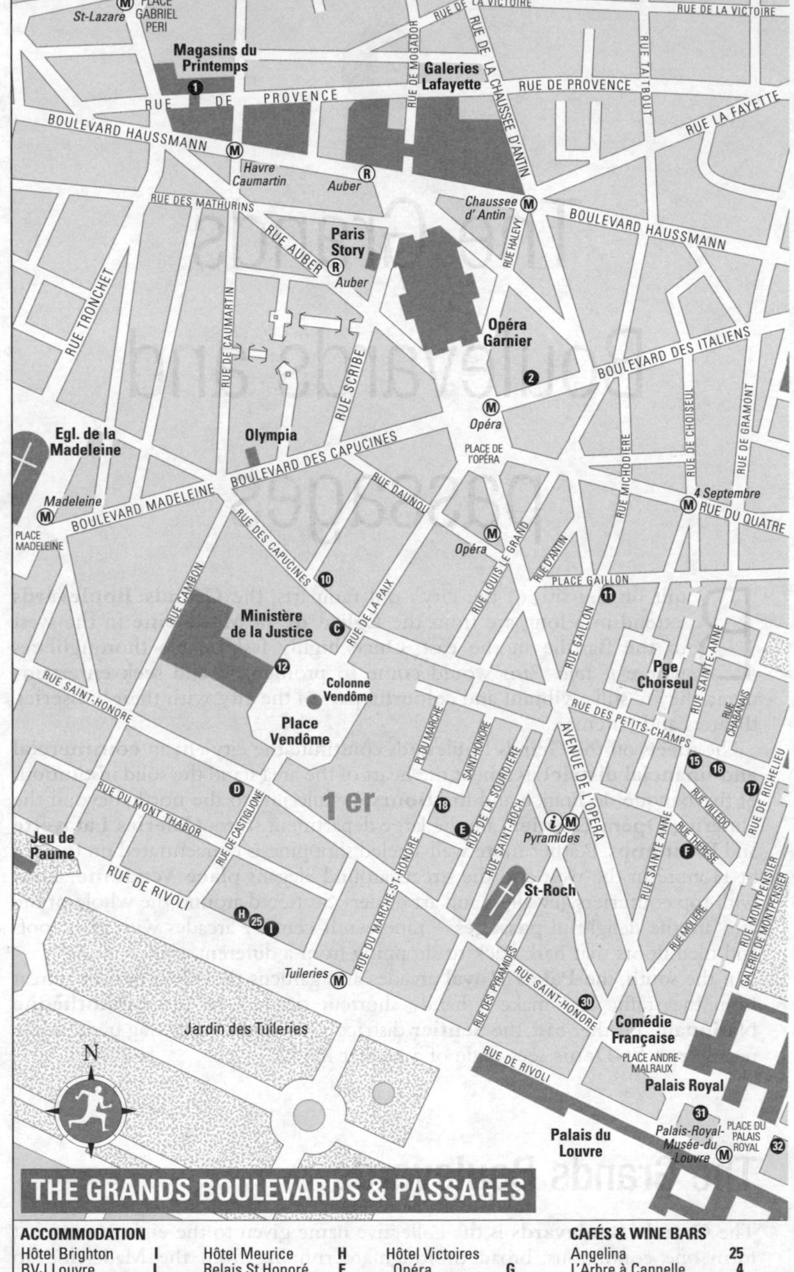

ACCOMMODATION					
Hôtel Brighton	I	Hôtel Meurice	H	Hôtel Victoires Opéra	G
BVJ Louvre	L	Relais St Honoré	E	Hôtel Vivienne	B
Hôtel Costes	D	Hôtel Thérèse	F		
Hôtel de Lille	K	Hôtel Chopin	A		
Maison des Etudiants	M	Hôtel Mansart	C		
		Hôtel Tiquetonne	J		

CAFÉS & WINE BARS	
Angelina	25
L'Arbre à Cannelle	4
Le Bar de l'Entracte	19
Café de la Comédie	31
Le Dénicheur	28
Juvéniles	17

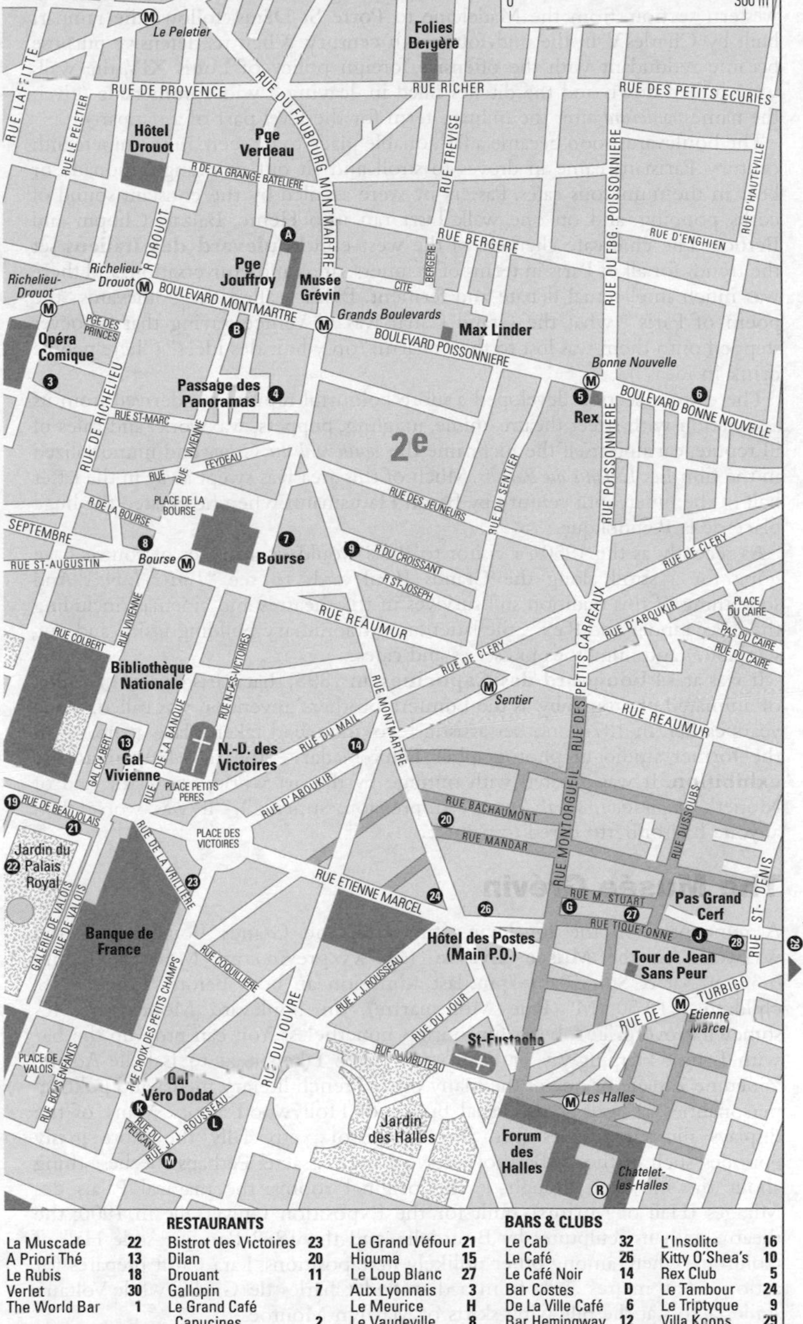
0
300 m
Le Peletier
Folies Bergère
RUE LAFFITTE
RUE DE PROVENCE
RUE DU FAUBOURG MONTMARTRE
RUE RICHER
RUE DES PETITS ECURIES
RUE LE PELETIER
Hôtel Drouot
Pge Verdeau
R DE LA GRANGE BATELIERE
RUE TREVISE
RUE DU FBG. POISSONNIERE
RUE D'HAUTEVILLE
R. DROUOT
RUE BERGERE
RUE D'ENGHIEN
Richelieu-Drouot
Pge Jouffroy
Musée Grévin
CITE
BERGERE
BOULEVARD MONTMARTRE
Grands Boulevards
PGE DES PRINCES
Opéra Comique
Max Linder
BOULEVARD POISSONNIERE
Bonne Nouvelle
Passage des Panoramas
Rex
BOULEVARD BONNE NOUVELLE
RUE ST-MARC
RUE DE RICHELIEU
RUE VIVIENNE
FEYDEAU
2e
RUE DU SENTIER
RUE POISSONNIERE
PLACE DE LA BOURSE
R DE LA BOURSE
RUE DES JEUNEURS
SEPTEMBRE
RUE ST-AUGUSTIN
Bourse
R DU CROISSANT
R ST-JOSEPH
RUE DE CLERY
RUE REAUMUR
RUE D'ABOUKIR
PLACE DU CAIRE
PAS DU CAIRE
RUE DU CAIRE
RUE COLBERT
Bibliothèque Nationale
RUE N.-D.-DES-VICTOIRES
RUE MONTMARTRE
Sentier
RUE DES PETITS CARREAUX
RUE DE LA BANQUE
RUE DU MAIL
Gal Vivienne
GAL COLBERT
N.-D. des Victoires
PLACE PETITS PERES
RUE MONTORGUEIL
RUE DE BEAUJOLAIS
RUE BACHAUMONT
RUE DUSSOUBS
PLACE DES VICTOIRES
RUE MANDAR
Jardin du Palais Royal
RUE DE LA VRILLIERE
RUE ETIENNE MARCEL
RUE M. STUART
Pas Grand Cerf
RUE ST-DENIS
RUE TIQUETONNE
Banque de France
GALERIE DE VALOIS
RUE DE VALOIS
Hôtel des Postes (Main P.O.)
Tour de Jean Sans Peur
RUE COQUILLIERE
RUE J. J. ROUSSEAU
RUE DE TURBIGO
Etienne Marcel
RUE CROIX DES PETITS CHAMPS
RUE DU JOUR
RUE DU LOUVRE
St-Eustache
RUE RAMBUTEAU
PLACE DE VALOIS
RUE BONS ENFANTS
Gal Véro Dodat
Les Halles
RUE DU PELICAN
Jardin des Halles
Forum des Halles
Chatelet-les-Halles
RESTAURANTS
La Muscade 22
A Priori Thé 13
Le Rubis 18
Verlet 30
The World Bar 1
Bistrot des Victoires 23
Dilan 20
Drouant 11
Gallopin 7
Le Grand Café Capucines 2
Le Grand Véfour 21
Higuma 15
Le Loup Blanc 27
Aux Lyonnais 3
Le Meurice H
Le Vaudeville 8
BARS & CLUBS
Le Cab 32
Le Café 26
Le Café Noir 14
Bar Costes D
De La Ville Café 6
Bar Hemingway 12
L'Insolite 16
Kitty O'Shea's 10
Rex Club 5
Le Tambour 24
Le Triptyque 9
Villa Koops 29

alluring or fashionable parts of Paris – though this was not always so. The western section, from the Madeleine to Porte St-Denis, follows the rampart built by Charles V in the mid-fourteenth century. When its defensive purpose became redundant with the offensive foreign policy of Louis XIV, the walls were pulled down and the ditches filled in, leaving a wide promenade (given the name *boulevard* after the military term for the level part of a rampart).

The boulevards soon became a fashionable place to be seen. In the nineteenth century Parisians came in droves to stroll and sit out drinking lemonade or beer in the numerous cafés. Passers-by were assailed by the constant sound of corks popping, and on one walk Liszt ran into Heine, Balzac, Chopin and Berlioz. The chic café clientele of the west-end **boulevard des Italiens** set the trends for all of Paris in terms of manners, dress and conversation, and there was much intellectual debate and ferment. Balzac called the boulevards "the poem of Paris", what the Grand Canal was to Venice, saying that whoever stepped onto them was lost to their charm: "on y boit des idées" ("here people drink in ideas").

The eastern section developed a more colourful reputation, derived from its association with street theatre, mime, juggling, puppets, waxworks and cafés of ill repute, earning itself the nickname the *boulevard du Crime* and immortalized in the film *Les Enfants du Paradis*. Much of this area was swept away in the latter half of the nineteenth century by Baron Haussmann when he created the huge place de la République.

As recently as the 1950s, a visitor to Paris would, as a matter of course, have gone for a stroll along the Grands Boulevards to see "*Paris vivant*". And something of this tradition still survives in the theatres and cinemas (including the Max Linder and Rex – the latter an extraordinary building inside and out, see p.367) and numerous brasseries and cafés.

It was at 14 **boulevard des Capucines**, in 1895, that Paris saw its first film, or animated photography, as the Lumière brothers' invention was called. Some years earlier, in 1874, another artistic revolution had taken place at no. 35 in the former studio of photographer Félix Nadar – the first **Impressionist exhibition**. It was greeted with outrage by the art world; one critic said of Monet's *Impression, soleil levant* ("Impression: sunrise"), "it was worse than anyone had hitherto dared to paint".

The Musée Grévin

A remnant from the fun-loving times on the Grands Boulevards is the waxworks in the **Musée Grévin** (Ⓦwww.grevin.com; Mon–Fri 10am–6.30pm, Sat & Sun 10am–7pm; last admission an hour before closing; €18, children €10.50; M° Rue Montmartre), on boulevard Montmartre. It's somewhat overpriced, but a fun outing nonetheless. You can prop up the bar with Ernest Hemingway or have your photo taken next to Isabelle Adjani, Zinedine Zidane or one of the many other French literary, media and political personalities, as well as the usual bunch of Hollywood actors. Many of the displays illustrate scenes from French history, especially the more grisly episodes such as the St Bartholomew's Day massacre. Perhaps the best thing about the museum, though, is the original rooms: the magical Palais des Mirages (Hall of Mirrors), built for the Exposition Universelle in 1900; the theatre with its sculptures by Bourdelle; and the 1882 Baroque-style Hall of Columns, where among other unlikely juxtapositions, Lara Croft prepares for action a few metres away from a dignified Charles de Gaulle, while Voltaire smiles across at the billowing skirts of Marilyn Monroe.

Opéra Garnier and around

Set back from the boulevard des Capucines is the dazzling Opéra de Paris – usually referred to as the **Opéra Garnier** (Ⓦwww.opera-de-paris.fr; M° Opéra) to distinguish it from the new opera house at the Bastille. Constructed between 1865 and 1872 as part of Napoléon III's vision for Paris, it crowns the avenue de l'Opéra, which was deliberately kept free of trees in order not to mask views of the building. The architect, Charles Garnier, whose golden bust by Carpeaux can be seen on the rue Auber side, was a relative unknown, determined to make his mark with something original. Drawing on a number of existing styles, he succeeded in creating a magnificently ornate building the like of which Paris had never seen before – when the Empress Eugénie asked in bewilderment what style it was, Garnier replied that it was "Napoléon III style". Certainly, if any building can be said to exemplify the Second Empire, it is this – in its show of wealth and hint of vulgarity. In the event, however, it was only completed in 1875 after the Empire had been swept away by the Third Republic, and even Garnier had to pay for his ticket on the opening night. Part of the reason construction took so long – fourteen years in all – was the discovery of a water table which had to be drained and replaced by a huge concrete well, giving rise to the legend of an underground lake, popularized by Gaston Leroux's *Phantom of the Opera*.

The theatre's **facade** is a fairy-tale concoction of white, pink and green marble, colonnades, rearing horses, winged angels and gleaming gold busts of composers. The group sculpture on the right of the entrance, Carpeaux's *La Danse*, caused a stir on unveiling for its frank sensuality; one outraged protestor went as far as to throw black ink over the fleshy thigh of the female nude dancer.

The opulent **interior**, with its spacious, gilded-marble and mirrored lobbies, was intended to give Second Empire society suitably grand spaces in which to meet and be seen. The auditorium itself is all red velvet and gold leaf, hung with a six-tonne chandelier; the colourful ceiling was painted by Chagall in 1964 and depicts scenes from well-known operas and ballets jumbled up with famous Parisian landmarks. You can **visit** the interior (daily 10am–5pm; €8), including the auditorium – as long as there are no rehearsals; your best chance is between 1 and 2pm. The entry ticket includes the **Bibliothèque-Musée de l'Opéra**, containing model sets, dreadful nineteenth-century paintings, and rather better temporary exhibitions on operatic themes. Amid the postcards and memorabilia in the **shop** is one of the city's most unusual souvenirs – honey collected from hives kept by former backstage worker Jean Paucton on the vast copper and zinc roof of the opera house; his 125,000 bees seek out nectar from parks, cemeteries and window boxes and produce up to 300kg of honey a year.

On the west side of the Opéra, at 11bis rue Scribe, is the **Paris-Story** multimedia show (daily with shows on the hour 10am–6pm; €10, children €6; M° Opéra), a partial and highly romanticized history of Paris "narrated" by Victor Hugo, with simultaneous translation in English. The fifty-minute film uses a kaleidoscope of computer-generated images and archive footage, set against a luscious classical-music soundtrack. You probably won't learn much you didn't already know, but it's quite enjoyable all the same.

Just to the north, on boulevard Haussmann, you'll find two of the city's big department stores, **Printemps** and **Galeries Lafayette** (M° Chausée d'Antin/Havre Caumartin; see pp.366–367 for reviews). Built in the latter half of the nineteenth century, they may have lost their grand central staircases, but they still sport their proud fin-de-siècle stained-glass domes. Printemps' dome is particularly splendid, coloured in glowing hues of green and blue, best appreciated from the brasserie beneath. Following in the stores' wake, a number of banks were built in the area. The Crédit Lyonnais at 19 boulevard des Italiens, south of boulevard Haussmann, is perhaps the most imposing, with its huge gold clock flanked by gigantic caryatids. Across the road at no. 20 the Banque Nationale de Paris occupies another striking building, with gilded wrought-iron balconies and finely sculpted friezes depicting hunting scenes. It used to be the *Maison Dorée*, a restaurant from the 1840s, where you might have bumped into Balzac, Hugo, Flaubert and Nerval, among other literary figures. At no. 16 is the bank's main building – a sleek 1930s Art Deco edifice. As you cross over rue Laffitte to reach it, you get a wonderful view of Notre Dame de Lorette, with the Sacré Coeur rearing up in the background.

The Eglise de la Madeleine

South of boulevard Haussmann, occupying nearly the whole of the place de la Madeleine, is the imperious-looking **Eglise de la Madeleine** (M° Madeleine), a favourite venue for society weddings. Modelled on the Parthenon, the building is surrounded by 52 Corinthian columns and fronted by a huge pediment depicting the Last Judgement; its facade is a near mirror image of the Assemblée Nationale, directly opposite, on the far side of the place de la Concorde – a fine vista best appreciated from the top of the Madeleine steps. Originally intended as a monument to Napoleon's army – a plan abandoned after the French were defeated by the Russians in 1812 – the building narrowly escaped being turned into a railway station before finally being consecrated to Mary Magdalene in 1845. Inside, a theatrical stone sculpture of the Magdalene being swept up to heaven by two angels draws your eye to the high altar. The half-dome above is decorated with a fresco by Jules-Claude Ziegler (1804–56), a student of Ingres; entitled *The History of Christianity*, it commemorates the concordat signed between the church and state after the end of the Revolution, and shows all the key figures in Christendom, with Napoleon centre-stage, naturally. The church's interior is otherwise rather dull and gloomy, heavy with gilt-edged marble. If you're lucky, the sombre atmosphere may be broken by the sound of the organ, reckoned to be one of Paris's best – the church is in fact a regular venue for recitals and choral concerts. Illustrious past organists include Saint-Saëns and Fauré, whose famous *Requiem* was premiered at the Madeleine in 1888 – to be heard here again at the composer's own funeral 36 years later.

If the Madeleine caters to spiritual needs, the rest of the square is given over to nourishment of a rather earthier kind, for this is where Paris's top **gourmet food stores** Fauchon and Hédiard (see box, p.398) are located. Their remarkable displays are a feast for the eyes, and both have restaurants where you can sample some of their epicurean treats. On the east side of the Madeleine church is one of the city's oldest flower markets dating back to 1832, open every day except Monday, while nearby some rather fine Art Nouveau public toilets, built in 1905, are definitely worth inspecting.

Place Vendôme and around

A short walk east of place de la Madeleine lies **place Vendôme**, one of the city's most impressive set pieces, built by Versailles architect Hardouin-Mansart during the final years of Louis XIV's reign. It's a pleasingly symmetrical, eight-sided *place*, enclosed by a harmonious ensemble of elegant mansions, graced with Corinthian pilasters, mascarons and steeply pitched roofs. Once the grand residences of tax collectors and financiers, they now house such luxury

△ Place Vendôme

establishments as the *Ritz* hotel (from where Di and Dodi set off on their last journey), Cartier, Bulgari and other top-flight jewellers, lending the square a decidedly exclusive air. The Ministry of Justice is also sited here, on the west side; its facade still has the marble plaque showing a standard metre put here in 1795 in order to familiarize Parisians with the new unit of measure. No. 12, on the opposite side, now occupied by Chaumet jewellers, is where Chopin died, in 1849. Somewhat out of proportion with the rest of the square, the centrepiece is a towering triumphal **column**, modelled on Trajan's column in Rome, and surmounted by a statue of Napoleon dressed as Caesar. It was raised in 1806 to celebrate the Battle of Austerlitz – bronze reliefs of scenes of the battle, cast from 1200 recycled Austro-Russian cannons, spiral their way up the column. The column that stands here today is actually a replica of the original, brought crashing down during the Commune in 1871 – the main instigator behind this act was the artist Gustave Courbet, who was imprisoned and ordered to pay for the column's restoration; he was financially ruined and lived the rest of his life in exile in Switzerland.

Rue St-Honoré and Eglise St-Roch

A healthy bank balance comes in handy if you intend to do more than window-shop in the streets around place Vendôme, especially ancient **rue St-Honoré**, a preserve of top fashion designers and art galleries; you can wonder at John Galliano's extravagant creations at no. 392 or join the style-conscious young Parisians perusing the latest designs at Colette concept store at no. 213 (see p.394).

East of place Vendôme, on rues **St-Roch** and **Ste-Anne**, in particular, the Japanese community has established a mini enclave; you'll find some good noodle and sushi bars here such as *Higuma* (see p.325), nearly always full to bursting at lunch.

On the corner of rue St-Roch and rue **St-Honoré** stands the **Eglise St-Roch**, begun in 1653 but not completed till 1740, as money kept running out. Its handsome honey-coloured classical facade was recently scrubbed clean and shows little sign of the battering it received in 1795 when the young Napoleon dispersed a Royalist uprising with cannons (or a "whiff of grapeshot", as he famously put it), and was rewarded with promotion to the rank of general. The St-Roch quartier was much more densely populated than it is now and boasted many illustrious parishioners, some of whom – Corneille, Diderot and Le Nôtre among them – are buried in the church. The nave is very long, almost as long as Notre-Dame's, filled with light and flanked with numerous side chapels richly decorated with paintings and sculpture by the likes of Coysevox and Coustou. A free leaflet detailing the artworks is available from the welcome desk. The church is also a regular venue for evening concerts, and holds free lunchtime song and chamber music recitals most Tuesdays from 12.15 to 1pm.

The Palais Royal

Following rue St-Honoré east you come to the **Palais Royal** (M° Palais-Royal-Musée-du-Louvre), a complex of handsome buildings and gardens. There are two main parts: the palace itself and, beyond it, galleries surrounding gardens on three sides. The palace, a fine colonnaded building, dates back to 1624, though has been much modified and renovated since. It was built for Cardinal Richelieu, who left it to the king, Louis XIV, then just a boy; he and his mother lived in the palace for a time, and Louis loved to play here with his toy soldiers and march up and down banging his drum. The palace later passed to his brother, the duc d'Orléans, and for a time provided sanctuary to Henrietta Maria, the widow of the executed English king, Charles 1. The palace is now occupied by various government departments and is rarely open to the public; an annexe to the side houses the **Comédie Française**, long-standing venue for the classics of French theatre. Beyond the palace lie sedate **gardens** lined with stately arcaded buildings, put up in the 1780s by Philippe-Egalité, a descendant of the duc d'Orléans. Desperate to pay off his debts, he let out the spaces under the arcades to shops. One of them, Guillaumot, founded in 1785 and selling antiquarian books mostly on genealogy and heraldry (153 **Galerie de Valois**), is still there today. Many of the other shops also specialize in antiques or quirky collectors' items, such as lead soldiers and medals – you can buy a Légion d'Honneur for around €150 at A Marie Stuart, no. 3 Galerie de

Montpensier. At no. 142 Galerie de Valois is an exquisite purple-panelled *parfumerie*, Les Salons du Palais Royal Shiseido, while the bright-red decor at Didier Ludot's La Petite Robe Noire (no. 125) sets off to advantage his wonderful collection of new and vintage little black dresses.

Past residents of the desirable flats above the arcades include Cocteau and Colette – the latter lived here until her death in 1954 and enjoyed looking out over the gardens when she was too crippled with arthritis to walk. It's certainly an attractive and peaceful oasis, with avenues of clipped limes, fountains and flowerbeds, and popular on weekends with newlyweds who come here to be photographed, though surprisingly unfrequented at other times. You'd hardly guess that for many years this was a site of gambling dens, brothels (it was to a prostitute here that Napoleon lost his virginity in 1787) and funfair attractions – there was even a *café mécanique*, where you sat at a table, sent your order down one of its legs, and were served via the other. As an 1815 guidebook put it: "There you can see everything, hear everything, know everything ... All the senses are aroused, all the passions are excited and a general intoxication of pleasure may be said to prevail in this enclosure of luxury." The clearing of Paris's brothels in 1829–31 and the prohibition on public gambling in 1838, however, put an end to the fun, and the Grands Boulevards took up the baton. Folly, some might say, has returned – in the form of Daniel Buren's black-and-white striped pillars, rather like sticks of Brighton rock, all of varying heights, dotted about the main courtyard in front of the palace. Installed in 1986 after the space was cleared of cars, they're a rather disconcerting sight, but are certainly popular with children and rollerbladers, who treat them as an adventure playground and obstacle course respectively.

The passages, Bibliothèque Nationale and Bourse

The 2e arrondissement is scattered with around twenty **passages**, or shopping arcades, that have survived from the early nineteenth century. In 1840 over a hundred existed, but most were later destroyed to make way for Haussmann's boulevards. After decades of decay and neglect, some have now been restored to something approaching their former glory and are being colonized by chic boutiques. Their entrances are easy to miss and where you emerge at the other end can be quite a surprise. Most are closed at night and on Sundays.

The following account takes you on a walking route around the best of the *passages*, including the elegant **Galerie Véro-Dodat** and **Galerie Vivienne**, the more neglected, but no less fascinating **Passage Choiseul** and **Passage des Panoramas**, and the **Passages Jouffroy and Verdeau** with their quirky boutiques and secondhand bookshops. En route you could make detours to the **Bibliothèque Nationale**, the National Library of France, and the **Bourse**, the city's stock exchange.

Galerie Véro-Dodat and the Bibliothèque Nationale

The most homogeneous and aristocratic of the *passages,* with painted ceilings and panelled mahogany shop fronts divided by faux marble columns, is **Galerie Véro-Dodat** (between rue Croix-des-Petits-Champs and rue Jean-Jacques

Rousseau; M° Palais-Royal-Musée-du-Louvre), named after the two pork butchers who set it up in 1824. Renovated in 1980, it's been largely colonized by smart design shops and art galleries, though some older businesses, such as R. F. Charle, at no. 17, specializing in the repair and sale of vintage guitars, mandolins and other stringed instruments, remain.

The **Banque de France** lies a short way northwest of Galerie Véro-Dodat. Rather than negotiating its massive bulk to reach the *passages* further north, it's more pleasant to walk through the garden of the Palais Royal via place de Valois. Rue de Montpensier, running alongside the gardens to the west, is connected to rue de Richelieu by several tiny *passages*, of which Hulot brings you out at the statue of Molière on the junction of rues Richelieu and Molière. A certain charm also lingers about rue de Beaujolais, bordering the northern end of the gardens, with its corner café looking out on the Théâtre du Palais-Royal, and with glimpses into the venerable *Grand Véfour* restaurant (see p.325), plus more short arcades leading up to rue des Petits-Champs.

On the other side of rue des Petits-Champs, just to the left as you come from rue de Beaujolais, looms the forbidding wall of the **Bibliothèque Nationale**, part of whose enormous collection has been transferred to the new François Mitterrand site in the 13e (see p.190). The library's origins go back to the 1660s, when Louis XIV's finance minister Colbert deposited a collection of royal manuscripts here, and it was first opened to the public in 1692. There's no restriction on entering the library, nor on peering into the atmospheric reading rooms; the central room, with its slender iron columns supporting nine domes, is a fine example of the early use of iron frame construction, though it looks strangely bereft now that its books have been transferred to the newer site. Visiting the library's excellent **temporary exhibitions** (Tues–Sat 10am–7pm, Sun noon–7pm; €7), which in 2007 included a major retrospective of Atget's photography, will give you access to the beautiful **Galerie Mazarine**, with its panelled ceilings painted by Romanelli (1617–62). It's also worth calling into the **Cabinet des Monnaies, Médailles et Antiques** (Mon–Fri 9am–6pm, Sat 9am–5pm; free), a permanent display of coins and ancient treasures built up by successive kings from Philippe-Auguste onwards. Exhibits include Etruscan bronzes, ancient Greek jewellery and some exquisite medieval cameos. One of the highlights is Charlemagne's ivory chess set, its pieces malevolent-looking characters astride elephants.

Galerie Colbert and Vivienne

Galerie Colbert, one of two *passages* linking rue Vivienne with rue des Petits-Champs, has been renovated and incorporated into the INHA (National Institute of Art History), under the umbrella of the Bibliothèque Nationale, and is out of bounds to the general public; on the corner of the *passage* and rue Vivienne is the 1830s-style brasserie, *Le Grand Colbert*, to which senior librarians and academics retire for lunch. The flamboyant decor of Grecian and marine motifs in neighbouring **Galerie Vivienne** establishes the perfect ambience in which to buy Jean-Paul Gaultier gear, or you can browse in the antiquarian bookshop, Librairie Jousseaume, dating back to the *passage*'s earliest days, and take a tea break in *A Priori Thé* (see p.325).

Passage Choiseul

Three blocks west from Galerie Vivienne along rue des Petits-Champs, lined with wine bars, delicatessens and design shops, lies **passage Choiseul**, alluringly dark and dingy-looking. It was here, in the early 1900s, that the author

Louis-Ferdinand Céline lived as a boy, and judging by his account of it in his autobiographical *Death on Credit*, it was none too salubrious a place: "The gas lamps stank so badly in the stagnant air of the *passage* that towards evening some women would start to feel unwell, added to which there was the stench of dogs' urine to contend with." Nowadays the only aromas you're likely to be assailed with come from the takeaway food shops, which keep company with discount clothes and book stores, bars, art galleries and Lavrut, at no. 52, a well-known supplier of artists' materials. Also here is an entrance to the théâtre des Bouffes Parisiens, where Offenbach conducted the first performance of *Orpheus in the Underworld*.

The Bourse and around

Exiting passage Choiseul onto rue St Augustin and turning right, you come to the **Bourse**, the Paris stock exchange, an imposing Neoclassical edifice built under Napoleon in 1808 and enlarged in 1903 with the addition of two side wings. To visit you'll need to book in advance on ⓣ01.49.27.55.55. Guided tours (€8.50) around the eerily quiet building (most of the action takes place online these days) last about an hour and include a presentation on how *Paris-bourse* works. Overshadowing the Bourse from the south is the antennae-topped building of AFP, the French news agency. Rue Réaumur, running east from here, used to be the Fleet Street of Paris, but all the newspapers have now moved elsewhere; the last to leave was *Le Figaro* in 2005.

Just up the road on the corner of rue du Croissant and rue Montmartre, the *Café du Croissant* was the scene of the assassination on July 31, 1914 of Jean Jaurès, the Socialist leader. He was shot by young French nationalist Raul Vilain, in protest at Jaurès's pacifism. Even if he had survived it seems unlikely that Jaurès could have held back the slide to war: just three days later Germany declared war on France.

Passage des Panoramas

The grid of arcades north of the Bourse, just off rue Vivienne, is known as the **passage des Panoramas**. It was around here, in 1817, that the first Parisian gas lamps were tried out. A little shabby and frayed around the edges, the *passage* combines old-fashioned chic and workaday atmosphere. Most of the eateries here – mainly Indian and Chinese restaurants – make no pretence at style, but one café, *L'Arbre à Cannelle* (see p.324), a former brasserie, has beautiful carved wood ornamentation and painted ceiling panels dating from the 1900s. Another place that's kept its original decor is the printshop, Stern, dating back to 1867. Most of the other outlets are given over to bric-a-brac, secondhand postcard, coin and stamp dealers, with serious collectors poring over catalogues.

Passages Jouffroy, Verdeau and des Princes and Hôtel Drouot

Across boulevard Montmartre, **passage Jouffroy** is full of the kind of stores that make shopping an adventure rather than a chore. One of them, M & G Segas, sells eccentric walking canes and theatrical antiques opposite Pain d'Epices (see p.434), a shop selling every conceivable fitting and furnishing for a doll's house. Near the romantic *Hôtel Chopin* (reviewed on p.298), Paul Vulin's secondhand books spill out into the passageway, and Ciné-Doc appeals to cinephiles with its collection of old film posters. Crossing rue de la Grange-Batelière, you enter equally enchanting **passage Verdeau**, sheltering antiquarian books and old prints.

At the top of rue Richelieu, the tiny **passage des Princes**, with its beautiful glass ceiling, stained-glass decoration and twirly lamps, has been taken over by the toy emporium JouéClub (see p.433). Its erstwhile neighbour, the passage de l'Opéra, described in surreal detail by Louis Aragon in *Paris Peasant*, was eaten up with the completion of Haussmann's boulevards.

While in this area, you could also take a look at what's up for auction at the Paris equivalent of Christie's and Sotheby's, the **Hôtel Drouot** (9 rue Drouot; M° Le Peletier/Richelieu-Drouot). To spare any fear of unintended hand movements landing you in the bankruptcy courts, you can simply wander round looking at the goods before the action starts (11am–6pm on the eve of the sale, 11am–noon on the day itself). Auctions are announced in the press, under "Ventes aux Enchères"; you'll find details, including photos of pieces, in the widely available weekly *Gazette de l'Hôtel Drouot* or on their website Ⓦwww.drouot.fr.

Sentier and around

At the heart of the 2e arrondissement lies the **Sentier** quartier, largely given over to the rag trade, and the frenetic trading and deliveries of cloth and the general to-ing and fro-ing make a lively change from the office-bound districts further west. On **place du Caire**, beneath an extraordinary pseudo-Egyptian facade of grotesque Pharaonic heads (a celebration of Napoleon's conquest of Egypt), an archway opens onto a series of arcades, the **passage du Caire**. This, contrary to any visible evidence, is the oldest of all the *passages* and entirely monopolized by wholesale clothes shops.

The garment business gets progressively more upmarket as you head west from the trade area. Louis XIV's attractive circular **place des Victoires**, adjoined to the north by the appealingly asymmetrical place des Petits-Pères, is full of designer clothes shops such as Kenzo and Cacharel. The trend continues on the upper stretch of **rue Etienne Marcel**, with young, hip fashion boutiques at the lower end.

Rue Etienne Marcel is roughly where the old medieval city wall used to run, and at no. 20 survives a rare vestige from this period: the **Tour Jean Sans Peur** (April–Oct Wed–Sun 1.30–6pm; Nov–March Wed, Sat & Sun 1.30–6pm; €5), a fine Gothic tower, the only remnant of a grand town house that used to straddle the old wall and was built by Jean Sans Peur, the Duc de Bourgogne. The duke had this tower erected as a place of refuge – he feared reprisal after having assassinated Louis d'Orléans, the king's brother – a murder that kicked off a thirty-year war between the Armagnacs and Burgundys. A spiral stone staircase (138 steps) climbs up inside the tower and ends with a beautiful vaulted roof decorated with intricate stone carvings of oak leaves, hawthorn and hops, all symbols of the Burgundy family. Various rooms off the staircase contain background information on the tower and the period.

Just north of M° Etienne-Marcel, between rue St-Denis and rue Dessoubs, arches the lofty, three-storey **passage du Grand-Cerf**, one of the most attractive of all the arcades. The wrought-iron work, glass roof and plain-wood shop fronts have all been cleaned, attracting stylish arts, crafts and contemporary design shops.

Rue St-Denis

Running north from rue Etienne Marcel, **rue St-Denis** is the city's centuries-old red-light area, where weary women wait in doorways between peepshows, striptease joints and sex shops. The area is changing, however, and some of the older outlets are closing down, partly because sex megastores have taken some of their business and partly because the 2e arrondissement *mairie* is attempting to clean up the area by encouraging new businesses to move in. Many of the independent streetwalkers – the native Parisian "traditionelles" – have also left, forced out by steep fines introduced by Sarkozy in his capacity as interior minister in 2002. Reactions to these changes have been mixed, with many locals lamenting that the street is being over-sanitized and in danger of losing its character, while *Le Parisien* newspaper has argued that the *traditionelles* are as Parisian as *steak-frites* and Gaulloises and that their disappearance from the city centre is a great loss to traditional Paris life.

Rue Montorgueil

The emphasis on rues Montmartre, Montorgueil and Turbigo, leading south from rue Réaumur, turns towards food as they approach Les Halles. Worth lingering over in particular is the picturesque pedestrianized market street **rue Montorgueil**, where grocers, horse butchers and fishmongers ply their trade alongside traditional restaurants, such as *L'Escargot*, serving snails since 1875, and trendy cafés catering to a cool crowd. Hard to pass by without stopping to gaze at its exquisite cakes and beautiful old decor is Stohrer's *patisserie*, in business since 1730; it seems Her Majesty Queen Elizabeth couldn't resist either – as postcards on sale at the shop record, she stopped off here during her Entente Cordiale centenary visit in April 2004 and was presented with a handmade chocolate Easter egg.

Rue Montmartre is characterized by its excellent kitchenware shops, such as MORA and Bovida (see p.400), stocking all the essential utensils for making the perfect *tarte tatin* or *coq au vin*.

5

Beaubourg and Les Halles

Straddling the third and fourth arrondissements, the **Beaubourg** quartier hums with lively cafés, shops and art galleries; at its heart stands the **Pompidou Centre**, one of the city's most popular attractions. The ground-breaking "inside-out" architecture of this huge arts centre provoked a storm of controversy on its opening in 1977, but since then it has won over critics and public alike, and become one of the city's most recognizable landmarks, drawing large numbers to its excellent modern art museum and high-profile exhibitions. By contrast, nearby **Les Halles**, a massive underground shopping complex built at around the same time as the Pompidou Centre to replace the centuries-old food market, has never really endeared itself to the city's inhabitants and is probably the least inspired of all the developments in the capital in the last thirty years; the good news is that it's soon to undergo a major revamp.

The Pompidou Centre

Celebrating its thirtieth anniversary in 2007 and attracting over five million visitors a year, the **Pompidou Centre** (ⓦwww.centrepompidou.fr; M° Rambuteau/Hôtel-de-Ville), known locally as Beaubourg, would seem to have fulfilled its founder Georges Pompidou's vision of a world-class modern art museum and multidisciplinary arts centre. Such is its popularity and success that in 2000 the building had to close for two years for major repair work from all the wear and tear. When the centre first opened, however, it met with a very mixed reception, with one critic dubbing it an oil refinery. The design is certainly radical. The architects, Renzo Piano and Richard Rogers, wanted to move away from the idea of galleries as closed treasure chests to create something more open and accessible, so they stripped the "skin" off the building and made all the "bones" visible. The infrastructure was put on the outside: escalator tubes and utility pipes, colour-coded according to their function, climb around the exterior, giving the building its crazy snakes-and-ladders appearance.

The centre's main draw is its modern art museum, the **Musée National d'Art Moderne**, on the fourth and fifth floors, with temporary exhibitions on

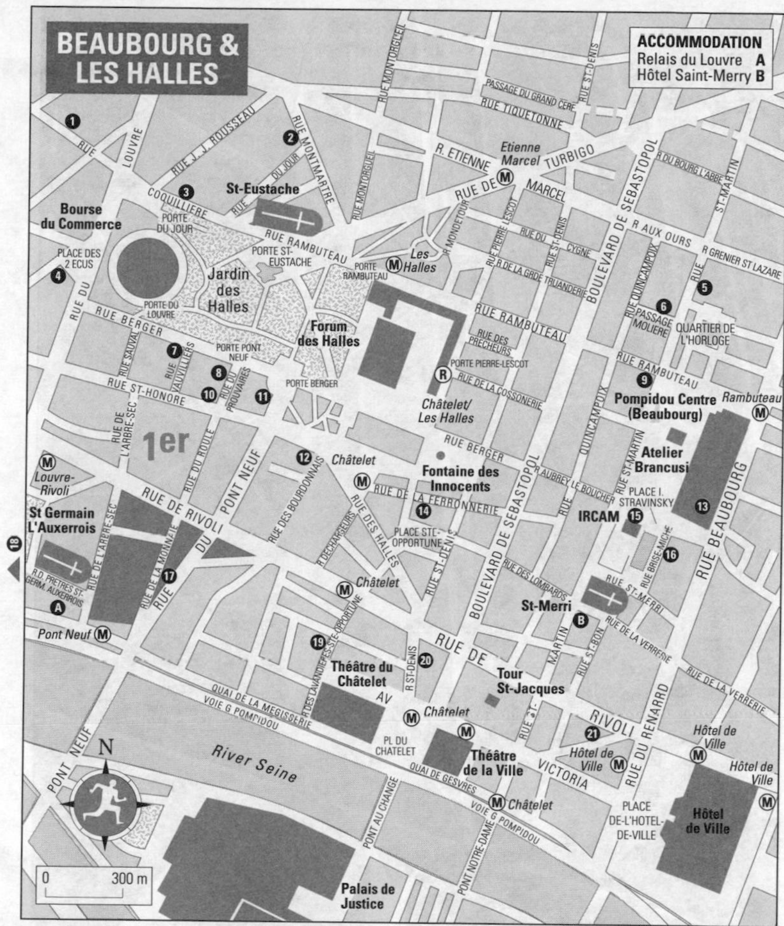

CAFÉS & WINE BARS
- Café Beaubourg 15
- Le Café des Initiés 4
- A la Cloche des Halles 1
- Dame Tartine 16
- Le Petit Marcel 9

RESTAURANTS
- Au Chien qui Fume 11
- La Coupe-Gorge 21
- Georges 13
- Le Gros Minet 10
- Au Pied de Cochon 3
- La Robe et le Palais 19
- La Tour de Montlhéry (Chez Denise) 8
- La Victoire Suprême du Cœur 12
- Au Vieux Mollère 6

BARS & CLUBS
- Banana Café 14
- Le Cochon à l'Oreille 2
- Le Comptoir 7
- Le Fumoir 18
- Kong 17
- Au Trappiste 20
- L'Unity Bar 5

the sixth floor. One of the added treats of visiting these is that you get to ascend the transparent escalator on the outside of the building, affording superb views over the city. Equally good is the vista from the sleek sixth-floor restaurant *Georges* (see p.327). On the lower floors there are cinemas, a performance space and the BPI or **Bibliothèque Publique** (Mon–Fri noon–10pm, Sat & Sun 11am–10pm; free), which has an impressive collection of 2500 periodicals, including international press, 10,000 CDs and 2200 documentary films.

Amid the centre's thirtieth anniversary celebrations plans were announced to open an annexe of the modern art museum in Shanghai. The centre is making

△ The Pompidou Centre

much of the benefits of cultural exchange, but the other major bonus is that the project will bring in much-needed revenue and help to finance the costly bill of maintaining the Pompidou Centre; those colourful exterior pipes are all very well but they require constant repainting, and the building itself consumes huge amounts of energy.

Musée National d'Art Moderne

Thanks to an astute acquisitions policy and some generous gifts, the **Musée National d'Art Moderne** (daily except Tues 11am–10pm; €10, under 18s free; free to all first Sun of the month; tickets bookable online) is a near-complete visual essay on the history of twentieth-century art and is so large that only a fraction of the 58,000 works are on display at any one time (they're frequently rotated). The fifth floor covers 1905 to 1960, while the fourth floor brings the collection from 1960 to the present day. Your ticket is valid for a single visit only, so you can't, for example, pop out for a break in one of the centre's cafés and re-enter. The collection is densely and efficiently organized, so, unlike many of the more unwieldy museums in Paris, half a day is probably enough for a comfortable, rewarding visit.

Fauvism, Cubism and Dada

The collection on floor five is organized more or less chronologically and starts in a blaze of colour with the **Fauvists – Braque**, **Derain**, **Vlaminck** and **Matisse**. Their vibrant works reflect the movement's desire to create form rather than imitate nature. Colour becomes a way of composing and structuring a picture, as in Braque's *L'Estaque* (1906), where trees and sky are broken down into blocks of vibrant reds and greens. Matisse's series of *Luxe paintings* also stands out, the colourful nudes recalling the primitive figures of Gauguin.

Shape is broken down even further in Picasso's and Braque's early **Cubist** paintings. Highlights include **Picasso**'s portrait of his lover Fernande (*Femme assise dans un fauteuil*; 1910), in which different angles of the figure are shown all at once, giving rise to complex patterns and creating the effect of movement. Hung alongside Picasso's works, and almost indistinguishable from them, are a number of **Braque**'s works, such as *Nature morte au violon* (1911) and *Femme à la guitare* (1913). The juxtaposition of these paintings illustrates the intellectual and artistic dialogue that went on between the two artists, who lived next door to each other at the Bateau-Lavoir in Montmartre.

Another artist heavily influenced by the new Cubism was **Fernand Léger**. In paintings such as *Femme en rouge et vert* (1914) and *Contraste de formes* (1913) Léger creates his own distinctive form of Cubism based on tubular shapes, inspired by the modern machinery of World War I in which he fought.

Reaction to the horror of the 1914–18 war gave rise to the nihilistic **Dada** movement, a revolt against petty bourgeois values; leading members included **Marcel Duchamp**, who selected everyday objects ("ready-mades") such as the *Hat Rack* (1917), and elevated them, without modification, to the rank of works of art, simply by taking them out of their ordinary context and putting them on display. As well as the *Hat Rack*, you can inspect Duchamp's most notorious ready-made – a urinal – which he called *Fontaine* and first exhibited in New York in 1917.

Abstract art

The museum holds a particularly rich collection of **Kandinskys**. His series entitled *Impressions*, *Improvisations* and *Compositions* consists of non-figurative shapes and swathes of colour, and heralds a move away from an obsession with subject towards a passion for the creative process itself. Fellow pioneering abstract artists **Sonia and Robert Delaunay** set the walls ablaze with their characteristically colourful paintings. In Sonia Delaunay's wonderfully vibrant

Marché de Minho (1916), the juxtaposition of colours makes some appear to recede and others come forward, creating a shimmering effect.

Surrealism and abstract expressionism

Surrealism, an offshoot of the Dada movement, dominates in later rooms with works by Magritte, Dalí and Ernst. Typical of the movement's exploration of the darker recesses of the mind, **Ernst**'s disturbing *Ubu Imperator* (1923) depicts a figure that is part man, part Tower of Pisa and part spinning top, and would seem to symbolize the perversion of male authority. A more ethereal, floating world of abstract associations is depicted in **Joan Miró**'s and **Jean Arp**'s canvases.

American **abstract expressionists** Jackson Pollock and Mark Rothko are also represented. In Pollock's splattery *No 26A, Black and white* (1948), the two colours seem to struggle for domination; the dark bands of colour in Rothko's large canvas *No. 14 (Browns over Dark)*, in contrast, draw the viewer in.

Matisse's later experiments with form and colour are usually on display. His technique of *découpage* (creating a picture from cut-out coloured pieces of paper) freed colour from drawing and line, and is perfected in his masterpiece *La Tristesse du roi* (1952), in which a woman dances while an elderly king plays a guitar, mourning his lost youth.

Contemporary art

The fourth floor is given over to **contemporary art**, as well as displays of architectural models and contemporary design. Of the more established artists, **Yves Klein** stands out for his series of "body prints", in which he turned female models into human paintbrushes, covering them in paint to create his artworks. Most of the prints are executed in International Klein Blue, a beautiful deep and luminous blue which the artist patented himself. Also known for their experiments with new methods and materials, the Nouveaux Réalistes **César** and **Dubuffet** are usually represented, César recognizable for his "compressions", striking sculptures of compressed cars and scrap metal.

Other established French artists you're likely to come across include Annette Messager, Sophie Calle, Christian Boltanski and Daniel Buren. **Christian Boltanski** is known for his large *mise-en-scène* installations, often containing veiled allusions to the Holocaust, while **Daniel Buren**'s works are easy to spot: they nearly all bear his trademark stripes, exactly 8.7cm in width. He caused a furore in 1986 with his installation of black-and-white, vertically striped columns in the courtyard of the Palais Royal, and his work was widely criticized and vilified by the press. Now, however, in his sixties, the one-time *enfant terrible* of the art world has become one of France's most respected living artists – a status confirmed by a one-man show at the Pompidou Centre in 2002.

Some space is dedicated to **video art**, with changing installations by artists such as Jean-Luc Vilmout, Dominique Gonzalez-Foerster, the up-and-coming Melik Ohanian and current star of the scene Pierre Huyghe, who in 2005–6 had solo exhibitions at London's Tate Gallery and Paris's Musée de l'Art Moderne de la Ville de Paris.

Atelier Brancusi

On the northern edge of the Pompidou Centre, down some steps off the piazza, in a small separate one-level building, is the **Atelier Brancusi** (daily except Tues 2–6pm; combined ticket with the Musée National d'Art Moderne). Upon his death in 1956, the sculptor **Constantin Brancusi** bequeathed the contents of his

15e arrondissement studio to the state, on the condition that it be reconstructed exactly as it was found. The artist had become obsessed with the spatial relationship of the sculptures in his studio, going so far as to supplant each sold work with a plaster copy, and the four interconnected rooms of the studio faithfully adhere to his arrangements. Studios one and two are crowded with fluid sculptures of highly polished brass and marble, his trademark abstract bird and column shapes, stylized busts and objects poised as though they're about to take flight. Unfortunately, the rooms are behind glass, adding a feeling of sterility and distance. Perhaps the most satisfying rooms are ateliers three and four, his private quarters, where his tools are displayed on one wall almost like works of art themselves.

Quartier Beaubourg and the Hôtel de Ville

The lively **quartier Beaubourg** around the Pompidou Centre also offers much in the way of visual art. The colourful, moving sculptures and fountains in the pool in front of Eglise St-Merri on **place Igor Stravinsky**, on the south side of the Pompidou Centre, were created by Jean Tinguely and Niki de St-Phalle; this squirting waterworks pays homage to Stravinsky – each fountain corresponds to one of his compositions (*The Firebird*, *The Rite of Spring*, etc) – but shows scant respect for passers-by. Stravinsky's music in many ways paved the way for the pioneering work of **IRCAM** (Institut de la Recherche et de la Coordination Acoustique/Musique), whose entrance is on the west side of the square. Founded by the composer Pierre Boulez, it's a research centre for contemporary music and a concert venue, much of it underground, with an overground extension by Renzo Piano. For more on IRCAM's activities see p.376.

To the north of the Pompidou Centre numerous commercial art galleries and the odd bookshop and *salon de thé* occupy the attractive *hôtels particuliers* of narrow, pedestrianized **rue Quincampoix**. A little further east of here, hidden on impasse Berthaud, off rue Beaubourg, is the **Musée de la Poupée** (daily except Mon 10am–6pm; €6, children €3; Ⓦ www.museedelapoupeeparis.com; M° Rambuteau), a doll museum certain to appeal to small children. In addition to the impressive collection of antique dolls, there are displays of finely detailed tiny irons and sewing machines, furniture and pots and pans and other minuscule accessories.

South of the Pompidou Centre, rue Renard runs down to the **Hôtel de Ville**, the seat of the city's government and a mansion of gargantuan proportions in florid neo-Renaissance style, built in 1882 and modelled pretty much on the previous building burned down in the Commune in 1871. An illustrated history of this edifice, always a prime target in riots and revolutions, is displayed along the platform of M° Châtelet on the Neuilly–Vincennes line. Those opposed to the establishments of kings and emperors created their alternative municipal governments in this building: the Revolutionaries installed themselves here in 1789, the poet Lamartine proclaimed the Second Republic here in 1848, and Gambetta the Third Republic in 1870. But, with the defeat of the Commune in 1871, the conservatives, in control once again, concluded that the Parisian municipal authority had to go if order was to be maintained and the people kept in their place. Thereafter Paris was ruled directly by the ministry of the interior until eventually, in 1977, the city was allowed to run its own affairs and Jacques Chirac was elected mayor.

The square in front of the Hôtel de Ville, once a notorious execution site, is the location of a popular **ice rink** from December to mid-March; it's particularly magical at night and is open till midnight on weekends. You can hire skates for €5.

Les Halles

Located right at the heart of the city is the sprawling underground shopping and leisure complex of **Les Halles**, built in the 1970s and now widely acknowledged as an architectural disaster – so much so, in fact, that plans are under way to give it a major facelift. Described by Zola as "the belly of Paris", the original Les Halles was Paris's main food market for over eight hundred years, until it was moved out to the suburbs in 1969. Victor Baltard's elegant nineteenth-century iron pavilions were destroyed (two were saved – one is in Nogent-sur-Marne, the other in Yokohama, Japan), despite widespread protest, to make way for an ugly, irretrievably Seventies glass-and-steel shopping mall, known as the **Forum des Halles**, and a huge metro station, the biggest in Europe. The working-class quarter, with its night bars and bistros for the market traders, was largely swept away, and though much of the area above ground was landscaped, providing some welcome green space, the gardens have developed an unsavoury reputation as the preferred hang-out of drug-dealers.

Very soon, however, the whole complex will undergo a major renovation, scheduled for 2008–12, which should transform it for the better. French architect David Mangin, who won the commission, plans to suspend a vast glass roof over the forum, allowing light to flood in, while overground redesigning the gardens and creating a wide promenade on the model of Barcelona's Ramblas. His plan was chosen as the most sensitive to local needs, though it's hard not to feel an opportunity has been missed to go for something really exciting and ambitious. Jean Nouvel, architect of the Institut du Monde Arabe, for example, put in a proposal for an enormous hanging garden, complete with a hundred-metre open-air swimming pool.

The Forum is spread over four levels. The bottom level is the metro/RER station, used by some half million commuters a day. The other levels accommodate numerous shops, housed in aquarium-like arcades around a sunken patio; they're mostly devoted to high-street fashion, though there's also a decent FNAC bookshop and the Forum des Créateurs (level -1), an outlet for young fashion designers. Leisure activities comprise a swimming pool (see p.415) and a number of cinemas, including the **Forum des Images**, which has four screens and a film archive of some 6,500 films, all connected with Paris and any of which you can watch in your own private booth. The Forum des Images comes out of a major revamp in autumn 2007, with more space and a new café.

St-Eustache

For an antidote to steel-and-glass troglodytism head for the soaring vaults of the beautiful church of **St-Eustache**, on the north side of the gardens. Built between 1532 and 1637, the church is Gothic in structure, with lofty naves and graceful flying buttresses, and Renaissance in decoration – all Corinthian columns and arcades. Molière, Richelieu and Madame de Pompadour were baptized here, while Rameau and Marivaux were buried here. The side chapels contain some minor works of art, including, in the tenth chapel in, the ambulatory, an early Rubens (*The Pilgrims at Emmaus*), and, in the sixth chapel on the north side, Coysevox's marble sculpture over the tomb of Colbert, Louis XIV's finance minister. In the Chapelle St-Joseph there is a naïve relief by British artist Raymond Mason, *The Departure of Fruit and Vegetables from the Heart of Paris, 28 February 1969*, showing a procession of market traders, resembling a funeral cortège, leaving Les Halles for the last time. The church has a long musical tradition and is a popular venue for concerts and organ recitals.

Fontaine des Innocents

Another remnant of the Renaissance can be seen on the other side of Les Halles in the shape of the perfectly proportioned **Fontaine des Innocents** (1549), adorned with reliefs of water nymphs. It looks slightly marooned amid the fast-food joints, tattoo parlours and shoe shops of the place Jean du Bellay; on warm days shoppers sit around its edge, drawn to the cool of its cascading waters. The fountain takes its name from the cemetery that used to occupy this site, the Cimetière des Innocents. Full to overflowing, the cemetery was closed down in 1786 and its contents transferred to the catacombs in Denfert-Rochereau.

Châtelet and around

The labyrinth of tiny streets southeastwards to **place du Châtelet** teems with jazz bars, nightclubs and restaurants, and is far more crowded at 2am than 2pm. One of these streets, narrow little rue de la Ferronerie, was the scene of Henri IV's assassination in 1610. A plaque at no. 11 marks the spot where Henri's carriage came to a standstill, caught in the seventeenth-century equivalent of a traffic jam, and giving his assassin, religious fanatic Ravaillac, the chance he was seeking to plunge his dagger into the king's breast.

Place du Châtelet, to the south, was once the site of a notorious fortress prison and is now a maelstrom of traffic overlooked by two grand theatres, the **Théâtre Musical de Paris** and the **Théâtre de la Ville** (both reviewed on p.107), built in the 1860s during Haussmann's *grands travaux*. The latter was formerly known as the Théâtre Sarah Bernhardt (changed to Théâtre des Nations during the German occupation on account of Bernhardt's Jewish origins) after the great actress bought it and regularly performed on stage here until her death in 1923.

One block north, on rue de Rivoli, stands the **Tour Saint Jacques**, currently undergoing restoration and closed to the public. Built in Flamboyant Gothic style and dating from the early sixteenth century, it's all that remains of the Eglise St-Jacques-de-la-Boucherie, built by butchers from nearby Les Halles and destroyed in the Revolution. The church used to be an important stopping point for pilgrims on their way to Santiago de Compostella. At the base of the tower a statue commemorates Blaise Pascal, who carried out experiments on atmospheric pressure here in the seventeenth century. The tower is now used as a weather station and monitors pollution and air quality.

West from the tower, busy rue de Rivoli is dominated by high-street clothing stores. One of the facades, no. 59, is likely to make you pull up short on account of its wacky decoration – two colourful giant faces made of recycled materials. This is **Electron Libre**, an artists' squat (or "squart"). The empty building, owned by Crédit Lyonnais, was occupied by artists in 1999, who were unable to afford the city's high rents. They opened up their *ateliers* to the public, and, with some 40,000 visitors a year, it became one of the capital's most important contemporary art spaces – so much so that the Paris authorities agreed to buy and renovate it. Since 2005 it's been closed while renovations are carried out and it should be open again in 2008, though access to the public may be more restricted.

Also closed for long-term renovation, a little further west on rue de Rivoli, is the **Samaritaine** department store, built in 1903 in pure Art Nouveau style; it's not due to reopen for a number of years (perhaps never, according to some rumours). The quayside just behind the Samaritaine is known as **Quai de la Mégisserie**, a reference to the treatment of animal skins in medieval times when this was an area of abattoirs; nowadays there are plants and pets for sale all along this stretch up to the Pont au Change.

6

The Marais

Located on the Right Bank, just west of the Bastille, the **Marais** is one of the most seductive areas of central Paris, perfect for idle wandering. Largely untouched by Baron Haussmann and modern development, it preserves its magnificent Renaissance *hôtels particuliers* (mansions) and enchanting narrow streets. The area was little more than a riverside swamp (*marais*) up until the thirteenth century, when the Knights Templar (see box, p.120) moved into its northern section, now known as the **quartier du Temple**, and began to drain the land. It became a magnet for the aristocracy in the early 1600s after the construction of the **place des Vosges** – or place Royale, as it was then known – by Henri IV in 1605. This golden age was relatively short-lived, however, for the aristocracy began to move away after the king took his court to Versailles in the latter part of the seventeenth century, leaving their grand houses to the trading classes, who were in turn displaced during the Revolution. From then on, the mansions became multi-occupied slum tenements and the streets degenerated into unserviced squalor – hard to believe, now that the Marais is one of the most desirable areas of the city.

Gentrification proceeded apace from the 1960s, and the quarter is now known for its exclusivity, sophistication and artsy leanings, and for being the neighbourhood of choice for gay Parisians. Renovated *hôtels particuliers*, with their intimate courtyards and sumptuous architectural detail, have become chic flats, boutiques and offices; some also provide splendid settings for a number of excellent museums, not least among them the **Musée Picasso**, the **Musée Carnavalet** history museum, to which entry is free, and the **Musée d'Art et d'Histoire du Judaïsme**.

The main artery running through the Marais, dividing it roughly north and south, is the busy **rue de Rivoli** and its continuation to the Bastille, rue St-Antoine. South of this line is the **quartier St-Paul-St-Gervais**, with its antique shops and atmospheric backstreets. To the north are most of the museums, place des Vosges and the quartier du Temple. Prime streets for exploration are **rue des Francs-Bourgeois**, lined with trendy fashion and interior-design boutiques; **rue des Rosiers**, the old Jewish quarter; and **rue Vieille-du-Temple** and **rue des Archives**, their terraced cafés and bars humming with life at all times of day and night. Every street has an abundance of colour and detail: magnificent *portes cochères* (huge double carriage gates), secluded cobbled courtyards, stone and iron bollards that protected pedestrians from ruthless carriage drivers, elegant iron railings and gates, sculpted house fronts, chichi boutiques and ethnic grocers.

The Marais, incidentally, is one of the few areas of the city where most shops, cafés and restaurants remain open on a **Sunday** (usually 2–6pm) – many Parisians come here for brunch (see pp.327–330) and spend the afternoon

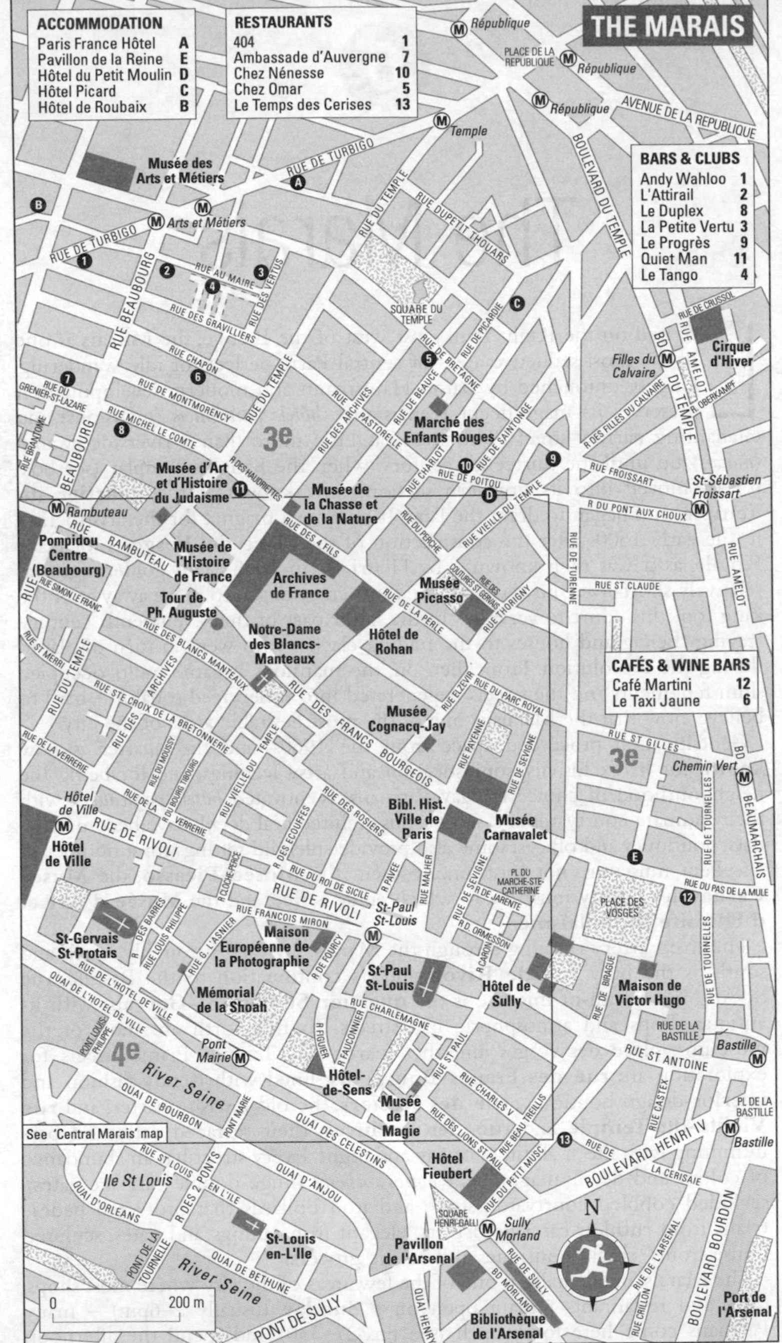
THE MARAIS
ACCOMMODATION
Paris France Hôtel A
Pavillon de la Reine E
Hôtel du Petit Moulin D
Hôtel Picard C
Hôtel de Roubaix B
RESTAURANTS
404 1
Ambassade d'Auvergne 7
Chez Nénesse 10
Chez Omar 5
Le Temps des Cerises 13
BARS & CLUBS
Andy Wahloo 1
L'Attirail 2
Le Duplex 8
La Petite Vertu 3
Le Progrès 9
Quiet Man 11
Le Tango 4
CAFÉS & WINE BARS
Café Martini 12
Le Taxi Jaune 6
République
PLACE DE LA REPUBLIQUE
AVENUE DE LA REPUBLIQUE
Temple
Musée des Arts et Métiers
Arts et Métiers
RUE DE TURBIGO
BOULEVARD DU TEMPLE
RUE DU TEMPLE
RUE DUPETIT THOUARS
SQUARE DU TEMPLE
Cirque d'Hiver
Filles du Calvaire
Marché des Enfants Rouges
3e
Musée d'Art et d'Histoire du Judaisme
Musée de la Chasse et de la Nature
St-Sébastien Froissart
Rambuteau
Pompidou Centre (Beaubourg)
Musée de l'Histoire de France
Archives de France
Tour de Ph. Auguste
Musée Picasso
Notre-Dame des Blancs-Manteaux
Hôtel de Rohan
Musée Cognacq-Jay
Chemin Vert
Bibl. Hist. Ville de Paris
Musée Carnavalet
Hôtel de Ville
RUE DE RIVOLI
PLACE DES VOSGES
St-Paul St-Louis
St-Gervais St-Protais
Maison Européenne de la Photographie
Mémorial de la Shoah
Hôtel de Sully
Maison de Victor Hugo
Bastille
RUE ST ANTOINE
Pont Marie
4e
River Seine
Hôtel-de-Sens
Musée de la Magie
PL DE LA BASTILLE
See 'Central Marais' map
Hôtel Fieubert
BOULEVARD HENRI IV
Ile St Louis
SQUARE HENRI-GALLI
Sully Morland
St-Louis en-L'Ile
Pavillon de l'Arsenal
Bibliothèque de l'Arsenal
Port de l'Arsenal
BOULEVARD BOURDON
PONT DE SULLY
0 200 m
N

browsing the shops and strolling around place des Vosges. The main **métro stops** for the area are M° Hotel de Ville and, a little further east, M° St-Paul.

Place des Vosges and around

As you approach via the narrow streets from the Bastille or from the north or west, nothing quite prepares you for the size and grandeur of the **place des Vosges** (M° Bastille/Chemin Vert/St-Paul), a magnificent square bordered by arcaded pink-brick and stone mansions, with a formal garden at its centre. A masterpiece of aristocratic elegance and the first example of planned development in the history of Paris, the square was commissioned in 1605 by Henri IV, and was inaugurated in 1612 for the wedding of Louis XIII and Anne of Austria; it is Louis's statue – or, rather, a replica of it – that stands hidden by chestnut trees in the middle of the gardens. Originally called place Royale, it was renamed Vosges in 1800 in honour of the *département*, the first to pay its share of the expenses of the revolutionary wars.

Royal patronage of the area goes back to the days when a royal palace, the Hôtel des Tournelles, stood on the north side of what is now the place des Vosges. It remained in use until 1559, having served also as the residence of the Duke of Bedford when he governed northern France in the name of England in the 1420s. Catherine de Médicis had the Hôtel des Tournelles demolished after the death of her husband Henri II in 1559 and the vacant space became a huge horse market, trading between one and two thousand horses every Saturday. So it remained until Henri IV decided on the construction of his place Royale.

Through all the vicissitudes of history, the *place* has never lost its cachet as a smart address. Today, well-heeled Parisians pause in the arcades to look at art, antique and fashion shops, and lunch alfresco at the restaurants while buskers play classical music and jazz. In the garden, toddlers, octogenarians, workers and schoolchildren on lunch breaks sit or play in the only green space of any size in the locality – unusually for Paris, you're allowed to sprawl on the grass.

Among the many celebrities who made their homes here was Victor Hugo; the second-floor apartment, at no. 6, where he lived from 1832 to 1848 and wrote much of *Les Misérables*, is now a museum, the **Maison de Victor Hugo** (Tues–Sun 10am–6pm; closed hols; free). Hugo's life, including his nineteen years of exile in Jersey and Guernsey, is evoked through a somewhat sparse collection of memorabilia, portraits, photographs and first editions of his works. What you do get, though, is an idea of Hugo's prodigious creativity: as well as being a prolific writer, he drew – a number of his ink drawings are exhibited – and designed his own Gothic-style furniture, in which he let his imagination run riot, as seen in some of the pieces displayed; he even put together the extraordinary Chinese-style dining room re-created in its entirety here and originally designed for the house of his lover Juliette Drouet in Guernsey. Among the family portraits is one by Auguste Chatillon of Hugo's daughter, Léopoldine, shown holding a Book of Hours open at the Dormition of the Virgin – a somewhat poignant detail, given that eight years later at the age of 19 she drowned, along with her husband of just six months. Her loss inspired some of Hugo's most moving poetry, including well-known *Demain dès l'aube*.

From the southwest corner of the place des Vosges, a door leads through to the formal château garden, orangerie and exquisite Renaissance facade of the

△ Café Les Philosophes, rue Vieille-du-Temple

Hôtel de Sully. The garden, with its park benches, makes for a peaceful rest-stop; it's also a handy shortcut through to rue St-Antoine. Temporary photographic exhibitions, usually with social, historical or anthropological themes, are mounted in the *hôtel* by the Jeu de Paume (Tues–Fri noon–7pm, Sat & Sun 10am–7pm; €5; Ⓦwww.jeudepaume.org). The attached bookshop has an extensive collection of books on Paris, some in English.

A short distance back to the west along rue St-Antoine, almost opposite the sixteenth-century **church of St-Paul-St-Louis**, which was inaugurated by Cardinal Richelieu, you'll find another square. A complete contrast to the imposing formality of the place des Vosges, the tiny **place du Marché-Ste-Catherine** is a perfect example of that other great French architectural talent: an unerring eye for the intimate, the small-scale, the apparently accidental and the irresistibly charming.

Rue des Francs-Bourgeois

Running west from the Place des Vosges, the main lateral street of the northern part of the Marais is the narrow **rue des Francs-Bourgeois**, full of fashion and design shops. Beatnik Jack Kerouac translated it as "the street of the outspoken middle classes", which is a fair description of the contemporary residents, though the name in fact means "people exempt from tax", in reference to the penurious inmates of a medieval almshouse that once stood on the site of no. 34.

Along or just off this street lie some of the Marais' finest mansions, including the superb **Musée Carnavalet**, tracing the history of Paris; the bijou **Musée Cognacq-Jay**, devoted to eighteenth-century art and decorative arts; the engaging **Musée d'Art et d'Histoire du Judaïsme**; and the **Musée de l'Histoire de France**, the state archives museum, housed in one of the grandest mansions of all.

The Musée Carnavalet and around

The **Musée Carnavalet** (daily except Mon 10am–6pm; free; M° St-Paul), its entrance at 23 rue de Sévigné, off rue des Francs-Bourgeois, is a fascinating museum that charts the history of Paris from its origins up to the belle epoque through an extraordinary collection of paintings, sculptures, decorative arts and archeological finds. The museum's setting, in two beautiful Renaissance mansions – Hôtel Carnavalet and Hôtel Le Peletier – surrounded by attractive gardens, makes a visit worthwhile in itself. There are 140 rooms in all, impossible to visit in one go, so it's best to pick up a floor plan and decide which areas you'd like to concentrate on.

The **ground floor** displays nineteenth- and early twentieth-century shop and inn signs and engrossing models of Paris through the ages, along with maps and plans, showing how much Haussmann's boulevards changed the face of the city. The renovated **orangerie** houses a significant collection of Neolithic finds, including a number of wooden pirogues (dug-out canoes) unearthed during the redevelopment of the Bercy riverside area in the 1990s.

On the **first floor**, decorative arts feature strongly, with numerous re-created salons and boudoirs full of richly sculpted wood panelling and tapestries from the time of Louis XII to Louis XVI, rescued from buildings that had to be destroyed for Haussmann's boulevards. Room 21 is devoted to the famous letter-writer **Madame de Sévigné**, who lived in the Carnavalet mansion from 1677 until her death in 1696 and wrote a series of letters to her daughter, which vividly portray her privileged lifestyle under the reign of Louis XIV. You can see her Chinese lacquered writing desk, as well as portraits of her and various contemporaries, such as Molière and Corneille. Rooms 128 to 148 are largely devoted to the **belle epoque** (early twentieth century), evoked through

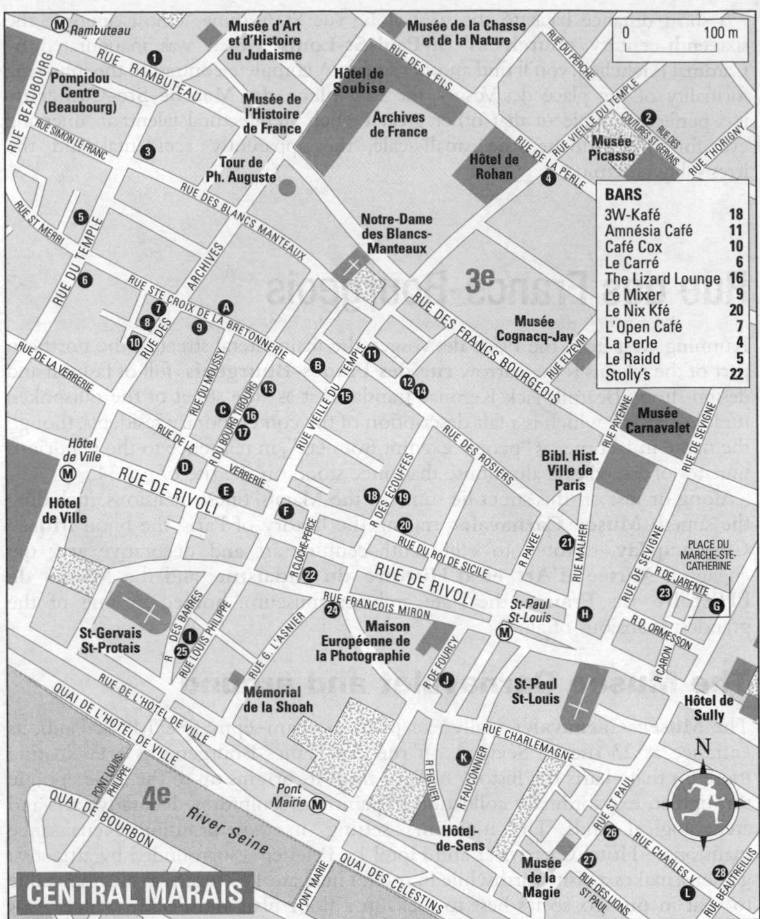

ACCOMMODATION
- Hôtel du Bourg Tibourg C
- Hôtel de la Bretonnerie A
- Caron de Beaumarchais F
- Hôtel Central Marais B
- Le Fauconnier K
- Le Fourcy J
- Grand Hôtel Jeanne d'Arc G
- Grand Hôtel du Loiret D
- Maubuisson I
- Hôtel de Nice E
- Hôtel St-Louis Marais L
- Hôtel Sévigné H

RESTAURANTS
- Auberge de Jarente 23
- Au Bourguignon du Marais 24
- B4 Le Resto 8
- Chez Marianne 12
- Le Colimaçon 3
- Le Coude Fou 17
- L'Enoteca 26
- Piccolo Teatro 19
- Le Potager du Marais 1
- Le Rouge Gorge 27
- Au Vin des Pyrénées 28

CAFÉS & WINE BARS
- L'Apparemment Café 2
- L'As du Falafel 14
- L'Ebouillanté 25
- Le Loir dans la Théière 21
- Mariage Frères 13
- Le Petit Fer à Cheval 15

numerous paintings of the period and some wonderful **Art Nouveau** interiors, among which is the sumptuous peacock-green interior designed by Alphonse Mucha for Fouquet's jewellery shop in the rue Royale. Also well preserved is José-Maria Sert's **Art Deco** ballroom, dating from the 1920s, with its extravagant gold-leaf decor and grand-scale paintings, including one of the Queen of Sheba with a train of elephants. Nearby is a section on literary life at the beginning of the twentieth century, including a reconstruction of Proust's modestly furnished bedroom (room 147), with its cork-lined walls, designed to muffle external noise and allow the writer to work in peace – he spent most of his last three years closeted away here, penning his great novel.

The **second floor** has rooms full of mementos of the **French Revolution**: models of the Bastille, original declarations of the Rights of Man and the Citizen, sculpted allegories of Reason, and crockery with revolutionary slogans and glorious models of the guillotine. There are also execution orders to make you shed a tear for the royalists, and one of the rooms of the Temple prison (see p.121) where Louis XVI and his family were locked up has been re-created, complete with the king's chess set and the Dauphin's toy tin soldiers.

The post-Revolution and **Napoleonic period** is covered on the ground floor, in rooms 115–121; look out for Napoleon's favourite canteen, which accompanied him on his military exploits (and also followed him into exile on St Helena), consisting of 110 pieces ingeniously contained within a case no bigger than a picnic hamper. Among the items is a full set of gold cutlery, a gold-handled toothbrush, two candelabras and a dinky geometry set – everything an emperor could possibly need while on campaign.

The Bibliothèque Historique de la Ville de Paris

Just across from the Musée Carnavalet on rue des Francs-Bourgeois stands the **Bibliothèque Historique de la Ville de Paris**, housed in the splendid sixteenth-century Hôtel Lamoignon and safeguarding centuries' worth of texts and picture books about the city (see p.413 for opening times). Next to the Lamoignon, on rue Pavée – so called because it was among the first of Paris's streets to be paved, in 1450 – was the site of **La Force prison**, where many of the Revolution's victims were incarcerated, including the Princesse de Lamballe, who was lynched in the massacres of September 1792 and her head presented on a stake to her friend Marie-Antoinette.

The Musée Cognacq-Jay

At 8 rue Elzévir, one block west of the Musée Carnavalet, lies the **Musée Cognacq-Jay** (daily except Mon 10am–5.40pm; free; M° St-Paul/Chemin-Vert), occupying the fine Hôtel Donon. The Cognacq-Jay family built the Samaritaine department store and were noted philanthropists, as well as lovers of eighteenth-century European art. Their small collection of pieces on show includes a handful of works by Canaletto, Fragonard, Rubens and Quentin de la Tour, as well as an early Rembrandt and an exquisite still life by Chardin, displayed in beautifully carved wood-panelled rooms filled with Sèvres porcelain and Louis XV furniture.

The Musée de l'Histoire de France

At the western end of the rue des Francs-Bourgeois there once stood a magnificent early eighteenth-century palace complex, filling the entire block from rue des Quatre Fils and rue des Archives, and from rue Vieille-du-Temple to rue des Francs-Bourgeois. Only half remains today, but it is utterly splendid, especially the grand colonnaded courtyard of the Hôtel Soubise, with its fabulous rococo interiors, paintings by Boucher and vestigial fourteenth-century towers on rue des Quatre Fils. The *hôtel* houses the city archives and the **Musée de l'Histoire de France** (Mon–Fri 10am–12.30pm & 2–5.30pm, Sat & Sun 2–5.30pm; €3; M° Rambuteau/St-Paul), which mounts changing exhibitions drawn from its extensive holdings, such as the fascinating one in 2007 displaying the last letters and journals written by Marie-Antoinette before her execution.

The *hôtel*'s ground-floor Chambre du Prince is the scene of **chamber music recitals** (€10), held here most Saturdays, usually at 6pm. The adjacent **Hôtel de Rohan**, currently closed for renovation, is also part of the archives complex and has more fine interiors, including the Chinese-inspired Cabinet des Singes, whose walls are painted with monkeys acting out various aristocratic scenes.

Opposite the Hôtel Soubise, at the back of a driveway for the Crédit Municipal bank, stands a pepperpot tower that formed part of the **city walls**; these were built by King Philippe-Auguste early in the thirteenth century to link up with his new fortress, the Louvre. Further east, past several more imposing facades, you can admire the delicate filigree ironwork of the balcony above the main entrance to the **Hôtel d'Albret** (no. 31), built in 1740 and now home to the cultural department of the mayor of Paris.

The Musée de la Chasse et de la Nature

Just behind the Musée de l'Histoire de France at 60 rue des Archives is the **Musée de la Chasse et de la Nature** (Tues–Sun 11am–6pm; €6, under-18s free; Ⓦwww.chassenature.org; M° Rambuteau), devoted largely to hunting. Housed in the beautiful Hôtel Guénégaud and recently extended into the neighbouring Hôtel Mongelas, the museum has had a good go at dusting off its slightly fusty image and has opened a series of new rooms, each devoted to a particular animal connected with the hunt, such as the wild boar, wolf and dog. In each room a wooden "cabinet of curiosities" invites you to pull open drawers and discover miscellaneous bits and bobs, such as paw prints, animal droppings and drawings, and you can look through eyeglasses and watch a video of the animal in its natural habitat – all quite appealing to children in particular. The rest of the museum's collection includes a formidable array of stuffed animals, including a giant polar bear, weapons ranging from prehistoric stone arrowheads to highly decorative crossbows and guns, and paintings by French artists, such as Desportes, romanticizing the chase.

Musée d'Art et d'Histoire du Judaïsme

Two blocks further west, at 71 Rue du Temple, stands the attractively restored Hôtel de Saint-Aignan, now home to the **Musée d'Art et d'Histoire du Judaïsme** (Mon–Fri 11am–6pm, Sun 10am–6pm; €6.80; Ⓦwww.mahj.org; M° Rambuteau). Opened in 1998, it's mostly a combination of the collections of the now closed Musée d'Art Juif in Montmartre, of Isaac Strauss, conductor of the Paris Opera orchestra during the Second Empire, and the Dreyfus archives, a gift to the museum from Dreyfus's grandchildren. The museum traces the culture, history and artistic endeavours mainly of the **Jews in France**, though there are also many artefacts from the rest of Europe and North Africa. The result is a very comprehensive collection, as educational as it is beautiful. Free audioguides in English are available and well worth picking up if you want to get the most out of the museum.

Highlights include a Gothic-style Hanukkah lamp, one of the very few French Jewish artefacts to survive from the period before the expulsion of the Jews from France in 1394; an Italian gilded circumcision chair from the seventeenth century; and a completely intact late nineteenth-century Austrian *Sukkah*, decorated with paintings of Jerusalem and the Mount of Olives and built as a temporary dwelling for the celebration of the Harvest. Other artefacts include Moroccan wedding garments, highly decorated marriage contracts from eighteenth-century Modena and gorgeous, almost whimsical, spice containers.

The Dreyfus Affair

The **Dreyfus Affair** was one of the biggest crises to rock the Third Republic. It centred on Alfred Dreyfus, a captain in the French army and a Jew, who was arrested and convicted of spying for the Germans in 1894 on the flimsiest of evidence – his handwriting was said to resemble that on documents detailing French armaments found in the German embassy. In a humiliating public ceremony of "dégradation" in the courtyard of the Ecole Militaire his epaulettes were torn from his uniform and his sword broken, while anti-Semitic slogans were chanted by crowds outside. He was then sent to the notorious penal colony of Devil's Island, off Guyana. His family, convinced of his innocence, began campaigning for a retrial. Two newspapers, *L'Eclair* and *Le Matin*, questioned the evidence and in 1897 Colonel Georges Picquart, the new head of the Statistical Section, discovered a document which suggested that the true culprit was Major Ferdinand Walsin-Esterhazy. Esterhazy was perfunctorily tried by the Ministry of War, and let off. The government, keen to uphold the army's authority and reputation, acquiesced to the verdict, and Colonel Picquart was packed off to Tunisia. However, a storm broke out when shortly afterwards writer Emile Zola published his famous open letter, titled *J'accuse...!*, to the President of the Republic in the *Aurore* newspaper on January 13, 1898. In it he denounced the army and authorities and accused them of a cover-up. Zola was convicted for libel and sentenced to a year's imprisonment, which he avoided by fleeing to England. The article triggered a major outcry and suddenly the *affaire* was the chief topic of conversation in every café in France. French society divided into two camps: Dreyfusards and anti-Dreyfusards. The former, convinced the army was guilty of a cover-up, comprised republicans committed to equal rights and the primacy of parliament and included many prominent intellectuals and left-wing figures such as Jean Jaurès, Anatole France, Léon Blum, Georges Clemenceau and Marcel Proust. Ranked among the anti-Dreyfusards were clerics, anti-Semitic newspapers such as *La Libre Parole*, monarchists and conservatives, all suspecting a Jewish conspiracy to tarnish the army's reputation. The former clamoured for justice, while the latter called for respect and order.

In June 1897, the secret dossier that convicted Dreyfus was finally re-examined; there was a retrial and, again, Dreyfus was convicted of treason, but was quickly pardoned by the president Loubet, desperate to draw a line under the whole affair. Finally, in 1906, Dreyfus, his health broken by hard labour, was granted a full pardon and awarded the *légion d'honneur*. The matter was formally closed, but the repercussions of the affair were deep and long-lasting; it had revealed fundamental divisions in French society, and split the country along lines that would determine France's development in the twentieth century.

Appropriately enough, one room is devoted to the notorious **Dreyfus affair** (see box above), documented with letters, photographs and press clippings; you can read Emile Zola's famous letter "*J'accuse…!*" in which the novelist defends Dreyfus's innocence, and the letters that Dreyfus sent to his wife from prison on Devil's Island in which he talks of *épouvantable* ("terrible") suffering and loneliness.

There's also a significant collection of paintings and sculpture by **Jewish artists** – Marc Chagall, Samuel Hirszenberg, Chaïm Soutine and Jacques Lipchitz – who came to live in Paris at the beginning of the twentieth century. The Holocaust is only briefly touched on, since it's dealt with in depth by the Musée de la Shoah (see p.122). The main reference is an installation by contemporary artist Christian Boltanski; one of the exterior walls of a small courtyard is covered with black-bordered death announcements printed with the names of the Jewish artisans who once lived in the building, a number of whom were deported.

The Jewish quarter: rue des Rosiers

One block south of the rue des Francs-Bourgeois, the area around narrow, pedestrianized **rue des Rosiers** has traditionally been the **Jewish quarter** of the city ever since the twelfth century. Although the hammam is now a design shop, and many of the little grocers, bakers, bookshops and cafés are under pressure to follow suit, the area just about manages to retain its Jewish identity, with a number of kosher food shops and Hebrew bookstores. There's also a distinctly Mediterranean flavour to the quartier, testimony to the influence of the **North African Sephardim**, who, since the end of World War II, have sought refuge here from the uncertainties of life in the French ex-colonies. They have replenished Paris's Jewish population, depleted when its Ashkenazim, having escaped the pogroms of Eastern Europe, were rounded up by the Nazis and the French police and transported back east to concentration camps.

Musée Picasso

On the northern side of rue des Francs-Bourgeois, rue Payenne leads up to the lovely gardens and houses of **rue du Parc-Royal** and on to **rue de Thorigny**. Here, at no. 5, the magnificent classical facade of the seventeenth-century **Hôtel Salé**, built for a rich salt-tax collector, conceals the **Musée Picasso** (daily except Tues: April–Sept 9.30am–6pm; Oct–March 9.30am–5.30pm; €6.50, free on the first Sun of the month; ⓦwww.musee-picasso.fr; M° Chemin Vert/St-Paul). It's the largest collection of Picassos anywhere, representing almost all the major periods of the artist's life from 1905 onwards. Many of the works were owned by Picasso and on his death in 1973 were seized by the state in lieu of taxes owed. The result is an unedited body of work, which, although not among the most recognizable of Picasso's masterpieces, nevertheless provides a sense of the artist's development and an insight into the person behind the myth. In addition, the collection includes paintings Picasso bought or was given by contemporaries such as Matisse and Cézanne; his African masks and sculptures; his Communist party membership cards and sketches of Stalin; and photographs of him in his studio taken by Brassaï.

The **exhibition** unfolds chronologically, starting with the artist's blue period, studies for the *Demoiselles d'Avignon*, and his experiments with Cubism and Surrealism. It then moves on to his larger-scale works on themes of war and peace (eg, *Massacre in Korea*, 1951) and his later preoccupations with love and death, reflected in his Minotaur and bullfighting paintings. Perhaps some of the most engaging works, though, are his more personal ones – those of his children, wives and lovers – such as *Olga pensive* (1923), in which his first wife is shown lost in thought, the deep blue of her dress reflecting her mood. The breakdown of their marriage was probably behind the Surrealist-influenced *Femme dans le fauteuil rouge*: the violent clash of colours and the woman's grotesquely deformed body tell of acute distress.

Portraits of later lovers, Dora Maar and Marie-Thérèse, show how the two women inspired Picasso in very different ways: they strike the same pose, but Dora Maar is painted with strong lines and vibrant colours, suggesting a passionate, vivacious personality, while Marie-Thérèse's muted colours and soft contours convey serenity and peace.

The museum also holds a substantial number of Picasso's **engravings**, **ceramics** and **sculpture**, reflecting the remarkable ease with which the artist moved from one medium to another. Some of the most arresting sculptures are those he created from recycled household objects, such as the endearing *La Chèvre* (Goat), whose stomach is made from a basket, and the *Tête de taureau*, an ingenious pairing of a bicycle seat and handlebars. Another striking work is the huge bronze *L'Homme au mouton* (1943), showing a man carrying a struggling sheep, as though offering it for sacrifice.

The haut Marais

The northern part of the Marais, often referred to as the "haut Marais" (the "upper Marais"), encompasses the **Quartier du Temple**, named after the Knights Templar's stronghold that once stood at its heart, and the city's original **Chinatown**, concentrated on the upper end of rue du Temple and the streets west. Here the aristocratic stone facades of the lower Marais give way to the more humble, though no less attractive, stucco, paint and thick-slatted shutters of seventeenth- and eighteenth-century streets. Some bear the names of old rural French provinces: Beauce, Perche, Saintonge, Picardie. Formerly a quiet backwater, traditionally working-class and multicultural, the area has recently been attracting an arty, hip crowd, as numerous contemporary art galleries, design shops and chichi fashion boutiques have sprung up, especially along **rue Charlot** and rue de Poitou, edging out the older businesses, such as rag-trade leather workshops and printers.

Typical of the trendy shops that are opening up in this area are Galerie Dansk, at 31 rue Charlot, devoted to Scandinavian design from the 1950s to 1970s, and cutting-edge fashion designer Gaspard Yurkievich, at no. 43. At no. 9 you could check out what's happening at the art gallery, **Passage de Retz** (daily except Mon 10am–7pm; €8; Ⓦwww.passagederetz.com; M° Filles-du-Calvaire), which stages changing exhibitions of fine art and design from young artists and is attractively set in an old mansion; there's also a bookshop and café.

Opposite, in the dead-end **ruelle de Sourdis**, one section of the street has remained unchanged since its construction in 1626. Further along, on the corner of **rue du Perche**, a little classical facade on a leafy courtyard hides the **Armenian church of Ste-Croix**, testimony to the many Armenians who sought refuge here from the Turkish pogroms of World War I. Further still, on the left and just short of the vibrant rue de Bretagne, is the easily missed entrance to the **Marché des Enfants-Rouges**, one of the smallest and oldest food markets in Paris (Tues–Sat 8.30am–1pm & 4–7.30pm, Sun 8.30am–2pm), dating back to 1616, and purveying mostly traditional produce, though there's also a stall selling Moroccan specialities including delicious mint tea, which you can drink at tables set out alongside. **Rue de Bretagne** itself has an agreeable provincial air and is full of old-fashioned food shops such as cheesemongers, bakeries and coffee merchants. Off to the right, rue de Picardie leads up to the Carreau du Temple.

The Quartier du Temple

The **Quartier du Temple** designates the area that was once occupied by the Knights Templar's central stronghold, bounded by rue de Bretagne, rue du Temple, rue de Béranger and rue de Picardie. Nothing of the complex, which included a tower and church, remains beyond the name "Temple", preserved in the **Square du Temple** gardens and the **Carreau du Temple**, a clothes market with a heavy preponderance of leather gear (Tues–Sun mornings) housed in a fine *halles*-like structure. **Rue de la Corderie**, a pretty little street on the north side, opening into an otherworldly *place*, has a couple of pleasant cafés under the trees.

Chinatown and the Musée des Arts et Métiers

A couple of blocks to the west, on and around the top end of **Rue du Temple**, lies Paris's original **Chinatown** district. The area was settled during World War I when Chinese immigrants came over to fill the gap in the workforce left by the departure of French troops for the front. Rue du Temple, lined with many beautiful houses dating back to the seventeenth century (no. 41, for instance, the Hôtel Aigle d'Or, is the last surviving coaching inn of the period), is full of Chinese-run wholesale businesses trading in leather and fashion accessories.

The streets to the west of rue du Temple are narrow, dark, and riddled with passages, the houses half-timbered and bulging with age. At no. 51 rue Montmorency is Paris's oldest house, built in 1407 for the alchemist Nicolas Flamel, whose name will ring a bell with Harry Potter fans; the building is now a restaurant, *Auberge Nicolas Flamel*.

West of rue Volta is the **Musée des Arts et Métiers** (daily except Mon 10am–6pm, Thurs until 9.30pm; €6.50; ⓦ www.arts-et-metiers.net; M° Arts-et-Métiers), at 60 rue de Réaumur. This fascinating museum of technological

The Knights Templar

The military order of the Knights Templar was established in Jerusalem at the time of the Crusades to protect pilgrims to the Holy Land. Its members quickly became exceedingly rich and powerful, with some nine thousand commands spread across Europe. They acquired land in the *marais* in Paris around 1140, and began to build. After the loss of Palestine in 1291, this fortress property, which covered the area now bounded by rues du Temple, Bretagne, Picardie and Béranger and constituted a separate town outside the city walls, became their international headquarters, as the seat of their Grand Master.

They came to a sticky end, however, early in the fourteenth century, when King Philippe le Bel, alarmed at their power and in alliance with Pope Clement V, had them tried for sacrilege, blasphemy and sodomy. Fifty-four of them were burnt, including, in 1314, the Grand Master himself, in the presence of the king. Thereafter the order was abolished.

The Temple buildings continued to exist until the Revolution, with about four thousand inhabitants: a mixed population, consisting of artisans not subject to the city's trade regulations, debtors seeking freedom from prosecution, and some rich residents of private *hôtels*. Louis XVI and the royal family were imprisoned in the keep in 1792 (see box opposite). It was finally demolished in 1808 by Napoleon, determined to eradicate any possible focus for royalist nostalgia.

The Temple and Louis XVI

Louis XVI, Marie-Antoinette, their two children and immediate family were imprisoned in the keep of the Knights Templar's ancient fortress in August 1792 by the revolutionary government. By the end of 1794, when all the adults had been executed, the two children – the teenage Marie-Thérèse and the 9- or 10-year-old Dauphin, now, in the eyes of royalists, Louis XVII – remained there alone, in the charge of a family called Simon. Louis XVII was literally walled up, allowed no communication with other human beings, not even his sister, who was living on the floor above. He died of tuberculosis in 1795, a half-crazed imbecile, and was buried in a public grave.

At least that is what appeared to be his fate. A number of clues, however, point to hocus-pocus. The doctor who certified the child's death kept a lock of his hair, but it was later found not to correspond with the colour of the young Louis XVII's hair, as remembered by his sister. Mme Simon confessed on her deathbed that she had substituted another child for Louis XVII. And a sympathetic sexton admitted that he had exhumed the body of this imbecile child and reburied it in the cloister of the Eglise Ste-Marguerite in the Faubourg St-Antoine (see p.214), but when this body was dug up it was found to be that of an 18-year-old.

A plausible theory is that the real Louis XVII died early in 1794. But since Robespierre needed the heir to the throne as a hostage with which to menace internal and foreign royalist enemies, he had Louis disposed of in secret and substituted the idiot. Taking advantage of this atmosphere of uncertainty, 43 different people subsequently claimed to be Louis XVII. After centuries of speculation, all rumours were put to rest in the spring of 2000 when DNA from the child who died of TB was found to match samples obtained from locks of Marie-Antoinette's hair, and also that of several other maternal relatives.

innovation is part of the Conservatoire des Arts et Métiers and incorporates the former Benedictine priory of St-Martin-des-Champs, its original chapel dating from the fourth century. Extensively revamped a number of years ago, the museum happily combines creaky old floors and spacious rooms with high-tech, twenty-first-century touches. Its most important exhibit is Foucault's pendulum, which the scientist used to demonstrate the rotation of the earth in 1851, a sensational event held at the Panthéon and attended by a huge crowd eager to "see the earth go round". The orb itself, a hollow brass sphere, is under glass in the chapel and there's a working model set up nearby.

Other exhibits include the laboratory of Lavoisier, the French chemist who first showed that water is a combination of oxygen and hydrogen and, hanging as if in mid-flight, above the grand staircase is the elegant "Avion 3", a flying machine complete with feathered propellers, which was donated to the Conservatoire after several ill-fated attempts to fly it.

South of the rue de Rivoli: Quartier Saint Paul

The southern part of the Marais, the **Quartier Saint Paul**, between the rue de Rivoli/St Antoine and the Seine, is less buzzy than the rest of the district, its quiet, atmospheric streets lined with attractive old houses. The chief sights are the moving **Mémorial de la Shoah**, with its museum documenting the fate of French Jews in the last war; the **Maison Européenne de la Photographie**, which hosts exhibitions by contemporary photographers; and the **Pavillon de l'Arsenal**, a showcase for the city's current architectural projects. The area is also a good hunting ground for antiques, concentrated mostly in the **Village St-Paul** and rue Saint-Paul.

The first landmark you come to, starting at the western end of the distict, near the Hôtel de Ville, is the church of **St-Gervais-St-Protais** (M° Hôtel de Ville). There's been a church on this site since the sixth century; the current building was started in 1494, though not completed until the seventeenth century, which explains the mismatched late-Gothic interior and Classical exterior. There's some lovely stained glass inside, sixteenth-century carved misericords and a seventeenth-century organ, one of Paris's oldest and played on by eight generations of the Couperin family, including the famous François Couperin. The third chapel down on the right commemorates the hundred-odd victims of a German shell that hit the church on Good Friday 1918 and caused part of the nave to collapse.

Exiting the church round the altar at the back, you enter cobbled **rue des Barres**, a picturesque little street, filled with the scent of roses from nearby gardens in summer and a nice setting for the outdoor terrace of *L'Ebouillanté* café (see p.328).

The Mémorial de la Shoah

A little further east, at 17 rue Geoffroy l'Asnier, the grim fate of French Jews in World War II is commemorated at the **Mémorial de la Shoah** (daily except Sat 10am–6pm, Thurs till 10pm; free; Ⓦwww.memorialdelashoah.org; M° St-Paul/Pont-Marie), within the Centre de Documentation Juive Contemporaine, access to which usually involves queuing, as visitors and bags are scanned at the entrance. President Chirac opened a new museum here in January 2005 and, alongside the sombre Mémorial du Martyr Juif Inconnu (Memorial to the Unknown Jewish Martyr), unveiled a Wall of Names; ten researchers spent two and a half years trawling Gestapo documents and interviewing French families to compile the list of the 76,000 French Jews – around a quarter of the wartime population – sent to death camps from 1942 to 1944. Chirac, in 1995, was the first French president to formally acknowledge that France was involved in systematically persecuting Jews during World War II. In most instances, it was the French police, not the Nazi occupiers, who rounded up the Jews for deportation. The most notorious case was in July 1942, when 13,152 Jews (including over 4000 children) were rounded up in the Vel d'Hiv bicycle stadium in Paris and sent to death camps.

This episode, along with much else, is documented in the excellent new **museum**, with plenty of information in English. Its main focus is events in France leading up to and during World War II, but it also gives lots of useful background on the history of Jews in France and in Europe as a whole. Individual stories are illustrated with photos, ID cards, letters and other documents. You learn about model citizens such as the Javel family, who were all deported and died in the camps, their long-established residence in France and distinguished record of military service counting for naught in the relentless Nazi drive to exterminate all Jews. Others, such as the Lifchitz family, who fled pogroms in Russia and settled in France in 1909, managed to survive the war – in this case by going into hiding and obtaining false ID as Orthodox Christians. There are some drawings and letters from Drancy, the holding station outside Paris, from which French Jews were sent on to camps in Germany; in one letter a woman urges her elderly mother left behind to be "courageuse et forte" ("brave and strong") and to look after her daughter. One chilling letter in 1942 from the Comité des Questions Juives issues a cold refusal to a request by the chief of police to free twenty non-Jews who had donned the yellow star – presumably as a form of protest and solidarity. The museum ends with the Mémorial des Enfants, an overwhelming collection of photos of 2500 French children, each marked with the date of their birth and the date of their deportation.

The Maison Européenne de la Photographie

Between rues Fourcy and François-Miron (entrance at 4 rue de Fourcy), a gorgeous Marais mansion, the early eighteenth-century Hôtel Hénault de Cantobre, has been turned into the **Maison Européenne de la Photographie** (Wed–Sun 11am–8pm; €6, free Wed after 5pm; Ⓦwww.mep-fr.org; M° St-Paul/Pont-Marie), dedicated to the art of contemporary photography. Temporary shows combine with a revolving exhibition of the Maison's permanent collection; young photographers and news photographers get a look-in, as well as artists using photography in multimedia creations or installation art. A library and *vidéothèque* can be freely consulted, and there's a stylish café.

The Village St-Paul and around

Shift eastwards to the next tangle of streets and you'll find chic, modern flats in the "**Village St-Paul**" (M° St-Paul/Pont-Marie), with clusters of antique shops in the courtyards. This part of the Marais suffered a postwar hatchet job, and, although seventeenth- and eighteenth-century magnificence is still in evidence (there's even a stretch of the city's defensive wall dating from the early thirteenth century in the lycée playground on rue des Jardins St-Paul), it lacks the architectural cohesion of the Marais to the north. The fifteenth-century **Hôtel de Sens**, on the rue du Figuier, looks bizarre in its isolation. The public library it now houses, the **Bibliothèque Forney**, filled with volumes on fine and applied arts, makes a good excuse to explore this outstanding medieval building. See p.413 for the library's opening hours.

Amid the antique shops on nearby rue St-Paul is the **Musée de la Magie** (Wed, Sat & Sun 2–7pm; €7, children €5; Ⓦwww.museedelamagie.com; M° St-Paul/Sully-Morland) at no. 11, a delightful museum of magic and illusion. A few tricks are explained, but don't expect to glean all the answers. Automatas, distorting mirrors and optical illusions, things that float on thin air, a box for sawing people in half – they're all on view, with examples from the eighteenth and nineteenth centuries, as well as contemporary magicians' tools and plenty of hands-on exhibits for children. The best fun is a live demonstration of the art (every 30min from 2.30–6pm) by a skilled magician. The museum shop sells books on conjuring and magic cards, wands, boxes, scarves and the like. Groups of schoolchildren tend to visit on Wednesday, so it's better to visit at weekends.

The Pavillon de l'Arsenal and around

Further east, on rue du Petit-Musc, there's an entertaining combination of 1930s Modernism and nineteenth-century exuberance in the Hôtel Fieubert (now a school). Diagonally opposite, at 21 boulevard Morland, is the **Pavillon de l'Arsenal** (Tues–Sat 10.30am–6.30pm, Sun 11am–7pm; free; Ⓦwww.pavillon-arsenal.com; M° Sully-Morland). A fine example of the city's art of self-promotion, the *pavillon* is an exhibition centre that presents the capital's current **architectural projects** to the public, such as Frank Gehry's exciting project in the Jardin d'Acclimatation, the Fondation Louis Vuitton contemporary arts centre. There's also a permanent exhibition on Paris's architectural development, "Paris, visite guidée", including a huge interactive model of the city.

The **southeast corner of the 4e arrondissement**, jutting out into the Seine, has its own distinct character. It's been taken up since the nineteenth century by the Célestines barracks and was previously the site of the Arsenal, which used to overlook a third island in the Seine. Boulevard Morland was built in 1843, covering over the arm of the river that formed the Ile de Louviers. The deranged poet Gérard de Nerval escaped here as a boy and lived for days in a log cabin he made with wood scavenged from the island's timberyards. In the 1830s, his more extrovert contemporaries – Victor Hugo, Liszt, Delacroix, Alexandre Dumas and co – were using the library of the former residence of Louis XIV's artillery chief as a meeting place. While the literati discussed turning art into a revolutionary form, the locals were on the streets giving the authorities reason to build more barracks.

7

The Quartier Latin

The traditional heartland of the **Quartier Latin** lies between the river and the Montagne-Ste-Geneviève, a hill once crowded with medieval colleges and now proudly crowned by the giant dome of the **Panthéon**. In medieval times, the name "Latin quarter" was probably a simple description, as this was the area whose inhabitants – clergymen and university scholars for the most part – ordinarily spoke Latin. These days, it's an ill-defined area, sometimes used as shorthand for the whole central area of the Left Bank below the Ile de la Cité, sometimes, as here, used to mean the modern 5e arrondissement, an area defined by the boulevard St-Michel, to the west; the river, to the north; and the great inner ring of boulevards to the south and east.

The students may no longer speak Latin, but it's still a deeply scholarly area. In the northern half of the arrondissement alone are the famous **Sorbonne** and Jussieu campuses, plus two of France's most élite lycées and a cluster of stellar academic institutes. Few students can afford the rents these days, but they still maintain the quarter's traditions in the cheaper bars, cafés and *bistrots*, decamping to the Luxembourg gardens, over in the 6e arrondissement (see p.145) on sunny days.

The quarter's medieval heritage is superbly displayed in the Roman and sixteenth-century buildings housing the **Musée National du Moyen Age**, worth visiting for the stunning tapestry series, the *Lady with the Unicorn*, alone. Out towards the eastern end of the 5e, the theme is more Arabic than Latin in the brilliantly designed **Institut du Monde Arabe** and **Paris mosque**, while nearby are the flowerbeds, zoo and natural history museum of the leafy **Jardin des Plantes**. The southern half of the 5[e] arrondissement is less interesting, though the ancient, romantic thoroughfare of the **rue Mouffetard** still snakes its way down to the boundary of the 13[e] arrondissement, at Les Gobelins (see p.188).

Place St-Michel and around

The pivotal point of the Quartier Latin is **place St-Michel**, where the tree-lined boulevard St-Michel begins. The name is redolent of student chic, though these days dull commercial outlets have largely taken over the famous "boul' Mich". Nevertheless, the cafés and shops around the square are constantly jammed with young people: either students or, in summer, foreign backpackers. A favourite meeting point is the fountain at the back end of the *place*, which

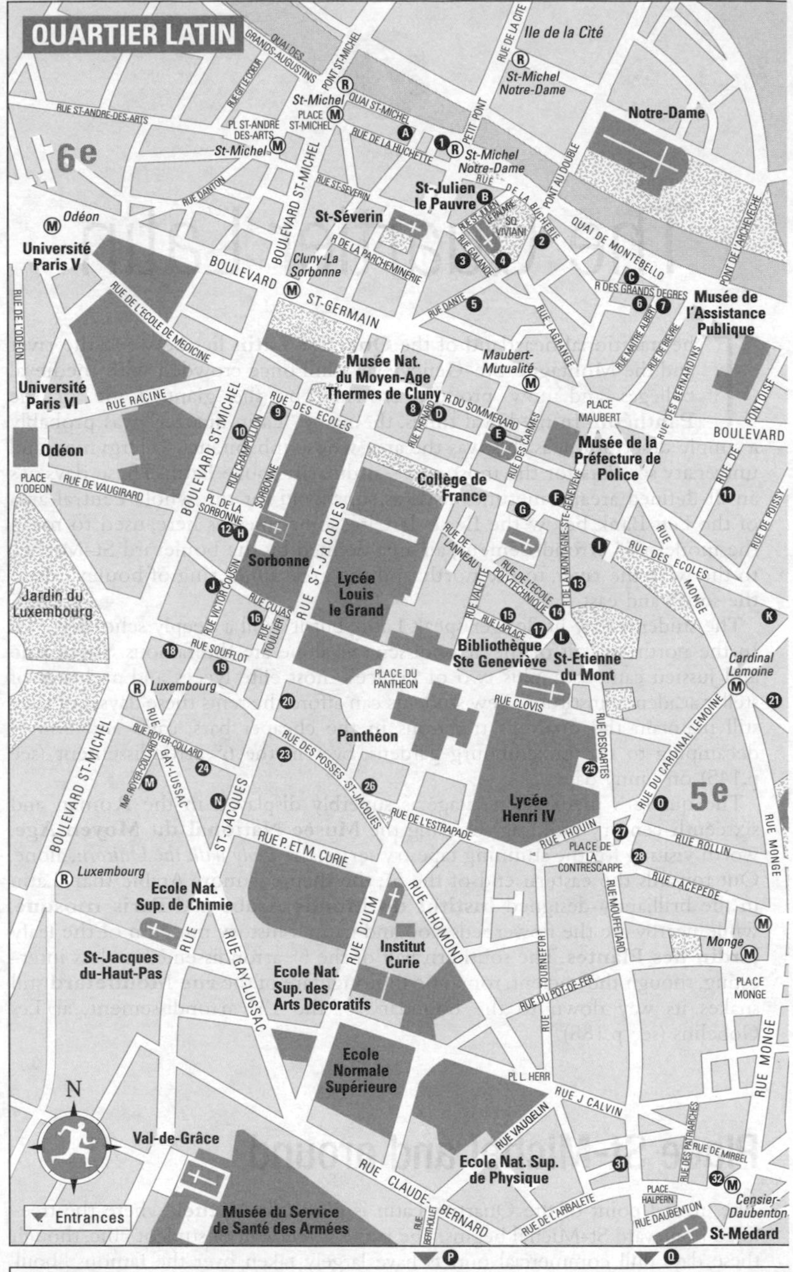

RESTAURANTS

L'Atelier Maître Albert	7	Le Buisson Ardent	22	Coco de Mer	33	L'Ecurie	17
Au Bistrot de la Sorbonne	16	Les Cinq Saveurs d'Anada	27	Les Degrés de Notre-Dame	C	Les Fontaines	19
Brasserie Balzar	9	Au Coin des Gourmets	5			Le Grenier de Notre-Dame	2

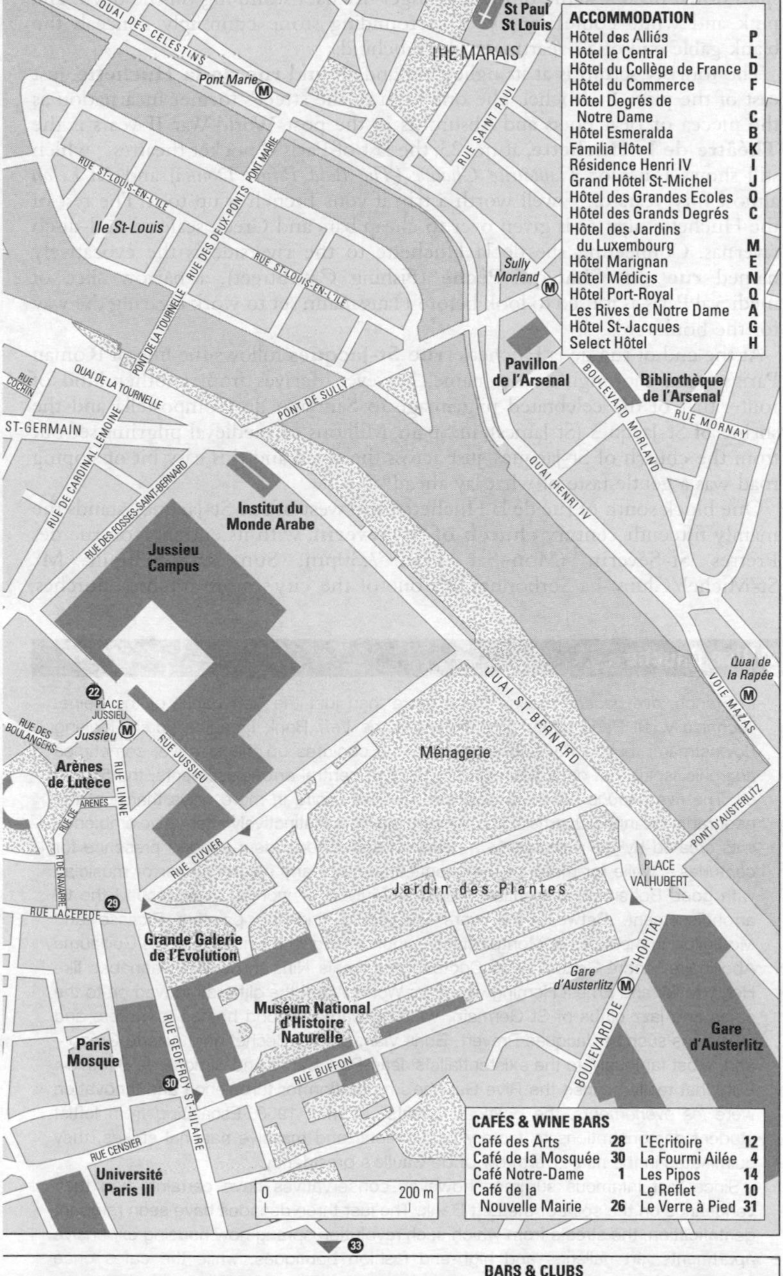

33

BARS & CLUBS

Au Jardin des Pâtes	29	La Petite Légume	21	Le Pré-Verre	8	Le Bateau Ivre	25	Le Piano Vache	15
Mavrommatis	32	Pho 67	3	Le Reminet	6	La Gueuze	18	Le Violon Dingue	13
Perraudin	20	Le Petite Pontoise	11	Tashi Delek	23	Le Pantalon Bar	24		

spills down from a statue of the archangel Michael stomping on the devil. The pink and white confectionery of surrounding stone cunningly conceals the blank gable end of an apartment block behind.

The touristy scrum is at its ugliest on and around **rue de la Huchette**, just east of the place St-Michel. The only sign of the street's former incarnation as the mecca of Beat poets and Absurdists in the post-World War II years is the **Théâtre de la Huchette**, at no. 23, the last of Paris's "pocket theatres", which still shows Ionesco's *Cantatrice Chauve* (*The Bald Prima Donna*) and *La Leçon* almost fifty years on – well worth a trip if your French is up to it. The rest of the Huchette quarter is given over to cheap bars and Greek seafood-and-disco tavernas. Connecting rue de la Huchette to the riverside is the evocatively named **rue du Chat-qui-Pêche** (Fishing Cat Street), a narrow slice of medieval Paris as it used to look before Haussmann set to work clearing the way for the boulevards.

At the end of rue de la Huchette, **rue St-Jacques** follows the line of Roman Paris's main thoroughfare. Its name, however, derives from another kind of route: that of the celebrated pilgrimage to Santiago de Compostella and the shrine of St-Jacques (St James), in Spain. Millions of medieval pilgrims set out from the church of St-Jacques, just across the river, and this easy bit of sloping road was a gentle taste of what lay ahead.

One block south of rue de la Huchette, and west of rue St-Jacques, stands the mainly fifteenth-century **church of St-Séverin**, with its entrance on rue des Prètres St-Séverin (Mon–Sat 11am–7.30pm, Sun 9am–8.30pm; M° St-Michel/Cluny-La Sorbonne). It's one of the city's more intense churches,

Rive Gauche

In French, *rive gauche* means much more than just the "left bank" of the Seine. Technically, all Paris south of the river is the Left Bank (imagine you're looking downstream), but to Parisian ears the name conjures up the creative, sometimes anarchic, spirit that once flourished in the two central arrondissements, the 5e and 6e. The *rive gauche* has long opposed the *rive droite* in more ways than just the geographical: in the Quartier Latin, around the 5e, a distinctively alternative ambience was created by the university – a powerful and independent-minded presence for centuries – while for much of the twentieth century any painter, writer or musician with good Bohemian credentials would have lived or worked in or around the 6e arrondissement. Between the wars you could find the painters Picasso and Modigliani in the cafés of Montparnasse, hobnobbing with writers such as Guillaume Apollinaire, André Breton, Jean Cocteau and Anaïs Nin, and expat wannabes like Henry Miller and Ernest Hemingway. After World War II the glitterati moved on to the cafés and jazz clubs of St-Germain, which became second homes to writers and musicians such as Jacques Prévert, Boris Vian, Sidney Bechet and Juliette Gréco – and, most famously, to the existentialists Jean-Paul Sartre and Simone de Beauvoir. But what really defined the Rive Gauche's reputation for turbulence and innovation were *les évènements*, the political "events" of May 1968. Escalating from leftist student demonstrations to factory occupations and massive national strikes, they culminated in the near-overthrow of de Gaulle's presidency.

Since that infamous summer, however, conservatives have certainly had their vengeance on the spirit of the Left Bank. The last three decades have seen rampant gentrification, the streets from which such revolution sprang now housing expensive apartments, art galleries and high-end fashion boutiques, while the cafés once frequented by penniless intellectuals and struggling artists are filled with designers, media and political magnates, and scores of well-heeled foreign residents.

its interior seemingly focused on the single, twisting, central pillar of the Flamboyant choir. The effect is heightened by deep stained glass designed by the modern French painter Jean Bazaine. The flame-like carving that gave the *flamboyant* ("flaming") style its name flickers in the window arch above the entrance while, inside, the first three pillars of the nave betray the earlier, thirteenth-century origins of the church. Outside, on the south side of the church, you can see the remains of what looks like a cloister enclosing a modest courtyard garden on two sides; this was in fact a **charnel house** for the mortal remains of fifteenth-century parishioners. Today, it's the last surviving one anywhere in the city.

One block to the south of the church, **rue de la Parcheminerie** is where medieval scribes and parchment sellers used to congregate. It's worth cricking your neck to look at the decorations on the facades, including that of no. 29, where you'll find the Canadian-run Abbey Bookshop.

The riverside

Just east of rue St-Jacques, and back towards the river, the little patch of green that is **square Viviani** provides the most flattering of all views of Notre-Dame. The three-quarters-dead tree propped on a couple of concrete pillars is reputed to be Paris's oldest, a false acacia brought over from Guyana in 1680. The mutilated and disfigured church behind is **St-Julien-le-Pauvre** (daily 9.30am–12.30pm & 3–6.30pm; M° St-Michel/Maubert-Mutualité). The same age as Notre-Dame, it used to be the venue for university assemblies until rumbustious students tore it apart in 1524. For the last hundred years it has belonged to a Greek Catholic sect, hence the unexpected iconostasis screening the sanctuary. The hefty slabs of stone by the well at the entrance are all that remain of the Roman thoroughfare now overlain by rue St-Jacques. It's a quiet and intimate place, ideal for a moment's pause.

A few steps from square Viviani, on the river bank, rue de la Bûcherie is the home of the historic American-run English-language bookshop **Shakespeare and Co** (daily noon–midnight; M° St-Michel). In fact, the original Shakespeare and Co, owned by the American Sylvia Beach, long-suffering publisher of James Joyce's *Ulysses*, was on rue de l'Odéon, over in St-Germain. Under George Whitman, octogenarian friend of the Beat poets and widely touted (but not actual) grandson of Walt, this "new" incarnation has played host to plenty of literati since it opened in 1951. In 1957, when Allen Ginsberg, William Burroughs and Gregory Corso were living in the so-called Beat Hotel, over on rue Gît-le-Cœur, they'd read their poems on the street outside the store. These days, it's staffed by young would-be Hemingways who sleep upstairs, borrow freely from the library and pay their rent by manning the tills, cleaning – and leaving a photo and a brief autobiography on departure. More books, postcards, prints and assorted goods are on sale from the **bouquinistes**, who display their wares in green padlocked boxes hooked onto the parapet of the **riverside quais**. If you can manage to ignore the traffic and dwell on images from the countless films shot here instead, you'll find the *quais* a romantic place for a stroll.

A little further upstream, the seventeenth-century Hôtel de Miramion, at 47 quai de la Tournelle, provides a handsome riverfront facade for the **Musée de l'Assistance Publique-Hôpitaux de Paris** (Tues–Sun 10am–6pm; closed

Aug; €4; M° Maubert-Mutualité), a museum recounting the history of Paris's hospitals through paintings, sculptures, pharmaceutical containers, surgical instruments and so on. It's not a thrilling visit, though there are some beautiful old ceramic jars for recherché medicaments such as *sang de dragon* (dragon's blood), and a number of curious sentimental paintings among the portraits of medical worthies.

Close by, the **Pont de l'Archevêche** – the archbishop's bridge – leads across the Seine to the lovely green area behind Notre-Dame, offering fine views of the sunlit apartment buildings marshalled along the south-facing fringe of the Ile-St-Louis. One block south, **place Maubert** has a good food market on Tuesday, Thursday and Saturday mornings, stocking anything from fine cheeses to basic salad vegetables. Just beyond the square, to the south, the ugly modern police building houses the **Musée de la Préfecture de Police** (Mon–Fri 9am–5pm, Sat 10am–5pm; free), at 1bis rue des Carmes. The history of the Paris police force, as presented in this collection of uniforms, arms and papers, is dry stuff, but the murder weapons used by legendary criminals may titillate, and voluntarily walking into a working Paris police station has its own peculiar frisson.

The Musée National du Moyen Age

West of place Maubert, the broad boulevard St-Germain leads back to boulevard St-Michel, fronting which are the remains of the walls of the third-century **Roman baths**. Behind, on rue du Sommerard, stands the **Hôtel de Cluny**, a sixteenth-century mansion built by the abbots of the powerful Cluny monastery in Burgundy as their Paris pied-à-terre. The *hôtel* now houses the richly rewarding **Musée National du Moyen Age** (daily except Tues 9.15am–5.45pm; €7.50; Ⓦ www.musee-moyenage.fr; M° Cluny-La Sorbonne). The two-level museum is a treasure house of medieval art and tapestries, its masterpiece being the wonderful tapestry series of *La Dame à la licorne* (*The Lady with the Unicorn*). The building provides a perfect setting for the art – from the huge carved-stone medieval fireplaces and perfect little chapel, to the cool, intricately bricked Gallo-Roman baths filled with sculptural fragments. A pamphlet in English provides a plan of the museum, and while you're wandering around look out for the laminated information sheets in English provided in some rooms.

There's no charge for entry to the beautiful, shady courtyard or to the grounds running along boulevard St-Germain, where you'll find lawns, benches and a children's playground. Excellent **concerts** of medieval music, often featuring vocal groups backed by outlandish-sounding instruments, are usually held inside the museum on Friday lunchtimes (12.30pm) and Saturday afternoons (4pm). Call Ⓣ01.53.73.78.16 for programme information.

Ground floor

Seemingly the backdrop to the artefacts on display, the **tapestries** that hang in most rooms are in fact the highlight of the collection. In room 2, there's an exquisite Resurrection scene embroidered in gold and silver thread, with sleeping guards in medieval armour, and a fourteenth-century embroidery of two leopards in red and gold. Scenes of manorial life are hung in room 3: these sixteenth-century Dutch tapestries are full of flowers and birds, and include scenes such as a woman spinning while her servant patiently holds the threads for her, a lover making advances, a woman in her bath which is overflowing into a duck pond, and a hunting party leaving for the chase.

Room 5 holds attractively naïve wood and alabaster **altarpiece plaques** found in homes and churches all over Europe and produced in England by the Nottingham workshops. Adjacent (room 6) are some wonderful backlit fragments of **stained glass** from the Sainte Chapelle, moved here during the chapel's mid-nineteenth-century renovation. It's fascinating to see the workmanship close up, particularly in bizarre little scenes such as one of Samson having his eyes gouged out.

Down the steps, in the modern structure built around the old baths, room 8 houses the 21 thirteenth-century heads of the **Kings of Judea** from the west front of Notre-Dame, lopped off during the Revolution in the general iconoclastic frenzy, and only discovered in a 1977 excavation near the Opéra Garnier. The blurred, eroded faces and damaged crowns of the Old Testament kings are lined up in a melancholy row of fallen nobility, next to a stage of headless robed figures. Arching over the *frigidarium* (room 9), the cold room of the **Gallo-Roman baths**, the vaults are preserved intact – though temporarily protected by corrugated sheets and scaffolding to enable a study to be carried out on the age of the bricks and plaster. They shelter two beautifully carved first- and second-century capitals, the so-called *Seine Boatmen's Pillar* and the *Pillar of St-Landry*, which has animated-looking gods and musicians adorning three of its faces. From the Roman baths it's a smooth transition to room 10, with its (modern) vaulting and mainly Romanesque works, notably two harrowing wooden *Crucifixions*. Three alarmingly fish-eyed heads, detached from the portals of the royal basilica at St-Denis, guard the entrance to room 11, with its Gothic sculptures of saints and biblical figures.

First floor

Undisputed star of the collection is the truly exquisite **Lady with the Unicorn tapestry series**, displayed in a specially darkened, chapel-like chamber (**room 13**) on the first floor. Dating from the late fifteenth century, the highly allegorical tapestries were probably made in Brussels for the Le Viste family, merchants from Lyon, perhaps to celebrate the family acquiring its own coat of arms – three crescents on a diagonal blue stripe, as shown on the flags floating in various scenes. Each tapestry centres on a woman, a lion and a unicorn, set against a deep red background worked with a myriad of tiny flowers, birds, plants and animals. The tapestries are allegories of the five senses: the richly dressed young woman takes a sweet from a proffered goblet (taste); plays a portable organ (hearing); makes a necklace of carnations (smell); holds a mirror up to the unicorn who whimsically admires his own reflection (sight); and strokes the unicorn's horn with one hand (touch). The final panel, entitled *A Mon Seul Désir* ("To My Only Desire") and depicting the woman putting away her necklace into a jewellery box held out by her servant, remains ambiguous. Some authorities think it represents the dangerous passions engendered by sensuality – the open tent behind is certainly suggestive – others that it shows the sixth "moral sense" that guards against such sinfulness.

The rest of the first floor is an amazing ragbag of carved choir stalls, altarpieces, ivories, stained glass, illuminated Books of Hours, games, brassware and all manner of precious objets d'art. Ecclesiastical gold and enamels fill room 16, notably some seventh-century Visigothic votive crowns and the delicate, long-stemmed **Golden Rose of Basel**, a papal gift dating from 1330. From room 17 onwards you're back in the Hôtel de Cluny section. The bright tapestries, beams and carved fireplaces make it possible to forget you're in a museum, especially in the *hôtel*'s original Flamboyant **chapel** (room 20), which preserves its remarkable vault splaying out from a central pillar.

The Sorbonne and around

"Making it" in France has always meant going to Paris, and it's as true for students as for social climbers. In the heart of the Quartier Latin, on the south side of rue des Ecoles, cluster the modern heirs of the colleges that once sat atop the Montagne-Ste-Geneviève, attracting the finest scholars from all over medieval Europe. Paris doesn't have quite the same world-beating status now, but the Lycée Louis-le-Grand attracts the cream of France's would-be students, the Sorbonne remains one of France's top universities for the arts, while the Collège de France is the leading research institution for the humanities. If you're bright enough, you need never leave the quartier.

From rue des Ecoles, **rue Champollion**, with its huddle of arty cinemas and cinema café, *Le Reflet* (see p.331), leads to the **place de la Sorbonne** (M° Cluny-La Sorbonne). It's a peaceful place to sit, in a café or just under the lime trees, listening to the play of the fountains and watching students toting their books about. Overshadowing the graceful ensemble is the **Chapelle Ste-Ursule**, built in the 1640s by the great Cardinal Richelieu, whose tomb it contains. A building of enormous influence in its unabashed emulation of the Roman Counter-Reformation style, it helped establish a trend for domes, which mushroomed over the city's skyline in the latter part of the century. It is certainly the most architecturally distinctive part of the **Sorbonne**, as the university buildings were entirely (and unfortunately) rebuilt in the 1880s. Sadly, in the era of anti-terrorism measures – or "*plans vigipirates*", as they're known in France – you're now unable to look into the Sorbonne's main **courtyard** unless you can produce some kind of student ID and bluff convincingly in French. It's a shame, as it's a historic as well as a handsome spot: it was here, on May 3, 1968, that a riot broke out after police violently intervened to break up a political meeting – in contravention of centuries of tradition separating the university and civic authorities. The faculty buildings were occupied by furious radicals and the college briefly became the flashpoint of France's student-led rebellion against institutional stagnation, housing a vibrant, anarchic commune before finally being stormed by the police on June 16. The shake-up in the higher education system that followed transformed the Sorbonne into the more prosaic Paris IV (though the old name is still used unofficially), largely attended by arts and social science students.

The foundation of the **Collège de France**, alongside, was first mooted by the Renaissance king François I, in order to establish the study of Greek and Hebrew in France. Its modern incarnation, as a research institution, has attracted intellectual giants such as Michel Foucault and Claude Lévi-Strauss. Behind it, on rue St-Jacques, the **Lycée Louis-le-Grand** numbers Molière, Robespierre, Sartre and Victor Hugo among its former pupils. In some ways it's an ordinary *lycée*, or secondary school, but it's also a portal to academic and political success, hothousing some of France's brightest students for their entry exams to the *grandes écoles*, France's most élite colleges of higher education. The study programme is renowned for reducing the most brilliant pupils to stressed-out wrecks; just one in ten get through.

The Panthéon and St-Etienne-du-Mont

The most visible of the Left Bank's many domes graces the hulk of the **Panthéon** (daily: April–Sept 9.30am–6.30pm; Oct–March 10am–6.15pm; €6.40; RER Luxembourg/M° Cardinal-Lemoine), the towering mausoleum which tops the Montagne Ste-Geneviève. It was originally built as a church by Louis XV, on the site of the ruined Ste-Geneviève abbey, to thank the saint for curing him of illness and to emphasize the unity of the church and state, troubled at the time by growing divisions between Jesuits and Jansenists – not only had the original abbey church entombed Geneviève, Paris's patron saint, but it had been founded by Clovis, France's first Christian king. The building was only completed in 1789, whereupon the Revolution promptly transformed it into a mausoleum, adding the words "*Aux grands hommes la patrie reconnaissante*" ("The nation honours its great men") underneath the pediment of the giant portico. The remains of French heroes such as Voltaire, Rousseau, Hugo and Zola are now entombed in the vast, barrel-vaulted crypt below, along with more recent arrivals: Marie Curie (the only woman), with her husband Pierre (1995), writer and landmark culture minister André Malraux (1996), and the novelist Alexandre Dumas (2002), the last to be *panthéonizé* here, with much fanfare. There's also a plaque to Saint-Exupéry, author of the much-loved *Petit Prince*. He'd have a full-scale monument, but because his plane was lost at sea he fell foul of the rule that without a body part to inter you cannot be pantheonized.

The Panthéon's **interior** is rather bleak, but worth a visit for its oddly secular frescoes and sculptures, and monumental design, originally conceived as a combination of the virtues of Classical Greek and Gothic construction. You can also see a working model of **Foucault's Pendulum** swinging from the dome (the original is under glass at the Musée des Arts et Métiers – see p.120). The French physicist Léon Foucault devised the experiment, conducted at the Panthéon in 1851, to demonstrate vividly the rotation of the earth. While the pendulum appeared to rotate over a 24-hour period, it was in fact the earth beneath it turning. The demonstration wowed the scientific establishment and the public alike, with huge crowds turning up to watch the ground move beneath their feet. In summer (June–Sept 10am–5.30pm; free), you can join regular guided tours, which take small groups up into the vertiginous cupola and out onto the high **balcony** running round the outside of the dome; as you'd expect, the views are spectacular.

Sloping downhill from the main portico of the Panthéon, broad rue Soufflot entices you west towards the Luxembourg gardens (see p.145). On the east side of the Panthéon, however, peeping over the walls of the Lycée Henri IV, look out for the lone Gothic tower which is all that remains of the earlier church of Ste-Geneviève. The saint's remains, and those of two seventeenth-century literary greats who didn't make the Panthéon, Pascal and Racine, lie close at hand in the church of **St-Etienne-du-Mont** (Mon noon–7.45pm, Tues–Fri 8.45am–noon & 2–7.30pm, Sat 8.45am–noon & 2–7.45pm, Sun 8.45am–12.15pm & 2.30–7.45pm; RER Luxembourg/M° Cardinal-Lemoine), on the corner of rue Clovis. The church's facade is a bit of a hotch-potch, but it conceals a stunning and highly unexpected interior. The transition from Flamboyant Gothic choir to sixteenth-century nave would be startling if the eye wasn't distracted by a strange high-level catwalk which springs from pillar to pillar before transforming itself into a rood screen which arches across the width of the nave. This last feature is highly unusual in itself; most French rood screens were destroyed by Protestant iconoclasts, reformers or revolutionaries. Exceptionally tall windows flood the church with light, while the west end of the nave is filled by an elaborate carved organ loft.

Further down rue Clovis, a huge piece of Philippe-Auguste's early thirteenth-century **city wall** emerges from among the houses.

Mouffetard

East of the Panthéon, the villagey **rue de la Montagne-Ste-Geneviève** descends towards place Maubert, passing the pleasant cafés and restaurants around rue de l'Ecole-Polytechnique. Heading uphill from the rue de la Montagne-Ste-Geneviève, rue Descartes climbs past a landmark blue **mural** of a tree, by the Belgian artist Pierre Alechinsky – a tree which the accompanying poem by Yves Bonnefoy invites passers-by to contemplate – before suddenly arriving at the oasis of **place de la Contrescarpe**. This intimate, pleasingly run-down square has long been the hub of the Mouffetard quarter's café life. On its sunny side, the *Café Delmas* was once the famous – and much less swanky – café *La Chope*, as described by Ernest Hemingway in *A Moveable Feast*. He knew it well, as he lived just round the corner on the fourth floor of 74 rue Cardinal Lemoine, in a miserable flat largely paid for by his wife's trust fund. Just to the east of the square, the curved frontage of a municipal crèche on rue Lacépède was inspired by the shape of a pregnant belly.

Place de la Contrescarpe once stood at the edges of the medieval city. Passing through Philippe-Auguste's fortress walls, travellers would leave Paris along the narrow, ancient incline of **rue Mouffetard**, which followed the line of the old Roman road to Italy. "La Mouffe", as it's known to locals, was for generations one of the great **market streets** of Paris. These days, its top half is given over to tacky eating places and touristy shops, especially around rue du Pot de Fer, but the market traditions still cling on at the southern end, where you'll find fruit and vegetable stalls in the mornings, shops selling fine cheeses and wines, and a couple of old-fashioned market cafés, notably *Le Verre à Pied* (see p.331). Some traces of the past can be found on the old shopfronts, most obviously the two cows adorning a former butcher's at no. 6, and no. 12's hand-painted sign depicting a black man in striped trousers waiting on his mistress, with the unconvincing legend, "*Au Nègre Joyeux*". At no. 69 there's a fine old carved oak tree, while no. 122, labelled "*La Bonne Source*" (the Good Spring), seems to advertise the fresh water – or possibly, more obliquely, the fresh produce – once available there.

At the foot of rue Mouffetard, just beyond the beautiful painted facade at no. 134, **St-Médard** (Tues–Sat 8am–12.30pm & 2.30–7.30pm, Sun 8.30am–12.30pm & 4–8pm; M° Censier-Daubenton) was once a country parish church, and only brought within the city walls during the reign of Louis XV. The church twice achieved notoriety: in 1561, when it was sacked by Protestant rioters in the so-called Tumult of St-Médard, and again in 1727, when fanatical supporters of François de Paris – a leading light in the reforming Jansenist movement, which had been condemned by pope and king alike but drew massive popular support in Paris – gathered at his fresh grave. Rumours of miracles led crowds of "*convulsionnaires*" into collective hysteria, rolling on the ground around their saint's tomb, eating the earth and even wounding or crucifying themselves in sado-masochistic frenzies. These excesses helped split the Jansenist movement,

△ Rue Mouffetard market

and led the authorities to post armed guards at the church gates in 1732, beside a sign reading "*De par le roi, défense à Dieu/De faire miracle en ce lieu*" (By order of the king, God is forbidden to work miracles in this place). The church today preserves its simple, narrow Gothic nave and more elaborate late sixteenth-century choir, with fine fluted columns in the ambulatory. The organ loft is astounding, and not just for its size – it's topped by noble statues carved by the great Renaissance sculptor Germain Pilon in the 1640s.

Below St-Médard lay the marshy ground of the now-covered **River Bièvre**, where tanners and dyers worked in the Middle Ages – which may explain the origin of the name Mouffetard, from a slang term for "stinking". Today, Avenue des Gobelins leads into the 13ᵉ arrondissement, passing the Gobelins tapestry workshops (see p.188) on the way up to busy place de l'Italie.

Val-de-Grâce

West of rue Mouffetard, you quickly leave other tourists behind as you penetrate the academic heart of the Quartier Latin, lorded over by the Curie and oceanographic institutes and the élite **Ecole Normale Supérieure**, on rue d'Ulm. Definitely more *supérieure* than *normale*, its students – dubbed *normaliens* – are France's academic elite, bred for the top arts and humanities jobs in universities and lycées.

It's a closed world to outsiders, however, and there's not much point in visiting this corner of the city unless it's to see the magnificent Baroque church of **Val-de-Grâce**, set just back from rue St-Jacques. Built by Anne of Austria as an act of pious gratitude following the birth of her first son in 1638, it's a suitably awesome monument to the young prince who went on to reign as Louis XIV, with its dome and double-pedimented facade thrusting skywards.

You can only enter via the **Musée du Service de Santé des Armées** (Tues, Wed, Sat & Sun noon–6pm; €5; RER Luxembourg), which occupies the old Benedictine convent adjoining the church to the south. Part of a modern hospital complex, the museum is a wearyingly thorough history of military medicine, and its mock-ups of field hospitals and gory details of prosthetic limbs and reconstructive plastic surgery aren't for the faint-hearted. The church, properly known as the **Chapelle St-Louis**, is reached via a curved iron grille behind which the Benedictine nuns once watched the Mass. It isn't quite as large as you'd imagine after seeing the grandiose exterior, but still staggeringly impressive in the Roman Baroque manner. Inside the dome, Pierre Mignard's wonderful trompe-l'oeil fresco of Paradise depicts Anne of Austria offering a model of the church up to the Virgin.

Around the corner from the hospital, the busy **boulevard de Port-Royal** forms the boundary with the 13ᵉ arrondissement; from here it's just a short step west to the bright lights and brasseries of Montparnasse (see p.339).

The Paris mosque and Jardin des Plantes

East of rue Mouffetard, across rue Monge, lie some of the city's most agreeable surprises. Just beyond place du Puits de l'Ermite stand the gate and crenellated walls of the **Paris mosque** (daily except Fri & Muslim holidays 9am–noon & 2–6pm; €3; M° Jussieu), which was built by Moroccan craftsmen in the early 1920s. You're free to walk from cloister to tiled cloister, admiring the sunken garden, but non-Muslims are asked not to enter the prayer room. No-one seems to mind, however, if you watch from a discreet distance during prayers. Towards the back of the building, on the rue Geoffroy St-Hilaire side, lies a simple monument to the Algerian scholar and national hero Abd el-Kader, who led the resistance against French invasion before finally being forced to surrender in 1847. The gate on the southeast corner of the mosque complex, on rue Daubenton, leads into a lovely **tearoom** with a garden (see p.338), and an atmospheric **hammam** (see p.416).

Behind the mosque, the **Jardin des Plantes** (daily: April–Aug 7.30am–8pm; Sept–March 8am–dusk; free; Ⓦwww.mnhn.fr; M° Austerlitz/Jussieu/Monge) was founded as a medicinal herb garden in 1626 and retains a scientific botanical role. It has always had another, more leisured side, however, and its hothouses, shady avenues of trees, lawns, museums and zoo make it a favourite oasis for Parisians. There's an entrance at the corner of rues Geoffroy-St-Hilaire and Buffon; other entrances are further north on the corner with rue Cuvier, the main gate on rue Cuvier itself, and on quai St-Bernard. If you enter by the rue Cuvier gate and climb the little hillock on the right up to an ironwork gazebo, you can then descend along pleasant winding paths past a stately cedar of Lebanon planted in 1734; keep straight ahead on the main path leading in from the gate and you'll pass some fine plane trees a mere half-century younger. In the nearby physics labs overlooking the gardens, Henri Becquerel discovered radioactivity in 1896, and two years later the Curies discovered radium.

Magnificent, varied floral beds make a fine approach to the collection of buildings that form the **Muséum National d'Histoire Naturelle**. Skip the musty museums of paleontology, anatomy, mineralogy, entomology and paleobotany in favour of the **Grande Galerie de l'Evolution** (daily except Tues 10am–6pm; €8), housed in a dramatically restored nineteenth-century glass-domed building (the entrance is off rue Buffon). You can't fail to be wowed by the sheer scale of the interior, where the story of evolution and the relations between human beings and nature is told with the aid of stuffed animals (rescued from the dusty old zoology museum and restored to such spruceness that they look alive) and a combination of clever lighting effects, ambient music and birdsong, videos and touch-screen databases. If you really want to do something as old-fashioned as reading, there are wooden lecture boards in English to accompany the aurals and visuals. On the lower level, submarine light suffuses the space where the murkiest deep-ocean creatures are displayed. Above, glass lifts rise silently from the savannah, where a closely packed line of huge African animals, headed by an elephant, look as if they're

Lamarck and the theory of evolution

Outside the paleontology museum in the Jardin des Plantes a statue rises above the proud legend "Founder of the Doctrine of Evolution". The fact that the man portrayed is one **Jean-Baptiste Lamarck** rather than a certain rather more celebrated Englishman says a lot about cultural perspectives. Born in 1744, Lamarck began his career as an assistant at Paris's **Jardin des Plantes**. When the Musée National d'Histoire Naturelle was set up after the Revolution, he was promoted to the proud post of professor of worms and insects. By 1809, the same year Charles Darwin was born, he had worked out a radical theory that animal species could adapt in response to environmental pressures. But his work received only moderate recognition, and he died blind and poor (and surrounded by daughters from four marriages) in 1829 – two years before Darwin set sail in the *Beagle*. Many of Lamarck's ideas have been disproved or abandoned – notably that traits acquired during an animal's lifetime can be inherited – but he was nevertheless the first scientist to give birth to the great evolutionary idea. As such, the title under his statue couldn't be more apt.

stepping onto Noah's ark. It's all great fun for children, and there's even a small interactive centre for kids on the first floor (see p.431).

Live animals can be seen in the small **ménagerie** across the park to the northeast near rue Cuvier (summer Mon–Sat 9am–6pm, Sun 9.30am–6.30pm; winter daily 9am–5pm; €7). Founded just after the Revolution, it is France's oldest zoo – and looks it. The old-fashioned iron cages of the big cats' *fauverie*, the stinky vivarium and the unkempt, glazed-in primate house are frankly depressing, though these animals will at least be spared the fate of their predecessors during the starvation months of the 1870 Prussian siege. Thankfully, most of the rest of the zoo is pleasantly park-like and given over to deer, antelope, goats, buffaloes and other marvellous beasts that seem happy enough in their outdoor enclosures. In the **Microzoo** you can inspect headlice and other minuscule wonders through a microscope.

The surprisingly large – and remarkably well-hidden – open space of the **Arènes de Lutèce** lies a short distance away to the northwest, with entrances in rue de Navarre, rue des Arènes and another through a passage on rue Monge. A few ghostly rows of stone seats are all that's left of the Roman amphitheatre that once amused ten thousand here; the entertainment is now provided by the old men playing boules in the sand below. Benches, gardens and a kids' playground stand behind.

Institut du Monde Arabe

To the north of the Arènes de Lutèce and Jardin des Plantes, a great chunk of the quartier is swallowed up by the much-loathed **Jussieu campus** building, an uncompromising structure built entirely in metal and glass around notoriously windswept internal courtyards. Built to house the baby-boomers coming of university age in the late 1960s – and to thwart any unseemly outbreaks of student rebellion with its single entrance – its population has since outgrown it once again, and it has decamped upstream to a new site (see p.191). At the time of writing, the brutal skyscraper of the main Tour Zamansky stood empty, denuded of its glass cladding while vast amounts of asbestos were stripped out.

A more recent and vastly more successful piece of modern metal-and-glass architecture stands immediately to the north. The **Institut du Monde Arabe** (Tues–Sun 10am–6pm; Ⓦwww.imarabe.org; M° Jussieu/Cardinal-Lemoine) is a stunning and radical piece of architectural engineering, designed by the architect of the moment, Jean Nouvel, who subsequently built the ambitious Fondation Cartier (see p.177) and the brand-new Musée du Quai Branly (see p.159). Its broad southern facade comprises thousands of tiny light-sensitive shutters which modulate the light levels inside while simultaneously mimicking a *moucharabiyah*, the traditional Arab latticework balcony. Unfortunately, the computer system operating the little steel diaphragms has a habit of crashing, so you may not get to see the full effect. On the riverfront side of the building, a boldly curving curtain wall of glass seems to symbolize the transition from the glass box behind to the flowing water at its feet. To the north, the **Pont de Sully** cuts across to the tip of the Ile-St-Louis, providing a fine view downstream towards Notre-Dame.

Inside the Institute, hit exhibitions and concerts pull in the curious, open-minded visitors sought by its creators – the Mitterrand government in collaboration with the Arab League. A sleek permanent **museum** (€5) begins on the seventh floor, using an array of exquisite artefacts to trace the evolution of the arts and sciences in the Islamic world. The topmost level, dedicated to pre-Islamic finds, is somewhat surprising, as the Carthaginian sculptures and pottery display a distinctly Roman influence, while a beautiful seventh-century Tunisian mosaic hails from an early church. One floor down, brass celestial globes, astrolabes, compasses and sundials illustrate the cutting-edge Arab research that so influenced the West in the Middle Ages, along with illustrated manuscripts, weights and measures, and the grinding and mixing implements for medicines. But the museum's treasures are kept on the lowest floor, with exquisitely crafted ceramics, metalwork and carpets from all over the Muslim world – from Spain to Central Asia.

On other levels there are a library and multi-media centre for scholars, a space for temporary exhibitions, a specialist bookshop that sells good Arab music CDs, and an auditorium for regular films and concerts, often featuring leading performers from the Arab world. Up on the ninth floor, the terrace offers brilliant **views over the Seine** towards the apse of Notre-Dame. At the adjacent **café-restaurant** you can drink mint tea and nibble on cakes; for something more substantial there's the self-service restaurant *Le Moucharabieh* where you can tuck into a plate of couscous while marvelling at the aperture action of the windows.

St-Germain

St-Germain is one of the most picturesque and lively quarters in the city. Encompassing the 6e arrondissement and the eastern fringe of the 7e, it has all the sophistication of the Right Bank – and, these days, most of the same shops too – but a certain easy-going, thoughtful chic makes it uniquely appealing. The quartier has moved ever further upmarket since the postwar era, when it was the natural home of arty mould-breakers and trendsetters, but it still clings to its offbeat charm. Broadly speaking, the further west you go the posher the shops, houses and restaurants become.

Historically, St-Germain has stood outside the city proper for most of its life. From the sixth century onward, its fields and riverine meadows fell under the sway of the giant Benedictine abbey of **St-Germain des Prés** – "St Germain of the Fields" – of which just the church remains today. Marie de Médicis built the **Palais du Luxembourg**, now the Senate, in the early seventeenth century, but the area only became urbanized a hundred years later, as aristocrats migrated across the Seine from the Marais in search of new, spacious plots of land for their fine mansion *hôtels*. The **Faubourg St-Germain** thus created became one of Europe's most fashionable districts, its heyday only eclipsed by the Revolution.

The now-celebrated **boulevard St-Germain** was driven right through the heart of the quarter by Baron Haussmann in the mid-nineteenth century, but it became famous in its own right after the war, when the cafés **Flore** and **Les Deux Magots** attracted the resurgent Parisian avant-garde – Sartre debated existentialism with de Beauvoir and Boris Vian sang in smoky cellar jazz bars. As Guy Béart and, later, Juliette Gréco sang, "*il n y a plus d'après à Saint-Germain-des-Prés*" – there's no tomorrow in St-Germain.

Of course, there was – even if an older Juliette Gréco tried to fight it with her movement SOS St-Germain in the late 1990s. The glitterati may still prefer the Left Bank – apart from Gréco, **Serge Gainsbourg** lived here until his death in 1991 – but high-rolling publishers, designers and politicians have long since shouldered out boho intellectuals and musicians. **Fashion**, now, is king. The streets around the Carrefour de la Croix-Rouge and place St-Sulpice, in particular, swarm with internationally known clothes boutiques, while a little further west the historic Bon Marché department store stocks an ever-classier range. Towards the river, it's antique shops and **art dealers** that dominate, with one pricey cluster around rue Jacob and rue Bonaparte, and another in the "Carré Rive Gauche", the three blocks south of Quai Voltaire. After shopping, eating and drinking are the main attractions, though, once again, the scene is distinctly chichi these days. Well-heeled foodies now flock to the gastronomic **restaurants** of celebrity chefs like Hélène Darroze and Joël Robuchon, and foreign visitors fill the *bistrots* around Mabillon.

There are excellent markets and cafés to take in as you shop or stroll, as well as some fine buildings – from the domed **Collège de France**, by the river, to the churches of St-Germain-des-Prés and **St-Sulpice** – the latter recently featuring as a key location in a certain best-selling thriller. Two small, single-artist museums, the **Musée Maillol** and **Musée Delacroix**, make intimate antidotes to the grand Right Bank institutions, while the art exhibitions at the **Musée du Luxembourg** are regularly among the city's most exciting. And of course there's the **Musée d'Orsay**, at the western edge of the quarter, loved as much for its stunning railway-station setting as its Impressionist collection. But St-Germain's most beguiling attraction lies in the southeastern corner of the quarter, hard up against the Quartier Latin. Notoriously romantic, and often packed with students, the **Jardin du Luxembourg** is one of the largest and loveliest green spaces in the city.

The Institut de France

From the Right Bank and the Louvre, the pedestrian **Pont des Arts** entices you across the river and into St-Germain. It's the most charming of all the city's bridges and a classic place to loiter, taking in the view upstream to the Ile de la Cité and, on fair days, basking in the heat that seems to soak into its wooden planking. The bridge owes its name not to the artists who have long sold their work here but to the institute that sits under the elegant dome on the St-Germain side. This is the **Collège des Quatre-Nations**, seat of the **Institut de France**. Of the Institut's five academies of arts and sciences, the most famous is the **Académie Française**, an august body of writers and scholars whose mission is to award literary prizes and defend the integrity of the French language against Anglo-Saxon invasion. Recent creations include the excellent word *courriel* for "email", but rearguard actions against English terms in science, management and webspeak have been hopelessly ineffective. Becoming an *Académicien* is the ultimate accolade, and the chosen few are known as *Immortels* – though ironically, by the time they have accumulated enough prestige to be elected, most are not long for this world. The list of *Immortels* is hardly avant garde: among the forty-strong group at the time of writing, one was a cardinal and just four were women.

You'd need an invitation to attend one of the Institut's lectures, but if you ask politely at the gate and present ID and a couple of photos, you may be given a visitor's pass for the exquisite **Bibliothèque Mazarine** (Mon–Fri 10am–6pm; free; M° Mabillon/Pont Neuf), where scholars of religious history sit in hushed contemplation of some of the 200,000 sixteenth- and seventeenth-century volumes, surrounded by *rocaille* chandeliers, marble busts and Corinthian columns.

Next door to the Institut, at 11 quai de Conti, is the **Hôtel des Monnaies**. In the late eighteenth century this was the Mint, but it's now reduced to housing the **Musée de la Monnaie** (Tues–Fri 11am–5.30pm, Sat & Sun noon–5.30pm; €5). Its dry collection of coins and coin-making tools might, at a pinch, appeal to those deeply nostalgic for the franc, or Balzac-lovers curious to see the actual coins that slipped so easily through the fingers of young Rastignac, from the gold *Louis* to the humble *sou*. To the west of the Institut lies the **Ecole des Beaux-Arts**, the School of Fine Art, whose glory days gave its name to an entire epoch. It's occasionally open for exhibitions of work by its students.

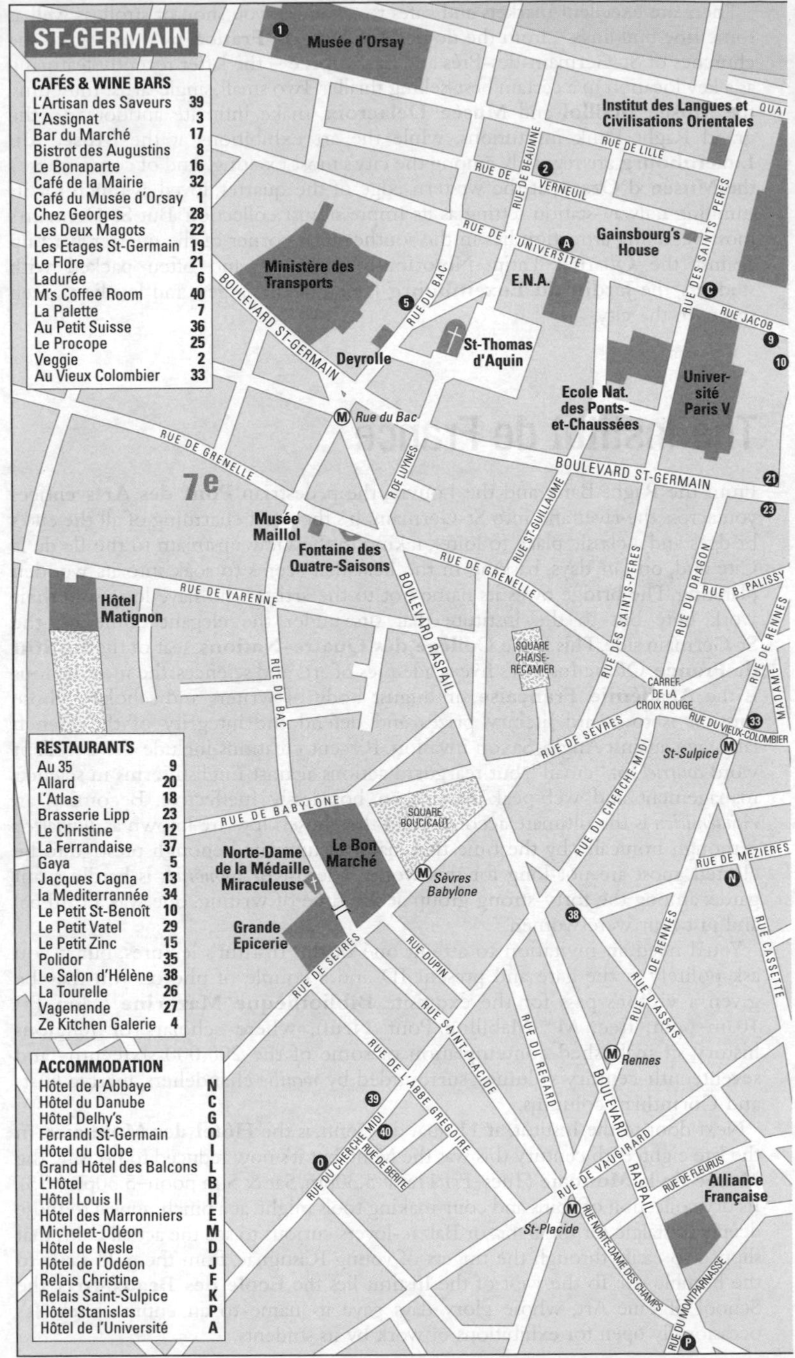
ST-GERMAIN
CAFÉS & WINE BARS
L'Artisan des Saveurs 39
L'Assignat 3
Bar du Marché 17
Bistrot des Augustins 8
Le Bonaparte 16
Café de la Mairie 32
Café du Musée d'Orsay 1
Chez Georges 28
Les Deux Magots 22
Les Etages St-Germain 19
Le Flore 21
Ladurée 6
M's Coffee Room 40
La Palette 7
Au Petit Suisse 36
Le Procope 25
Veggie 2
Au Vieux Colombier 33
RESTAURANTS
Au 35 9
Allard 20
L'Atlas 18
Brasserie Lipp 23
Le Christine 12
La Ferrandaise 37
Gaya 5
Jacques Cagna 13
la Mediterrannée 34
Le Petit St-Benoît 10
Le Petit Vatel 29
Le Petit Zinc 15
Polidor 35
Le Salon d'Hélène 38
La Tourelle 26
Vagenende 27
Ze Kitchen Galerie 4
ACCOMMODATION
Hôtel de l'Abbaye N
Hôtel du Danube C
Hôtel Delhy's G
Ferrandi St-Germain O
Hôtel du Globe I
Grand Hôtel des Balcons L
L'Hôtel B
Hôtel Louis II H
Hôtel des Marronniers E
Michelet-Odéon M
Hôtel de Nesle D
Hôtel de l'Odéon J
Relais Christine F
Relais Saint-Sulpice K
Hôtel Stanislas P
Hôtel de l'Université A
Musée d'Orsay
Institut des Langues et Civilisations Orientales
QUAI
RUE DE LILLE
RUE DE BEAUNNE
RUE DE VERNEUIL
RUE DES SAINTS PERES
RUE DE L'UNIVERSITE
Gainsbourg's House
Ministère des Transports
E.N.A.
BOULEVARD ST-GERMAIN
RUE DU BAC
RUE JACOB
St-Thomas d'Aquin
Deyrolle
Univer-sité Paris V
Ecole Nat. des Ponts-et-Chaussées
Rue du Bac
RUE DE GRENELLE
R. DE LUYNES
7e
Musée Maillol
Fontaine des Quatre-Saisons
RUE ST-GUILLAUME
RUE DE GRENELLE
RUE B. PALISSY
RUE DE VARENNE
Hôtel Matignon
BOULEVARD RASPAIL
RUE DES SAINTS-PERES
RUE DU DRAGON
RUE DE RENNES
SQUARE CHAISE-RECAMIER
CARREF. DE LA CROIX ROUGE
MADAME
RUE DU BAC
RUE DE SEVRES
RUE DU VIEUX-COLOMBIER
St-Sulpice
RUE DU CHERCHE-MIDI
RUE DE BABYLONE
SQUARE BOUCICAUT
Norte-Dame de la Médaille Miraculeuse
Le Bon Marché
Sèvres Babylone
RUE DE MEZIERES
Grande Epicerie
RUE DE SEVRES
RUE DUPIN
RUE SAINT-PLACIDE
RUE DU REGARD
RUE DE RENNES
RUE D'ASSAS
RUE CASSETTE
Rennes
RUE DE L'ABBE GREGOIRE
RUE DU CHERCHE MIDI
RUE DE BERITE
BOULEVARD RASPAIL
RUE DE VAUGIRARD
RUE DE FLEURUS
Alliance Française
St-Placide
RUE NOTRE-DAME DES CHAMPS
RUE DU MONTPARNASSE
Gare Montparnasse

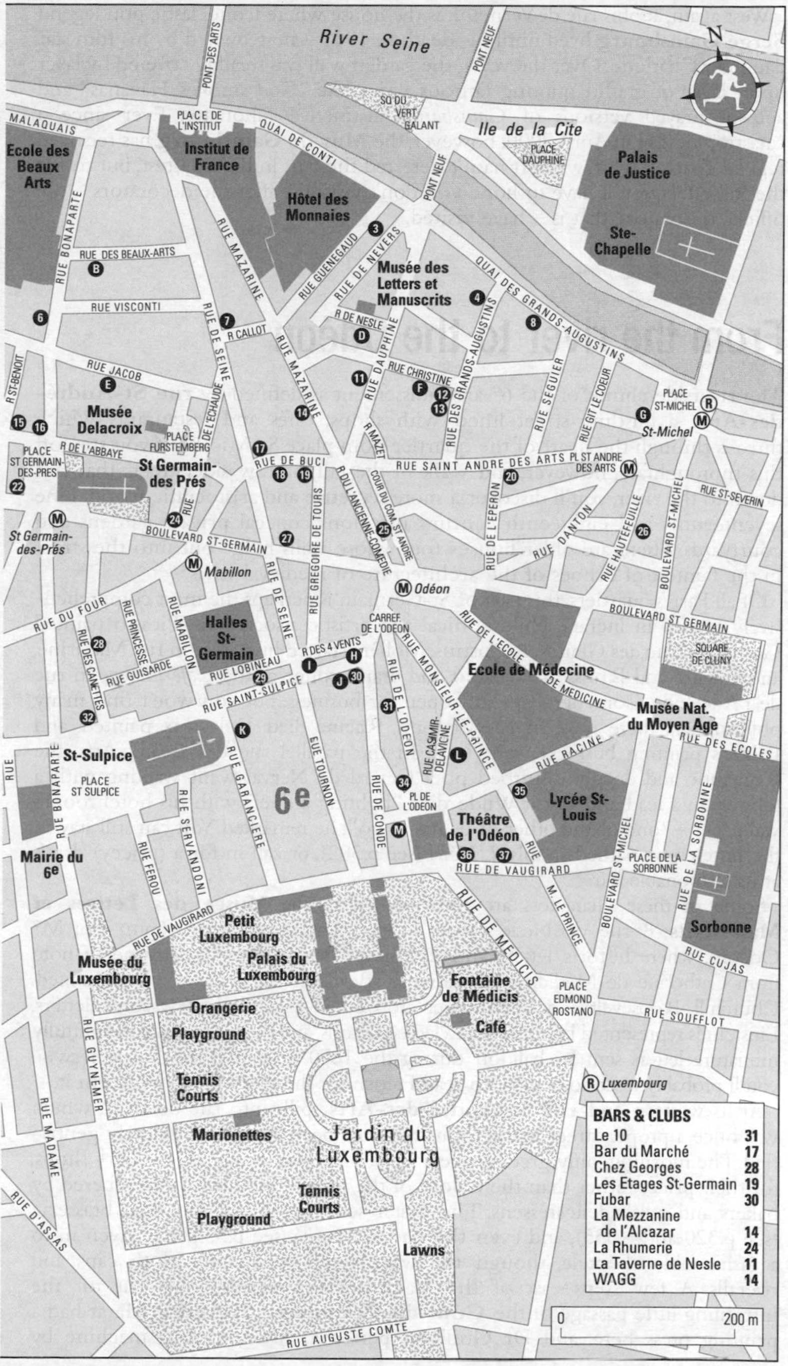
River Seine
PONT DES ARTS
PONT NEUF
SQ DU VERT GALANT
Ile de la Cite
PLACE DAUPHINE
Palais de Justice
Ste-Chapelle
MALAQUAIS
PLACE DE L'INSTITUT
QUAI DE CONTI
Ecole des Beaux Arts
Institut de France
Hôtel des Monnaies
RUE BONAPARTE
RUE DES BEAUX-ARTS
RUE MAZARINE
RUE GUENEGAUD
RUE DE NEVERS
Musée des Letters et Manuscrits
QUAI DES GRANDS-AUGUSTINS
RUE VISCONTI
RUE DE SEINE
R CALLOT
R DE NESLE
RUE DAUPHINE
RUE CHRISTINE
RUE DES GRANDS-AUGUSTINS
RUE SEGUIER
RUE GIT LE COEUR
PLACE ST-MICHEL
St-Michel
R ST-BENOIT
RUE JACOB
Musée Delacroix
RUE DE L'ECHAUDE
R MAZET
PLACE FURSTEMBERG
R DE L'ABBAYE
PLACE ST GERMAIN-DES-PRES
St Germain-des Prés
RUE DE BUCI
RUE SAINT ANDRE DES ARTS
PL ST ANDRE DES ARTS
R DE L'ANCIENNE-COMEDIE
COUR DU COM. ST ANDRE
RUE DE L'EPERON
RUE DANTON
RUE HAUTEFEUILLE
BOULEVARD ST-MICHEL
RUE ST-SEVERIN
St Germain-des-Prés
BOULEVARD ST-GERMAIN
Mabillon
RUE GREGOIRE DE TOURS
Odéon
BOULEVARD ST GERMAIN
RUE DU FOUR
RUE PRINCESSE
RUE MABILLON
Halles St-Germain
CARREF DE L'ODEON
RUE DE L'ECOLE DE MEDICINE
SQUARE DE CLUNY
RUE DES CANETTES
RUE GUISARDE
RUE LOBINEAU
R DES 4 VENTS
RUE MONSIEUR-LE-PRINCE
Ecole de Médecine
RUE SAINT-SULPICE
RUE DE L'ODEON
RUE CASIMIR-DELAVIGNE
Musée Nat. du Moyen Age
RUE DES ECOLES
St-Sulpice
PLACE ST SULPICE
RUE GARANCIERE
EUE TOURNON
RUE RACINE
6e
RUE DE CONDE
PL DE L'ODEON
Lycée St-Louis
RUE DE LA SORBONNE
RUE SERVANDONI
Théatre de l'Odéon
Mairie du 6e
RUE FEROU
RUE DE VAUGIRARD
PLACE DE LA SORBONNE
M. LE PRINCE
Sorbonne
RUE DE MEDICIS
RUE DE VAUGIRARD
Petit Luxembourg
Palais du Luxembourg
Musée du Luxembourg
Fontaine de Médicis
RUE CUJAS
PLACE EDMOND ROSTANO
RUE SOUFFLOT
Orangerie
Café
Playground
RUE GUYNEMER
Tennis Courts
Luxembourg
RUE MADAME
Marionettes
Jardin du Luxembourg
RUE D'ASSAS
Tennis Courts
Playground
Lawns
RUE AUGUSTE COMTE
0
200 m
BARS & CLUBS
Le 10 31
Bar du Marché 17
Chez Georges 28
Les Etages St-Germain 19
Fubar 30
La Mezzanine de l'Alcazar 14
La Rhumerie 24
La Taverne de Nesle 11
WAGG 14

West again, at 5bis rue de Verneuil, is the house where iconoclastic pop legend **Serge Gainsbourg** lived until his death in 1991 – now owned by his film star daughter Charlotte. Over the years, the garden wall was steadily covered by layer upon layer of graffiti quoting famous lyrics like "God smokes Havanas" and aerosol-sprayed versions of *Gainsbarre*'s distinctive silhouette. Ever since a catastrophic day in April 2000, however, the **Mur de Gainsbourg** has received regular coats of whitewash. It hasn't deterred the fans in the slightest, but to get the full effect you'll have to hope you don't visit just after the decorators – the official decorators, that is – have visited.

From the river to the Odéon

The riverside chunk of the 6e arrondissement is defined by **rue St-André-des-Arts**, a bustling street lined with shops, cafés and restaurants which threads through the heart of the quartier from place St-Michel. If you step off this thoroughfare, however, and walk in the tall, narrow side streets that run down to the river, you'll discover a more secretive and aristocratic world. Fine seventeenth- and eighteenth-century mansions conceal private gardens and courtyards. There are older houses too, whose walls bulge out into the street in the faintest of echoes of the architecture of medieval Paris.

Of all Paris's quartiers, this part of St-Germain is perhaps the most comprehensively soaked in literary, philosophical and artistic associations. Picasso painted *Guernica* in rue des Grands-Augustins, Molière started his career in rue Mazarine, and Voltaire and Rousseau debated and drank coffee at the *Café Procope* in rue de l'Ancienne-Comédie – it's still open for business, but you won't find many philosophers there now. In rue Visconti, Racine died, Delacroix painted, and Balzac's printing business went bust. In the parallel rue des Beaux-Arts, the Romantic and deeply disturbed poet Gérard de Nerval went walking with a lobster on a lead and Oscar Wilde died "fighting a duel" with his hotel room's wallpaper – "one or the other of us has to go", he remarked. You can still stay in the hotel, now named simply *L'Hôtel* (see p.302), or call in for a (pricey) drink at its fashionable bar.

Some of these characters are remembered in the **Musée des Lettres et Manuscrits**, 8 rue de Nesle (Wed 1–9pm, Thurs–Sun 10am–6pm; €6; M° Odéon), where historic letters and documents handwritten by anyone of note from Catherine de Médicis to Simone de Beauvoir are permanently exhibited. Churchill, Roosevelt and Eisenhower crop up in a handful of wartime letters, Einstein is represented by some scrawled equations, and there are some delightfully miniature letters sent by balloon during the 1870 siege of Paris, but otherwise you'll probably need to be able to read French for the entry fee to be worth it.

At its western end, **rue St-André-des-Arts** spills into rue de Buci, which was once a proper street market, but has now been almost completely gentrified. The morning-only greengrocers' stalls – known locally as jewellery shops, for their prices rather than the colour of the fruits – are now outnumbered by bakers and swish delicatessens. The oyster-seller works for the *Atlas* brasserie (see p.320 and p.335), and even the *Bar du Marché* (see p.334) has given in to a fashionable clientele, though the waiters still wear natty cloth caps and overalls. A few steps east of the main Buci crossroads, look out for the intriguing little passage of the **Cour du Commerce St André**. Marat had a printing press here, and Dr Guillotin perfected his notorious machine by

Paris architecture – the shock of the new

Viewed from the top of the Eiffel Tower, Paris looks astonishingly uniform. Squint, or go on a rainy day, and those endless lead roofs could almost be a choppy sea, its silver-grey surface broken only by the arrow-straight boulevards – urban canyons that fill with green leaves in spring and cold winds in winter. Rising from this sea, however, are the great hulls and masts of Paris's monuments. Some – Notre-Dame, the Louvre, the Panthéon – are so familiar it's hard to imagine they were ever new. Others are as shocking today as when they were first built.

▲ Haussmann apartment buildings

Haussmann's brave new Paris

The sheer harmoniousness of modern Paris is the legacy of a uniquely energetic age. From 1853, the overgrown and insanitary medieval capital was ruthlessly transformed into an urban utopia. In half a century, half of Paris was rebuilt. Napoléon III's authoritarian government provided the force – land was compulsorily purchased and boulevards bulldozed through old quarters – while banks and private speculators provided the cash. The poor, meanwhile, either provided the labour or were cleared out to the suburban badlands.

The presiding genius was the emperor's chief of works, **Baron Haussmann**. In his brave new city, every apartment building was seven stories high. Every facade was built in golden limestone, often quarried from under the city itself, with unobtrusive Neoclassical details sculpted around the windows. Every second and fifth floor had its wrought-iron balcony and every lead roof sloped back from the streetfront at precisely 45 degrees. It would all have been inhumanly regular if it hadn't been for the ground-floor shops, which have provided Paris's streets with a more varied face ever since.

◄ Eiffel Tower

Eiffel's modern world

Some extravagant new buildings were erected in and after the Haussmann era, notably the magnificent **Opéra Garnier** and the blanched bulbosity of the **Sacré-Cœur**, atop Montmartre. But the era of the outrageous, epoch-defining structure really began in 1889, when Eiffel's ironwork rocket landed on the Left Bank. With a loud bang of hammer on rivet, the industrial world had arrived. Parisians were outraged. Artists and writers protested against the "gigantic black factory chimney" which would see "all our monuments humiliated, all our architecture belittled". But the new **Eiffel Tower** anchored its feet foursquare in the Champ de Mars and resisted all its critics.

In 1900, the giant glass aviaries of the **Grand** and **Petit Palais** pointed the way towards a more feminine modernity, as did a less visible but more pervasive symbol of the new era, the **métro**, whose sinuous signage helped launch Art Nouveau on the rest of Europe.

Filling holes in the 1970s

▼ Pompidou centre

Parisians had most of the new century to get used to their new city – thankfully, the Nazi plan to reduce Paris to rubble was thwarted. The unrest of 1968, however, brought more than just political change: within a few years, a glass tower scraped the skies of Montparnasse, and the stately ironwork halls that had long sheltered Paris's central marketplace, **Les Halles**, had been demolished. "The belly of Paris", as Zola had called the market, stood empty for a decade, and only in 1979 did the **Forum des Halles** fill the gap, its curving glass arcades pouring down into a giant pit of a shopping centre and transport interchange. Far more successful was its close neighbour and contemporary, Renzo Piano and Richard Rogers' **Pompidou Centre**. Wearing its insides on its outside, it presented a postmodern face of blue and green pipes that vied for room with red lifts and grey steel cabling. Critics called it a giant petrol refinery. Parisians, with a mixture of irony and fondness, adopted the name of an adjacent street and dubbed it Beaubourg – or "Prettytown".

Presidential passions: the "Big Projects"

Ambitious as they were, the schemes of the 1970s were just warm-up acts for the **Grands Projets** of Socialist president François Miterrand. Between 1981 and 1995, Paris spawned a whole clutch of new cultural centres, including a radical geometric structure in the very middle of the Louvre's courtyard. With I.M. Pei's glass **Pyramide**, some muttered that Mitterrand was trying to outdo the Pharoahs.

◀ Louvre Pyramid

Cynics compared the Grands Projets to the medieval frenzy for cathedral construction, with culture as the new state religion and the taxpayer footing the 35 billion-franc bill. Some buildings have worn better than others. The **Institut du Monde Arabe** has become a well-loved classic, while the **Cité de la Musique** attracts concert-goers and architectural plaudits alike, and the Pyramide has become a symbol of Paris as potent as the Louvre itself. The **Bibliothèque Nationale**, however, has been beset by technical problems, while the **Grande Arche de la Défense** feels emptily overweening rather than triumphal. As for the unhappy **Bastille Opéra**, it has been compared to a hospital, an elephant and, according to Parisian writer Edmund White, "a cow palace in Fort Worth".

Landmarks of the future

Vanity-fuelled cultural legacies aren't the exclusive province of the Left. Outgoing president Jacques Chirac bequeaths the splendid **Musée du Quai Branly**, a signature work by the darling of contemporary French architecture, Jean Nouvel. Its radical lines are offset by a certain grace and modesty – qualities unlikely to appear in the latest addition to Paris's architectural roster, Frank Gehry's **Fondation Louis Vuitton pour la Création**, supposed to be finished by 2010. It will stand in the Bois de Boulogne's Jardin d'Acclimation and, judging by the plans, will bear more than a passing resemblance to a lunatic glass armadillo which has burst out of its own skin.

A different kind of architectural ambition will soon take shape as the **Tour Phare**, a boldy curvaceous eco-scraper in the Défense business district that, by 2012, will rival the height of the Eiffel Tower. Far more significant, if less self-promoting, will be the new, made-over **Les Halles**. The old, murky underground halls are soon to be transformed by architect David Mangin into light-filled spaces under a giant glass roof.

▼ Musée du Quai Branly

lopping off sheep's heads in the loft next door. Backing onto the street is *Le Procope* – Paris's first coffee house, which opened its doors in 1686. A couple of smaller courtyards open off the alleyway, revealing another stretch of Philippe-Auguste's twelfth-century city wall.

At its southern end, the Cour du Commerce opens out at the **Carrefour de l'Odéon**, known for its cinemas and now for its infamous Starbucks too – when it opened in early 2004, along with another branch on Avenue de l'Opéra, this apparently innocuous coffee shop was widely regarded in Paris as the vanguard of the long-feared American corporate invasion of Parisian café culture. Climbing southeast towards the Sorbonne, **rue Monsieur le Prince** is lined with budget and ethnic restaurants, of which the best is the classic bistrot, *Polidor* (see p.337). At this eastern edge of St-Germain you start to feel the gravitational pull of the university, and indeed this area is sometimes considered to be part of the Quartier Latin. Around the **Ecole de Médicine**, university bookshops display skeletons and instruments of medical torture, and the restaurants become steadily less expensive as they aim towards the shallower pockets of a student clientele.

The defining landmark of the area is the recently restored **Théâtre de l'Odéon**, its proud Doric facade fronting a handsome semicircular plaza. Designed as a replacement home for the Comédie Française (see p.94), this was one of the learned King Louis XVI's last projects before the Revolution, a revolutionary all-seater design with a then unheard-of capacity of 1900.

Jardin du Luxembourg

Hemingway liked to claim he fed himself in Paris by shooting pigeons in the **Jardin du Luxembourg**, immediately south of the Odéon theatre. These lovely gardens belong to the **Palais du Luxembourg**, which fronts onto the eastern end of rue de Vaugirard, Paris's longest street. Today, palace and garden alike belong to the French Senate, but they were originally built for Marie de Médicis, Henri IV's widow, as a distant northern echo of the Palazzo Pitti and Boboli gardens of her native Florence.

The **gardens** (open roughly dawn to dusk; RER Luxembourg/M° Odéon) are the Left Bank's heart and quite possibly its lungs as well. They get fantastically crowded on summer days, when the most contested spots are the shady **Fontaine de Médicis** in the northeast corner and the tail of the gardens that points south towards the Paris observatory – the latter being the only place where you're allowed to sit out on the **lawns**. Everywhere else you'll have to settle yourself on the heavy, sage-green metal chairs, which are liberally distributed around the gravel paths. Alternatively, there's a delightful tree-shaded **café** roughly 100m northeast of the central pond.

Children rent toy yachts to sail on the pond, but the western side is the more active area, with **tennis courts** (see p.420), donkey rides, a marionette show for children (see p.327), a large playground and the inevitable sandy area for boules. **Sculptures** are scattered around the park, including an 1890 monument to the painter Delacroix by Jules Dalou and a suitably bizarre homage to the Surrealist poet Paul Eluard by the sculptor Ossip Zadkine, more of whose works can be seen in the nearby Musée Zadkine (see p.176). In the quieter, wooded, western section of the park you can also find one of Paris's miniature versions of the Statue of Liberty, just bigger than human-size, and cast in bronze. The southwest corner ends in a miniature orchard of elaborately espaliered pear trees whose fruits grace the tables of senators or, if surplus to requirements, are given to associations for the homeless.

In the last week of September, the half-glazed **Orangerie**, just west of the main palace, is the venue for the annual "Expo-Automne", which shows off the garden's finest fruits and floral decorations. For the rest of the winter, it shelters scores of exotic trees – palms, bitter oranges, oleanders and pomegranates, some over two hundred years old – which are grown in giant pots so that every winter they can be wheeled indoors, and then wheeled out again the following spring.

The north–south spine of the gardens extends down into a tail pointing towards the Paris observatory, following the line of the old Paris meridian (see p.179). At the extreme southern end of the gardens, the circular **Fontaine de l'Observatoire** symbolizes Paris's historic self-conception as the very navel of the world, with Jean-Baptiste Carpeaux's fine sculptures of the four continents supporting a mighty iron globe.

St-Sulpice

North of the Jardin du Luxembourg, the streets around the **church of St-Sulpice** (daily 7.30am–7.30pm; M° St-Sulpice) are calm and classy. Broad place St-Sulpice should be enchanting, with its lion fountain and chestnut trees, but it's currently slightly spoiled by major restoration works on the north tower, which are set to continue for an astonishingly long time – 2011 is the estimated completion date. It's not as long as the south tower has had to wait, however – if you look closely you can see uncut masonry blocks at the top, still attending the sculptor's chisel.

The church itself is an overbearingly muscular classical edifice erected either side of 1700. For decades, the gloomy **interior** was best known for three **Delacroix murals** found in the first chapel on the right, and a monstrously huge, five-manual eighteenth-century **organ**, which is put through its paces at regular recitals. Since the publication of *The Da Vinci Code*, however, St-Sulpice's visitors have come for one thing alone: the **gnomon**. A lens in the south transept window, long since removed, once focused the sun's rays on a narrow strip of brass, which still runs right across the floor of the nave to an obelisk on the north side. At its winter low, the sun would exactly crown the stone pillar at noon; at its summer height, it would burn down on the start of the brass line. As a printed notice wearily points out, it's an "instrument of astronomy" designed in 1727 by an English clock-maker called Henry Sully to measure the exact time of the winter and summer solstices, and from it "no mystical notion can be derived". And the brass strip does not follow any "Rose Line", nor even the Paris meridian – though it runs close by.

The fact that the actress Catherine Deneuve has an apartment on place **St-Sulpice** is a good clue to its character. On the sunny north side of the square, the outside tables at the *Café de la Mairie* hum with trendy chatter on fine days, but the main attractions here are the fashion boutiques, like the very elegant **Yves Saint Laurent Rive Gauche**, on the corner of the ancient rue des Canettes – though Yves himself has finally quit.

A few steps south of the church, rue Férou leads to the **Musée du Luxembourg**, at 19 rue de Vaugirard (hours and prices vary; M° St-Sulpice/RER Luxembourg). Some of Paris's biggest and most exciting art exhibitions are held here throughout most of the year, often causing long queues to form alongside the giant railings of the Jardin du Luxembourg – recent successes have included twentieth-century self-portraits and "Veronèse profane". Most shows are well advertised across Paris, or you can check what's showing online at ⓦwww.museeduluxembourg.fr.

Mabillon and St-Germain-des-Prés

North of St-Sulpice, pretty **rue Mabillon** passes the **Marché St-Germain**, a 1990s reconstruction of a covered market originally built in the early nineteenth century. The site is more ancient still, having been the venue for the raucous

△ Yves Saint Laurent Rive Gauche, place St-Sulpice

St-Germain fair, held at the gates of the abbey in medieval times. The creamy stone arches of the modern *halles* are very successful in architectural terms, but sadly the market stalls have been replaced by boutique shops and a swimming pool and gym complex.

The area around the Marché, on rues Princess, Lobineau, Guisarde and des Canettes, is something of a hub for eating and drinking. There are one or two good addresses, notably the wine bar *Chez Georges* (see p.334), but many of the restaurants are surprisingly disappointing, given how promising they look from the outside.

The **boulevard St-Germain** was bulldozed right through the Left Bank under Baron Haussmann (see p.453). For much of its length, it looks much the same as any of Paris's great avenues, but a short stretch around **place St-Germain-des-Prés** (M° St-Germain des Prés) forms the very heart of the quarter. The famous **Deux Magots** café stands on one corner of the square, while the equally celebrated **Flore** lies a few steps further along the boulevard. Both are chiefly celebrated for the postwar writers and philosophers who drank and debated there – most famously the philosopher-novelist Simone de Beauvoir and her existentialist lover, Jean-Paul Sartre. Although both cafés charge high prices and attract plenty of tourists, they're still genuine St-Germain institutions – albeit patronized by designers and directors rather than writers these days. The cognoscenti judge *Flore* to have maintained that edge of authenticity. *Brasserie Lipp*, across the boulevard, is another longtime haunt of moneyed intellectuals, and maintains its traditions proudly. All three are reviewed on pp.334–336.

The powerful tower dominating the square belongs to the **church of St-Germain-des-Prés**, which is all that remains of an enormous Benedictine monastery whose lands once stretched right across the Left Bank. Having survived a post-Revolution stint as a saltpetre factory, the church itself is one of twenty-first-century Paris's oldest surviving buildings, a rare Romanesque structure that dates back to the late tenth and early eleventh centuries. The choir, however, was rebuilt in the fashionable Gothic style in the mid-twelfth century – work that's just about visible under the heavy greens and golds of nineteenth-century paintwork. The marble columns of its middle triforium level date from an even earlier church on this site, erected in the sixth century, which housed the remains of the Merovingian kings. A later tomb, a simple slab engraved with the name René Descartes, can be found in the last chapel on the south side. Outside the church, on the corner of rue de l'Abbaye and rue Bonaparte, there's a pretty little garden with some strange fragments of Gothic stonework. These, along with a single stained-glass window in the apse of the main church, are the melancholy last remains of a thirteenth-century chapel. They make a perfect backdrop to the Picasso statue of a woman's head which also stands here, dedicated to the memory of the poet Apollinaire.

Musée Delacroix

Hidden away round the back of St-Germain-des-Prés, off rue Jacob, **place de Furstemberg** is one of Paris's most lovable squares, huddling round the trees and candelabra-like street lamp planted at its centre. Tucked into its northwest corner is the **Musée Delacroix**, 6 rue de Furstemberg (daily except Tues 9.30am–5pm; €5; M° Mabillon/St-Germain des Prés), a charming miniature museum displaying sketches by the artist and various personal effects. Delacroix lived and worked in the house here from 1857 until his death in 1863, watched over by Jenny Le Guillou, who'd been his servant since 1835. You can visit the bedroom where he died, now graced by Jenny's portrait, while the little sitting room houses the museum's only really interesting work, the intense *Madeleine au désert*, presented at the Salon of 1845. Delacroix had his studio built outside, its large window overlooking a hidden garden. Today, watercolours and a few more substantial works are hung here, alongside temporary exhibitions, but for Delacroix's major work you'll have to visit the Louvre and Musée d'Orsay, or head over to the murals at nearby St-Sulpice (see p.146).

At the southern end of the rue de Furstemberg looms the imposing **Palais Abbatial**, built for Charles de Bourbon, the powerful abbot of St-Germain, in the late sixteenth century in an early version of what became the Louis XIII style. Today, it still belongs to the Catholic Church, housing an institute for Augustinian studies.

Around Sèvres-Babylone

The area around **Sèvres-Babylone** métro station, at the western end of the 6e arrondissement and the eastern fringe of the 7e, is one of Paris's most promising for **shopping**. You might not find the most exclusive Right Bank designers or the more alternative-minded Marais and Montmartre boutiques, but rues Bonaparte, Madame, de Sèvres, de Grenelle, du Vieux-Colombier, du Dragon, du Four and des Saints-Pères are lined with designer and high-street names, from Agnès B on rue du Vieux-Colombier to Zara on rue de Rennes.

It's hard to imagine now, but smack in the middle of all this, at the **carrefour de la Croix Rouge**, there was a major barricade in 1871, fiercely defended by Eugène Varlin, one of the leading lights of the Commune (see box, p.197). He was later betrayed by a priest, half-beaten to death and shot by government troops on Montmartre hill. These days you're more likely to be suffering from till-shock than shell-shock, though César's four-metre statue of a **Centaure**, cast in homage to Picasso in 1983, is distinctly alarming. It surveys the cross-roads with ferocity, and two sets of genitals. If you need to retreat, make for the small, friendly American bookstore, The Village Voice (see p.395), where you can browse through the latest literature and journals.

On Sunday mornings, the celebrated **Marché Bio**, or organic food market, lines the boulevard Raspail between the Sèvres-Babylone and Rennes métro stations. Attracting both out-of-town farmers and chic shoppers, it offers plenty of opportunities for people-watching, even if you don't plan to buy any of the colourful, excellent produce.

Just over the boundary with the 7e arrondissement, at the far side of the green square Boucicaut, stands the city's oldest department store, **Le Bon Marché** (see p.386). The name means "inexpensive" in French, but these days it's one of Paris's best and most upmarket department stores. The original shop was a simple drapery emporium on rue du Bac, but exploded in size under the entrepreneurial and socially conscientious Aristide Boucicaut, becoming one of the great Parisian institutions of the era and the setting for Zola's novel *Au Bonheur des dames*. The building itself is palatial, the star team of Gustave Eiffel and Louis-Auguste Boileau responsible for the 1879 extension on rue de Babylone. With a canny sense of commercialism, the architects wanted to show off the goods to best advantage by making the interior spaces, in their own words, "as gay, resonant and well-furnished as if they were in the pure daylight of the outside". An annex, added on the west side of rue du Bac by Boileau's son in 1923, now houses the luxurious **Grande Epicerie**, or "big grocer's", on the ground floor.

If you stand outside the Bon Marché, especially on a Sunday, you'll notice that a surprisingly large proportion of people among the crowds isn't here for the shopping. The reason lies down an alley hidden behind 140 rue du Bac, just north of the aerial bridge joining the two wings of the Bon Marché. Tucked away at its end is a little chapel with the unwieldy name of **Notre-Dame de la Médaille Miraculeuse**. It was here, in 1830, that a 24-year-old nun called Catherine Laboure had visions of the Virgin Mary dressed in silk, with her feet resting on a globe. A voice told Catherine to "have a medal struck like this – those who wear it will receive great graces". The nuns duly obeyed, and have been quite literally coining it ever since. You can buy a souvenir medal and visit the chapel, which was rebuilt to accommodate huge pilgrim congregations in 1930.

If you're heading southwest towards the stylish, Art Deco Vaneau métro station, check out the bizarre **Fontaine du Fellah**, adjacent. Built in 1807, with two jets of water spouting from a statue of an ancient Egyptian-style water-carrier, it's a product of the fad for all things Egyptian that swept France in the wake of Napoleon's campaigns of 1798–99.

Musée Maillol and Deyrolle

North of Sèvres-Babylone, boulevard Raspail marches grandly towards the junction with boulevard St-Germain. Just short of the Rue-du-Bac métro stop, a handsome eighteenth-century house at 61 rue de Grenelle has been turned into the **Musée Maillol** (daily except Tues 11am–6pm; €8; Ⓦ www.museemaillol.com; M° Rue-du-Bac), a tiny building gloriously overstuffed with post-Impressionist sculptor Aristide Maillol's endlessly buxom female nudes – copies of which stand in the Louvre's Jardin du Carrousel. Maillol's most famous work, the dumpily curvacious *Mediterranean*, sits on the first floor at the top of the stairs. The exhibits belong to Dina Vierny, Maillol's former model and inspiration, and works by other contemporaries are also collected here, including drawings by Matisse, Dufy and Bonnard, for whom Dina also modelled, and a room full of Poliakoff's jaggedy abstracts on the second floor. The museum also organizes excellent exhibitions of twentieth-century art, recent shows featuring Robert Rauschenberg and Raoul Dufy. A few steps east of the museum stands the **Fontaine des Quatre-Saisons**, less a fountain than a piece of early eighteenth-century architectural theatre. At the centre of the curved stone arcade sits the City of Paris herself, flanked by two sinuous figures representing the rivers Seine and Marne.

You might not normally go out of your way to visit a taxidermist's, but **Deyrolle**, 46 rue du Bac (Mon 10am–1pm & 2–7pm, Tues–Sat 10am–7pm; free), just north of the Rue-du-Bac métro, should be an exception. The chichi garden tool shop below is a mere front for the real business upstairs, in a room perfumed with the sharp, clean, coal-tar smell of taxidermy. Giant, antique wooden display cases are stuffed with pinned butterflies and shards of prehistoric trilobytes, while above and all around them, and covering the walls, are scores of stuffed rabbits, ducks, sheep, deer, boars, bears and even big cats. A lion or an entire polar bear – both on open display – could be yours for around €10,000, or you can pick up a fossil for a couple of euros. Children, in particular, tend to be fascinated by the place.

The Musée d'Orsay

As it penetrates the 7e arrondissement, boulevard St-Germain swings up towards the river disgorging its traffic across the Pont de la Concorde onto the Right Bank. On the east side of this wedge of the city are the expensive art and antiques shops of the **Carré Rive Gauche**, between rue de l'Université and the Quai Voltaire. To the west, facing the Tuileries gardens across the river, is the **Musée d'Orsay**, with its entrance on rue de la Légion de l'Honneur (Tues, Wed, Fri & Sat 9.30am–6pm, Thurs 9.30am–9.45pm, Sun 9am–6pm; €7.50, free to under-18s and on first Sun of the month; ⓦ www.musee-orsay.fr; M° Solférino/RER Musée-d'Orsay). The museum's collection of the electrifying works of the **Impressionists** and post-Impressionists has made it one of Paris's most-visited attractions. There's more to it than just Monet and Renoir, however. The collection covers the artistically revolutionary era between 1848 and 1914 – between the end of the Louvre's Classical traditions and the start of the modern era, as represented in the Pompidou Centre.

The **building** itself was inaugurated as a railway station for the 1900 World Fair. It spans the worlds of nineteenth-century Classicism and industrial modernity brilliantly, its elegant, formal stone facade cunningly disguising the steel-and-glass construction of the railway arch within. It continued to serve the stations of southwest France until 1939, but its platforms became too short for postwar trains and it fell into disuse. De Gaulle made it the backdrop for the announcement of his coup d'état of May 19, 1958, but such was the site's degradation by the 1960s that Orson Welles thought it the perfect location for his film of Kafka's *The Trial*, filling the high, narrow corridors with filing cabinets to create a nightmarishly claustrophobic setting. Despite this illustrious history, the station was only saved from destruction by the backlash of public opinion that followed the demolition of Les Halles. The job of redesigning the interior as a museum was given, in 1986, to the fashionable Milanese architect Gae Aulenti. Hers is a considered, beautiful design with one major drawback: the Impressionist section is crammed under the roof, putting the biggest crowds in the most cramped area.

Taken at an easy pace, you could easily spend half a day, if not a whole one, meandering through the rooms in their numbered, chronological order, but the **layout** makes it easy to confine your visit to a specific section, each of which has a very distinctive atmosphere. The collection begins on the ground floor, under the huge vault of steel and glass, then continues up to the attics of the upper level, before ending with the terraces of the middle level, overlooking the main chamber.

The **café** on the upper level of the museum – with its summer terrace and wonderful view of Montmartre through the giant railway clock – and the resplendently gilded restaurant and tea room on the middle level, are great spots to recuperate. Tea and a cake will set you back around €10.

Ground floor

The **ground floor**, under the great glass arch, is devoted to pre-1870 work, with a double row of sculptures running down the central aisle like railway tracks, and paintings in the odd little bunkers on either side. Chief among the **mid-nineteenth-century sculptors** in the central aisle is Carpeaux, whose *Ugolin* shows the damned Count Ugolino, from Dante's *Divine Comedy*, gnawing at his fingers with pain and hunger as he contemplates consuming the bodies of his dying children. The original plaster of the *Four Quarters of the World Bearing the Celestial Sphere*, the bronze version of which lies at the foot of the Jardin du Luxembourg, is also his. Nearby stand Charles Cordier's bizarre polychrome busts of black Africans, in bronze and coloured stone.

On the south side of this level, towards rue de Lille, the first set of rooms (1–3) is dedicated to **Chassériau**, **Gérôme**, **Delacroix** – the bulk of whose work is in the Louvre – and the serious-minded works of the painters acceptable to the mid-nineteenth-century salons; just beyond (rooms 11–13) are the relatively wacky works of Puvis de Chavannes, Gustave Moreau and the younger Degas.

The influential **Barbizon school** and the **Realists** are showcased on the Seine side (rooms 4–7), with canvases by Daumier, Corot and Millet, which were some of the first to break with the established norms of moralism and idealization of the past. The soft-toned landscapes by Millet and Corot, and quickly executed scenes by Daubigny, such as his *La Neige*, were influential on later, avowed Impressionists, as can be seen in two paintings by **Monet** and **Manet** both entitled *Déjeuner sur l'herbe*, or *The Picnic* (both in room 6). Manet's version caused outrage at the 1863 Salon des Refusés – the show of works rejected by the judges of the official exhibition which is often said to mark the beginning of the **Impressionist** movement. The problem wasn't so much the female figure's nudity, as this was a standard Classical theme, but rather the fact that Manet had juxtaposed her with male figures in modern dress. Manet's provocative *Olympia* (1863), close at hand in room 14, is another work said to have heralded the movement's arrival. It was as controversial in its day for its colour contrasts and sensual surfaces as for the portrayal of Olympia as a high-class whore who returns the stares of her audience with a look of insolent defiance.

In room 15, just across the nave, on the Seine side of the gallery, Courbet's *L'Origine du monde* has the power to shock even contemporary audiences. The explicit, nude female torso was acquired from psychoanalyst Jacques Lacan, who had had it screened behind a decorative panel. It sits oddly among Courbet's brooding portraits. The adjacent rooms 19, 20, 22 and 23 are dedicated to early Impressionist landscapes by **Sisley**, **Monet** and **Pissarro**, among others. Don't miss Monet's well-loved *Coquelicots* ("Poppies"), in room 20.

Upper level: Impressionism and Post-Impressionism

To continue chronologically, proceed straight to the **upper level**, whose rooms have a more intimate feel, done up almost like a suite of attic studios. After the initial shock of room 29 – where the relatively monochrome, realist portraits by **Eugène Carrière** and **Henri Fantin-Latour** prove that not everbody at this time was painting light and colour – you arrive in deep Impressionist territory. In this section of the museum you'll have to fight off the persistent sense of familiarity or recognition – Degas' *L'Absinthe*, Renoir's *Bal du Moulin de la Galette*, Monet's *Femme a l'ombrelle* – in order to appreciate Impressionism's vibrant, experimental vigour.

There's a host of small-scale landscapes and outdoor scenes by Renoir, Sisley, Pissarro and Monet in rooms 30–32, paintings which owed much of their brilliance to the novel practice of setting up easels in the open – often as not, on the banks of the Seine. Less typical works include Degas' ballet-dancers, which demonstrate his principal interest in movement and line as opposed to the more common Impressionist concern with light, and *Jeune Femme en toilette de bal* (1879), by Berthe Morisot, the first woman to join the early Impressionists. More heavyweight masterpieces can be found in rooms 34 and 39, devoted to **Monet** and **Renoir** in their middle and late periods. The development of Monet's obsessions is shown with five of his Rouen cathedral series, each painted in different light conditions. Room 35 is full of the fervid colours and disturbing rhythms of **Van Gogh**, while **Cézanne**, another step removed from the preoccupations of the mainstream Impressionists, is superbly represented in room 36.

Passing the café and the little rooms (37 and 38) housing **Degas**' atmospheric pastels, you arrive at a dimly lit, melancholy chamber (40) devoted to more **pastels**, by Redon, Manet, Mondrian and others. The next and final suite of rooms on this level is given over to the various offspring of Impressionism, and has an edgier, more modern feel, with a much greater emphasis on psychology. It begins with Rousseau's dreamlike *La Charmeuse de serpent* (1907) and continues past **Gauguin**'s ambivalent Tahitian paintings to **Pointillist** works by Seurat (the famous *Cirque*), Signac and others. There are also some iconic caricatures by **Toulouse-Lautrec**, including the splendidly smoky *Danse Mauresque*, which depicts the celebrated cancan dancer, La Goulue, entertaining an audience of lowlifes including a corpulent Oscar Wilde.

Middle level

Don't miss the covetable Kaganovitch collection (rooms 49 & 50) – small, but strong on the post-Impressionists – on your way down to the **middle level**, where the flow of the painting section continues with **Vuillard** and **Bonnard** (rooms 70–72), tucked away behind Pompon's irresistible sculpture of a polar bear, on the rue de Lille side of the railway chamber. Vuillard and Bonnard began their careers as part of an Art Nouveau group known as the **Nabis**, and strong Japanese influences can be seen in Vuillard's decorative screen, *Jardins publics* (1894) and Bonnard's *La Partie de croquet* (1892). The Impressionist interest in light is still evident, but it seems subservient to a highly distinctive palette, with colours that are at once muted and intense.

On the far side of this level, overlooking the Seine (rooms 55–58), you can see a less familiar side of late-nineteenth-century painting, with large-scale, epic, naturalist works such as Detaille's stirring *Le Rêve* (1888) and Cormon's *Caïn* (1880), as well as the famously effete *Portrait de Marcel Proust* (1892) by Jacques-Emile Blanche. The painting collection ends with a troubling handful of international **Symbolist** paintings; room 60, overlooking the Seine, is dominated by the almost formless wash of leaves and petals that constitutes Klimt's *Rosiers sous les arbres*.

On the parallel **sculpture terraces**, nineteenth-century marbles on the Seine side face early twentieth-century pieces across the divide, but the **Rodin terrace** bridging the two puts almost everything else to shame. Rodin's *Ugolin* is even grimmer than Carpeaux's, immediately below, while his *Fugit amor*, a response to his pupil and lover Camille Claudel's *L'Age mûr*, adjacent, is a powerful image of the end of their liaison. It's a pity, but few visitors will have energy left for the half-dozen rooms (61–66) of **Art Nouveau** furniture and objets d'art.

The Eiffel Tower quarter

Standing sentinel over a great bend in the Seine as it flows southwest out of Paris is the monumental flagpole that is the **Eiffel Tower**. It surveys the most relentlessly splendid of all Paris's districts, embracing the palatial heights of the Trocadéro, on the Right Bank, and the wealthy, western swathe of the **7e (septième) arrondissement**, on the Left. These are street vistas planned for sheer magnificence; as you look out across the river from the terrace of the **Palais de Chaillot** to the Eiffel Tower and the huge **Ecole Militaire**, or let your gaze run from the ornate **Pont Alexandre III** past the parliament building to the vast **Hôtel des Invalides**, you are experiencing city design on a truly monumental scale.

Sparsely populated by diplomats, ministers and members of the old and new aristocracies, the area is nevertheless home to some compelling **museums**. Newest on the block in the Septième is the museum of "primitive" (or non-Western) art at **Quai Branly**, built at extravagant expense at the foot of the Eiffel Tower. At the other end of the scale, though close at hand, the city's museum of the sewer system is indeed found down in the **sewers**. A little further east, the huge military complex of Les Invalides is home to a gigantic **war museum**, while nearby the sculptor **Rodin** has a beautiful private house entirely devoted to his works. Across the river, in the **Trocadéro** quarter of the 16e arrondissement, the **Musée Guimet** displays a sumptuous collection of Asian Buddhist art, while the landmark Neoclassical palaces of **Tokyo**, **Chaillot** and **Galliera**, on the elevated north bank of the Seine, house museums devoted to modern and contemporary art, maritime life, fashion and architecture.

But for all the pomp and history, corners of neighbourhood life do exist – along **rue de Babylone**, for example, and in the wedge of homely streets between the Invalides and the Champ de Mars, centred on the **rue Cler** market. And however tired of mega-monuments you may be, the **Eiffel Tower** remains endlessly inspirational. No matter how many pictures, photos, models or glimpses from elsewhere in the city you may have seen, it is still, when you get up close, an amazing structure.

The 7e

The proudest possession of the **7e (septième) arrondissement**, the **Eiffel Tower**, lies at its westernmost edge. It offers the most exhilarating vistas in the city, while the area at its feet, to the east, is worth exploring for the classy shops and restaurants around **rue Cler** and the lavish new museum of "primitive" art, the **Musée du Quai Branly**. Much of the rest of this quarter is dominated by monumental government buildings and the military edifices of the **Ecole Militaire** and **Hôtel des Invalides**, the latter housing the impressive war museum and, appropriately enough, the **tomb of Napoleon**. Tucked away in the streets towards St-Germain, the **Musée Rodin** shows off the sculptor's works in the intimate surroundings of a handsome private *hôtel*, or mansion house. Note that the easternmost end of the 7e, including the Musée d'Orsay, is covered in chapter 8 (see p.140).

The Eiffel Tower

It's hard to believe that the **Eiffel Tower** (RER Champ de Mars-Tour Eiffel), the quintessential symbol both of Paris and the brilliance of industrial engineering, was designed to be a temporary structure for a fair. Late nineteenth-century Europe had a taste for giant-scale, colonialist–capitalist extravaganzas, but Paris's 1889 Exposition Universelle was particularly ambitious: when completed, the tower, at 300m, was the tallest building in the world. Outraged critics protested against this "grimy factory chimney". "Is Paris," they asked, "going to be associated with the grotesque, mercantile imaginings of a constructor of machines?" Eiffel himself thought it was a piece of architectural perfection. "The basic lines of a structure must correspond precisely to its specified use," he said. "To a certain extent the tower was formed by the wind itself."

Curiously, this most celebrated of landmarks was only saved from demolition by the sudden need for "wireless telegraphy" aerials in the first decade of the twentieth century. The tower's role in telecommunications – its only function apart from tourism – has only become more important, and the original crown is now masked by an efflorescence of antennae. Over the last century, the structure has seen some surprising cosmetic changes; the original deep red paint scheme has been covered up with a sober, dusty-chocolate brown since the late 1960s – at least the city is spared the canary yellow that covered the tower for most of its first decade. The only structural maintenance it has ever needed was carried out in the 1980s, when one thousand tonnes of metal were removed to make the tower ten percent lighter, and the frame was readjusted to remove a slight warp.

Outside daylight hours, distinctive sodium **lights** now light up the structure, and a double searchlight was added for the millennium celebrations, making its first sweep at midnight on December 31. Its twin xenon arc-lamps have turned the tower into an oversized urban lighthouse. For the first ten minutes of every hour thousands of effervescent lights now scramble and fizz about the structure, defining the famous silhouette in luminescent champagne.

Going up (daily: mid-June to Sept 9–12.45am; Sept to mid-June 9.30am–11.45pm) costs €11.50 (for the top; access closes at 11pm), €7.80 (second level) or €4.50 (first level); you can also climb the stairs as far as the second level for a mere €4, though note that from September to mid-June access to the stairs closes at 6pm. Paris looks surreally microscopic from the top and the views are

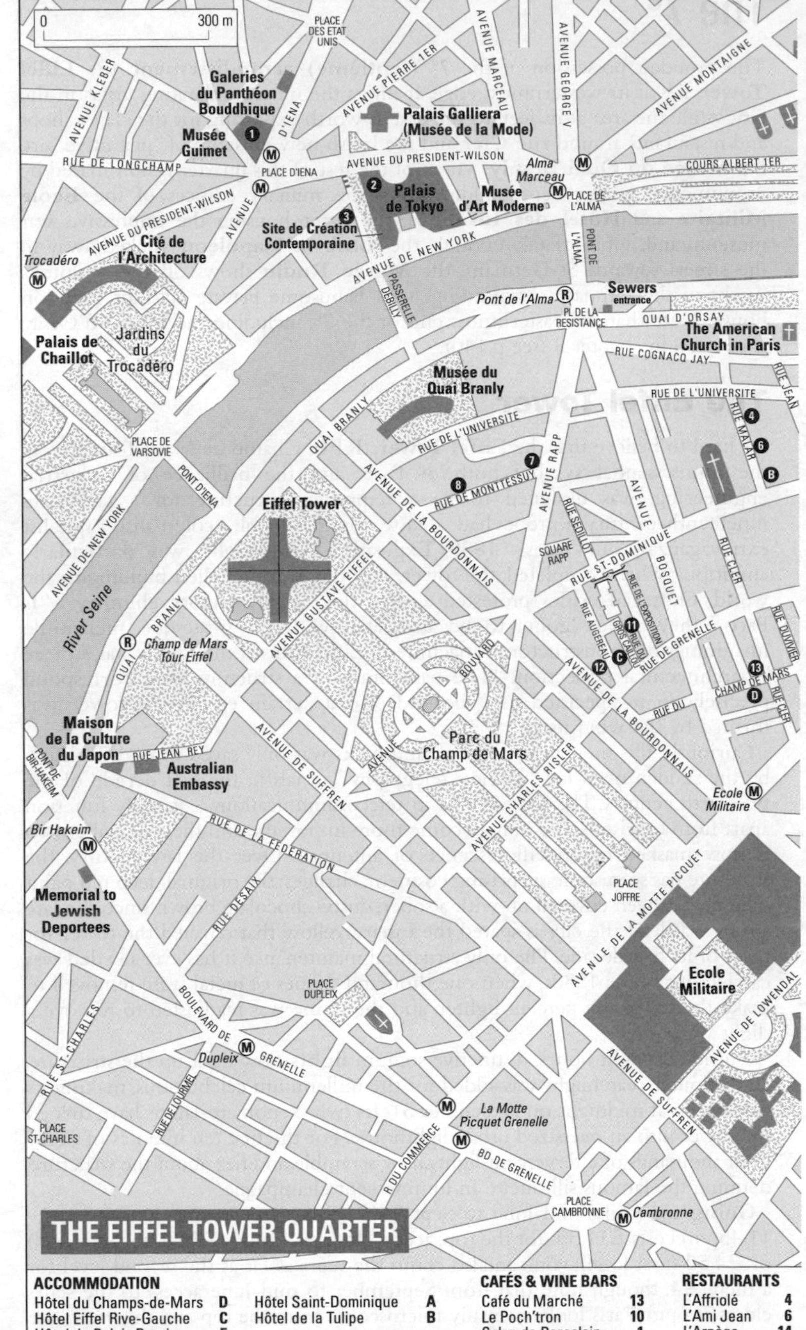

ACCOMMODATION				CAFÉS & WINE BARS		RESTAURANTS	
Hôtel du Champs-de-Mars	D	Hôtel Saint-Dominique	A	Café du Marché	13	L'Affriolé	4
Hôtel Eiffel Rive-Gauche	C	Hôtel de la Tulipe	B	Le Poch'tron	10	L'Ami Jean	6
Hôtel du Palais Bourbon	E			Salon de Porcelain	1	L'Arpège	14

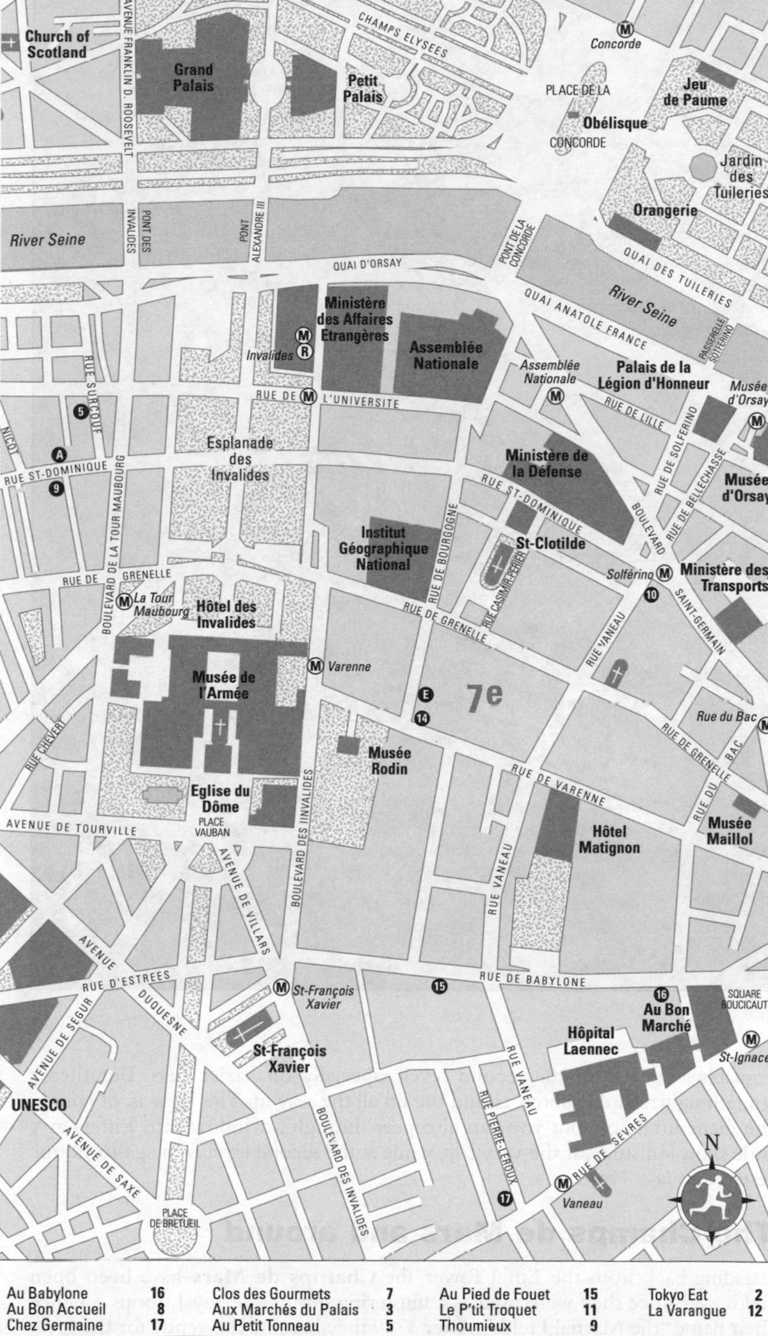
Church of Scotland
Grand Palais
Petit Palais
CHAMPS ELYSEES
Concorde
PLACE DE LA CONCORDE
Obélisque
Jeu de Paume
Jardin des Tuileries
Orangerie
AVENUE FRANKLIN D. ROOSEVELT
River Seine
PONT DES INVALIDES
PONT ALEXANDRE III
PONT DE LA CONCORDE
QUAI D'ORSAY
QUAI DES TUILERIES
QUAI ANATOLE FRANCE
PASSERELLE SOLFERINO
Ministère des Affaires Etrangères
Invalides
Assemblée Nationale
Palais de la Légion d'Honneur
Musée d'Orsay
RUE DE L'UNIVERSITE
RUE DE LILLE
RUE SURCOUF
NICOT
RUE ST-DOMINIQUE
Esplanade des Invalides
Ministère de la Défense
RUE DE SOLFERINO
RUE DE BELLECHASSE
BOULEVARD SAINT-GERMAIN
Institut Géographique National
RUE DE BOURGOGNE
St-Clotilde
RUE CASIMIR-PERIER
Solférino
Ministère des Transports
RUE DE GRENELLE
BOULEVARD DE LA TOUR MAUBOURG
La Tour Maubourg
Hôtel des Invalides
Varenne
Musée de l'Armée
7e
RUE VANEAU
Rue du Bac
RUE DU BAC
RUE CHEVERT
Musée Rodin
RUE DE VARENNE
Eglise du Dôme
PLACE VAUBAN
AVENUE DE TOURVILLE
BOULEVARD DES INVALIDES
AVENUE DE VILLARS
Hôtel Matignon
Musée Maillol
RUE DE BABYLONE
RUE D'ESTREES
AVENUE DUQUESNE
St-François Xavier
Au Bon Marché
SQUARE BOUCICAUT
Hôpital Laennec
St-Ignace
AVENUE DE SEGUR
UNESCO
AVENUE DE SAXE
RUE PIERRE-LEROUX
RUE DE SEVRES
Vaneau
PLACE DE BRETEUIL
N
Au Babylone 16
Au Bon Accueil 8
Chez Germaine 17
Clos des Gourmets 7
Aux Marchés du Palais 3
Au Petit Tonneau 5
Au Pied de Fouet 15
Le P'tit Troquet 11
Thoumieux 9
Tokyo Eat 2
La Varangue 12

△ The Eiffel Tower

arguably better from the second level, especially on hazier days. But there's something irresistible about taking the lift all the way up. The view is, of course, the main attraction, but you can also peer through a window into Eiffel's airy little show-off study, at the very top, while at the second level is the gastronomic restaurant, *Jules Verne*.

The Champs de Mars and around

Parading back from the Eiffel Tower, the **Champs de Mars** have been open fields ever since they were used as a mustering ground for royal troops – hence their name "the Martial Fields". After 1789 they became the venue for the great revolutionary fairs, including Robespierre's vast "Fête of the Supreme Being" in 1794, while the Second Empire turned them into a giant industrial exhibition area, which explains the location of the Eiffel Tower. At the far southern end lie the eighteenth-century buildings of the **Ecole Militaire**, originally founded in 1751 by Louis XV for the training of aristocratic army officers – including the "little corporal", Napoleon Bonaparte.

The quartier surrounding the Ecole Militaire is expensive, elegant and classic. The Y-shaped **UNESCO building** (M° Ecole Militaire) is the controversial exception. It was built in reinforced concrete in 1958 by, appropriately, an international team, and was designed from the outset to showcase art and culture. You can tour the building if you book in advance and bring ID and two passport photos (Tues at 3pm in English; free; call ⓣ01.45.68.16.42). You get to see artworks by Giacometti, Calder, Le Corbusier, Miró and Picasso, as well as the Noguchi Garden of Peace, which contains the Nagasaki angel – a rare survivor of the atomic atrocities of August 1945. Alternatively, come for one of the regular exhibitions or evening concerts, which could take in anything from "colours and impressions of Albania" and "three days of Bolivian crafts and culinary delights" to Algerian *çan'a* music and Tchaikovsky dances.

Behind the UNESCO building, the Avenue de Saxe continues the grand line on to the southeast towards the giant Necker hospital, passing through the **Place de Breteuil**, a huge roundabout – even by Parisian standards – centred on a **monument to Louis Pasteur**, the much-loved discoverer of vaccination and, of course, pasteurization. A modest figure seated and wrapped in a cloak, Pasteur seems overawed by his situation, uncertain whether to look back towards the Ecole Militaire, or north up the other grand axis towards Les Invalides. His role as the saver of millions of lives is represented by the Grim Reaper cowering beneath him, while healthy lambs and children gambol all around. You can visit a museum devoted to him about ten minutes' walk south, in the 15e (see p.175).

Musée du Quai Branly

A short distance upstream of the Eiffel Tower, the brash new **Musée du Quai Branly** (Tues, Wed & Fri–Sun 10am–6.30pm, Thurs 10am–9.30pm; €8.50; ⓦwww.quaibranly.fr; M° Iéna/RER Pont de l'Alma) cuts a postmodern swathe along the riverbank. Even if you're not interested in non-Western art, it's well worth visiting for Jean Nouvel's exciting architecture. As with his other Parisian buildings, the Fondation Cartier (see p.176) and Institut du Monde Arabe (see p.138), Nouvel's design plays with the divide between structure and outside world. Fronting the riverbank is a tall glass wall, which turns the garden into a half-indoor space. The building itself unfurls in a long curve through the middle of the garden – in fact the garden actually runs underneath it at one point – and the outline is self-consciously broken up by greenhouse-like sections. Elsewhere, brightly coloured stretches of red, purple and brown panelling reveal sudden cavities or box-like swellings that pop outwards from the skin of the structure.

Parisians have rather taken to Nouvel's design. The museum, however, has proved deeply controversial. When commissioned, it was the pet project of then-president Jacques Chirac, who has a passion for non-Western art. Ethnographers bewailed the plundering of existing collections while art-lovers decried the whole quasi-colonial enterprise of ethnography. Certainly, there is something dubious about lumping together folk artefacts from every part of the world except Europe and North America, and the truth is that the museum is founded on a collection of what used to be called Art Premier or "Primitive Art" – a term that's rightly enough no longer considered acceptable.

Inside the museum, the objects are arranged by their place of origin, as if this was ethnography. But they're dramatically lit by spotlights as if to underline their art status (or as if to emphasize some sort of ethnic spookiness – throughout the museum, you follow a trail in semi-darkness on blood-red flooring between curving "mud" walls in brown leather). Unfortunately, the ambient lighting makes it hard to read the too-brief explanatory panels, and while occasional screens show film footage collected in the field by anthropologists and other agents of imperialism, it feels like a token effort. Carping aside, the actual artefacts (or artworks) are stunning. Even if their original contexts aren't always made clear, it's hard not to be moved by the potency and craftsmanship of – to follow the museum's own example and take a few random examples – Papua New Guinean full-body masks which tread a fine line between the anthropomorphic and the monstrous, Aboriginal Australian dot-paintings which illustrate the journeys of different ancestral spirits, exquisite Indonesian gold jewellery, or man-sized wooden statues of the spirits of god-kings from Abomey, in West Africa.

The sewers

A little way east of the quai Branly site, on the northeast side of the busy junction of place de la Résistance, is the entrance to the **sewers**, or **les égouts** (Sat–Wed: May–Sept 11am–5pm; Oct–April 11am–4pm; €4.10). They're dark, damp and noisy with gushing water, but not all that smelly. The main part of the visit runs along a gantry walk poised alarmingly above a main sewer, where bilingual displays of photographs, engravings, dredging tools, lamps and other flotsam and jetsam turn the history of the city's water supply and waste management into a surprisingly fascinating topic. A good companion guide might be Victor Hugo's *Les Misérables*: he turns the history of the sewer system – "a dread sink-hole which bears the traces of the revolutions of the globe as of the revolutions of man, and where are to be found vestiges of all cataclysms from the shells of the Deluge to the rag of Marat" – into a magnificent lecture, throwing in a diatribe on the waste of human excrement. Twenty-five million francs' worth of manure were apparently lost to the city in the 1860s alone.

The visit is more than half a publicity exercise by the sewage board, showing the natural water cycle becoming disrupted by the city's over-dense population, then slowly controlled by increasingly good management. What it doesn't tell you is that the work isn't quite finished. Almost all the effluent from the sewers goes to the Achèves treatment plant, northwest of Paris, but around thirty times a year parts of the system get overloaded with rainwater, and the sewer workers have to empty the excess – waste and all – straight into the Seine.

Rue Cler and the Quai d'Orsay

A few steps southeast of the sewers and Musée du Quai Branly sits an attractive, villagey wedge of early nineteenth-century streets between avenue Bosquet and the Invalides. This miniature quartier contrasts starkly with the grand austerity of much of the rest of the Septième. At its heart is the lively market street **rue Cler**, whose cross-streets, rue de Grenelle and rue St-Dominique, are full of neighbourhood shops, posh *bistrots* and little hotels. The daily **market** is a well-to-do affair – as much permanent delicatessens as fruit stalls on barrows.

Modern architecture in the Septième

The Septième is renowned for its grand state monuments and extravagant aristocratic mansions, which mostly date from the seventeenth and eighteenth centuries, but you can also seek out a trio of the city's most exciting **Art Nouveau** apartment buildings, the work of Jules Lavirotte at the turn of the nineteenth century. From the **contemporary era**, the new museum at Quai Branly is the most trumpeted representative, but hidden away nearby is a fascinating example of the postmodernist architecture of Christian de Portzamparc.

29 avenue Rapp (RER Pont de l'Alma). Art Nouveau to the extreme, complete with turbaned women adorning the sinewy doorway, and colourful glazed ceramic tiles. Designed by Jules Lavirotte in 1901.

3 square Rapp, off avenue Rapp (RER Pont de l'Alma). More of Lavirotte's extravagant Art Nouveau work, dating from 1900. There's also a fine trellis trompe l'oeil alongside.

12 rue Sédillot (RER Pont de l'Alma). From the studio of Lavirotte in 1899, featuring Art Nouveau and Art Deco elements, with superb dormers and wrought-iron balconies.

Conservatoire de Musique Erik Satie, 7 rue Jean-Nicot (M° Invalides). The architect Christian de Portzamparc plays with a half-peeled tube of a tower in this building dating (very much) from 1988.

Back on the riverbank, immediately north, the pale neo-Gothic tower and copper spire of the **American Church** stand out on the **quai d'Orsay.** Together with the American College nearby at 31 avenue Bosquet, it plays a key role in the busy life of Paris's large expat American community. Newspapers reporting on French foreign policy use "the quai d'Orsay" to refer to the Ministère des Affaires Etrangères (Ministry of Foreign Affairs), which sits next to the Esplanade des Invalides and the Palais Bourbon, home of the **Assemblée Nationale**. Napoleon, never a great one for democracy, had the riverfront facade of the Palais Bourbon done to match the pseudo-Greek of the Madeleine. The result is an entrance that sheds little light on what's happening within.

The eastern end of the quai d'Orsay opens out into a grand esplanade. Parading across the river towards the giant conservatories of the Grand and Petit Palais is the **Pont Alexandre III**. The vista here was so cherished that when this bridge was built it was set as low as possible above the water so as not to get in the way of the view. That said, it's surely the most extravagant bridge in the city, its single-span metal arch stretching 109m across the river. It was unveiled in 1900, just in time for the Exposition Universelle, its name and elaborate decoration symbolizing Franco–Russian friendship – an ever-more important alliance, in the face of fast-growing German power. The nymph stretching out downstream represents the Seine, matched by Petersburg's River Neva facing upstream; atop the giant columns on each bank, a gilded figure of Fame holds the winged horse Pegasus.

The Hôtel des Invalides

On the Left Bank of the Pont Alexandre III, the green **Esplanade des Invalides** parades down towards the resplendently gilded dome of the **Hôtel des Invalides**. Despite its palatial appearance, it was built as a home for wounded soldiers in the reign of Louis XIV – whose foreign wars gave the building a constant supply of residents and whose equestrian statue lords it over a massive central arch. Architecturally, the building is a kind of barracks version of the awesome spirit of Versailles, stripped of finer flourishes – other than the gilded dome – but crushingly grand nonetheless. Even the cobbles on the esplanade seem made for giants' feet.

The Musée de l'Armée

Les Invalides today houses the vast **Musée de l'Armée** (daily: April–Sept 10am–5.30pm; Oct–March 10am–4.30pm; €7 ticket also valid for Napoleon's tomb, see opposite; Ⓦwww.invalides.org; M° La Tour-Maubourg/Varenne), the national war museum. The moat around the whole Invalides complex means you can only approach from the north or south ends of the building; the ticket office is in the southwest wing, where it faces in towards the Eglise du Dôme.

The most interesting section of the museum, also in the southwest wing, begins with Prussia's annexation of Alsace-Lorraine in 1871 and ends with the defeat of the Third Reich in 1945. It thus implicitly signs up to the ultra-traditionalist view of modern French history: that, after a seventy-year struggle with the German aggressor, *la Patrie* finally emerged victorious. The museum tells its story using original uniforms and real weapons alongside photographs, maps, paintings, contemporary sound recordings, film footage and explanatory panels in French and English. The coverage of **World War I** focuses more on strategy than the well-known horrors of that conflict; there's a fascinating video projection of troop movements during the crucial battle of the Marne, for instance, but the war's ten million dead soldiers – 1.37 million of them French, alongside almost five million wounded – are only really represented by the artefacts that killed them: gas shells, machine guns and an entire wall of grenades. The section on **World War II** is more stirringly presented. The battles, the resistance and the slow liberation are documented through imaginatively displayed war memorabilia combined with gripping film reels (most of which have an English-language option). You leave shocked, stirred, and with the distinct impression that de Gaulle was personally responsible for the liberation of France.

By comparison, the vast collection of armour, uniforms and weapons that makes up the northern half of the museum, on either side of the front court, is probably best left to tin-soldier fanatics or military history buffs. That said, this entire section of the museum will reopen following a complete refit in 2009 or 2010. It's likely to liven up what was previously a rather dull exhibition on the French armed forces between Louis XIV and Napoléon III; the large collection of **Napoleon**'s personal effects – notably his horse (stuffed), campaign tent and trademark hat and coat – should at least be worth seeing. A few sections of this part of the museum are already open. Some children will love the gorier sections in the **west wing**, where the old arsenal has been filled with **medieval** and **Renaissance** weaponry and armour, most of it laid out as if ready for use. Highlights include the extraordinary mail made for François I, a big man for his time, and a dimly lit chamber of beautifully worked Oriental weaponry.

Up under the roof of the east wing, the super-scale models of French ports and fortified cities in the **Musée des Plans-Reliefs** (same hours and ticket as Musée de l'Armée above) are crying out for a few miniature armies. Essentially giant three-dimensional maps, they were created to plan defences or plot potential artillery positions. The collection was begun in 1668 by Louvois, Louis XIV's war minister, and was classed a historic monument in 1927 – the plans' usefulness had only been made redundant by the technological advances of World War I. With the eerie green glow of their landscapes only just illuminating the long, tunnel-like attic, the effect is rather chilling.

Eglise des Soldats

At the core of the Invalides complex is a double church, built by Jules Hardouin-Mansart in the 1670s. The giant **Eglise du Dôme**, to the south, was formerly the Eglise Royale, intended for the private worship of Louis XIV and the royal family, while the relatively spartan northern section is known as the **Eglise des Soldats**. A glass wall divides the two churches, a design innovation which would have allowed worshippers to share the same high altar without the risk of coming into social contact. The door to the Soldier's Church (no ticket required) is in the main northern courtyard of Les Invalides. Inside it's bright and airy, the high walls lined with almost a hundred banners captured by the French army over the centuries. The collection once numbered three thousand trophies at its peak, but was largely destroyed in 1817 by a governor of Les Invalides too proud to see them fall back into the hands of Napoleon's triumphant enemies. A commemorative Mass is still said here on May 5, the anniversary of the emperor's death.

Eglise du Dôme and Napoleon's tomb

The **Eglise du Dôme** (same hours and ticket as Musée de l'Armée, opposite) has a separate entrance on the south side of the complex. Unlike its northern twin, the Soldiers' Church, it's a supreme example of architectural pomp, with Corinthian columns and pilasters, and grandiose frescoes in abundance. Napoleon lies in a giant hole in the floor in a sarcophagus of deep red quartzite, surrounded by giant guardian statues representing his military victories. Around the outside of the enclosure runs a circular gallery decorated with friezes representing the emperor's civic triumphs, captioned with quotations of awesome (and occasionally accurate) conceit such as "By its simplicity my code of law has done more good in France than all the laws which have preceded me"; and "Wherever the shadow of my rule has fallen, it has left lasting traces of its value". Napoleon's shadow still fell heavily on Paris on December 14, 1840, the day on which his ashes, freshly returned from St Helena, were carried through the streets from the newly completed Arc de Triomphe to Invalides. Even though Louis-Philippe, a Bourbon, was on the throne, and Napoleon's nephew, Louis-Napoléon, had been imprisoned for attempting a coup four months earlier, the Bonapartists came out in force – half a million of them – to watch the emperor's last journey. Victor Hugo commented that "it felt as if the whole of Paris had been poured to one side of the city, like liquid in a vase which has been tilted".

More affecting than Napoleon's tomb is the simple memorial to **Maréchal Foch**, commander in chief of the allied forces at the end of World War I,

Bonaparte's bones

In 2002 a French historian asked for Napoleon's ashes to be exhumed for DNA testing, claiming that the remains had been swapped for those of his *maître d'hôtel* on St Helena, one Jean-Baptiste Cipriani. Apparently, a witness at the original 1821 burial observed that the great man's teeth were "most villainous", whereas at the exhumation it was reported that they were "exceptionally white". There is some reason for suspicion, as the last round of tests – on a lock of the emperor's hair – suggested he had died of arsenic poisoning, not cancer, as the British claimed (though the traces may in fact have been caused by the green – and therefore arsenic-laced – pigment in the imperial wallpaper). To date, the mystery remains unresolved, as the French defence ministry refuses to give up the ashes for testing.

which stands in the side chapel by the stairs leading down to the crypt. The marshal's effigy is borne by a phalanx of bronze infantrymen displaying a soldierly grief, the whole chamber flooded by blue light from the stained-glass windows.

The Musée Rodin

Immediately east of Les Invalides is the **Musée Rodin**, on the corner of rue de Varenne, at no. 77 (daily except Mon: April–Sept 9.30am–5.45pm, garden closes at 6.45pm; Oct–March 9.30am–4.45pm, garden closes at 5pm; €6, garden only €1; Ⓦ www.musee-rodin.fr; M° Varenne). The museum's setting is superbly elegant, a beautiful eighteenth-century mansion which the sculptor leased from the state in return for the gift of all his work upon his death. Bronze versions of major projects like *The Burghers of Calais*, *The Thinker*, *The Gate of Hell* and *Ugolino and His Sons* are exhibited in the garden – the latter forming the centrepiece of the ornamental pond.

Things get even better inside – the vigorous energy of the sculptures contrasting with the worn wooden panelling of the *boisieries* and the tarnished mirrors and chandeliers. It's usually very crowded with visitors eager to see much-loved works like *The Hand of God* and *The Kiss*, which was originally designed to portray Paolo and Francesca da Rimini, from Dante's *Divine Comedy*, in the moment before they were discovered and murdered by Francesca's husband. Rodin once self-deprecatingly referred to it as "a large sculpted knick-knack following the usual formula"; art critics today like to think of it as the last masterwork of figurative sculpture before the whole art form was reinvented – largely by Rodin himself. Paris's *Kiss* is one of only four marble versions of the work, but hundreds of smaller bronzes were turned out as money-spinners.

It's well worth lingering over the museum's vibrant, impressionistic clay works, small studies that Rodin took from life. In fact, most of the works here are in clay or plaster, as these are considered to be Rodin's finest achievements – after completing his apprenticeship, he rarely picked up a chisel, in line with the common nineteenth-century practice of delegating the task of working up stone and bronze versions to assistants. Instead, he would return to his plaster casts again and again, modifying and refining them and sometimes deliberately leaving them "unfinished". On the ground floor, there's a room devoted to Camille Claudel, Rodin's pupil, model and lover. Among her works is *The Age of Maturity*, symbolizing her ultimate rejection by Rodin, and a bust of the artist himself. Claudel's perception of her teacher was so akin to Rodin's own that he considered it his self-portrait.

The rest of rue de Varenne and the parallel rue de Grenelle is full of aristocratic and ministerial mansions, including the **Hôtel Matignon**, the prime minister's well-guarded residence, with its giant garden stretching south as far as rue de Babylone. Overlooking the corner of rue Monsieur, at 57bis rue de Babylone, are the Chinese-style roofs of **La Pagode**, originally built as a fashionable toy for the wife of a director of the Bon Marché department store, and later turned into a historic cinema – in 1959 it premiered Cocteau's *Le Testament d'Orphée*. Following a superb renovation, it is now once again one of the most enjoyable art-house cinema venues in the city.

To the east, the area becomes steadily more human in scale, with increasing numbers of shops, apartment buildings and restaurants as you approach the Solférino, Rue du Bac and Sèvres-Babylone métro stations. This eastern fringe of the 7e is covered in the St-Germain chapter (see pp.140–153).

Over the river: the Trocadéro

Back on the western side of the Eiffel Tower area, the **Trocadéro** quarter lies on the elevated northern bank of the Seine. The river forms little barrier to a visit, however, as there's a picturesque above-ground métro line (line 6, which crosses the river on the Pont Bir-Hakeim, offering excellent views of the Eiffel Tower). The entire quartier is also connected to the Septième by three fine bridges: the businesslike Pont de l'Alma, anchored beside the entrance to the Sewers; the graceful Passarelle Debilly, a peaceful footbridge leading from the Musée du Quai Branly to the Modernist Palais de Tokyo; and the handsome Pont d'Iéna, which marches north under the very legs of the Tower towards the breathtakingly ugly **Palais de Chaillot**. Built in the 1930s, Chaillot is now home to museums of naval history and anthropology, and will soon add the state-of-the-art **Cité de l'Architecture et du Patrimoine** to the collection. To the east, the **Palais de Tokyo** houses the even more cutting-edge **Site de Création Contemporaine**, an exhibition space for contemporary art, as well as the **Musée d'Art Moderne de la Ville de Paris**, the municipal-run museum of modern art. Between the two palaces, the superbly revamped **Musée Guimet** boasts a stunning display of Oriental and especially Buddhist art, while the Palais Galliera puts on high-quality shows of historical fashions in its role as the **Musée de la Mode et du Costume**.

The Palais de Chaillot

The **Palais de Chaillot** stands on a site favoured by imperialist-minded rulers ever since Catherine de Médicis constructed one of her playpens here in the early sixteenth century. Napoleon planned to build a palace here for his short-lived son, the so-called King of Rome, but the project was never completed. In 1878, under the Third Republic, an Oriental-style confection was erected – and, thankfully, soon after demolished. The current bastardized Modernist-Neoclassical monster went up in 1937 as part of the globalist-minded Exposition Universelle. Adorned as it is with golden statues and acres of marble paving, it wouldn't look out of place in Fascist Rome. Quite what it's doing in Paris is another matter, though the two curving wings do neatly embrace the shadow of the Eiffel Tower, which falls across the river and onto the palace's elaborate gardens and ponds on sunny mornings.

The entire Chaillot complex wore a forlorn air for many years, a hang-out for local skateboarders and bewildered-looking tourists coming down from a trip up the Eiffel Tower and looking for a photo opportunity. It has acquired new vigour, however, since the opening of the **Cité de l'Architecture et du Patrimoine**. Underneath the central terrace lies the **Théâtre National de Chaillot**, which stages diverse and usually radical productions; its entrance is via the northern wing.

The Musée de l'Homme and Musée de la Marine

Sadly, almost all of the **Musée de l'Homme**'s (Mon & Wed–Fri 9.45am–5.15pm, Sat & Sun 10am–6.30pm; closed public hols; €7; M° Trocadéro) ethnographical collection has been moved across the river to Chirac's folly on quai Branly (see p.159), leaving behind a depleted and depressing rump exhibition on human evolution and diversity in the **southern wing**. The museum may yet shut for a couple of years for renovation and renewal then reopen as an annex of the Museum of Natural History; it may equally be closed down altogether.

On the ground floor of the same wing, the rather specialized **Musée de la Marine** (daily except Tues 10am–6pm; €7) traces French naval history using models of ships and their accoutrements. It's also home to the original Jules Verne trophy, awarded for nonstop round-the-world sailing – a hull-shaped streak of glass invisibly suspended by magnets within its cabinet.

The Cité de l'Architecture

The **northern wing** of the palace is occupied by the **Cité de l'Architecture et du Patrimoine** (Mon, Wed & Fri noon–8pm, Thurs noon–10pm, Sat & Sun 11am–7pm; free), a combined institute, library and **museum of architecture**. The long and lofty **Galerie des Moulages**, on the ground floor, displays giant plaster casts of sections of great French buildings. The basic idea – to tell the story of French architecture from the Middle Ages through to the end of the eighteenth century – dates back to the 1880s, when the great restorer and antiquarian Viollet-le-Duc pioneered the rescue and restoration of France's decaying churches and monuments, and argued for a giant "museum of comparative sculpture". Most of the moulds exhibited here were created for that very museum, which long stood on this site. To see French architecture laid out as a kind of grand historical panorama is as eye-opening now as it was for the original, Victorian curiosity-seekers. On the second floor, the **Galerie d'Architecture Moderne et Contemporaine** represents the nineteenth and twentieth centuries. The collection has a more thoughtful scheme, taking in not just the development of architecture itself but of its social role as well. Among the scores of photographs, designs and original architectural models you'll find a fascinating reconstruction of an apartment from Le Corbusier's infamous Cité Radieuse, in Marseille. The smaller **Galerie des Peintures Murales et des Vitraux** occupies the central pavilion on the second and third floors. In the same spirit as the *moulages* gallery, it displays life-size copies of French wall paintings and frescoes created by sixteen artists in the postwar period. A number of the ceiling paintings re-create the original architectural setting in three dimensions, and there are also four stunning copies of medieval stained-glass windows.

Excellent **temporary exhibitions** (€5) take place in separate galleries on the upper floors. The inaugural exhibitions included a retrospective of the work of Christian de Portzamparc, and a series of fascinating short films showing the development of new sites – from breaking the ground to the finished structure. A separate space, the Galeries d'Actualité, houses exhibitions on the theme of innovative, utopian or futuristic schemes. Even if you're not studying its collections, the library on the first floor is worth visiting for its ceiling mural, a life-size copy of a Romanesque painting from the nave vault of the church of St-Savin-sur-Gartempe.

Musée Guimet and Musée de la Mode

As you head east and downhill from Trocadéro, a couple of excellent, rather specialized museums stand within a stone's throw of each other. The first, on place d'Iéna, is the wonderful **Musée National des Arts Asiatiques-Guimet** (daily except Tues 10am–6pm; €6.50; Ⓦ www.museeguimet.fr; M° Iéna), whose breathtaking roofed-in courtyard provides an airy, modern space in which to show off the museum's world-renowned collection of **Khmer sculpture** – from the civilization that produced Cambodia's Angkor Wat. The museum winds round four floors groaning under the weight of statues of Buddhas and gods, some fierce, some meditative, all of them dramatically lit and imaginatively displayed on plinths or in sometimes surprising niches and cabinets. Each room is devoted to a different country of origin, stretching from Afghanistan to China. The Buddhist statues of the **Gandhara civilization**, on the first floor, betray a fascinating debt to Greek sculpture, while the fierce demons from Nepal, the many-armed gold gods of South India or the pot-bellied Chinese Buddhas are stunningly exotic. Ceramics, paintings and other objets d'art are scattered among the statuary, and on the third floor is a rotunda used by the collection's founder, **Emile Guimet**, for the first Buddhist ceremony ever held in France. A great collector and patron of the arts, Guimet came from a family of enormously wealthy industrialists and espoused the Christian-socialist-egalitarian theories about society, class and government proposed by Fournier, Saint-Simon and, in Britain, Robert Owen. Above the rotunda, two beautiful Chinese lacquer screens crown the topmost floor.

Guimet's original collection, which he brought back from his travels in Asia in 1876, is exhibited nearby in the **Galeries du Panthéon Bouddhique**, at 19 avenue d'Iéna (daily except Tues 9.45am–5.45pm; free). While far smaller and more modest, in some ways it's a more satisfying affair than the museum, as the gilded ranks of Buddhas are presented with a Buddhist's eye rather than an art collector's, arranged according to their religious significance rather than their provenance. At the back of the museum is a small Japanese garden, complete with bamboo, pussy willow and water.

A little further to the east, opposite the Palais de Tokyo, set in small gardens at 10 avenue Pierre 1er de Serbie, stands the grandiose Palais Galliera, home to the **Musée de la Mode et du Costume** (daily except Mon 10am–6pm; €7.50; M° Iéna/Alma-Marceau). The museum's magnificent collection of clothes and fashion accessories from the eighteenth century to the present day is exhibited in temporary, themed shows of which there are two or three a year – during changeovers the museum is closed.

Palais de Tokyo

The entrance to the **Palais de Tokyo** is on its north side, on avenue du Président-Wilson, but most people seem to approach from the south, where the opening of the Musée du Quai Branly (see p.159) has brought new life to this area. It's a pleasant walk across the pedestrian **Passerelle Debilly**, which, rather surprisingly, given its modern looks, is a contemporary of its near neighbour, the profoundly more ornate Pont Alexandre III (see p.161) – both bridges were opened in 1900, in time for the Exposition Universelle.

The Palais de Tokyo dates from a later exhibition, the tension-filled 1937 world fair, at which the German and Russian pavilions faced each other across the Seine in an architectural version of a Mexican standoff. **Antoine Bourdelle**'s bronze statue of "Eternal France", which surveys the central terrace of the Tokyo building, is a living reminder of the fervid nationalism of those times. The palace was always intended to be a gallery of modern art, however, and most of its decoration takes a more consciously artistic theme; Alfred Auguste Janniot's vast Art Deco bas-reliefs, which frame the central staircase, represent the nine muses. The colonnaded building itself is simple and beautiful. It's also a perfect suntrap, and much favoured by skateboarders and graffiti artists.

On Wednesday and Saturday mornings a bustling **market** takes over avenue Président Wilson, from Iéna métro station down to the palace. You'll find organic meats and cheeses and craft jewellery alongside ordinary fruit and veg, and cheap clothing.

The Musée d'Art Moderne de la Ville de Paris

The east wing of the Palais de Tokyo houses the **Musée d'Art Moderne de la Ville de Paris** (Tues–Sun 10am–6pm; closed Mon & public hols; free; ⓦwww.mam.paris.fr; M° Iéna/Alma-Marceau). The collection can't rival the Pompidou Centre's, but it's free, relatively empty and the environment is far more contemplative – and architecturally more fitting when it comes to works by early twentieth-century artists. The ground floor, by the entrance, is given over to temporary exhibitions.

The museum has two enormous and marvellous centrepieces. Just above the main stairs leading down to the permanent collections, a vast, curving chamber provides wall-space for Raoul Dufy's mural *La Fée Electricité* ("The Electricity Fairy"). Originally designed for the Electricity Pavilion in the 1937 Exposition Universelle, its 250 vivid, cartoon-like panels tell the story of electricity from the earliest experimenters to the triumph of industrialization that was the power station. Facing the stairs as you descend, the chapel-like **salle Matisse** is devoted to Matisse's *La Danse de Paris*, beginning with an incomplete early version and progressing through to the finished work, displayed high on the wall, its sinuous figures seemingly leaping through colour. Daniel Buren's *Mur de Peintures* (1995–2006), in his trademark stripes, is displayed in the same room.

The main permanent collection is chronologically themed, starting with Fauvism and Cubism, and progressing through to Dada and the Ecole de Paris, and beyond. Most artists working in France – Braque, Chagall, Delaunay, Derain, Duchamp, Dufy, Klein, Léger, Modigliani, Picasso and many others – are represented, and there is a strong Parisian theme to many of the works. The collection is kept up to the minute by an active buying policy, and some bold acquisitions of sculpture, painting and video by contemporary artists are displayed in the final suite of rooms. Look out in particular for the intimate scrapbook works of Annette Messager, Jean-Marc Bustamente's chilly photography, Christian Boltanski's sinister photographs and harrowing installations of old clothing and phone books, and, towards the end, Philippe Parreno's mesmerizing video works.

Site de Création Contemporaine

In the western wing of the palace, the **Site de Création Contemporaine** (Tues–Sun noon–midnight; €6; ⓦwww.palaisdetokyo.com) has staged a number of avant-garde exhibitions and endless events, talks, installations and projections since it opened in 2002, including a show of works by Paris-born Louise Bourgeois and a temporary occupation by squatter-artists. The distressed, semi-derelict interior has been deliberately left untouched to create a sense of "work in progress", while the young French artists working and hanging out in the bar/restaurant, bookshop and library add to the arty, informal ambience. The hippy-pattern floor painting in the downstairs café, by the Paris-based Taiwanese artist Michael Lin, and the giant, Benetton-like photo-portrait windows in the restaurant, *Tokyo Eat* (see p.328), by Swiss photographer Beat Streuli, are the gallery's sole permanent exhibits – though the small row of allotment **gardens** alongside the museum on rue de la Manutention apparently counts, too, as it was conceived by the artist Robert Milin. Signs planted in each allotment tell you a little bit about the gardener who tends it, and when they like to visit.

Place and Pont de l'Alma

A few steps upstream of the Palais de Tokyo, on **place de l'Alma**, stands a full-scale, golden replica of the flame from the Statue of Liberty. It was given to

France in 1987 as a symbol of Franco-American relations but is now an unofficial memorial to **Princess Diana**, whose Mercedes crashed in the underpass beneath. The authorities clean up the site regularly, but you'll often find bunches of withered flowers and graffiti messages along the lines of "Maria love you Diana".

The **Pont de l'Alma**, which crosses the Seine towards the Sewers, is a rather brutal 1970s steel-and-concrete affair. It's worth taking a peek at its celebrated **zouave**, however, which hides away by the waterline, on the upstream side. The name comes from the north African soldiers who fought in the French army during the Crimean War, and it was one of four military statues that adorned the previous Alma bridge. It has long served as Parisians' yardstick for describing the Seine's flooding. In 1910, for instance, the water came up to the zouave's shoulders. On the new bridge, he actually stands slightly higher than he used to, so even a knee-high flood is a fairly serious event.

10

Montparnasse and southern Paris

The swathe of cafés, brasseries and cinemas that runs through the heart of modern **Montparnasse** has long been a honeypot for pleasure-seekers, as well as a kind of border town dividing the lands of well-heeled St-Germain from the amorphous populations of the three arrondissements of **southern Paris**, the **13e**, **14e** and **15e**. Overscale developments from the 1950s to the present day have scarred parts of this southern side of the city, but there are three great parks – **André Citroën** (with its very own tethered balloon), **Georges-Brassens** and **Montsouris** – and some enticing pockets of Paris that have been allowed to evolve in a happily patchy way. Lively areas such as **Pernety** and **Plaisance** in the 14e, the **quartier du Commerce** in the 15e, and the **Butte-aux-Cailles** quartier in the 13e are pleasant places to explore, and well off the tourist track.

For **transport** through the outer 15e, 14e and 13e arrondissements, bus #62 plies a useful route along rues de la Convention, Alésia and Tolbiac.

Montparnasse and the 14^{e}

Before it was levelled in the early eighteenth-century, the story goes that students used to drink and declaim poetry from the top of a pile of spoil deposited from the Denfert-Rochereau quarries, calling the mound "Mount Parnassus" after the legendary home of the muses of poetry and song, and of drunken Bacchus. This may or may not be how the area got its name, but the reputation of **Montparnasse** for carousing persists to this day, though its status as a nightspot really stems from the construction of the Mur des Fermiers Généraux in 1784, or "Customs Wall", which split the high-taxed city from the poorer, less regulated township areas beyond. Bohemians and left-leaning intellectuals abandoned the staid city centre for Montparnasse's inexpensive cafés and nightspots; among them Verlaine and Baudelaire in the nineteenth century, and Trotsky, Hemingway, Sartre and de Beauvoir in the twentieth. Montparnasse's lasting fame, however, rests on the patronage of artists, especially during the 1920s, following the exodus from Montmartre. Picasso, Matisse, Kandinsky, Man Ray, Modigliani, Giacometti and Chagall were all habitués of the celebrated cafés around **Place Vavin**, and many were buried in **Montparnasse cemetery**. Still more bones lie nearby in the grim **catacombs**.

The area immediately around Montparnasse's railway station is dominated by the gigantic **Tour Montparnasse**, which you can ascend for a superb view of the city. In the tower's shadow, a handful of **artists" museums** recall Montparnasse's traditions, while the **Fondation Cartier** showcases contemporary art and architecture. South of the station, the **14e** is one of the most characterful of the outer arrondissements. The old-fashioned networks of streets still exist in the **Pernety** and **Plaisance** quartiers, where many artists chose to live in the affordable *villas* (similar to mews) built in the 1920s and 1930s. Down in the southeast corner of the arrondissement you'll find plenty of green space in the **Parc Montsouris** and the giant student campus of the **Cité Universitaire**.

The station and Tour Montparnasse

The interior of the **Gare Montparnasse** is a modernist confusion of railway platforms and levels of concrete and glass built over one of the city's largest métro interchanges. Until recently, many Parisians would go out of their way to avoid changing métro lines here, but the advent of a new, high-speed **tapis roulant**, or "rolling carpet" between the two main junctions of lines 4 and 12, and lines 6 and 13, has sped things up considerably – to an alarmingly rapid 9km per hour, to be exact, or three times the speed of a normal travelator. Children love it, but note that it's often closed for lack of supervision in quieter periods, including weekends.

Outside, the station's arch gives onto a broad concrete esplanade surrounded by traffic, the prospect of the city blocked by the brown glass blade of the **Tour Montparnasse**. At the time of its deeply controversial construction, this was one of Paris's first skyscrapers, defying the problem of the city's quarried-out limestone bedrock with 56 massive piles driven into a chalk layer over 40m below ground. Few Parisians have a good word to say for such a monolithic landmark, but the **view from the top** (daily: May–Sept 9.30am–11.30pm; Oct–April 9.30am–10.30pm; €8.50) is arguably better than the one from the Eiffel Tower – it has the Eiffel Tower in it, after all, plus there are no queues and it costs less to ascend. Elevators on the north side of the tower – allegedly the fastest in Europe – take you up to the open, often windy rooftop platform. You can also make for the 56th-floor café and gallery room, but it's just not the same as being outside, for all the banks of multimedia displays. Sunset is the best time to visit. It's probably worth checking in advance if the top levels are open – asbestos is being stripped out floor by floor over the next few years; call ⓣ01.45.38.52.56 for **information** or check online at ⓦwww.tourmontparnasse56.com.

Boulevard Edgar Quinet runs east of the tower towards the cemetery (see p.177), and is entirely taken over by a lively food **market** on Wednesday and Saturday mornings. Leading off the boulevard to the south, **rue de la Gaité**, the street where Trotsky lived, is a slice of turn-of-the-twentieth-century theatreland, with the Théâtre Montparnasse facing the Théâtre Gaité-Montparnasse at the bottom of the street. At the northern end, the **Comédie Italienne** advertises its diet of Goldoni and the like with a wonderfully camp, golden exterior painted with commedia dell'arte scenes – you'd never know it used to be a police station.

The Jardin Atlantique

With its connections to the western ports, Montparnasse was once the great arrival and departure point for boat travellers across the Atlantic, whether

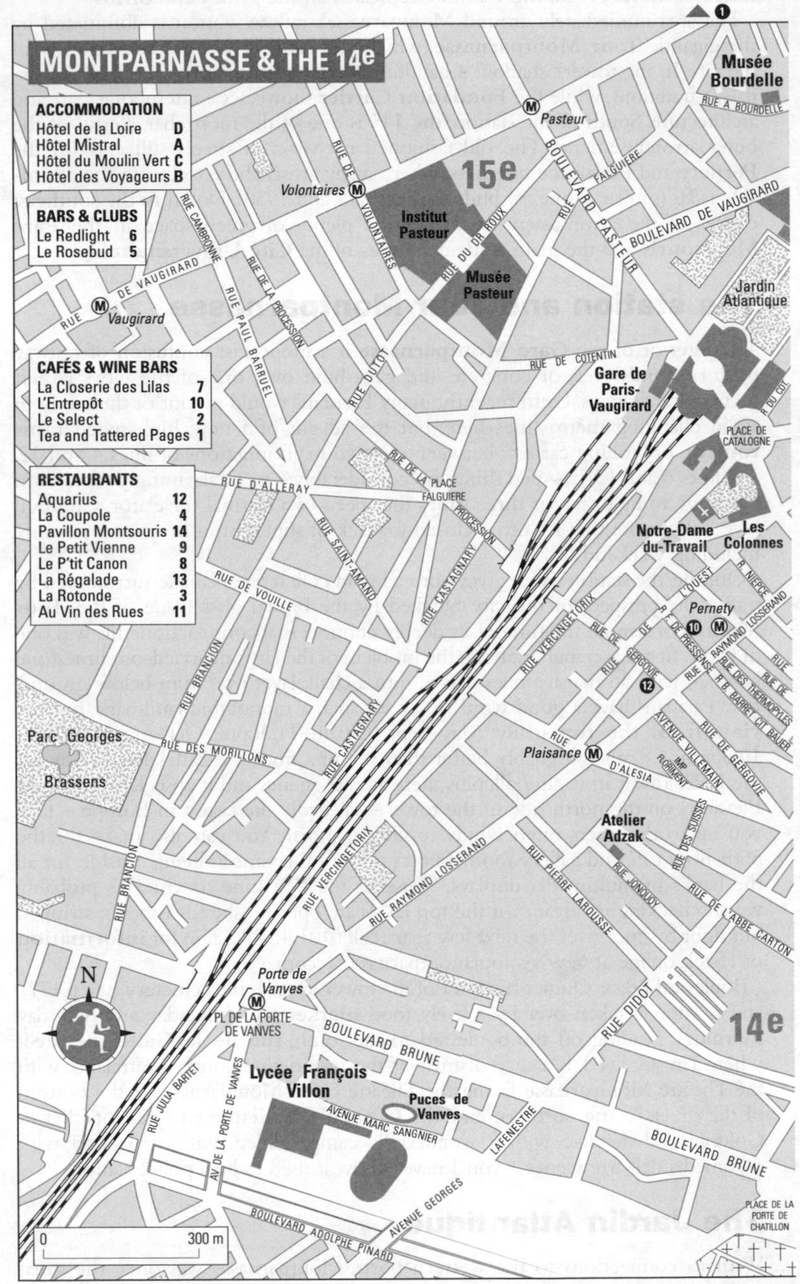
MONTPARNASSE & THE 14e
ACCOMMODATION
Hôtel de la Loire D
Hôtel Mistral A
Hôtel du Moulin Vert C
Hôtel des Voyageurs B
BARS & CLUBS
Le Redlight 6
Le Rosebud 5
CAFÉS & WINE BARS
La Closerie des Lilas 7
L'Entrepôt 10
Le Select 2
Tea and Tattered Pages 1
RESTAURANTS
Aquarius 12
La Coupole 4
Pavillon Montsouris 14
Le Petit Vienne 9
Le P'tit Canon 8
La Régalade 13
La Rotonde 3
Au Vin des Rues 11
Musée Bourdelle
Institut Pasteur
Musée Pasteur
15e
14e
Jardin Atlantique
Gare de Paris-Vaugirard
Notre-Dame du-Travail
Les Colonnes
Parc Georges Brassens
Atelier Adzak
Lycée François Villon
Puces de Vanves
Pasteur
Volontaires
Vaugirard
Pernety
Plaisance
Porte de Vanves
BOULEVARD PASTEUR
BOULEVARD DE VAUGIRARD
RUE DE VAUGIRARD
RUE DE COTENTIN
RUE D'ALLERAY
RUE DES MORILLONS
RUE VERCINGETORIX
RUE RAYMOND LOSSERAND
BOULEVARD BRUNE
BOULEVARD ADOLPHE PINARD
AVENUE MARC SANGNIER
PLACE DE CATALOGNE
PL DE LA PORTE DE VANVES
PLACE DE LA PORTE DE CHATILLON
0
300 m
N

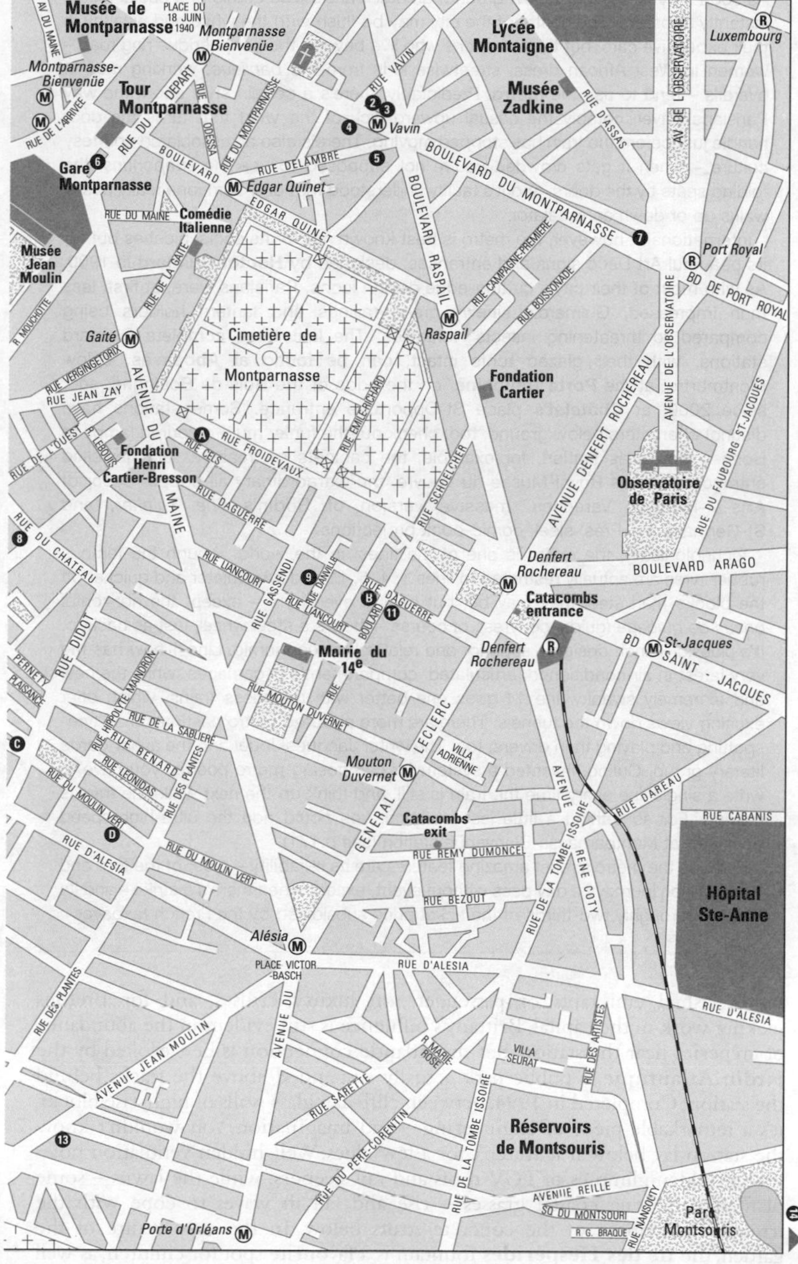
Musée de Montparnasse
Tour Montparnasse
Gare Montparnasse
Comédie Italienne
Musée Jean Moulin
Lycée Montaigne
Musée Zadkine
Cimetière de Montparnasse
Fondation Cartier
Fondation Henri Cartier-Bresson
Observatoire de Paris
Catacombs entrance
Mairie du 14e
Catacombs exit
Hôpital Ste-Anne
Réservoirs de Montsouris
Parc Montsouris
Montparnasse Bienvenüe
Vavin
Edgar Quinet
Raspail
Gaité
Port Royal
Luxembourg
Denfert Rochereau
St-Jacques
Mouton Duvernet
Alésia
Porte d'Orléans
BOULEVARD DU MONTPARNASSE
BOULEVARD RASPAIL
AVENUE DU MAINE
AVENUE DENFERT ROCHEREAU
BOULEVARD ARAGO
BD SAINT-JACQUES
AVENUE JEAN MOULIN
RUE D'ALESIA
RUE DE LA TOMBE ISSOIRE
AVENUE RENE COTY
AVENUE REILLE

The métro

As soon as you set foot below ground, greater Paris's true ethnic and social mix is instantly apparent. The centre of the city may be flush with the white and wealthy in their expensive cars, but the *franciliens* who live beyond the périphérique ring road – women in West African dress, streetwise kids from the *banlieue*, working men in overalls – tend to use the **métro**. Predictably, there's a certain style about the way Parisians travel, notably the casual upward flick of the wrist that turns the door handle just before the train has stopped moving. There's also an associated courtesy culture – when it gets crowded you're not supposed to use the *strapontins*, the folding seats by the doors, and it's tacitly understood that only someone really pushy walks up or down an escalator.

Internationally, however, the métro is best known not for its social niceties but for its beautiful Art Deco signs and entrances, designed by **Hector Guimard** in 1900. As with most of their city's cutting-edge design icons, Parisians were, at first, less than impressed, Guimard's sinewy green railings and lantern holders being compared to threatening insects' tentacles. The last three complete Guimard stations, with their glazed roofs intact, can be found at **Abbesses**, below Montmartre; at the **Porte Dauphine**, on the edge of the Bois de Boulogne; and, since 2000, at **Châtelet**'s place St-Opportune entrance. Some stations have distinct characters below ground, too: check out the funky multi-coloured lamps at Bonnes Nouvelles station, for example, the cabinets of treasures and jewelled entrance at Palais Royal-Musée du Louvre, the extraordinary all-copper decor of Arts-et-Métiers, Varennes' massive version of Rodin's *The Thinker*, and St-Germain-des-Prés' sleek comic-book projections.

Technologically, the métro is one of the finest in the world, though the famous rubber tyres are actually restricted to lines 1, 4, 6, 11 and 14. Quieter and quicker off the blocks than steel they may be, but behind every tyre – except the horizontal *pneus de guidage* (guidance tyres), of course – there's a steel wheel, just as backup. It's classic French design – superior and relatively uneconomic. Line 1 now has the very latest in air-conditioned, articulated, compartmentless carriages, while the new and extremely swanky line 14 goes one better with driverless trains, which offer exciting views down the tunnels. There are more elevated métro pastimes than tyre-spotting and playing train drivers, too. The writer Jacques Jouet and the avant-garde literary group, Oulipo, invented a system for composing métro poems; you have to write a single line every time the train is still, and think up the next while the train is moving. For something a little less cerebral, you could ride the ultra-high-speed travelator at Montparnasse-Bienvenüe station (see p.171).

Perhaps the métro's most amazing features are its reliability – most of the four and a half million journeys a day pass without event, except when there's a strike – and its cost, with roughly two-thirds of the ticket price subsidized by the French taxpayer.

impoverished emigrants or passengers on luxury cruises, and for Bretons seeking work in the capital. Brittany's influence is still evident in the abundance of crêperies near the station, but the Atlantic connection is best evoked by the **Jardin Atlantique**, a public park actually suspended above the tracks behind the station. Completed in 1994, between cliff-like glass walls of high-rise blocks, it's a remarkable piece of engineering – and imagination. You wouldn't know the station lay below if it weren't for a few clues. Well-hidden ventilation holes reveal sudden glimpses of TGV roofs and rail sleepers, while the lawns – some planted with long coastal grasses – rise and fall in waves to cope with the irregular placement of the concrete struts below. In the very centre of the garden, the **Ile des Hespérides** fountain is a favourite spot for children, as well as a giant-scale disguised weather station. The centrepiece column beside the large mirror is in fact a thermometer, though it hasn't worked since the record-breaking summer of 2003 caused it to burst way beyond its 40°C maximum. Access is via lifts on rue Cdt. R. Mouchotte and boulevard Vaugirard, or by the stairs alongside platform #1.

Facing out onto the garden, the tiny **Musée Jean Moulin** (daily except Mon 10am–6pm; €4) may be worth stopping in at if you're waiting for a train to Chartres. It gives a rather dry potted history of the Resistance illustrated by a few photos, posters and newspapers, with a special section on Jean Moulin, wartime prefect of Chartres and hero of the Resistance.

Montparnasse museums

North and west of Montparnasse station are three little-visited yet beguiling **museums**. At 21 avenue du Maine, beyond the raised slip road of rue de l'Arrivée, a piece of Montparnasse's illustrious artistic heritage has been saved from demolition. A half-hidden, ivy-clad alley leads to what was once the Russian painter Marie Vassilieff's studio, now converted into the **Musée du Montparnasse** (Tues–Sun 12.30–7pm; €5; Ⓦwww.museedumontparnasse.net; M° Montparnasse-Bienvenüe/Falguière), hosting temporary exhibitions based on Montparnasse artists past and present. Vassilieff lived here between 1912 and 1929, during which time many leading contemporary artists (Picasso, Léger, Modigliani, Chagall and Braque, among others) visited to wine, dine and dance with her. Architects' offices now occupy many of the studios nearby, but there's also a private art gallery and a flower shop whose blooms spill out into the alley.

On rue Antoine-Bourdelle, opposite the Musée du Montparnasse, a garden of sculptures invites you into the **Musée Bourdelle** (Tues–Sun 10am–6pm; free; M° Montparnasse-Bienvenüe/Falguière), a museum built around the artist's former studio. As Rodin's pupil and Giacometti's teacher, Bourdelle bridged the period between naturalism and a more geometrically conceived style. His monumental sculptures take pride of place in the chapel-like, modernist grand hall, but other, more intimate areas of the museum are just as rewarding. The sculptor's atmospheric old **studio**, musty with the smells of its ageing parquet floor and greying plaster, is littered with half-complete works that face a chilly northern light. Elsewhere, there's a wonderful series of Beethoven busts and masks, sculpted between 1887 and 1929, and a basement extension in which you can see studies for the sculptor's greatest works, the muscular *Monument à Mickiewicz* and *Monument au Général Alvear*. On the far side of the garden, Bourdelle's living quarters have been preserved complete with shabby bed, stove and some sombre paintings from his private collection.

Just around the corner to the right, on rue Falguière, the bold facade of the Ile-de-France urban-planning department veers up and away from the line of the street in the smoothest of curves, like the hull of a fantasy spaceship.

Between rue du Docteur-Roux and rue Falguière, the **Institut Pasteur** is renowned for its research into AIDS, a specialism that grew out of the work of its founder Louis Pasteur, who proved that disease is caused by germs and created the first vaccine for rabies. For the last few years of his life, after he had finally won the recognition and the laboratory he deserved, Pasteur lived and worked in the house built for him by public subscription at 25 rue du Docteur-Roux, now the **Musée Pasteur** (guided tours in French and English Mon–Fri 2–5.30pm, closed Aug; €3; Ⓦwww.pasteur.fr; M° Pasteur). You have to register first with a piece of ID – this is a cutting-edge research laboratory, after all. The tour takes you first to a room of scientific memorabilia, then through the Pasteurs' private apartments, whose nineteenth-century interiors are perfectly preserved, right down to the gas light and heated towel cabinet in the bathroom. The final touch is the lavish, Byzantine-style mausoleum erected to Pasteur by his wife, in 1896. Designed by the architect of the Petit Palais, Charles Girault, its walls and ceiling are covered in golden, Symbolist-style mosaics which show a boy wrestling a rabid dog, along with the unusual quartet of Faith, Hope, Charity and Science.

Boulevard du Montparnasse

Most of the life of the Montparnasse quartier is concentrated on **boulevard du Montparnasse**. The numerous **cinemas** here – six on the boulevard alone – are almost all of the multi-screen variety, specializing in mass-market French and US films. The liveliest point of the boulevard is around Vavin métro, where you'll find Rodin's **Balzac** ruminating over the crossroads, and a cluster of celebrated cafés: the *Select*, *Coupole*, *Dôme* and *Rotonde*. Their heyday was in the 1910s and 1920s, when artists and poets such as Apollinaire, Chagall, Leger, Modigliani, Picasso and Zadkine rubbed shoulders with exiled revolutionaries, including Lenin and Trotsky, paying a few centimes to occupy tables for hours on end. Even by the 1930s, the fashionable intelligentsia were moving on to St-Germain, but the brasseries remain proudly Parisian classics – if no longer Bohemian haunts – and this stretch of the boulevard still stays up late.

Most of the cafés have moved upmarket, leaving only the *Select* as a traditional café. The swankiest literary relic by far, however, is the brasserie **Closerie des Lilas**, which sits on the corner of the tree-lined avenue de l'Observatoire. In the days when it was a cheap café, Hemingway wrote most of *The Sun Also Rises* here. The café's most stirring historical association, however, is with Napoleon's legendarily brave Marshal Ney, whose sword-wielding statue now marks the spot on the pavement where he died at the hands of a royalist firing squad.

The Musée Zadkine and Fondation Cartier

Just north of the boulevard du Montparnasse, and within a few minutes' walk of the Jardin du Luxembourg (see p.145), is the tiny **Musée Zadkine**, at 100bis rue d'Assas (Tues–Sun 10am–6pm; free; M° Vavin/RER Port-Royal). The museum occupies the Russian-born sculptor **Ossip Zadkine**'s studio-house, where he lived and worked from 1928 – after a spell at La Ruche (see p.182) – until his death in 1967. In the garden, enclosed by ivy-covered studios and dwarfed by tall buildings, his angular Cubist bronzes seem to struggle for light – one of the most compelling, *Orphée*, is half buried among the bushes. Inside is a collection of his gentler wooden torsos, along with smaller-scale bronze and stone works, notably *Femme à l'éventail*. Studies for the renowned *La Ville détruite*, whose twisted, agonized torso was intended to express the horror of aerial bombing, can be seen inside and in the garden.

Taking a shortcut down rue Campagne-Première leads through to boulevard Raspail and the **Fondation Cartier pour l'Art Contemporain**, at no. 261 (Tues–Sun noon–8pm; €6.50; ⓦ www.fondation.cartier.fr; M° Raspail), a ten-minute walk away. The foundation is housed in a stunning glass-and-steel construction designed in 1994 by Jean Nouvel, architect of the Institut du Monde Arabe (see p.138). A glass wall follows the line of the street like a false start to the building proper, leaving space for the Tree of Liberty planted by Chateaubriand during the Revolution to grow in the garden behind. The glass of the building itself cleverly suggests a kind of fade-out into the air. Inside, all

Montparnasse architecture

Dominated as it is by the skyscraping blade of its tower, the busy boulevards, and the large-scale developments around the station, Montparnasse can feel a little inhuman and over-modernized. Wandering down the backstreets, however, you can find some kindlier examples of **architecture**, ranging from the playful lines of early Art Deco to the diaphanous contemporary glasswork of Jean Nouvel's Fondation Cartier.

26 rue Vavin, 6e. M° Vavin. A block of flats decked in white and blue tiles, with terraced balconies stepping back to allow terrace gardens to flourish in the light. Built by Henri Sauvage in 1912.

Rue Schoelcher and rue Froidevaux, 14e. M° Raspail/Denfert-Rochereau. A parade of varied nineteenth- and early twentieth-century styles. Check out 5 rue Schoelcher, especially, for its beautiful Art Deco balconies and windows, dating from 1911 (Picasso had his studio at 5bis for a short time in 1916). The artists' studios at 11 rue Schoelcher are just sixteen years younger, but the transformation to modernity is complete. Also worth seeing are 11 and 23 rue Froidevaux, the last being a 1929 block of artists' studios, with huge windows for northern light and fabulous ceramic mosaics.

266 boulevard Raspail, 14e. M° Raspail/Denfert-Rochereau. A recently completed private architecture and interior design academy with a marked Beaubourg influence, notably the external stairs and blue pipe columns in front. The original Ecole Spéciale d'Architecture building, at no. 254, dates from 1904.

31 rue Campagne-Première, 14e. M° Raspail. Myriad shell-like, earthenware tiles by Alexandre Bigot encrust the concrete structure of André Arfvidson's utterly desirable 1912 *appartements*, with their huge, iron-framed studio windows. Man Ray had a studio here in the early 1920s.

Fondation Cartier, 261 bd Raspail, 14e. M° Raspail. One of Jean Nouvel's most successful airy, postmodern steel-and-glass structures. For a full account, see p.176.

Passage d'Enfer, 14e. M° Raspail. Parallel to rue Campagne Première, this narrow, cobblestoned street – whose name translates as "Hell Alley" – was once a Cité Ouvrière, or cul-de-sac of nineteenth-century workers' housing. The unusually small, terraced buildings are now utterly covetable.

kinds of contemporary art – installations, videos, multimedia – often by foreign artists little known in France, are shown in temporary exhibitions that use the light and very generous spaces to maximum advantage.

Montparnasse cemetery

To the east of the station, the daily **food market** on boulevard Edgar-Quinet provides the cafés in the surrounding streets with their down-to-earth clientele, in marked contrast to the historic establishments a stone's throw away on boulevard du Montparnasse. On Sundays (10am–dusk), over a hundred craftworkers take over the market; photographers jostle with potters, clothes designers with painters, and it's a great place to browse away the day.

Just to the south is the main entrance to **Montparnasse cemetery** (March 16–Nov 5 Mon–Fri 8am–6pm, Sat 8.30am–6pm, Sun 9am–6pm; Nov 6 to March 15 closes 5.30pm; free; M° Raspail/Gaîté/Edgar Quinet). Second in size and celebrity to Père-Lachaise (see p.238), it's nevertheless an impressive space, sheltering in the lee of the Tour Montparnasse behind high walls. In the

△ Montparnasse cemetery

southwest corner, the old, sail-less windmill was once one of the taverns whose literary-minded customers are said to have given the Montparnasse district its name.

If you want to track down the cemetery's illustrious residents you can pick up a leaflet and map from the guardhouse by each entrance. The joint grave of Jean-Paul Sartre and Simone de Beauvoir lies immediately right of the entrance on boulevard Edgar-Quinet – Sartre lived out the last few decades of his life just a few metres away on boulevard Raspail. Down avenue de l'Ouest, which follows the inside western wall of the cemetery, you'll find the tombs of Baudelaire (who has a more impressive cenotaph by rue Emile-Richard, on the cemetery's avenue Transversale), the sculptor Zadkine (see p.176) and the Fascist Pierre Laval, who was executed for treason. As an antidote, you can pay homage to Proudhon, the anarchist who coined the phrase "Property is theft!"; he lies in Division 2, by the central roundabout, near the great photographer of Paris, Brassaï. In the adjacent Division 1, the tomb of singer Serge Gainsbourg is regularly festooned with métro tickets – the "lilacs" of his ticket-punching song *Le Poinçonneur des lilas* – and packets of Gitanes cigarettes, these being Serge's own, preferred brand.

Grave-hunting aside, it's worth seeking out some of the cemetery's finer monuments. Horace Daillion's 1889 winged bronze, *Le Génie du sommeil éternel*, dominates the central roundabout, but far more moving is the tragic sculptural scene *La Séparation du Couple*, which stands a short distance below the windmill (in Division 4, beside the Allée de Sergeants de la Rochelle). A giant bird created by the sculptor Niki de Saint-Phalle in mirrored mosaic hovers in the northeast corner of Division 18, next to the Avenue de l'Est; the title reads "to my friend Jean-Jacques: a bird who has flown too soon". The most touching monument of all is found in the eastern angle of the cemetery, on the other side of rue Emile-Richard; in the far northern corner of this section is a tomb crowned with a version of Brancusi's sculpture *The Kiss* – an utterly poignant statement of grief. Seekers of the bizarre should make for the inside wall of this part of the cemetery, along avenue du Boulevard (parallel to boulevard Raspail), where you can see the inventor of a safe gas lamp, Charles Pigeon, in bed next to his sleeping wife, reading a book by the light of his invention.

The catacombs

You won't find any celebrity dead in the nearby **catacombs** (Tues–Sun 10am–5pm; €7; M° Denfert-Rochereau), only row on row of anonymous human bones. The entrance is a few steps southeast of the cemetery on **place Denfert-Rochereau** – formerly place d'Enfer, or "Hell Square". This underground warren of tunnels was originally part of the gigantic quarry network underlying Paris (see box on p.180). From 1785, a use was found for all that empty space, when it was realized that the city's graveyards and charnel houses were fast becoming unhealthily over-full. For the next eighty years, the stony corridors were gradually filled with skeletal remains, and it's estimated that the remains of six million Parisians are interred here – more than double the population of the modern city not counting the suburbs. Lining the passageway, the long thigh bones are stacked end-on, forming a wall to keep in the smaller bones, which can just be seen heaped higgledy-piggledy behind. These high femoral walls are further inset with skulls and plaques carrying light-hearted quotations such as "happy is he who always has the hour of his death in front of his eyes, and readies himself every day to die". Older children often love the whole experience, though there are a good couple of kilometres to walk, and it can quickly become claustrophobic, especially in the busier afternoon period when, if you're unlucky, you might find yourself in a bottlenecked queue of shrieking teenagers. It also gets fairly cold and a touch squidgy underfoot, so flip-flops and a T-shirt aren't a great idea. Spare a thought for the uniformed *gardiens*, placed here to obstruct trophy-hunters and to prevent local youths of a Gothic bent slyly losing themselves and regrouping for midnight parties.

The area just west of Denfert-Rochereau is worth exploring. There's a busy **food market** on rue Daguerre, and some interesting architecture (see box, p.177) in the area around the cemetery.

Observatoire de Paris

About 500m northeast of the catacombs, on avenue de l'Observatoire, the classical **Observatoire de Paris** sat precisely on 0° longitude from the 1660s, when it was constructed, until 1914, when France finally gave in and agreed to recognize the Greenwich Meridian as the standard. The Observatoire itself is rarely open to visitors, but you can check out a couple of commemorative bronze medallions set in the pavement on either side of the front gate. Similar discs run right through the city, marking the old meridian, now named the **Arago line** after the early nineteenth-century astronomer. (Dan Brown fans should note that it was never called the "Rose Line", at least not before *The Da Vinci Code.*) The building itself was the work of Claude Perrault, brother of the more famous Charles, the original author of *Sleeping Beauty*. It's a graceful structure, and the telescope cupola perched on the east tower adds an exotic touch.

On the other side of the boulevard de Port-Royal, the green avenue de l'Observatoire stretches due north into the Jardin du Luxembourg (see p.145).

Around place de Catalogne

Just south of Montparnasse station, the circular **place de Catalogne** is filled with a giant, flat disc of a fountain designed by the Israeli artist Shamaï Haber,

Undergound Paris

In September 2004, while on a training exercise in a group of tunnels underneath the Palais de Chaillot, the Parisian police stumbled upon a clandestine underground cell. Nothing to do with terrorism, this one, but an actual subterranean chamber, 400 square metres in size, which had been fitted out as a cinema by a dedicated club of *film noir* lovers. As the story hit the press, a band of troglodytes emerged blinking into the full beam of the media spotlight. Since the 1980s, it turned out, hundreds of these "*cataphiles*" had been holding anything from underground parties and art exhibitions to festivals and, it was rumoured, orgies. Experienced tunnel-goers talked of elaborate graffiti murals and a huge, pillared party room known as "La Plage".

In fact, the tunnels underneath Chaillot form only a small part of a vast network that dates back to the medieval era, when the stone for building Paris was quarried out from its most obvious source, immediately underfoot – almost as if Paris were matched by a negative image of itself below ground. Today, over 300km of underground galleries lie beneath the city, especially on the Left Bank's 5e, 6e, 14e and 15e arrondissements, where the Grand Réseau Sud runs for over 100km. Another separate network lurks beneath the 13e arrondissement, while in the 16e, it's said that the rock is like a gruyère cheese. In the 1770s, worried by teetering or even collapsing buildings, a royal commission was set up to map the old quarries and shore up the most precarious foundations. Great galleries were cut along the lines of the roads and the material used to infill the worst voids. Today, some of these underground "streets" still exist, while those above have disappeared. Some attribute modern Paris's relative lack of skyscrapers to doubts about the quality of the city's foundations.

In the nineteenth century, many tunnels were used for mushroom cultivation (the everyday supermarket variety is still known in France as the *champignon de Paris*), others for growing endives or brewing, while Carthusian monks even practised distillation under the modern-day Jardin du Luxembourg. The most creative scheme, however, involved the hygienic storage of human remains. From the 1780s, the contents of Paris's unhealthily overcrowded cemeteries were slowly transferred underground. In Montparnasse, one bone-lined section of the catacombs can still be visited (see p.179) but, otherwise, "penetrating into or circulating within" the network has been illegal since 1955. You can always get down into the métro (see p.174), of course, while at the Égouts de Paris (see p.160) you can descend into a part of the city's 2300km of sewers. But it would be foolish to try anything more adventurous. In 1993, one *cataphile* apparently disappeared into the labyrinth, never to return.

and surrounded by **Ricardo Bofill**'s housing development, a gargantuan exercise in postmodern Classicism. To the northwest, **place des 5 Martyrs du Lycée Buffon** runs right through the buildings behind the Jardin Atlantique, offering a little-known view down the horse-chestnut-lined slope of boulevard Pasteur towards the Eiffel Tower, apparently floating over the city below.

East of the *place*, you can thread your way through the backstreets to the tiny Impasse Lebouis, where the slender steel-and-glass front of the new **Fondation Henri Cartier-Bresson** (Tues–Sun 1–6.30pm, Wed 1–8.30pm, Sat 11am–6.45pm, closed Aug; €5; Ⓦ www.henricartierbresson.org; M° Gaîté) is hidden away. The foundation houses the archive of the grand old photographer of Paris, who died shortly after its opening, in August 2004. There's also a permanent photography exhibition space. Fascinating, often intimate shows of the work of Cartier-Bresson and his contemporaries alternate with exhibitions promoting younger photographers, including the winner of the foundation's annual prize.

South of place de Catalogne, Rue Vercingétorix runs between the two great wings of the Bofill complex – one oval, the other squared off – past the **church of Notre-Dame du Travail**, which was built at the end of the nineteenth century to cater for a congregation swollen by the men employed in building the Eiffel Tower and the surrounding exhibition palaces for the Exposition Universelle. The stone came from the Cloth Pavilion and the slender metal columns of the interior – a fascinating industrial take on Gothic – from the Palace of Industry.

Pernety to the Puces de Vanves

The southwestern swathe of the 14e arrondissement is deeply residential, often village-like in atmosphere, especially around the **Pernety** métro station. The number of prizes won by the bakery La Fournée d'Augustine, in the heart of things at 96 rue Raymond Losserand, is some indication of the old-fashioned values proudly maintained in this quartier. Nearby, a number of good neighbourhood restaurants and friendly hotels make this an excellent area to stay in if you want to taste old-fashioned Paris life.

Wandering around Cité Bauer, rue des Thermopyles and rue Didot reveals adorable houses, secluded courtyards and quiet mews, and on the corner of rue du Moulin Vert and rue Hippolyte-Maindron you'll find **Giacometti**'s ramshackle old studio and home. Cinema has one of its best Parisian venues at **L'Entrepôt**, 7–9 rue Francis-de-Pressensé, with spaces for talks, meals and drinks, and even a garden. South again, **rue d'Alésia**, the main east–west route through the 14e, has a small **food market** every Thursday and Sunday between the Plaisance métro and rue Didot. At the junction with rue des Plantes, there's a delightful example of an old-style mews, the **Villa d'Alésia**.

Just south of rue d'Alésia, at 3 rue Jonquoy, the **Atelier Adzak** (usually open Sat & Sun 3–7pm during exhibitions; ring in advance for information or to visit at other times ☎01.45.43.06.98; free; M° Plaisance) is a showcase for the work of British sculptor Roy Adzak, and a living and working space for contemporary artists. Adzak, who is best known for his comment "good art is not what it looks like, but what it does to us", built the studio with his own hands in the 1980s, along with the permanent sculpture garden, and there are frequent temporary exhibitions by associated artists.

At the weekend it's worth heading out to the southern edge of the arrondissement for one of the city's best **flea markets**, known as the **Puces de Vanves** (see p.181). Starting at daybreak, it spreads along the pavements of avenues Marc-Sangnier and Georges-Lafenestre, petering out at its western end in place de la Porte-de-Vanves, where the city fortifications used to stand until the 1920s.

Parc Montsouris and the Cité Universitaire

In the southeastern corner of the arrondissement, there are still more artistic and historic associations; the artists Dal' and Jean Lurcat, and expat writers Henry Miller and Lawrence Durrell lived in the miniature enclosed street of **Villa Seurat**, off rue de la Tombe-Issoire – Miller wrote *Tropic of Cancer* there; Lenin and his wife, Krupskaya, lodged across the street at 4 rue Marie-Rose; Le Corbusier built the studio at 53 avenue Reille, close to the secretive and verdant square du Montsouris which links with rue Nansouty; and Georges Braque's home was in the cul-de-sac now named after him off this street. The nearby **Parc Montsouris** (RER Cité-Universitaire) is a pleasant place to wander, with its unlikely contours, winding paths and waterfall above the lake – even the RER tracks cutting right through it fail to dent its charm. More surprising features include a meteorological office, a marker of the old meridian line, near boulevard Jourdan, and, by the southwest entrance, a kiosk run by the French Astronomy Association.

On the other side of boulevard Jourdan, several thousand students from more than a hundred different countries live in the curious array of buildings of the **Cité Universitaire**. The central Maison Internationale resembles a traditional French château, while the styles of the others are designed to represent the home nations of those who come to study here: the red brick of the Collège Franco-Britannique, for instance, all too accurately recalls Britain's institutional buildings. Two of the most remarkable buildings were designed by Le Corbusier; the graceful suspended shoebox of the Pavillon de la Suisse (1931–33) is one of his major works, and still has original mural paintings inside; the more brutal Pavillon du Brésil (1957–59) recalls Le Corbusier's famous Cité Radieuse in Marseille, and was a co-creation with the architect Lúcio Costa, the so-called "father of Bras'lia". The Cité puts on films, shows and other events (check the notice boards in the Maison Internationale or online at Ⓦwww.ciup.fr), and the cafeterias offer an inexpensive meal if you have a student card.

The 15e

Though it's the largest and most populous of them all, the **15e arrondissement** falls off the agenda for most visitors as it lacks even a single important building or monument. If the area has a heart it's the surprisingly provincial **rue du Commerce**. In the southern corners are two modern and attractive **parks** that are especially good for kids: the **Parc André-Citroën**, built over the old Citroën works, and the **Parc Georges-Brassens**, on the site of a former abattoir. Elsewhere in the 15e there are some pleasant areas to wander around, many with offbeat associations, such as the island **Allée des Cygnes**, and the artist colony known as **La Ruche**.

The riverbank

Heading south from the Eiffel Tower, the first landmark on the city's southwestern **riverbank** front is the glass **Maison de la Culture du Japon à Paris**, at 101 quai Branly (Tues–Sat noon–7pm, Thurs till 8pm; Ⓦwww.mcjp.asso.fr; M° Bir-Hakeim). A symbol of prosperous Franco–Japanese relations, it puts on excellent programmes of Japanese theatre, dance and cinema, and offers the opportunity to take part in a Japanese tea ceremony (Wed 3pm & 4pm; book two weeks in advance on Ⓣ01.44.37.95.30; €7).

Immediately south, you can watch the métro trains trundling across to Passy on the top level of the two-decker **Pont de Bir-Hakeim**, a lovable structure dating from 1902. Up on the adjacent, raised walkway, at the beginning of boulevard de Grenelle, a bronze sculptural group stands in memorial to the notorious **rafle du Vel d'Hiv**, the mass arrest of 13,152 Parisian Jews in July 1942. Nine thousand people, including four thousand children, were interned for a week at the cycle track which once stood here, before being carted off to the death camps. Only thirty adults survived.

One of Paris's most curious walks leads down from the very middle of the Pont de Bir-Hakeim, along the **Allée des Cygnes**, a narrow, midstream island built up on raised concrete embankments. It's a strange place – one of Samuel Beckett's favourites – with just birds, trees and a path to walk along, and, at its furthest point downstream, a smaller-scale version of the **Statue of Liberty**, or *Liberty Lighting the World*, to give it its full title. This was one of the four preliminary models constructed between 1874 and 1884 by sculptor Auguste Bartholdi, with the help of Gustave Eiffel, before the finished article (originally intended for Alexandria in Egypt) was presented to New York. Contemporary photos show the final version, assembled in Bartholdi's rue de Chazelles workshop, towering over the houses of the 17e like a bizarre female King Kong.

The facing riverfront of the 15e arrondissement, right down to the edge of the city at Pont du Garigliano, bristles with office blocks and miniature apartment skyscrapers, the shabby fruits of a 1960s and 1970s development programme called the **Front de Seine**. There's little reason to penetrate this maze unless you're a particular fan of postwar architecture, or perhaps raised pedestrian walkways. Even the distinctively slender, white skylon-like tower turns out to be nothing more interesting than a central-heating chimney.

Parc André-Citroën

The **Parc André-Citroën** (Mon–Fri 8am to dusk, Sat & Sun 9am to dusk; M° Javel-André Citroën/Balard), on the banks of the Seine, between Pont du Garigliano and Pont Mirabeau, is not a park for traditionalists. The central grassy area is straightforward enough, but around it you'll find futuristic terraces and concrete-walled gardens with abstract themes. It's as much a sight to visit in its own right as a place to lounge around or throw a frisbee.

At the top end, away from the river, are two large glass **hothouses**, one housing mimosa, fish-tailed palms and other sweet smelling shrubbery, the other used for temporary exhibitions. On hot days, however, the most tempting feature is the large platform between them, which sprouts a capricious set of automated **fountain** jets, luring children and occasionally adults to dodge the sudden spurts of water. On either side of the greenhouses, the White and Black Gardens are for plants that show off the two extreme colours, but the most exciting themed gardens lie along the northern side of the park, where high walls surround the **Serial Gardens**. Here, the Green Garden is dedicated to sound, with bubbling water and *Miscanthus sinensis* grasses rustling dryly in the wind; the Blue Garden is for scent, planted with wisteria and strong-smelling herbs; the Orange Garden, for touch, is highly textured; and there are Red, Silver and Gold gardens too. At the foot of this section, towards the river, is the Garden in Movement, whose semi-wild, constantly changing plants are broken up by miniature greenhouses, and a long stone staircase flowing with water. Best of all, perhaps, is the **tethered balloon**, which rises and sinks regularly on calm days, taking small groups 150m above the ground – higher than the second level of the Eiffel Tower – for great views of the city (daily from 9am to 30min before the park closes; call to check weather conditions on the day ⓣ01.44.26.20.00; Mon–Fri €10, Sat & Sun €12, children aged 3–11 €5/6).

The quartier du Commerce

The best way to get the flavour of the **quartier du Commerce** is to start walking down **avenue de la Motte-Picquet**, where the Champ de Mars meets the Ecole Militaire. At the corner, the brasseries throng with officers from the Ecole, and the hundred-odd antique shops in the snooty **Village Suisse** (all open Thurs–Mon; ⓦwww.theswissvillage.com) display endless chandeliers and

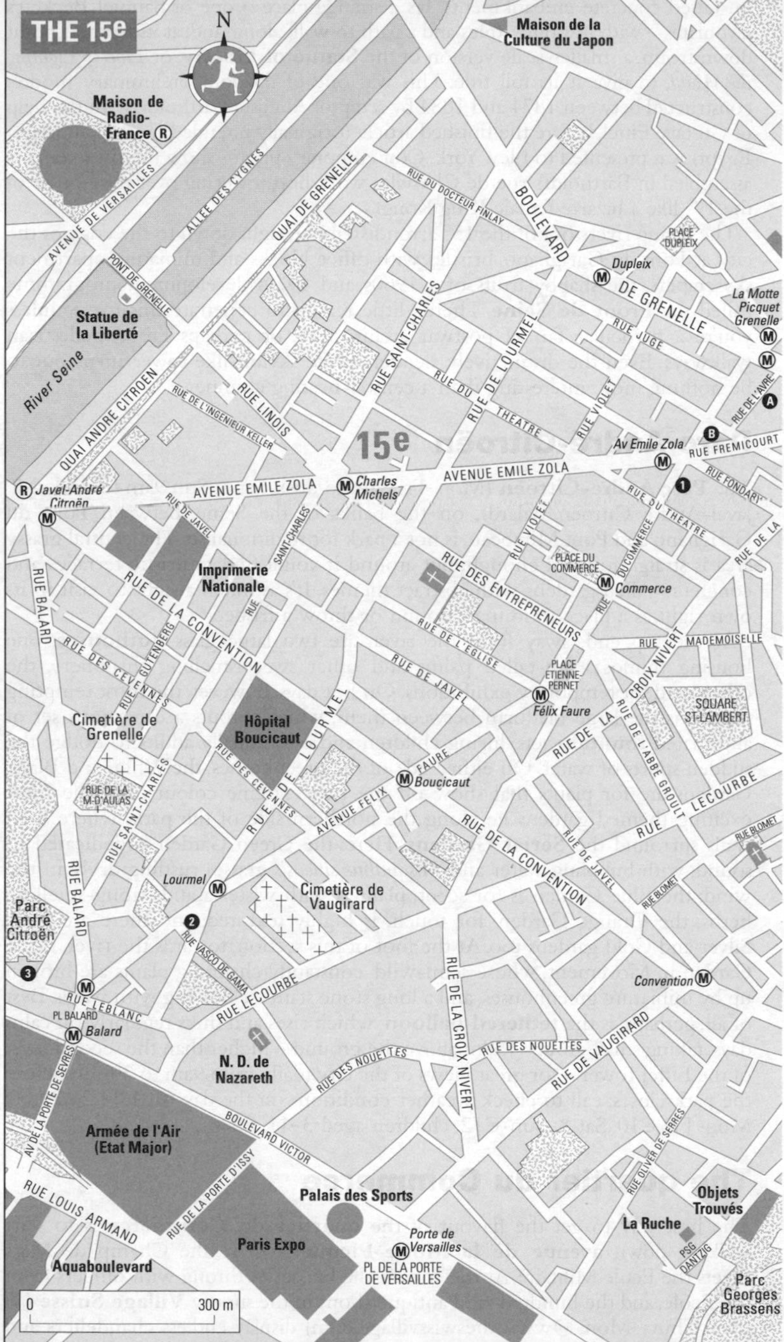

THE 15e
N
Eiffel Tower
Maison de la Culture du Japon
Maison de Radio-France
Statue de la Liberté
River Seine
15e
Imprimerie Nationale
Hôpital Boucicaut
Cimetière de Grenelle
Cimetière de Vaugirard
Parc André Citroën
N. D. de Nazareth
Armée de l'Air (Etat Major)
Palais des Sports
Paris Expo
Aquaboulevard
La Ruche
Objets Trouvés
Parc Georges Brassens
SQUARE ST-LAMBERT
Dupleix
La Motte Picquet Grenelle
Av Emile Zola
Charles Michels
Javel-André Citroën
Commerce
Félix Faure
Boucicaut
Lourmel
Balard
Convention
Porte de Versailles
AVENUE DE VERSAILLES
ALLEE DES CYGNES
QUAI DE GRENELLE
PONT DE GRENELLE
QUAI ANDRE CITROEN
RUE DU DOCTEUR FINLAY
BOULEVARD DE GRENELLE
PLACE DUPLEIX
RUE JUGE
RUE DE L'AVRE
RUE SAINT-CHARLES
RUE DE LOURMEL
RUE DU THEATRE
RUE VIOLET
RUE LINOIS
RUE DE L'INGENIEUR KELLER
RUE FREMICOURT
RUE FONDARY
AVENUE EMILE ZOLA
RUE DE JAVEL
RUE DU COMMERCE
PLACE DU COMMERCE
RUE DE LA CONVENTION
RUE DES ENTREPRENEURS
RUE DE L'EGLISE
RUE MADEMOISELLE
RUE BALARD
RUE DES CEVENNES
RUE GUTENBERG
PLACE ETIENNE-PERNET
RUE DE LA CROIX NIVERT
RUE DE L'ABBE GROULT
RUE LECOURBE
RUE BLOMET
AVENUE FELIX FAURE
RUE DE LA M-D'AULAS
RUE VASCO DE GAMA
RUE LEBLANC
PL BALARD
RUE DES NOUETTES
RUE DE VAUGIRARD
AV DE LA PORTE DE SEVRES
BOULEVARD VICTOR
RUE DE LA PORTE D'ISSY
RUE LOUIS ARMAND
RUE OLIVIER DE SERRES
PL DE LA PORTE DE VERSAILLES
PSG DANTZIG
0
300 m

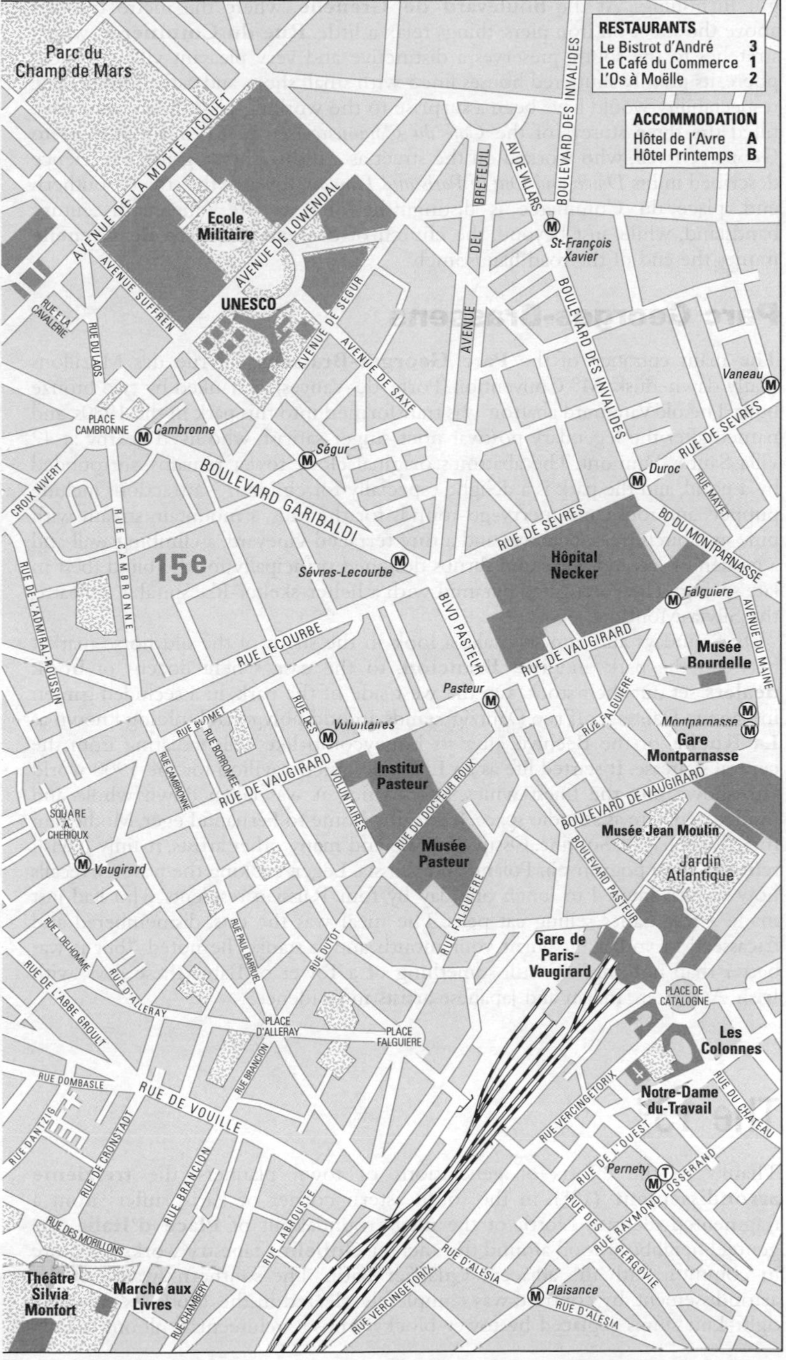
RESTAURANTS
Le Bistrot d'André 3
Le Café du Commerce 1
L'Os à Moëlle 2
ACCOMMODATION
Hôtel de l'Avre A
Hôtel Printemps B
Parc du Champ de Mars
Ecole Militaire
UNESCO
AVENUE DE LA MOTTE PICQUET
AVENUE DE LOWENDAL
AVENUE SUFFREN
AVENUE DE SEGUR
AVENUE DE SAXE
AVENUE DE BRETEUIL
AV DE VILLARS
BOULEVARD DES INVALIDES
St-François Xavier
Vaneau
RUE DE SEVRES
Duroc
Ségur
Cambronne
PLACE CAMBRONNE
BOULEVARD GARIBALDI
Sèvres-Lecourbe
15e
Hôpital Necker
BD DU MONTPARNASSE
Falguière
Musée Bourdelle
AVENUE DU MAINE
RUE DE VAUGIRARD
RUE LECOURBE
BLVD PASTEUR
Pasteur
Volontaires
Institut Pasteur
Musée Pasteur
Montparnasse
Gare Montparnasse
BOULEVARD DE VAUGIRARD
Musée Jean Moulin
Jardin Atlantique
Gare de Paris-Vaugirard
PLACE DE CATALOGNE
Les Colonnes
Notre-Dame du-Travail
Vaugirard
SQUARE A. CHERIOUX
PLACE D'ALLERAY
PLACE FALGUIERE
RUE DE VOUILLE
RUE D'ALLERAY
RUE DE L'ABBE GROULT
RUE DOMBASLE
RUE DE CRONSTADT
RUE BRANCION
RUE LABROUSTE
RUE D'ALESIA
Plaisance
Pernety
RUE RAYMOND LOSSERAND
RUE VERCINGETORIX
RUE DE L'OUEST
RUE DU CHATEAU
Théâtre Silvia Monfort
Marché aux Livres

gilt furnishings. At the **boulevard de Grenelle**, where the métro trundles above the street on iron piers, things relax a little. **Rue du Commerce**, which stretches to the south, preserves a distinctive and very pleasant village atmosphere, its prettily shuttered houses lined with small shops and cafés. This upscale respectability would have been a surprise to the working-class diners who once filled the three storeys of the *Café du Commerce* (see p.321 and p.341), or to George Orwell, who worked on the street as a dishwasher, a gritty experience described in his *Down and Out in Paris and London*. Towards the street's southern end, place du Commerce is distinguished by its late nineteenth-century bandstand, while, just beyond, the church of **St-Jean Baptiste de Grenelle** frames the end of the road handsomely.

Parc Georges-Brassens

The main entrance of the **Parc Georges-Brassens**, on rue des Morillons (daily dawn–dusk; M° Convention/Porte-de-Vanves), is flanked by two bronze bulls. The old Vaugirard abattoir was transformed into this park in the 1980s, and named after the legendary postwar poet-singer-satirist, who lived nearby at 42 villa Santos-Dumont. The abattoir's original clock tower remains, surrounded by a pond, and the park is a delight, especially for children – attractions include puppets and rocks and merry-go-rounds for the kids, a mountain stream with pine and birch trees, beehives and a tiny terraced vineyard, a climbing wall and a garden of scented herbs and shrubs designed principally for the blind (best in late spring). The corrugated pyramid with a helter-skelter-like spiral is a theatre, the Silvia-Montfort.

On Saturdays and Sundays, take a look in the sheds of the old horse market between the park and **rue Brancion**, to the east, where dozens of **book dealers** set out their stock. On the west side of the park, in a secluded garden in passage Dantzig, off rue Dantzig, stands an odd polygonal building known as **La Ruche**, or the Beehive, after its honeycomb-like cells radiating from the central staircase. It started life as an Eiffel-designed pavilion for the 1900 world fair, showcasing the finest wines, after which it was taken down whole and resurrected here as a studio space. It became home to Fernand Léger, Modigliani (briefly), Chagall, Soutine, Ossip Zadkine and many other artists, mainly Jewish refugees from pogroms in Poland and Russia. Léger, evoking the poverty, recalls how he was invited to lunch one day by four Russian residents who had just made a few francs selling cat pelts. The meal was the cats, dismembered and fricasséed in vodka. "It burnt your mouth and it stank," he noted, "but it was better than nothing." It's still something of a Tower of Babel these days, with Irish, American, Italian and Japanese artists in residence.

The 13e

Thanks to the efforts of generations of town planners, the **treizième arrondissement** (**13e**), in the southeastern corner of Paris, suffers from a fragmented identity. North of the mega-roundabout of **Place d'Italie**, the genteel neighbourhood around the ancient **Gobelins** tapestry works has more in common with the adjacent Quartier Latin. The southern swathe of the arrondissement, by contrast, was completely cleared in the 1960s, its crowded, tight-knit slums replaced by tower blocks whose architectural gloom is only

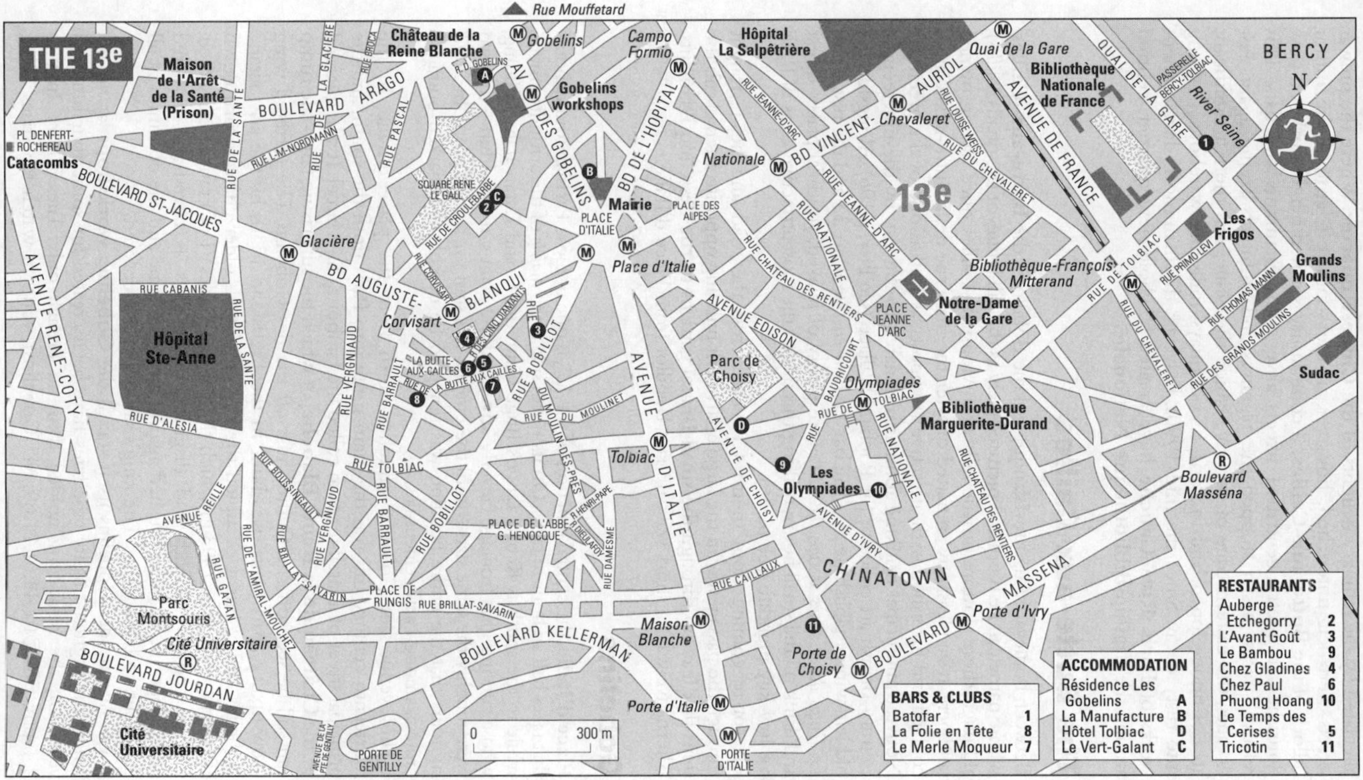

THE 13e
Rue Mouffetard
BERCY
N
13e
Maison de l'Arrêt de la Santé (Prison)
Château de la Reine Blanche
Gobelins
Gobelins workshops
Campo Formio
Hôpital La Salpêtrière
Quai de la Gare
Bibliothèque Nationale de France
River Seine
PASSERELLE BERCY-TOLBIAC
QUAI DE LA GARE
AVENUE DE FRANCE
AURIOL
BD VINCENT- Chevaleret
Nationale
Les Frigos
Grands Moulins
Sudac
RUE PRIMO LEVI
RUE THOMAS MANN
RUE DES GRANDS MOULINS
RUE DE TOLBIAC
RUE DU CHEVALERET
RUE LOUISE WEISS
Bibliothèque-François-Mitterand
Notre-Dame de la Gare
PLACE JEANNE D'ARC
RUE JEANNE-D'ARC
RUE NATIONALE
RUE CHATEAU DES RENTIERS
AVENUE EDISON
BAUDRICOURT
Olympiades
TOLBIAC
Bibliothèque Marguerite-Durand
Les Olympiades
Parc de Choisy
AVENUE DE CHOISY
AVENUE D'IVRY
CHINATOWN
MASSENA
Boulevard Masséna
Porte d'Ivry
BOULEVARD
Porte de Choisy
RUE CAILLAUX
Maison Blanche
Porte d'Italie
PORTE D'ITALIE
AVENUE D'ITALIE
Tolbiac
Place d'Italie
PLACE D'ITALIE
Mairie
PLACE DES ALPES
BD DE L'HOPITAL
AV DES GOBELINS
R. D. GOBELINS
PL DENFERT-ROCHEREAU
Catacombs
BOULEVARD ARAGO
RUE DE LA SANTE
RUE DE LA GLACIERE
RUE BROCA
RUE PASCAL
RUE L-M-NORDMANN
SQUARE RENE LE GALL
RUE DE CROULEBARBE
BOULEVARD ST-JACQUES
Glacière
BD AUGUSTE-BLANQUI
RUE CORVISART
Corvisart
RUE DES CINQ DIAMANTS
LA BUTTE-AUX-CAILLES
RUE DE LA BUTTE AUX CAILLES
RUE BOBILLOT
RUE DU MOULINET
RUE DU MOULIN-DES-PRES
RUE BARRAULT
RUE VERGNIAUD
RUE CABANIS
Hôpital Ste-Anne
RUE D'ALESIA
AVENUE RENE-COTY
RUE TOLBIAC
RUE BOUSSINGAULT
PLACE DE L'ABBE G. HENOCQUE
R. HENRI-PAPE
R. DIEULAFOY
RUE DAMESME
AVENUE REILLE
RUE GAZAN
RUE DE L'AMIRAL-MOUCHEZ
RUE BRILLAT-SAVARIN
PLACE DE RUNGIS
BOULEVARD KELLERMAN
Parc Montsouris
Cité Universitaire
BOULEVARD JOURDAN
AVENUE DE LA PTE DE GENTILLY
PORTE DE GENTILLY
0 300 m
BARS & CLUBS
Batofar 1
La Folie en Tête 8
Le Merle Moqueur 7
ACCOMMODATION
Résidence Les Gobelins A
La Manufacture B
Hôtel Tolbiac D
Le Vert-Galant C
RESTAURANTS
Auberge Etchegorry 2
L'Avant Goût 3
Le Bambou 9
Chez Gladines 4
Chez Paul 6
Phuong Hoang 10
Le Temps des Cerises 5
Tricotin 11

alleviated by the culinary delights of the **Chinese quarter**. Where the prewar streets were left untouched, however, in the southwest, around the minor hillock of the **Butte-aux-Cailles**, a community-spirited neighbourhood now flourishes, its pretty, gentrified streets alive with restaurants and bars. This relative success hasn't stopped the planners and architects trying again. For decades, the eastern edge of the 13^{e}, beside the Seine, was the last significant area of undeveloped land in Paris, its old quays, mills and warehouses lapsing into rusty decay. Since the mid-1990s, however, the mammoth development works of **Paris Rive Gauche** have created a whole new quartier, centred around the flagship **Bibliothèque Nationale**.

The Butte-aux-Cailles

Between boulevard Auguste-Blanqui and rue Bobillot is the **Butte-aux-Cailles**, whose name can be translated picturesquely as the hill (*butte*) of the quails (*cailles*), although there is more prosaic talk of a Monsieur Cailles once having owned land here. It's a pleasantly animated quarter, the main rue de la Butte-aux-Cailles cobbled and furnished with attractive lampposts, as well as one of the green Art Nouveau municipal drinking fountains donated to the city by the nineteenth-century British art collector Sir Richard Wallace (see box, p.196). Alongside the old left-wing establishments – the bar *La Folie en Tête* at no. 33 and the restaurant *Le Temps des Cerises* at nos. 18–20 – are plenty of relaxed, youthful places to eat and drink till the small hours, making this one of the most attractive areas of Paris for low-key nightlife (see p.356).

If you're coming from métro Corvisart, cross the road and head straight through the passageway in the large apartment building opposite, then climb the steps that lead up through the small Brassaï gardens to rue des Cinq Diamants. Alternatively, it's a short walk up rue Bobillot from Place d'Italie.

Gobelins

Place d'Italie, the central junction of the 13^{e}, is one of those Parisian roundabouts that takes half an hour to cross. On its north side is the *mairie* of the arrondissement, while to the south is Kenzo Tange's huge Gaumont Grand Ecran Italie building, whose curving glass frontage cleverly advertised the giant screen within – the two were roughly the same size – until the cinema was shut for lack of profit. In 2007, rumours that the entire building was going to be demolished sparked outraged protests among Paris's cinéphiles.

The avenue des Gobelins stretches north from the place d'Italie. In the fourteenth century, this was the main route into Paris from the south, and the principal street of a satellite town called the Faubourg St-Marcel. It was guarded by the **Château de la Reine Blanche**, of which the surprising fairy-tale rump can still be seen off rue Geffroy, just off rue des Gobelins. The turreted wing (now luxury apartments) was built in the 1520s and 1530s by the aristocratic Gobelins family, but it occupied the site of a much older château torn down after a tragic party in 1393 in which the young Charles VI of France nearly died. Charles and five friends had disguised themselves as tarred-and-feathered savages but one of them brushed against a candle flame and the costumes of all five went up like torches. The king's sanity never recovered.

On Avenue des Gobelins itself stands the **Gobelins workshops**, at no. 42, where the highest-quality tapestries have been created for some four hundred years. On the hour-long guided tour (in French only; Tues–Thurs 2pm & 2.45pm; €8; ⓣ01.44.61.21.69; M° Gobelins), you can watch tapestries being made by painfully slow traditional methods; each weaver completes between one and four square metres a year. The designs are now exactingly specified by contemporary artists, and almost all of the dozen or so works completed each year are destined for French government offices.

The site of the works owes everything to the presence of the river Bièvre, whose course is still marked by the curves of rues Berbier-du-Mets and Croulebarbe. Once a hellish ditch polluted by tanners and dye-makers, the river was finally covered over in 1910. The green space of the **Square René-le-Gall** was once an island between two branches of the river – known as the Ile aux Singes for the jugglers' monkeys that once lived there. A row of poplars now marks the course of the Bièvre; plans to uncover the river for the first time in a hundred years have, to date, come to nothing. A short distance west, the métro station **Glacière** ("icebox" in French) gets its name from the Bièvre's winter overflow, which attracted hundreds of skaters in the nineteenth century.

Over to the east, towards the **gare d'Austerlitz**, the ornate, bourgeois boulevards St-Marcel and Vincent-Auriol are dominated by the immense **Hôpital de la Salpêtrière**, built under Louis XIV to dispose of the dispossessed, and later used as a psychiatric hospital; today it's a general hospital. Jean Charcot, who believed that susceptibility to hypnosis proved hysteria, staged his theatrical demonstrations here, with Freud as one of his fascinated witnesses.

Chinatown and Tolbiac

The area between rue de Tolbiac, avenue de Choisy and boulevard Masséna is what is known as the **Chinatown** of Paris, despite the fact that it was founded by Vietnamese refugees in the late 1970s, and is now home to several other east Asian communities. Avenues de Choisy and d'Ivry are full of Vietnamese, Thai, Cambodian and Laotian restaurants and food shops, as is **Les Olympiades**, a pedestrian area bizarrely suspended between giant tower blocks. One escalator leads up to it from 66 avenue d'Ivry, next door to a slip road leading down to an underground car park; halfway down this access road lurks a tiny **Buddhist temple** and community centre, advertised by a pair of red Chinese lanterns dimly visible in the gloom. On Monday, Wednesday and Friday afternoons, from around 2.30pm, there are informal **concerts** of Chinese music; the rest of the time elderly Chinese people play games and doze quietly on rickety sofas. As you step out into avenue d'Ivry, you'll find the huge Tang Frères **Chinese supermarket** (see p.400), a former railway warehouse now stocked with an incredible variety of Asian goods and foodstuffs.

On the north side of **rue de Tolbiac**, the **parc de Choisy** offers outdoor ping-pong tables with concrete nets and shady trees. There are some interesting modern buildings near here, including Christian de Portzamparc's humanely scaled public housing estate on rue des Hautes-Formes, with its curious little gantries (1979), and, at 106 rue du Château-des-Rentiers, a ten-storey block of public flats whose facade, on rue Jean-Colly, has a map of the quartier in coloured tiles, with pipes to show the métro lines. Serious **Le Corbusier** fans could make the long slog down rue Cantagrel, where his colourful Cité de Refuge (1933), or Salvation Army building, stands at no. 12.

Bibliothèque Nationale

The easternmost edge of the treizième, between the river and the Austerlitz train tracks, has been utterly transformed in recent years as part of the **Paris Rive Gauche** development (see p.190). The star architectural attraction, which

Mitterrand managed to inaugurate though not open just before his death in 1996, is the **Bibliothèque Nationale de France**, accessible from the métro stations at Quai de la Gare or Bibliothèque-François Mitterrand, on the swanky new line 14 – which is worth visiting on its own account. There are regular exhibitions – typically serious, arty and high-quality – and the **reading rooms** on the "haut-jardin" level, along with their unrivalled collection of foreign newspapers, are open to everyone over 16 (Tues–Sat 10am–7pm, Sun 1–7pm; €3.30 for a day pass; Ⓦwww.bnf.fr). The garden level, below, is reserved for accredited researchers only, while the garden itself is completely out of bounds.

The four enormous L-shaped towers at the corners of the site were intended to look like open books, but attracted widespread derision after shutters had to be added behind the glazing in order to protect the collections from sunlight. Once you mount the dramatic wooden steps surrounding the library, however, the perspective changes utterly. Now you're looking down into a huge sunken pine wood, with glass walls that filter light into the floors below your feet; it's like standing at the edge of a secret ravine. The concept is startlingly original, and almost fulfils architect Dominique Perault's intention to seek "a kind of sensibility capable of combining rigour and emotion, which will generate a sense of dignity, a well-tempered soul for the buildings of the French Republic". Cynics might find the steel stays added to stop the trees blowing over less than dignified, but it's undoubtedly a fascinating structure.

Paris Rive Gauche

From the Gare d'Austerlitz right down to the *boulevard périphérique*, almost every stick of street furniture and every square metre of tarmac in the **Paris Rive Gauche** area is shiny, spanking new. Ultra-modern traffic lights and provisional road signs, and still-underpopulated cafés and apartment blocks give the area a frontier-town feel that's strange so near to the centre of Paris, the other-worldly impression exacerbated by the quarter's isolation between rail tracks and river. That said, the railway lines are slowly being roofed over, and a new €21 million footbridge, the **Passerelle Simone de Beauvoir**, now spans the Seine between the Bibliothèque Nationale and the Parc de Bercy in a futuristic double-ribbon design. Built by the Eiffel company – a descendant of the original – it had an early case of the wobbles but is now an exciting (and now stable) addition to Paris's fine roster of bridges.

The most recent development is the northernmost of all: the former warehouses on the Quai d'Austerlitz are currently being transformed into **Docks en Seine**, a fashion, shopping and entertainment space. The structure will be typical of current trends, with lots of glass and open space, including a piazza and a "vegetalized" terrace on the top, which is expected to house restaurants and bars. A projected fashion institute inside is still on the drawing board. Heading upstream, a new swimming pool, the **Piscine Josephine Baker**, actually floats in the Seine between the Pont de Bercy and the Passerelle Simone de Beauvoir. Upstream of the new footbridge come two unusual **barges** which have made the area a nightlife attraction in its own right. The ex-lighthouse boat called *Batofar* (see p.360), and the Chinese barge *La Guinguette Pirate*, in particular, are excellent venues for a gig or a night's low-key clubbing. And just west of the library, near métro Chevaleret, a few small but cutting-edge art galleries are now well settled on **rue Louise Weiss** and round the corner on rue Chevaleret.

South of Mitterrand's library, the brash new apartments and offices gradually fade out into busy building sites towards the *périphérique*. Only a handful of landmark industrial buildings survive. Immediately south of rue Tolbiac, the giant, decaying warehouse of **Les Frigos** was once used for cold-storage of meat and fish destined for Les Halles, but was taken over immediately after the market's closure by artists and musicians and has been run as an anarchic studio space ever since, with open-door exhibitions once or twice a year, a bar/restaurant for the artists and an on-site gallery. The site's recent purchase by the city of Paris is supposed to guarantee its future in the face of the brave new commercial world that now hems it in.

South again, the massive **Grands Moulins de Paris** and Halle aux Farines have been ambitiously rebuilt for the University Denis Diderot, aka "Paris 7", which has flown from its cramped, decrepit old site in the Quartier Latin (see p.138). Just short of the *périphérique*, another early twentieth-century industrial-era site, the handsomely arched **SUDAC** compressed-air building, is now the home of a new school of architecture.

11

Montmartre and northern Paris

Stacked on its hilltop in the northern part of Paris, **Montmartre** sets itself apart from the city at its feet. Its chief landmark, visible from all over the city, is the all-white church of **Sacré-Coeur**, crowning the Butte as if an overenthusiastic pâtissier had run riot with an icing gun. The slopes below preserve something of the spirit of the little village that once basked here, but unlike most villages Montmartre has a very diverse and dynamic population, by turns lefty, trendy, arty and sleazy. Some of the city's hippest and most individualistic clothes shops, cafés and restaurants are hidden away in the streets around **Abbesses** métro, a quartier within a quartier that seems to become more fashionable every year.

Between Montmartre and the Grands Boulevards, which define the edge of the city centre proper, stretch the twin arrondissements of the 9e (neuvième) and 10e (dixième). While both were born in the same nineteenth-century era, and their architecture and almost total lack of green space make them look superficially quite similar, in other ways they couldn't be more different; where the 9e arrondissement is largely genteel and well groomed, the 10e is rough, boisterous and shabby. In the heart of the 9e you'll find some exceptionally graceful architecture, especially around **place St-Georges**, as well as two beguiling museums devoted to the nineteenth-century artistic heyday, the **Musée Moreau** and **Musée de la Vie Romantique**. In keeping with its period mores, however, the 9e also has a darker side. The area around **Pigalle**, along the northern fringe of the arrondissement just below the Butte Montmartre, is famous for its cabarets and sex shows.

As for the 10e, while many visitors arrive there – at the **Gare du Nord**, one of the two northern stations that dominate the quarter – few stay long. There are one or two low-key sights, such as the **Portes St-Martin and St-Denis**, standing sentinel at the foot of the faubourgs, but otherwise the main attractions are two beautiful nineteenth-century brasseries, *Flo* and *Julien*, and a lively immigrant quarter that is slowly being infiltrated by waves of what Parisians call "bourgeois-bohemians", or *bobos*.

The far **north** of the city has less still to offer the visitor. East of Montmartre, you could explore the poor, largely African **Goutte d'Or** quartier. Alternatively, you could enjoy the cafés and restaurants of pleasantly bourgeois **Batignolles**, just west of Montmartre. Just outside the official city limits, beyond the so-called "plain of Montmartre", sprawls the **St-Ouen market**, a segregated empire of antiques and curios.

Montmartre

In spite of being one of the city's chief tourist attractions, **Montmartre** retains something of the quiet, almost secretive, air of its rural origins. Incorporated into the city only in the mid-nineteenth century, its population was swollen by the poor communities displaced by Haussmann's rebuilding programme. Its heyday was from the last years of the century to World War I, when its rustic charms and low rents attracted crowds of artists. Since then, the quartier's physical appearance has changed little, thanks largely to the warren of **plaster-of-Paris quarries** that perforate its bowels and render the ground too unstable for new building. Tiny squares still give way to sudden vistas south over the rooftops of central Paris, and the occasional studio window is a tangible reminder of Montmartre's illustrious artistic past.

In the second half of the twentieth century, the Butte, along with Pigalle at its foot (see p.200), slumped into a sleazy half-life of porn shows and semi-genteel poverty, but both neighbourhoods have undergone a radical makeover in recent years. The boom in property prices has brought wholesale gentrification of formerly crumbling apartment blocks, fashionable nightspots have driven out the sex shows, and moneyed *bobos* have replaced artists, transvestites and prostitutes. The heart of the action is around **Abbesses** métro, extending right down to Pigalle, with **rue des Martyrs** as the chief artery of cool. Local regulations are currently being adjusted to allow Sunday trading, as part of the creation of a "tourist zone" that it's hoped will rival the Marais. If it's successful, expect crowds of fashionable Sunday brunches and browsers – Parisians as much as tourists – and don't visit on a dead Monday. Non-local cars are already banned from the Butte all day on Sunday (8am–6.30pm).

Most visitors make straight for the landmark church of **Sacré-Coeur** via the steps or funicular railway (covered by ordinary métro tickets) immediately below. But for a less touristy approach, head up via place des Abbesses, currently one of the liveliest areas in the city, full of trendy **clothes shops** (see box on p.386) and bijou cafés and restaurants.

Abbesses

You could almost be persuaded that pretty, tree-shaded **Place des Abbesses** was a village square – if it weren't for its centrepiece, one of Guimard's rare, canopied Art Nouveau métro entrances (there are only two others in the city – see box, p.174). The métro canopy isn't in fact an authentic Abbesses sight, as it was transferred from the Hôtel de Ville, complete with its glass porch,

Montmartrobus

The diminutive size of the **Montmartrobus** is designed to help it negotiate the twisting streets of the Butte, but its eccentric shape and determinedly ecological electric engine also make it fit right in with the quartier's spirit. If you don't want to walk, taking this bus is probably the best way of doing a Montmartre tour, and certainly the cheapest, as normal métro/bus tickets are valid. Starting at place Pigalle, the route heads up rue des Martyrs and west along rue des Abbesses, then follows the curve of rue Lepic to rue des Saules and rue Caulaincourt. On the return leg it heads down rue Lamarck past Sacré-Coeur and the *funiculaire*, before heading back to Pigalle via Abbesses and rue Houdon.

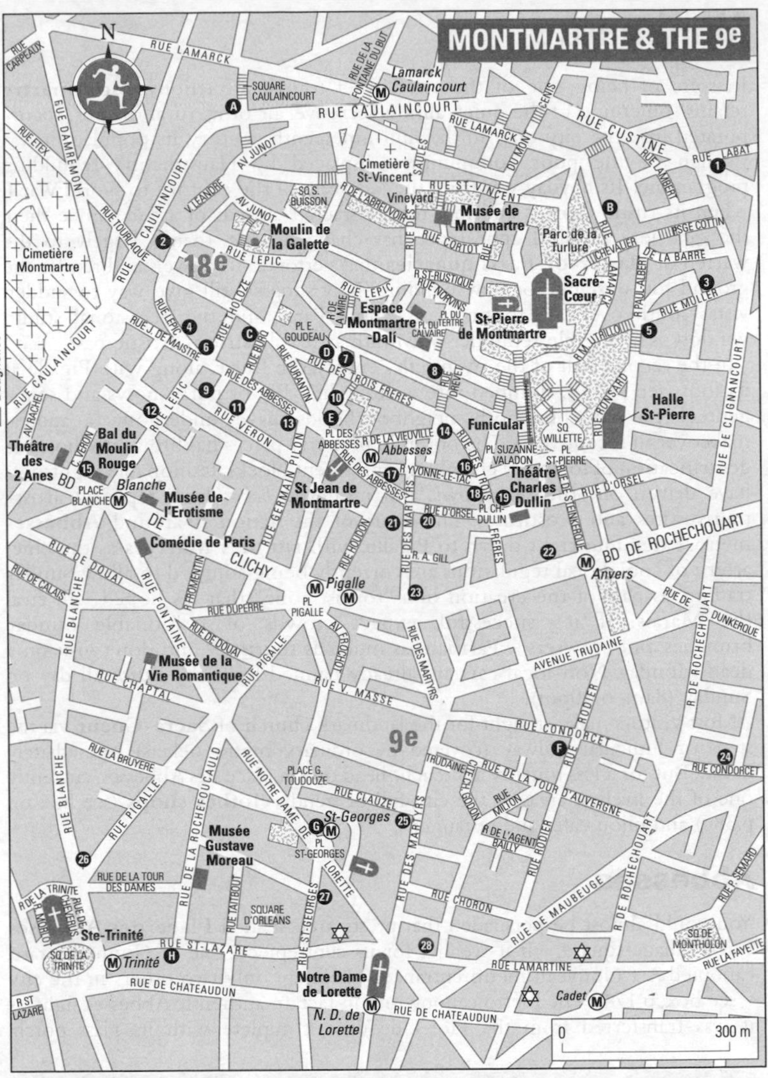

ACCOMMODATION

Hôtel Bonséjour Montmartre	C	Ermitage	B	Lorette Opéra	G	Hôtel Regyns Montmartre	E
Hôtel Caulaincourt Square	A	Hôtel Langlois	H	Perfect Hotel	F	Timhotel Montmartre	D

RESTAURANTS

Le XVIIIème Barathym	3
L'Alsaco	24
Le Bistro des Deux-Théâtres	26
Casa Olympe	27
L'Entracte	19
Au Grain de Folie	14
Haynes	25
L'Homme Tranquille	21
Kokolion	20
Le Mono	9
A la Pomponnette	6
Au Refuge des Fondus	16
Le Relais Gascon	17
Le Restaurant	11
Velly	28
Au Virage Lepic	2

CAFÉS & WINE BARS

Le Bar du Relais	7
Café des Deux Moulins	12
L'Eté en Pente Douce	5
La Fourmi Café	23
Aux Négociants	1
Le Progrès	18
Le Sancerre	13
Un Zèbre a Montmartre	4

BARS & CLUBS

Le Bar du Relais	7
Chez Camille	10
Elysée Montmartre	22
La Fourmi Café	23
La Loco	15
Au Rendez-Vous des Amis	8

tendril-like railings and obscene-looking lanterns – but it looks perfectly at home here in the square.

For **shopping** and **eating**, the area around Abbesses is one of the most satisfying in Paris, though note that most places are closed on Mondays. A few peeling, shuttered-up old shops and the odd unreconstructed workers' café survive from the old Montmartre, but these days most have been turned into restaurants or jazzy little boutiques. Still, the unusual number of high-quality, artisan boulangeries is proof that the quarter has held on to its residential roots – you'll find three on rue des Abbesses alone, and two more on rue Caulaincourt. Some of the best addresses are listed in the Shopping chapter (see p.398), but you can let your eye for fashion guide you round rue de Martyrs, rue des Trois Frères, rue de la Vieuville, rue Houdon and rue Durantin. Heading west from the métro, **rue des Abbesses** is best for cafés, especially the popular suntrap of *Le Sancerre* (see p.343).

On the downhill side of place des Abbesses, the red-brick church of **St-Jean de Montmartre** is well worth putting your nose inside for its radical construction, dating from the early 1900s. The incredibly slender pillars and broad vaulting were only made possible by the experimental use of reinforced concrete, a material that was, as the church's architect Anatole de Baudot claimed, both the bones and the skin.

East from the *place*, at the Chapelle des Auxiliatrices in rue Yvonne-Le-Tac, Ignatius Loyola founded the **Jesuit** movement in 1534. This is also supposed to be the spot where **St Denis**, the first Bishop of Paris, had his head chopped off by the Romans around 250 AD. He's said to have carried it until he dropped, on the site of the cathedral of St-Denis (see p.261). One block south, rue d'Orsel makes the transition from chichi Montmartre to cheap Barbès, with trendy clothes shops at its top end, near Abbesses, and cheap fabric shops at the bottom. Towards its western end is the picturesque **place Charles Dullin**, centred on the small Théâtre de l'Atelier (Ⓣ01.46.06.49.24, Ⓦwww.theatre-atelier.com), where the great mime Jean-Louis Barrault – the inimitable Baptiste in *Les Enfants du Paradis* – made his debut.

The Butte

At 130m, the "Mound", or **Butte Montmartre**, is the highest point in Paris. The various theories as to the origin of its name all have a Roman connection: it could be a corruption of *Mons Martyrum* – "the Martyrs' hill", the martyrs being St Denis and his companions; on the other hand, it might have been named *Mons Mercurii*, in honour of a Roman shrine to Mercury; or possibly *Mons Martis*, after a shrine to Mars.

If you're in any doubt about finding your way **up the Butte**, just keep heading uphill – the area is so charming that there's no such thing as a wrong turn. Still, two of the quietest and most attractive paths begin at place des Abbesses. You can climb **rue de la Vieuville** and the stairs in rue Drevet to the minuscule **place du Calvaire**, which has a lovely view back over the city; alternatively, go up rue Durantin, then right on rue Tholozé and right again on rue Lepic into rue des Norvins. Along rue Lepic, you'll pass the **Moulin de la Galette**, a lone survivor of Montmartre's forty-odd windmills whose famous dances were immortalized by Renoir in his *Bal du Moulin de la Galette*, now hanging in the Musée d'Orsay.

Rue Poulbot, at the beginning of rue des Norvins, leads round to the underground **Espace Montmartre-Salvador Dal'**, at no. 9–11 (daily 10am–6pm; €10; Ⓦwww.daliparis.com; M° Abbesses). With its giant souvenir shop and

Wallace's fountains

After the Prussian siege and the bloody fighting of the Commune (see box opposite), Paris was physically and emotionally scarred, and badly in need of succour. In 1872, a wealthy British resident of the city called Richard Wallace came up with the perfect symbol of renewal. He gave the city fifty cast-iron drinking fountains, each topped with a kind of miniature temple designed by the sculptor Charles-Auguste Lebourg, its roof supported by four caryatids representing Simplicity, Temperance, Charity and Goodness. More fountains were added in later years, and today some 65 still stand in the city. Painted in lustrous green, their usefulness is limited these days by the loss of the cups once permanently attached to them. All the same, *les fontaines wallace* remain quintessential symbols of Paris. (Curiously, the fountains have an unusual status in the French language, too, being one of few French words to begin with "w"; like *le whisky*, *le weekend* and *le walkman*, they are a treasured import.)

collection of limited-edition sculptures and etchings, many created towards the end of the artist's life when he was quite frankly cashing in, this museum lives up to the anagram that André Breton made of Dal"s name: Avida Dollars.

Artistic and literary associations abound hereabouts. Zola, Berlioz, Turgenev, Seurat, Degas and Van Gogh lived in the area, while in 1904 Picasso took up a studio in an old piano factory known as the **Bateau-Lavoir**, on the tiny place Emile-Goudeau. He stayed for the best part of a decade, painting *Les Demoiselles d'Avignon* and sharing loves, quarrels and opium trips with Braque, Juan Gris, Modigliani, Max Jacob, Apollinaire and others both famous and obscure. It was on the place Emile-Goudeau that he had his first encounter with the beautiful Fernande Olivier, thrusting a kitten into her hand as she passed by. "I laughed," she said, "and he took me to see his studio." Fernande became his model and lover. Although the original building burnt down some years ago, the modern reconstruction still provides studio space for artists, and you wouldn't notice any change on the square itself. Even the graceful **Wallace fountain** (see box above) is still in place.

The winding contours of **rue Lepic**, at the western side of the Butte, recall the lane that once served the plaster quarry wagons. A resolutely ordinary food market occupies the lower part of the street, but once above rue des Abbesses it becomes progressively more tranquil and elegant. Round the corner, above rue Tourlaque, a flight of steps sneaks between gardens to avenue Junot and the secluded and exclusive cul-de-sac **Villa Léandre**, just round to the left. To the right, the Cubist house of Dadaist poet Tristan Tzara stands on the corner of another exclusive enclave of houses and gardens, the **Hameau des Artistes**. Higher up the street the square Suzanne-Buisson provides a gentle haven, with a sunken boules pitch overlooked by a statue of St Denis clutching his head to his breast.

Place du Tertre and Sacré-Coeur

The core of old Montmartre, **place du Tertre**, would be incredibly pretty if it hadn't so completely fallen victim to its own fame. Today, it's jammed with tour groups, souvenir stalls and street artists knocking up lurid oils of Paris landmarks from memory. Even the famous trees – planted here in the seventeenth century – aren't authentic; after surviving numerous attempts to remove them, no fewer than seventeen trees were cut down overnight in November 1991 – apparently on the grounds that they were diseased. The new trees planted in their stead are flourishing, but it'll take more than this to give the *place* its heart back.

If you want to seek sanctuary from the commercial hustle, head for the **church of St-Pierre**, between place du Tertre and the Sacré-Coeur, which rivals St-Germain-des-Prés for the title of oldest church in Paris. It once served a Benedictine convent which occupied the Butte Montmartre from the twelfth century onwards, and though much altered, with modern stained glass throughout, it still retains its Romanesque and early Gothic structures. More ancient still are four columns inside the church, two by the west door and two in the choir; they probably date from a Roman shrine that stood on the hill, though their capitals were carved in Merovingian times.

Crowning the Butte is the **Sacré-Coeur** (daily 6.45am–10.30pm; free; M° Abbesses/Anvers), a weird confection of French and Byzantine architecture whose pimply tower and white ice-cream dome has somehow become an essential part of the Paris skyline – Parisian poet Jacques Roubaud has compared it to a big baby's bottle for the angels to suck. Construction was started in the 1870s on the initiative of the Catholic Church to atone for the "crimes" of the Commune (see box below). The thwarted opposition, which included

The Paris Commune

In March 1871, **Montmartre** saw the first sparks fly in what would become the great conflagration of the **Paris Commune**. After Napoléon III's disastrous campaign against the Prussians in the summer of 1870, and the declaration of the Third Republic in September of the same year, Paris finally fell to the Prussian army on January 28, 1871, after a four-month siege. Peace terms were agreed by the end of February, and the Prussians withdrew, leaving the new Republic in the hands of a shaky conservative administration. Paris's situation was least secure of all, as the city's workers – and their armed representatives in the National Guard – had been disenfranchised by the February settlement, and were not inclined to respect it. The new Prime Minister, Adolphe Thiers, dispatched a body of regular troops under General Lecomte to take possession of 170 guns which the National Guard controlled on the high ground of the Butte Montmartre. Although the troops seized the guns easily in the darkness before dawn, they had failed to bring any horses to tow them away. That gave the revolutionary Louise Michel time to raise the alarm.

An angry crowd of workers and National Guard members quickly gathered. They persuaded the troops to take no action and arrested General Lecomte, along with another general, Clément Thomas, who was notorious for the part he had played in the brutal repression of the 1848 republican uprising. The two generals were shot and mutilated in the garden of no. 36 rue du Chevalier-de-la-Barre, behind the Sacré-Coeur. Across the city, soldiers and National Guard members joined the rebellion, and, by the following morning, a panicking government had decamped to Versailles, leaving the Hôtel de Ville and the whole of the city in the hands of the National Guard. The rebels quickly proclaimed a revolutionary Commune, decreeing the separation of church and state, the enfranchisement of women and numerous measures to protect workers' rights.

By the beginning of April, the Communards were under attack from Thiers' army, its numbers newly swelled by prisoners of war helpfully released by the Prussians. Isolated and ill-equipped, they didn't stand a chance. In the notorious *semaine sanglante*, of May 21–28, something like 25,000 Communards died – no-one knows the exact figure – with some 10,000 executed or deported. The cost to Paris was also severe; the Hôtel de Ville and Tuileries palace (see p.60) were reduced to smouldering ashes. Today the Communards are commemorated in Père Lachaise cemetery (see p.238), and in the continuing fervour of the French Left; since 1871, not to be revolutionary has somehow seemed a betrayal of the dead.

△ Sacré-Coeur, Montmartre

Clemenceau, eventually got its revenge by naming the space at the foot of the monumental staircase **square Willette**, after the local artist who turned out on inauguration day to shout "Long live the devil!" The interior is more neo-Byzantine nonsense, and apart from its carillon of bells – the largest bell in France, at 19 tonnes, swings here – the only exciting thing about the Sacré-Coeur is the **view from the top** (daily: April–Sept 9am–7pm; Oct–March 9am–6pm; €4.50). It's almost as high as the Eiffel Tower, and you can see the layout of the whole city – a wide, flat basin ringed by low hills, with stands of high-rise blocks in the southeastern corner, on the heights of Belleville, and at

La Défense in the west. The tall tower block in the middle of the city is the Tour Montparnasse and beyond, in the hazy distance, are the high, flat faces of southern suburban *cités*.

The northern side of the Butte

Rue des Saules tips steeply down the north side of the Butte past the terraces of the tiny **Montmartre vineyard**, which is lovingly tended by an association of local grandees. The annual harvest in mid-September yields an extraordinary 1500kg of grapes, producing in the region of 1500 bottles of Clos du Montmartre wine. It's a pretty rough beverage, yet few wine buffs would be hard-hearted enough to resist having at least a bottle in the cellar. A small festival celebrates the *vendange* on the first weekend of October. The picturesque house standing opposite the lowest corner of the vineyard is the cabaret club **Au Lapin Agile** (ⓦ www.au-lapin-agile.com), made famous by the Montmartre artists who drank there in the 1900s – among them Picasso, whose fifty-million-dollar self-portrait as a harlequin is set inside. The "nimble rabbit" is still alive today and still serving up classic French chanson, though age has made it somewhat less sprightly and given it a distinctly nostalgic mind-set.

To the right, **rue Cortot** cuts through to the water tower, whose distinctive, white, lighthouse-like form is one of the landmarks of the city's skyline, together with the Sacré-Coeur.

The elegant old house at 12 rue Cortot is particularly rich in artistic associations, having been home, at various times, to Auguste Renoir, Raoul Dufy, and Suzanne Valadon and her troubled son Maurice Utrillo. It's now the **Musée de Montmartre** (Wed–Sun 11am–6pm; €7; ⓦ www.museedemontmartre.fr; M° Lamarck-Caulaincourt), whose low-key exhibits attempt to re-create the atmosphere of Montmartre's heyday via a selection of Toulouse-Lautrec posters, mock-ups of various period rooms – including a bar complete with original *zinc*, or pewter top – and painted impressions of how the Butte once looked. It's not terribly gripping, but the museum does offer a magnificent view from the back over the hilly northern reaches of the city and the vineyard, and the shop usually has a few bottles of Montmartre wine.

Berlioz lived with his English wife in the corner house on the steps of rue du Mont-Cenis, from where there's a breathtaking view northwards along the canyon of the steps, as well as back up towards place du Calvaire. The steps are perfect sepia-romantic Montmartre – a double handrail runs down the centre, with the lampposts between – and the streets below are among the quietest and least touristy in Montmartre.

The Halle St-Pierre

To the south and east of the Sacré-Coeur, the slopes of the Butte drop steeply down towards boulevard Barbès and the Goutte d'Or quarter (see p.205). Directly below are the gardens of square Willette, milling with tourists. To avoid the crowds, make instead for the quiet gardens to the north of the Sacré-Coeur, the **Parc de la Turlure**, or head down the steeply stepped rue Utrillo, turning right at the pleasant café, *L'Eté en Pente Douce* (see p.342), which has outdoor tables on the corner of rue Paul Albert. From here, more steps lead down along the edge of the gardens to rue Ronsard, where you can see the (sealed) entrances to the quarries where the original plaster of Paris was extracted.

The circular **Halle St-Pierre** (daily 10am–6pm; €7; ⓦ www.hallesaintpierre.org; M° Anvers), at the bottom of rue Ronsard, was once a market building but is now an exhibition space dedicated to Art Brut, or works by artists – often autodidacts – that mainstream galleries won't touch. The biannual exhibitions encompass anything from naïve paintings to sci-fi sculptures. The diet is usually visionary and alternative, often fascinating and sometimes indigestible; a recent exhibitor was H.R. Giger, the artist behind the film *Alien*, for example. On the ground floor is a selection of works by young, semi-professional artists that changes every fortnight. The Halle is energetically run by a charitable association, with evening concerts (mostly classical, mostly on Thursdays), kids' workshops, book readings and a café with good cakes and teas.

Montmartre cemetery

West of the Butte, near the beginning of rue Caulaincourt in place Clichy, lies the **Montmartre cemetery** (March 16–Nov 5 Mon–Fri 8am–6pm, Sat from 8.30am, Sun from 9am; Nov 6–March 15 closes 5.30pm; M° Blanche/Place-de-Clichy). Tucked down below street level in the hollow of an old quarry, it's a tangle of trees and funerary pomposity, more intimate and less melancholy than Père-Lachaise or Montparnasse. The entrance is on avenue Rachel, underneath the bridge section of rue Caulaincourt. A few metres inside the gates, watch out for the antique cast-iron poor-box (*Tronc pour les Pauvres*).

The illustrious dead at rest here include Stendhal, Berlioz, Degas, Feydeau, Offenbach, Nijinsky and François Truffaut, as well as La Goulue, the dancer at the Moulin Rouge immortalized by Toulouse-Lautrec. In division 15, left of the entrance, lies Alphonsine Plessis, the real-life model for the consumptive courtesan Marguerite, the "Dame aux Camélias" of Alexander Dumas' novel and, later, the original "Traviata". Liszt, who became her lover after Dumas, called her "the most absolute incarnation of Woman who has ever existed". Dumas lies on the other side of the cemetery, in division 21. Beside the roundabout, near the entrance, is the grave of another great writer, Emile Zola, though his remains have been transferred to the Panthéon (see p.133). There's also a large Jewish section by the east wall.

The 9e

Immediately south of Montmartre, the **9e** (neuvième) **arrondissement** is rarely visited. It's as if the broad and busy east–west roads that frame it – seedy and shabby on the northern fringe around **Pigalle**, handsome and expensive to the south, around the Opéra – form an invisible barricade. Lurking inside these limits, however, is a handsome, distinctly urban residential district with a powerful nineteenth-century atmosphere, especially around **place St-Georges**, and some excellent theatres and restaurants. The southernmost strip of the arrondissement, next to the Opéra and Grands Boulevards, is covered in Chapter 4 (see p.87).

Blanche and Pigalle

From place de Clichy in the west to Barbès-Rochechouart in the east, the hill of Montmartre is underlined by the sleazy **boulevards de Clichy** and **de Rochechouart**. The pedestrianized centre of the boulevards was occupied by dodgem cars and other tacky sideshows for most of the twentieth century, but Montmartre's upward mobility seems to be dragging its shabby hem along with it. The traffic-choked roads have now been "civilized", as the Paris planners put it, with bus and cycle lanes, and lots more greenery. It remains to be seen whether or not they will be recolonized by the sophisticated strollers, or *flâneurs*, that defined them in the late nineteenth century. At the eastern **Barbès** end, where the métro clatters by on iron trestles, the crowds teem round the Tati department store, the cheapest in the city, while the pavements are thick with Arab and African street vendors hawking watches, trinkets and textiles.

At the **place de Clichy** end, tour buses from all over Europe feed their contents into massive hotels. In the middle, between **place Blanche** and **place Pigalle**, sex shows, sex shops and prostitutes – male and female – vie for the custom of *solitaires* and couples alike. It's an area in which respectability and sleaze rub very close shoulders. One of the city's most elegant *villas* (private streets), **avenue Frochot**, leads off place Pigalle itself. In the adjacent streets – rues de Douai, Victor-Massé and Houdon – specialist music and hi-fi shops jostle with exploitative "hostess" bars.

Perfectly placed amongst all the sex shops and shows is the **Musée de l'Erotisme** at 72 boulevard de Clichy (daily 10am–2am; €8; Ⓦ www.musee-erotisme.com; M° Blanche), testament to its owner's fascination with sex as expressed in folk art. The ground floor and first floor are awash with model phalluses, fertility symbols and intertwined figurines from all over Asia, Africa and pre-Columbian Latin America. The European pieces tend to the satirical or plain smutty, with lots of naughty nuns and priests caught in compromising situations. The rest of the floors upstairs are devoted to intriguing temporary exhibitions. A few steps west, the photogenic **Moulin Rouge** still thrives on place Blanche. Once Toulouse-Lautrec's inspiration, it's now a mere shadow of its former self (see box below).

Pigalle cabarets

For many foreigners, entertainment in Paris is still synonymous with cabaret, especially that mythical name, Pigalle's **Moulin Rouge**, at 82 boulevard de Clichy (Ⓣ 01.53.09.82.82, Ⓦ www.moulinrouge.fr). Unlike the **Folies Bergère**, further south at 32 rue Richer (Ⓣ 08.92.68.16.50, Ⓦ www.foliesbergere.com), which has gone for a relatively mixed programme of musicians, belly-dancers and circus acts, the Moulin Rouge still trades on its traditional, bare-breasted, can-canning "Doriss Girls", although the accompanying sound-and-light show is very flashy these days. The evening is a very expensive one at around €90, or €150 with dinner, but the show is as glitzy as you'd expect, full of special effects and nodding feathers. For similar alternatives, try the **Lido** (116bis av des Champs-Elysées, 8e, Ⓣ 01.40.76.56.10, Ⓦ www.lido.fr), best known for its "Bluebell Girls" and high-excitement, high-tech, Vegas-style shows; or the **Crazy Horse** (12 av George V, 8e, Ⓣ 01.47.23.32.32, Ⓦ www.lecrazyhorseparis.com), where the performances are relatively arty and theatrical – and totally nude.

Audiences are mainly made up of package tourists whose deal includes a ticket. To get away from the crowds, as long as you don't mind roughing it, you could visit one of the pair of tiny **transvestite cabarets** on rue des Martyrs, just up from Pigalle métro. At its best, *Chez Michou*, at no. 80 (Ⓣ 01.46.06.10.04, Ⓦ www.michou.fr; show-only €35), is like a scene from an Almodóvar film, with transvestites masquerading as various female celebrities, singing classic songs and teasing the audience, but you'll need to know French pop culture very well to get much out of it. The similar *Chez Madame Arthur*, at 75bis (Ⓣ 01.42.54.40.21; €47–91 with dinner), has a historic pedigree, but you're obliged to have a poor-value dinner beforehand. Both can be outrageously camp good fun, or rather desperate on a quiet night, and your bill is likely to be much larger than you might expect.

Around St-Georges

The heart of the 9e arrondissement was first developed in the early nineteenth century as a fashionable suburb. It was soon dubbed the **Nouvelle Athènes**, or New Athens, after the Romantic artists and writers who came to live here made it the centre of a minor artistic boom. The handsome centrepiece of the quartier is the circular **place St-Georges**. At its centre, the fountain – still with its horse trough – is topped by a bust of Paul Gavarni, a nineteenth-century cartoonist who made a speciality of lampooning the mistresses that were *de rigueur* for bourgeois males of the time. This was the mistresses' quarter – they were known as *lorettes*, after the nearby church of **Notre-Dame de Lorette**, built in the 1820s in the Neoclassical style. On the east side of place St-Georges, the **Hôtel de la Païva** was built in the 1840s in an extravagant French Renaissance style for Thérèse Lachman, a famous Second Empire courtesan who married a Marquis. On the west side, the **Hôtel Thiers** was destroyed by the Communards in 1871 but quickly rebuilt; it now houses the Dosne-Thiers foundation, with a huge library specializing in nineteenth-century French history.

In the immediate vicinity of the square, **place Toudouze** and **rues Clauzel**, **Milton** and **Rodier** are worth wandering along for their elegantly ornamented facades. A short distance southwest of St-Georges, the serene **square d'Orléans** is an 1829 development that aped the designs of Regency London. The project was a great success, attracting Chopin, Alexandre Dumas *fils* and George Sand as early residents. Some of the *hôtels*, or fine town houses, of the original Nouvelle Athènes scheme can still be spotted just to the west, along the south side of **rue de la Tour des Dames**.

Rue St-Lazare is a welcome swathe of activity amid the residential calm, winding its way towards the Gare St-Lazare, passing the bulbous church of **La Sainte-Trinité**, whose single, over-size French Renaissance-style tower is its most exciting feature. Inside, the vast space under the barrel vault feels cold and sterile – hard to imagine that the deeply spiritual composer Oliver Messiaen was organist here for the best part of half a century.

Musée de la Vie Romantique and Musée Moreau

To get the full flavour of the neuvième's nineteenth-century heyday, make for the **Musée de la Vie Romantique**, at 16 rue Chaptal (daily except Mon 10am–6pm, closed public hols; €9 during exhibitions, otherwise free; M° St-Georges/Blanche/Pigalle), which sets out to evoke the Romantic period in what was once the painter Ary Scheffer's house. The shuttered building is a delightful surprise, facing onto a cobbled courtyard at the end of a private alley, while the interior preserves the rich colours of a typical bourgeois home of the nineteenth century. George Sand used to visit here, and the ground floor consists mainly of bits and pieces associated with her, including jewels, locks of hair and a cast of her lover Chopin's surprisingly small hand. Scheffer was art tutor to Louis-Philippe's children, and upstairs are a number of his hideously sentimental aristocratic portraits.

A short way south down rue de la Rochefoucauld, you'll find the curious and little-visited **Musée Moreau** (daily except Tues 10am–12.45pm & 2–5.15pm; €5; Ⓦwww.musee-moreau.fr; M° St-Georges/Blanche/Pigalle), dedicated to the fantastical Symbolist paintings of **Gustave Moreau**. The museum's design was conceived by Moreau himself, to be carved out of the house he shared with his parents for many years; you can visit their tiny, stuffy apartment rooms, crammed with furniture and trinkets. The paintings get more room – two huge, studio-like spaces connected by a beautiful spiral staircase – but the effect is no less cluttered. Moreau's canvases hang cheek-by-jowl, every surface crawling with figures and decorative swirls – literally crawling in the case of *The Daughters of Thespius* – or alive with deep colours and provocative symbolism, as in the museum's *pièce de résistance*, *Jupiter and Sémèle*. For all the rampantly decadent symbolism, some viewers haven't been quite convinced. Degas, for one, commented that Moreau was "a hermit who knows the train timetable".

The 10e and the Goutte d'Or

The rue du Faubourg Poissonnière separates the 9e from its grittier twin, the 10e (dixième) **arrondissement**. At its upper end the **northern stations** dominate, while to the south lies the gritty but fascinating quarter of the **faubourgs St-Denis** and **St-Martin**. In the far north, just inside the 18e, east of Montmartre, lies the African quarter of the **Goutte d'Or**. The prettier eastern end of the arrondissement, on the far side of the Canal St-Martin, is covered in Chapter 13 (see p.222).

The northern stations

The life of the 10e is coloured by the presence of the big **northern stations**. Most travellers scarcely give them a glance, intent on hurrying off to more salubrious parts of the city, but the station buildings are in fact very beautiful, closer to Classical orangeries in style than icons of the industrial age. The **Gare du Nord** (serving all places north, including the high-speed train lines to Germany and London) was built by the architect Hittorff in the early 1860s, and is aggressively dominated by its three giant arches, crowned by eight statues representing the original terminus towns, from Amsterdam and Berlin to Vienna and Warsaw. Facing the boulevard de Strasbourg, the slightly earlier **Gare de l'Est** (serving northeastern and eastern France and Eastern Europe) is more delicate, though when its central arch was open to the elements, as it was when originally built, the steam and smoke billowing out would have had a powerful effect.

The area around the stations is mostly gritty and unappealing, the major traffic thoroughfares of boulevard de Magenta and boulevard de Strasbourg both noisy and dull. Beside the Gare de l'Est, however, a high wall encloses the gardens of **square Villemin** (entrance on rue des Récollets and avenue de Verdun), which provides a welcome haven in this otherwise unrelievedly stony quarter of the city. The garden once belonged to the **Couvent des Récollets**, one much-restored, seventeenth-century wing of which still stands on rue du Faubourg-St-Martin. After stints as a hospital and an architecture school, this former convent has now become a centre for cultural exchanges, housing artists and researchers working in Paris. Further east again, the **Canal St-Martin** (covered in Chapter 13, see p.222) is an even more tranquil place to escape the city hustle. Just south of the Gare de l'Est, the **church of St-Laurent** has a handsome choir dating from the fifteenth century. Thanks to Haussmann, who thought its original facade irritatingly off-centre, the church's Gothic-looking west front actually dates from the same era as the Gare du Nord.

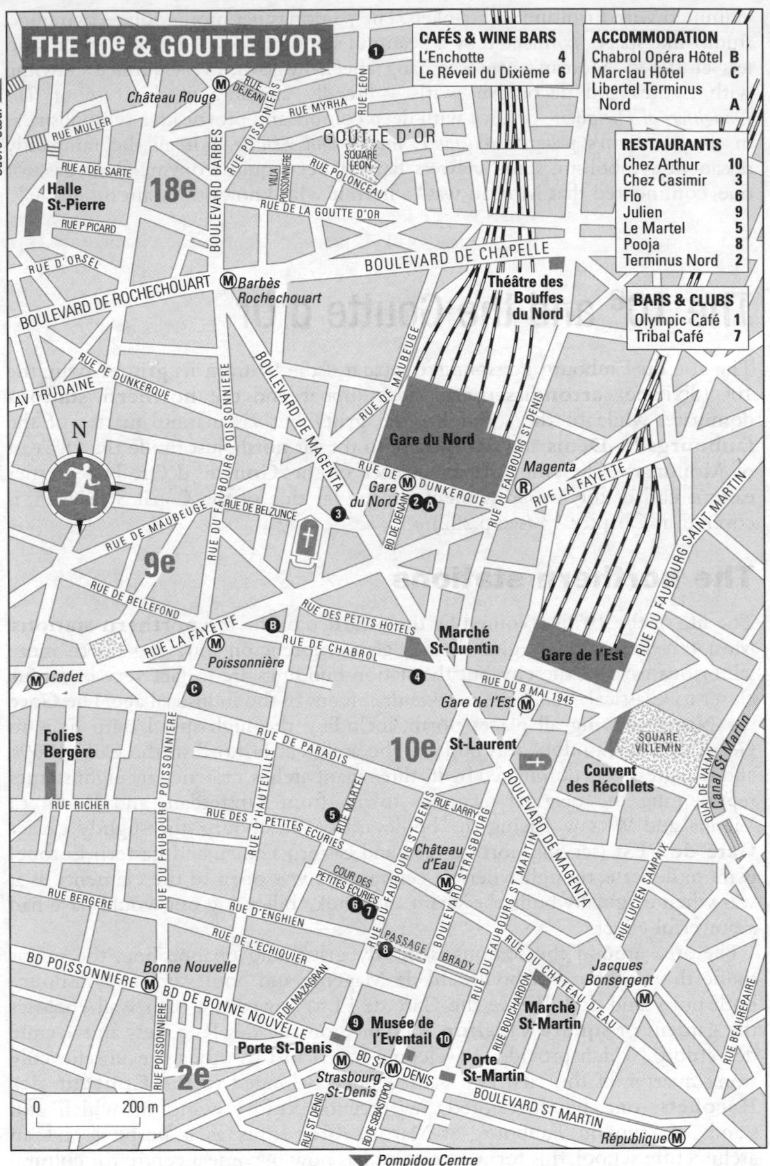

The faubourgs

The southern end of the 10^e arrondissement is its liveliest, a poor but vibrant quarter that has become home to Indian, black African, and Near Eastern communities as well as, in recent years, a small vanguard of young, trendy Parisians. The two main thoroughfares, the rue du Faubourg-St-Denis and rue du

Faubourg-St-Martin, bear the names of the **faubourgs**, or suburbs, that once stood just outside the town walls. For once, you can still get a vivid sense of the old city limits, as two triumphal arches stand at either end of the boulevard St-Denis, now looking oddly out of place in the midst of motor traffic and shop hoardings. The **Porte St-Denis** was erected in 1672 to celebrate Louis XIV's victories on the Rhine – below the giant letters spelling out Ludovico Magno, or "Louis the Great", are the bas-reliefs *The Crossing of the Rhine* (on the south side) and *The Capture of Maastricht* (on the north). With France's northern frontier secured, Louis ordered Charles V's city walls to be demolished and replaced by leafy promenades; they became known as the *boulevards* after the Germanic word for an earth rampart, a *bulwark*. Two hundred metres east, the more graceful **Porte St-Martin** was built two years after its sibling, in celebration of further victories in Limburg and Besançon. Louis planned a veritable parade of these arches, but the military adventures of the latter part of his reign, the Wars of the League of Augsburg and Spanish Succession, proved much less successful for France.

Halfway between the two arches, the **Musée de l'Eventail**, at 2 boulevard de Strasbourg (Mon–Wed 2–6pm; closed Aug; €6; M° Strasbourg-St-Denis), is a curious port of call. In a workshop and showroom dating from the end of the nineteenth century, Anne Hoguet continues the family tradition of lace fan-making, almost exclusively for customers from the worlds of haute couture or theatre. There are frequent exhibitions and displays drawing on a selection of the museum's nine hundred-strong collection of fans.

At its lower end, the **rue du Faubourg-St-Denis** is full of charcuteries, butchers, greengrocers and ethnic delicatessens, as well as a number of restaurants, including the historic **brasseries** *Julien* and *Flo* (see p.345). The latter is tucked away in an attractive old stableyard, the cour des Petites-Ecuries, one of a number of hidden lanes and covered passages that riddle this corner of the city. Probably the best known, if not the easiest to find, is the glazed-over **Passage Brady**, the hub of Paris's "Little India", lined with identikit curry houses and Indian barbers' and grocers' shops. The passage runs through to **rue du Faubourg-St-Martin**, crossing the busy boulevard de Strasbourg and coming out just south of the impressive neo-Gothic **town hall** of the 10e arrondissement.

To the west of rue du Faubourg-St-Denis, rues d'Enghien and de l'Echiquier are quieter but have several restaurants, cafés and shops serving the area's Turkish community. Rue des Petites Ecuries is known for the large jazz and world music nightclub, the *New Morning* (see p.364), while on the next street north, at 18 rue de Paradis, is the magnificent mosaic and tiled facade of Monsieur Boulanger's Choisy-le-Roi **tileworks** shop; it's closed to the general public, but you can peer through the gate and admire more exuberant ceramics featuring peacock tails and flamingos on the stairs and floors.

The Goutte d'Or

The wide, grotty boulevard de la Chapelle forms the northern boundary of the 10e arrondissement, its only beacon the gloriously delapidated **Théatre des Bouffes du Nord** (see p.205), energetically run by British director Peter Brook since 1974. Immediately north of the boulevard, the poetically named quartier of the **Goutte d'Or** stretches between boulevard Barbès and the Gare du Nord rail lines. The setting for Zola's classic novel of gritty realism, *L'Assommoir*, its name – the "Drop of Gold" – comes from a vineyard which stood here in medieval times. After World War I, when large numbers of North Africans were imported to restock the trenches, it gradually became an immigrant ghetto.

For years, the streets languished in a lamentable state of decay, but a major renovation programme has dramatically changed the area's character. While the quartier remains poor, it is home to a host of vibrant mini-communities, now predominantly – and colourfully – West African and Congolese, rather than North African, but with pockets of South Asian, Haitian, Turkish and other ethnicities as well.

On the rue de la Goutte d'Or itself, you could seek out one of the city's **Wallace fountains** (see box, p.196), on the corner with the rue de Chartres, but the main sight is a few steps north on rue Dejean, where the **Marché Dejean** (daily except Sun afternoon & Mon; M° Château-Rouge) heaves with African groceries and thrums with shoppers, including lots of women in technicolour African dress. You can pick up imported African beers and drinks and, if you're self-catering, vegetables like plantains, yams and taro roots, or packets of bamboo-leaf-wrapped manioc called *coangas*, as well as warm-water fish from barracuda to the delicious tilapia. Another, more general market takes place in the mornings twice weekly (Wed & Sat) underneath the métro viaduct on the **boulevard de la Chapelle**.

Most of the quartier's cafés and bars tend to be very local in flavour and may not appeal to outsiders, but the *Olympic Café*, a bar, café-théâtre and world music venue (see p.365), is splendidly welcoming.

Batignolles

West of Montmartre cemetery, in a district bounded by the St-Lazare train lines, marshalling yards and avenue de Clichy, lies the "village" of **Batignolles** – sufficiently conscious of its uniqueness to have formed an association for the preservation of its *caractère villageois*. Its heart is the attractive **place du Dr F. Lobligeois**, framing the elegant Neoclassical church of **Ste-Marie-des-Batignolles**. On the corners of the *place*, a handful of modern bars and restaurants attracts the young, bourgeois parents of the neighbourhood while, behind, the green **square des Batignolles** is filled with prams, pushchairs and handsome old plane trees.

The poet Verlaine was brought up on the **rue des Batignolles**, which runs southeast past the Mairie of the 17e arrondissement to the junction with **rue des Dames**. This narrow but lively thoroughfare winds its way east from the flamboyant food and clothes market of the **rue de Lévis** (daily except Mon), beside the Villiers métro stop, to the avenue de Clichy. Just below lies the traffic- and neon-filled roundabout of the **place de Clichy**, dominated by its Pathé cinema and classic old brasserie, *Wepler* (see p.321 and p.346). Northeast of Ste-Marie-des-Batignolles, the long **rue des Moines** runs past a bustling and price-conscious covered market, the **Marché des Batignolles**, into an increasingly working-class area, all small, animated, friendly shops, low apartment blocks in shades of peeling grey and modest, local bars.

The pet cemetery

Right at the frontier of the 17e, under the *périphérique*, lies the little-visited **Cimetière des Batignolles**, with the graves of André Breton, Verlaine and Blaise Cendrars (M° Porte-de-Clichy). A great deal more curious, and more lugubrious, is the **pet cemetery** (daily except Mon: mid-March to mid-Oct 10am–5.30pm, rest of year 10am–4.30pm; €3; M° Mairie-de-Clichy), on the

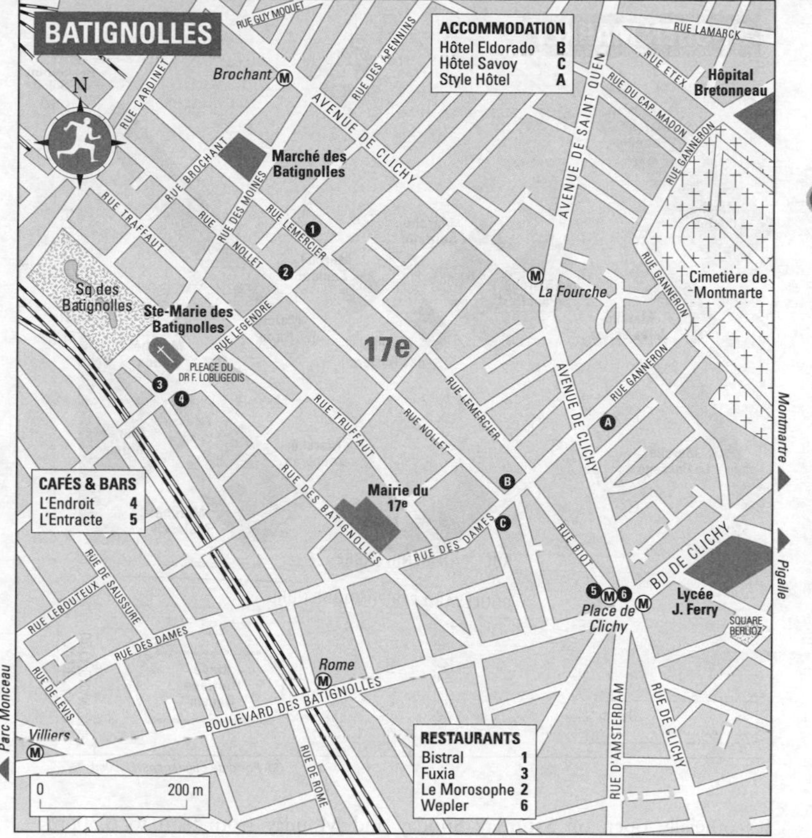

banks of the Seine at Asnières, one métro stop beyond Porte de Clichy. It's outside the city proper but accessible on the métro line 13, about fifteen minutes' walk from M° Mairie-de-Clichy along rue Martre, then left at the far end of Pont de Clichy. Privately owned, and beautifully kept, this Cimetière des Chiens occupies a tree-shaded ridgelet that was once an island in the river. Most of its tiny graves decked with plastic flowers, some going back as far as 1900, belong to dogs and cats, many with epigraphs of the kind: "To Fifi, the only consolation of my wretched existence". Among the more exotic cadavers are a Muscovite bear, a wolf, a lioness, the 1920 Grand National winner, and that Hollywood megastar of the 1920s – the German Shepherd Rin Tin Tin.

St-Ouen market

The **St-Ouen market**, sometimes called the Clignancourt market, is located just outside the northern edge of the 18e arrondissement, in the suburb of St-Ouen.

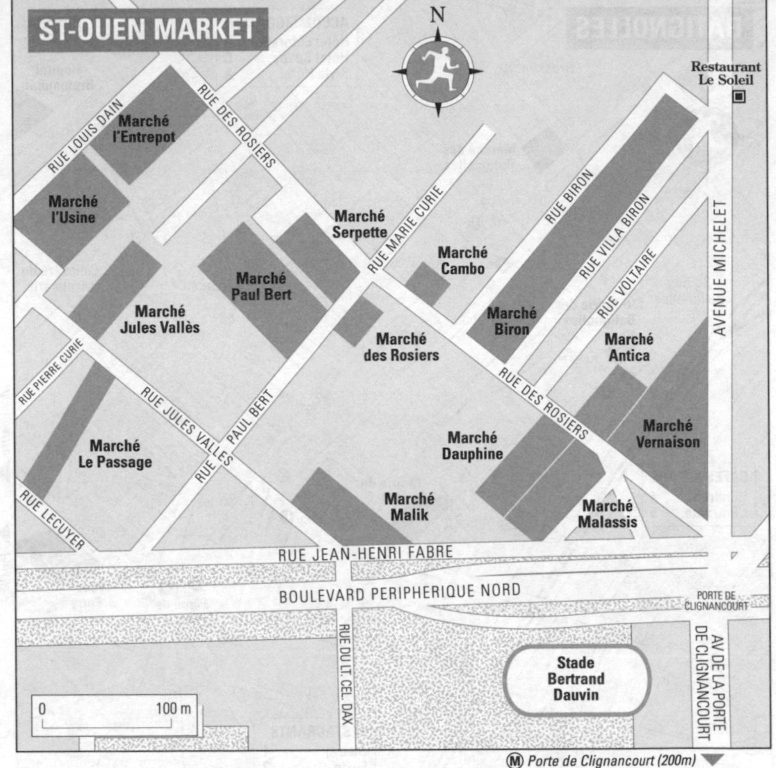

It's officially open on Saturday, Sunday and Monday from 9am to 6.30pm – although this can vary depending on the weather, and many stands are closed on Monday. Its popular name of **les puces de St-Ouen**, or the "St-Ouen flea market", dates from the days when secondhand mattresses, clothes and other infested junk was sold here in a free-for-all zone outside the city walls. Nowadays, however, it's predominantly a proper – and very expensive – **antiques** market, selling mainly furniture, but also old zinc café counters, telephones, traffic lights, posters, jukeboxes and so on.

The closest **métro stop** is Porte-de-Clignancourt (line 4), from where it's a five-minute walk up the busy avenue de la Porte-de-Clignancourt. For a slower but quieter approach, you can go to the Porte de St-Ouen stop (line 13) and walk north along the avenue de la Porte de St-Ouen, turning right after the *périphérique* flyover, and continuing along rue du Dr Babinski for about ten minutes until it meets rue Jean-Henri-Fabre.

Coming from either direction, you have to pass through the market's genuinely flea-bitten fringe before you get to the real thing. Shaded by the flyover, **rue Jean-Henri-Fabre** is the heart of this light-fingered area, lined with stalls flogging cheap jeans and leather jackets, rip-off DVDs, sunglasses, household cleaning products with inscrutable foreign labels, and African souvenirs. Watch your wallet, and don't fall for the gangs pulling the three-card monte or cup-and-hidden-ball scams.

Should hunger overtake you, there are plenty of **cafés** on rue Paul Bert and rue des Rosiers, or you could brave the rather touristy *buvette* buried at the end of Marché Vernaison's Allée 10, *Chez Louisette*. The great gypsy jazz guitarist, Django Reinhardt, sometimes played here, but these days singers belt out Parisian chansons with keyboard backing every Saturday afternoon. For a proper **restaurant** meal, book a table in advance at *Le Soleil*, 109 ave Michelet (☎01.40.10.08.08; Mon–Wed & Sun noon–2pm, Thurs–Sat noon–2.30pm & 7.30–10.30pm), where you'll pay around €30–45 a head for unfussy but excellent French cuisine.

The markets

The official complex lies just beyond rue Jean-Henri-Fabre, with over a dozen separate markets covering some two thousand shops. Most have their entrances on **rue des Rosiers**, the main thoroughfare, but a few lie on **rue Jules-Vallès**. For the chance to buy something you could feasibly carry home by yourself, restrict yourself to one of three markets. Marché **Vernaison**, the oldest in the complex, is the closest thing to a real flea market. Its maze-like, creeper-covered alleys are great fun to wander along, threading your way between stalls selling all kinds of bric-a-brac. Marché **Jules-Vallès** is smaller but similar, stuffed with books and records, vintage clothing, colonial knick-knacks and other curiosities. While you won't find any breathtaking bargains, there's plenty to titillate the eye at both. Marché **Malik** stocks mostly discount and vintage clothes and bags, as well as some high-class couturier stuff.

For casual browsing of antiques and curios, try Marché **Dauphine**, whose glazed roof shelters an eclectic mix of decorative antique furniture, vintage fashions and rare books, and Marché **Malassis**, where you'll find all kinds of little boutiques specializing in anything from maritime ephemera or jewellery to imaginatively restored eighteenth-century pieces and twentieth-century designer *objets*. For furnishings, the least expensive is Marché **Paul-Bert**, which offers furniture, china and the like, often unrestored and straight from the auction houses. **Le Passage** has lots of fine furnishings and *objets d'art*, including new pieces by contemporary designers.

The rest of the markets in the complex are seriously posh collections of antiques shops, aimed as much at professionals as at private clients. Marché **Biron** is the most luxurious of all, full of eighteenth- and nineteenth-century gilt and crystal. Marché **Antica** and Marché **Cambo** are similar, the latter with an Art Deco area on the gallery level, while Marché **des Rosiers** concentrates on top-flight late nineteenth- and early twentieth-century glass, bronzes and ornaments. Marché **Serpette** covers seriously expensive twentieth-century collectors' furnishings, especially Art Deco and Art Nouveau. **L'Entrepôt** houses large-scale antiques, from whole staircases to *boiserie* panelling and cast-iron gates. **L'Usine** is restricted to dealers only.

12

The Bastille and around

A symbol of revolution since the famous toppling of the Bastille prison in 1789, the **Bastille quarter** used to belong in spirit and in style to the working-class districts of eastern Paris. Since the construction of the new opera house in the 1980s, however, it has become a magnet for artists, fashion folk and young people who have brought with them trendy shops and an energetic nightlife, making this one of Paris's central hot spots. Much of the action takes place on **rue de Lappe**, continuing a tradition that goes back to the nineteenth century when immigrants from the Auvergne colonized this street and set up dancehalls and music clubs. Cocktail haunts and theme bars now dominate the street and the surrounding area, edging out the old tool shops, cobblers and ironmongers. Some of the working-class flavour lingers on, though, especially along **rue de la Roquette** and in the furniture workshops off **rue du Faubourg St-Antoine**, east of the Bastille, testimony to a long tradition of cabinet-making and woodworking in the district. The area was outside the city limits until the 1780s, and so, away from the restrictions of the city guilds, the Faubourg St-Antoine workers enjoyed a measure of independence and free thinking, given full expression during the 1789 Revolution.

South of the Bastille, the relatively unsung **twelfth arrondissement** offers an authentic slice of Paris, traditionally working-class and full of neighbourhood shops and bars. Much is changing here too, though, and a fashionable crowd is moving in, attracted by new developments, such as the landscaping of a large park in the **Bercy** riverside area and the conversion of the old Bercy wine warehouses into attractive cafés and shops. One of the most imaginative projects has been the creation of the **Promenade Plantée**, an ex-railway line turned into an elevated walkway, running from the Bastille right across the twelfth arrondissement to the green expanse of the **Bois de Vincennes**. Elsewhere, large pockets of the 12e remain resolutely unchanged, such as the traditional **place d'Aligre market**.

Place de la Bastille

Place de la Bastille, a vast, traffic-choked square, is indissolubly linked with the events of July 14, 1789, when the Bastille prison fortress was stormed, triggering the French Revolution and the end of feudalism in Europe. Bastille Day (July 14) is celebrated throughout France and the square is the scene of dancing and partying on the evening of July 13. The prison itself no longer stands – its only visible remains have been transported to square Henri-Galli at the end of boulevard Henri-IV. A Société Générale bank is situated on the site of the prison and the place de la Bastille is where the fortress's ramparts would have been. A gleaming gold statue, a winged figure of Liberty, stands atop a bronze column at the centre of the square. The plinth on which it stands was once intended to hold quite a different monument – Napoleon had wanted a giant elephant fountain to stand here, with a spiral staircase inside one leg and viewing platform on top. The project never came to fruition, but the full-scale model that was made became a curiosity in its own right and stood for a while near the Gare de Vincennes (Gavroche in Victor Hugo's *Les Miserables* sought shelter in it). After 35 years it was sold for 3833 francs. The same architect who had worked on the elephant built the present column, which was erected to commemorate the July Revolution of 1830, and which replaced the autocratic Charles X with the "Citizen King" Louis-Philippe. When Louis-Philippe fled in the more significant 1848 Revolution, his throne was burnt beside the column and a new inscription added. Four months later, the workers again took to the streets. All of eastern Paris was barricaded, with the fiercest fighting on rue du Faubourg-St-Antoine, until the rebellion was quelled with the usual massacres and deportation of survivors. The square is still an important rallying point for political protest.

Opéra Bastille

The Bicentennial of the French Revolution in 1989 was marked by the inauguration of a new opera house on place de la Bastille, the **Opéra Bastille** (for information on performances see p.379), one of François Mitterrand's pet projects. Filling almost the entire block between rues de Lyon, Charenton and Moreau, it has shifted the focus of place de la Bastille, so that the column is no longer the pivotal point; in fact, it's easy to miss it altogether when dazzled by the night-time glare of lights emanating from the Opéra. One critic described it as a "hippopotamus in a bathtub", and you can see his point. The architect, Uruguyan Carlos Ott, was concerned that his design should not bring an overbearing monumentalism to place de la Bastille. The different depths and layers of the semicircular facade do give a certain sense of the building stepping back, but self-effacing it is not. With time, use and familiarity, Parisians seem to have become reconciled to it, and people happily sit on its steps, wander into its shops and libraries, and camp out all night for the free performance on July 14.

The Port de l'Arsenal and Maison Rouge

Just south of the place de la Bastille is the **Port de l'Arsenal** marina, occupying part of what was once the moat around the Bastille. The Canal St-Martin starts here, flowing underneath the square and emerging much further north, just past place de la République, a route plied by canal pleasure boats run by Canauxrama (see p.411). Some two hundred boats are moored up in the marina, and the landscaped banks, with children's playgrounds, make it quite a pleasant spot for a wander.

One of the former industrial spaces bordering the Arsenal, at 10 blvd de la Bastille, has been converted into a light and spacious contemporary art gallery, called the **Maison Rouge – Fondation Antoine de Galbert** (Wed–Sun 11am–7pm, Thurs till 9pm; €6.50; ⓦwww.lamaisonrouge.org;

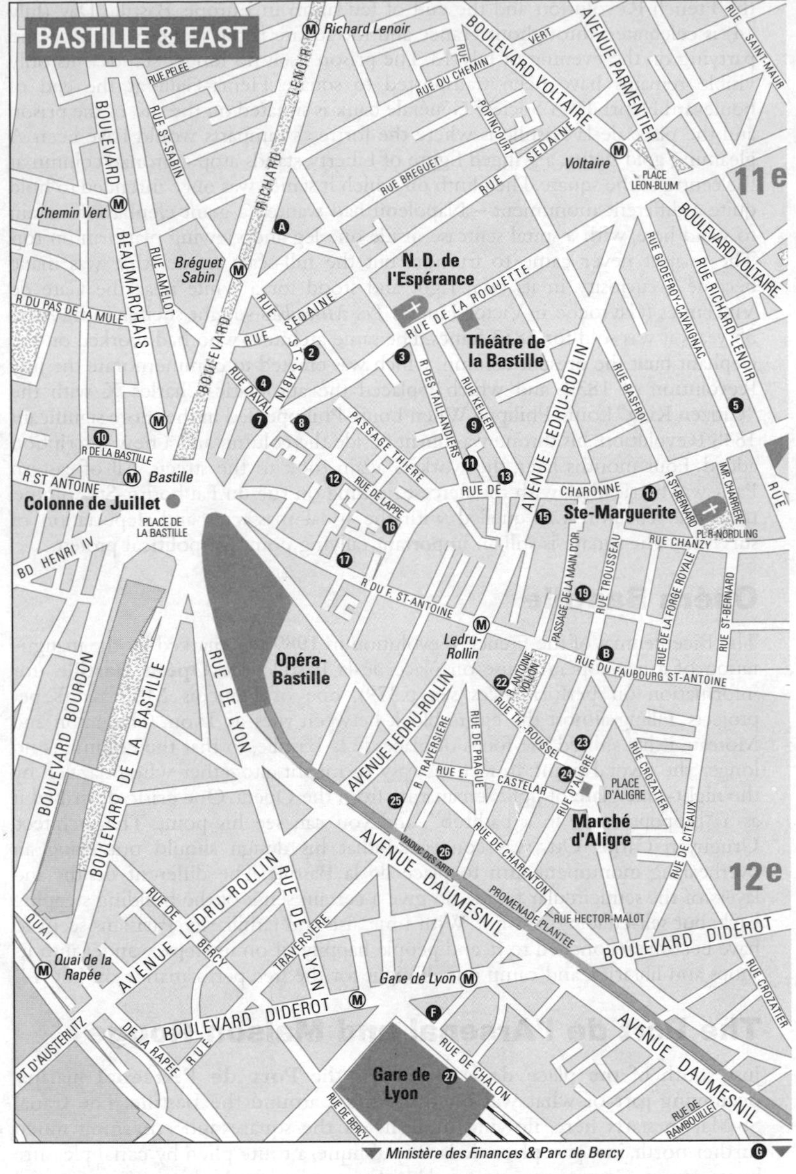

M° Bastille/Quai de la Rapée). Founded in 2004 by collector Antoine de Galbert, the Maison Rouge, which takes its name from the bright-red pavilion at the centre of the building, holds changing exhibitions, either devoted to an individual artist or a private collection, such as the recent exhibition of Belgian Sylvio Perlstein's collection of art and photography from the Dada movement up to the present day.

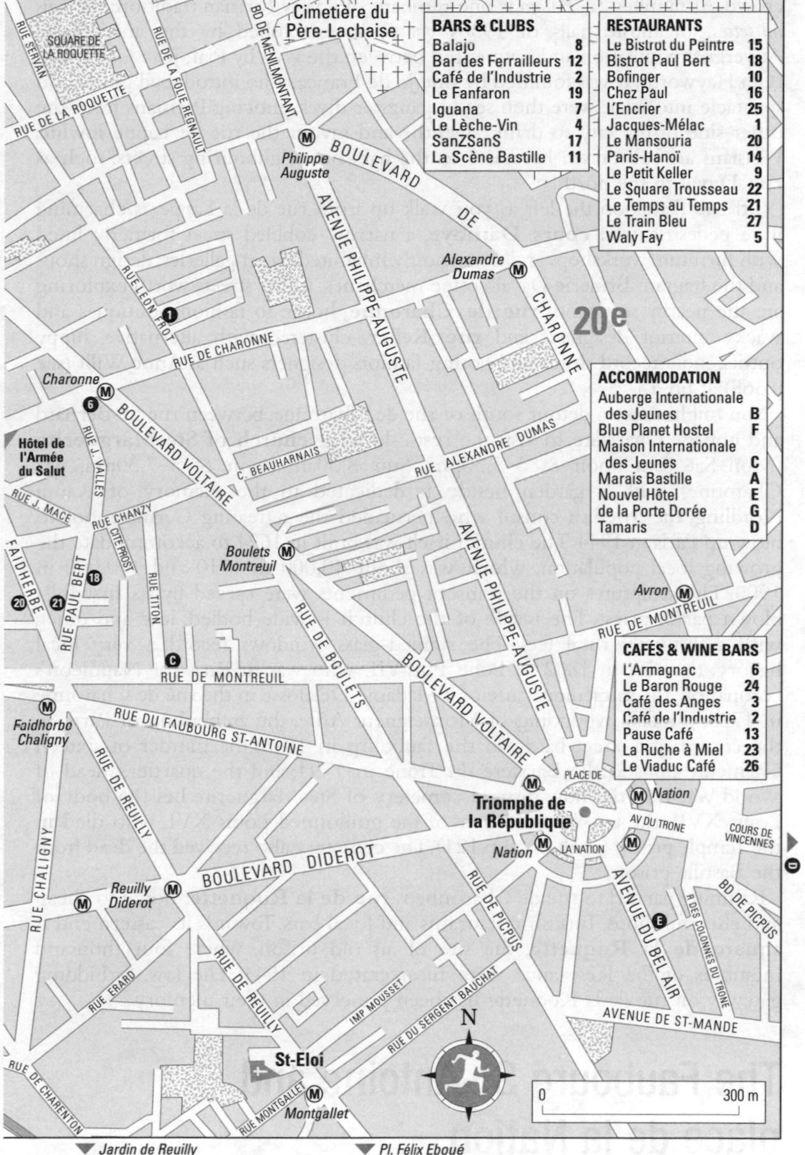

Rue de Lappe and rue de Charonne

Northeast of place de la Bastille, off rue de la Roquette, narrow, cobbled **rue de Lappe** is a lively nightspot, crammed with bars drawing a largely teen crowd. At number 32, *Balajo* is one remnant of a very Parisian tradition: the *bals musettes*, or music halls of 1930s *gai Paris*, established by the area's large Auvergnat population and frequented between the wars by Piaf, Jean Gabin and Rita Hayworth. It was founded by one Jo de France, who introduced glitter and spectacle into what were then seedy gangster dives, enticing Parisians from the other side of the city to drink absinthe and savour the rue de Lappe lowlife. Parisians are still drawn here and to the bars on neighbouring streets, such as **rue Daval** to the north.

Off rue Daval, on the left as you walk up from rue de la Lappe, is charming little pedestrianized **cours Damoye**, a narrow cobbled street formerly lined with furniture workshops and now mostly inhabited by art galleries, design shops and the fragrant Brûlerie Daval coffee merchant's. Other streets worth exploring are the nearby section of **rue de Charonne**, home to fashion boutiques and wacky interior designers; and **rue Keller**, clustered with alternative, hippy outfits, indie record stores and young fashion designers such as Anne Willi (see p.368) at no. 13.

You might make a detour south of rue de Charonne, between rue St-Bernard and impasse Charrière, to visit the rustic-looking **church of Ste-Marguerite** (Mon–Sat 8am–noon & 3–7.30pm, Sun 8.30am–noon & 5–7.30pm; M° Charonne), with a garden beside it dedicated to the memory of Raoul Nordling, the Swedish consul who persuaded the retreating Germans not to blow up Paris in 1944. The church itself was built in 1624 to accommodate the growing local population, which was about 40,000 in 1710 and 100,000 in 1900. The sculptures on the transept pediments were carved by its first full-blown parish priest. The inside of the church is wide-bodied, low and quiet, with a distinctly rural feel. The stained-glass windows record a very local history: the visit in 1802 of Pope Pius VII, who was in Paris for Napoleon's coronation; the miraculous cure of a Madame Delafosse in the rue de Charonne in 1725; the fatal wounding of Monseigneur Affre, the archbishop of Paris, in the course of a street battle in the faubourg in 1848; the murder of sixteen Carmelite nuns at the Barrière du Trône in 1794; and the quartier's dead of World War I. In the now disused cemetery of Ste-Marguerite lies the body of Louis XVII, the ten-year-old heir of the guillotined Louis XVI, who died in the Temple prison (see box on p.121). The cemetery also received the dead from the Bastille prison.

Running parallel to rue de Charonne is **rue de la Roquette**, home to cheap and cheerful shops, Turkish restaurants and local bars. Towards its eastern end is **square de la Roquette**, the site of an old prison, where four thousand members of the Resistance were incarcerated in 1944. The low, forbidding gateway on rue de la Roquette has been preserved in their memory.

The Faubourg St-Antoine and place de la Nation

After Louis XI licensed the establishment of craftsmen in the fifteenth century, the **rue du Faubourg-St-Antoine**, running east from place de la Bastille, became the principal working-class quartier of Paris, cradle of revolutions and mother of street-fighters. From its beginnings, the principal trade associated with it has been **furniture-making**, and this was where the classic styles of French furniture – Louis XIV, Louis XV, Second Empire – were developed.

There are still quite a few furniture shops on the street, and a number of workshops, as well as related trades such as inlayers, stainers and polishers, still inhabit the maze of interconnecting yards and *passages* that run off the faubourg, especially at the western end. One of the most attractive courtyards is at no. 56, the Cours du Bel Air, with its lemon trees, and ivy- and rose-covered buildings.

To the east, rue du Faubourg-St-Antoine ends at **place de la Nation**. The *place* is adorned with the "Triumph of the Republic", a monumental bronze group topped with a stately female figure personifying the republic. To the east, framing the avenue du Trône, are two tall Doric columns, surmounted by statues of medieval monarchs, looking very small and insignificant. During the Revolution, when the old name of place du Trône became place du Trône-Renversé ("the overturned throne"), more people were guillotined here than on the more notorious execution site of place de la Concorde.

Place d'Aligre market

Just to the south of the rue du Faubourg-St-Antoine is the **place d'Aligre market** (M° Ledru-Rollin), a lively, raucous affair, held every morning except Monday, and particularly animated on Saturdays and Sundays. The square itself is given over to clothes and bric-a-brac stalls, selling anything from old gramophone players to odd bits of crockery. There's also a covered food market with the usual line-up of *fromageries* and *charcuteries*, plus more unusual stalls such as Sur les Quais, selling numerous varieties of olive oil. It's along the adjoining rue d'Aligre, however, where the market really comes to life, the vendors, many of Algerian origin, doing a frenetic trade in fruit and veg. As the market winds down, you could follow the locals to the old-fashioned *Baron Rouge* wine bar (see p.347) for a glass of wine and *saucisson*, or drink in the North African atmosphere at the *Ruche à Miel* café (see p.348) at 19 rue d'Aligre and order some mint tea with sticky cakes. Before leaving the area it's also worth taking a look at the old-style boulangerie on the corner of rues Charenton and Emilio-Castelar, with its beautiful painted glass panels, the queue of shoppers outside testifying to the excellence of its bread and pâtisseries.

The Promenade Plantée and around

The **Promenade Plantée** (M° Bastille/Ledru-Rollin), also known as the Coulée Verte, is an excellent way to see a little-visited part of the city – and from an unusual angle. This disused railway viaduct, part of the old Paris–Cherbourg line, has been ingeniously converted into an elevated walkway and planted with a profusion of trees and flowers – cherry trees, maples, limes, roses and lavender. The walkway starts near the beginning of **avenue Daumesnil**, just south of the Bastille opera house, and is reached via a flight of stone steps – or lifts – with a number of similar access points further along. It takes you to the Parc de Reuilly then descends to ground level and continues nearly as far as the *périphérique*, from where you can follow signs to the Bois de Vincennes. Plans are afoot to extend the *promenade* so that it takes you directly to the Bois. The whole walk is around 4.5km long, but if you don't feel like doing the entire thing you could just walk the first part, along the viaduct – a twenty-minute stroll – which also happens to be the most attractive stretch, running past venerable old mansion blocks and giving you a bird's-eye view of the street below. Small architectural details such as decorative mouldings and elaborate wrought-iron balconies that you wouldn't normally notice at street level come to light – the oddest sight is the series of caryatids adorning the police station at the end of the avenue Daumesnil.

Underneath, the red-brick arches of the viaduct itself have been converted into attractive spaces for artisans' studios and craft shops, collectively known as the **Viaduc des Arts**. The workshops house a wealth of creativity: furniture and tapestry restorers, interior designers, cabinet-makers, violin- and flute-makers, embroiderers and fashion and jewellery designers. The viaduct ends around halfway down avenue Daumesnil, but the Promenade Plantée continues, taking you to the **Jardin de Reuilly**, an old freight station, now an inviting, circular expanse of lawn, popular with picnickers on sunny days, and bordered by terraces and arbours. The open-air café here makes a good refreshment halt if you're walking the length of the *promenade*. You can also choose to bypass the park altogether by taking the gracefully arching wooden footbridge that spans it. The next part of the walkway – the **allée Vivaldi** – is a rather nondescript road lined with modern blocks, but then you enter a tunnel and emerge at the other end in the old railway cutting, a delightful stretch that meanders through a canopy of trees and flowers, below the level of the surrounding streets. At this point the path divides into two – one for pedestrians, the other for cyclists – landscaped all along, taking you through a series of ivy-draped, ex-railway tunnels and shadowing the rue du Sahel for most of the way. The walk comes to an end at the *boulevard périphérique*. Take the wrought-iron spiral staircase up to road level, turn right onto the ring road, and then left under the flyover. A right turn will take you onto busy boulevard de la Guyane, and a short walk along here will eventually bring you to the **Bois de Vincennes** and the **Porte Dorée** métro station (turn right onto avenue Daumesnil at the end of boulevard de la Guyane and the métro station is a five-minute walk along the avenue).

Around the Jardin de Reuilly

North of the Jardin de Reuilly, on place M. de Fontenay (M° Montgâllet), lies the peculiar church of **St-Eloi**, built in 1968 to a ground plan of a right-angled triangle with the altar positioned at one of the non-right-angled corners. It all feels more like an industrial building than a place of worship; both outside and inside are clad with lacquered aluminium leaves, in honour of St Eloi, patron saint of jewellers and iron-workers who lived in this area in the seventeenth century. Close by the church, on the other side of rue de Reuilly, is one of the most perfect *villas* (mews) in Paris, the **impasse Mousset**. Roses, clematis, wisteria and honeysuckle wind across telegraph lines and up the whitewashed walls of its tiny houses; a rusted hotel sign advertising wines and liqueurs, as well as beds, still hangs from one of the houses; and you can hear children playing in hidden gardens. There are no designer offices here, just homes, the odd artist's studio and a small printworks.

Another unusual church lies southeast of the Jardin de Reuilly – about a twenty-minute walk down avenue Daumesnil, on the other side of place Félix Eboué, on the right. An extremely narrow brickwork facade, topped by the tallest bell tower in Paris, conceals the vast cupola – filling the whole block behind the street – of the **Eglise du Saint-Esprit**, built in 1931 in memory of the colonial missionaries. The Roman Catholic Church was worried by the possible reaction of the anticlerical, Communist sympathies of the local residents, hence the disguise of its enormous dimensions.

Bercy

Over the last decade or so, the former warehouse district of **Bercy**, along the Seine just east of the Gare de Lyon, has been transformed by a series of ambitious, ultra-modern developments designed to complement the grand-scale "Seine Rive Gauche" project (see p.190) on the opposite bank. As you emerge from Bercy métro station, one of the first things you notice is the **Ministère des Finances**, a monster of a building, constructed in 1990 to house the treasury staff after they had finally agreed to move out of the Richelieu wing of the Louvre. Housing some 4700 employees, it stretches like a giant loading bridge from above the river (where higher bureaucrats and ministers arrive by boat) to rue de Bercy, a distance of some 400m.

A little east of here squats the charmless **Palais Omnisports de Bercy**. Built in 1983, its concrete bunker frame clad with grass covers a vast arena used for sporting and cultural events (see p.410 for more details). Beyond it, the area that used to house the old Bercy warehouses, where for centuries the capital's wine supplies were unloaded from river barges, is now the extensive **Parc de Bercy**. Here, the French formal garden has been given a modern twist with geometric lines and grid-like flowerbeds, but it also cleverly incorporates elements of the old warehouse site such as disused railway tracks and cobbled lanes. The western section of the park is a fairly unexciting expanse of grass with a huge stepped fountain (popular with children) set into one of the grassy banks, but the area east has arbours, rose gardens, lily ponds, an orangerie and

△ Bercy village

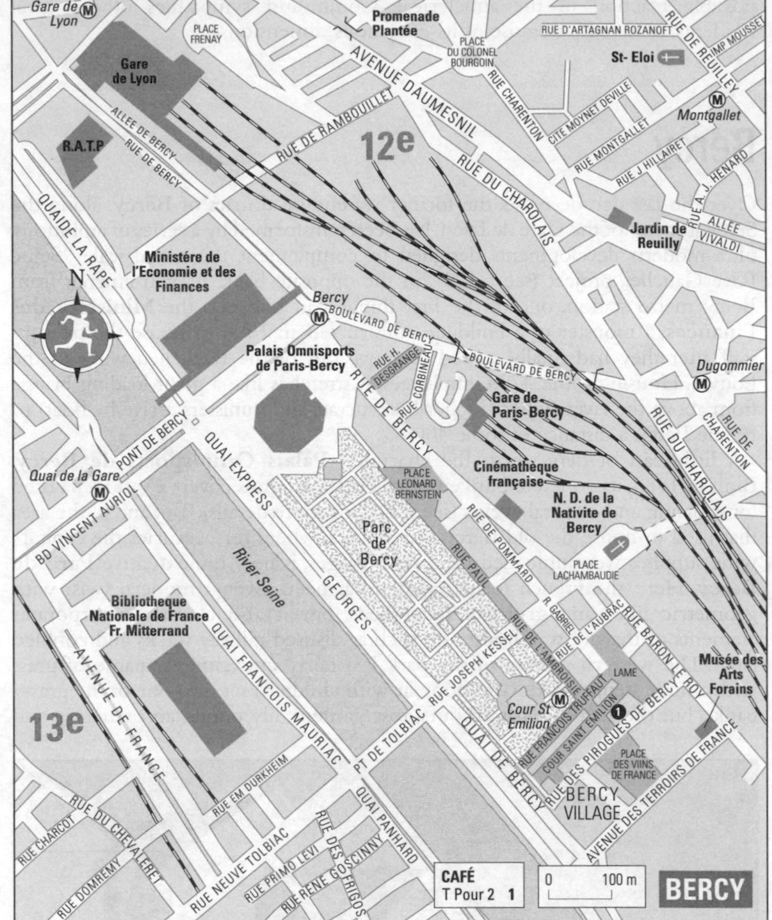

a **Maison du Jardinage** (March–Oct Tues–Fri 1.30–5.30pm, Sat & Sun 1.30–6.30pm; Nov–Feb Tues–Sat 1.30–5pm), which provides information on all aspects of gardening.

Of the new buildings surrounding the park, the most striking, at 51 rue de Bercy, on the north side, is the **Cinémathèque** (Ⓦwww.cinematheque.fr; M° Bercy), recently transferred here from the Palais de Chaillot. Designed by Guggenheim architect Frank O. Gehry, it's constructed from zinc, glass and limestone and resembles a falling pack of cards – according to Gehry, the inspiration was Matisse's collages, done "with a simple pair of scissors". On site there's a huge archive of films dating back to the earliest days of cinema, and regular retrospectives of French and foreign films are screened in its four cinemas. It also has an engaging **museum** (Mon, Wed–Fri noon–7pm, Thurs till 10pm, Sat & Sun 10am–8pm; €4), tracing the history of cinema, with lots of early cinematic equipment, magic lanterns, silent-film clips and costumes from films, such as the dress worn by Vivienne Leigh in *Gone with the Wind* and outfits from Eisenstein's *Ivan the Terrible*.

A little east of here, arched footbridges take you over the busy rue Kessel into the eastern extension of the park and the adjoining **Bercy village** (M° Cour Saint-Emilion), the hub of which is the **Cour Saint Emilion**, a pedestrianized, cobbled street lined with former wine warehouses that have been stylishly converted into shops, restaurants and wine bars – popular places to come before or after a film at the giant Bercy multiplex cinema at the eastern end of the street. Another set of old stone wine warehouses at no. 53 avenue des-Terroirs-de-France now houses the privately owned funfair museum, the **Musée des Arts Forains** (Ⓣ01.43.40.16.15; €12, children €4), with its collection of nineteenth- and early twentieth-century funfair rides (which you're even allowed to try out), fairground music and Venetian carnival rooms. It's open to groups only, though individuals can join a tour (in French, lasting 90min) – you just need to ring in advance.

Vincennes

Beyond the 12e arrondissement, across the *boulevard périphérique*, lies the **Bois de Vincennes**, a favourite family Sunday retreat and the largest green space that the city has to offer, aside from the Bois de Boulogne in the west. The Bois de Vincennes' main draw is the **Parc Floral**, an attractive park with an adventure playground. To the east is the **Cartoucherie de Vincennes**, an old ammunitions factory, home to four theatre companies, including the radical Théâtre du Soleil (see p.372), while bordering the Bois to the north stands the **Château de Vincennes**, the country's only surviving medieval royal residence. West of the Bois de Vincennes is a new museum, the **Cité nationale de l'histoire de l'immigration**, devoted to the history of immigration in France.

The Bois de Vincennes

The extensive **Bois de Vincennes** was once a royal hunting ground roamed by deer; nowadays, unfortunately, it's so crisscrossed with roads that countryside sensations don't stand much of a chance, but it has some pleasant corners, such as the Parc Floral and the two lakes. Sights are quite a long distance from each other, so to avoid a lot of footslogging you may want to just target one or two, or you could rent a bike quite cheaply from near the Lac des Minimes, at the Porte Jaune (Wed, Sat, Sun & hols) or from the outlet on the Esplanade St-Louis (April–Oct Sun & hols 10am–6pm), near the Parc de Floral entrance; bring your passport in case you're asked to leave something as security. The three main métro stops giving access to the park are M° Porte-Dorée, M° Porte-de-Charenton and M° Château-de-Vincennes, and it's also served by buses #46 and #86.

If you've only got a limited amount of time, you should make for the **Parc Floral** (daily: summer 9.30am–8pm; winter 9.30am–dusk; €1; Ⓦwww.parcfloraldeparis.com; M° Château-de-Vincennes, then bus #112 or a short walk), just behind the Fort de Vincennes. This is one of the best gardens in Paris – flowers are always in bloom in the Jardin des Quatres Saisons, you can picnic beneath pines, then wander through concentrations of camellias, rhododendrons,

cacti, ferns, irises and bonsai trees. Between April and September there are art and horticultural exhibitions in several pavilions, free jazz and classical music concerts, and numerous activities for children including a mini-golf of Parisian monuments (see p.423 for more information on activities for children).

If you're after a lazy afternoon in the park, you could go boating on the **Lac Daumesnil**, near the Porte Dorée entrance, or feed the ducks on the **Lac des Minimes** (bus #112 from Vincennes métro), on the other side of the wood. North of the Lac Daumesnil, at 53 avenue de St-Maurice, is the city's largest **zoo** (daily 9am–5.30pm; €5; M° Porte Dorée), though only parts of it are open at the moment, as a much-needed restoration is under way to restore its fake rocks, now some seventy years old and falling apart. Many of the larger animals have been transferred to other zoos while renovations are carried out.

The fenced enclave on the southern side of Lac Daumesnil harbours a **Buddhist centre**, with Tibetan temple, Vietnamese chapel and international pagoda; all occasionally visitable (information on ⓣ01.43.41.54.48). As far as real woods go, the *bois* comes into its own once you're east of avenue de St-Maurice. Boules competitions are popular – there's usually a collection of devotees between route de la Tourelle and avenue du Polygone.

Château de Vincennes

On the northern edge of the Bois stands the **Château de Vincennes** (daily: May–Oct 10am–noon & 1–6pm, Sept–April 10am–noon & 1–5pm; ⓦwww.chateau-vincennes.fr; M° Château-de-Vincennes), enclosed by a high defensive wall and surrounded by a moat, no longer filled with water. The château – erstwhile royal medieval residence, then state prison, porcelain factory, weapons dump and military training school – is still undergoing restoration work started by Napoléon III. Highlights are the Flamboyant-Gothic **Chapelle Royale**, completed in the mid-sixteenth century and decorated with superb Renaissance stained-glass windows, and the lofty fourteenth-century **donjon** (keep), built by Charles V and about to reopen at the time of writing after a ten-year restoration. It was here in Charles's bedchamber that the English king Henry V died in 1422, shortly before he was to join forces with his Burgundian allies. Visits are with a **guided tour**; two circuits are available, one lasting forty-five minutes (€5), the other an hour and fifteen minutes (€6.50).

Cité nationale de l'histoire de l'immigration

Just outside the Bois de Vincennes, across the way from the Porte Dorée entrance, at 293 avenue Daumesnil, a huge Art Deco building, the Palais de la Porte Dorée, is at the time of writing about to accommodate a new museum, the **Cité nationale de l'histoire de l'immigration** (Tues–Fri 10am–5.30pm, Sat & Sun 10am–7pm; €3; Ⓦ www.histoire-immigration.fr; Mº Porte Dorée), dealing with the history of immigration to France over the last two centuries (15 million French citizens have foreign roots) through a collection of photographs, artefacts, illustrations and contemporary artworks. The decision to locate it here, in a building erected for the 1931 Colonial Exhibition and sporting a vast and somewhat dubious bas-relief illustrating the former French colonies, suggests the museum will be challenging and thought-provoking, encouraging visitors to confront awkward episodes in French history. On the lower ground floor you'll still be able to visit the popular **aquarium** with its large collection of tropical fish and crocodile pit, left over from the palais' previous incarnation as the Musée des Arts Africains et Océaniens (whose exhibits have been transferred to the new Musée du Quai Branly).

13

Eastern Paris

The **Canal St-Martin**, running from the Bastille in the south to the place de la Bataille de Stalingrad in the north, effectively marks the boundary between central and **eastern Paris**. The area east of the canal has traditionally been the home of the working classes, and during the Industrial Revolution in the mid-nineteenth century, the old villages of **Belleville**, **Ménilmontant** and **Charonne** were colonized by the French rural poor. These populations supplied the people-power for the insurrections of 1830, 1832, 1848 and 1851, and the short-lived Commune of 1871, which divided the city in two, with the centre and west battling to preserve the status quo against the oppressed and radical east. Indeed, for much of the nineteenth century, the establishment feared nothing more than the "descente de Belleville" – the descent from the heights of Belleville of the revolutionary mob. It was in order to contain this threat that so much of the Canal St-Martin, a natural line of defence, was covered over by **Baron Haussmann** in 1860.

Today only a few reminders of these turbulent times survive, such as the Mur des Fédérés in **Père-Lachaise cemetery** recording the deaths of 147 Communards, and a few streets bearing the names of popular leaders. Some of the old working-class character of the district lives on in places: narrow streets and artisans' houses survive in Belleville, Ménilmontant and off the Canal St-Martin. Much of the area, however, has undergone redevelopment over the last few decades. Crumbling, dank and insanitary houses were replaced by shelving-unit apartment blocks in the Sixties and Seventies, giving way in recent years to more imaginative and attractive constructions. The biggest development was the conversion of the old meat market area of **La Villette** in the 1980s into a futuristic science museum and park.

In places, redevelopment has inevitably shifted older populations further out into the suburbs; the Canal St-Martin for example has now been colonized by the new arty and media intelligentsia. Further east, in Ménilmontant and Belleville, rents remain relatively low, attracting significant numbers of students and artists, who have created a thriving, alternative scene. These areas have also been settled by sizeable **ethnic populations**, especially North Africans, Malians, Turks, Yugoslavs and Chinese, making it one of the most diverse areas of the city and a good place for sampling exotic cuisine.

The Canal St-Martin and around

Completed in 1825, the **Canal St-Martin** was built so that river traffic could short-cut the great western loop of the Seine around Paris. As it happened, it also turned out to be a splendid natural defence for the rebellious quarters of eastern Paris: the canal was spanned by six swing-bridges, which could easily be drawn up to halt the advance of government troops. Napoléon III's solution was simply to cover over the lower stretch in the latter half of the nineteenth century; the canal now runs underground at the Bastille, emerging after a mile and a half near the rue du Faubourg-du-Temple, and continuing up to the **place de la Bataille de Stalingrad**. The canal hasn't completely lost its radical associations: in December 2006 it hit the news when up to three hundred homeless people camped out along its banks for several months in order to raise awareness of homelessness in France (a huge problem, with around a million homeless throughout the country). With an election looming, the government

△ The Canal St-Martin

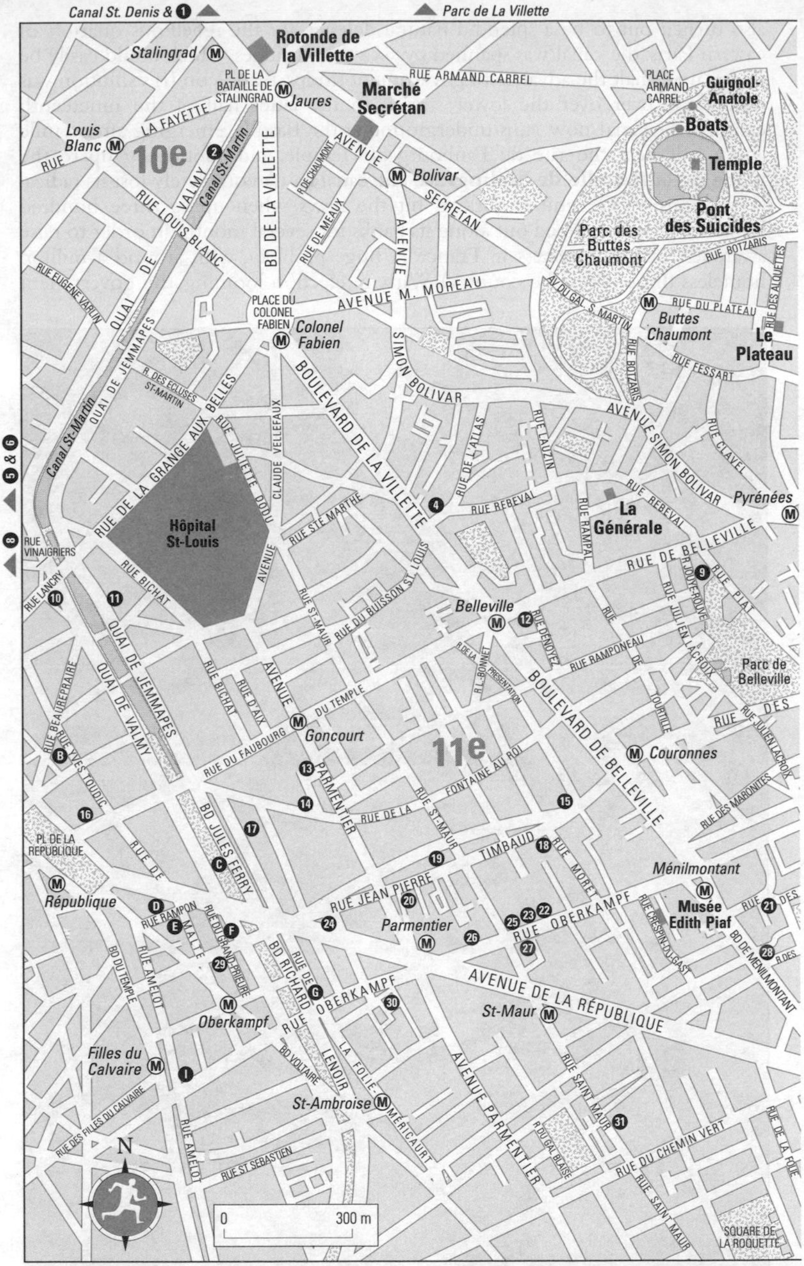

Canal St. Denis & 1 ▲ ▲ Parc de La Villette

RESTAURANTS

Restaurant	No.	Restaurant	No.	Restaurant	No.	Restaurant	No.
Assoce	31	Le Baratin	9	Chez Imogène	29	Au Rendez-Vous de la Marine	1
Astier	24	Le Bistrot du Parisien	18	L'Homme Bleu	20	Restaurant de Bourgogne	8
L'Auberge Pyrénées Cévennes	17	Le Châteaubriand	13	Ile de Gorée	19	Le Sporting	6
				Lao Siam	3		

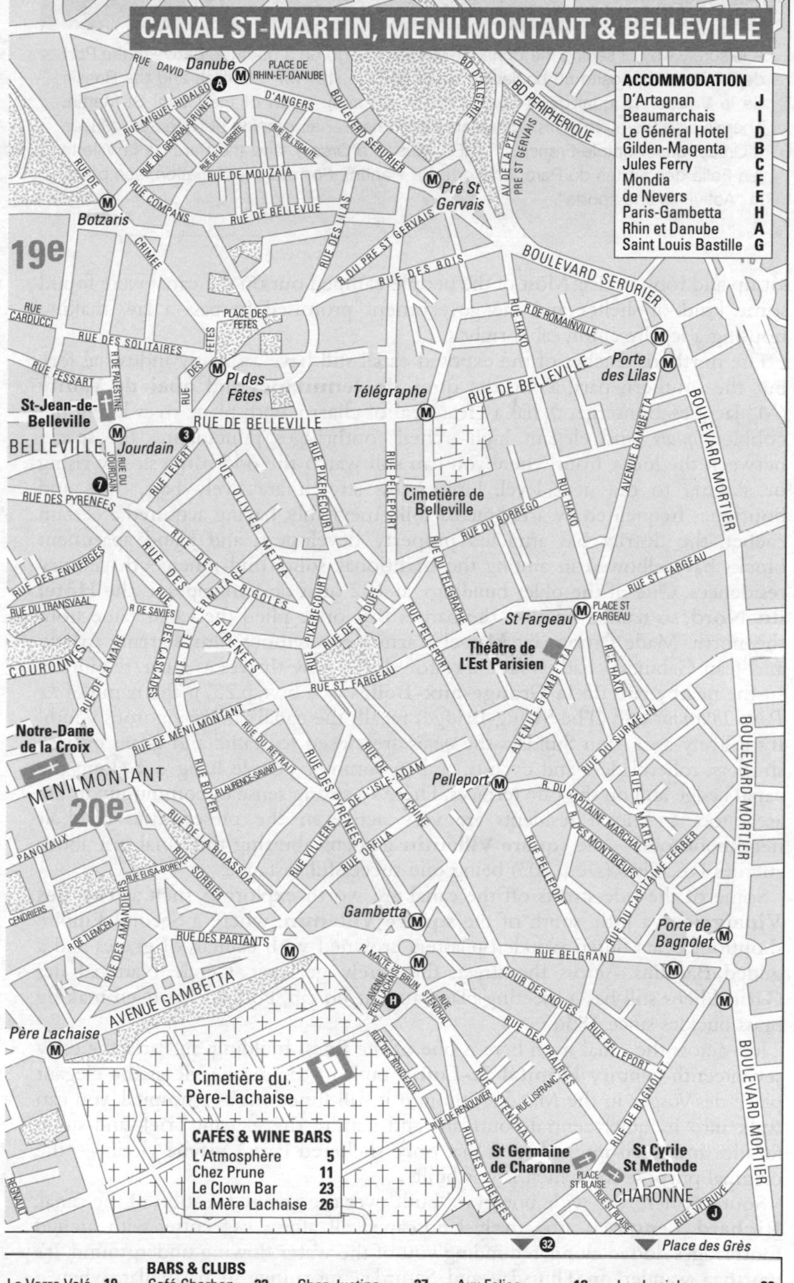

BARS & CLUBS

Le Verre Volé	10	Café Charbon	22	Chez Justine	27	Aux Folies	12	Les Lucioles	28
Le Villaret	30	Café Chéri	4	Favela Chic	16	Le Jemmapes	11	Le Nouveau Casino	25
Le Zéphyr	7	Le Cannibale	15	La Flèche d'Or	32	Lou Pascalou	21	Point Ephémère	2
		La Caravane	14						

Canal boat trips

A leisurely way of seeing the Canal St-Martin is to go on a boat trip between the Port de l'Arsenal, opposite 50 boulevard de la Bastille, 12e (M° Bastille), and the Bassin de la Villette, 13 quai de la Loire, 19e (M° Jaurès), north of the Canal St-Martin. There's also the more stylish catamaran of Paris-Canal, running between the Musée d'Orsay, quai Anatole-France, 7e (RER Musée d'Orsay), and the Parc de la Villette (La Folie des Visites du Parc; M° Porte-de-Pantin). For more information, see p.411 in "Activities and sports".

sat up and took notice. Most of the people camped out on the canal were found some kind of shelter and the government promised to pass a law making housing a legally enforceable right.

The northern reaches of the exposed canal still have a slightly industrial feel, but the southern part, along the **quai de Jemmapes** and **quai de Valmy** (M° Jacques-Bonsergent), has a great deal of charm, with plane trees lining the cobbled *quais*, and elegant high-arched footbridges punctuating the spaces between the locks, from where you can still watch the odd barge slowly rising or sinking to the next level. Lining this stretch are lively bars, cafés and boutiques frequented by artsy, media folk. Inevitably, having acquired a certain cachet, the district has attracted property developers, and bland apartment blocks have elbowed in among the traditional, solid, mid-nineteenth-century residences. One of the older buildings, at 102 quai de Jemmapes, is the **Hôtel du Nord**, so named because the barges that once plied the canal came from the north. Made famous by Marcel Carné's eponymous film, starring Arletty and Jean Gabin, it's had its facade restored and now thrives as a bar/restaurant. In the nearby **rue de la Grange-aux-Belles** (see box, p.227), the name of *Le Pont-Tournant* café (The Swing-Bridge) recalls the canal's more vigorous youth. It's a lively area – on Sundays the *quais* are closed to traffic and given over to strollers, rollerbladers and cyclists, and in summer people hang out along the canal's edge and on the café terraces. There's a strong sense of community in the area, too, and local residents are very active in the preservation of their neighbourhood – the **square Villemin** gardens abutting the canal just above rue des Récollets (see p.203) being one successful instance.

Some of the side streets off the canal are worth exploring, such as **rue des Vinaigriers**, a little south of the **square Villemin**, where a Second Empire shopfront bears fluted wooden pilasters crowned with capitals of grapes and a gilded Bacchus. Across the street, the surely geriatric Cercle National des Garibaldiens still has a meeting place and, at no. 35, Poursin has been making brass buckles since 1830.

Just across the canal from here is one of the finest buildings in Paris, the early seventeenth-century **Hôpital St-Louis**, built in the same style as the elegant place des Vosges in the Marais. Although it still functions as a hospital, you can walk into its quiet central courtyard and admire the elegant brick-and-stone facades and steep-pitched roofs that once sheltered Paris's plague victims – the original purpose for which it was built.

South of here, the wide boulevard built over the covered section of the canal, **Richard Lenoir**, is attractively landscaped all along its centre, with arched footbridges dotted along, reminding you of the water flowing underground. It's worth a wander on Thursday and Saturday mornings in particular, when a traditional **food market**, known for its choice range of regional produce, sets up on the lower stretch, near the Bastille.

Place de la Bataille de Stalingrad and Bassin de la Villette

The Canal St-Martin goes underground again at the busy **place de la Bataille de Stalingrad**, dominated by the Neoclassical **Rotonde de la Villette**, a handsome stone rotunda fronted with a portico, inspired by Palladio's Villa de la Rotonda in Vicenza. This was one of the toll houses designed by the architect Ledoux as part of Louis XVI's scheme to tax all goods entering the city. At that time, every road out of Paris had a customs post, or *barrière*, linked by a six-metre-high wall, known as "Le Mur des Fermiers-Généraux" – a major irritant in the run-up to the Revolution. Cleaned and restored, the *rotonde* is currently being turned into an arts and exhibition centre. Backing the toll house is an elegant aerial stretch of métro, supported by Neoclassical iron and stone pillars. The area has a slightly dodgy reputation at night, as it's a known haunt of drug dealers.

Beyond here the canal widens out into the **Bassin de la Villette**, built in 1808. The recobbled docks area today bears few traces of its days as France's premier port, its dockside buildings now offering **canal boat trips** (see box below), and boasting a multiplex cinema, MK2 (see p.368), with a popular waterfront brasserie (see p.350). On Sundays and holidays people stroll along the *quais*, play boules, fish or take a rowing boat out in the dock, but despite the clean-up the area retains a slightly industrial and seedy feel.

Three blocks west of the basin, another major renovation project is under way at **104 rue d'Aubervilliers** (M° Ricquet) – to convert a former, rather grand funeral parlour, built in the 1870s, into a multimedia arts space, covering some 28,000 square metres. The "104" is due to open to the public in summer 2008 and promises to be well worth a visit, with thirty-odd established and new artists due to take up residence, performance and exhibition spaces, shops and cafés.

Parc de la Villette

All the meat for Paris used to come from the slaughterhouses in **La Villette**, an old village that was annexed to the city in the mid-nineteenth century. Slaughtering and butchering, and industries based on the meat markets' by-products, provided plenty of jobs for its dense population, whose recreation time was

The Montfaucon gallows

Long ago, **rue de la Grange-aux-Belles**, on the north side of the Hôpital St-Louis, was a dusty track leading uphill, past fields, en route to Germany. Where no. 53 now stands, a path led to the top of a small hillock. Here, in 1325, on the king's orders, an enormous **gallows** was built, consisting of a plinth 6m high, on which stood sixteen stone pillars each 10m high. These were joined by chains, from which malefactors were hanged in clusters. They were left there until they disintegrated, by way of example, and they stank so badly that when the wind blew from the northeast they infected the nostrils of the still far-off city. The practice continued until the seventeenth century. Bones and other remains from the pit into which they were thrown were found during the building of a garage in 1954.

LA VILLETTE & AROUND

RESTAURANTS & BARS

Abracadabar	2
Bar Ourcq	1
Au Rendezvous de la Marine	3

Cité des Sciences et de l'Industrie
Cabaret Sauvage
Parc de la Villette
Géode
Zénith
Canal de L'Ourcq
Grande Halle
Cité de la Musique
Conservatoire de Paris
Cemetery
Le 104
Bassin de la Villette
Rotonde de la Villette
Corentin Cariou
Crimée
Riquet
Ourcq
Laumière
Stalingrad
Pte de Pantin
Place de la Porte de Pantin
Boulevard Macdonald
Boulevard Peripherique
Boulevard Serurier
Boulevard d'Indochine
BD d'Indochine
Avenue Jean Jaures
Avenue Jean Lolive
Avenue de Flandre
Avenue de Laumiere
Avenue de la Porte Chaumont
Avenue de Laporte Brunet
Avenue du Gal Leclerc
Rue de Crimee
Rue de l'Ourcq
Rue Manin
Rue Curial
Rue de Cambrai
Rue Archereau
Rue Riquet
Rue de Tanger
Rue d'Aubervilliers
Rue Raymond Radiguet
Rue Marthis
Rue de Joinville
Rue de Meaux
Rue Cavendish
Rue Euyale
Dehaynin
Rue de la Lorraine
Rue Petit
Rue de Solidarite
Rue de la Prevoyance
Allee Darius
Allee A Honegger
Allee du Zenith
Allee du Belvedere
Galerie de la Villette
Quai de Metz
Quai de la Marne
Quai de Loire
Quai de la Seine
Rue Edgar Varese
Rue Beranger
Rue des Cheminets
Rue Lamartine
Rue Franklin
Rue des Sept Arpents
Rue d'Estienne d'Orves
Rue J B Semanaz
Rue a France
Rue Auger
Rue Honche
Rre des Petits Ponts
0 200 m
N

spent betting on cockfights, skating or swimming, and eating in the numerous local restaurants famed for their fresh meat. In the 1960s, vast sums of money were spent building a huge new abattoir. Yet, just as it neared completion, the emergence of new refrigeration techniques rendered the centralized meat industry redundant. The only solution was to switch course entirely; billions continued to be poured into La Villette in the 1980s, with the revised aim of creating a **music, art and science complex** to blow the mind.

The end result, the **Parc de la Villette** (Ⓦwww.villette.com), which opened in 1986, is enormous in scope and volume. There's so much going on here, most

Visiting the Parc de la Villette

The Parc de la Villette is accessible from M° Porte-de-la-Villette at the northern end by avenue Corentin-Cariou and the Cité des Sciences et de l'Industrie; from the Canal de l'Ourcq's quai de la Marne to the west; or from M° Porte-de-Pantin, on avenue Jean-Jaurès, at the southern entrance by the Cité de la Musique. There's an **information centre** at the southern entrance, which will help you get your bearings. The park's key attractions are listed below.

Cité des Sciences et de l'Industrie

A huge science museum, with a special section for children, the **Cité des Enfants**. The complex also includes the **Cinaxe** cinema which shows 3D films, the **Géode** Imax film theatre and a decommissioned naval submarine, the **Argonaute**.

Cité de la Musique

The city's music academy, which puts on regular concerts (see p.232) and incorporates a superb museum, covering the history of Western music.

Gardens

As well as large expanses of lawn, the park has ten themed gardens, including the Garden of Mirrors, of Shadows and of Dunes, all linked by a walkway called the Promenade des Jardins. See p.426 of "Kids' Paris" for more information.

Entertainment

The park has a number of distinguished music, arts and theatre venues; all performances are detailed in *Pariscope* (see p.46).

Cabaret Sauvage A venue for live music and avant-garde circus performances.

Festival du Cinéma en Plein Air On sticky summer nights you can join the crowds lounging on the acres of grass known as "prairies" for a movie in the open air (see also p.370).

Grande Halle The elegant old iron-framed beef market hall hosts large-scale art exhibitions and the annual **La Villette jazz festival** in September (see p.382).

Théâtre National de la Langue Française A small theatre specializing in works from French-speaking parts of the world such as Tahiti and Togo. See p.373.

Théâtre Paris-Villette A theatre that encourages young talent and puts on mostly contemporary works. See p.373.

Trabendo A live music venue for jazz, world music and rock.

Zénith Rock concerts are staged at this inflatable concert hall (see p.365).

Cafés and restaurants

Aux pains perdus (Cité des Sciences); Tues–Sun 8.30am–6.30pm.

Le hublot (Cité des Sciences); Tues–Sun noon–2.30pm.

Café de la Géode Tues–Sun 10am–9pm.

Café de la Musique Daily 9am–2am.

Quick Hamburger restaurant Near the Cinaxe. Daily 10.30am–10.30pm.

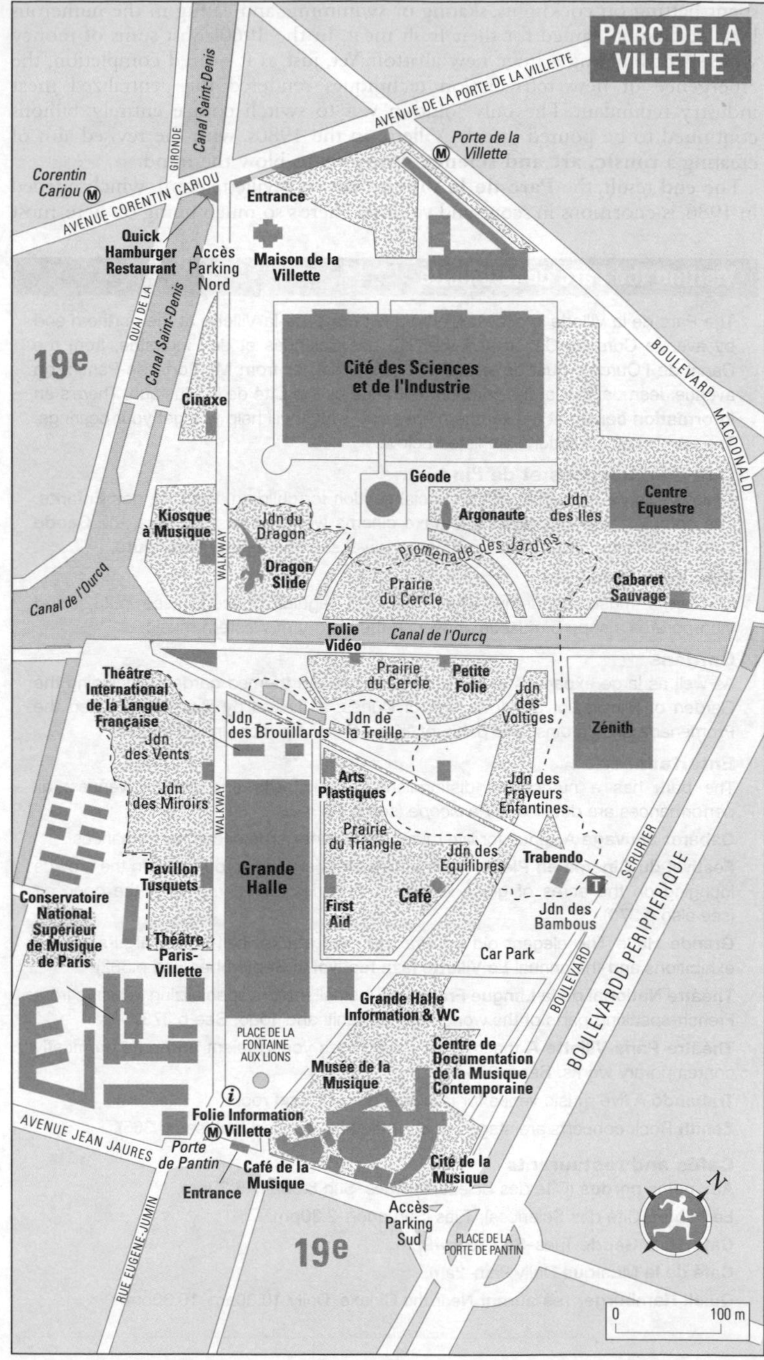
PARC DE LA VILLETTE
AVENUE DE LA PORTE DE LA VILLETTE
Canal Saint-Denis
GIRONDE
Porte de la Villette
Corentin Cariou
AVENUE CORENTIN CARIOU
Entrance
Quick Hamburger Restaurant
Accès Parking Nord
Maison de la Villette
QUAI DE LA
Canal Saint-Denis
19e
Cité des Sciences et de l'Industrie
BOULEVARD MACDONALD
Cinaxe
Géode
Kiosque à Musique
Jdn du Dragon
WALKWAY
Argonaute
Jdn des Iles
Centre Equestre
Promenade des Jardins
Dragon Slide
Prairie du Cercle
Cabaret Sauvage
Canal de l'Ourcq
Folie Vidéo
Canal de l'Ourcq
Théâtre International de la Langue Française
Prairie du Cercle
Petite Folie
Jdn des Voltiges
Jdn des Brouillards
Jdn de la Treille
Zénith
Jdn des Vents
Jdn des Miroirs
Arts Plastiques
Jdn des Frayeurs Enfantines
Prairie du Triangle
SERURIER
Jdn des Equilibres
Trabendo
Pavillon Tusquets
Grande Halle
Conservatoire National Supérieur de Musique de Paris
Café
First Aid
Jdn des Bambous
BOULEVARDD PERIPHERIQUE
Théâtre Paris-Villette
Car Park
BOULEVARD
Grande Halle Information & WC
PLACE DE LA FONTAINE AUX LIONS
Musée de la Musique
Centre de Documentation de la Musique Contemporaine
Folie Information
Villette
AVENUE JEAN JAURES
Porte de Pantin
Café de la Musique
Cité de la Musique
Entrance
N
Accès Parking Sud
PLACE DE LA PORTE DE PANTIN
19e
RUE EUGENE-JUMIN
0
100 m

of it stimulating and entertaining, but it's all so disparate and disconnected, with such a clash of styles, that it can feel more overwhelming than inspiring. According to the park's creators, this is all intentional, and philosophically justified. It was conceived by Bernard Tschumi as a futuristic "activity" park that would dispel the eighteenth- and nineteenth-century notion of parks and gardens as places of gentle and well-ordered relaxation. Instead, we're offered a landscape that backs off from the old-fashioned idea of unity, meaning and purpose, that "deconstructs" the whole into its fragmented elements, thereby opening up numerous possible interpretations. Yet there's something vaguely disconcerting about the setting. The 900-metre straight **walkway**, with its wavy shelter and complicated metal bridge across the Canal de l'Ourcq, seems to insist that you cover the park from end to end, and there's something too dogmatic about the arrangement of the bright red **follies** like chopped-off cranes, each slightly different but all spaced exactly 120m apart. The park's focal point, the **Cité des Sciences et de l'Industrie**, is alarming for its sheer bulk.

The Cité des Sciences et de l'Industrie

The park's dominant building is the enormous **Cité des Sciences et de l'Industrie** (Tues–Sat 10am–6pm, Sun 10am–7pm; €8 includes admission to Explora, certain temporary exhibitions and the Louis-Lumière 3D Cinema; Ⓦwww.cite-sciences.fr; M° Porte-de-la-Villette), an abandoned abattoir redesigned by architect Adrien Fainsilber and transformed into a high-tech museum. Four times the size of the Pompidou Centre, from the outside it appears fortress-like, despite the transparency of its giant glass walls beneath a dark blue lattice of steel, reinforced by walkways that accelerate out towards the Géode across a moat level with the underground floors. Once you're inside, however, the solidity of first impressions is totally reversed by the three themes of water (around the building), vegetation (in the greenhouses) and light – with which the building is flooded, from vast skylights as well as the glass facade.

This is the science museum to end all science museums, and worth visiting for the interior of the building alone: all glass and stainless steel, crow's-nests and cantilevered platforms, bridges and suspended walkways, the different levels linked by lifts and escalators around a huge central space open to the full forty-metre height of the roof. It may be colossal, but you are more likely to lose yourself mentally rather than physically, and come out after several hours reeling with images and ideas about DNA, quasars, bacterial reproduction, curved space or rocket launching. Entry to the building itself is free, as are some of the facilities within – the cafés, aquarium, *médiathèque*, and viewing of documentaries (in French) in the Salle Jean-Painlevé and in the auditorium. The ticket for Explora (the permanent exhibition) is valid all day, but for four entries only. For details of the **Cité des Enfants**, which is designed for children, see p.432.

The exhibition space, **Explora**, is ranged across the top two floors (pick up a detailed plan in English from the welcome desk on level 0) and includes both temporary shows and a permanent exhibition divided into twenty units, many accompanied by English translations. These cover a variety of subjects, among them water, oceans, the universe, automobiles, aeronautics, energy, images, genes, sound, mathematics, light and matter, and there's also a section on current scientific developments. As the name suggests, the emphasis is on exploring, and the means used are interactive computers, multimedia displays, videos, holograms, animated models and games.

On **level 1**, a classic example of chaos theory introduces the **maths section**; La Fontaine Turbulente is a wheel of glasses rotating below a stream of water in which the switch between clockwise and anticlockwise motion is unpredictable beyond two minutes. An "inertial carousel" – a revolving drum (2–6pm only) – provides a four-minute insight into the strange transformations of objects in motion. In **Les Sons** (sounds), you can watch a video of an X-rayed jaw and throat talking, or sit in a cubicle and feel your body tingle with physical sensations as a rainstorm crashes around you. Videos in **L'homme et les gènes** trace the development of an embryo from fertilization to birth, while in **Images** you can use computer simulation to manipulate Mona Lisa's smile.

On **level 2**, the **Jeux de Lumière**, especially popular with children, is a whole series of experiments to do with colour, optical illusions, refraction and the like. You can have your head spun further by a session in the **planetarium** (around six shows daily; €3 supplement).

Back on the ground floor, the **Cinéma Louis-Lumière** shows short stereoscopic (3D) films every half hour or so, for which you'll have to queue. General documentaries in French only and more serious scientific documentaries are shown in **Salle Jean-Painlevé** (level –1; free). In the **Médiathèque** (levels –1 & –2; Tues noon–7.45pm, Wed–Sun noon–6.45pm; free), a multimedia library, you can select from over four thousand films (some in English) at individual consoles, as well as consult educational software, books and magazines. On level –1 the **Cité des Métiers** (Tues–Fri 10am–6pm, Sat noon–6pm) provides free access to information on finding work, changing careers, training, creating your own employment, and working conditions in different countries. It even offers an on-the-spot consultancy with a careers adviser. Finally, on the lowest floor (–2), you can eat and drink beside an **aquarium** filled with Mediterranean sea life.

The Géode, the Cinaxe and the Argonaute

In front of the museum complex floats the **Géode** (hourly shows daily; €9; ⓦwww.lageode.fr), a bubble of reflecting steel dropped from an intergalactic boules game into a pool of water that ripples with the mirrored image of the Cité. Inside, the sphere holds a screen for Imax films and 3D films, not noted for their plots but a great visual experience. Or there's the **Cinaxe**, between the Cité and the Canal St-Denis (screenings every 15min daily; €4.80 with Explora ticket), combining 70mm film shot at thirty frames a second with seats that move, so that a bobsleigh ride down the Cresta Run, for example, not only looks unbelievably real, but feels it, too. You can clamber around a real 1957 French military submarine beside the Géode, the **Argonaute** (Mon–Fri 10.30am–5.30pm, Sat & Sun 11am–6.30pm; €3), and view the park through its periscope.

The Cité de la Musique

Crossing the Canal de l'Ourcq south of the Géode, a walkway leads past the Grande Salle to the **Cité de la Musique** (ⓦwww.cite-musique.fr), housed in two complexes either side of the Porte-de-Pantin entrance. To the west, the waves and funnels, irregular polygons and non-parallel lines of the Conservatoire de Paris, the city's music academy, make abstract sense: windows in sequences like musical notation; the wavy roof, which, according to the architect, Christian de Portzamparc, is like a Gregorian chant, but could equally suggest the movement of a dancer or a conductor's baton; and the crescendo of the rising curves of the facade.

The wedge-shaped complex to the east contains the public spaces, which include the excellent Musée de la Musique, the chic *Café de la Musique*, a music and dance information centre, and a concert hall whose ovoid dome rises like a perfect soufflé from the roof line. The harsh semi-exterior element of a girdered "arrow" pointing down to the entrance arch pretending to be another red folly hides an unexpectedly sensual interior. A glass-roofed arcade spirals round the auditorium, the combination of pale-blue walls, a subtly sloping floor and the height to the ceiling creating a sense of calm and uplift.

The Musée de la Musique

The **Musée de la Musique** (Tues–Sat noon–6pm, Sun 10am–6pm; €7; M° Porte-de-Pantin) presents the history of music from the end of the Renaissance to the present day, both visually, exhibiting some 4500 instruments, and aurally, via headsets (available in English; free) and interactive displays. Glass case after glass case holds gleaming, beautiful instruments – jewel-inlaid crystal flutes and a fabulous lyre-guitar, all made in Paris in the early 1800s, are some impressive examples. The instruments are presented in the context of a key work in the history of Western music; as you step past each case, the headphones are programmed to emit a short scholarly narration, followed by a delightful concert. It's a truly transporting – and educational – experience to gaze at the grouping of harps, made in Paris between 1760 and 1900, and hear an excerpt of music as heavenly as the instruments you're looking at.

The museum also includes an **auditorium**, where regular concerts are held, in addition to a huge archive of documents and sound recordings, and spaces for workshops, films and audiovisuals.

Belleville, Ménilmontant and Charonne

The old villages of **Belleville**, **Ménilmontant** and **Charonne**, only incorporated into the city in 1860, are strung out along the western slopes of a ridge that rises steadily from the Seine at Bercy to an altitude of 128m near Belleville's place des Fêtes, the highest point in Paris after Montmartre. The area is a bit run-down in parts, but there are pockets of charm here and there, especially around the attractive **Parc des Buttes-Chaumont** and **Parc de Belleville**, and it's home to what is probably one of the most diverse populations in the city: a mix of traditional working class, various ethnic communities and a good number of students, artists and other creative types, making this area quite a trendy hang-out. The quickest and easiest way to get out here is to take a trip on the #26 **bus** from the Gare du Nord, getting on and off at strategic points along the **avenue de Simon-Bolivar** and **rue des Pyrénées**, which between them run the whole length of the ridge to Porte de Vincennes.

Parc des Buttes-Chaumont and around

The delightful, hilly **Parc des Buttes-Chaumont** (daily: May & mid-Aug to end Sept 7am–9pm; June to mid-Aug 7am–10pm; Oct–April 7am–8pm; M° Buttes-Chaumont/Botzaris), north of the Belleville heights, was constructed under Haussmann in the 1860s to camouflage what until then had been a desolate warren of disused quarries, rubbish dumps and shacks. Out of this rather unlikely setting, a fairy-tale-like park was created – there's a grotto with a cascade and artificial stalactites, and a picturesque lake from which a huge rock rises up, topped with a delicate Corinthian temple. You can cross the lake via a suspension bridge, or take the shorter **Pont des Suicides**. This, according to Louis Aragon, the literary grand old man of the French Communist Party, "before metal grilles were erected along its sides, claimed victims even from passers-by who had had no intention whatsoever of killing themselves but were suddenly tempted by the abyss . . ." (*Le Paysan de Paris*). From the temple you can see the Sacré-Coeur, and you can also go boating on the lake. Unusually for Paris, you're not cautioned off the grass.

There are some rather desirable residences around the park, especially to the east, between rue de Crimée and **place de Rhin-et-Danube**; little cobbled *villas* (tiny streets, a bit like mews), lined with ivy-strewn houses, their little gardens full of roses and lilac trees, can be found here, off rue Miguel-Hidalgo, rue du Général-Brunet, rue de la Liberté, rue de l'Egalité and rue de Mouzaïa.

One block south of the park, at 33 rue des Alouettes, is a small contemporary art centre, **Le Plateau** (Wed–Fri 2–7pm, Sat & Sun noon–8pm; Ⓦwww.fracidf-leplateau.com; M° Jourdain), set up after a vigorous campaign by local residents, who successfully acquired the space after fighting off property developers. Exhibitions tend to focus on experimental, cutting-edge French and international artists.

Belleville

Belleville is not exactly "belle", but it's certainly vibrant and happening, thanks to its diverse population. Successive waves of immigrants have settled in the area – Jews, Poles, Greeks and Armenians in the 1920s and 1930s, followed by Spaniards and Portuguese, then Tunisian Jews and Muslims from Algeria. The most recent arrivals are Chinese, who have established a mini Chinatown around the lower slopes of rue de Belleville. The quarter is known for its strong left-wing and community spirit, with organizations such as La Bellevilleuse campaigning to preserve the area from property developers. The availability of affordable and large spaces, ideal for *ateliers*, has attracted many artists to the area. The best opportunity to view their work is during the **Journées portes ouvertes ateliers d'artistes de Belleville** in mid-May (for exact dates see Ⓦwww.ateliers-artistes-belleville.org), when around 240 artists living or working in Belleville open their doors to the public. A number of derelict buildings have also been taken over and turned into art squats, which regularly host exhibitions.

For a chance to meet some of Belleville's artists and see little-known parts of the quartier you could join a tour run by "**Belleville ça se visite**" (€12; Ⓣ01.48.06.27.41, Ⓦwww.ca-se-visite.fr), an organization set up by locals. Tours on different themes, such as "Belleville d'hier et d'aujourd'hui", take place most

La descente de la Courtille

The name *Courtille* comes from *courti*, "garden" in the Picard dialect. The heights of Belleville were known as La Haute Courtille in the nineteenth century, while the lower part around rue du Faubourg-du-Temple and rue de la Fontaine-au-Roi was La Basse Courtille. Both were full of boozers and dancehalls, where people flocked from the city on high days and holidays.

The wildest revels of the year took place on the night of Mardi Gras, when thousands of masked people turned out to celebrate the end of the *carnaval*. Next morning – Ash Wednesday – they descended in drunken procession from Belleville to the city, in up to a thousand horse-drawn vehicles: *la descente de la Courtille*.

Claude Chappe and the rue du Télégraphe

The rue du Télégraphe, running south off the eastern end of rue de Belleville alongside the Cimetière de Belleville, is named in memory of Claude Chappe's invention of the **optical telegraph**. Chappe first tested his device here in September 1792, in a corner of the cemetery. When word of his activities got out, he was nearly lynched by a mob that assumed he was trying to signal to the king, who was at that time imprisoned in the Temple (see box, p.121). Eventually, two lines were set up, from Belleville to Strasbourg and the east, and from Montmartre to Lille and the north. By 1840, it was possible to send a message to Calais in three minutes, via 27 relays, and to Strasbourg in seven minutes, using 46 relays. Chappe himself did not live to see the fruits of his invention; his patent was contested in 1805 and, distraught, he threw himself into a sewer (his grave is in nearby Père-Lachaise).

Saturdays at 2pm (and occasionally on Wednesdays and Fridays); they're designed for five to eight people and usually involve a visit to some artists' studios. They're mostly in French, but tours in English can also be arranged for groups of a minimum of eight people.

Rue de Belleville and around

Belleville's main artery is **rue de Belleville**. Its lower end is liveliest, with numerous Chinese restaurants and *traiteurs* doing a brisk trade, while adjoining **boulevard de Belleville** is home to Algerian pastry shops and grocers and *shisha* cafés. The boulevard is lined with dramatic new architecture, employing jutting triangles, curves, and the occasional reference to the roof lines of nineteenth-century Parisian blocks. It's particularly lively on Tuesday and Friday mornings when the **market** sets up, stretching the whole length of the boulevard. Kosher food shops and cafés, belonging to Sephardic Jews from Tunisia, are also in evidence here and on **rue Ramponeau**, running parallel to the rue de Belleville. It was at the junction of rue Ramponeau and rue de Tourtille that the very last barricade of the Commune was defended single-handedly for fifteen minutes by the last fighting Communard in 1871. A combative spirit lives on here at **La Forge**, nos. 23–25, an abandoned smithy squatted by artists in the 1990s and whose cause was successfully taken up by local community associations. It now houses around thirty artists' studios, open to the public during the Journées Portes Ouvertes (see opposite) and for other occasional exhibitions.

Just the other side of rue de Belleville, down rue Rampal, is the city's biggest art squat, **La Générale** (Ⓦwww.lagenerale.org), set in an old school, at 10–14 rue du Général Lasalle. Around 125 artists, photographers and fashion designers work here and there's usually something worthwhile going on in one of the three exhibition spaces (generally open Wed–Sun 3–7pm), such as the recent Outre Part show, featuring unsettling installations, videos, photographs and paintings designed to challenge the viewer's perception of reality. Uncertainty and challenge lie ahead for the squat itself, as the authorities are threatening eviction, though it seems likely that the artists will be offered an alternative space elsewhere.

Further up rue de Belleville, a turn to the right on cobbled **rue Piat** will take you past the beautiful wrought-iron gate of the jungly **Villa Otoz** to the **Parc de Belleville**, created in the mid-1990s. From the terrace at the junction with rue des Envierges, there's a fantastic view across the city, especially at sunset. At your feet, the small park descends in a further series of terraces and waterfalls. There's a little exhibition/educational centre, geared towards children in particular, the **Maison de l'Air** (Tues–Fri 1.30–5pm, Sat & Sun 1.30–6.30pm; €3.35, children €1.60), with lots of information on air quality and meteorology, including live satellite pictures of the weather across Europe.

A path crosses the top of the park past a minuscule vineyard and turns into steps that drop down to **rue des Couronnes** (which leads back to boulevard de Belleville). Some of the adjacent streets are worth a wander for a feel of the changing times – rue de la Mare (site of the headquarters of the Ateliers d'artistes de Belleville at no. 32), rue des Envierges, rue des Cascades – with two or three beautiful old houses in overgrown gardens, alongside new housing that follows the height and curves of the streets and *passages* between them.

The upper stretch of rue de Belleville is not as distinctive as its lower end and could be the busy main street of any French provincial town, with its boulangeries and charcuteries. On the wall of no. 72, a plaque commemorates the birth of the legendary chanteuse, **Edith Piaf**; the story goes that she was born under a street lamp just here. One of Piaf's favourite hang-outs is not far from here, at 105 rue du Faubourg-du-Temple, on rue de Belleville's busy lower extension: *La Java*, a former *bal musette* venue whose original dancehall interior is still intact, though the dancing and music are now distinctly Latino.

Ménilmontant

Like Belleville, much of **Ménilmontant**, to the south, aligns itself along one straight, steep, long street, the **rue de Ménilmontant** and its lower extension rue Oberkampf. Although seedy and dilapidated in parts, its popularity with artists and young professionals, or *bobos* (*bourgeois-bohémiens*), as they're often referred to, has helped to revitalize the area. Alternative shops and trendy bars and restaurants have elbowed in among the grocers and cheap hardware stores, especially along **rue Oberkampf**, which now hosts a vibrant bar scene

The bygone eastern villages

Before redevelopment, the superb hillside location, combined with cobbled lanes, individual gardens, numerous stairways, and local shops and cafés perfectly integrated with human-scale housing, gave the area around Belleville and Ménilmontant a unique charm – quite the equal of Montmartre, but without the touristy commercialism.

For a picture of what it was like, there's no more evocative record than Willy Ronis's atmospheric photographs in *Belleville Ménilmontant*. But there's still on-the-ground evidence, in addition to the little cul-de-sacs of terraced houses and gardens east of rue des Pyrénées. There are alleys so narrow that nothing but the knife-grinder's tricycle could fit down them, like passage de la Duée, 17 rue de la Duée, and little detached houses, like 97 rue Villiers-de-l'Isle-Adam. You can also see the less romantic side of life in the grim neo-Gothic fortress housing estates of 140 rue de Ménilmontant, built in 1925 for the influx of rural populations after World War I, and the 1913 Villa Stendhal, off rue Stendhal, east of the southern section of rue des Pyrénées, in the Charonne area. In marked contrast is the housing right over to the east, near the Porte de Bagnolet, provided for workers in 1908 and almost unmatched in the city. From place Octave-Chanute, wide stone steps bordered by lanterns lead up to a miraculous little sequence of streets of terraced houses and gardens, some with Art Nouveau glass porches, fancy brickwork and the shade of lilac and cherry trees.

(see p.359): some of the most popular hang-outs are *Café Charbon*, a renovated dancehall, the nearby *Cithéa* club and *La Mercerie*. **Boulevard Ménilmontant**, west of Père-Lachaise, is also prime bar-crawling territory, with places like *La Mère Lachaise* (see p.350) and *Les Lucioles* (see p.359) drawing a cool crowd. The upper reaches of rue de Ménilmontant, above rue Sorbier, are quieter, and looking back you find yourself dead in line with the rooftop of the Pompidou Centre, a measure of how high you are above the rest of the city.

Like Belleville itself, the area closest to boulevard de Belleville, centred on rue des Amandiers, has been almost completely demolished and rebuilt – on a small scale, around courtyards with open spaces for kids to play. **Rue Elisa-Borey** turns into steps alongside the extraordinary France Telecom building, topped with great bunches of masts, which faces a lovely small park on rue Sorbier.

Cross the park, take a right, then a left into rue Boyer, and you'll find the splendid mosaic and sculpted constructivist facade of **La Bellevilloise** (Ⓦwww.labellevilloise.com) at no. 19, built for the PCF (French Communist Party) in 1925 to celebrate fifty years of work and science. Saved from demolition by a preservation order, it is now a thriving little arts and community centre, hosting regular concerts and exhibitions.

A short way before it, a delightful lane of village houses and gardens, **rue Laurence-Savart**, climbs up to rue du Retrait. The latter street ends on rue des Pyrénées opposite the poetically named alley of sighs, the "*passage des Soupirs*". **Rue des Pyrénées**, the main cross-route through this quartier, is itself redolent of the provinces, getting busier as it approaches place Gambetta. The post office at no. 248 has a big ceramic wall-piece by the sculptor Zadkine. Close by place Gambetta, on rue Malte-Brun, is the glass frontage of the **Théâtre National de la Colline**. You can snack in its **cafeteria** and pick up brochures on current productions.

Just 200m west of the place Gambetta is the Père-Lachaise cemetery (see p.238). There's more melancholy to be found near the northwest corner of the cemetery, where the **street names** echo the long-vanished orchards and rustic pursuits of the villagers: Amandiers (almond trees), Pruniers (plum trees), Mûriers (mulberry trees), Pressoir (wine press). Further west, across boulevard de Ménilmontant, another era is captured in the **Musée Edith Piaf**, at 5 rue Crespin-du-Gast (Mon–Thurs 1–6pm; closed Sept; admission by appointment only on Ⓣ01.43.55.52.72; donation; M° Ménilmontant/St-Maur). Piaf was not an acquisitive person; the few clothes (yes, a little black dress), letters, toys, paintings and photographs that she left are almost all here, along with every one of her recordings. The venue is a small flat lived in by her devoted friend Bernard Marchois, and the "Amis d'Edith Piaf" will show you around and tell you stories about her life.

Charonne

With its perfect little Romanesque church, St-Germain-de-Charonne, and the cobbled street of rue St-Blaise, **Charonne** retains its village-like atmosphere. To get to this unexpected and little-visited corner of the city, take the southwest radial, avenue du Père-Lachaise, from place Gambetta, and then turn left along rue des Rondeaux, the street that follows the Père-Lachaise cemetery wall. Cross rue des Pyrénées by the bridge in rue Renouvier, turn right on rue Stendhal (Villa Stendhal is opposite – see box, p.236) past the underground reservoir that serves as a gigantic header tank for the stopcocks that wash the city's gutters, and go down the steps at the end to rue de Bagnolet.

To the left, in place St-Blaise, stands **St-Germain-de-Charonne** (M° Porte de Bagnolet/Gambetta), which has changed little, and its Romanesque belfry not at all, since the thirteenth century. It's one of only two Paris churches to have its own graveyard (the other is St-Pierre in Montmartre) – several hundred Communards were buried after being accidentally disinterred during the construction of a reservoir in 1897. Elsewhere in Paris, charnel houses were the norm, with the bones emptied into the catacombs as more space was required. It was not until the nineteenth century that public cemeteries appeared on the scene, the most famous being **Père-Lachaise** (see below).

Opposite the church, the old cobbled village high street, **rue St-Blaise**, pedestrianized to place des Grès, was once one of the most picturesque in Paris, and still has a measure of charm, with its wooden shuttered houses, cafés and artists' *ateliers*. Turning right at place des Grès onto rue Vitruve and walking two blocks, you'll find lurking round the corner of rue R.A. Marquet, on the left, a large sculpted **salamander** and its footprints, mounted high up on the side of a building. Engraved above the street sign are the words: "A legend is told that a salamander, after passing by the square where it would have left a long trail, set off towards rue R.A. Marquet and stopped to rest on a corner of rue Vitruve."

Père-Lachaise cemetery

Final resting place of a host of French notables, as well as a fair number of illustrious foreigners, **Père-Lachaise** (Mon–Fri 8am–5.30pm, Sat 8.30am–5.30pm, Sun 9am–5.30pm; free; M° Père-Lachaise/Phillipe-Auguste) is one of the world's most famous cemeteries and draws around two million visitors a year. Sited on a hill commanding grand views of Paris, it extends across some 47 hectares, making it one of the world's largest cemeteries. In fact, it's a bit like a miniature town in itself with its grid-like layout, cast-iron signposts and neat cobbled lanes – a veritable "city of the dead". Size aside, it's surely also one of the most atmospheric cemeteries – an eerily beautiful haven, with terraced slopes and magnificent old trees (there are around six thousand) that spread their branches over the moss-grown tombs as though shading them from the outside world.

Finding individual graves can be a tricky business. The **map** overleaf and the free plans given out at the entrance will point you in the right direction, but it's worth buying a slightly more detailed map as it's easy to get lost; the best one is published by Editions Métropolitain Paris (around €2) and should be available in the newsagents and florists near the **main entrance** on boulevard de Ménilmontant.

Père-Lachaise was opened in 1804 and turned out to be an incredibly successful piece of land speculation. Nicolas Frochot, the urban planner who bought the land, persuaded the civil authorities to have **Molière**, **La Fontaine**, **Abélard** and **Héloïse** reburied in his new cemetery, and it began to acquire cachet, but it really took off when Balzac set the last scene of his 1835 novel *Le Père Goriot* here. Ironically, Frochot even sold a plot to the original owner for considerably more money than the price he had paid for the entire site. Even today, the rates are extremely high.

Among the most visited graves is that of **Chopin** (Division 11), who has a willowy muse mourning his loss and is often attended by groups of Poles laying wreaths and flowers in the red and white colours of the Polish flag. Many other musicians repose nearby, among them Bellini, Cherubini, the violinist Kreutzer, whose commemorative column leans precariously to one side, and the more recently deceased French jazz pianist, Michel Petrucciani. **Rossini** is honoured with a spot on the *avenue principale*, though in fact his remains have been transferred to his native Italy. Swarms also flock to the grave of ex-Doors lead singer **Jim Morrison** (Division 6), who died in Paris in 1971 at the age of 28. Once graffiti-covered and wreathed in marijuana fumes, it has been cleaned up and is watched over by a security guard to ensure it stays that way, though this hasn't stopped fans placing flowers, candles and cigarette butts on his tomb and scribbling messages in praise of love and drugs on other graves, and trees, nearby. In fact things got so bad some years ago that relatives of undistinguished Frenchmen interred nearby signed a petition asking for the singer's body to be exhumed and sent home, but the grave, unlike many here, is on a perpetual lease, so Jim is here to stay.

Another tomb that attracts many visitors is **Oscar Wilde**'s (Division 89), the base of which is covered in graffiti and lipstick kisses left by devoted fans. It's topped with a sculpture by Jacob Epstein of a mysterious Pharaonic winged messenger (sadly vandalized of its once prominent member, which was last seen being used as a paper weight by the director of the cemetery). The inscription behind is a grim verse from *The Ballad of Reading Gaol*.

Most of the celebrated dead have unremarkable tombs. Femme fatale **Colette**'s tomb, close to the main entrance in Division 4, for example, is very plain, though always covered in flowers. The same holds true for the divine **Sarah Bernhardt**'s (Division 44) and the great chanteuse **Edith Piaf**'s (Division 97). **Marcel Proust** lies in his family's black-marble, conventional tomb (Division 85). Just across the way is the rather incongruous-looking **Crematorium** (Division 87), crudely modelled on the Aghia Sophia in Istanbul, with domes and minarets. Here among others of equal or lesser renown lie the ashes of Max Ernst, Georges Pérec, Stéphane Grappelli and American dancer Isadora Duncan, who was strangled when her scarf got tangled in the rear axle of her open-top car. Maria Callas has a plaque here, too, though her ashes were removed and scattered in the Aegean.

In contrast to these modest monuments, in Division 48 a now-forgotten French diplomat, Félix de Beaujour, is marked with an enormous tower, rather like a lighthouse. To the north in Division 86, one **Jean Pezon**, a lion-tamer, is shown riding the pet lion that ate him. In Division 71, two men lie together hand in hand – Crocé-Spinelli and Sivel, a pair of balloonists who went so high they died from lack of oxygen. In Division 92, journalist **Victor Noir** – shot at the age of 22 in 1870 by Prince Napoleon for daring to criticize him – is portrayed at the moment of death, flat on his back, fully clothed, his top hat fallen by his feet. However, it's not as a magnet for anti-censorship campaigners that his tomb has become famous, but as a lucky charm – a prominent part of his anatomy has been worn shiny by the touch of infertile women, hoping for a cure.

Other bed scenes include **Félix Faure** (Division 4), French president, who died in the arms of his mistress in the Elysée palace in 1899; draped in a French flag, his head to one side, he cuts rather a romantic figure. **Géricault** reclines on cushions of stone (Division 12), paint palette in hand, his face taut with concentration; below is a sculpted relief of part of his best-known painting *The Raft of the Medusa*. Close by is the relaxed figure of **Jean Carriès**, a model-maker, in felt hat and overalls, holding a self-portrait in the palm of his hand.

Among other illustrious representatives of the arts, **Corot** (Division 24) and **Balzac** (Division 48) both have fine busts, as does poet **Alfred de Musset**, near Rossini on the *avenue principale*, and buried, according to his wishes, under

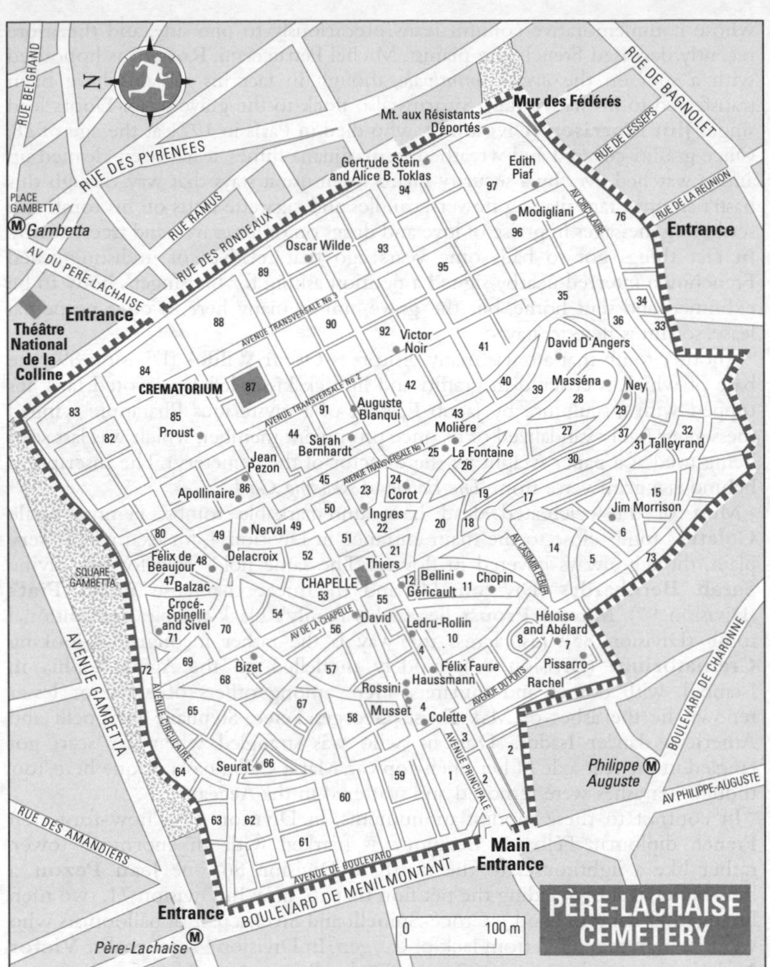

a willow tree. **Delacroix** lies in a sombre sarcophagus in Division 49, while Jacques-Louis **David**'s heart rests in Division 56 (the rest of him is buried in Belgium, where he died). His pupil **Ingres** reposes in Division 23. In Division 96, you'll find the grave of **Modigliani** and his lover Jeanne Herbuterne, who killed herself in crazed grief a few days after he died in agony from meningitis. Impressionist painter **Camille Pissarro** lies among the sober, unadorned tombs of the Jewish plot near the main entrance, as does the beautiful nineteenth-century actress **Rachel**, known for one of the pithiest love-letter exchanges in history; after seeing her on stage, Prince de Joinville sent her his card with the note "Où? Quand? Combien?", to which Rachel scribbled back, "Chez toi. Ce soir. Pour rien."

Notable politicians include **Auguste Blanqui** (Division 91), after whom so many French streets are named. Described by Karl Marx as the nineteenth century's greatest revolutionary, he served his time in jail – 33 years in all – for political activities that spanned the 1830 Revolution to the Paris Commune. South from Blanqui's grave, in Division 76, lie **Laura Marx**, Karl's daughter, and her husband **Paul Lafargue**, who committed suicide together in 1911.

It is the monuments to the collective, violent deaths, however, that have the power to change a sunny outing to Père-Lachaise into a much more sombre experience. In Division 97, in what's become known as the "coin des martyrs", you'll find the memorials to the **victims of the Nazi concentration camps**, to executed **Resistance fighters** and to those who were never accounted for in the genocide of World War II. The sculptures are relentless in their images of inhumanity, of people forced to collaborate in their own degradation and death.

Marking one of the bloodiest episodes in French history is the **Mur des Fédérés** (Division 76), the wall where the last troops of the Paris Commune were lined up and shot in the final days of the battle in 1871. A total of 147 were rounded up and killed, after a frenetic chase through the tombstones, and the remains of around a thousand other Communards were brought here and thrown into a grave-pit. The wall soon became a place of pilgrimage for the Left, and remains so today. The man who ordered the execution, **Adolphe Thiers**, lies in the centre of the cemetery in Division 55.

14 Western Paris

Western Paris consists of the well-manicured 16^{e} and 17^{e} arrondissements, often referred to as the **Beaux Quartiers**. The 16e is aristocratic and rich; the 17e, or at least the southern part of it, bourgeois and rich, embodying the staid, cautious values of the nineteenth-century manufacturing and trading classes. The area is mainly residential with few specific sights as such, the chief exception being the **Musée Marmottan**, known for its impressive collection of Monets. The northern half of the 16e, towards place Victor-Hugo and place de **l'Etoile**, is leafy though still distinctly metropolitan in feel. The southern part, around the old villages of **Auteuil** and **Passy**, is particularly pleasant for strolling. It has an almost provincial air, with its tight knot of streets and charming *villas* – leafy lanes of attractive old houses, fronted with English-style gardens, full of roses, ivy and wisteria. Although they're often closed off to non-residents, should you find the access gate open, no-one seems to mind if you wander in. Auteuil and Passy were only incorporated into the city in 1860, and soon became the capital's most desirable districts. Well-to-do Parisians commissioned new houses here, and as a result, the area is rich in fine examples of **early twentieth-century architecture**: Hector Guimard, designer of the swirly green Art Nouveau métro stations, worked here, and there are some rare Parisian examples of work by interwar architects Le Corbusier and Mallet-Stevens, who created the first "Cubist" buildings.

Auteuil

The **Auteuil** district is now completely integrated into the city and has become quite built up, but there's still a villagey feel about its streets, and it has some charming little *villas* not to mention some notable examples of early twentieth-century architecture. The ideal place to start an exploration of the area is the **Eglise d'Auteuil** métro station. Nearby are several of Hector Guimard's **Art Nouveau** buildings: at 34 rue Boileau, 8 avenue de la Villa-de-la-Réunion, 41 rue Chardon-Lagache, 142 avenue de Versailles, and 39 boulevard Exelmans.

The house at no. 34 **rue Boileau** was one of Guimard's first commissions, in 1891. To reach it from the Eglise d'Auteuil métro, head directly west along rue d'Auteuil for 200m, then turn left (south) into Boileau. A high fence and wisteria obscure much of the view, but you can see some of the decorative tile-work under the eaves and around the doors and windows. Further down the street, just before you reach boulevard Exelmans, the Vietnamese embassy

Auteuil bus routes

Handy bus routes for exploring Auteuil are the #52 and the #72. The #52 runs between M° Opéra in the centre and M° Boulogne-Pont-de-St-Cloud near the Parc des Princes, stopping at rue Poisson en route, while the #72's route extends between M° Hôtel-de-Ville in the Marais and M° Boulogne-Pont-de-St-Cloud, stopping en route by the Exelmans crossroads near some of Guimard's buildings on avenue de Versailles.

at no. 62 successfully combines 1970s Western architecture with the traditional Vietnamese elements of a pagoda roof and earthenware tiles. Continue south for 0.5km along rue Boileau beyond boulevard Exelmans, turn right onto rue Parent de Rosan and you'll find a series of enchanting *villas* off to the right, backing onto the Auteuil cemetery.

Rue Boileau terminates on avenue de Versailles, where you can turn left and head back to the Eglise d'Auteuil métro via the Guimard apartment block at 142 avenue de Versailles (1905), with its characteristic Art Nouveau flower motifs and sinuous, curling lines. It's just by the Exelmans crossroads (on bus #72's route). You can then cut across the **Jardin de Ste-Périne**, once the rural residence of the monks of Ste Geneviève's abbey, established here in 1109, to get back to the métro. The entrances to the garden are opposite 135 avenue de Versailles and alongside the hospital on rue Mirabeau, just north of the rue Chardon-Lagache junction.

For more of the life of the quartier, follow the old village high street, **rue d'Auteuil**, west from the métro exit to **place Lorrain**, which hosts a Saturday market. From here you could take rue de la Fontaine for some more Guimard buildings and the Maison de Radio-France or, if the bulgy curves of Art Nouveau make you feel queasy, head up rue du Dr-Blanche for the cool, rectilinear lines of Cubist architects Le Corbusier and Mallet-Stevens (see p.245).

Rue de la Fontaine and the Maison de Radio-France

Rue de la Fontaine runs northeast from place Lorrain to the Radio-France building and has Guimard buildings at nos. 14, 17, 19, 21 and 60. Of these, no. 14 is the most famous: the "Castel Béranger" (1898), with exuberant Art Nouveau decoration and shapes in the bay windows, the roofline and the chimney. At no. 65 there's a huge block of artists' studios by Henri Sauvage (1926) with a fascinating colour scheme, bearing signs of a Cubist influence. The **Maison de Radio-France**, its entrance at 116 avenue du Président Kennedy, is the national radio headquarters; you can visit for free concerts (see p.243) or take a guided tour through the **Musée de Radio-France** (Mon–Fri 10–11am & 2.30–4pm; €5; RER Av-du-Prés-Kennedy–Maison-de-Radio-France/M° Ranelagh), which illustrates the history of broadcasting through a wide collection of equipment including some early Marconi radios.

From place Lorrain to the Musée Marmottan

Just off place Lorrain, in rue Poussin (on bus #52's route), carriage gates open onto **Villa Montmorency**, one of the grander *villas* – more like an exclusive estate (with a security guard on the gate). The writer André Gide, and the Goncourt brothers of Prix Goncourt fame, lived in this one. Behind it, in a cul-de-sac off rue

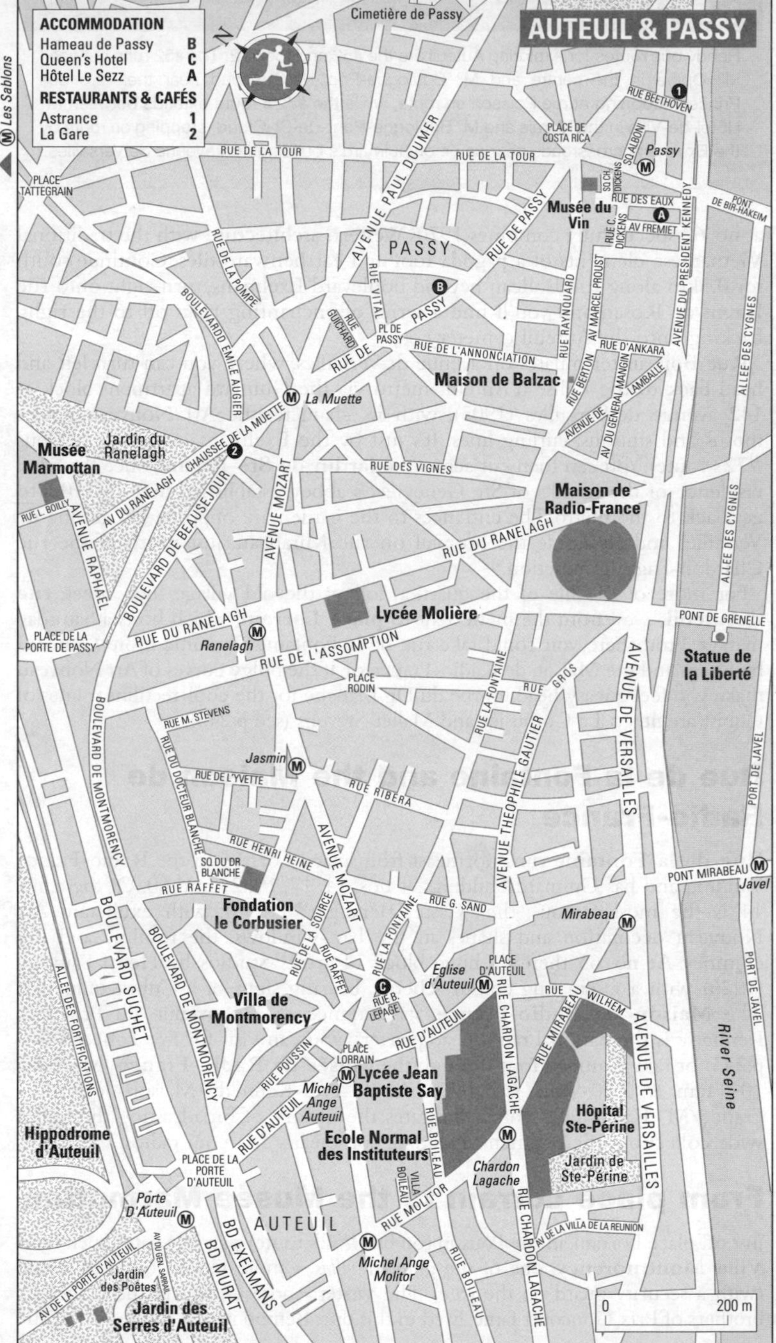
AUTEUIL & PASSY
ACCOMMODATION
Hameau de Passy B
Queen's Hotel C
Hôtel Le Sezz A
RESTAURANTS & CAFÉS
Astrance 1
La Gare 2
Cimetière de Passy
PASSY
Musée du Vin
Maison de Balzac
Maison de Radio-France
Musée Marmottan
Jardin du Ranelagh
Lycée Molière
Statue de la Liberté
Fondation le Corbusier
Villa de Montmorency
Lycée Jean Baptiste Say
Ecole Normal des Instituteurs
Hôpital Ste-Périne
Jardin de Ste-Périne
Hippodrome d'Auteuil
AUTEUIL
Jardin des Poètes
Jardin des Serres d'Auteuil
River Seine
Les Sablons
Passy
La Muette
Ranelagh
Jasmin
Javel
Mirabeau
Eglise d'Auteuil
Michel Ange Auteuil
Chardon Lagache
Michel Ange Molitor
Porte D'Auteuil
Porte de St-Cloud & Parc des Princes
0 200 m

du Dr-Blanche, are **Le Corbusier**'s first private houses (1923), the Villa Jeanneret and the Villa La Roche, now in the care of the Fondation Le Corbusier. You can visit one of the houses, the **Villa La Roche** (Mon 1.30–6pm, Tues–Thurs 10am–12.30pm & 1.30–6pm, Fri 10am–12.30pm & 1.30–5pm, Sat 10am–5pm, closed Aug; €3; Ⓦ www.fondationlecorbusier.fr; M° Jasmin), built in strictly Cubist style, very plain, with windows in bands, the only extravagance a curved frontage. They look commonplace enough now from the outside, but were a great contrast with anything that had gone before, and once you're inside the spatial play still seems ground-breaking. The interior is appropriately decorated with Cubist paintings.

Further north along rue du Dr-Blanche and off to the right, the tiny **rue Mallet-Stevens** was built entirely by the architect of the same name, also in Cubist style. No. 12, where Robert Mallet-Stevens had his offices, has been altered, along with other houses in the street, but you can still see the architectural intention of sculpting the entire street space as a cohesive unit. Continue to the end of rue du Dr-Blanche, turn left and then right onto boulevard Beauséjour; a shortcut immediately opposite rue du Ranelagh across the disused Petite Ceinture rail line takes you to shady avenue Raphaël, which runs alongside the pretty **Jardin du Ranelagh** (with a rather engaging sculpture of the fabulist La Fontaine with an eagle and fox) and on to the Musée Marmottan.

The Musée Marmottan

The **Musée Marmottan** (daily except Mon 10am–6pm; €8; Ⓦ www.marmottan.com; M° Muette), 2 rue Louis-Boilly, is best known for its excellent collection of **Monet paintings**, bequeathed to the museum by the artist's son. Among them is *Impression, soleil levant*, a canvas from 1872 of a misty Le Havre morning, and whose title the critics usurped to give the Impressionist movement its name. The painting was stolen from the gallery in October 1985, along with eight other paintings. After a police operation lasting five years, which extended as far afield as Japan, the paintings were discovered in a villa in southern Corsica, and were put back on show with greatly increased security. There's also a dazzling selection of canvases from Monet's last years at Giverny; these paintings show the increasingly abstract quality of the artist's later work and include several *Nymphéas* (Waterlilies), *Le Pont japonais*, *L'Allée des rosiers* and *La Saule pleureur*, where rich colours are laid on in thick, excited whorls and lines. The collection also features some of Monet's contemporaries – Manet, Renoir and **Berthe Morisot**. Morisot, who lived most of her life in Passy and is buried in the Cimetière de Passy, is particularly well represented, with two rooms devoted to her wonderfully summery canvases; her work is characterized by vigorous, almost aggressive, brushwork, seen to best effect in paintings such as *Branches of an orange tree* (1889) and *Garden at Bougival* (1884).

In addition, the museum displays some splendid examples of First Empire pomposity: chairs with golden sphinxes for armrests, candelabra of complicated headdresses and twining serpents, and a small and beautiful collection of thirteenth- to sixteenth-century **manuscript illuminations** – look out for the decorated capital R framing an exquisitely drawn portrait of St Catherine of Alexandria.

West of Auteuil

West of place de la Porte d'Auteuil are two gardens: the **Jardin des Poètes** (daily 9am–6pm; free), with its entrance on avenue du Général Sarrail, and the adjoining **Jardin des Serres d'Auteuil** (daily 10am–6pm, closes 5pm in winter; free; M° Porte d'Auteuil), its main entrance at 3 avenue de la Porte d'Auteuil (or you can enter from the Jardin des Poètes). You can't escape the traffic noise completely, but the Jardin des Poètes is extremely tranquil. Famous French poets are each remembered by a verse (of a mostly pastoral nature) engraved on small stones surrounded by little flowerbeds. A statue of Victor Hugo by Rodin stands in the middle of this very informal garden. Approaching the Auteuil garden and the greenhouses (*serres*) from the Jardin des Poètes, you pass the delightful potting sheds with rickety wooden blinds. Then you're into a formal garden, beautifully laid out around the big old-fashioned metal-frame greenhouses. Among them is a palm house containing two hundred tropical species and a greenhouse devoted entirely to flora rarely seen outside their native New Caledonia. There may also be a special exhibition on – azaleas in April, for example.

Directly beyond the Jardin des Serres d'Auteuil is the **Stade Roland Garros**, venue for the French tennis championships (see p.422 for information about watching a tournament). A **tennis museum** (Tues–Sun 10am–6pm; €7.50; M° Porte-d'Auteuil) fills you in on the history of the game and its development from *jeu de paume*, or "real tennis"; Paris boasted over a hundred real tennis courts under Henri IV, a keen player himself, while in Orléans in 1656 students were spending so much time hitting a ball around that the only way to get them back to their studies was to close the courts down. Most of the rest of the museum is given over to photos and footage of mainly French tennis stars, such as René Lacoste and Yannick Noah.

The **Jardins Albert Kahn** (Tues–Sun: May–Sept 11am–7pm; Oct–April 11am–6pm; garden & museum entry €3.30; M° Boulogne-Pont-de-St-Cloud/ M° Marcel-Semblat) at 14 rue du Port, to the south in the neighbouring suburb of Boulogne-Billancourt, consists of a very pretty garden and a small museum dedicated to temporary exhibitions of "*Les Archives de la Planète*" – photographs and films collected by banker and philanthropist Albert Kahn between 1909 and 1931 to record human activities and ways of life that he knew would soon disappear for ever. His aim in the design of the garden was to combine English, French, Japanese and other styles to demonstrate the possibility of a harmonious, peaceful world. It's an enchanting place, with rhododendrons and camellias under blue cedars, a rose garden and an espaliered orchard, a forest of Moroccan pines and streams with Japanese bridges beside pagoda tea houses, Buddhas and pyramids of pebbles. A palm hothouse has been turned into a very chic *salon de thé*, serving such delights as pear liqueur and *marrons glacés* sorbet.

Passy

Northeast of Auteuil, the area around the old village of **Passy**, too, offers scope for a good meandering walk, from La Muette métro, through old characterful streets like rue de l'Annonciation, to Balzac's house, and through more cobbled streets to the Seine and Pont de Bir-Hakeim near Passy métro.

From La Muette to the Maison de Balzac

From **La Muette** métro, head east along the old high street, **rue de Passy**, past an eye-catching parade of boutiques, until you reach **place de Passy** and the crowded but leisurely terrace of *Le Paris Passy* café. From the *place*, stroll southeast along cobbled, pedestrianized **rue de l'Annonciation**, a pleasant blend of down-to-earth and genteel well-heeled which gives more of the flavour of old Passy. You may no longer be able to have your Bechstein repaired here or your furniture lacquered, but the food shops that now dominate the street have delectable displays guaranteed to make your mouth water.

When you hit rue Raynouard, cross the road and veer to your right, where at no. 47 you'll discover the **Maison de Balzac** (Tues–Sun 10am–6pm; free; Ⓦ www.balzac.paris.fr; M° Av-du-Prés-Kennedy–Maison-de-Radio-France/ M° Passy), a delightful, summery little house with pale-green shutters and a decorative iron entrance porch, tucked away down some steps among a tree-filled garden. Balzac moved to this secluded spot in 1840 in the hope of evading his creditors. He lived under a pseudonym, and visitors had to give a special password before being admitted. Should any unwelcome callers manage to get past the door, Balzac would escape via a backdoor and go down to the river via a network of underground cellars. It was here that he wrote some of his best-known works, including *La Cousine Bette* and *Le Cousin Pons*. The museum preserves his study, simple writing desk and monogrammed cafetière – frequent doses of caffeine must have been essential during his long writing stints, which could extend up to sixteen or eighteen hours a day for weeks on end. One room is devoted to the development of ideas for the creation of a monument to Balzac, resulting in the famously blobby Rodin sculpture of the writer; caricatures of the sculpture by cartoonists of the time are on display here. Other exhibits include letters to Mme Hanska, whom he eventually married after an eighteen-year courtship, and a highly complex family tree of around a thousand of the four thousand-plus characters that feature in his *Comédie Humaine*. Outside, the shady, rose-filled garden is a serene haven and a pleasant place to dally on wrought-iron seats amid busts of the writer.

Behind Balzac's house, and reached via some steps descending from rue Raynouard, **rue Berton** is a cobbled path with gas lights still in place, blocked off by the heavy security of the **Turkish embassy**. The building, an eighteenth-century château shrouded by greenery and screened by a high wall and guards, was once the home of Marie-Antoinette's friend, the Princesse de Lamballe, who met a grisly fate at the hands of revolutionaries in 1792. Later, it became a private asylum where the pioneering Dr Blanche treated patients with serious nervous disorders. The poet Gérard de Nerval was admitted in 1854, driven insane partly by the task of translating Goethe's *Faust* into French. Four years later, Charles Gounod, while working on the score for his opera *Faust*, based on Nerval's translation, was also treated here. And in 1892, Maupassant, suffering serious mental illness brought on by syphilis, was committed in a straitjacket; he died a year later on the upper floor. You can get a better view of the building from cobbled **rue d'Ankara**, reached by heading down avenue de Lamballe and then right into avenue du Général-Mangin.

East to the Musée du Vin and Pont de Bir-Hakeim

From rue d'Ankara, head northeast along avenue Marcel-Proust, turn right and then left onto rue Charles Dickens and follow it until it hits rue des Eaux. Rue des Eaux was where fashionable Parisians used to come in the eighteenth century for the therapeutic benefits of the once-famous iron-rich and sulphuric Passy waters. Today, the street is enclosed by a canyon of moneyed apartments, which dwarf the eighteenth-century houses of **square Charles-Dickens**. In one of them, burrowing back into the cellars of a vanished, fourteenth-century monastery, which produced wine until the Revolution, is the **Musée du Vin** (daily except Mon 10am–6pm; €8.90, admission includes a glass of wine; Ⓦwww.museeduvinparis.com), an exhibition of viticultural bits and bobs about as exciting as flat champagne, though the cellar bar is an atmospheric place for a glass of wine or lunch. Extensive stone-vaulted cellars and passages lead off from here to the ancient quarry tunnels – not visitable – from which the stone for Notre-Dame was hewn.

Back on rue Raynouard, head northeast to place du Costa-Rica, take the first right into rue de l'Alboni and go down the steps into square Alboni, a patch of garden enclosed by tall apartment buildings as solid as banks. Here the métro line emerges from what used to be a vine-covered hillside for the Passy stop – more like a country station – before rumbling out across the river by the **Pont de Bir-Hakeim**, the distinctive bridge famously featured in the racy Bertolucci film *Last Tango in Paris*, starring Marlon Brando. From here you're well placed to hop back onto the métro, or cross the bridge and head north along the water to the Eiffel Tower about 500m along.

Bois de Boulogne

The **Bois de Boulogne**, running all the way down the west side of the 16e, was designed by Baron Haussmann and supposedly modelled on London's Hyde Park – though it's a very French interpretation. The *bois*, or "wood", of the name is somewhat deceptive, though the extensive parklands (just under 900 hectares) do contain some remnants of the once great Forêt de Rouvray. As its location would suggest, the Bois was once the playground of the wealthy, although it also established a reputation as the site of illicit sex romps; it was popularly said that "Les mariages du bois de Boulogne ne se font pas devant Monsieur le Curé" – "Unions cemented in the Bois de Boulogne do not take

△ Parc de Bagatelle rose garden

place in the presence of a priest". Today's unions are no less disreputable – the area is a favoured haunt for prostitutes and accompanying kerb-crawlers who, despite an obvious police presence and the night-time closure of certain roads, still do business along its periphery. Accompanying the sex trade is a certain amount of crime; the park is a very unwise choice for a midnight promenade.

By day, however, the Bois de Boulogne is a delightful retreat from the city. While entry to the overall park is free, there are several attractions within it that have entry fees or limited opening times: the **Jardin d'Acclimatation**, which is aimed at children (see p.424 for more information); the beautiful floral displays of the Parc de Bagatelle; and the **racecourses** at Longchamp and Auteuil. You can also partake of a wealth of activities: there's a **riding** school, a **bowling** alley, **bike rental** (for which you'll need to leave your passport as security) at the entrance to the Jardin d'Acclimatation and 14km of cycling routes; and **boating** on the Lac Inférieur. More details of sporting and leisure activities in the park are given on p.419 and p.422. The best, and wildest, part for **walking** is towards the southwest corner. On avenue du Mahatma Gandhi, inside the Jardin d'Acclimataion, building has started on the Fondation Louis Vuitton pour la Création, a contemporary arts space, designed by Frank Gehry and due for completion in 2010.

Spread out to the south and west of the *bois* is the **Parc de Bagatelle** (daily 9am–7pm; €3; M° Porte-Maillot, then bus #244, which takes you to the entrance on allée de Longchamp; there's also an entrance on route de Sèvres à Neuilly). Comprising a range of garden styles from French and English to Japanese, its most famous feature is the stunning **rose garden** of the charming Château de Bagatelle. The château was designed and built in just over sixty days in 1775 as a wager between Comte d'Artois, the owner, and his sister-in-law Marie-Antoinette, who said it could not be achieved in less than three months. The best time for the roses is June, while in other parts of the garden there are beautiful displays of tulips, hyacinths and daffodils in early April, irises in May, and waterlilies in early August. The park's attractive orangerie is the setting for candlelit recitals of Chopin's music during the Festival Chopin in late June (see p.381).

Bang in the middle of the Bois de Boulogne, the Pré Catalan park is famous for its huge beech tree and, outside an open-air theatre, its **Jardin Shakespeare**, where you can study the herbs, trees and flowers referred to in the bard's plays.

Exiting the park at Porte Dauphine, Avenue Foch runs northeast from the Bois de Boulogne to Etoile through the 16e. Two blocks east of here is the beginning of rue de la Faisanderie, where at no. 16 you'll find one of Paris's oddest museums, the **Musée de la Contrefaçon** (Tues–Sun 2–5.30pm; €4; M^{o} Porte-Dauphine), set up to deliver an anti-counterfeiting message. Examples of imitation products, labels and brand marks trying to pass themselves off as the genuine article are all on display, in most cases alongside the real thing.

The suburbs

The outskirts of Paris have been swallowed up by the capital's expansion, but, despite a bland proliferation of industrial buildings and modern flats, many towns, especially to the south and west, retain their identities and links with the past. Royal or noble châteaux dedicated to hunting and other leisured pursuits once studded the region, and it's surprisingly easy to escape the city on a day-trip to take a stroll in the **gardens**, **parks and forests** that surround them. The most renowned château by far, on the very edge of the Paris conurbation, is **Versailles**, an overwhelming monument to the reigns of Louis XIV, who built it, and Louis XVI, whose furniture now fills it. The much more modest **Malmaison** preserves the exquisite Empire furnishings of Napoleon's wife, Josephine. Artists have also traditionally sought an escape in the countryside around Paris; **Meudon**, for example, was Rodin's final home and resting place. Quite the reverse of a bucolic retreat is **La Défense**, Paris's gleaming modern business district, graced with the stunning **Grande Arche**.

The northern and eastern suburbs have more than their fair share of *cités* (high-rise housing estates), but are punctuated by distractions. At **St-Denis**, the impressive Gothic basilica was the wellspring of the Gothic style, and the burial place of almost all the French kings; these days, it stands proudly at the centre of a fascinating multi-ethnic suburb. Whether the various suburban museums deserve your attention will depend on your degree of interest in the subjects they represent: air and space travel at **Le Bourget**; contemporary art in Vitry-sur-Seine's **Mac/Val**; and the authoritative collection of china at **Sèvres**.

All of the sights listed in this section are easily accessible by RER, métro and bus. Sights further afield, for which you'll need to take a train or have access to a car, are covered in Chapter 16 (see p.267). For other attractions in Ile-de-France, the tourist office (Espace Tourisme d'Ile-de-France, ⓦ www.paris-ile-de-france.com, see p.46) in the Carrousel du Louvre is a good source of information.

La Défense

A mini Manhattan of towering glass and concrete blocks, **La Défense**, just west of the city, is Paris's prestige **business district**. Its most dazzling sight is **La Grande Arche**, built in 1989 to mark the bicentenary of the Revolution. This beautiful and astounding structure, a 112-metre hollow cube clad in white marble, is a conscious echo of the Arc de Triomphe, visible 6km away at the far end of the Voie Triomphale; the Grande Arche closes the western axis of this

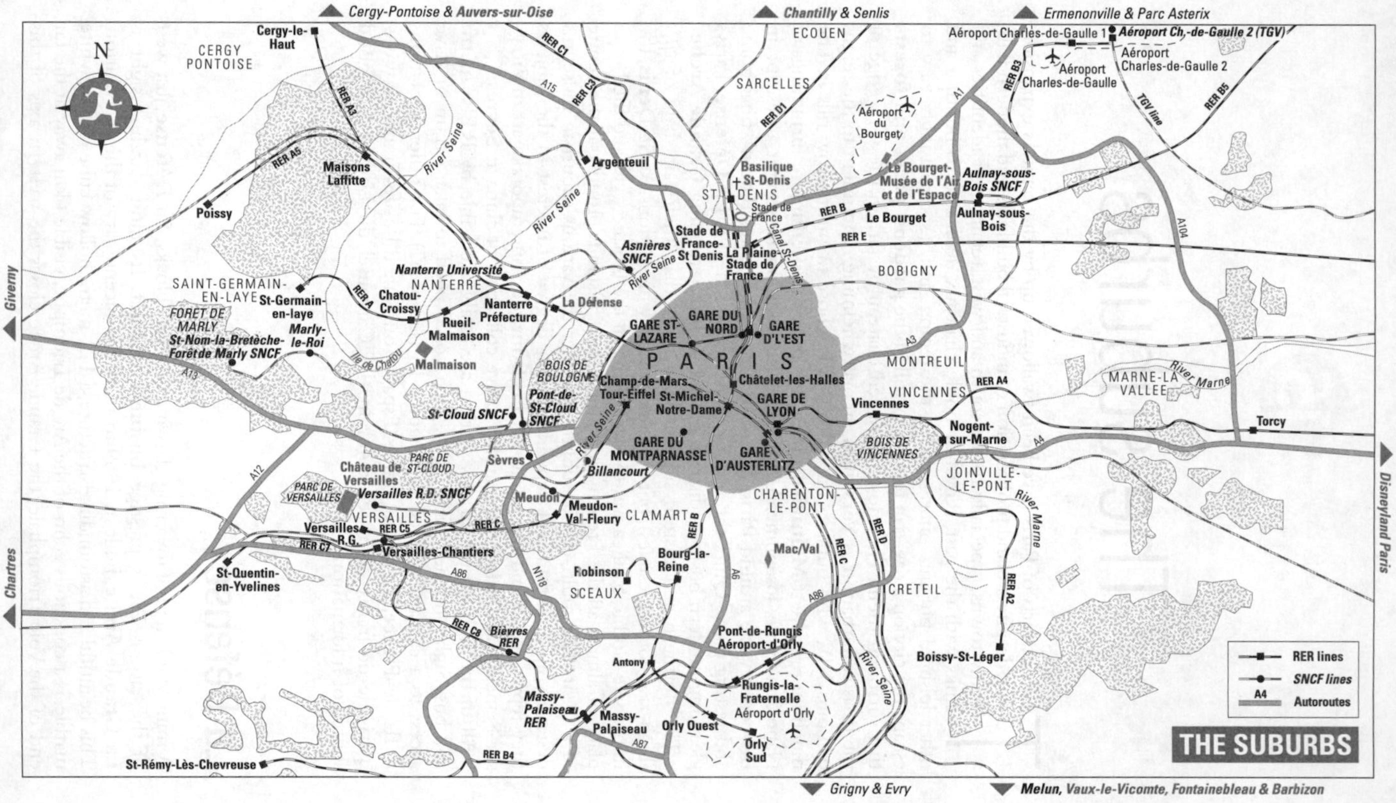

THE SUBURBS

RER lines
SNCF lines
A4 Autoroutes

Cergy-Pontoise & Auvers-sur-Oise
Chantilly & Senlis
Ermenonville & Parc Asterix
Disneyland Paris
Melun, Vaux-le-Vicomte, Fontainebleau & Barbizon
Grigny & Evry
Chartres
Giverny

N

CERGY PONTOISE
Cergy-le-Haut
Poissy
Maisons Laffitte
Argenteuil
ECOUEN
SARCELLES
ST DENIS
Basilique St-Denis
Stade de France
Aéroport du Bourget
Le Bourget-Musée de l'Air et de l'Espace
Le Bourget
Aéroport Charles-de-Gaulle 1
Aéroport Ch.-de-Gaulle 2 (TGV)
Aéroport Charles-de-Gaulle
Aéroport Charles-de-Gaulle 2
TGV line
Aulnay-sous-Bois SNCF
Aulnay-sous-Bois
BOBIGNY
Stade de France-St Denis
La Plaine-Stade de France
Canal St-Denis
Asnières SNCF
River Seine
Nanterre Université
NANTERRE
SAINT-GERMAIN-EN-LAYE
St-Germain-en-laye
Chatou-Croissy
Rueil-Malmaison
Nanterre Préfecture
La Défense
FORET DE MARLY
St-Nom-la-Bretèche-Forêt de Marly SNCF
Marly-le-Roi
Ile de Chatou
Malmaison
BOIS DE BOULOGNE
St-Cloud SNCF
Pont-de-St-Cloud SNCF
PARIS
GARE ST-LAZARE
GARE DU NORD
GARE D'L'EST
Châtelet-les-Halles
Champ-de-Mars-Tour-Eiffel
St-Michel-Notre-Dame
GARE DE LYON
GARE DU MONTPARNASSE
GARE D'AUSTERLITZ
MONTREUIL
VINCENNES
Vincennes
BOIS DE VINCENNES
MARNE-LA VALLEE
River Marne
Torcy
Nogent-sur-Marne
JOINVILLE-LE-PONT
CHARENTON-LE-PONT
Sèvres
PARC DE ST-CLOUD
Billancourt
Château de Versailles
PARC DE VERSAILLES
Versailles R.D. SNCF
VERSAILLES
Meudon
Meudon-Val-Fleury
CLAMART
Versailles R.G.
Versailles-Chantiers
St-Quentin-en-Yvelines
Robinson
Bourg-la-Reine
SCEAUX
Mac/Val
CRETEIL
Boissy-St-Léger
Bièvres RER
Antony
Pont-de-Rungis Aéroport-d'Orly
Rungis-la-Fraternelle
Aéroport d'Orly
Orly Ouest
Orly Sud
Massy-Palaiseau RER
Massy-Palaiseau
St-Rémy-Lès-Chevreuse
RER A
RER A2
RER A3
RER A4
RER A5
RER B
RER B3
RER B4
RER B5
RER C
RER C1
RER C3
RER C5
RER C7
RER C8
RER D
RER D1
RER E
A1
A3
A4
A6
A12
A13
A15
A86
A87
A104
N118

monumental east–west vista and is cleverly positioned at a slight angle so as to allow an uninterrupted view all the way to the Louvre's Cour Carré. The only thing that slightly mars the grace of the arch is a fibreglass "cloud" canopy, suspended within its hollow, large enough to enclose Notre-Dame with ease. The architect was a little-known Danish professor, Johann Otto von Spreckelsen, whose previous projects amounted to no more than three churches and a house, and who tragically died before the arch's completion.

The arch houses a government ministry, international businesses, an information centre on the European Union ("Sources d'Europe"; Mon–Fri 10am–6pm) and, in the roof section, the Fondation Internationale des Droits de l'Homme, which stages exhibitions and conferences on issues related to human rights. Transparent lift shafts make for a thrilling ride to the top. The **lift** (daily 10am–8pm; closes an hour earlier in winter; €7.50), however, is pricey, and the views no more impressive than from the series of steps that leads up to the base of the arch, itself a popular meeting and viewing point – on a clear day, you can scan from the marble path on the parvis below you to the Arc de Triomphe, and beyond to the Louvre.

Around La Grande Arche

From the Grande Arche to the river extends the main artery of La Défense, the pedestrianized **Esplanade du Général de Gaulle**, bristling with shiny office towers, apartment blocks and modern artworks. It has to be said, however, that fifty years on from its beginnings, and despite such sleek edifices as the EDF building on place de la Défense, the district is starting to look a little tired – a widely recognized fact that has prompted a major facelift and a new wave of building. Foremost among the projects is the **Tour Phare**, a three-hundred-metre-high gleaming, sinuous skyscraper which is due to be completed in 2012 and is the brainchild of top American architect Thomas Mayne. It will rival the Eiffel Tower in height and is designed to match buildings such as London's "Gherkin". It's also notable for its green credentials – it will have a wind farm on top of its roof and a "double skin" around it which will reduce the heat from direct sunlight through the windows.

To see the plans for the tower and other new developments call into the little **museum** downstairs at **Info Défense** (April–Oct daily 10am–6pm; Nov–March Mon–Fri 9.30am–5.30pm; free), on the main place de la Défense. Also worth a look are displays of some of the early projects that were put forward for La Défense in the 1930s, such as Le Corbusier's huge *Metropolis*-like high-rises, and the gigantic Victory Angel once considered in place of the Grande Arche. While here it's worth picking up a map, showing all La Défense's main buildings and outdoor **sculptures** (of which there are around fifty altogether).

The oldest work of art is just behind Info Défense, perched on a concrete plinth in front of a coloured plastic water sculpture: Barrias's bronze *La Défense de Paris*, dating from the 1880s and depicting a soldier defending a woman who symbolizes Paris. It commemorates the **defence of Paris** against the Prussians in 1870 and is the origin of the district's name.

The first building to go up at La Défense was the undulating **CNIT building**, to the right of the Grande Arche, erected in the 1950s as a trade exhibition centre and the first intimation of the area's modernist architectural future. The floor of the hangar-like building, all gleaming granite, is softened by slender bamboo trees; the serious activity takes place off in the far corners, where it seems every major computer company has an office. There's also a FNAC store, and a selection of cafés and brasseries. Across the

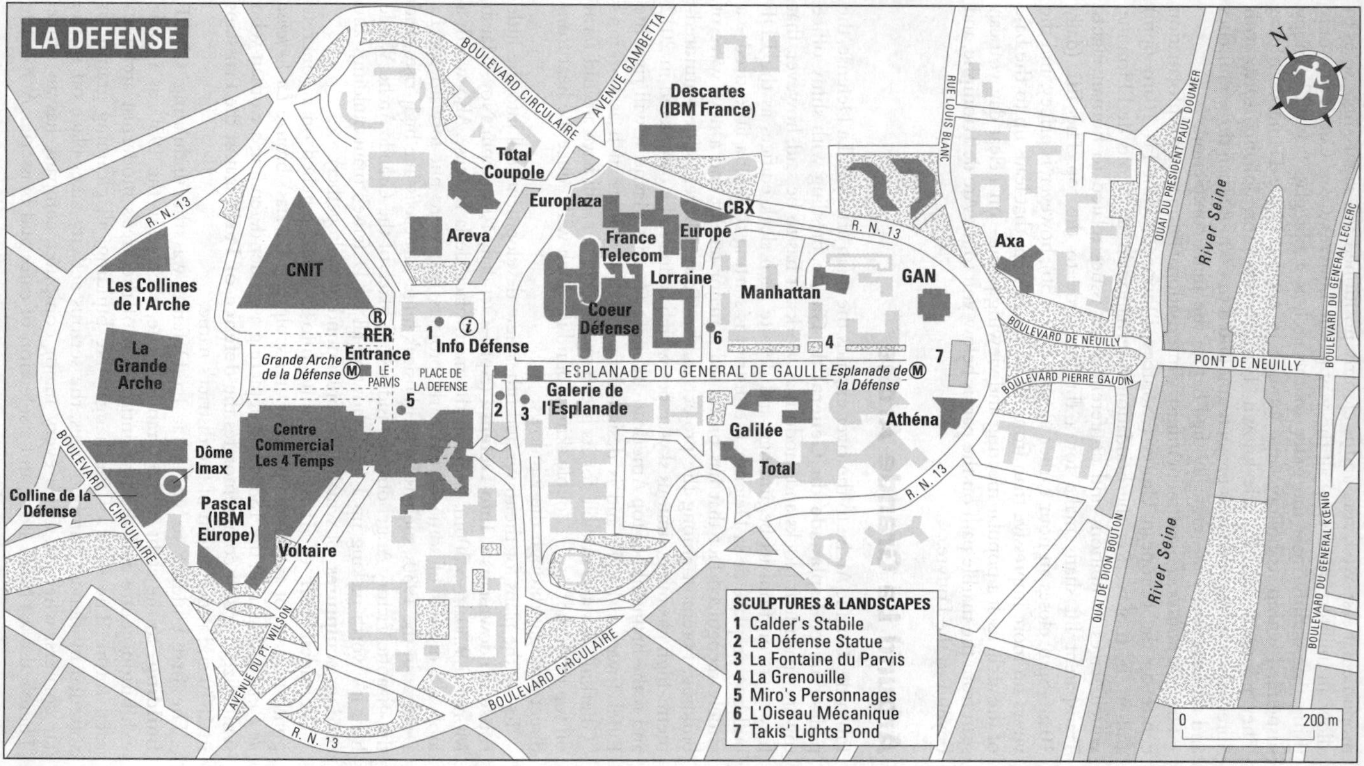

LA DEFENSE

Boulevard Circulaire
Avenue Gambetta
Descartes (IBM France)
Rue Louis Blanc
Quai du President Paul Doumer
River Seine
Boulevard du General Leclerc
Total Coupole
Europlaza
CBX
R. N. 13
Axa
Areva
France Telecom
Europe
Lorraine
Manhattan
GAN
Les Collines de l'Arche
CNIT
Coeur Défense
Boulevard de Neuilly
Pont de Neuilly
RER Entrance
1
Info Défense
6
4
7
La Grande Arche
Grande Arche de la Défense
Le Parvis
Place de la Défense
Esplanade du General de Gaulle
Esplanade de la Défense
Boulevard Pierre Gaudin
5
2
3
Galerie de l'Esplanade
Athéna
Centre Commercial Les 4 Temps
Galilée
Dôme Imax
Total
Colline de la Défense
Pascal (IBM Europe)
Voltaire
Quai de Dion Bouton
Avenue du Pt. Wilson
Boulevard Circulaire
Boulevard du General Kœnig
0 200 m

SCULPTURES & LANDSCAPES

1 Calder's Stabile
2 La Défense Statue
3 La Fontaine du Parvis
4 La Grenouille
5 Miro's Personnages
6 L'Oiseau Mécanique
7 Takis' Lights Pond

way sprawls the **Quatre-Temps commercial centre**, one of the biggest of its ilk in Europe with some 250 shops on three levels. On the south side of the arch is the globe of the **Dôme-Imax**, one of the world's largest cinema screens.

Over a hundred thousand people come to La Défense to work during the week, and it's often a popular and animated place at weekends, too, although the bustle of the daytime melts away to leave everywhere rather empty by night.

The **closest station** is M°/RER Grande-Arche-de-la-Défense, though for the most dramatic approach to the Grande Arche it's worth getting off a stop early, at M° Esplanade-de-la-Défense, from where it's a twenty-minute walk to the arch.

Versailles

Twenty kilometres southwest of Paris, the royal town of **VERSAILLES** is renowned for the **Château de Versailles**, the enormous palace built for Louis XIV which is today one of the most visited monuments in France. It was inspired by the young Louis XIV's envy of his finance minister's château at Vaux-le-Vicomte (see p.271), a construction which he was determined to outdo. He recruited the design team of Vaux-le-Vicomte – architect Le Vau, painter Le Brun and gardener Le Nôtre – and ordered something a hundred times the size (the palace has 700 rooms, 67 staircases and 352 fireplaces). Versailles is the apotheosis of French regal indulgence and, even if the extravagant, self-aggrandizing decor of the "Sun King" is not to your liking, the palace's historical significance and anecdotes will enthral, and its park is a delight.

Since 2003, the palace has been the focus of a great **restoration project**, "La Grande Versailles", initiated by Jacques Chirac and on a par with Mitterrand's "Grand Louvre". The first phase of development will be complete by 2010 and includes renovation of the facades, the Grande Galerie des Glaces, and the **Petit Trianon** and the rest of **Marie-Antoinette's estate** – much of it not previously open to visitors. The gardens will also be replanted according to the original designs, and the Grille Royale – a three-metre-high gilded fence – will be reconstructed (the original went missing during the revolutionary period) and returned to the inner Cour de Marbre.

The château

A great sloping sweep of cobbled courtyard, backed by the old stables, forms a suitably grand prelude to the **château**. It was never meant to be a home. Second only to God, and the head of an immensely powerful state, its master, Louis XIV, was an institution as much as a private individual. His risings and sittings, comings and goings, were minutely regulated and rigidly encased in ceremony, attendance at which was an honour much sought-after by courtiers. Versailles was the headquarters of every arm of the state, and the entire court of around 3500 nobles lived in the palace (in a state of unhygienic squalor, according to contemporary accounts).

Construction began in 1664 and lasted virtually until Louis XIV's death in 1715, after which the château was abandoned for a few years before being reoccupied by Louis XV in 1722. It remained a residence of the royal family until the

Versailles practicalities

To **get to Versailles**, take the RER line C5 to Versailles-Rive Gauche (40min; €2.60); turn right out of the station and then take the first left on to avenue de Paris, which leads to the palace – a five-minute walk. The château is **open** throughout the year, except on Mondays, public holidays and during occasional state events (April–Oct 9am–6.30pm; Nov–March 9am–5.30pm; Ⓦwww.chateauversailles.fr).

The easiest, if not the cheapest, way to visit the château and grounds is to buy the **Passeport Versailles** (April–Oct weekdays €20, Sat, Sun & hols €25; Nov–March €16; under-18s free all year round), a one-day pass which you can buy in advance and saves you having to queue for a ticket on the day. It gives you access to all the main sights, including the main showcase rooms of the State Apartments and Galerie des Glaces, the gardens, the Grand Trianon and Marie-Antoinette's estate, and includes free audioguides. You can buy the pass in advance from any branch of FNAC (see p.396) and the tourist office at the Carrousel du Louvre (see p.46). It's also available at the château itself up until 2pm on the day, though this means queuing with everyone else. You can also get a combined rail and Passeport ticket from any RER station, such as Invalides.

While the château's huge forecourt, the Cour Royale, undergoes extensive renovation, usual ticket and entry points to the château have been disrupted. The following information was correct at the time of writing, but may change sometime in 2009 or 2010 when restoration is complete. Passeport and Paris Museum Pass holders can bypass the **ticket** queues and go straight to door H to access the château. Visitors without tickets, wishing to visit the **château** only, including the State Apartments and Galerie des Glaces, have to queue at the information point, to the left as you enter; tickets cost €13.50 and come with free audioguide. Under-18s get in free, but have to pay €6 for an audioguide (€10 on weekends April–Sept). If you just want to visit Marie-Antoinette's estate (**"Domaine de Marie-Antoinette"**), you can go straight there and buy tickets (April–Oct noon–7.30pm €9; Nov–March access to gardens and Grand Trianon only noon–5.30pm €5; under-18s free all year round; gardens open 8am till dusk, free); the queues aren't generally very long. Note that both the château and Domaine de Marie-Antoinette tickets are also available in advance from branches of FNAC.

A number of **guided tours** (prices vary) are available throughout the day, including English-language tours, which take you to wings of the palace that can't otherwise be seen; they can all be booked in the morning at the information point – turn up reasonably early in the day to make sure of a place. It's well worth taking at least one tour if only for the guides' commentaries, which are usually extremely well informed – though some anecdotes should be taken with a pinch of salt. Don't set out to see the whole palace in one day – it's not possible.

Revolution of 1789, when the furniture was sold and the pictures dispatched to the Louvre. Thereafter Versailles fell into ruin until Louis-Philippe established his giant museum of French Glory here; it still exists, though most is mothballed. In 1871, during the Paris Commune, the château became the seat of the nationalist government, and the French parliament continued to meet in Louis XV's opera building until 1879. Restoration only began in earnest between the two world wars, but today it proceeds apace, the château's management scouring the auction houses of the world in the search for original furnishings from Louis XVI's day. Ironically, they have been helped in the task by the efforts of the revolutionaries, who inventoried all the palace's furnishings before they were auctioned off in 1793–4, a process that took a year.

The rooms you can visit without a guide are known as the **State Apartments**, as they were used for all the king's official business. The route leads past the **royal**

chapel, a grand structure that ranks among France's finest Baroque creations. From there, a procession of gilded drawing rooms leads to the king's throne room and the dazzling **Galerie des Glaces** (Hall of Mirrors), where the Treaty of Versailles was signed after World War I. Under the golden barrel ceiling, with its paintings by Charles Le Brun showing the glories of Louis XIV, Georges Clemenceau finally won his notorious "war guilt" clause, which blamed the entire conflict on German aggression. The *galerie* underwent extensive restoration in 2004–7; mouldings were regilded, the lapis lazuli (a very expensive blue pigment) of the paintings retouched and the lustre restored to the 357 mirrors. It's best viewed at the end of the day, when the crowds have departed and the setting sun floods it from the west, across the park. More fabulously rich rooms, this time belonging to the **queen's apartments**, line the northern wing, beginning with the queen's bedchamber, which has been restored exactly as it was in its last refit, of 1787, with hardly a surface unadorned with gold leaf. At the end of the visit, the staircase leads down to the **Hall of Battles**, whose oversize canvases unashamedly blow the trumpet for France's historic military victories; be thankful that most of the rest of Louis-Philippe's historical museum is out of bounds.

The Domaine de Marie-Antoinette

Hidden away in the northern reaches of the park is the **Domaine de Marie-Antoinette** (Marie-Antoinette's estate), the queen's country retreat, centred on the Petit Trianon palace, where she could find some relief from the stifling atmosphere and etiquette of the court. Here she commissioned some dozen or so buildings, sparing no expense and imposing her own style and tastes throughout (and gaining herself a reputation for extravagance that wouldn't do her any favours in the long run). She also had a bucolic park created in the fashionable English style, and a miniature farm. The whole estate has been undergoing restoration funded by the Swiss watchmakers Breguet, reviving a link with the queen that goes back to 1783 when Breguet's founder was commissioned to make her a watch with workings so complex it was never completed in her lifetime. The gardens (badly damaged in the devastating December 1999 storm) are being replanted and restored along original lines, and most of the *domaine*'s sights should be fully open to the public by April 2008, some of them accessible for the first time ever, affording a fascinating glimpse into the private pursuits and passions of the last French queen.

The Petit Trianon

The estate's centrepiece is the elegant and restrained Neoclassical **Petit Trianon** palace, built by Gabriel in the 1760s for Louis XV's mistress, Mme de Pompadour, and given to Marie-Antoinette by her husband Louis XVI as a wedding gift. The interior boasts a fine stone and wrought-iron staircase, sculpted wood panelling, period furniture and the intriguing *cabinet des glaces montantes*, the queen's elegant pale-blue salon, fitted with sliding mirrors that could be moved by a sophisticated mechanism to conceal the windows, creating a more intimate space.

The gardens and the rest of the domaine

West of the palace are formal gardens (the **Jardin français**) with pavilions such as the octagonal **Pavillon français**, sporting a gold and marble interior and a frieze of sculpted swans, ducks and other wildfowl, which would have been farmed on the estate. More impressive still is the deceptively plain-looking **Petit Théâtre**, built for the queen in 1778–79 and lavishly decorated inside in blue and gold. Marie-Antoinette loved the theatre and regularly performed here in her favourite plays with the Troupe des Seigneurs before the king and members of her inner circle, often taking the role of a shepherdess or maid.

On the other side of the palace lies the much more informal **Jardin anglais**, with its little winding stream, grassy banks dotted with forget-me-nots and daisies, classical temple (Le Temple d'Amour), fake waterfall and grotto with belvedere. It's all impossibly picturesque and idyllic. Further east lies the equally enchanting, if rather bizarre, **Hameau de la Reine**, a play village and thatch-roofed farm where Marie-Antoinette could indulge the fashionable Rousseau-inspired fantasy of returning to the natural life. The farm, with its cows, goats, pigs and hens, has been re-created (much to the delight of children), and vineyards are being replanted.

The Grand Trianon

Included in the ticket for the Domaine de Marie Antoinette is the Italianate, pink-marble **Grand Trianon** palace, a little to the west, designed by Hardouin-Mansart in 1687 as a "country retreat" for Louis XIV. Its two wings are linked by a colonnaded portico, with formal gardens to the rear. Napoleon stayed here intermittently between 1805 and 1813 and had the interior refurbished in Empire style. Nowadays it's often used by the French president when entertaining foreign dignitaries.

The park

You could spend the whole day just exploring the **park** at Versailles (daily: April–Oct 8am–8.30pm; Nov–March 8am–6pm; free), consisting of perfectly symmetrical gardens with grand vistas, designed by André Le Nôtre, numerous statues of nymphs and gods, fifty fountains, 34 pools, a Grand Canal and, on the outer limits, woods, and fields grazed by sheep. In the summer months, the **fountains** dance elaborately to the tune of classical music (April–Sept Sat & Sun 11am–noon & 3.30–5pm, plus occasional evening shows; €7, evenings €17), a spectacle known as the **Grandes Eaux Musicales**.

Distances in the park are considerable. If you can't manage them on foot, you could hop on the **petit train**, which shuttles between the terrace in front of the château and the Trianons (€3.50 one-way); it runs about every fifteen minutes in summer. Another option is to hire a **buggy**, for which you'll need a driving licence. You can rent **bikes** at the Grille de la Reine, Porte St-Antoine and by the Grand Canal, and **boats** on the Grand Canal, next to a pair of **café-restaurants**. There are plenty of little kiosks where you can get takeaway sandwiches, too.

The Town

If you've time and energy left after touring the château it's worth having a look round the town and taking in its sights, one of the most interesting of which is the **Potager du Roi** (April–Oct Tues–Sun 10am–6pm; Nov–March Tues–Fri 10am–6pm; Tues–Fri €4.50, Sat & Sun €6.50), the king's kitchen-garden; to reach it turn right as you exit the château's main gate and it's a five-minute walk away on rue Joffre. Nine hectares were under the care of the head gardener, Jean-Baptiste La Quintinie, who managed to produce strawberries and melons in March and asparagus in December; the best of the fruit and vegetables produced here was sent by the king to those in favour. Louis XIV was proud of his *potager* and used to visit often, sometimes even asking La Quintinie for gardening lessons. A statue of La Quintinie stands on the raised terrace watching over his plot, a great sunken square of espaliered fruit trees and geometrically arranged vegetables in the lee of the stately church of St-Louis. Some of the 150 varieties of apples and pears, and fifty types of vegetables, are sold in the little farm shop.

The king indulged another of his passions nearby, at the Grand Ecurie du Roy, or royal stables, opposite the main entrance to the château. Louis XIV installed six hundred horses here, and the stables soon became a setting for equestrian displays and other grand spectacles. After nearly two centuries, the building is once again open to the public and now houses the **Académie du spectacle équestre** (Ⓦwww.acadequestre.fr), which puts on highly choreographed theatrical shows of horsemanship. Performances take place on weekends (usually Sat 8.30pm, Sun 3pm; €21; check the website for latest information) and some weekday evenings. You can also watch the horses being put through their paces at a training session (usually Sat & Sun 10.30am & 11.15am & more frequently during hols, see website; €9.50).

The fate of the French monarchy was sealed a little south of here on rue du Jeu de Paume at the **Salle du Jeu de Paume** (April–Oct Sat & Sun 12.30–6.30pm; free), the tennis court where the representatives of the Third Estate set the Revolution in progress.

Other parts of the town worth exploring are **place Notre-Dame**, with its lively food market (Tues, Fri & Sun 7.30am–1.30pm), the surrounding streets full of buzzy cafés, and the little cobbled **rue du Bailliage** and adjoining **passage de la Geôle**, lined with over fifty antique shops (Fri, Sat & Sun 10am–7pm; Ⓦwww.antiques-versailles.com), selling anything from tin soldiers to antiquarian books, paintings and ceramics.

Practicalities

The **tourist office** (April–Sept daily 9am–7pm; Oct–March Mon & Sun 11am–5pm, Tues–Sat 9am–6pm; Ⓣ01.39.24.88.88, Ⓦwww.versailles-tourisme.com) is at 2bis avenue de Paris, on the left as you approach the château, and gives out a free map of the town.

The best located of the **hotels** is the *Hotel de France* (Ⓣ01.30.83.92.23, Ⓦwww.hotelfrance-versailles.com; doubles cost €137–141), a stone's throw from the château's gate, on 5 rue Colbert; rooms have nice fabrics and decor, all in keeping with the style across the way. A cheaper option, near place Notre-Dame, at 18 rue André-Chénier, is the quiet *Hotel du Cheval Rouge* (Ⓣ01.39.50.03.03, Ⓦwww.chevalrouge.fr.st; doubles €73), former livery stables, with clean, modern, if rather bland, rooms, and secure parking.

The area around Marché Notre-Dame is good for **restaurants**. The emphasis at long-established *Valmont* (closed Sun eve & Mon), at 20 rue au Pain, is on fish, with mains at around €28 and a set evening menu at €31. Next door, at no. 20, is *Au Carré* (closed Sun eve), a smart modern bistrot, offering a set evening menu for €28, with a Mediterranean influence.

Malmaison

The relatively small and enjoyable **Château de Malmaison** (April–Sept Mon & Wed–Fri 10am–5.45pm, Sat & Sun 10am–6.15pm; Oct–March Mon & Wed–Fri 10am–12.30pm & 1.30–5.15pm, Sat & Sun 10am–12.30pm & 1.30–5.45pm;

€4.50; Ⓦ www.chateau-malmaison.fr) is set in the beautiful landscaped grounds known as the **Bois-Préau**, about 15km west of central Paris.

This was the home of the Empress Josephine. During the 1800–1804 Consulate, Napoleon would drive out at weekends, though by all accounts his presence was hardly guaranteed to make the party go with a bang. Twenty minutes was all the time allowed for meals, and when called upon to sing in party games, the great man always gave a rendition of "Malbrouck s'en va-t'en guerre" ("Malbrouck Goes to War"), out of tune. A slightly odd choice, too, when you remember that it was Malbrouck, the Duke of Marlborough, who had given the French armies a couple of drubbings a hundred years earlier. According to his secretary, Malmaison was "the only place next to the battlefield where he was truly himself". After their divorce, Josephine stayed on here, building up her superb rose garden and occasionally receiving visits from the emperor until her death in 1814.

Visitors today can see the official apartments, which perfectly preserve the distinctive First Empire style, as well as Josephine's clothes, china, glass and personal possessions. During the Nazi occupation, the imperial chair in the library was rudely violated by the fat buttocks of Reichsmarschall Goering, dreaming perhaps of promotion or the conquest of Egypt. There are other Napoleonic bits in the nearby Bois-Préau museum, currently closed for renovation with no opening date in sight.

To **reach** Malmaison, take the métro line 1 (or RER A) to La Défense, then the fairly frequent bus #258 to Malmaison-Château.

Meudon and Sèvres

The tranquil suburb of **MEUDON**, 10km southwest of Paris, was where **Rodin** spent the last years of his life. His house and studio, the **Villa des Brillants**, is at 19 avenue Rodin (April–Sept Fri–Sun 1–6pm; €2) and is worth a visit for its wealth of preparatory sketches, plaster casts and studies. The studies, figuring many of his most famous works, were donated to the state in 1916 by Rodin and have the distinction of being the primary material, in direct contact with Rodin's hand, something that can't be said of the finished product (see p.164). It was in this house that he lived with his companion, Rose Beuret, and here that he married her, after fifty years together, just a fortnight before her death in February 1917. His own death followed in November, and they are buried together on the terrace below the house, beneath a bronze version of *The Thinker*. The classical facade behind masks an enormous pavilion that once housed a landmark Rodin retrospective at the Exposition Universelle of 1901; today it contains plaster versions of his most famous works.

To **get to** Rodin's house at Meudon, take RER line C to Meudon-Val Fleury, from where it's a fifteen-minute walk along avenues Barbusse and Rodin, or a short ride by bus (#169; Paul Bert stop).

A couple of kilometres west, Meudon's neighbour, **SEVRES**, has been manufacturing some of the world's most renowned **porcelain** since the eighteenth century. The style, with its painted coloured birds, ornate gilding and rich polychrome enamels, was so beloved by Louis XV's mistress, Madame de Pompadour, that two new colours, *rose Pompadour* and *bleu de roi*, were named after the couple in 1757. The compliment paid off: two years later, when the factory fell into financial trouble, the king bought up all the shares to guarantee its future, and it remained in royal hands until the Revolution. Since the beginning of the nineteenth century the factory has been home to the **Musée National de la Céramique** (daily except Tues 10am–5pm; €4.50; Ⓦwww.musee-ceramique-sevres.fr). A ceramics museum may possibly seem a bit too rarefied an attraction to justify a trip out of Paris but, if you do have the time, there is much to be savoured; with fifty thousand pieces, the collection is in fact the third-largest in the world, after Taipei and Istanbul. Inevitably, displays centre on Sèvres ware, but there are also collections of Islamic, Chinese, Italian, German, Dutch and English pieces.

Right by the museum is the **Parc de St-Cloud**, good for fresh air and visual order, with a geometrical sequence of pools and fountains. You could, if you wanted, take a train from St-Lazare to St-Cloud and head south through the park to the museum. A more direct way **to get here** would be to take the métro to the Pont-de-Sèvres terminus, then cross the bridge and spaghetti junction; the museum is the massive building facing the river bank on your right. Alternatively, Meudon and Sèvres are conveniently connected by bus #389 (from stop "Paul Besnard" to "Pont-de-Sèvres"; roughly twenty minutes' journey) making a combined afternoon or day-trip a possibility.

St-Denis

For most of the twentieth century, **ST-DENIS**, 10km north of the centre of Paris and accessible by métro (M° St-Denis-Basilique), was one of the most heavily industrialized communities in France, and a bastion of the Communist party. Since those days, factories have closed, unemployment is rife and immigration has radically altered the ethnic mix. For bourgeois Parisians, the political threat of the *banlieue rouge* ("red suburbs") has become the social threat of the *banlieue chaude* ("hot suburbs"). Visitors, however, are likely to find a poor but buoyant community, its pride buttressed by the town's twin attractions: the ancient **basilica of St-Denis** and the hyper-modern **Stade-de-France**, seat of the 1998 World Cup final.

The basilica

Close by the St-Denis-Basilique métro station, the **Basilique St-Denis** (April–Sept Mon–Sat 10am–6pm, Sun noon–6pm; Oct–March Mon–Sat 10am–5pm, Sun noon–5pm, but closed during weddings and funerals) is generally regarded as the birthplace of the Gothic style in European architecture. The basilica was built in the first half of the twelfth century by Abbot Suger,

The legend of St Denis

The first church at St-Denis was probably founded by an early (mid-third-century) Parisian bishop known by the name of St Denis, or St Dionysius in English. The legend goes that after he was decapitated for his beliefs at Montmartre – supposedly so-called because it is the "Mount of the Martyr" – he picked up his own head and walked all the way to St-Denis, thereby indicating the exact spot where his abbey should be built. It's not in fact all that far – just over 5km – though as a friend of Edward Gibbon's once remarked, "the distance is nothing, it's the first step that counts".

friend and adviser to kings, on the foundations of an earlier abbey church. With its two towers (the northern one collapsed in 1837), three large sculpted portals and high rose window, the west front set the pattern of Gothic facades to come, while the high, light-filled choir made a deep impression on the bishops attending the dedication service – in the next half century they went on to build most of the great Gothic cathedrals in France. Suger's innovatory design can still be traced in the lowest storey of the choir, notably the ambulatory space, which allowed pilgrims to process easily around the relics held in the choir. The novel rib vaulting allowed the walls to be no more than an in-filling between a stone skeleton, making huge, luminous windows possible. Today, the upper storeys of the choir are still airier than they were in Suger's day, having been rebuilt in the mid-thirteenth century, at the same time as the nave – you can

△ St-Denis market

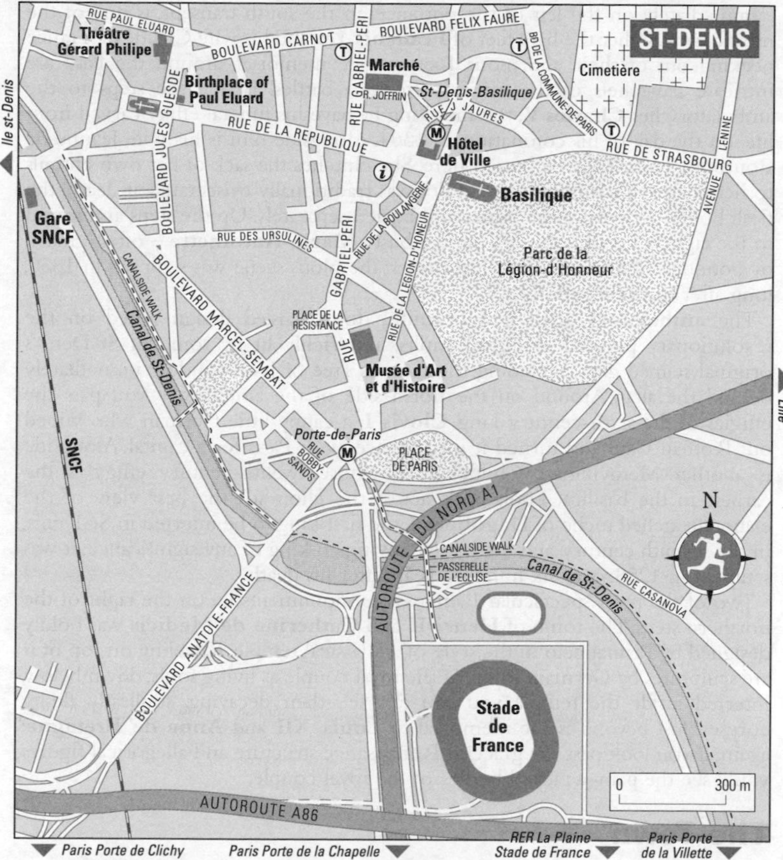

still see the odd angle where the old, narrow choir was broadened to fit the new, wider design of the transepts. The newer, upmost clerestory level is almost entirely made of glass, a flat sheet of light soaring above the deep, opaque nave arcade, with the narrow, half-open triforium level holding the two styles in balance. It was a brilliant architectural idea, defining the mature Rayonnant style which dominated church architecture for the next century and a half.

A good way to appreciate the atmosphere in the basilica is during the **St-Denis Festival** (end of June; Ⓣ01.48.13.06.07, Ⓦwww.festival-saint-denis.fr) when it plays host to various classical concerts, with an emphasis on choral music.

The necropolis

The site's **royal history** began with the coronation of Pepin the Short in 754, but it wasn't until the reign of Hugues Capet, in 996, that it became the customary burial place of the kings of France. Since then, all but three of France's kings have been interred here, and their fine tombs and effigies are distributed about the **necropolis** (€6.50; closed during services) in the transepts and ambulatory, which is entered separately via the south portal.

Immediately on the left of the entrance, in the south transept, is one of the most bizarre sights: the bare feet of **François 1er** and his wife Claude de France peeking out of their enormous Renaissance memorial; around the base are intricate bas-reliefs of the king's victorious battles. Beside the steps to the ambulatory lies **Charles V**, the first king to have his funeral effigy carved from life, on the day of his coronation in 1364. Alongside him is his wife Jeanne de Bourbon, the first queen buried here. She clutches the sack of her own entrails to her chest – a reminder that royalty was traditionally eviscerated at death, the flesh boiled away from the bones and buried separately. Up the steps and round to the right, a florid Louis XVI and a busty **Marie-Antoinette** – often graced by bouquets of flowers – kneel in prayer; the pious scene was sculpted in 1830, long after their execution.

The **ambulatory** itself is a beautiful double-aisled design raised on the revolutionary pointed or ogival vaults, and richly lit by some of St-Denis's original stained glass, including the famous Tree of Jesse window immediately behind the altar. Around on the north side of the ambulatory you pass the effigies of the sixth-century king **Clovis I**, a canny little German who wiped out Roman Gaul and turned it into France, with Paris for a capital. Alongside is another Merovingian, Childebert I, whose twelfth-century effigy is the earliest in the basilica. Look back across the choir for the best view of the elaborate arched niche of **Dagobert I**, the first king to be interred in St-Denis, in the seventh century, and the last Merovingian king of any significance; it was sculpted in 1258, over six hundred years after his death.

Two of the most spectacular Renaissance monuments lie on the right of the northern steps. The tomb of **Henri II** and **Catherine de Médicis** was boldly designed by Primaticcio in the style of a Classical temple. Kneeling on top of it are sculptures by Germain Pilon of the royal couple as living souls; down below, interred inside the temple you can just see their decaying, soullessly fleshy corpses. Just beyond is the memorial to **Louis XII** and **Anne de Bretagne**; again, if you look past the graceful Renaissance structure and allegorical figures you'll see the pain-wracked bodies of the royal couple.

The Town

The **tourist office** (April–Sept Mon–Sat 9.30am–1pm & 2–6pm, Sun 10am–1pm & 2–4pm; Oct–March Mon–Sat 9.30am–1pm & 2–6pm, Sun 10am–2pm; Ⓣ01.55.87.08.70, Ⓦwww.saint-denis-tourisme.com), opposite the basilica at 1 rue de la République, sells tickets for the St-Denis festival and can provide maps of the town.

Although the centre of St-Denis still retains traces of its small-town origins, the area immediately abutting the basilica has been transformed into an extraordinary fortress-like housing and shopping complex, where local youths hang out on mopeds and skateboards, women shop for African groceries and men, fresh from the latest conflict zone, beg for a few cents. The thrice-weekly **market**, in the main place Jean-Jaurès (Tues, Fri & Sun mornings), peddles vegetables at half the price of Parisian markets, as well as cheap curios, clothes and fabrics. Adjacent, off rue Dupont, are the covered *halles*, a multi-ethnic affair where the quantity of offal on the butchers' stalls – ears, feet, tails and bladders – shows this is not rich folks' territory.

About five minutes' walk south of the basilica is the **Musée d'Art et d'Histoire de la Ville de St-Denis** (Mon, Wed & Fri 10am–5.30pm, Thurs 10am–8pm, Sat & Sun 2–6.30pm; €4; Ⓦwww.musee-saint-denis.fr), housed in a former Carmelite convent on rue Gabriel-Péri. The quickest route is along rue de la Légion-d'Honneur, then third right. The exhibits on display are not of spectacular interest, though the presentation is excellent. The local archeology collection is good, and there are some interesting paintings of nineteenth- and twentieth-century industrial landscapes, including the St-Denis canal. The one unique collection is of documents relating to the Commune: posters, cartoons, broadsheets, paintings, plus an audiovisual presentation. There's also an exhibition of manuscripts and rare editions of the Communist poet, Paul Eluard, native son of St-Denis.

About ten minutes' further down rue Gabriel-Péri you come to the métro stop St-Denis Porte-de-Paris. Just beyond it, a broad footbridge crosses the motorway and Canal St-Denis to the **Stade de France** (Ⓦwww.stadedefrance.fr), scene of France's World Cup victory in 1998. At least €430 million was spent on the construction of this stadium, whose elliptical structure is best appreciated at night when lit up. If there isn't a match or a mega-rock event on, you can visit its grounds, facilities and a small museum about the stadium's brief but eventful history (daily 10am–5pm; €10).

From the northern side of the stadium's footbridge it's possible to **walk back to Paris** all the way along the **canal towpath**. Parts of the canalside are being rehabilitated and may necessitate a slight detour, and there are decaying, semi-abandoned stretches where it may feel as if you're not supposed to be there, but press on regardless and you'll eventually fetch up at Porte de la Villette, after no more than two hours. The walk is only picturesque in patches, but it's a fascinating way to probe Paris's forgotten, rusting underbelly.

Le Bourget – Musée de l'Air et de l'Espace

Five kilometres east of St-Denis, a short hop up the A1 motorway, is **Le Bourget** airport. Until the development of Orly in the 1950s it was Paris's principal gateway and is closely associated with the exploits of France's pioneering aviators – Lindbergh landed here after his epic first flight across the Atlantic.

Today Le Bourget is used only for internal flights, while some of the older buildings have been turned into a museum of powered flight, the **Musée de l'Air et de l'Espace** (Tues–Sun: April–Sept 10am–6pm; Oct–March 10am–5pm; €7; Ⓦwww.mae.org). It consists of five adjacent hangars and a large exhibition space, the Grande Galerie, with displays ranging from early flying machines through to the latest spacecrafts. The first set of displays, dedicated to the Montgolfier brothers, inventors of the first successful hot-air balloon, shows society going balloon crazy. Displays of aeroplanes begin in the Grande Galerie: the first contraption to fly 1km, the first cross-channel flight, the first aerobatics – successes and failures are all on display here.

Drancy

At **Drancy**, near Le Bourget airport, the Germans and the French Vichy regime had a transit camp for Jews en route to Auschwitz – this was where the poet Max Jacob, among many others, died. A cattle wagon and a stone stele in the courtyard of a council estate commemorate the nearly 100,000 Jews who passed through here. Only 1518 returned.

The **Grande Galerie** also showcases World War I planes, while highlights of World War II aircraft are housed along with the first **Concorde** prototype, first flown in 1969 and finally retired in 2003. Hangars C and D cover the years from 1945 to the present day with France's high-tech achievements represented by the super-sophisticated, best-selling Mirage fighters and two Ariane space-launchers, Ariane I and the latest, Ariane V (both parked on the tarmac outside). Hangar E contains light and sporty aircraft, and Hangar F, nearest to the entrance, is devoted to space, with rockets, satellites, space capsules and the like. Some are mock-ups, some the real thing. Among the latter are a Lunar Roving Vehicle, the Soyuz craft in which a French astronaut flew and France's own first successful space rocket. Everything is accompanied by extremely good explanatory panels – though in French only.

To **get to** the Musée de L'Air et de l'Espace from Paris, take RER line B from Gare du Nord to Gare du Bourget (or métro line 7 to La Courneuve), then bus #152 to Le Bourget/Musée de l'Air. Alternatively, take bus #350 from Gare du Nord, Gare de l'Est or Porte de la Chapelle, or #152 from Porte de la Villette.

The Mac/Val

The **Mac/Val** (Tues–Sun noon–7pm, Thurs till 9pm; €4, under 18s free; Ⓦ www.macval.fr), in Vitry-sur-Seine, south of Paris, is a new contemporary art museum, opened in 2006 and dedicated mainly to French art from the last fifty years. Its collection numbers some thousand works, many drawn from the local council's own collection, which it had been quietly building up for years. The building itself, a low-slung glass structure that you might easily miss among all the surrounding high-rises, is pretty low-key – certainly no Guggenheim. The interior is light and airy and sets off the artworks to good advantage. Around a quarter of the collection is on display at any one time and there's a new hanging every year, organized around an abstract theme, such as 2007's "Etre présent au monde".

Established artists you might come across include Daniel Buren, Jean Dubuffet, video artists Jean-Luc Wilmouth and Pierre Huyghe, and Christian Boltanski, known for his large-scale installations on themes related to the Holocaust. Among a younger generation beginning to make their mark, worth looking out for are video artists such as **Bertrand Lamarche**, whose thirty-two minute *Le Terrain Ombelliférique* (2005) takes you on a close-up journey through a garden of giant hogweed, shot in black and white and conveying a vague mood of threat; and **Melik Ohanian**, who creates installations on political-social themes, such as *The Hand* (2002), consisting of nine monitors each showing a pair of clapping hands, belonging to unemployed people from Armenia, their energetic, rhythmic sound a kind of appeal and demonstration of their potential for work. Photography is represented by young artists such as **Valérie Belin**, whose striking black-and-white photos play with the theme of absence and presence, as in *La Mariée Marocaine* (2000), "The Moroccan Bride", who seems to disappear behind her magnificent costume.

In the museum's foyer there's a bookshop with plenty of books on contemporary art, and you can get refreshments at the restaurant on the ground floor. To **get to the museum** take the métro to Porte de Choisy and then bus #183 (the bus stop is right by the métro entrance on avenue de Choisy), direction Orly Terminal Sud, and get off at the Moulin de Saquet-Pelletan stop (a fifteen-minute journey).

16

Day-trips from Paris

In the further reaches and beyond the boundaries of Ile-de-France lie exceptional towns and sights that are still accessible as day-trips from Paris, and are worth making the effort to visit. An excursion to **Chartres** can seem a long way to go just to see one building; but then you'd have to go a very long way indeed to find a building to beat it. Of the **châteaux** that abound in this region, we describe only a select few: **Chantilly**, with its wonderful art museum; **Vaux-le-Vicomte**, the envy of Louis XIV; and **Fontainebleau**, the most elegant of Renaissance palaces. **Monet's garden** at Giverny, the inspiration for all his waterlily canvases in the Marmottan and Musée d'Orsay, is perenially popular; it's bright and vibrant in spring, hauntingly melancholy in autumn. The peaceful village of **Auvers-sur-Oise** was the inspiration for a number of Van Gogh's lonesome and turbulent landscape studies – and site of the verdant fields where he took his own life.

Travel details are given at the end of each account. Return train tickets cost €10–25, depending on how far you're going. For Auvers-sur-Oise, Fontainebleau and – usually – Chantilly as well you can save a few euros by buying a combined train and château entry ticket ("Forfait Loisirs") at the station before you leave. To check times of specific trains, contact the national train carrier, the SNCF (ⓣ08.92.35.35.35, ⓦwww.sncf-voyages.com) or visit the websites of Transilien (ⓦwww.transilien.com), for the Paris region, or the RATP (ⓦwww.ratp.fr), for the city of Paris proper. **Tourist information** on the region surrounding Paris, the Ile-de-France, can be found at ⓦwww.pidf.com.

Auvers-sur-Oise

On the banks of the River Oise, about 35km northwest of Paris, **AUVERS-SUR-OISE** makes an attractive rural excursion. It's the place where, in 1890, **Van Gogh** spent the last two months of his life, in a frenzy of painting activity, producing more canvases than the days of his stay – 76 in all. The quaint landscape of small, stone-and-plaster houses on the river banks has changed little since. The church at Auvers, the portrait of Dr Gachet, black crows flapping across a wheat field – these and many more of Van Gogh's best-known works belong to this period. He died in his brother's arms, after an incompetent attempt to shoot himself, in the tiny attic room he rented in the **Auberge Ravoux**. The auberge still stands on the main street, and a visit to Van Gogh's room (March–Oct Wed–Sun 10am–6pm; €6) is movingly modest. You can watch a short video about his time in Auvers, but you might get more out of

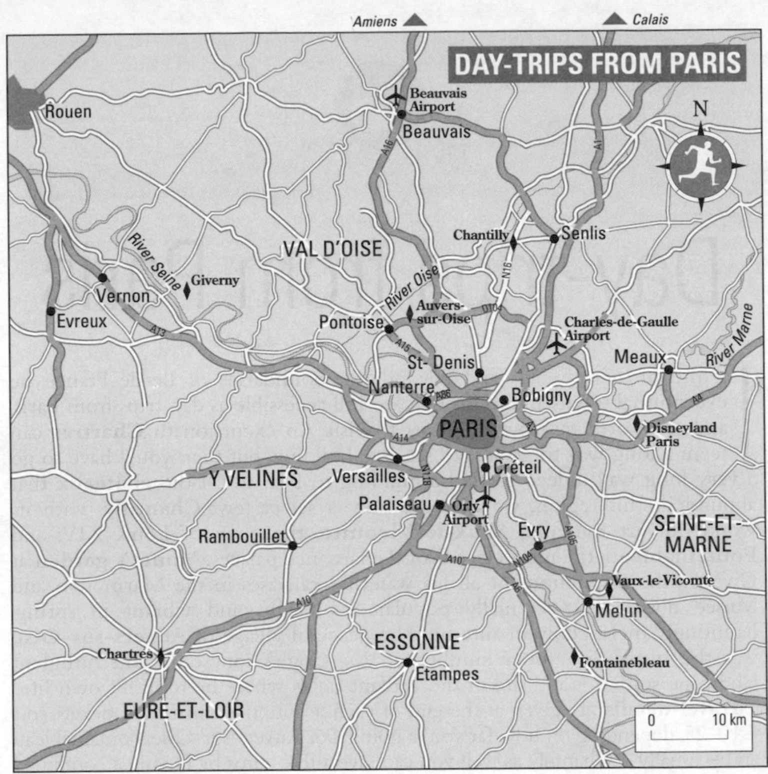

dining in the restaurant – it has been very sympathetically restored and serves an excellent "seven-hour" leg of lamb.

The **Musée de l'Absinthe** (mid-June to mid-Sept Wed–Fri 1.30–6pm, Sat & Sun 11am–6pm, March–Nov Sat & Sun 11am–6pm; €4.50) is devoted to the cloudy, aniseed-flavoured, wormwood-based liqueur, banned in France since 1915 for its poisonous properties, but much loved by writers and artists such as Van Gogh for its supposed stimulation of creativity. Inside the museum, there's a mock-up of a typical bar of the era, along with the various implements – glasses, holed spoons – associated with the ritual of drinking it. You can't try the stuff on the spot, but the shop is allowed to sell various brands in sealed bottles, and they have a few miniatures. Luckily (or sadly, depending on your point of view), the modern versions derive from a related type of wormwood that has less of the active toxin, a nerve poison called alpha-thujone.

At the entrance to the village is the handsome but undistinguished **Château d'Auvers**, which offers an expensive multimedia tour of the world the Impressionists inhabited (Tues–Sun: April–Sept 10.30am–6pm; Oct–March 10.30am–4.30pm, Sat & Sun till 5.30pm; €10.50; Ⓦwww.chateau-auvers.fr). As you wander through the various rooms mocked-up as cafés, period trains and so on, with cinema-style projections and special effects, headphones relay evocative music and a commentary on hundreds of canvases. If you really want to conjure up the Impressionists' world, however, simply take a **walk** through the old part of the village, past the church and the red lane into the famous wheat field and up the hill to the cemetery where, against the far left wall in a humble, ivy-covered grave, the Van Gogh brothers lie side by side.

Auvers boasts further artistic connections – most notably with Van Gogh's predecessor **Daubigny**, a contemporary of Corot and Daumier best known for his depictions of Seine riverscapes. A modest **museum** (Easter–Oct Thurs–Sun 2–6.30pm, closed mid-July to mid-Aug; €5), dedicated to Daubigny and other artists, can be visited above the tourist office. Daubigny's **studio-house** (April–Oct Thurs–Sun 2–6.30pm; €5), built to his own specifications and elegantly frescoed by the owner and his artist friends, can also be visited at 61 rue Daubigny. From here, Daubigny would go off in his floating studio for weeks at a time to paint – hence the boat sitting in the garden which is, in fact, a replica of a smaller craft once owned by Monet.

To reach Auvers **by road**, take the autoroute A15 towards Cergy-Pontoise, the exit for Saint-Ouen-l'Aumône, then turn off on the D928 to Auvers-sur-Oise. Hourly **trains** depart from the Gare du Nord, changing at Valmondois (1hr–1hr 15min); there is sometimes a direct service as well, leaving in the morning, but whether or not it runs may vary from year to year. A slightly quicker but more awkward alternative route is to take the RER A to Cergy Préfecture, then pick up bus #45 to the Gare SNCF at Pontoise, and get the train on to Auvers from there.

Chantilly

The main associations with **CHANTILLY**, a small town 40km north of Paris, are horses, cream and the Aga Khan. Scores of thoroughbreds can be seen thundering along the forest rides of a morning, and two of the season's classiest flat races are held here – the Jockey Club and the Prix de Diane, held on the first and second Sundays in June. The **château**, which rises romantically from the centre of a lake amid gardens and a forested park, has stables almost as grand as the main building; they are still in use today, as the **museum of the horse**. In 2005, it was announced that the Aga Khan – spiritual leader of the world's fifteen million Ismaili Muslims and local resident – would donate €40 million of his estimated €6 billion fortune to help **restore** the house and estate. It was, he said, "a special gesture in favour of the population in whose midst I have lived for several years". A major restoration is now in progress, so expect certain areas of the château and park to be closed for works – and, as time goes on, expect new rooms in the château to open for the first time. As for **cream**, the Chantilly recipe is basically whipped and sugared and delicious, and you can try it in the café in the Hameau, the rustic faux-village within the château grounds.

The château

The Chantilly estate used to belong to two of the most powerful clans in France: first to the Montmorencys, then, through marriage, to the Condés. The present **château** (daily except Tues: château open April–Oct 10am–6pm, Nov–March 10.30am–5pm; park open April–Oct 10am–8pm, Nov–March 10.30am–6pm; château and park €9; park only €5; Ⓦ www.chateaudechantilly.com) was put up in the late nineteenth century. It replaced a palace, destroyed in the Revolution, which had been built for the Grand Condé, who smashed Spanish military power for Louis XIV in 1643. It's a beautiful structure, graceful and romantic, surrounded

A man of honour

Chantilly is perhaps most famous as the venue for a single notorious incident: **the suicide of Vatel**. The story is widely retold to illustrate the otherwordly moral code of the *ancien régime*. Major-domo to the nobility, (supposed) inventor of Chantilly cream and orchestrator of financier Fouquet's fateful supper party in 1661 (see p.271), François Vatel was justifiably proud of his status. In April 1671, the Prince de Condé set him to organize a feast for three thousand guests, in honour of Louis XIV. On the opening evening, two tables went without meat thanks to unexpected arrivals. "I cannot endure such a humiliation," Vatel was heard to say, over and over again. At four in the morning, the distraught maître d' was seen wandering the corridors of the palace, where he met a fish supplier with two baskets of fish. "Is that all there is?", he asked, in horror. Not knowing that Vatel had sent for supplies from all over France, the man replied "yes". Dishonoured, Vatel played the Roman and ran upon his sword.

by water and looking out in a haughty manner over a formal arrangement of pools and pathways created by the busy André Le Nôtre, the designer of the gardens at Versailles (and indeed at every other seventeenth-century château with pretensions to grandeur).

The entrance is across a moat, past two realistic bronzes of hunting hounds. The visitable parts mainly consist of the **Musée Condé**, the largest collection of Classical art in France outside the Louvre, owned outright by the Institut de France (see p.141). Stipulated to remain exactly as organized by Henri d'Orléans, the son of France's last king and the donor of the château, the arrangement is haphazard by modern standards but immensely satisfying to eclectic appetites. Some highlights can be found in the Rotunda of the picture gallery – Piero di Cosimo's *Simonetta Vespucci* and Raphael's *La Vierge de Lorette* – and in the so-called Sanctuary, with Raphael's *Three Graces* displayed alongside Filippo Lippi's *Esther et Assuerius* and forty miniatures from a fifteenth-century Book of Hours attributed to the great French Renaissance artist Jean Fouquet. Pass through the Galerie de Psyche with its series of sepia stained glass illustrating Apuleius' *Golden Ass*, to the room known as the Tribune, where Italian art, including Botticelli's *Autumn*, takes up two walls, and Ingres and Delacroix have a wall each.

A free, 45-minute guided tour (French only) will take you round the apartments of the sixteenth-century wing known as the Petit Château. The first port of call is the well-stocked library, where a facsimile of the museum's single greatest treasure is on display, **Les Très Riches Heures du Duc de Berry**, the most celebrated of all the Books of Hours. The illuminated pages illustrating the months of the year with representative scenes from contemporary (early 1400s) rural life – like harvesting and ploughing, sheep-shearing and pruning – are richly coloured and drawn with a delicate naturalism. The remaining half-dozen rooms on the tour mostly show off superb furnishings, with exquisite *boisieries* panelling the walls of the **Singerie**, or Monkey Gallery, wittily painted with allegorical stories in a pseudo-Chinese style. A grand parade of canvases in the long gallery depicts the many battles won by the Grand Condé.

The Musée Vivant du Cheval

Five minutes' walk back towards town along the château drive stands the colossal stable block, which has been transformed into a museum of horses and horsemanship, the **Musée Vivant du Cheval** (April–Oct daily except Tues

10.30am–6.30pm; Nov–March Mon & Wed–Fri 2–5pm, Sat & Sun 10.30am–6.30pm; €9, or €16 combined ticket with château and park; Ⓦwww.museevivantducheval.fr). The building was erected at the beginning of the eighteenth century by the incumbent Condé prince, who believed he would be reincarnated as a horse and wished to provide fitting accommodation for 240 of his future relatives.

In the vast, barrel-vaulted main hall, horses of different breeds from around the world are stalled, with a central ring for equestrian **demonstrations** (April–Oct daily 11.30am, 3.30pm & 5.15pm; Nov–March Sat & Sun 11.30am & 3.30pm, Mon–Fri 3.30pm; spectacle first Sun of the month 3.30pm; free with entry ticket) of the Spanish Riding School type. In the further wing, life-size model horses draw various chariots, carts and drays, and wear saddles and harnesses built for racing, polo, bullfighting and other activities for which horses are used. Off to the sides a handful of rooms are devoted to other horsey specialisms, the one for veterinary medicine proudly displaying a real horse's diseased intestine.

Potager des Princes

The newest of Chantilly attractions is the lush **Potager des Princes**, or "kitchen garden of the princes" (April–Oct daily except Tues 2–7pm; €7.50; Ⓦwww.potagerdesprinces.com). A horticultural haven of herbs, salad plants and meticulously planted vegetables, it's set a few hundred metres down from the stables. The luscious orchard, until recently abandoned and overgrown with rural blight, was designed for the Grand Condé by the ubiquitous Le Nôtre. Today, the garden is almost restored to its former glory, complete with fowl, goats and the occasional recording of period poetry, piped into the centre of the garden.

Chantilly practicalities

Trains run almost every hour from Paris's Gare du Nord to Chantilly (30min). Free shuttle buses to the château meet some but not all trains – you can ring the Chantilly **tourist office** on Ⓣ03.44.67.37.37 for details, but in any case it's a pleasant two-kilometre stroll through the forest; turn right outside the station, then left at the major roundabout on the signposted **footpath**. A good, reasonably priced meal can be had in the attractive, vaulted-ceilinged surroundings of the *Capitainerie*, located in the Château itself (daily except Tues; *menus* from €22).

Vaux-le-Vicomte

Of all the great mansions within reach of a day's outing from Paris, the Classical château of **Vaux-le-Vicomte** (April to mid-Nov Mon–Fri 10am–1pm & 2–6pm, Sat & Sun 10am–6pm; €12.50; Ⓦwww.vaux-le-vicomte.com), 46km southeast of Paris, is the most architecturally harmonious, the most aesthetically pleasing and the most human in scale. It stands isolated in the countryside amid fields and woods, and its gardens make a lovely place to picnic.

The château was built between 1656 and 1661 for Nicolas Fouquet, Louis XIV's finance minister, by the finest design team of the day – architect Le Vau, painter-designer Le Brun and landscape gardener Le Nôtre. The result was magnificence and precision in perfect proportion, and a bill that could only be paid by someone who occasionally confused the state's accounts with his own. Fouquet, however, had little chance to enjoy his magnificent residence. On August 17, 1661, he invited the king and his courtiers to a sumptuous house-warming party. Three weeks later he was arrested – by d'Artagnan of Musketeer fame – charged with embezzlement, of which he was certainly guilty, and clapped into jail for the rest of his life. Thereupon, the design trio was carted off to build the king's own piece of one-upmanship, the palace of Versailles.

Stripped of much of its furnishings by the king, the château remained in the possession of Fouquet's widow until 1705, when it was sold to the Maréchal de Villars, an adversary of the Duke of Marlborough in the War of Spanish Succession. In 1764 it was sold, again, to the Duc de Choiseul-Praslin, Louis XV's navy minister. His family kept it until 1875, when, in a state of utter dereliction – the gardens had vanished completely – it was taken over by Alfred Sommier, a French industrialist, who made its restoration and refurbishment his life's work. It was finally opened to the public in 1968. Today, work continues on restoring more and more public rooms to their original grandeur.

The château and gardens

Seen from the entrance, the **château** is a rather austerely magnificent pile surrounded by an artificial moat. It's only when you go through to the south side, where the gardens decline in measured formal patterns of grass and water, clipped box and yew, fountains and statuary, that you can look back and appreciate the very harmonious and very French qualities of the building – the combination of steep, tall roof and bulbous central dome with classical pediment and pilasters.

As to the interior, the predominant impression is inevitably of opulence and monumental cost. The main artistic interest lies in the work of **Le Brun**. He was responsible for the two fine **tapestries** in the entrance, made in the local workshops set up by Fouquet specifically to adorn his house, and subsequently removed by Louis XIV to become the famous Gobelins works in Paris (see p.188). Le Brun also painted numerous **ceilings**, notably in Fouquet's bedroom, the Salon des Muses, his *Sleep* in the Cabinet des Jeux, and the so-called "king's bedroom", whose decor is the first example of the ponderously grand style that became known as Louis XIV. Other points of interest are the cavernous **kitchens**, which have not been altered since construction, and a room displaying letters in the hand of Fouquet, Louis XIV and other notables. One, dated November 1794 (mid-Revolution), addresses the incumbent Duc de Choiseul-Praslin as *tu*. "Citizen," it says, "you've got a week to hand over one hundred thousand pounds . . .", and signs off with "Cheers and brotherhood". You can imagine the shock to the aristocratic system.

The **Musée des Equipages** in the stables comprises a collection of horse-drawn vehicles, complete with model horses. On summer evenings (May–Sept Sat 8pm–midnight; mid-July to Aug also Fri 8pm–midnight; €15.50) the **state rooms** are illuminated with a thousand candles, as they probably were on the occasion of Fouquet's fateful party, with classical music in the gardens adding to the effect. The **fountains** and other waterworks can be seen in action on the second and last Saturdays of each month (3–6pm).

Vaux-le-Vicomte practicalities

By road, Vaux-le-Vicomte is 7km east of Melun, which is itself 46km southeast of Paris by the A4 autoroute (exit Melun-Sénart) or a little further by the A6 (exit Melun). **By train** there are regular services from the Gare de Lyon as far as Melun (40min), from where a rather sparse shuttle-bus service (€7 return) covers the journey to the château on weekends. Otherwise, short of walking, the only means of covering the last 7km is **by taxi** (around €15 one-way). There's a taxi rank on the forecourt of the train station, with telephone numbers to call if there are no taxis waiting.

Fontainebleau

The **château of Fontainebleau** (daily except Tues: June–Sept 9.30am–6pm; Oct–May 9.30am–5pm; €8; ⓦwww.musee-chateau-fontainebleau.fr; info on access or guided tours ⓣ01.60.71.50.70), 60km south of Paris, owes its existence to its situation in the middle of a magnificent forest, which made it the perfect base for royal hunting expeditions. A lodge was built here as early as the twelfth century, but its transformation into a luxurious palace only took place in the sixteenth century on the initiative of François I, who imported a colony of Italian artists to carry out the decoration, most notably Rosso Fiorentino, Primaticcio and Niccolò dell'Abate. The palace continued to enjoy royal favour well into the nineteenth century; Napoleon spent huge amounts of money on it, as did Louis-Philippe. And, after World War II, when it was liberated from the Germans by General Patton, it served for a while as Allied military HQ in Europe. The town in the meantime has become the seat of the prestigious INSEAD business school – a hothouse for future directors of Tesco and the like.

The **buildings**, unpretentious and attractive despite their extent, have none of the unity of a purpose-built residence like Vaux-le-Vicomte. In fact, their chief architectural delight is the gloriously chaotic profusion of styles. From the expanse of the **Cour du Cheval Blanc**, built as a humble *basse cour* or working courtyard in the 1530s, you progress up a seventeenth-century horseshoe staircase into a confusion of wings, courtyards and gardens. At the very heart of the palace, the secretive and splendidly asymmetrical **Cour Ovale** conceals a twelfth-century fortress keep, jarringly but pleasingly flanked by fine Renaissance wings on either side.

The palace's highlights, however, are the sumptuous **interiors** worked by the Italians, chiefly the dazzlingly frescoed **Salle de Bal** and the celebrated **Galerie François I**, which is resplendent in gilt, carved, inlaid and polished wood, and adorned down its entire length by intricate stucco work and painted panels covered in vibrant Mannerist brushwork. The paintings' Classical themes all celebrate or advocate wise kingship, and had a seminal influence on the development of French aristocratic art and design. Utterly contrasting in style is the sobre but elegant decor of Napoleon's **Petits Appartements**, the private rooms of the emperor, his wife, and their intimate entourage. Like the **Musée Napoléon**, which displays a wide variety of souvenirs – some very personal, some official – of Napoleon's life, the Petits Appartements can only be visited as part of a guided tour (€12.50; includes château entry). The **Musée Chinois** (free), which is only open when there's enough staff, shows off the Empress Eugénie's private collection of Chinese and Thai *objets d'art* in their original Second Empire setting.

The **gardens** are equally splendid and in the summer months you could do worse than play owl and pussycat on the *Etang des Carpes*, a pleasant pond where you can rent boats. If you want to escape into the relative wilds, head for the surrounding **Forest of Fontainebleau**, which is full of walking and cycling trails, all marked on Michelin map #196 (*Environs de Paris*). Its rocks are a favourite training ground for Paris-based climbers.

Fontainebleau practicalities

Getting to Fontainebleau from Paris is straightforward. **By road** it's 16km from the A6 autoroute (exit Fontainebleau). **By train**, it's forty minutes from the Gare de Lyon to Fontainebleau-Avon station, from where buses #A or #B will take you to the château gates in fifteen minutes.

Barbizon

Ten kilometres northwest of Fontainebleau on the other side of the forest, the country town of **BARBIZON** is easily accessible from Fontainebleau by car but not by public transport – the bus service is infrequent and only runs on Sundays in summer. The local landscape and rural lifestyle inspired painters such as Rousseau and Millet to set up camp here, initiating an artistic movement, the Barbizon group. More painters followed as well as writers and musicians, all attracted by the lifestyle and community. The *Auberge du Père Ganne*, on the main road, became the place to stay, not unrelated to the fact that the generous owner accepted the artists' decorations of his inn and furniture as payment. Now home to a **museum** (daily except Tues 10am–12.30pm & 2–5.30pm; €3), the Impressionist inn still contains its original painted furniture, as well as many Barbizon paintings.

Chartres

When King Philip-Auguste visited **CHARTRES** to mediate between church and townsfolk after the riots of October 1210, the cathedral chapter noted that "he did not wish to stay any longer in the city but, so as to avoid the blasphemous citizens, stayed here only for one hour and hastened to return". Chartres' modern visitors often stay little longer, but if you've come all the way from Paris, a journey of 80km, the modest charms of the little town at the cathedral's feet may persuade you to linger. One of the world's most astounding buildings, the cathedral is best experienced early or late in the day, when the low sun transmits the stained-glass colours to the interior stone and the quiet scattering of people leaves the acoustics unconfused.

The cathedral

Built between 1194 and 1260, the Gothic **cathedral** (daily 8.30am–7.30pm; free) was one of the quickest ever constructed and, as a result, preserves a uniquely harmonious design. An earlier Romanesque structure burnt down in 1194, but the church's holiest relic – the **Sancta Camisia**, supposed to have been the robe Mary wore when she gave birth to Jesus – was discovered three days later, miraculously unharmed. It was a sign that the Virgin wanted her church lavishly rebuilt, at least so said the canny medieval fundraisers.

The cathedral's official name, Notre-Dame (Our Lady), and its staggering size and architectural richness are entirely owed to the Sancta Camisia. Hordes of pilgrims would stop here on their way south to the shrine of Santiago de

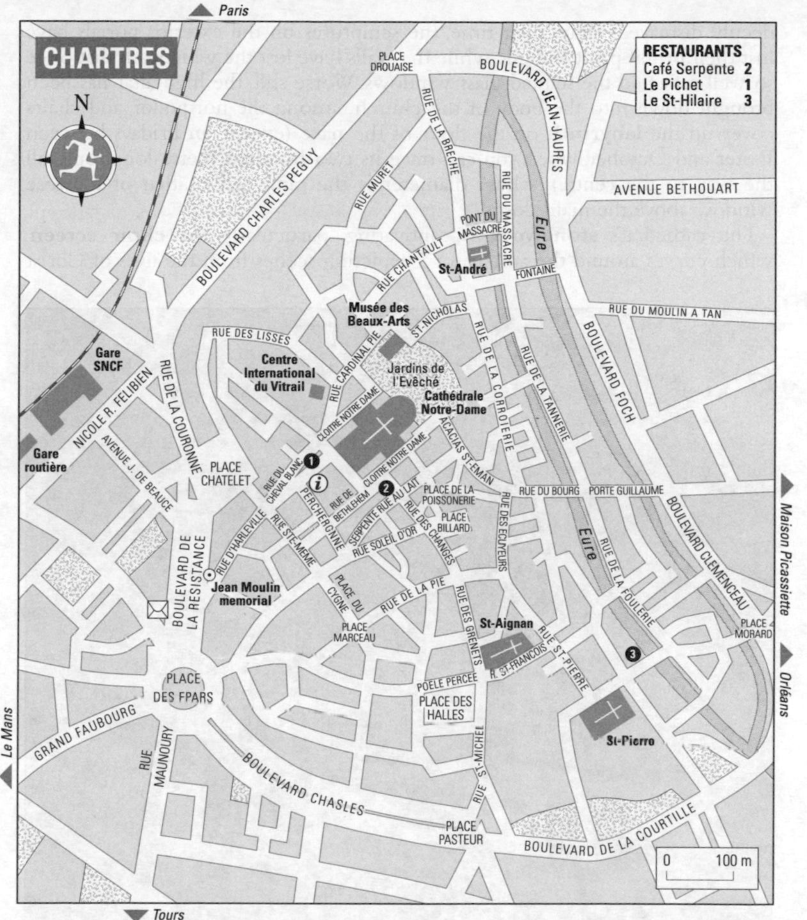

Compostela, in Spain, and the church needed to accommodate them with a sizeable crypt, for veneration of the relic, and a nave large enough to sleep hundreds – the sloping floor evident today allowed for it to be washed down more easily. The Sancta Camisia still exists, though after many years on open display it has recently been carefully rolled up and put into storage. It may yet be restored to the cathedral.

The geometry of the building is unique in being almost unaltered since its consecration, and virtually all of its stained glass is original – and unsurpassed – thirteenth-century work. Many of the windows in the nave were donated by craft guilds and merchants, whose symbols can often be seen in the bottommost pane. Some of the stories fit the donors' work, such as the carpenters' window showing Noah's ark. The superb, largely twelfth-century "**Blue Virgin**" window, in the first bay beyond the south transept, is filled with a primal image of the Virgin that has been adored by pilgrims for centuries.

Chartres may be the best-preserved medieval cathedral in Europe, but if a group of medieval pilgrims suddenly found themselves here they would be deeply dismayed. Since their time, the sculptures on the exterior portals have lost their bright paint and gilt, while the walls have lost the whitewash that once so well reflected the stained-glass windows. Worse still, the high altar has been brought down into the body of the church, among the hoi polloi, and chairs cover up the **labyrinth** on the floor of the nave (except on Fridays between Easter and October, when you can trace its two-hundred-metre-long route all the way to the centre), whose diameter is the same size as that of the rose window above the main doors.

The cathedral's **stonework** is captivating, particularly the **choir screen**, which curves around the ambulatory, depicting scenes from the lives of Christ

△ Chartres cathedral

Cathedral tours

A good way to appreciate the detail of Chartres cathedral is to join one of Malcolm Miller's **guided tours** (April–Nov Mon–Sat noon & 2.45pm; days and times vary in winter; or reserve for private tours on ⓣ02.37.28.15.58, ⓔmillerchartres@aol.com; €10), starting just inside the west door. His is no ordinary patter, but a guided lecture by someone who has studied Chartres for decades, with fascinating digressions into the significance of the building's symbols, shapes and numbers.

and the Virgin. Its sculptor, Jehan de Beauce, was also responsible for the design of the Flamboyant Gothic north spire. Outside, hosts of sculpted figures stand like guardians at each entrance portal. Like the south tower and spire which abuts it, the mid-twelfth-century Royal Portal actually survives from the earlier Romanesque church, and it's interesting to compare its sometimes awkward, relatively stylized figures with the more completely Gothic sculptures on the north and south porches, completed half a century later.

Crowds permitting, it's worth climbing the three hundred steps up the **north tower** for its bird's-eye view of the sculptures and structure of the cathedral (May–Aug 9am–6pm, Sun 1–6.30pm; Sept–April Mon–Sat 9.30–11.30am & 2–4.30pm, Sun 2–4.30pm; free). The **gardens** behind the cathedral, meanwhile, are a perfect spot for contemplation of the flying buttresses. There are a couple of paying extras, including the crypt and a collection of ecclesiastical treasures, but they're relatively unimpressive.

The rest of town

Though the cathedral is the main attraction, a wander round the town of Chartres also has its rewards. Occasional exhibitions of stained glass take place in a medieval wine and grain store, now the **Centre International du Vitrail**, at 5 rue du Cardinal-Pie on the north side of the cathedral (Mon–Fri 9.30am–12.30pm & 1.30–6pm, Sat & Sun 10am–12.30pm & 2.30–6pm; €4; ⓦwww.centre-vitrail.org). The **Musée des Beaux Arts** (May–Oct Mon & Wed–Sat 10am–noon & 2–6pm, Sun 2–6pm; Nov–April Mon & Wed–Sat 10am–noon & 2–5pm, Sun 2–5pm; €2.80), in the former episcopal palace just north of the cathedral, has some beautiful tapestries, a room full of the French Fauvist Vlaminck, and the Spanish Baroque painter Zurbarán's *Sainte Lucie*, as well as good temporary exhibitions.

Behind the museum, rue Chantault leads past old town houses to the river Eure and Pont du Massacre. You can follow this reedy river lined with ancient wash houses upstream via rue du Massacre on the right bank. The cathedral appears from time to time through the trees and, closer at hand, on the left bank, is the Romanesque church of **St-André**, now used for art exhibitions, jazz concerts and so on.

A left turn at the end of rue de la Tannerie, then third right, will bring you to one of Chartres' more eccentric tourist attractions. The quirky **Maison Picassiette**, at 22 rue du Repos (April–Nov Mon & Wed–Sat 10am–noon & 2–6pm, Sun 2–6pm; €4.40), has been entirely coated with mosaics using bits of pottery and glass and is a fine example of Naïve art. Back at the end of rue de la Tannerie, the bridge over the river brings you back to the **medieval town**. At the top of rue du Bourg there's a turreted staircase attached to a house, and at the eastern end of place de la Poissonnerie, a carved salmon decorates a sixteenth-century house. The **food market** takes place on place

Billard and rue des Changes, and there's a **flower market** on place du Cygne (Tues, Thurs & Sat).

At the edge of the old town, on the junction of boulevard de la Résistance and rue Collin-d'Arleville (to the right as you're coming up from the station), stands a memorial to **Jean Moulin**, Prefect of Chartres until he was sacked by the Vichy government in 1942. When the Germans occupied the town in 1940, Moulin refused to sign a document attributing Nazi atrocities to Senegalese soldiers in the French army. He later became de Gaulle's number one man on the ground, coordinating the Resistance, and died at the hands of Klaus Barbie in 1943.

Chartres practicalities

Trains run from the Gare du Montparnasse at least every hour on weekdays, but note that there are slightly fewer trains at weekends, especially on Sundays; the journey takes roughly one hour. The station is just five minutes' walk from the **tourist office** (April–Sept Mon–Sat 9am–7pm, Sun 9.30am–5.30pm; Oct–March Mon–Sat 10am–6pm, Sun 10am–1pm & 2.30–4.30pm; ⓣ02.37.18.26.26), which is right by the cathedral.

For a snack, there are lots of places with outside tables opposite the south side of the cathedral, on rue Cloître-Notre-Dame; try the *Café Serpente*. For a proper **restaurant** meal, *Le Pichet*, 19 rue du Cheval Blanc, almost under the northwest spire (ⓣ02.37.21.08.35; closed Wed, Tues eve & Sun eve), has a cosy interior full of gingham and bric-a-brac, and serves simple, inexpensive dishes like steak or Greek salad. The genteel *St-Hilaire*, 11 rue du Pont St-Hilaire (ⓣ02.37.30.97.57; closed Mon & Sun), serves refined regional cuisine (menus €25–40) in a sweet little upstairs dining room.

Giverny

Claude Monet considered his **gardens at Giverny** to be his greatest masterpiece (April–Oct Tues–Sun 9.30am–6pm; €5.50; ⓦwww.fondation-monet.com). They're way out in Normandy, 65km from Paris in the direction of Rouen, but well worth the trip. Monet lived in Giverny from 1883 till his death in 1926, painting and repainting the effects of the changing seasonal light on the gardens he laid out between his house and the river. Every month from spring to autumn has its own appeal, but May and June, when the rhododendrons flower round the lily pond and the wisteria bursts into colour over the famous Japanese bridge, are the prettiest months to visit – though you'll have to contend with crowds photographing the waterlilies and posing on the bridge. **Monet's house** stands at the top of the gardens, an idyllic pastel-pink building with green shutters. Inside, the rooms are all painted different colours, exactly as they were when Monet lived here, and the painter's original collection of Japanese prints, including wonderful works by Hokusai and Hiroshige, still hangs on the walls.

Just up rue Claude Monet from the gardens is the well-funded **Musée d'Art Américain** (April–Oct Tues–Sun 10am–6pm; €5.50; ⓦwww.maag.org). The display rotates pictures from the Terra Foundation for the Arts collection, which includes paintings by John Singer Sargent and James Whistler, as well as lots of works by various American Impressionists who lived in the small colony that grew up around Claude Monet, notably the Japanese-influenced Mary Cassatt.

Temporary exhibitions, usually high-quality, spin variations on Franco–American influences, Japanese art and Impressionism.

Giverny practicalities

Without a car, the easiest **approach to Giverny** is by train to Vernon from Paris-St-Lazare (4–5 daily; 45min). **Buses** meet each train for the six-kilometre ride to the gardens, or you can rent a **bike** (around €12) from the *Café du Chemin de Fer*, opposite the station. Failing that, you can **walk** (1hr), in which case cross the river and turn right on the D5; take care as you enter Giverny to follow the left fork, otherwise you'll make a long detour to reach the garden entrance. If you're **driving**, Giverny is just an hour's jaunt from Paris; take the A13, direction Vernon/Giverny to exit 14.

There are lots of indifferent tea shops in town, or, for something more substantial **to eat**, try the *charcuterie* at 60 rue Claude-Monet, which does good sandwiches. Note, however, that picnicking in the gardens is forbidden and the countryside around the village isn't particularly picnic-friendly. For a full meal, walk up beyond the Musée d'Art Américain to the *Ancien Hôtel Baudy* at 81 rue Claude Monet (closed Sun eve, Mon & Nov–March); once a lodging house for international artists, it now serves salads and decent lunch *menus* for under €20.

Disneyland Paris

Children will love **Disneyland Paris** – there are no two ways about it. What their minders will think of it is another matter, though a cartoon moment will still cadge a smile from most grown-ups, and you can terrify yourself on a roller coaster at any age. There is the question of whether it's worth it. Quite why American parents might bring their charges here is hard to fathom; even British parents might well decide that it would be better to buy a family package to Florida, where sunshine is assured, Disney World has better rides, and where the conflict between enchanted kingdom and enchanting city does not arise.

Carping aside, at a distance of just 25km east of the capital, it's easy to visit in a day-trip from Paris, and, since the opening of Space Mountain and the Rock 'n' Roller Coaster, Disneyland Paris has a variety of good fear-and-thrill rides. There's a much wider choice of things to do than at a funfair or ordinary theme park, too, and many of the sets are incredibly detailed. The complex is divided into three areas: **Disneyland Park**, the original Magic Kingdom, with most of the big rides; **Walt Disney Studios Park**, a more technology-based attempt to re-create the world of cartoon film-making, along with a few rides; and **Disney Village** and the hotels, where you can eat and sleep if you're determined to see both the other attractions. For all the omnipresent Americana, occasional French elements do creep through: science-fiction writer Jules Verne appears in a couple of Discoveryland rides; Sleeping Beauty's Castle is partly based on an illustration in the medieval manuscript *Les Très Riches Heures du Duc de Berry* (see p.270); and there's a faintly discernible French slant to some of the cinema-themed attractions in Walt Disney Studios. Otherwise, that's about it, and the food throughout the resort is almost all Stateside fare. That said, the commentaries or scripts in the more theatrical attractions are almost always in French, though there are sometimes disappointing translated summaries displayed on a caption board, and, in the most audience-focused attractions, you'll always find an English-language headset to don.

The best **time to go** is on an off-season weekday, when you'll probably get round every ride you want, though queuing for and walking between rides is purgatorial in wet or very cold weather. At other times, longish waits for the popular rides are common in the middle of the day, though the most popular attractions use the "Fastpass" pre-booked timeslot scheme (see box on p.283).

Getting there

From London, there are direct **Eurostar** trains to Disneyland, but it can sometimes be less expensive to change onto the TGV at Lille; all these trains arrive at Marne-la-Vallée/Chessy station, right outside the main entrance. If

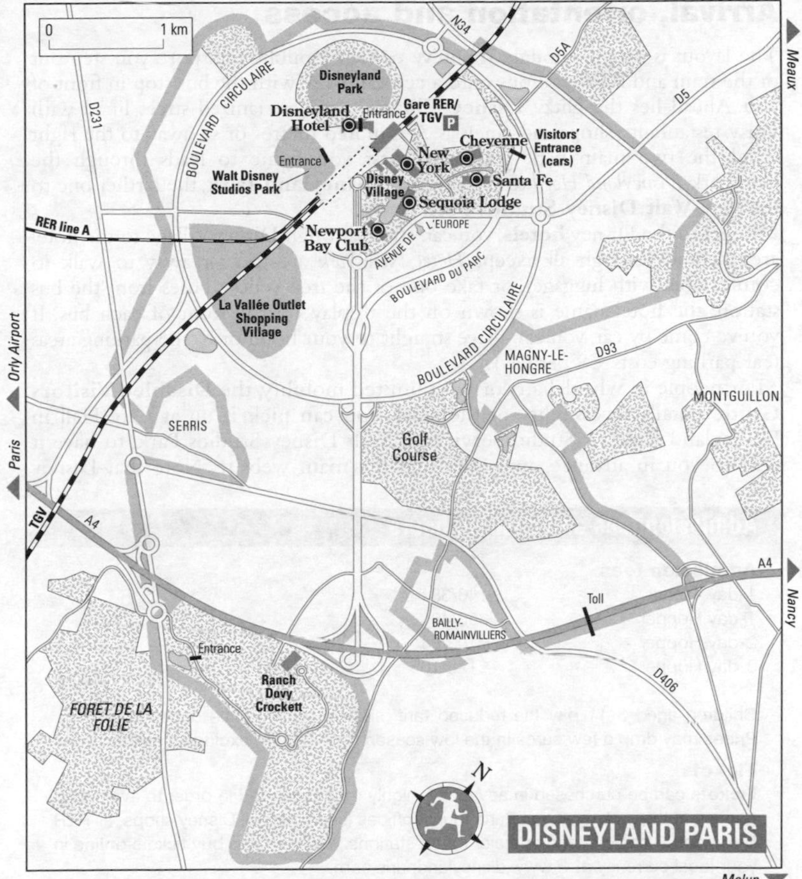

you're coming straight **from the airport**, there are shuttle buses from both Charles de Gaulle and Orly, taking 45 minutes from both airports (roughly every 30min from 8.30am to 7.45pm; for recorded information call ⓣ01.72.30.10.25 or consult ⓦwww.vea.fr/uk for timetables and pickup points). Tickets cost €16 one-way, but children under 12 pay €13, and under-3s go free.

From Paris, take RER line A (from Châtelet-Les Halles, Gare-de-Lyon or Nation) to Marne-la-Vallée/Chessy station, which is right next to the train terminal, and opposite the main park gates. The journey takes around 35 minutes and costs €12.50 round-trip (children under 12 €6.20, under-3s free). For prices of Mobilis travel cards, including Disneyland Paris, see p.28.

By car, the park is a 32-kilometre drive east of Paris along the A4; take the Porte de Bercy exit off the *périphérique*, then follow "direction Metz/Nancy", leaving at exit 13 for Ranch Davy Crockett or exit 14 for Parc Disneyland and the hotels. From Calais follow the A26, changing to the A1, the A104 and finally the A4.

Arrival, orientation and access

The layout is simple enough. If you've come by public transport, you step out of the train and RER stations onto a central plaza, with the bus stop in front of you. Ahead lies the glitzy **Disney Village**, a pedestrianized street lined with noisy restaurants, shops and cinemas. A hundred metres or so away to the right stand the two main park gates. The first you come to leads through the landmark *Disneyland Hotel* to the original **Disneyland Park**; the farther one to the new **Walt Disney Studios Park**.

To get to the Disney **hotels**, you can stroll through Disney Village to the hotel area behind (though all except *Hotel New York* are too far away to walk to comfortably with luggage), or take one of the free yellow buses from the bus station; the hotel name is shown on the display on the front of each bus. If you've come by car, you can drive straight to your hotel or to the parking areas (car parking costs €8 per day).

For people in wheelchairs or with limited mobility, the **Disabled Visitors Guide** details accessibility of the rides. You can pick it up at City Hall in Disneyland Park, or Studio Services in Walt Disney Studios Park; to have it sent to you in advance, apply through the main website. Note that Disney

Admission fees and opening hours

Admission fees

1-day 1-park	€46/38
1-day Hopper	€56/48
2-day Hopper	€103/84
3-day Hopper	€128/105

Children aged 3–11 pay the reduced tariff shown above, while under-3s go free. Prices may drop a few euros in the low season (Oct–March, excluding holidays).

Tickets

Tickets can be purchased in advance – highly recommended in order to avoid long queues at the park itself – at Paris tourist offices (see p.46), all Disney shops, all RER line A and B stations and at major métro stations. You can also buy tickets **online** in your local currency at Ⓦwww.disneylandparis.com.

The **one-day one-park pass** allows you to visit either the main Disneyland Park or the Walt Disney Studios Park. You can't swap between both areas. Otherwise, you can come and go during the day – your wrist is stamped with invisible ink when you leave the park, allowing you to return. If you buy a **Hopper pass** or *passe-partout* you can move freely between both park areas. If you buy a two- or three-day Hopper you don't have to use the ticket on consecutive days.

Opening hours

Opening hours vary depending on the season and whether it's a weekend, but opening times are either 9am or 10am, while the gates close at either 6pm or 8pm – or 11pm in mid-summer. Check when you buy your ticket.

Special packages

If you plan to stay at a Disneyland hotel, it's worth booking one of their special **accommodation and entry packages** in advance. From the UK, for example, you can get a three-day pass, with a return ticket on Eurostar and two nights' accommodation at the *Hotel Santa Fe* (see p.290) for something like £250 per adult and £150 per child. For details look online or call Ⓣ00 33.1.60.30.60.81 from the US, Ⓣ0870/503 0303 in the UK, and Ⓣ01.60.30.60.53 in France, or from other countries.

Queues and Fastpass

One-hour waits for the popular rides are not uncommon – don't be fooled by the length of the visible queues; they often snake for a further 100m or more inside.

Realistic wait times are posted at the entry to most rides (eg 20 minutes, 50 minutes) and actual times are often slightly shorter, which makes for a pleasant surprise. Bring sunhats or umbrellas, and make sure your kids have all been to the toilet recently before you begin to queue as, once you're in, it's very hard to get out; keep snacks and drinks handy, too. A number of rides use the **Fastpass** scheme, in which you insert your entry card into a ticket machine by the entrance to the ride; the machine then spews out a time at which you should come back and join the much shorter Fastpass queue.

staff aren't allowed to lend assistance in getting into and out of the less accessible rides, but all the loos, phones, shops and restaurants have wheelchair access.

Disneyland Park

The introduction to Disneyland Paris is the same as in Florida, LA and Tokyo. **Main Street USA** is a mythical vision of a 1900s American town, and it leads up to **Central Plaza**, the hub of the park. Clockwise from Main Street are Frontierland, Adventureland, Fantasyland and Discoveryland. The **castle**, directly opposite Main Street across Central Plaza, belongs to Fantasyland. A steam-train **Railroad** runs round the park with stations at each "land" and at the main entrance.

The listings on pp.285–288 are a selection of the best and worst rides, with some warnings about suitability. Apart from some height restrictions, Disney offers little guidance about suitability, and indeed it's surprisingly difficult to tell what one child will find exhilarating and another upsetting. For the youngest kids, **Fantasyland** is likely to hold the most thrills. There are no height restrictions here, and rides are mostly gentle. Each of the other three themed areas offers a landmark roller coaster and a theme; **Adventureland** has the most outlandish, jungly sets, **Frontierland** is set in the Wild West, while **Discoveryland** emphasizes technology and the space age.

Eating and drinking

As you'd expect, there's a lot of overpriced American junk **food** in Disneyland Paris. It's probably safest to avoid the swankier restaurants in Disney Village and go for hamburger-style snacks at the various themed eateries around the park. If you want to sit down to a proper meal, the fixed price, "all-you-can-eat" buffet-style restaurants are not a bad deal, with their large salad bars. Adults can drink wine or beer at any of the park's restaurants.

Officially, you're not supposed to bring any refreshments into the park, but you could always eat a good Parisian breakfast and bring some discreet snacks. Whether Goofy will turn nasty if he sees you eating a brand name not on the list of Disney sponsors is anyone's guess.

The parades

The main "Once Upon a Dream" **Parade** happens every day at 4pm and lasts for half an hour. This is not a bad time to make for the most popular rides, but if you have kids they will no doubt force you to press against the barriers for the ultimate Disney event. One of the best vantage spots is on the queuing ramp for *It's a Small World*, right by the gates through which the floats appear. From here, the parade progresses, very slowly, to Town Square. The best seating is in front of the Fantasyland Castle, one of the points where the floats stop and the characters put on a performance. The parade floats represent all the top box-office Disney movies and characters – *Mickey and Minnie Mouse*, *Donald Duck*, *Snow White*, *Cinderella*, *Peter Pan*, *Mary Poppins*, *Toy Story*, *The Lion King*, *Pirates of the Caribbean*. Everyone waves and smiles, and characters on foot shake hands with the kids who've managed to get to the front.

Smaller events such as costumed Dixie bands and jungle-themed hoedowns take place throughout the day, while on summer and Halloween-period nights at 7.30pm, elaborately lit floats and dancing characters trace the main route.

Firework displays happen about twice a week during the summer. Check with the programme available at City Hall for dates and times.

Though there are a few green patches, there is no lawn to sprawl about on. Opportunities for afternoon naps are limited, which shows by late afternoon in the general frayed tempers; renting a pushchair (see below) for even an older child might be a good idea.

Information and practicalities

Passing underneath the wedding-cake *Disneyland Hotel*, you enter the park underneath Main Street Station, on the internal railroad system. **City Hall** is to the left, where you can get **information** about the day's programme of events, and retrieve **lost property**. You can enquire about lost children here, too, and there's a dedicated **Lost Children** area in the First Aid complex by the *Plaza Gardens Restaurant* on Central Plaza (in the block between Main Street and Discoveryland). Next door, you can change nappies, breastfeed and heat baby food in the **Baby Care Centre**, sponsored by the ever-thoughtful Nestlé corporation. **Luggage** can be left in lockers in "Guest Storage" under Main Street Station (€1.50). You can rent wheelchairs and **pushchairs** (€7.50) in the building opposite City Hall.

Main Street USA

Main Street is really just a giant mall for Disney sponsors only. See if you can get down it without buying one of the following: a balloon, a hat with your name embroidered on it, an ice cream, silhouette portraits of your kids, the *Wall Street Journal* of 1902, a Disney version of a children's classic in hardback, a video camera and tripod, an evening dress and suit and tie, a Donald Duck costume, some muffins, a Coke and a complete set of Disney characters in ceramics, metal, plastic, rubber or wool. Leaving Main Street is quickest on foot (crowds permitting), although omnibuses, trams, horse-drawn streetcars, fire trucks and police vans are always on hand, plus the Disney *pièce de résistance*, the Railroad, for which **Main Street Station** has the longest queues.

Discoveryland

Autopia Miniature futuristic cars to drive on rails. Good fun, especially for little kids, but there's no possibility of any race-day stratagems. Minimum height to drive is 1.32m.

Buzz Lightyear Laser Blast Inspired by *Toy Story 2*, an interactive cart ride through a black-light universe. You shoot at threatening space creatures, helping Buzz and his friendly three-eyed Martians save the galaxy. Good for little kids. Uses Fastpass.

Honey, I Shrunk The Audience Visitors enter the "Imagination Institute" wearing 3D glasses to meet Eric Idle, host of the "Inventor of the Year Awards". The audience is then dive-bombed by Rick Moranis and "shrunk" using his "shrinking machine", a process that involves loud music, clever 3D and film effects, and general mayhem. Not exactly scary, but overwhelming and therefore not recommended for young children.

Les Mystères du Nautilus A rather disappointing stroll through a mock-up of the *Nautilus* submarine – Captain Nemo's vessel in *20,000 Leagues Under the Sea*. What's supposed to impress you is the faithfulness of the decor to the original Disney set, though there is a fishy surprise inside.

Orbitron The "rockets" on this ride go round and round fairly slowly and go up (at your control) to a daring 30 degrees above the horizontal. Suitable for small kids and for those who hate more violent rides.

Space Mountain Not for the faint-hearted. You're catapulted upwards, suspended weightless and then spun through an interstellar world at speeds of up to 40km, with a 360-degree sidewinder loop and corkscrew loop. Minimum height 1.40m, and pregnant women and people with health problems are advised not to ride. Uses the Fastpass scheme.

Space Mountain Mission 2 The new star attraction provides 1.3G of horrifying speed and a moment of weightlessness, all in an elaborately lit – meteor storms, rushing star clusters – ambience. The same restrictions apply as at the original Space Mountain. Uses the Fastpass scheme.

Star Tours Giddy, simulated ride in a spacecraft (with sixty other people all in neat rows) piloted by friendly, incompetent C3PO of *Star Wars* fame. The projection of what you're supposed to be careering through is actually from the film, which pleases fans. Pregnant women and those with health problems are advised not to board. Using Fastpass skips the queues.

Videopolis This vast fast-food restaurant and theatre combined is currently showing musical highlights from the *Legend of the Lion King* show (5 times per day; first show at noon). The singing and dancing "African villager" cast has a special-effects backup rarely seen in rural Tanzania. Tickets are free and should be collected approximately 2 hours before show time at the Discoveryland Station. Not all shows are in English, but as the dialogue is minimal, the singing is English-language and the dancing and decor don't need translation anyway, it's not something to worry about too much. Check the programme guide for schedules.

Le Visionarium 360-degree film presented by a robotic timekeeper host. The story involves travelling through time and picking up Jules Verne at the 1900 Exposition Universelle in Paris just as he and H. G. Wells, played by Jeremy Irons, are discussing time travel. They show Jules all the wonders of contemporary life – TGVs and Mirage jets mainly. Headphones for English translation provided.

Fantasyland

Alice's Curious Labyrinth A giant maze with surprises. There are passages that only those under 1m can pass through and enough false turns and exits to make it an irritatingly good labyrinth. Takes fifteen to twenty minutes, though there is the option to exit at the halfway point.

Blanche-Neige et les Sept Nains This *Snow White and the Seven Dwarfs* ride takes you through lots of menacing moving trees, swinging doors and cackling witches, recreating scenes from the classic Disney film. Can frighten smaller kids.

Le Carrousel de Lancelot A stately merry-go-round, whose every horse has its own individual medieval equerry in glittering paint.

Dumbo the Flying Elephant Dumbo and his clones provide a safe, slow, aerial ride in

Roller coasters

Each of the park's areas, apart from the tinies-focused Fantasyland, centres on its roller coaster. The runaway train on Frontierland's **Big Thunder Mountain** and the mine-carts of Adventureland's **Indiana Jones and the Temple of Peril: Backwards!** are fast and exciting, but the emphasis is on thrills rather than sheer terror – you can tell that things aren't going to be too bad because you're kept in your seat by a bar, rather than being fully strapped in. **Space Mountain** and its newer sibling **Space Mountain Mission 2**, in Discoveryland, and the **Rock 'n' Roller Coaster Starring Aerosmith**, over in the Walt Disney Studios section, are a different matter altogether. Their upside-down loops, corkscrews and terrifying acceleration require a lock-in padded brace to keep you in place, and you'll need a strong constitution to really enjoy it.

All four rides have different height restrictions, and as you queue for the latter two you'll be bombarded with warnings to discourage pregnant women or people with neck or back problems. You can avoid queues on all of them by using the Fastpass scheme, and arriving early can also be a good strategy, but be warned: the experience can be so intense that the park's gentler rides may seem disappointing. Children, in particular, may want to return again and again.

When you emerge from the exit gates, video screens show close-up images of terrified faces captured moments before. While it's fun to hang around until you spot your own twisted visage, buying a photographic copy is fairly expensive and the quality is poor.

which you can regulate the rise and fall of the revolving elephants yourself with a lever. One of the most popular rides in Fantasyland, though it only lasts a measly 25 seconds.

It's a Small World This is a quintessential Disney experience; there's one in every Disneyland, and Walt considered it to be the finest expression of his corporation's philosophy. Your boat rides through a polystyrene and glitter world, where animated dolls in national/ethnic/tribal costumes dance beside their most famous landmarks or landscapes, singing the song *It's a Small World*. Some children seem to enjoy the sugar-coated fantasy.

Mad Hatter's Tea Cups Great big whirling teacups slide past each other on a chequered floor. Again, not a whizzy ride, but fun for younger ones.

Le Pays des Contes de Fées A boat ride through cleverly miniaturized fairy-tale scenes: *Alice in Wonderland*, *Pinocchio*, etc. Fine for little kids.

Peter Pan's Flight The very young seem to really enjoy this jerky ride above Big Ben and the lights of London to Never-Never Land. Uses Fastpass.

Sleeping Beauty's Castle The castle stands at the entrance to Fantasyland, just off the central plaza at the end of Main Street. There's little to see inside other than a few bits of plasticky vaulting, naff stained glass and cartoon tapestries, though a huge animated dragon lurks in the dungeon.

Adventureland

Adventureland Bazaar A clever bit of shopping mall disguised as a *souk*, with traditional Arab latticed walls, desert pastel colours, and all sorts of genuine Hollywood details.

Adventure Isle Not a ride, but a sort of playground of caves, bouncy bridges, huge boulders, trees, tunnels and waterfalls built on two small islands in the middle of Adventureland. Parents of over-tired children and those who need a break from the queues should not underestimate the thrill of just being able to wander around unfettered.

La Cabane des Robinson The 27-metre mock banyan tree at the top of Adventure Isle is one of Disneyland Paris's most obsessively detailed creations, complete with hundreds of thousands of false leaves and blossoms. It's reached by walkways and a series of more than 170 steps, so it's best avoided by pram-pushers and toddler-haulers.

Indiana Jones and the Temple of Peril: Backwards! A fast and quite violent roller coaster through a classic Indy landscape, made all the more frightening by the fact that it's done backwards. The minimum height for the ride is 1.40m. Children under about 8 years old, pregnant women and people with health problems should steer clear. Queues can be avoided by using Fastpass.

Pirates of the Caribbean This satisfyingly long ride is one of the finest, consisting of an underground ride on water and down waterfalls, past scenes of evil piracy. The animated automata are the best yet – be warned that they set small children whimpering and crying immediately. Battles are staged across the water, skeletons slide into the deep, parrots squawk, chains rattle and a treasure trove is revealed.

△ Sleeping Beauty's Castle

Frontierland

Big Thunder Mountain A proper scream-out-loud funfair thrill, this is a roller coaster mimicking a runaway mine train round a "mining mountain". There are wicked twists and turns, sudden tunnels and hairy moments looking down on the water, but no violent upside-down or corkscrew stuff. Minimum height 1.02m; not suitable for small children. Use Fastpass.
The Chapparal Theater Shows seasonal theatrical spectaculars featuring all the usual Disney suspects. Times are displayed outside, and on the back of the main park map.
Phantom Manor *Psycho*-style house on the outside and Hammer Horror Edwardian mansion within. Holographic ghosts appear before cobweb-covered mirrors and ancestral portraits, but nothing actually jumps out and screams at you. Probably too frightening for young children nevertheless.
Rustler Roundup Shootin' Gallery There's a fee (€2) for this attraction, apparently because without some check people stay for hours and hours shooting infrared beams at fake cacti.
Thunder Mesa Riverboat Landing A rather pointless cruise around the lake, but the paddleboat steamer is carefully built to offer lots of antique-style curiosities, and it's fun to watch the roller coaster rattle around the rocks of Big Thunder Mountain.

Walt Disney Studios Park

Other than the "Rock 'n' Roller Coaster Starring Aerosmith", a terrifyingly fast, corkscrew-looping, Metal-playing white-knuckler, the new **Walt Disney Studios Park** complex rather lacks the mega-rides offered by its older, larger neighbour. That said, a major new attraction, the **TwilightZone Tower of Terror** – complete with a terrifying elevator ride with the provisional (and self-explanatory) title of **The Big Drop** – was almost finished at the time of writing. In some ways this side of the park is a more satisfying affair, however, focusing on what Disney was and is still renowned for – animation. You can try your hand at drawing, there are mock film and TV sets where you can be part of the audience, and the special effects and stunt shows are impressive in their way, although probably not as impressive as just going to the movies.

Rides and shows

Animagique Disney characters in full fluffy costumes act out classic scenes from Disney films.
Armageddon Special Effects Your group of fifty or so is ushered into a circular chamber decked out as a space station. As meteors rush towards the screens on all sides, the whole ship seems about to break up. Less cynical children may find the whole experience overwhelming.
Art of Disney Animation You progress through two mini-theatres, one showing famous moments from Disney cartoons, the next with a "cartoonist" having a conversation with an on-screen animated creation, explaining to the creature how it came to look as it did. In the lobby area, children are taught to draw identical Mickey Mouse faces.
Cars Race Rally An all-new, Cars-inspired ride on the lines of a destruction derby. The ride is real enough, though sedate – the hell-raising element is engineered using special effects.
Cinémagique A theatrical screening of a century of movie moments, with actors appearing to jump into and out of the on-screen action, helped by special effects.
Crush's Coaster The theme of this gentle coaster is taken from Finding Nemo. You're taken into a virtual underwater world on the back of a turtle, then into a minute-long

roller-coaster section which isn't especially fast but features an unusual spinning mechanism. Minimum height 1.04m.

Flying Carpets over Agrabah A good, solid fairground ride where the carpet-shaped cars wheel around the central lamp for a disappointingly short time. Very popular with smaller children, especially the lever which makes their carpet rise up and down. Using Fastpass can avoid the long queues.

Moteurs ... Action! Stuntshow Spectacular Decked out like a Mediterranean village, a big arena is the scene for some spectacular stunts: jumping rally cars, sliding motorbikes, leaping jet skis, stuntmen falling from heights and so on. Various timed shows throughout the day.

Rock 'n' Roller Coaster Starring Aerosmith A real heart-stopper, reaching 5G at one point. There are corkscrews, loops and violent lurches, and the whole thing takes place in a neon-lit and hard-rock-soundtracked darkness that makes it all the more alarming. It's all over in less than two minutes. Uses Fastpass. Minimum height 1.2m; entirely unsuitable for small children.

Stitch Encounter A theatrical-type experience in which children talk and play with the virtual reality alien Stitch who, despite being on-screen, manages to interact with the audience.

Studio 1 For "boulevard of dreams", read row of shops and restaurants. Not a ride, though it's listed on the map.

Studio Tram Tour Featuring Catastrophe Canyon An electric tram takes you on a sedate circuit of various bits and pieces of film set. The high point is the halt among the Wild West rocks of Catastrophe Canyon – sit on the left for the scariest ride.

Walt Disney Television Studios Television shows are produced here with the help of a ready-to-hand live audience. It's moderately entertaining to watch how it's all done, with cameras, chatty compères and so on.

Disney Village and the hotels

The **Disney Village** entertainment and restaurant complex, opposite the RER and train stations, is basically a street lined with expensive shops and restaurants. The work of architect Frank Gehry, it looks like a circus-top tent that has had its top carried off by a bomb, with a pedestrian street driven through the middle of it. *Buffalo Bill's Wild West Show*, with guns, horses, bulls and bison, *Billy Bob's Country Western Saloon*, *Hurricanes* disco, the new multiplex cinema, *Annette's Diner*, *Rock 'n' Roll America* and a *Planet Hollywood Restaurant* await you, with live music on summer nights and various sideshows.

When you're nearing exhaustion from so much enchantment, you can return to your **hotel** and have a sauna, Jacuzzi or whirlpool dip and be in bed in time to feel fresh and fit to meet Mickey and Minnie again over breakfast. In the hotel area of the resort, you can play **golf** (27-hole course), skate (in winter), sail (in summer) and jog on a special "health circuit". In reality, all these activities are secondary to the main attraction, and they're expensive.

Disneyland hotels

Disney's six themed **hotels** are a mixed bag of hideous eyesores and over-ambitious kitsch designed by some of the world's leading architects – Michael Graves, Antoine Predock, Robert Stern and Frank Gehry. For all the dramatically themed exteriors and lobbies, the rooms are much the same inside: comfortable, well furnished and distressingly huge.

The hotels are only worth staying in as part of a multi-day package including park entry, which you can book through Disney (see box on p.282) or major travel agents. If you book directly it will turn out much more expensive. **Prices** vary hugely according to season, and which package you book. Winter, obviously, is cheaper than summer, but even within these periods there are low and high seasons; prices are highest throughout July and August.

Most rooms are family rooms with two double beds; on selected "kids free" dates in winter, children aged 3–11 stay for free, while in summer there's usually a supplement of around €100 per child per night. The hotels below are listed in order of price, starting with the most expensive.

The budget alternative, as long as you have a car, is the park's *Davey Crockett Ranch*, a fifteen-minute drive away, with self-catering log cabins. To really economize, you could **camp** at the nearby *Camping du Parc de la Colline*, Route de Lagny, 77200 Torcy (Ⓣ01.30.58.56.20, Ⓦwww.camping-de-la-colline.com), which is open all year; prices vary throughout the year, but a family of four staying in two tents will usually pay under €50.

Free bright-yellow **shuttle buses** run between the hotels and the single stop for the train station and both park entrances.

Hotel Cheyenne Along with *Sante Fe*, the *Cheyenne* is broken up into attractively small units: the film-set buildings of a Western frontier town, complete with wagons, cowboys, a hanging tree and scarecrows. With its Wild West theme and bunk beds in all the rooms, this is a good hotel for children.

Davy Crockett Ranch Prices range from €55 to €130 per person for a self-catering "bungalow" or log cabin (4–6 people) in a wooded, Wild West-themed setting – there's even a high-wire treetop assault course. The ranch is a fifteen-minute drive from the park, with no shuttle service laid on, so you'll need your own transport.

Disneyland Hotel Situated right over the entrance to the park with wings to either side, the large, frilly, pastel-pink *Disneyland Hotel* is decked out in glitzy Hollywood style. It's the most upmarket and best located by far.

Hotel New York Outside, the hotel is a plasticky, post-modern attempt at conjuring up the New York skyline, while the furnishings within are pseudo Art Deco with lots of apples. Comfortable, but showing its age. In winter, the outdoor ice rink makes it a good option for children.

Newport Bay Club This "New England seaside resort circa 1900" spreads like a game of dominoes. Blue-and-white-striped canopies over the balconies fail to give it that cosy guesthouse feel, but some rooms have the benefit of looking out over the lake.

Hotel Santa Fe Accommodation takes the form of smooth, mercifully unadorned, imitation sun-baked mud buildings in various shapes and sizes. Between them are tasteful car wrecks, a cactus in a glass case, strange geological formations and other products of the distinctly un-Disney imagination of New Mexican architect Antoine Predock. A scowling cheroot-chewing Clint Eastwood creates the drive-in movie entrance.

Sequoia Lodge Built around the theme of the "mountain lodge" typically found in the National Parks of the western United States, but on a giant scale.

La Vallée Outlet Shopping Village

Even if you're not going to Disneyland Paris itself, you might want to visit **La Vallée Outlet Shopping Village** (Mon–Fri 10am–7pm, Sat 10am–8pm, Sun 11am–7pm), an outdoor shopping mall that's designed to look like a village, standing just inside the Disney complex's boundaries. It's best for discounted labelled clothing, with the previous season's collections sold on at discounts of a third or more. Agnès b, Armani, Burberry, Cacharel, Christian Lacroix, Diesel, Givenchy, Reebok, Tommy Hilfiger and Versace are just a few of the international brands found here, each represented by their own individual shop. For a full list, see the official website, Ⓦ www.lavalleevillage.com. To get to La Vallée Outlet from Paris, take RER line A4 to the Val d'Europe/Serris-Montévrain stop, from where you can get a ride on a shuttle bus. From the Disney hotels there are regular park shuttles.

Listings

Listings

18

Accommodation

Accommodation in Paris is often booked up well in advance, especially in the spring and autumn peak seasons. It's wise to **reserve** a place as early as you can, particularly if you fancy staying in one of the more characterful places. You can simply call – all receptionists speak some English – but bear in mind that more and more hotels offer **online booking** as well, sometimes at discounted prices. In fact, it's always worth asking for a discount on the advertised rate; in August and from November to March (apart from Christmas) you can often negotiate reductions of ten to twenty percent or more. If you book by phone, many places will ask for a credit card number, others for written or faxed confirmation, while a few inexpensive places may even ask for a deposit to be sent in the post.

If you find yourself stuck on arrival, the main **tourist office** (see p.46) at rue des Pyramides and the branches at the Gare de Lyon and Eiffel Tower will find you a room in a hotel or hostel free of charge. The tourist office also offers a free **online reservation service** (Ⓦwww.paris-info.com), with good discounts on many hotels. The online agency Ⓦwww.ratestogo.com offers discounts on last-minute bookings.

Bed and breakfasts, apartment-hotels, hostels and campsites are listed separately on pp.308–311.

Hotels

Paris has an enormous range of **hotels** to suit all tastes and budgets, from well-worn cheapies, just a step up from youth hostels, to palatial establishments like the Ritz. Chains have taken over many smaller family-run hotels, pushing them upmarket, but it's still possible to find independently run, characterful places at reasonable prices. A growing number are restyling themselves as "design hotels" – some coolly minimalist, others fabulously elegant. Rooms are typically small – cramped, even – in all but the most expensive categories.

The **star system** provides some clues as to the pretensions of a hotel, particularly its **price**, but little else – a two-star hotel might have lovely rooms but fail to be awarded a third star because its staff don't speak enough languages, or its foyer is small. A double room in an old-fashioned two-star will cost between €60 and €90, though don't expect much in the way of decor at the lower end of the scale. For something with a bit more class – whether that means a touch of character, smooth efficiency or a minibar – you'll pay upwards of €90; in swankier areas, expect to pay €120 or more. At the luxury end of the scale the sky's the limit, with prices at €300–400 and upwards not uncommon. It is possible to find a double room in a central location for around €40, sometimes even less, though at this level you will probably have to accept a room with just a sink (*lavabo*) and a shared bathroom on the landing (*dans le palier*) – and a few such places still charge for use of the shower.

Even within one hotel, rooms can vary considerably, and it's worth asking what's available – almost all hoteliers speak at least enough English to get by. Rooms at the back, overlooking an internal courtyard (*côté cour/jardin*) can be dark; rooms on the street (*côté rue*) tend to be larger and lighter, but noise can be a problem if there isn't double-glazing. Certain standard terms recur: *douche/WC* and *bain/WC* mean that you have a shower or bath as well as toilet in the room. A room with a *grand lit* (double bed) is invariably cheaper than one with *deux lits* (two separate beds). Many hotels offer de luxe or *supérieure* rooms as well as those in a *standard* or *classique* class; a superior room in a less expensive hotel can often be better value than a standard one in a pricier establishment.

Breakfast (*petit déjeuner*) is sometimes included (*compris*) in the room price but is normally extra (*en sus*) – around €6–10 per person. Always make it clear whether you want breakfast or not when you take the room. Either way, it's usually an indifferent continental affair of croissant/baguette, orange juice and coffee.

One of the best central **areas for budget-priced hotels** is the 10e, especially around place de la République. Quieter districts, further out, where you can get some good deals are the 13e and 14e, south of Montparnasse, and the 17e and 20e, on the western and eastern sides of the city respectively.

Our hotel recommendations are listed by area, following the same chapter divisions used in the guide. Most hotels have a selection of rooms – singles, doubles, twin-bedded and triples – at different prices. In our listings we give **prices for doubles** and also cite tariffs for **single rooms** where these are particularly good value.

The Islands

The hotels in this section are marked on the map on pp.50–51.

Henri IV 25 place Dauphine, Ile de la Cité, 1er ⓣ01.43.54.44.53. An ancient and well-known cheapie on a beautiful square right in the centre of Paris. A squeaky, narrow staircase winds its way up to twenty rooms spread over five storeys (no lift). It's best to go for one of the renovated rooms with shower, as the rest come with nothing more luxurious than a cabinet de toilette and are very run-down. It's advisable to book well in advance and ring to confirm nearer the time. Doubles €50–62. M° Pont-Neuf/Cité.

Hôtel de Lutèce 65 rue St-Louis-en-l'Ile, 4e ⓣ01.43.26.23.52, ⓦwww.paris-hotel-lutece.com. Twenty-three tiny but appealing wood-beamed rooms are eked out of this narrow seventeenth-century town house, located on the most desirable island in France. All the rooms have recently been tastefully renovated in contemporary style in shades of terracotta and cream, and come with modern, sparkling-white bathrooms. Doubles are €195. M° Pont-Mairie.

The Champs-Elysées and around

The hotels in this section are marked on the map on pp.76–77.

Le Bristol 112 rue du Faubourg St-Honoré, 8e ⓣ01.53.43.43.25, ⓦwww.hotel-bristol.com. The city's most luxurious and spacious hotel manages to remain discreet and warm. Some of the rooms come with Gobelins tapestries and private roof gardens; there's also a large colonnaded interior garden, as well as the expected swimming pool, health club and gourmet restaurant. Doubles start at €710. M° Miromesnil.

Hôtel des Champs-Elysées 2 rue d'Artois, 8e ⓣ01.43.59.11.42, ⓦwww.champselysees-paris-hotel.com. The rooms at this well-located two-star are small but clean and decorated in warm reds and yellows; all come with modern bathrooms (either shower or bath), plus satellite TV, minibar, hairdryer and safe. Breakfast is served in a cool, relaxing converted stone cellar. Doubles start from €102, and are pretty good value for the area. M° St-Philippe-du-Roule.

Hôtel de l'Elysée Faubourg Saint Honoré 12 rue des Saussaies, 8e ⓣ01.42.65.29.25, ⓦwww.france-hotel-guide.com/h75008efsh.htm. This plush three-star, a mere chandelier swing from the Elysée Palace, has sixty rooms decorated in traditional style, with *toile de Jouy* wallpaper, solid mahogany furniture and jacquard bedspreads. Doubles from €150. M° Miromesnil/Champs-Elysées-Clémenceau.

Hôtel Lancaster 7 rue de Berri, 8e ⓣ01.40.76.40.76, ⓦwww.hotel-lancaster.fr. The rooms in this elegantly restored nineteenth-century town house retain original features and are chock full of Louis XVI and rococo antiques, but with a touch of contemporary chic. The hotel was the pied-à-terre for the likes of Garbo, Dietrich and Sir Alec Guinness, and is still a favourite hideout today for those fleeing the paparazzi. A small interior zen-style garden and pleasant service make for a relaxing stay, and there's an excellent restaurant under triple-Michelin-starred chef Michel Troisgros. Doubles start at €480, though it's worth checking their site for special offers. M° George-V.

L'Hotel Pergolèse 3 rue Pergolèse, 16e ⓣ01.53.64.04.04, ⓦwww.hotelpergolese.com. A classy four-star boutique hotel in a tall, slender building on a quiet side street near the Arc de Triomphe. The decor is all contemporary – wood floors, cool colours, chic styling – but without chilliness; sofas and friendly service add a cosy touch. Rooms on six floors (facing the street or the internal courtyard) are comfortable and well appointed, with great designer bathrooms. Doubles start from €220, but frequent special deals bring prices well down below advertised rates. M° Argentine.

Hôtel de Sers 41 av Pierre 1er de Serbie, 8e ⓣ01.53.23.75.75, ⓦwww.hoteldesers.com. A chic and luxurious boutique hotel, just off the Champs-Elysées, offering rooms in minimalist style, with rosewood furnishings and decor in white, grey, deep reds and pinks; facilities include CD/DVD player and huge TV. The two suites on the top floor have fabulous panoramic terraces. Doubles from €480. M° George-V.

The Tuileries and Louvre

The hotels in this section are marked on the map on pp.88–89

Hôtel Brighton 218 rue de Rivoli, 1er ⓣ01.47.03.61.61, ⓦwww.paris-hotel-brighton.com. An elegant hotel dating back to the late nineteenth century and affording magnificent views of the Tuileries gardens from the front-facing rooms on the upper floors – if your budget stretches to it, go for one with a balcony right at the top. Most of the 65 rooms have recently been renovated and have a certain period charm. Doubles €168–246. M° Tuileries.

Costes 239 rue St-Honoré, 1er ⓣ01.42.44.50.00, ⓦwww.hotelcostes.com. A favourite with media and fashion celebrities, this luxury hotel, marrying Second Empire style with all up-to-date amenities, is postmodern decadence perfected. Beautiful people saunter about plush red velvet interiors under dim lighting, making you feel you're in an élite, invitation-only French bordello. Doubles run at €550–750. M° Tuileries.

Hôtel de Lille 8 rue du Pélican, 1er ⓣ01.42.33.33.42. A small, old-fashioned budget hotel on a quiet street, just a couple of blocks from the Louvre. The rooms, some en suite, are basic, though not unappealing, decorated with a nod to belle époque style. Non-en-suite rooms have access to a shower on the landing for an extra €2. There's no lift to serve the five floors, and no breakfast, and the walls are rather thin. The minuscule singles cost €38; doubles €50–65. M° Palais-Royal-Musée-du-Louvre.

Hôtel Meurice 228 rue de Rivoli, 1er ⓣ01.44.58.10.10, ⓦwww.meuricehotel.com. Palatial opulence in the style of Louis XVI, with unsurpassed vistas over Paris. You'll be so busy having tea in the winter garden or taking a Turkish bath that the delights of Paris just on your doorstep are likely to go ignored. Doubles start at €620. M° Tuileries.

Relais St Honoré 308 rue St Honoré, 1er ⓣ01.42.96.06.06, http://sainthonore.free.fr. A snug little hotel, set in a stylishly renovated seventeenth-century town house. The pretty wood-beamed rooms are done out in warm colours and quality fabrics. Facilities include free broadband Internet access and flat-screen TVs. Doubles cost from €196. M° Tuileries.

Hôtel Thérèse 5–7 rue Thérèse, 1er ⓣ01.42.96.10.01, ⓦwww.hoteltherese.com. A very attractive boutique hotel, on a quiet street within easy walking distance of the Louvre, offering small, cosy rooms, decorated in contemporary style with soothing beige, pale greens or reds, dark woods and prints, and equipped with marble bathrooms. Book well in advance as it's very popular, especially during the fashion shows. Doubles from €145. M° Palais Royal-Musée du Louvre.

The Grands Boulevards and passages

The hotels in this section are marked on the map on pp.88–89.

Hôtel Chopin 46 passage Jouffroy, 9e; entrance on bd Montmartre, near rue du Faubourg-Montmartre ⓣ01.47.70.58.10, ⓦwww.bretonnerie.com. A charming, quiet hotel set in an atmospheric period building hidden away at the end of a picturesque 1850s passage. Rooms are pleasantly furnished, though the cheaper ones are on the small side and a little dark. Doubles at €81–92. M° Grands-Boulevards.

Hôtel Mansart 5 rue des Capucines, 1 er ⓣ01.42.61.50.28, ⓦwww.paris-hotel-mansart.com. This gracious hotel is situated on the corner of place Vendôme, just a stone's throw from the Ritz, but with rooms at a fraction of the price, and while they're not quite in the luxury bracket they're very agreeably decorated in Louis XIV style, with plenty of antique furniture, old prints and quality fabrics, and most are fairly spacious by Parisian standards. Doubles range from €180 to €315, with the more expensive rooms looking out onto the square. M° Opéra/Madeleine.

Hôtel Tiquetonne 6 rue Tiquetonne, 2e ⓣ01.42.36.94.58. Located on a characterful pedestrianized street a block away from Montorgueil street market and around the corner from the rue St-Denis red-light district, this excellent-value budget hotel is pleasantly old-fashioned, dating back to the 1920s and looking as though it's probably changed little since. Colour-clash decor notwithstanding, the rooms are nice enough and well maintained, many quite spacious, though walls are thin. Non-en-suite rooms are equipped with a sink and bidet. There are no TVs and breakfast is served in your room. Singles €30, doubles €40–50. M° Etienne-Marcel.

Hôtel Victoires Opéra 56 rue de Montorgueil, 2e ⓣ01.42.36.41.08, ⓦwww.hotelVictoiresOpera.com. A stylish boutique hotel on the lovely pedestrianized Montorgueil market steet. The rooms are furnished in contemporary style and warmly decorated in chocolate-brown and coffee tones; the walls are hung with prints of Modigliani drawings. Posted rates for doubles are €214–275, though check the website for special offers. M° Les Halles/Etienne-Marcel.

Hôtel Vivienne 40 rue Vivienne, 2e ⓣ01.42.33.13.26, ⓔparis@hotel-vivienne.com. A ten-minute walk from the Louvre, this is a friendly, family-run place, with very clean, good-sized, cheery rooms and modern bathrooms. Ten have Internet capability, and the foyer also has a terminal with free access for guests. Doubles with shower only and shared WC €73; doubles with full bath €85–112. The single rooms are a decent size and well priced at €58. M° Grands-Boulevards/Bourse.

Beaubourg and Les Halles

Unless otherwise indicated, the hotels in this section are marked on the map on p.101.

Relais du Louvre 19 rue des Prêtres St-Germain l'Auxerrois, 1er ⓣ01.40.41.96.42, ⓦwww.relaisdulouvre.com. A discreet hotel with eighteen rooms set on a quiet backstreet opposite the church of St-Germain l'Auxerrois; you can admire the flying buttresses from the front-facing rooms. The decor is traditional but not stuffy, with rich, quality fabrics, old prints, Turkish rugs and solid furniture. There are also two comfy suites and an apartment on the top floor. All rooms have cable TV and wi-fi access; the cheaper ones are rather small. The relaxed atmosphere and charming service attract a faithful clientele. Doubles €160–198. M° Palais-Royal-Musée-du-Louvre.

Hôtel de Roubaix 6 rue Greneta, 3e ⓣ01.42.72.89.91, ⓦwww.hotel-de-roubaix.com. See map on p.110. An old-fashioned, family-run two-star. The 53 rooms are small and done out with floral wallpaper and slightly rickety furniture, but they're good value when you consider the location, just five minutes' walk from the Pompidou Centre. Breakfast (€4) – a crusty piece of bread and a hot drink – is included in the price whether you want it or not. Doubles €55. M° Réaumur-Sébastopol/Arts-et-Métiers.

Hôtel Saint-Merry 78 rue de la Verrerie, 4e ⓣ01.42.78.14.15, ⓔhotelstmerry@wanadoo.fr. Live out your Gothic medieval fantasies in this quirky little hotel in the former presbytery attached to Eglise Saint-Merry, run by friendly and helpful staff. The small rooms feature dark-wood furniture in Gothic style, exposed stone walls and decorative wrought iron; room 9, incorporating a flying buttress, is the most popular (and possibly most unusual hotel room in Paris). Possible minus points are the absence of a lift and TVs (apart from in the suite). Breakfast is served in your room. Rooms €160–230, suite €335. M° Rambuteau.

The Marais

The hotels in this section are marked on the maps on p.110 and 114.

Hôtel du Bourg Tibourg 19 rue du Bourg-Tibourg, 4e ⓣ01.42.78.47.39, ⓦwww.hoteldubourgtibourg.com. Oriental meets medieval, with a dash of Second Empire, at this sumptuously designed boutique hotel. Rooms are tiny, but cosseted with rich velvets, silks and drapes. A perfect romantic hideaway. Wi-fi in the rooms. Singles €150, doubles €220–250. M° Hôtel-de-Ville.

Hôtel de la Bretonnerie 22 rue Ste Croix de la Bretonnerie, 4e ⓣ01.48.87.77.63, ⓦwww.bretonnerie.com. A charming place on one of the Marais' liveliest streets; the rooms, all different, are decorated with exquisite care with quality fabrics, oak furniture and, in some cases, four-poster beds. The beamed attic rooms on the fourth floor are particularly appealing. The location's perfect for exploring the Marais, though front-facing rooms may suffer from street noise at night. Doubles from €116. M° Hôtel-de-Ville.

Caron de Beaumarchais 12 rue Vieille-du-Temple, 4e ⓣ01.42.72.34.12, ⓦwww.carondebeaumarchais.com. Named after the eighteenth-century French playwright Beaumarchais, who would have felt quite at home here: all the furnishings – the original engravings and Louis XVI furniture, not to mention the piano forte in the foyer – evoke the refined tastes of high-society pre-Revolution Paris. Rooms overlooking the courtyard are petite, while those on the street are more spacious, some with a small balcony. Book well in advance. Doubles €125–162. M° Hôtel-de-Ville.

Hôtel Central Marais 33 rue Vieille-du-Temple, 4e ⓣ01.48.87.56.08, ⓦwww.hotelcentralmarais.com. The only self-proclaimed gay hotel in Paris, whose famously popular gay bar, Le Central, is just downstairs. Six small boxy rooms with shared bathrooms, and only one with en-suite bath and WC. The entrance is on Rue Sainte-Croix-de-la-Bretonnerie. Doubles €87. M° Hôtel-de-Ville.

Grand Hôtel Jeanne d'Arc 3 rue de Jarente, 4e ⓣ01.48.87.62.11, ⓦwww.hoteljeannedarc.com. A welcoming budget hotel in an old Marais town house, just off lovely place du Marché Sainte-Catherine. The rooms, though nothing special, are well maintained and clean and come with cable TV and nicely tiled bathrooms. The triple at the top has good views over the rooftops. Doubles €84. M° St-Paul.

Grand Hôtel du Loiret 8 rue des Mauvais-Garçons, 4e ⓣ01.48.87.77.00, ⓔhotelduloiret@hotmail.com. A simple budget hotel, grand in name only. The rooms are essentially uneventful and very small, but acceptable for the price; cheaper ones have washbasin only, all have TV and telephone. The two triples on the top floor have views of Sacré-Coeur. Doubles €45 with shared toilet, €60–80 with en-suite. M° Hôtel-de-Ville.

Hôtel de Nice 42bis rue de Rivoli, 4e ⓣ01.42.78.55.29, ⓦwww.hoteldenice.com. A delightful old-world charm pervades this six-storey establishment, its small, pretty rooms hung with old prints and furnished with deep-coloured fabrics and Indian-cotton bedspreads. The rue de Rivoli is very busy, though, and traffic noise can be a problem despite the double-glazing. M° Hôtel-de-Ville. Singles €75; doubles €105; triple €130.

Paris France Hôtel 72 rue de Turbigo, 3e ⓣ01.42.78.00.04, ⓦwww.paris-france-hotel.com. Near the noisy intersection of rue de Turbigo and rue du Temple, but in an animated quartier off the beaten track. Rooms are fairly basic, with Ikea-style furniture, but clean and comfortable. Singles €62, doubles €76–86. M° Temple/République.

Hôtel Pavillon de la Reine 28 place des Vosges, 4e ⓣ01.40.29.19.19, ⓦwww.pavillon-de-la-reine.com. A perfect honeymoon or romantic-weekend getaway in a beautiful ivy-covered mansion secreted away off the Place des Vosges. It preserves an intimate ambience, with friendly, personable staff. The rooms mostly have a distinctively 1990s "hip hotel" feel, and could probably use another makeover. Doubles start at €415 and range up to €810 for the contoured, urbane Victor Hugo Suite. M° Bastille.

Hôtel du Petit Moulin 29–31 rue du Poitou, 3e ⓣ01.42.74.10.10, ⓦwww.paris-hotel-petitmoulin.com. A glamorous boutique hotel, set in an old bakery and designed top to bottom by Christian Lacroix. The designer's hallmark *joie de vivre* reigns in the seventeen rooms, each a fusion of different styles, from elegant Baroque to Sixties kitsch; shocking pinks and lime greens give way to *toile de Jouy* prints, while pod chairs rub up alongside antique dressing tables and old-fashioned bathtubs. Doubles from €180. M° Saint Sébastien Froissart/Filles du Calvaire.

Hôtel Picard 26 rue de Picardie, 3e ⓣ01.48.87.53.82, ⓦwww.france-hotel-guide.com/h75003picard.htm. In a quiet part of the Marais, this is a clean, friendly two-star establishment with decent-sized rooms, many of which have recently been renovated, though in rather old-fashioned style and with little thought for colour coordination. Nice, good-value breakfast for €4.50. Ten percent reduction if you produce your Rough Guide. €47 for simple doubles with basin (an extra €3 to use the shower on the landing), €72 with shower. M° Temple/République.

Hôtel St-Louis Marais 1 rue Charles-V, 4e ⓣ01.48.87.87.04, ⓦwww.saintlouismarais.com. Formerly part of the seventeenth-century Célestins Convent, this characterful place retains its period feel, with stone walls, exposed beams and tiled floors. Rooms are cosily done out with terracotta-coloured fabrics and old maps of Paris, and have wi-fi access; the bathrooms are attractive and modern. There's no lift, but the staff help with carrying luggage. A major plus is its location on a very quiet road, just a short walk from all the Marais action further north, and the Left Bank is easily reached over the Pont de Sully. Doubles cost €115 and €140; the cheaper ones are very small. M° Sully-Morland.

Hôtel Sévigné 2 rue Malher, 4e ⓣ01.42.72.76.17, ⓦwww.le-sevigne.com. A comfortable, pleasant hotel, just off rue de Rivoli. The rooms are small and simple but have been recently renovated and are double-glazed, and all have either full bath or shower. Good value for the area. Doubles €77–88. M° St-Paul.

Quartier Latin

The hotels in this section are marked on the map on pp.126–127.

Hôtel des Alliés 20 rue Berthollet, 5e ⓣ01.43.31.47.52, ⓦwww.alliesparishotel.com. Plain, rather dull rooms, but the place is clean and well run, and the price is a bargain. Rooms with bathroom are very spacious. Doubles €45–69. M° Censier-Daubenton.

Hôtel le Central 6 rue Descartes, 5e ⓣ01.46.33.57.93. This tiny hotel is a classic cheapo: shabbily furnished, set in a typically Parisian house above a café on a little square, and run rather sleepily by a couple living on the first floor. If you can get one of the half-dozen double rooms facing onto the street (€49), this is a great budget option, but the rooms on the internal courtyard (€44) are very sombre and have unmodernized bathrooms. Most rooms are singles (€36), so if you want a double you'll need to book months in advance. M° Maubert-Mutualité/Cardinal-Lemoine.

Hôtel du Collège de France 7 rue Thénard, 5e ⓣ01.43.26.78.36, ⓦwww.hotel-collegedefrance.com. This big, family-run hotel has a great situation on a street corner in the heart of the Quartier Latin – which means it has lots of bright street-front rooms. The decor is rather plain, but it's clean, well-kept and unfussy, and €97 for a double is a fair price. M° Cluny–La Sorbonne.

Hôtel du Commerce 14 rue de la Montagne-Ste-Geneviève, 5e ⓣ01.43.54.89.69, ⓦwww.commerce-paris-hotel.com. This brightly renovated budget hotel is aimed at backpackers and families. Rooms range from washbasin-only cheapies in the gloomy courtyard annex (€40, or €30 for one person) up to simple, modern en suites (€60–70) and three- and four-bed rooms. The feel is businesslike rather than warm, but the communal kitchen and dining area are handy, and the price at this central location is excellent. No credit cards. M° Maubert-Mutualité.

Hôtel Degrés de Notre Dame 10 rue des Grands Degrés, 5e ⓣ01.55.42.88.88, ⓦwww.lesdegreshotel.com. Just ten rooms make up this welcoming and superbly idiosyncratic hotel, so you'll need to book well in advance. The building is ancient and the rooms all very different, with prices corresponding to size (€115–170). Unique, personal touches are everywhere: hand-painted murals of clouds, antique mirrors, ancient beams and curious nooks and crannies. Perhaps the loveliest room of all is the one under the roof, which has its own stairs. M° St-Michel/Maubert-Mutualité.

Hôtel Esmeralda 4 rue St-Julien-le-Pauvre, 5e ⓣ01.43.54.19.20, ⓕ01.40.51.00.68. Dozing in an ancient house on square Viviani, this rickety old hotel offers cosily unmodernized en-suite rooms (€65) with a deeply old-fashioned feel – some are done up head to toe in faded red velvet. A few rooms have superb views of Notre-Dame, and there's a trio of very basic washbasin-only singles (€35). M° St-Michel/Maubert-Mutualité.

Familia Hôtel 11 rue des Ecoles, 5e ⓣ01.43.54.55.27, ⓦwww.hotel-paris-familia.com. Friendly, family-run hotel in the heart of the quartier. Rooms are small but characterful, with beams, elegant *toile de Jouy* wallpaper and pretty murals. Doubles cost €99–109; some top-floor rooms have views of nearby Notre-Dame, and others have their own balcony (€119) with table and chairs. The slightly more expensive Minerva, a three-star next door, has the same owners. M° Cardinal-Lemoine/Maubert-Mutualité/Jussieu.

Grand Hôtel St-Michel 19 rue Cujas, 5e ⓣ01.46.33.33.02, ⓦwww.grand-hotel-st-michel.com. This large three-star on a corner overlooking the Sorbonne has an appealing atmosphere of cosseted luxury. The rooms (up to €170) are pleasant, cheerful and well-kept, and have air-conditioning. RER Luxembourg.

Hôtel des Grandes Ecoles 75 rue du Cardinal-Lemoine, 5e ⓣ01.43.26.79.23, ⓦwww.hotel-grandes-ecoles.com. A cobbled private alleyway leads through to a big surprise: a large and peaceful garden, right in the heart of the Quartier Latin. Rooms (€135) are pretty in a modest way, with floral wallpaper and old-fashioned furnishings, and the welcome is homely and sincere. Reservations are taken three and a half months in advance. M° Cardinal-Lemoine.

Hôtel Résidence Henri IV 50 rue des Bernardins, 5e ⓣ01.44.41.31.81, ⓦwww.residencehenri4.com. Set back from busy rue des Ecoles on a cul-de-sac, this hotel is discreet and elegant. The eight rooms are classically styled, and some have original features like fireplaces; all have miniature kitchenettes, reflecting the hotel's longer-stay clientele. Prices can vary from €200 right down to €80 in quiet periods, so ask if there are any offers going. M° Maubert-Mutualité.

Hôtel des Jardins du Luxembourg 5 impasse Royer-Collard, 5e ⓣ01.40.46.08.88, ⓦwww.les-jardins-du-luxembourg.com You could almost throw a stone into the Luxembourg gardens from this peaceful, genteel hotel. The decor sometimes tries to look more expensive than it actually is, but the facilities are three-star, with air-conditioning throughout, and a little sauna. Rooms cost €140–150 – the nicest ones have balconies overlooking the street. RER Luxembourg, M° Cluny-La Sorbonne.

Hôtel Marignan 13 rue du Sommerard, 5e ⓣ01.43.54.63.81, ⓦwww.hotel-marignan.com. One of the better bargains in town, with breakfast thrown in. Totally sympathetic to the needs of rucksack-toting foreigners, with free laundry and ironing facilities, plus a room to eat your own food in – plates, fridge and microwave provided – and rooms for up to five people. Doubles from €60–100, depending on the season and the facilities – the least expensive have shared bathrooms. M° Maubert-Mutualité.

Hôtel Médicis 214 rue St-Jacques, 5e ⓣ01.43.54.14.66, ⓔhotelmedicis@aol.com. Basic, unmodernized hotel, but the low prices make it very popular with hard-up backpackers, and the owners are charming, even when they're slumbering on the couch. Doubles cost €35 and singles €20, but book or get here early to be sure of a room. RER Luxembourg.

Hôtel Port-Royal 8 bd Port-Royal, 5e ⓣ01.43.31.70.06, ⓦwww.hotelportroyal.fr. A one-star hotel at its very best, this friendly address has been in the same family since the 1930s. Double rooms (€78.50) are fairly large, immaculately clean and attractive; fifteen rooms are available with shared bathroom facilities (€52.50, but showers cost €2.50 extra). It's located out at the southern edge of the quartier, at the rue

Mouffetard end of the boulevard, but near the métro. No credit cards. M° Gobelins.

Les Rives de Notre Dame 15 quai Saint Michel, 5e ⓣ01.43.54.81.16, ⓦwww.rivesdenotredame.com. Just ten spacious and attractively fresh-feeling rooms look directly onto the quai St-Michel and the Seine, an obviously perfect location. The official rate is somewhat steep, at €245 and up for a double, but prices can drop as much as half off-season or if some rooms are vacant, so try asking for a discount. RER/M° St-Michel.

Hôtel St-Jacques 35 rue des Ecoles, 5e ⓣ01.44.07.45.45, ⓦwww.paris-hotel-stjacques.com. This pretty hotel in the heart of the district combines original nineteenth-century features, including a wrought-iron staircase and decorative ceiling mouldings, with modern comforts. The rooms are spacious, some with sashes draping the beds, decorous velvet settees and balconies offering great views of the Panthéon. Doubles at €100. M° Maubert-Mutualité/Odéon.

Select Hôtel 1 place de la Sorbonne, 5e ⓣ01.46.34.14.80, ⓦwww.selecthotel.fr. Situated right on the *place*, this hotel has had the full designer makeover, with exposed stone walls, leather and recessed wood trim much in evidence. The helpful staff are pleasantly un-snooty. Doubles from €150. M° Cluny-Sorbonne.

St-Germain

The hotels in this section are marked on the map on pp.142–143.

Hôtel de l'Abbaye 10 rue Cassette, 6e ⓣ01.45.44.38.11, ⓦwww.hotelabbayeparis.com. An atmosphere of hushed, luxurious calm presides over this hotel – there's even a fair-sized courtyard garden and conservatory out back. Rooms (doubles from €220) are characterized by swathes of floral fabric and brass fittings. M° St-Sulpice.

▽ L'Hôtel, 6e

Hôtel du Danube 58 rue Jacob, 6e ⓣ01.42.60.34.70, ⓦwww.hoteldanube.fr. Refined but friendly hotel in a very posh area, with a luxuriantly floral decor. The standard rooms (€120–155) are small and fairly attractive, but the *supérieures* (€170) are the ones to go for: unusually large, each with a pair of handsome, tall windows. M° Rue-du-Bac.

Hôtel Delhy's 22 rue de l'Hirondelle, 6e ⓣ01.43.26.58.25, ⓕ01.43.26.51.06. Hidden away in an ancient house in a tiny street just off place St-Michel, the location is the draw at this hotel, rather than the rooms – which are well maintained but unprepossessing. Around €80 for a double with shared bathroom facilities, or a few euros more en suite. M° St-Michel.

Ferrandi St-Germain 92 rue du Cherche-Midi, 6e ⓣ01.42.22.97.40, ⓔhotel.ferrandi@wanadoo.fr. Genteel, independent hotel with a timeless feel, hidden away in a residential corner of St-Germain. Rooms are charmingly homely, and cost €140–190, depending on size. M° Vaneau/St-Placide.

Hôtel du Globe 15 rue des Quatre-Vents, 6e ⓣ01.43.26.35.50, ⓦwww.hotel-du-globe.fr. Welcoming hotel in a tall, narrow, seventeenth-century building decked out with an appealingly eccentric medieval theme: four-posters, stone walls, roof beams and even a suit of armour. Rooms can be small, but aren't expensive for the location – doubles (no twins) cost around €140, depending on season. M° Odéon.

Grand Hôtel des Balcons 3 rue Casimir-Delavigne, 6e ⓣ01.46.34.78.50, ⓦwww.balcons.com. An appealing and comfortable hotel, thoroughly modernized but with some pleasing Art Deco details. It's fair value at €110–140 for a double, and in a lovely location near the Odéon and Luxembourg gardens. The balconies are all small, decorative affairs, except on the fifth floor. M° Odéon.

L'Hôtel 13 rue des Beaux-Arts, 6e ⓣ01.44.41.99.00, ⓦwww.l-hotel.com. Extravagantly styled and fashionable designer hotel, with twenty sumptuous rooms accessed by a wonderful spiral staircase, and with a tiny pool in the basement. Oscar Wilde died here, "fighting a duel" with his wallpaper, and he's now remembered by a room with a "Wilde" theme. Prices start in the high €200s. M° Mabillon/St-Germain-des-Prés.

Hôtel Louis II 2 rue St-Sulpice, 6e ⓣ01.46.33.13.80, ⓦwww.hotel-louis2.com. A great location between the Odéon and Jardin de Luxembourg means rates are fairly high, at around €190 for a double, but the warm, plush decor lives up to the price. It's more Louis XIV than Louis II, with plenty of gilt and swish red carpeting – plus flat-screen TVs, air-conditioning and Wi-Fi. M° St-Sulpice.

Hôtel des Marronniers 21 rue Jacob, 6e ⓣ01.43.25.30.60, ⓦwww.hotel-marronniers.com. A romantic address, with small rooms swathed in deep velvet curtains and fabric wallcoverings (doubles at €160). The breakfast room gives onto an unusually pleasant pebbled courtyard garden. M° St-Germain-des-Prés.

Hôtel Michelet-Odéon 6 place de l'Odéon, 6e ⓣ01.53.10.05.60, ⓦwww.hotelmicheletodeon.com. For a double room, €100 isn't much when you're this close to the Jardin de Luxembourg – and the rooms facing onto the *place*, especially the corner rooms, are genuinely attractive. Most rooms are slightly larger than the usual shoebox, too, and freshly redecorated. A few triples, quads and apartments are also available. M° Odéon.

Hôtel de Nesle 7 rue de Nesle, 6e ⓣ01.43.54.62.41, ⓦwww.hoteldenesleparis.com. Eccentric, offbeat hotel with historical- or literary-themed rooms, some decorated with wacky cartoon murals you'll either love or hate. Doubles are well priced at €75–100. M° St-Michel.

Hôtel de l'Odéon 13 rue St-Sulpice, 6e ⓣ01.43.25.70.11, ⓦwww.paris-hotel-odeon.com. Old-fashioned luxury: flowers, antique furniture, some four-poster beds, and great service. Doubles €130–250, depending on season. M° St-Sulpice/Odéon.

Relais Christine 3 rue Christine, 6e ⓣ01.40.51.60.80, ⓦwww.relais-christine.com. This deeply romantic four-star is set in a sixteenth-century building set around a deliciously hidden courtyard. Rooms are usually in the €300s, but at this level it's well worth paying the 20 percent premium for one of the *supérieure* rooms. If they freshened up the decor a little, this would be the perfect luxury Parisian hotel. M° Odéon/St-Michel.

Relais Saint-Sulpice 3 rue Garancière, 6e ⓣ01.46.33.99.00, ⓦwww.relais-saint-sulpice.com. Set in a beautiful, aristocratic town house on a side street immediately behind St-Sulpice's apse, this is a discreetly classy hotel with well-furnished rooms painted in cheery Provençal colours. Comes with all mod-cons, including a sauna off the dining room. Doubles from €175. M° St-Sulpice/St-Germain-des-Prés.

Hôtel Stanislas 5 rue du Montparnasse, 6e ⓣ01.45.48.37.05, ⓦwww.hotel-stanislas.com. This family-run two-star is closer to the bright lights of Montparnasse – you can hear the rumble of the métro – than the chichi north of St-Germain, but the price is correspondingly good value, at €65. Rooms are clean and welcoming enough, in a frumpily provincial sort of way. M° Notre-Dame des Champs/St-Placide.

Hôtel de l'Université 22 rue de l'Université, 7e ⓣ01.42.61.09.39, ⓦwww.hoteluniversite.com. Gorgeously cosy three-star with two-dozen rooms filled with antique details, from the stone-vaulted basement lounge to the beamed ceilings and fireplaces in the larger rooms, and the carefully chosen furnishings throughout. Doubles at €170, or €180 with a private terrace. M° Rue-du-Bac.

The Eiffel Tower quarter

The hotels in this section are marked on the map on pp.156–157.

Hôtel du Champs-de-Mars 7 rue du Champs-de-Mars, 7e ⓣ01.45.51.52.30, ⓦwww.hotel-du-champ-de-mars.com. Friendly and well-run hotel in a handsome area just off the rue Cler market. The rooms are decidedly cosy, with colourful fabrics adorning the bedheads, curtains and chairs. Excellent value at €85 for a double. M° Ecole-Militaire.

Hôtel Eiffel Rive-Gauche 6 rue du Gros-Caillou, 7e ⓣ01.45.51.24.56, ⓦwww.hotel-eiffel.com. A refurbishment has introduced modern furnishings to this traditional two-star, and the price of €75–125 for a double is reasonable for this attractive area. There's a tiny but cheerfully painted covered courtyard. The best rooms are at the top, with close-up views of the Eiffel Tower. M° Ecole-Militaire.

Hôtel du Palais Bourbon 49 rue de Bourgogne, 7e ⓣ01.44.11.30.70, ⓦwww.hotel-palais-bourbon.com. A substantial, handsome old building in the hushed, posh district near the Musée Rodin offers unusually spacious and prettily furnished double rooms that are a bargain at €130. As fits a homely, family-run hotel, there are parquet floors and lots of period details – and there's also air-conditioning in most rooms. Family rooms are available for around €185, as well as one tiny double and a few miniature, unmodernized singles that are a steal at €80. M° Varenne.

Hôtel Saint-Dominique 62 rue Saint-Dominique, 7e ⓣ01.47.05.51.44, ⓦwww.hotelstdominique.com. Welcoming hotel in the heart of this upmarket, villagey neighbourhood, which sits in the shadow of the Eiffel Tower. The smallish but tastefully wallpapered rooms (€93–121 for a double) are arranged around a bright little courtyard with tables and chairs amid the greenery. M° Invalides/La-Tour-Maubourg.

Hôtel de la Tulipe 33 rue Malar, 7e ⓣ01.45.51.67.21, ⓦwww.hoteldelatulipe.com. Attractively chintzy and cottage-like three-star with exposed-stone walls and flagstones recalling its former life as a convent. There's a miniature patio for summer breakfasts and drinks, but you pay for the location – €150 for a double. M° Invalides/La-Tour-Maubourg.

Montparnasse and southern Paris

Montparnasse and the 14e

The hotels in this section are marked on the map on pp.172–173.

Hôtel de la Loire 39bis rue du Moulin Vert, 14e ⓣ01.45.40.66.88, ⓦwww.hoteldelaloire-paris.com. Behind the pretty blue shutters lies a delightful family hotel with a genuinely homely feel. Rooms all have charming personal touches and spotless bathrooms, and are a real bargain at €59, or €52 for the slightly darker rooms in the annex, which runs the length of the garden. M° Pernety/Alésia.

Hôtel Mistral 24 rue de Cels, 14e ⓣ01.43.20.25.43, ⓦwww.hotel-mistral-paris.com. Welcoming and pleasantly refurbished hotel on a very quiet street, with a little courtyard garden and breakfast room behind. The good-value rooms come with showers and shared WC facilities (€60), or en suite (€75). M° Pernety/Alésia.

Hôtel du Moulin Vert 74 rue du Moulin Vert, 14e ⓣ01.45.43.65.38, ⓦwww.hotel-moulinvert.com. At €95 for a double, this isn't especially good value, but if you're looking for a peaceful, independent hotel with cosy, well-equipped rooms, it fits the bill. Good location on a green corner of this attractive neighbourhood. M° Pernety/Alésia.

Hôtel des Voyageurs 22 rue Boulard,14e ⓣ01.43.21.08.20, ⓦhttp://hotelvoyageursparis.free.fr. A friendly and great-value (all rooms €50) Montparnasse establishment with an original, warm spirit – there are paintings all over the walls and cultural events in the back garden. Rooms are modern and comfortable, with air-conditioning and free, Internet-ready terminals. M° Denfert-Rochereau.

The 15e

The hotels in this section are marked on the map on pp.184–185.

Hôtel de l'Avre 21 rue de l'Avre, 15e ⓣ01.45.75.31.03, ⓦwww.hoteldelavre.com. Within striking distance of the Eiffel Tower, this hotel lies just off the rue du Commerce – but you could be forgiven for thinking you were in the provinces. The fresh, pastel-coloured rooms have floral accents and wicker furniture, and some have balconies over the garden. The multilingual staff is cheery and welcoming. Doubles cost €77–87, or €92 with a garden view. M° La-Motte-Picquet-Grenelle.

Hôtel Printemps 31 rue du Commerce, 15e ⓣ01.45.79.83.36, ⓔhotel.printemps.15e@wanadoo.fr. Cheap furnishings and ageing decor don't stop this being a good budget choice for its neighbourhood location and friendly welcome. Rooms are clean and well priced at €43 with private bathrooms, €34 without, and the nicer ones have small balconies. Popular with backpackers. M° Emile-Zola/La-Motte-Picquet-Grenelle.

The 13e

The hotels in this section are marked on the map on p.187.

Résidence Les Gobelins 9 rue des Gobelins, 13e ⓣ01.47.07.26.90, ⓦwww.hotelgobelins.com. A pleasantly old-fashioned and quiet establishment within walking distance of the Quartier Latin's rue Mouffetard. With its large, simple but comfortable rooms going for €87, this is a well-known bargain, so book far in advance. M° Gobelins.

La Manufacture 8 rue Philippe de Champagne, 13e ⓣ01.45.35.45.25, ⓦwww.hotel-la-manufacture.com. The fifty-odd rooms at this smart, modeish hotel are trimmed in warm colours. Helpful staff, wooden flooring and rooms looking onto the Mairie justify the price – doubles at around €145. M° Place d'Italie.

Hôtel Tolbiac 122 rue de Tolbiac, 13e ⓣ01.44.24.25.54, ⓦwww.hotel-tolbiac.com. This big but friendly budget hotel has been newly refitted with a bright colour scheme and floorboards or wood-style lino throughout. There's free parking, free Internet and wi-fi, and the prices are good: €36 with shared shower room, or €45 en suite. The only drawback is the situation on a noisy junction. M° Tolbiac.

Le Vert-Galant 41 rue Croulebarbe, 13e ⓣ01.44.08.83.50, ⓦwww.vertgalant.com Set on a quiet backwater overlooking the verdant Square René-le-Gall, with a large garden behind, this family-run hotel seems to belong to a provincial French town rather than Paris – they'll even do your laundry and let you park your car on-site, and in the evening you can eat downstairs at the *Auberge Etchegorry* (see p.341). The rooms (€90) are modern but pleasantly airy; those giving onto the garden (€120) come with French windows and kitchenettes. M° Gobelins.

Montmartre and northern Paris

Montmartre

The hotels in this section are marked on the map on p.194.

Hôtel Bonséjour Montmartre 11 rue Burq, 18e ⓣ01.42.54.22.53, ⓕ01.42.54.25.92. Set in a marvellous location on a quiet, untouristy street on the slopes of Montmartre, this hotel is run by friendly and conscientious owners, and the rooms, which are basic but clean and spacious, are one of Paris's best deals – €29 for a simple double room with just a sink, or €45 with a private shower. Ask for the corner rooms 23, 33, 43 or 53, which have balconies. M° Abbesses.

Hôtel Caulaincourt Square 2 sq Caulaincourt (by 63 rue Caulaincourt), 18e ⓣ01.46.06.46.06, ⓦwww.caulaincourt.com. You can have shower-only (€63) or en-suite (€73) rooms at this friendly budget hotel on the heights above Montmartre, and there's also a hostel section with dorms (€25 a night). Private and dorm rooms alike are small and faintly shabby but decent enough, and Internet access and the fine views are both free. M° Lamarck-Caulaincourt.

Ermitage 24 rue Lamarck, 18e ⓣ01.42.64.79.22 ⓦwww.ermitagesacrecoeur.fr. One of the highest-altitude hotels in Paris, this discreet family-run establishment has rooms caught in time, characterfully decorated with florals in deep colours and antique *objets d'art*. Only a stone's throw from the Sacré-Coeur, but it's best to approach via M° Anvers and the funiculaire to avoid the steep climb. Doubles cost around €90 – no credit cards. M° Lamarck-Caulaincourt/Château-Rouge.

Hôtel Regyns Montmartre 13 place des Abbesses, 18e ⓣ01.42.54.45.21, ⓦwww.paris-hotels-montmartre.com. Friendly, tidy rooms with country-style decor, a number of which give onto the quiet place des Abbesses. If available, get one of the six rooms on the top floors, which have grand views of either the city or Sacré-Coeur. Doubles at €86, though you pay a €30 premium for a view. M° Abbesses.

Timhotel Montmartre place Emile-Goudeau, 11 rue Ravignan, 18e ⓣ01.42.55.74.79, ⓦwww.timhotel.com. Rooms are modern, comfortable and freshly decorated in a nondescript chain-hotel way. The location, however, is unbeatable – on the beautiful shady square where Picasso had his studio in 1900, with views across the city from the more expensive rooms. Doubles start at €130, running to €160 for the larger rooms with vistas. M° Abbesses/Blanche.

The 9e

The hotels in this section are marked on the map on p.194.

Hôtel Langlois 63 rue St-Lazare, 9e ⓣ01.48.74.78.24, ⓦwww.hotel-langlois.com. This superbly genteel hotel feels as if it has scarcely changed in the last century, though it has all the facilities you'd expect of a two-star. Every room is different, but they're all large and handsome with high ceilings, antique furnishings, fireplaces and other period details. Some have uniquely enormous bathrooms. There are only 27 rooms, with prices at €120–140, so book well in advance. M° Trinité.

Lorette Opéra 36 rue Notre Dame de Lorette, 9e ⓣ01.42.85.18.81, ⓦwww.astotel.com. Set in a great spot on place St-George between Opéra and Montmartre, this Best Western feels refreshingly unlike a chain. The warm, friendly, moderately stylish rooms are all well sized, while the tiled breakfast room with freestone arched ceiling makes a great place to start your day. Doubles around €170–220. M° Saint-Georges.

Perfect Hotel **39 Rue Rodier, 9e** **⊕01.42.81.18.86, ⓕ01.42.85.01.38.** This friendly, well-kept hotel on a lively street lined with restaurants sees many happy return visitors. Rooms are simple and clean, though the walls are notoriously paper-thin. While the hotel doesn't quite live up to its name, for the price it's a great find. Doubles without bath €25, otherwise €30. M° Anvers.

The 10e

The hotels in this section are marked on the map on p.204.

Hôtel Chabrol Opéra **46 rue de Chabrol, 10e** **⊕01.45.23.93.10, ⓦwww.hotelchabrol.com.** A reliable, welcoming little hotel within walking distance of the stations, and fairly recently renovated. Exposed roof beams add a warm note to the otherwise completely modernized rooms. Doubles cost €90. M° Poissonière/Gare-de-l'Est.

Libertel Terminus Nord **12 bd de Denain, 10e** **⊕01.42.80.20.00, ⓦwww.mercure.com.** A traditional-style luxury hotel that basks in its Victorian splendour right opposite the Gare du Nord – though it now bears the corporate imprint of the Libertel group. The prices and fittings are four-star, but you wouldn't chose to stay here unless you were looking for somewhere comfortable right next to the station. Doubles start at around €230, but bargains are to be had online. M° Gare-du-Nord.

Marclau Hôtel **78 rue du Faubourg Poissonnière, 10e ⊕01.47.70.73.50, ⓦwww.hotel-marclau .com.** Acceptable budget option situated on a quiet corner at the posher end of the quartier. Some frayed edges, but the rooms are large, clean and great value. The simplest singles go for €28, doubles for €31, with a few euros more for en-suite shower and /or toilet. M° Poissonnière.

Batignolles

The hotels in this section are marked on the map on p.207.

Hôtel Eldorado **18 rue des Dames, 17e** **⊕01.45.22.35.21, ⓦwww.eldoradohotel .fr.** Not quite the golden kingdom, but a superb address nonetheless. Idiosyncratic and enjoyable, this hotel has its own little wine bar and an attractive annex in a detached house at the back of its sizeable courtyard garden. Rooms (€50–70 for a double) are thoughtfully and charmingly decorated, with bright colour schemes and antique furnishings. A few simple shared-bath rooms are also available. M° Rome/Place-de-Clichy.

Hôtel Savoy **21 rue des Dames, 17e** **⊕01.42.93.13.47.** Basic but acceptable Paris cheapie. The reception is a bit musty but the rooms are clean and quite large, with recently refurbished bathrooms. Doubles cost €22 with shared bathrooms, or €45 en suite. M° Place-de-Clichy/Rome.

Style Hôtel **8 rue Ganneron (av Clichy end), 18e** **⊕01.45.22.37.59, ⓕ01.45.22.81.03.** Wooden floors, marble fireplaces, a secluded internal courtyard, and nice people. Simple, but great value, especially in the rooms with shared bathrooms. Doubles at €50, or €35 with shared facilities. No lift. M° Place-Clichy.

The Bastille and around

The hotels in this section are marked on the map on pp.212–213.

Hôtel Marais Bastille **36 bd Richard-Lenoir, 11e** **⊕01.48.05.75.00, ⓦwww.marais-bastille.com.** Taken over by the Best Western chain, but retaining much of its former character, this is a comfy three-star, handily located for the Marais and Bastille. Rooms are equipped with minibar, TV and wi-fi and are nicely furnished in light oak and muted colours. The rack rate is €145 for a double, though frequent special deals can bring the price down to around €120. M° Bréguet-Sabin/Bastille.

Nouvel Hôtel **24 av du Bel Air, 12e** **⊕01.43.43.01.81, ⓦwww.nouvel-hotel-paris .com.** A quiet, family-run hotel, with a faintly provincial air – lent partly by its charming little garden and patio, where guests can sit out in warm weather. The rooms are tiny, but immaculate and prettily decorated in pastels and white-painted furniture; number 9, opening directly onto the garden, is the one to go for. It's a bit out of the way, but the nearby RER gets you into the centre in no time. Doubles €78 (shower), €88 (bath). RER/M° Nation.

Hôtel de la Porte Dorée **273 av Daumesnil, 12e ⊕01.43.07.56.97, ⓦwww .hoteldelaportedoree.com.** A good-value two-star, renovated with care and taste by an American-French family. Traditional features such as ceiling mouldings, fireplaces and the elegant main staircase have been retained and many of the furnishings are antique. Facilities include wi-fi access, satellite TV and hairdryers in all the rooms. The Bastille is seven mintues away by métro or a pleasant twenty-minute walk along the Promenade Plantée. Doubles €70–78. M° Porte-Dorée.

Hôtel Tamaris 14 rue des Maraîchers, 20e ⓣ01.43.72.85.48 or toll free 0800.20.13.66, ⓦwww.hotel-tamaris.fr. A decent budget hotel run by friendly people. The plain rooms are clean and good value, starting at €38 for a single and €42 for a double with shower on the landing (€5). En-suite doubles cost €55–65. The neighbourhood's not very exciting, but you're only four métro stops from the Bastille and close to the terminus of bus route #26 from Gare du Nord. M° Porte-de-Vincennes.

Eastern Paris

The hotels in this section are marked on the map on pp.224–225.

Place de la République and the Canal St-Martin

Hôtel Beaumarchais 3 rue Oberkampf, 11e ⓣ01.53.36.86.86, ⓦwww.hotelbeaumarchais.com. A fashionable, funky and gay-friendly hotel with personal service and colourful Fifties-inspired decor; all 31 rooms are en-suite with air-conditioning, safes and cable TV. There's a little patio for breakfast (€10) on fine days. Singles €90, doubles €130. M° Filles-du-Calvaire/Oberkampf.

Le Général Hôtel 5–7 rue Rampon, 11e ⓣ01.47.00.41.57, ⓦwww.legeneralhotel.com. A cool design hotel, run by young, helpful staff, and located on a fairly quiet road. The colour pink features prominently in the lobby and common areas, though the rooms themselves are soberly and pleasantly decorated in contemporary style, with recently renovated bathrooms, and come with nice touches such as tea- and coffee-making facilities, as well as one or two quirkier features such as rubber ducks in the bath. Facilities include a sauna and fitness centre, and the breakfast area turns into a bar in the evenings. Doubles €235–265. M° République.

Hôtel Gilden-Magenta 35 rue Yves Toudic, 10e ⓣ01.42.40.17.72, ⓦwww.multi-micro.com/hotel.gilden.magenta. A friendly budget hotel, with fresh, colourful, if simple decor; rooms 61 and 62, up in the attic, are the best and have views of the Canal St Martin. Breakfast is served in a pleasant patio area. Doubles are €78, singles €65. M° République/Jacques-Bonsergent.

Hôtel Mondia 22 rue du Grand Prieuré, 11e, ⓣ01.47.00.93.44, ⓦwww.hotel-mondia.com. A welcoming budget place on a quietish street. The 23 old-fashioned rooms are modestly furnished in pastel colours and floral prints; those facing the street on the fifth floor have little balconies, and the two attic hideaways (nos. 602 and 603) have a certain charm. For stays of three nights or more in quieter periods you'll get a ten-percent reduction on presentation of your Rough Guide. Doubles €75. M° République/Oberkampf.

Hôtel de Nevers 53 rue de Malte, 11e ⓣ01.47.00.56.18, ⓦwww.hoteldenevers.com. The entrance to this hospitable one-star is patrolled by three smokey-grey cats. Needless to say, there's no room to swing one, but otherwise these are for the most part decent and cheerfully decorated rooms – the best are the en-suite doubles at the front, though there's a bit of traffic noise; courtyard-facing rooms are dark and pokey. When it's working, a rickety 1930s lift rumbles its way between the floors. Doubles €39–53. M° Oberkampf/République.

Hôtel Saint Louis Bastille 114 bd Richard Lenoir 11e ⓣ01.43.38.29.29, ⓦwww.saintlouisbastille.com. A smart new hotel, whose rooms are attractively decorated in soothing tones of dove grey, cream and beige, with rococo-style furnishings and Boucher prints on the walls, and sleek white bathrooms. The smaller rooms (€115) at the back are the ones to go for, as the larger, front-facing rooms (€135) suffer from considerable traffic noise. M° Oberkampf.

Belleville and Ménilmontant

Hôtel Paris-Gambetta 12 av du Père-Lachaise, 20e ⓣ01.47.97.76.57, ⓦwww.hotelparisgambetta.com. Located very near Père-Lachaise cemetery, this well-run hotel has recently been spruced up and renovated. Rooms are clean and well kept and have nice bathrooms, though the decor (floral pink wallpaper and busy carpets) is somewhat dated and unremarkable. All rooms come with cable TV and minibar, and there's an Internet point in the foyer. Front-facing rooms get some traffic noise from nearby place Gambetta. Singles €72–79, doubles €80–86. M° Gambetta.

Hôtel Rhin et Danube 3 place Rhin-et-Danube, 19e ⓣ01.42.45.10.13, ⓕ01.42.06.88.82. Sixteen good-value studio apartments with small kitchenettes, located northeast of the city centre, near the entrance to the Parc de la Villette on the airy heights of Belleville. Singles €46, doubles €61 and apartments sleeping from three to five people for €73–92. M° Danube.

Western Paris

The hotels in this section are marked on the map on p.244.

Hameau de Passy 48 rue Passy, 16e ⓣ01.42.88.47.55, ⓦwww.hameaudepassy.com. An utterly peaceful modern hotel with a country sensibility, set back from the main street. Rooms are on the small side, but are pleasantly decorated in bright hues of green and orange and look out onto a pretty tree-lined patio. Faultless service is assured by a charming, polyglot staff. Doubles €32. M° Muette/Passy.

Queen's Hotel 4 rue Bastien-Lepage, 16e ⓣ01.42.88.89.85, ⓦwww.queens-hotel.fr. A three-star hotel run by helpful staff and offering modern comfort on a lovely side street in the centre of old Auteuil. The 22 rooms, individually styled, come with some nice touches such as mahogany mirrors, and each is hung with a painting by a contemporary artist. Some rooms have showers, others have baths with Jacuzzi tubs. You'll pay €107 for doubles with showers, €131 with baths. M° Michel-Ange-Auteuil.

Hotel Le Sezz 6 av Frémiet, 16e ⓣ01.56.75.26.26, ⓦwww.hotelsezz.com. No humble receptionist, but a "personal assistant" welcomes you to this sleek boutique hotel, hidden behind a nineteenth-century facade on a quiet street near the place de Passy. The rooms are decorated with sober minimalism, veering on the austere (slate-grey stone walls, black wooden flooring, glass partitions and chrome furnishings), but with splashes of colour providing a touch of warmth. The standard rooms are smallish; the suites come with huge bathtubs big enough for two, and all rooms have flat-screen TVs, free wi-fi and CD/DVD player. Within easy walking distance of Trocadéro and the Eiffel Tower. Doubles from €320. M° Passy.

Apartments, apartment-hotels and bed and breakfast

Rented apartments and apartment-hotels – a hotel made up of mini apartments each with its own self-contained kitchen – are attractive alternatives for families with young children who want a bit more independence and the option to do their own catering, and also for visitors who are planning an extended stay. Staying on a **bed and breakfast** basis in a private house is also worth considering if you want to get away from the more impersonal set-up of a hotel, and is a reasonably priced option. The following is a list of recommended organizations. In addition, see the reviews of the *Hôtel Résidence Henri IV*, 5e, on p.301, the *Hôtel Michelet-Odéon*, 6e, on p.303, *Le Vert-Galant*, 13e, on p.305 and the *Hôtel Rhin et Danube*, 19e, above, which all offer apartments or rooms with kitchenettes on top of their standard rooms.

Alcôve & Agapes ⓦwww.bed-and-breakfast-in-paris.com. A family-run bed and breakfast organization that has a good selection of rooms on its books, most accommodating couples, but some able to welcome families. Some hosts offer extras, such as French conversation, wine tasting or cookery classes. Doubles range from €75 to €196 a night.

Citadines ⓦwww.citadines.com. A European-wide chain of apartment-hotels. Most of its seventeen Paris establishments are centrally located and offer high-standard, comfortable accommodation consisting of self-contained studios and apartments sleeping up to six, with well-equipped kitchen and bathroom. Offers all the usual amenities of a three-star hotel, plus parking, laundry facilities and the option of breakfast. Studios sleeping two cost from around €110 a night, apartments for four €195, though they sometimes have special offers and there are lower rates for long stays.

France Lodge 2 rue Meissonier, 17e ⓣ01.56.33.85.80, ⓦwww.apartments-in-paris.com. Offers bed-and-breakfast rooms inside and outside Paris. Prices start at €25 single or €40 double, plus a €15 booking fee. They can usually find something last minute, but reserve well in advance to be sure of something more special. They can also organize accommodation in furnished apartments by the week (from €400) or month (from €900).

Good Morning Paris 43 rue Lacépède, 5e ⓣ01.47.07.28.29, ⓦwww.goodmorningparis.fr. Bed-and-breakfast accommodation in central Paris, starting at €54 for a single room, €66 for a double. You have to stay at least two nights but there's no reservation fee – payment in full confirms your booking.

Lodgis 47 rue de Paradis, 10e ⓣ01.70.39.11.11, ⓦwww.lodgis.com. A well-run agency with over a thousand furnished flats on its books. A studio flat in the Latin Quarter starts from around €460 a week. Most places are available by the week, but some will consider stays of less than a week.

Paris B and B ⓣ1-800 872 2632, ⓦwww.parisbandb.com. US-based online bed-and-breakfast booking service. The rooms offered are on the luxurious side and start from $90 for a double. Apartments from $120.

Hostel groups

D'Artagnan 80 rue Vitruve, 20e ⓣ01.40.32.34.56, ⓕ01.40.32.34.55, ⓦwww.fuaj.fr. See map on pp.224–225. A colourful, funky, modern HI hostel, with a fun atmosphere and lots of facilities including a small cinema, restaurant and bar, Internet access, and a local swimming pool nearby. Located on the eastern edge of the city near Charonne, which has some good bars. Huge, but very popular so try to get here early – you can reserve online (ⓦwww.hihostels.com), by fax, or by calling the central reservations number on ⓣ01.44.89.87.27. Dorm beds cost €20 a night, and doubles (€26 per person), and rooms for three to five (€22 per person) are also available. M° Porte-de-Bagnolet.

BVJ Paris Quartier Latin 44 rue des Bernardins, 5e ⓣ01.43.29.34.80, ⓦwww.bvjhotel.com. See map on pp.126–127. Typically institutional UCRIF hostel, but spick and span and in a good location. Dorm beds (€28), plus single or double rooms (€30–40 per person), all with shared toilet. M° Maubert-Mutualité.

Le Fauconnier 11 rue du Fauconnier, 4e ⓣ01.42.74.23.45, ⓕ01.40.27.81.64. See map on p.114. MIJE hostel in a superbly renovated seventeenth-century building with a courtyard. Dorms (€28 per person) sleep four to eight, and there are some single (€45) and double rooms, too (€33 per person with shower). Breakfast is included. M° St-Paul/Pont-Marie.

Le Fourcy 6 rue de Fourcy, 4e ⓣ01.42.74.23.45. See map on p.114. Another MIJE hostel (same prices as *Le Fauconnier*, above) housed in a beautiful mansion, this one has a small garden and an inexpensive restaurant. Doubles and triples are available, as well as dorms. M° St-Paul.

Foyer International d'Accueil de Paris Jean Monnet 30 rue Cabanis, 14e ⓣ01.43.13.17.00, ⓦwww.fiap.asso.fr. See map on pp.172–173. A huge, efficiently run UCRIF hostel in a fairly sedate area, with singles (€56), doubles (€36.50 per person) and dorms (€26–33, depending on number of beds). Facilities include a disco; ideal for groups. M° Glacière.

Maubuisson 12 rue des Barres, 4e ⓣ01.42.74.23.45. See map on p 114. An MIJE hostel in a magnificent medieval building on a quiet street. Shared use of the restaurant at nearby Le Fourcy (see above). Dorms only, sleeping four (€28 per person). Breakfast included. M° Pont-Marie/Hôtel-de-Ville.

Maurice Ravel 6 av Maurice-Ravel, 12e ⓣ01.44.75.60.00, ⓦwww.cisp.asso.fr. This hostel, run by CISP (Centre International de Séjour de Paris), is some distance from central Paris, but close to the lovely Bois de Vincennes, and there's a swimming pool. Rooms come in a wide variety of sizes, from eight-bed dorms (€18.50 per person) to twins (€22.50) and singles (€25), but all share shower rooms. CISP has another hostel set in a park near the Porte-d'Italie, at the southern end of the 13e. M° Porte-de-Vincennes/Porte-Dorée.

Independent hostels

Aloha Hostel 1 rue Borromé, 15e ⓣ01.42.73.03.03, ⓦwww.aloha.fr. See map on pp.184–185. American-dominated hostel with the same management as *Three Ducks Hostel*, below. Jan–March €19, April–Dec €23 for a bed in a four-bed dorm, which can be booked in advance by credit card. Turn up at 8am for one of the double rooms, which cost €25 per person, or €23 Nov–Dec. M° Volontaires.

The Blue Planet Hostel 5 rue Hector Malot, 12e ⓣ01.43.42.06.18, ⓦwww.hostelblueplanet.com. See map on pp.212–213. Popular with backpackers and less of a party scene than some of the others, this family-run hostel charges €21 per night including breakfast. No curfew. M° Gare de Lyon.

BVJ Louvre 20 rue Jean-Jacques-Rousseau, 1er ⓣ01.53.00.90.90, ⓦwww.bvjhotel.com. See map on pp.88–89. A clean, modern and efficiently run hostel for 18- to 35-year-olds. Bookings can be made up to ten days prior to your stay. Accommodation ranges from single rooms to dorms sleeping eight, and there's a restaurant, open daily except Sunday. €27 for a dorm bed. M° Louvre/Châtelet-Les-Halles.

Hôtel Caulaincourt Square 2 sq Caulaincourt (by 63 rue Caulaincourt), 18e ⓣ01.46.06.46.06, ⓦwww.caulaincourt.com. See map on p.194. Friendly hostel and hotel at the very top of Montmartre with a useful dormitory section (€24 a night) from which there's a fine view over Paris; good value for the location. Doubles from €63. M° Lamarck-Caulaincourt.

Maison Internationale des Jeunes 4 rue Titon, 11e ⓣ01.43.71.99.21, ⓔmij.cp@wanadoo.fr. See map on pp.212–213. A clean, well-run establishment located between Bastille and Nation, geared to 18- to 30-year-olds for stays of between three and five days. Doors are open from 6am till 2am. Rooms range from doubles to dorms sleeping eight. €22.50 per person including shower, breakfast and sheets. Reservations should be made in advance and a fifty percent deposit is required. M° Faidherbe-Chaligny.

Peace and Love Hostel 245 rue La Fayette, 10e ⓣ01.46.07.65.11, ⓦwww.paris-hostels.com. See colour map 3 p.204. Tucked away at the top end of the 10e, but offering some of the least expensive beds in town, from €21 per person in a four-bed room up to a dizzy €25 per person in a twin room (prices fall by €4 Oct–March). The bargain-priced bar that's open till 2am gives a clue to the style of the place. Open 24hr. M° Jaurès.

Three Ducks Hostel 6 place Etienne-Pernet, 15e ⓣ01.48.42.04.05, ⓦwww.3ducks.fr. See map on pp.184–185. Private youth hostel very popular with Eurorailing students. In high season, beds cost €23 in dorm rooms (sleeping from four to ten people), €26 per person in a double; there are discounts in winter. Kitchen facilities as well as a bar with very cheap beer. Essential to book ahead between May and Oct; send the price of the first night or leave a credit card number online. Lockout 11am–4pm, curfew at 2am. M° Commerce/Félix-Faure.

Le Village Hostel 20 rue d'Orsel, 18e ⓣ01.42.64.22.02, ⓦwww.villagehostel.fr. See map on p.194. Brand-new hostel in an attractively renovated nineteenth-century building, with good facilities such as phones in the rooms. There's a view of the Sacré-Coeur from the terrace. Dorms (€23) or twin rooms (€27 per person); price includes breakfast. M° Anvers.

Woodstock Hostel 48 rue Rodier, 9e ⓣ01.48.78.87.76, ⓦwww.woodstock.fr. See map on p.194. A reliable hostel in the *Three Ducks* stable, with its own bar, and set in a great location on a pretty street, not far from Montmartre. Dorms €22/18, depending on season. Twin rooms available (€25/21); price includes breakfast. Book ahead, as the ethno-bop crowd fills up quickly here. M° Anvers/St-Georges.

Young and Happy Hostel 80 rue Mouffetard, 5e ⓣ01.47.07.47.07, ⓦwww.youngandhappy.fr. See map on pp.126–127. Noisy, basic and studenty independent hostel in a lively, if a tad touristy, position. Dorms, with shower, sleep four (€23 per person), and there are a few doubles (€26 per person). Curfew at 2am, lockout 11am–4pm. M° Monge/Censier-Daubenton.

Foyers

Cité Universitaire 19 bd Jourdan, 14e ⓣ01.44.16.64.41, ⓦwww.ciup.fr; Mon–Fri 9am–5pm. See map on pp.172–173. The student campus can provide a list of the different internationally themed maisons or fondations that let out rooms during the summer holidays, some April–Sept. Costs are usually around €20 a night, with a minimum stay of three nights, but you have to be a student, and may also have to show that you need to be in Paris to study. RER Cité-Universitaire.

Foyer Tolbiac 234 rue Tolbiac, 13e ⓣ01.44.16.22.22, ⓦwww.foyer-tolbiac.com. See map on p.187. Caters to women aged 18–25 only, and lets spartan but pleasant private rooms for short or long stays at very reasonable prices. Excellent facilities. M° Glacière.

Camping

The least expensive option is, of course, camping. With the exception of the one in the Bois de Boulogne, most of Paris's campsites are some way out of town, although those listed here are linked by public transport. Below is a selected list: for other possibilities, contact the tourist office or look online at ⓦwww.camping-fr.com.

Camping du Bois de Boulogne Allée du Bord-de-l'Eau, 16e ⓣ01.45.24.30.00, ⓦwww.campingparis.fr. Much the most central campsite, with space for 435 tents, next to the River Seine in the Bois de Boulogne, and usually booked out in summer. The ground is pebbly, but the site is well equipped and has a useful information office. Prices start at €16.50 for a tent with two people in high season; there are also bungalows for four to six people starting at €55.60 for four per night, which works out very inexpensively per person. M° Porte-Maillot then bus #244 to Moulins Camping (bus runs 6am–9pm). An extra shuttle bus runs regularly between the campsite and M° Porte-Maillot, usually from April to Sept.

Camping la Colline Route de Lagny, Torcy ⓣ01.60.05.42.32, ⓦwww.camping-de-la-colline.com. Pleasant wooded lakeside site to the east of the city near Disneyland (minibus shuttle to Disneyland costs €14 return), offering rental of anything from luxury tents to bungalows; erecting your own tent costs from €25.20 per night for two people. RER line A4 to Torcy, then take a shuttle bus.

Camping du Parc-Etang St-Quentin-en-Yvelines, Montigny-le-Bretonneux ⓣ01.30.58.56.20, ⓦwww.campeole.com. Adequately equipped large campsite in a leisure complex southwest of Paris; costs €15.20 for two people and a tent. RER line C St-Quentin-en-Yvelines.

19

Cafés and restaurants

The French seldom separate the major pleasures of eating and drinking, and there are thousands of establishments in Paris where you can both eat and drink. A restaurant may call itself a *brasserie*, *bistrot*, *café* or indeed *restaurant*; equally, a *café* can be a place to eat, drink, listen to music, dance or even watch theatre. To simplify matters, we've split our listings for each area into two parts: under **cafés and wine bars**, you'll find venues we recommend primarily for light snacks, and daytime or relaxed evening drinks; under **restaurants**, you'll find any establishment we recommend for a full meal. Of course, many if not most cafés and wine bars also serve meals, and if the cooking is what's specially good about a place, you'll find it listed under "restaurants". Equally, most cafés and some wine bars remain open until fairly late at night and are perfect for a beer, glass of wine or *digestif*; if you're looking for cocktails, pints or full-on **nightlife**, however, you'll find the best venues listed separately in Chapter 20, under "**bars**" (pp.353–359).

The listings are arranged in alphabetical order and correspond to the chapters of the main guide, where you'll find maps showing all the cafés, bars and restaurants reviewed in the area. If you're looking for a particular kind of cuisine (rather than searching by area), you'll also find boxes pointing you to our recommendations for **vegetarian** (p.315), **ethnic** (pp.318–319), late-night (pp.320–321) and **gourmet** (p.316) restaurants.

Cafés

The traditional Paris **café**, with zinc bar, tobacco-stained ceiling and neon lights, may soon be on the way out. Many neighbourhood caffs, particularly in the central arrondissements, are modernizing and going for the fashionable lounge-bar look, installing parquet floors, comfy velvet chairs and subtle lighting – and in the process are losing something of their diversity, attracting a more middle-class clientele. Despite their changing nature, however, cafés are still one of the mainstays of Parisian society, places where people come to gossip and discuss, pose and people-watch, or simply read a book, knowing that once they've bought their drink, the waiter will leave them undisturbed for hours at a stretch. The boulevards Montparnasse and St-Germain, on the Left Bank, are the historic haunts of café society. There you'll find the *Select*, *Coupole*, *Closerie des Lilas*, *Deux Magots* and *Flore* – the erstwhile hang-outs of Apollinaire, Picasso, Hemingway, Sartre and de Beauvoir, and mostly still popular today with the Parisian intelligentsia. The more vibrant and contemporary café culture is found on the Right Bank, around the Canal Saint Martin and Oberkampf, where many cafés have become exciting venues

Le snacking, takeaways and picnics

In the last few years a range of sophisticated snack bars has sprung up alongside the old stand-up sandwich bars as more and more Parisians abandon the traditional sit-down lunch for a quick bite in a trend known as le snacking. Cojean (17 bd Haussmann and many other branches; Ⓦwww.cojean.fr) is one successful example of this new breed of contemporary snack bar – sleek and hip, it's always full at lunch, serving homemade soups and salads made up of ingredients like quinoa and mangetout.

Traditional sandwiches such as the humble *sandwich jambon fromage* (cheese and ham) are of course still widely available; the chain "Paul" is reliable and easily found in railway stations and on main shopping streets. Boulangeries are also a good source of traditional takeaway fare – most sell savoury quiches and flans as well as breads and cakes. For picnics, head for a **charcuterie** or the delicatessen counter in a good supermarket, or *traiteurs* such as Fauchon (see box, p.398). Although specializing in cooked meats like hams and pâtés, most *charcuteries* also stock an excellent range of dressed salads and side dishes. You buy by weight, by the slice (*tranche*) or by the carton (*barquette*). Asian delis, especially Chinese, are a popular alternative in Paris, as are the rather rarer Jewish or Eastern European delis. Some of the city's most specialized or luxurious food shops are listed on pp.400–404 of the Shopping chapter.

For takeaway hot food, the indigenous offering is the crêperie, which sells *galettes* (wholewheat pancakes) and *gaufres* (waffles) as well as sweet and savoury *crêpes* (flat pancakes). More common are Turkish or North African kebab shops, the latter also serving couscous, which you can choose to have with *merguez* (spicy sausage), chicken or lamb, or indeed *royale* – with all three. Couscous always comes with a spicy, tomato-rich vegetable soup, while kebabs are usually served in a pitta bread with *frites* (French fries). Look a little harder and you may be able to find Middle Eastern *falafel* (deep-fried chickpea balls) with salad.

for exhibitions, live music and DJs. If it's nightlife you're after, see our listings under "bars" in Chapter 20.

In our "**cafés**" category, we've included all kinds of venues which we recommend primarily as places where you'd want to come and have a drink. If you want a full meal, you should probably look under "restaurants", listed separately below, but don't forget that most cafés do also serve **food**, from the simple pastries, *tartines* (open sandwiches) and toasted sandwiches often available in more basic places, to the dishes and full meals served in the larger cafés and **café-brasseries** – usually salads, a *plat du jour* (daily special), and perhaps a limited- or no-choice two-course *formule*. Alongside cafés, we've listed **wine bars** or *bistrots à vin* which may offer cheeses, cold meats and regional dishes to go with their fine wines by the glass. Also included in this category, you'll find genteel **salons de thé** (tea rooms), which typically serve tea, pastries and light meals.

Café prices

Prices have to be displayed in every café by law, usually without the fifteen percent service charge added, but detailing separately the prices for consuming at the bar (*au comptoir*), sitting down (*la salle*), or on the terrace (*la terrasse*) – each progressively more expensive. Addresses in the smarter or more touristy arrondissements set costs soaring – the Champs-Elysées and rue de Rivoli, for instance, are best avoided if you're on a tight budget – and you'll generally pay more on main squares and boulevards than on backstreets. At almost all cafés and bars, you're presented with a small bill along with your drinks, which you settle when you leave. At particularly busy night-time venues, however, or if your waiter is just going off shift, you may be asked to pay upfront.

Coffee and tea

Coffee is invariably made with an espresso machine and is very strong. *Un café* or *un express* is an espresso, *une noisette* is a macchiato (an espresso with a spot of milk) and *un crème* is a cappuccino. In the morning you could also ask for *un café au lait* – espresso in a large cup or bowl filled up with hot milk. *Un déca*, decaffeinated coffee, is widely available. *Chocolat chaud* (hot chocolate) can also be had in any café. Drinkers of **tea** (*thé*), nine times out of ten, have to settle for Lipton's teabags, served black. You can usually have a slice of lemon (*citron*) with it if you want; for some milk, ask for *un peu de lait frais*. *Tisanes* or *infusions* are the generic terms for **herb teas** – every café serves them. The more common ones are *verveine* (verbena), *tilleul* (lime blossom), *menthe* (mint) and *camomille*.

Drinks

All cafés and bars serve a full range of alcoholic and non-alcoholic drinks throughout the day. On the **soft drink** front, cafés generally offer bottled fruit juices and the usual cans, while *boulangeries* often stock the usual chilled fizzy drinks – *limonade*, *Coca*, *Orangina* – as well as *Minute Maid* canned fruit juices. At cafés you can also get a refreshing, freshly squeezed *orange pressé* or *citron pressé*, the latter of which brings lemon juice served in the bottom of a long ice-filled glass, with a jug of water and a sugar bowl so you can sweeten it to your taste. Particularly French are the various **sirops**, diluted with water to make cool, eye-catching drinks with traffic-light colours, such as *menthe* (peppermint) and *grenadine* (pomegranate).

Among **wines**, the astringent whites of the northern Loire – Quincy, Reuilly and Sancerre – have long been Parisian favourites, and a *kir*, a white wine with a dash of *cassis* (blackcurrant syrup), is another popular aperitif, sometimes with champagne substituted for white wine – *un kir royal*. The release of the new red wine from the Beaujolais – "*le Beaujolais Nouveau est arrivé*" – is a much-heralded event on November 15 every year. Champagne is drunk for simple pleasure as often as for celebration.

A characteristically French **apéritif** is the aniseed-flavoured *pastis* – Pernod and Ricard are the most common brands – which turns cloudy when diluted with water and ice cubes (*glaçons*). **Beers** are usually Belgian, German or Alsatian lagers, typically Kronenbourg. Most Parisians simply order *une pression*, or a glass of draught beer, but to be precise you could ask for

Breakfast and brunch

Most **cafés** advertise **snacks** or *un casse-croûte* (a quick bite), but even when they don't they may be able to make you up a filled baguette or a *tartine* on request. This is generally the best way to eat **breakfast**, and works out cheaper than the rate charged by most hotels (typically around €8–12). In the mornings, you may see a basket of croissants or some hard-boiled eggs on the counter. The drill is to help yourself – the waiter will keep an eye on how many you've eaten and bill you accordingly. **Brasseries** are also possibilities for cups of coffee, eggs, snacks and other breakfast-type food, while the concept of **le brunch** has taken Paris by storm in recent years, becoming a Sunday institution in areas like the Marais, although the Parisians' idea of brunch is really more like lunch – most places only serve it from midday onwards and it's often available until 4 or 5pm.

Paris for vegetarians

Paris's gastronomic reputation is largely lost on **vegetarians**. In most restaurants, aside from the usual salads and cheeses there is precious little choice for those who don't eat meat, as almost every dish, if not made almost entirely of beef, chicken, or fish, is invariably garnished with *lardons* (diced bacon), *anchois* (anchovies) or *jambon* (ham). That said, some of the newer, more innovative places will often have one or two vegetarian dishes on offer, and ethnic restaurants are always a good bet. *Salons de thé*, too, offer lighter fare such as soups and quiches or flans (*tartes*), which tend to be vegetarian. It's also possible to put together a meal at even the most meat-oriented brasserie by choosing dishes from among the starters (*crudités*, for example, are nearly always available) and soups, or by asking for an omelette. Useful French phrases to help you along are *Je suis végétarien(ne)* ("I'm a vegetarian") and *Il y a quelques plats sans viande*? ("Are there any non-meat dishes?").

The few purely vegetarian restaurants that do exist tend to be based on a healthy diet principle rather than haute cuisine, but at least you get a choice.

Vegetarian restaurants

Aquarius 40 rue de Gergovie, 14e; p.340.
L'Arpège 84 rue de Varenne, 7e; p.338.
Les Cinq Saveurs d'Anada 72 rue du Cardinal-Lemoine, 5e; p.332.
Au Grain de Folie 24 rue de La Vieuville, 18e; p.343.
Le Grenier de Notre-Dame, 18 rue de la Bûcherie, 5e; p.332.
La Petite Légume 36 rue Boulangers, 5e; p.332.
Piccolo Teatro 6 rue des Ecouffes, 4e; p.329.
Le Potager du Marais 22 rue Rambuteau, 4e; p.329.
La Victoire Suprême du Cœur 41 rue des Bourdonnais, 1er; p.327.

un demi (25cl). For a wider choice of draughts and artisan bottled beers you need to go to the special beer-drinking establishments, or the English- and Irish-style pubs found in abundance in Paris – for listings, see Chapter 20 (pp.353–359). As for the harder stuff, there are dozens of **eaux de vie** (brandies distilled from fruit) and **liqueurs**, in addition to the classic Cognacs or Armagnac. Measures are generous, but they don't come cheap; the same applies for imported spirits like whisky, usually referred to as *scotch*.

Restaurants

Most visitors come to Paris with an appetite, and high expectations. This is, after all, the city that invented the concept of the **restaurant**, and indeed of fine cooking. But while the city's celebrity art-chefs relentlessly pursue culinary perfection, and the avant-garde pace-setters operate at the very cutting edge of gastronomy, the **cuisine** at the average Parisian restaurant or simpler, more local **bistrot** is surprisingly conservative. In a recent survey, more than two-thirds of French people named a simple *steak-frites* as their favourite dish, after all, and out of the almost ten thousand restaurants in the city, almost ninety percent feature primarily **French cooking**. Quality and precision are typically valued over inventiveness and experimentation, and as such the real engines of the contemporary restaurant scene are the smaller local restaurants and bistrots, often run by committed enthusiasts for good food and wine whose stars tend to rise and fall in line with the exacting standards of their Parisian clientele. Still

Gourmet restaurants

With its concentration of top gourmet restaurants, Paris is the perfect place to blow out on the meal of a lifetime. Two of the most talked about chefs at the moment are young Pascal Barbot at *L'Astrance* (see p.351) and Yannick Alléno at *Le Meurice* (see p.323), both awarded three Michelin stars in 2007 for their bold and innovative cuisine. Also highly rated is *Alain Ducasse* at the *Plaza Athénée* hotel (see p.322); the first-ever chef to have been awarded six Michelin stars (shared between two restaurants), Ducasse swept like a tidal wave through the world of French cuisine in the early 1990s and hasn't looked back. Other greats include *Pierre Gagnaire* (see p.322), known for his experimental "molecular cuisine"; and more traditional *Taillevent* (see p.323), which dropped a Michelin star recently amid murmurs of surprise – after 33 years as a three-star it was regarded as "untouchable". Over on the Left Bank, you'll find Jacques Cagna's gastronomic restaurant (see p.336), along with two relatively unusual establishments: the *Restaurant d'Hélène* (see p.337) stands out in having a female chef, the Ducasse-trained *Hélène* Darroze, while Alain Passard's *L'Arpège* (see p.338) eschews most meat in favour of superb fish and vegetable dishes.

Prices at most of these restaurants are often cheaper if you go at midday during the week, and some offer a set lunch *menu* for around €70. In the evening, prices average at about €150, and there's no limit on the amount you can pay for top wines.

Recently, some of the star chefs have made their fine cuisine more accessible to a wider range of customers by opening up less expensive, more casual, but still high-quality establishments. In addition to presiding over the *Plaza-Athénée*, for example, Alain Ducasse also runs the cutting-edge restaurant *Spoon, Food & Wine* (see p.323) and *Aux Lyonnais* bistrot (see p.325). Hélène Darroze has her tapas-style *Salon d'Hélène* (see p.337) underneath the main restaurant, Pierre Gagnaire oversees the seafood restaurant Gaya (see p.336), and Guy Savoy has his rôtisserie, *L'Atelier Maître Albert* (see p.331).

The strain of having to produce consistently high-quality haute cuisine has been too much for some super chefs. Alain Senderens, for example, who used to run *Lucas Carton*, decided to give his three Michelin stars back and start again with a simpler, cheaper menu, renaming his restaurant *Senderens* (only to be awarded two Michelin stars just months later in the new guide).

more conservative are the Parisian institutions, the old-time **brasseries** and historic restaurants whose owners and chefs rarely dare to meddle with a decor – or indeed a style of cooking – that has been enjoyed by Parisians and visitors for generations.

That said, an openness to spicing and overseas techniques and ingredients – typically Asian – has been pioneered by **young chefs** in the last decade or so. Often working in smaller restaurants in the outer arrondissements, their ideas are now spreading more widely. The quality and profile of **ethnic restaurants** (see box, pp.318–319) is ever-growing, too. As well as the common, typically low-budget Chinese and Indian eateries, there are excellent restaurants specializing in the food of the former French colonies – notably Vietnamese, North African, Indian Ocean, Caribbean and West or Central African. Increasingly, you can also find Eastern European and Middle Eastern restaurants, while the cuisines of Japan and Tibet have strong followings in Paris.

Restaurant opening hours and reservations

Restaurant and bistrot **opening hours** are usually noon until 2pm, and 8pm until around 10pm. The **latest time** at which you can walk into a restaurant and order is generally about 9.30pm or 10pm, although once ensconced you can often remain well into the night. **Brasseries** serve quicker meals and at most hours of the day; they also serve meals later than restaurants, often till midnight or 1am, and because of this are popular places for a post-theatre or -opera dinner. Hours – last orders – are stated in the listings below, and unusually or specifically **late-night places** are included in the box, pp.320–321. After 9pm or so, some restaurants serve only *à la carte* meals, which invariably work out more expensive than eating the set menu.

For the more upmarket or trendy places, and at weekends, it's wise to make **reservations** – usually easily done on the same day, except for the most fashionable or gastronomically renowned places, for which you will need to book well in advance. At the élite, Michelin-starred end of the market, you'd be advised to **dress up**, too. Some more formal restaurants even insist on men wearing a tie.

Restaurant prices

There is often a choice between one or more fixed-price **menus** (simply called *le menu* in French – the French word for "menu" in the English sense is *la carte*), where the number of courses for the stated price is fixed and the choice accordingly limited. Lunchtime *menus* are particularly good value, typically priced at less than €20 even at quite classy restaurants, and as little as €12 for two courses at good inexpensive places. Top-notch gastronomic restaurants, too, typically offer a lunch *menu* for roughly half the price of the full evening experience.

If you just want a main course it's worth looking out for the *plat du jour* (chef's daily special). Eating *à la carte*, of course, gives you access to everything on offer, though you'll pay a fair bit more. The *à la carte* prices we give are generally for an average three-course meal with half a bottle of wine, but of course you can always restrain yourself to just one or two courses – there is never a minimum charge. **Service** is legally included in your bill at all restaurants, bars and cafés, but you may want to leave a few one- or two-euro coins as a **tip**. House **wines** are usually inexpensive, but a bottle of something interesting will usually add at least €15 to the bill, and potentially much, much more for a good bottle in a more expensive place.

Restaurant drinks

Wine (*vin*) is drunk at just about every meal or social occasion. In less expensive restaurants you can usually get a fairly good house wine by the *pichet* (carafe) – ask for *un quart* or *un demi*, a quarter- or half-litre. There is currently a vogue for less well-known, sometimes very interesting *vins du pays* (country wines), but you'll find the top-quality AOC (Appellation d'Origine Contrôlée) bottles on most menus. Wine is sometimes included in the price of the *menu*, though usually only on the most expensive tasting *menus*, where different wines are matched with each course.

Bottles of **mineral water** (*eau minérale*) are widely drunk, from the best-selling, naturally sparkling Badoit to the most obscure spa product. Ask for *eau gazeuse* for sparkling, *eau plate* (pronounced "platt") for still. That said, there's not much wrong with the tap water, which will always be brought free to your table if you ask for *une carafe d'eau du robinet*. You'll almost always be offered an **apéritif** at the beginning of a meal, and a *café* at the end – which invariably means an espresso.

Ethnic restaurants in Paris

Our selection of Paris's **ethnic restaurants** can only scratch the surface of what's available. **North African** places can be found throughout the city. **Indo-Chinese** restaurants are also widely scattered, with notable concentrations around avenue de la Porte-de-Choisy in the 13^{e} and in the Belleville Chinatown. At the south end of rue du Faubourg-St-Denis, there are numerous good snack bars and restaurants – mainly **Turkish and Kurdish** in rue d'Enghien and rue de l'Echiquier, and **Indian, Pakistani and Bangladeshi** around passage Brady. The majority of the city's **Greek** eateries are tightly corralled in the area around rue de la Huchette, in the 5e, and are mostly garish and overpriced – the better places are elsewhere in the city.

African (West and Central)

Ile de Gorée 70 rue Jean-Pierre-Timbaud, 11e. West African; p.350.

Le Mono 40 rue Véron, 18e. Togolese; p.343.

Waly Fay 6 rue Godefroy-Cavaignac, 11e. West African; p.347.

American

Haynes 3 rue Clauzel, 9e. American; p.344.

Eastern European and Jewish

L'As du Falafel 34 rue des Rosiers, 4e; p.328.

Chez Marianne 2 rue des Hospitalières-Saint-Gervais, 4e; p.328.

Greek

Mavrommatis 42 rue Daubenton, 5e; p.333.

Indian Ocean

Coco de Mer 34 bd Saint-Marcel, 5e. Réunionnais; p.332.

Italian

L'Enoteca 25 rue Charles-V, 4e; p.329.

Fuxia 69 place du Docteur Félix-Lobligeois, 17e; p.346.

Au Jardin des Pâtes 4 rue Lacépède, 5e; p.332.

Indian

Pooja 91 passage Brady, 10e; p.345.

The Islands

The listings in this section are marked on the map on pp.50–51.

Cafés and wine bars

Berthillon 31 rue St-Louis-en-l'Ile, Ile St-Louis, 4e. As the long queues outside attest, *Berthillon* serves the best ice cream and sorbets in Paris. They come in all sorts of unusual flavours, such as rhubarb, wild strawberry and glazed chestnut, and are also available at other island sites listed on the door. Wed–Sun 10am–8pm. M° Pont-Marie.

La Charlotte de l'Isle 24 rue Saint-Louis-en-l'Ile, 4^{e}. This enchanting little tea room with fairy-tale decor of marionettes and chocolate animals serves the most delicious hot chocolate – smooth and silky, it's made in a pan over a stove in the kitchen at the back and comes served in a white porcelain jug. Thurs–Sun 2–8pm; closed July & Aug.

Taverne Henri IV 13 place du Pont-Neuf, Ile de la Cité, 1er. An old-style wine bar that's probably changed little since Yves Montand used to come here with Simone Signoret. It's best to drop in at lunchtime when it's at its buzziest, usually full of lawyers from the nearby Palais de Justice. You can also get reasonably priced plates of meats and cheeses, as well as *tartines* (open sandwiches with a choice of cheeses, hams, pâté and *saucisson*). Mon–Fri 11.30am–9.30pm, Sat noon–5pm; closed Sun & Aug. M° Pont-Neuf.

Restaurants

Brasserie de l'Ile St-Louis 55 quai de Bourbon, Ile St-Louis, 4e ⓣ01.43.54.02.59. A long-established brasserie with a rustic, dark-wood

Indo-Chinese

Le Bambou 70 rue Baudricourt, 13e. Vietnamese; p.341.

Au Coin des Gourmets 5 rue Dante, 5e; p.332.

Lao Siam 49 rue de Belleville, 19e. Thai and Laotian; p.350.

Paris-Hanoï 74 rue de Charonne, 11e. Vietnamese; p.347.

Pho 67 59 rue Galande, 5e. Vietnamese; p.333.

Phuong Hoang Terrasse des Olympiades, 52 rue du Javelot, 13e. Vietnamese, Thai and Singaporean; p.342.

Salon de Porcelain place d'Iéna, 16e. Pan-Asian; p.337.

Tricotin Kiosque de Choisy, 15 av de Choisy, 13e. Thai, Vietnamese, Chinese and Cambodian; p.342.

Japanese

Higuma 32bis rue Ste-Anne, 1er; p.325.

Kurdish

Dilan 13 rue Mandar, 2e. Kurdish; p.326.

Lebanese

Al Ajami 58 rue François 1er, 8e; p.321.

North African

Au Bistrot de la Sorbonne 4 rue Toullier, 5e. North African and French; p.331.

Café de la Mosquée 39 rue Geoffroy-St-Hilaire, 5e. North African; p.330.

Chez Omar 47 Rue de Bretagne, 3e. North African; p.330.

La Mansouria 11 rue Faidherbe-Chaligny, 11e. Moroccan; p.348.

Le Martel 3 rue Martel, 10e. Moroccan; p.345.

Tibetan

Tashi Delek 4 rue des Fossés-St-Jacques, 5e; p.334.

interior and a sunny terrace with views of Notre-Dame, serving moderately priced Alsatian cuisine, such as sauerkraut with ham and sausage (around €17). Daily except Wed noon–midnight. M° Pont-Marie.

Mon Vieil Ami 69 rue St-Louis-en-l'Ile ⓣ01.40.46.01.35. Opened by Michelin-starred Alsatian chef Antoine Westermann in 2004, this charming little bistrot has lost no time in establishing itself as a firm favourite with locals and those in the know. The cuisine is bold and zesty, using seasonal ingredients, and the wine list includes a fine selection of Alsatian vintages. The minimalist decor of chocolate browns and frosted-glass panels makes a stylish backdrop. Reckon on around €40 for three courses. Wed–Sun noon–2pm & 8–10pm. M° Pont-Marie.

The Champs-Elysées and around

The listings in this section are marked on the map on pp.76–77.

The Champs-Elysées

Cafés and wine bars

Le Café Jacquemart-André 158 bd Haussmann, 8e. Part of the Musée Jacquemart André (see p.82) but with independent access, this is the most sumptuously appointed *salon de thé* in the city. Admire the ceiling frescoes by Tiepolo while savouring the fine pastries or salads. €8.50 for pastry and tea, lunch around €16. Daily 11.45am–5.30pm. M° St-Philippe-du-Roule/Miromesnil.

Le Dada 12 av des Ternes, 17e. This buzzy corner café, with modern decor, is especially busy at lunchtime when locals stream in for hearty servings of *steak-frites* or huge plates of salads, and waiters tear up and down the stairs, trying to keep pace with demand; the ground floor has a large bar and sunny outdoor terrace, and there's a cosy, low-lit upstairs room with leather stools. *Plat du jour* around €13. Mon–Sat 6–2am, Sun 6am–midnight. M° Ternes.

Le Fouquet's 99 av des Champs-Elysées, 8e ⓣ01.47.23.70.60. Dating from 1899, Le Fouquet's (you pronounce the "t") is the favourite venue for celebrations after the annual César film awards and is now such a well-established watering hole for the rich and famous that it's been classified a Monument Historique. (This was also where Sarkozy chose to celebrate after winning the presidential elections in 2007.) You can sit out on the terrace, a prime spot for people-watching on the Champs, or sink into a red velvet banquette in the plush café-brasserie. Coffee €7, caesar

Late-night Paris

Late-opening brasseries and restaurants are not unusual in Paris. You can eat till midnight or beyond at all the establishments listed below. The page references at the end of each listing point you to a fuller review in this chapter.

Champs-Elysées and around

Al Ajami 58 rue François 1er, 8e. Daily until midnight; p.321.

Le Fouquet's 99 av des Champs-Elysées, 8e. Daily until midnight; p.320.

La Maison de l'Aubrac 37 rue Marbeuf, 8e. Daily 24hr; p.322.

Grands Boulevards and around

Le Grand Café Capucines 4 bd des Capucines, 9e. Daily 24hr; p.324.

Beaubourg and Les Halles

Au Chien qui Fume 33 rue du Pont-Neuf, 1er. Daily until 1 or 2am; p.326.

Gallopin 40 rue Notre-Dame-des-Victoires, 2e. Daily until 1am; p.325.

Georges Centre Georges Pompidou, 4e. Daily except Tues until 1am; p.327.

Au Pied de Cochon 6 rue Coquillière, 1er. 24hr; p.327.

La Tour de Montlhéry (Chez Denise) 5 rue des Prouvaires, 1er. Mon–Fri until 5am; p.327.

Le Vaudeville 29 rue Vivienne, 2e. Daily until 1am; p.325.

Marais

Chez Marianne 2 rue des Hospitalières-Saint-Gervais, 4e. Daily until midnight; p.328.

The Quartier Latin

Coco de Mer 34 bd Saint-Marcel, 5e. Mon–Sat until midnight; p.332.

Les Degrés de Notre-Dame 10 rue des Grands Degrés, 5e. Mon–Sat until midnight; p.332.

L'Ecurie 58 rue de la Montagne Ste-Geneviève, 5e. Daily until midnight; p.332.

St-Germain

L'Atlas 11 rue de Buci, 6e. Daily until 1am; p.335.

Brasserie Lipp 151 bd St-Germain, 6e. Daily until 12.45pm; p.336.

Le Christine 1 rue Christine, 6e. Daily until midnight; p.336.

Ferrandaise 8 rue de Vaugirard, 6e. Fri & Sat until midnight; p.336.

Le Petit Zinc 11 rue St-Benoit, 6e. Daily until midnight; p.337.

Vagenende 142 bd St-Germain, 6e. Daily until 1am; p.337.

salad €18.50. Daily 8am–midnight. M° George-V.

Renoma Café Gallery 32 av George V, 8e ⓣ01.47.20.46.19, ⓦwww.renoma-cafe.fr. A trendy bar-café-restaurant hung with photos by avant-garde fashion designer Maurice Renoma. By day you can sit in the comfy lounge area and browse design and photo magazines, and by night chill out with a vodka cocktail (€14). 9–2am, closed Sat lunch & all day Sun. M° George-V.

Le Stübli 11 rue Poncelet, 17e. An authentic Austrian patisserie with a cosy little wood-panelled tea room on the upper floor where you can sample sachertorte, black forest gateau, apple strudel and an array of other delicious cakes. They also do savouries and a good daily brunch from €11. Tues–Sat 9am–7.30pm, Sun 9am–1pm. M° Ternes.

Restaurants

Al Ajami 58 rue François 1er, 8e ⓣ01.43.59.5.37. This top-notch Lebanese restaurant is a branch of the venerable Al Ajami in Beirut. Meat dishes include croquettes of minced lamb pounded together with cracked wheat and grated onion, a rarity on any menu outside the Middle East. There's plenty for

The Eiffel Tower quarter

Café du Marché 38 rue Cler, 7e. Mon–Sat until midnight; p.338.

Tokyo Eat Palais de Tokyo, 16e. Tues–Sun until 1am; p.338.

Montparnasse and southern Paris

Le Café du Commerce 51 rue du Commerce, 15e. Daily until midnight; p.341.

Chez Gladines 30 rue des Cinq-Diamants, 13e. Mon & Tues until midnight, Wed–Sun until 1am; p.342.

Chez Paul 22 rue Butte-aux-Cailles, 13e. Daily until midnight; p.342.

La Coupole 102 bd du Montparnasse, 14e. Daily until 1am; p.340.

L'Os à Moëlle 3 rue Vasco da Gama, 15e. Tues–Sun until midnight; p.341.

La Rotonde 105 bd du Montparnasse, 6e. Daily until 2am; p.340.

Montmartre and northern Paris

Le XVIIIème Barathym 2 rue Ramey, 18e. Daily until 2am; p.343.

L'Alsaco 10 rue Condorcet, 9e. Mon–Sat until midnight; p.344.

Le Bistro des Deux-Théâtres 18 rue Blanche, 9e. Daily until 12.30am; p.344.

Flo 7 cour des Petites-Ecuries, 10e. Daily until 1.30am; p.345.

Haynes 3 rue Clauzel, 9e. Tues–Sat until 12.30am; p.344.

Julien 16 rue du Faubourg-St-Denis, 10e. Daily until 1am; p.345.

Kokolion 62 rue d'Orsel, 18e. Tues–Sat until 1am; p.321.

Refuge des Fondus 17 rue des Trois Frères, 18e. Daily until 2am; p.344.

Le Relais Gascon 6 rue des Abbesses, 18e. Daily until 2am; p.344.

Terminus Nord 23 rue de Dunkerque, 10e. Daily until 1am; p.346.

Au Virage Lepic 61 rue Lepic, 18e. Mon & Wed–Sat until 2am; p.344.

Wepler 14 place de Clichy, 18e. Daily until 1am; p.346.

Bastille and around

Bofinger 7 rue de la Bastille, 3e. Daily until 1am; p.347.

Chez Paul 13 rue de Charonne, 11e. Daily until 12.30am; p.347.

Le Viaduc Café 43 av Daumesnil, 12e. Daily until midnight; p.349.

Eastern Paris

Le Villaret 19 rue Ternaux, 11e. Mon–Fri daily until midnight, Sat until 1am; p.351.

Western Paris

La Gare 19 Chaussée de la Muette, 16e. Daily until midnight; p.351.

Waiters, the bill and tipping

Waiters in Paris are considered to be professionals, and are paid as such, so **tipping** is a matter of leaving a few coins, perhaps €1–2, depending on the service. Many speak English and are eager to help, practise and/or show off, so try not to be offended if they shrug off your attempts in French. And never call a waiter *garçon*, whatever you were taught in school – *monsieur, madame/mademoiselle* or *s'il vous plaît* or *excusez-moi* are *de rigueur*. To ask for **the bill**, the phrase is *l'addition, s'il vous plaît*.

vegetarians, too: tabbouleh and *shanklish* (goat's cheese in olive oil chopped with tomato and onion), done to perfection; and exquisite *foul* (Egyptian dish of broad beans cooked with lemon/garlic) and *fttayer* (pastry triangles filled with spinach). Set menus range from €19 at lunch to a €41 *menu dégustation*, which lets you sample many different mezzes. *Á la carte* you're looking at €40–50. Daily noon–midnight. M° George-V.

Lasserre 17 av Franklin D. Roosevelt, 8e ⓣ01.43.59.53.43, ⓦwww.restaurant-lasserre.com. A classic haute cuisine restaurant with a beautiful belle époque dining room, decorated with flower-draped balustrades and fine ceiling frescoes – at the end of each meal and on balmy summer nights the roof is rolled back, with much rumbling and whirring, to reveal the Paris sky. The excellent cuisine is presided over by chef Jean-Louis Nomicos, trained by Alain Ducasse (see below); signature dishes include a sublime duck à l'orange and pigeon André Malraux, named after the Resistance hero and writer who used to dine here almost every day. *A la carte* you'll pay upwards of €120, not including wine, though you can eat more cheaply if you come at lunchtime and opt for the €75 *prix fixe menu*. Mon–Sat 7.30–10.30pm, plus Thurs & Fri noon–2pm; closed Aug. M° Franklin-D.-Roosevelt.

La Maison de l'Aubrac 37 rue Marbeuf, 8e ⓣ01.42.89.66.09. Large photographs of prize-winning cattle from the restaurant's own farm in the Auvergne leave you in little doubt as to what to expect at this all-night restaurant, with its cosy, ranch-style wooden cubicles: very meaty country cuisine, such as *pot-au-feu* and sausage with *aligot* (creamy mashed potato and cheese), while the most carnivorous of cravings should be satisfied by the *trilogie de viande* (*salade de boeuf*, *steak tartare* and *faux filet grillé sauce béarnaise*). There's also an impressive thousand-plus wines to choose from, with several available by the glass. Mains cost around €17. Daily 24hr. M° Franklin-D.-Roosevelt.

La Maison Blanche 15 av Montaigne, 8e ⓣ01.47.23.55.99, ⓦwww.maison-blanche.fr. The cool white decor of the aptly named *Maison Blanche*, at the top of the Théâtre des Champs-Elysées, exudes sophisticated chic, though it's the views of the city skyline from the restaurant's floor-to-ceiling windows that really impress. The refined cuisine, overseen by the Michelin-starred Pourcel brothers, is inventive and blends unusual flavours (eg collared dove with caramelized turnips with Sichuan pepper and liquorice morello syrup). The prices may take some swallowing (€100–150 a head), but it's a stylish place for a special night out. Mon–Fri noon–2am & 8–11pm, Sat & Sun 5–11pm. M° Alma-Marceau.

Pierre Gagnaire Hôtel Balzac, 6 rue Balzac, 8e ⓣ01.58.36.12.50, ⓦwww.pierre-gagnaire.com. Regularly judged among the top ten restaurants in the world by *Restaurant* magazine, *Pierre Gagnaire* is a gastronomic adventure. The *menu dégustation* (€225) has nine courses, featuring such treats as sea bass, Breton prawns, pomegranate, litchi, white cabbage and passion fruit (and that's just one course). *A la carte* around €250, lunch *menu* for €90. Mon–Fri noon–1.30pm & 7.30–9.30pm, Sun 7.30–9.30pm. M° George-V.

Plaza-Athénée Hôtel Plaza-Athénée, 25 av Montaigne, 8e ⓣ01.53.67.65.00. One of Paris's top haute cuisine temples, run by Alain Ducasse, whose sublime and inventive offerings are likely to revive even the most jaded palate. The menu might include Bresse chicken with truffle sauce or prawns with Iranian caviar. The decor is Louis XV with a modern gloss and the service is exceptional. From about €200 per head. Mon–Wed 7.45–10.15pm, Thurs & Fri 1–2.30pm & 7.45–10.15pm, closed Sat, Sun & mid-July to mid-Aug. M° Alma-Marceau.

Le Relais de l'Entrecôte 15 rue Marbeuf, 8e. Don't worry if a menu isn't forthcoming here – there isn't one. The only dish is *steak frites*, arguably the best in town and served with a delicious sauce, the ingredients of which are a closely kept secret. Make sure you leave room for seconds. Reckon on around €23 a head, including a salad first course, or a little extra with dessert (and these are well worth investigating). No reservations are taken so you may have to queue, or arrive early. Second branch at 20bis rue St-Benoit, 6e (M° St-Germain-des-Prés). Daily noon–2.30pm & 7–11.30pm. M° Franklin-D.-Roosevelt.

Rue Balzac 3 rue Balzac, 8e ☎01.53.89.90.91. This stylish, buzzing restaurant is the enterprise of singer Johnny Hallyday and chef Michel Rostang. The low lighting and subdued reds and yellows of the decor provide an atmospheric backdrop to classy cuisine, available in small or large servings ("*petit modèle*" and "*grand modèle*"); most people find the former filling enough. Three courses with wine comes to around €70. Mon–Fri 12.15–2.15pm & 7.30–11.30pm, Sat & Sun 7.30–11pm. M° George-V.

Les Saveurs de Flora 36 av George V, 8e ☎01.40.70.10.49. A stylish, romantic restaurant with an open fireplace and chandeliers, run by chef-owner Flora Mikula, who creates tasty, inventive dishes, drawing mainly on Mediterranean influences. The evening set menu at €36 is very good value, considering the high quality and upmarket location. Noon–2.30pm & 7–11pm; closed Sat lunch & all day Sun. M° George-V.

Spoon, Food and Wine 14 rue de Marignan, 8e ☎01.40.76.34.44, Ⓦwww.spoon.tm.fr. An innovative world-food bistrot run by star chef Alain Ducasse. The chic, minimalist decor and inventive cuisine, where you choose your own sauces and preparations, attract a fashionable crowd. Expect to pay around €70 a head without wine. Noon–2pm & 7.30–11pm; closed Sat, Sun & mid-July to mid-Aug. M° Franklin-D.-Roosevelt.

Taillevent 15 rue Lamennais, 8e ☎01.44.95.15.01, Ⓦwww.taillevent.com. It might have been downgraded from three to two stars by the Michelin guide in 2007, but Taillevent is still one of Paris's finest gourmet restaurants. The Provençal-influenced cuisine of Alain Solivérès is outstanding, with the emphasis on the classic rather than the experimental; sample dishes include spelt risotto with frogs' legs, and saddle of lamb with braised artichokes in wine. The main dining room is wood panelled and decorated in soothing colours, and the waiting staff manage to make you feel like special guests. Set menus cost €140 and €190, and there's also a special set lunch for €70. Wine starts from €28 a bottle and ranges up to €2000 for a 1934 Château Haut Brion. Mon–Fri noon–2.30pm & 7.30–11pm; closed Aug. M° George-V.

The Tuileries

Unless otherwise indicated, the listings in this section are marked on the map on pp.88–89.

Cafés and wine bars

Angelina 226 rue de Rivoli, 1er. This grand *salon de thé*, with its murals, gilded stucco work and comfy leather armchairs, does one of the best hot chocolates in town – a generous jugful with whipped cream on the side is enough for two. The other house speciality is the Mont Blanc, a chestnut cream, meringue and whipped cream dessert. It's also a good place for breakfast, with a wide range of pastries. Mon–Fri 8am–7pm, Sat & Sun 9.15am–7pm; closed Tues in July & Aug. M° Tuileries.

Café Véry (also known as Dame Tartine) Jardin des Tuileries, 1er; see map, pp.76–77. The best of a number of café-restaurants in the gardens, with tables outside under shady horse chestnuts, frequented by Louvre curators and other aesthetes. Snacks and more substantial meals available (€6–8). Daily noon–11pm. M° Concorde.

Le Rubis 10 rue du Marché-St-Honoré, 1er. One of the oldest wine bars in Paris, known for its excellent wines – mostly from the Beaujolais and Loire regions – and home-made *rillettes* (a kind of pork pâté). Very small and very crowded. *Plats du jour* around €10. Mon–Fri noon–10pm, Sat 9am–3pm; closed for around a week mid-Aug. M° Pyramides.

Restaurants

Le Meurice Hôtel Meurice 228 rue de Rivoli, 1er ☎01.44.58.10.55, Ⓦwww.meuricehotel.com.

Awarded three Michelin stars in 2007, this sumptuous restaurant decorated in Louis XVI style, complete with ornate gildings and marble, wows diners with its adventurous cuisine. You might start with duck foie gras poached in red wine, or gelée of whelk and sea urchin, followed by saddle of hare with pepper and paprika. *Menu dégustation* for €190, *à la carte* around €200, with drinks extra. Mon–Fri noon–2pm & 7.30–10pm. M° Tuileries/Concorde.

The Grands Boulevards and passages

Grands Boulevards

Unless otherwise indicated, the listings in this section are marked on the map on pp.88–89.

Cafés and wine bars

Ladurée 16 rue Royal, 8e. See map, pp.76–77. Ladurée tea room's melt-in-your-mouth macaroons are legendary – the chocolate and blackcurrant ones are the best. You can get a selection of four mini-macaroons (known as *gerbets*) for around €6. When you're done with the cakes, sit back and enjoy the luxurious interior of gilt-edged mirrors and ceiling frescoes, and count the Hermès scarves. Mon–Sat 8.30am–7pm. M° Madeleine.

The World Bar floor 5, Printemps de l'Homme, 64 bd Haussmann, 9e. British designer Paul Smith created the quirky decor of this bar on the fifth floor of Printemps' men's department. Newspapers from around the world plaster the walls and ceiling, while exposed concrete beams and metal workshop chairs lend an air of industrial-chic. A long zinc bar rounds off the masculine look. Mon–Sat 9.35am–7pm. M° Havre-Caumartin.

Restaurants

Drouant 16–18 place Gaillon, 2e ⓣ01.42.65.15.16. Legendary restaurant Drouant, the setting for the annual Goncourt prize, has been revitalized recently with a sleek makeover and a change of chef: Michelin-starred Antoine Westermann has taken over the reins and introduced some fun and creativity into the cooking. The main courses are well prepared, but it's really the starters and desserts that steal the show – you get four of each served in small portions and grouped around a theme, such as "four corners of the world". Starters cost €25, mains €30 (€20 at lunch), desserts €12, and there's a lunchtime menu for €45, as well as a €20 brunch on weekends. Daily noon–3pm & 7pm–midnight. M° Opéra.

Le Grand Café Capucines 4 bd des Capucines, 9e ⓣ01.43.12.19.00. A favourite post-cinema or -opera spot with fine belle époque decor and excellent seafood. The two-course special opera set menu costs €18.50 (before 7pm and after midnight). *A la carte*, mains cost €16–36. There's also a comfy café-brasserie area, ideal for boulevard people-watching and where you can get a light meal, such as *croque monsieur* or oysters, or just a drink. Daily 24hr. M° Opéra.

Passages and Palais-Royal

The listings in this section are marked on the map on pp.88–89.

Cafés and wine bars

L'Arbre à Cannelle 57 passage des Panoramas, 2e. Tucked away in an attractive *passage*, this early twentieth-century *salon de thé* with its exquisite wood panelling, frescoes and painted ceilings makes an excellent spot to treat yourself to salads (from €10), quiches, and desserts such as pear and chocolate tart (around €5–7). Mon–Sat 11.30–6pm. M° Grands-Boulevards.

Le Bar de l'Entracte cnr of rue Montpensier and rue Beaujolais, 1er. Theatre people, bankers and journalists come for quick snacks of Senegalese *gratin de pomme de terre* and Auvergnat ham in this almost traffic-free spot. Fills up to bursting before and after performances at the Palais-Royal theatre just down the road; you can scarf down a pre-theatre *tartine* and glass of wine for around €7, otherwise *plats* from €10. Mon–Fri 10–2am, Sat & Sun noon–midnight. M° Palais Royal-Musée du Louvre.

Café de la Comédie **153 rue St-Honoré, 1er.** A small, traditional café opposite the Comédie Française, serving excellent *tartines* and *croques monsieurs*. Tues–Sun 10am–midnight. M° Palais-Royal-Musée-du-Louvre.

Juvéniles **47 rue de Richelieu, 1er.** Unlike most wine bars in Paris, this very popular tiny place, run by a Scot, has wines from all around the world, not just France. Wine costs from €14 a bottle and there are usually around ten varieties available by the glass (from €3); *plats du jour* cost €12, and cheese plates and tapas-style dishes are also available. Tues–Sat 11am–11pm, Mon 4–11pm. M° Palais-Royal-Musée-du-Louvre.

La Muscade **67 Galerie de Montpensier, 1er.** A smart but relaxed café-restaurant in the Palais Royal gardens serving excellent hot chocolate, a variety of teas and cakes (afternoon tea served 3–6.15pm), as well as more substantial *plats du jour* for around €13. Seating in the gardens in nice weather. Tues–Sat 9.30am–8.30pm, Sun 9.30am–7pm. M° Palais-Royal-Musée-du-Louvre.

A Priori Thé **35 Galerie-Vivienne, 2e.** An attractive little *salon de thé* in a charming *passage*, with some tables spilling into the arcade itself. You can get crumbly home-made scones and tea, plus more substantial dishes at lunch. Mon–Sat 9am–6pm, Sun 12.30–6.30pm. M° Bourse.

Verlet **256 rue St-Honoré, 1er.** A wonderful aroma of coffee greets you as you enter this long-established coffee merchant's and café, with its wood furnishings, green-leather benches and caddies lining one wall. The menu features 25 varieties of coffee from around the world, including such quality beans as Mokka Harrar d'Ethiopie, and there's a good selection of teas and light snacks, too. Mon–Sat 9.30am–6.30pm. M° Palais-Royal-Musée-du-Louvre.

Restaurants

Bistrot des Victoires **6 rue de la Vrillère, 1er** **☎01.42.61.43.78.** Located just behind the chic place des Victoires, but very reasonably priced for the area, this charming, old-fashioned bistrot with zinc bar, mustard-coloured walls, globe lamps and dark-purple banquettes serves good old standbys such as *confit de canard* and *poulet rôti* for €9, as well as huge salads and hearty *tartines* for €8 – recommended is the savoyarde with bacon, potatoes and gruyère. Sun brunch for €13.50. Daily 9am 11pm. M° Bourse.

Gallopin **40 rue Notre-Dame-des-Victoires, 2e** **☎01.42.36.45.38.** An utterly endearing old brasserie, with all its original brass and mahogany fittings and a beautiful painted glass roof in the back room. The place heaves at lunchtime with journalists, business people and glamorous Parisiennes. The classic French dishes, especially the *foie gras maison*, are well above par, and *menus* range from €23 to €33.50. Daily noon–midnight. M° Bourse.

Le Grand Véfour **17 rue de Beaujolais, 1er** **☎01.42.96.56.27, ⓦwww.grand-vefour.com.** The carved wooden ceilings, frescoes, velvet hangings and late eighteenth-century chairs haven't changed since Napoleon brought Josephine here. Considering the luxury of the cuisine, the lunchtime *menu* for €78 is a cinch, though go *à la carte* and the bill could easily top €200. Mon–Thurs 12.30–2pm & 7.30–10pm, Fri 12.30–2pm. Closed Aug. M° Pyramides/Bourse.

Higuma **32bis rue Ste Anne, 1er** **☎01.47.03.38.59.** Authentic Japanese canteen with cheap, filling ramen dishes from €6.50 and a variety of set *menus* starting at €10.50. It's very popular and you may have to queue at lunch. Daily 11.30am–10pm. M° Pyramides.

Aux Lyonnais **32 rue St Marc, 2e** **☎01.42.96.65.04.** This venerable old bistrot, with its lovely belle époque tiles and mirrored walls, has been taken over by top chefs Alain Ducasse and Thierry de la Brosse. They've preserved the old-fashioned ambience and done wonders with the cuisine, serving up delicious Lyonnais fare – try the *quenelles* (light and delicate fish dumplings) followed by the heavenly Cointreau soufflé for dessert. Service is friendly and there's a buzzy atmosphere. Three-course set menu €30. Tues–Fri noon–2pm & 7.30–11pm, Sat 7.30–11pm. M° Bourse/Richelieu-Drouot.

Le Vaudeville **29 rue Vivienne, 2e** **☎01.40.20.04.62.** There's often a queue to get a table at this lively, late-night Art Deco brasserie, attractively decorated with marble and mosaics. Dishes include grilled cod with truffle sauce and *belle tête de veau*. Three-course set menu €30.50, €20.50 after 10.30pm. Daily noon–3pm & 7–1am; breakfast Mon–Sat 7–11am. M° Bourse.

Sentier

The listings in this section are marked on the map on pp.88–89.

Cafés and wine bars

Le Dénicheur 4 rue Tiquetonne, 2e ⓣ01.42.21.31.03. A small chic, gay-friendly café-restaurant. The place is a hodgepodge of wacky decor: bright-blue globes above, garden gnomes, and bin-shaped lampshades all about. Salads are the main event here, though you can find lasagne and *tartines* too, all at reasonable prices. Big, popular weekend brunches for €15. Tues–Sat 12.30–3.30pm & 7pm–midnight, Sun noon–4pm. M° Etienne-Marcel.

Restaurants

Dilan 13 rue Mandar, 2e ⓣ01.40.26.81.04. An excellent-value, popular Kurdish restaurant, with kilims strewn liberally across the benches and taped Kurdish music playing in the background. You can't really go wrong whatever you choose from the menu, but you could do worse than start with the melt-in-your-mouth *babaqunuc* (stuffed aubergines), followed by delicious *beyti* (spiced minced beef wrapped in pastry, with yoghurt, tomato sauce and bulgar wheat). Mains cost from €11.50; around €10 for half a litre of Kurdish wine. Mon–Sat noon–2.30pm & 7.30–11pm. M° Les Halles/Sentier.

Beaubourg and Les Halles

The listings in this section are marked on the map on p.101.

Cafés and wine bars

Café Beaubourg 43 rue St-Merri, 4e. A seat under the expansive awnings of this stylish café, bearing the trademark sweeping lines of designer Christian de Portzamparc, is one of the best places for people-watching on the Pompidou Centre's piazza. It's also a good place for a lazy Sun brunch, which costs €22 for the full works, taking in hash browns, sausage, scrambled eggs, bread and jams, and drinks. Mon–Thurs & Sun 8–1am, Sat 8–2am. M° Rambuteau/Hôtel-de-Ville.

Le Café des Initiés 3 place des Deux-Ecus, 1er. A smart yet intimate and comfortable café, with dark-red leather banquettes, wood floor and arty photos on the wall. Locals gather round the zinc bar or tuck into tasty dishes such as caramelized pork (€16.50) and home-made tiramisu. M° Châtelet-Les-Halles/Louvre.

Le Café Noir 65 rue Montmartre, 2e. **See p.354.**

A la Cloche des Halles 28 rue Coquillière, 1er. The bell hanging over this little wine bar is the one that used to mark the end of trading in the market halls, and the great ambience is due to the local vendors who spend their off-hours here. You are assured of some very fine wines, best sided with the *jambon d'Auvergne* or one of their delectable cheeses, all very reasonably priced. Open noon–10pm; closed Sat eve & Sun. M° Châtelet-Les-Halles/Louvre.

Dame Tartine 2 rue Brisemiche, 4e. Overlooking the Stravinsky fountain, with pleasant outdoor seating under shady plane trees, this popular café serves particularly cheap and tasty open toasted sandwiches, and children are catered for with a special set menu. Daily noon–11.30pm. M° Rambuteau/Hôtel-de-Ville.

Le Petit Marcel 63 rue Rambuteau, 4e. Speckled tabletops, mirrors and painted tiles, a cracked and faded ceiling and about eight square metres of drinking space. Friendly bar staff and "local" atmosphere. There's a dining area, too, where you can get cheap and filling dishes such as omelette and *frites*. Daily 10–1am. M° Rambuteau.

Restaurants

Au Chien qui Fume 33 rue du Pont-Neuf, 1er ⓣ01.42.36.07.42, ⓦwww.au-chien-qui-fume.com. Named after a local poodle who allegedly smoked a cigar, this extremely popular brasserie has quite literally been around for centuries. Tuxedoed waiters serve house favourites like fresh oysters, *langoustines fricassée volaille* (prawn fricasée) and *cuisse de canard en marmite et lentilles* (leg of duck with lentils). €29.80 set menu. Mon–Fri noon–1am, Sat & Sun noon–2am. M° Châtelet-Les-Halles.

Georges **Centre Georges Pompidou, 4e ☎01.44.78.47.99.** On the top floor of the Pompidou Centre, this trendy, ultra-minimalist restaurant with outdoor terrace commands stunning views over the rooftops of Paris and makes a stylish place for lunch or dinner; the fluid aluminum-swathed interior calls to mind a Frank Gehry museum. The French-Asian fusion cuisine is passable, though somewhat overpriced (main courses from €20), but then that's not the main reason you come. Reservations a must for dinner. Daily except Tues noon–1am. M° Rambuteau/Hôtel-de-Ville.

Le Gros Minet **1 rue des Prouvaires, 1er ☎01.42.33.02.62.** Relaxed, small restaurant with distinct charm and popular with families. The menu centres on duck, including *carpaccio de canard* (very thin slices of raw duck), but there are plenty of alternatives on offer. Around €25 a head. Mon–Sat 7.30–11.30pm, Tues–Fri noon–2pm. M° Châtelet-Les-Halles.

Au Pied de Cochon **6 rue Coquillière, 1er ☎01.40.13.77.00.** A Les Halles institution since 1946, this very typical brasserie is the place to go for extravagant middle-of-the-night pork chops, oysters and of course pigs' trotters. Lunchtime *formule* around €20. *A la carte* around €40. Daily 24hr. M° Châtelet-Les-Halles.

La Robe et le Palais **13 rue des Lavandières St-Opportune, 1er ☎01.45.08.07.41, ⓦwww.larobeetlepalais.com.** Small, busy *restaurant à vins* serving traditional cuisine and a *tête*-boggling selection of 250 wines *au compteur* (priced according to how much you consume). Although the food here can be rough on your cholesterol level, it is excellently prepared, and you'll want to take your time eating and soaking up the cool ambience of old Paris. Some of the great dishes include home-made foie gras, *risotto du champignon* and the chef's favourite, *grosse côte de cochon noir*, a delicious cut of the once-endangered Gascogne-bred boar, available in only a few Paris restaurants. Reckon on around €35 a head for three courses without wine. Mon–Sat noon–2.30pm & 7.30–11pm. M° Châtelet.

La Tour de Montlhéry (Chez Denise) **5 rue des Prouvaires, 1er ☎01.42.36.21.82.** An old-style, late-night Les Halles bistrot, packed with diners sitting elbow to elbow at long tables tucking into substantial meaty French dishes, such as *andouillette* (tripe) and steak, plus the odd fish dish, accompanied by perfectly cooked chips. Mains cost around €22. Booking advised. Mon–Fri noon–3pm & 7.30pm–5am; closed mid-July to mid-Aug. M° Louvre-Rivoli/Châtelet.

La Victoire Suprême du Cœur **41 rue des Bourdonnais, 1er ☎01.40.41.93.95.** Cheery vegetarian restaurant adored by herbivores everywhere. While the interior takes some getting used to – photos and drawings of Indian guru Sri Chimnoy plaster the place – the food is some of the best vegetarian in Paris. The menu offers a wide range of tasty salads, quiches and wholesome *plats du jour*, such as *roti champignons* with blackberry sauce, for €11.90. Good-value lunch *menu* at €12.50. Mon–Fri 11.45am–10pm, Sat noon–10pm. M° Louvre-Rivoli/Châtelet.

Au Vieux Molière **passage Molière, 157 rue Saint-Martin, 3e ☎01.42.78.37.87, ⓦwww.auvieuxmoliere.com.** French chansons playing softly in the background add to the mellow atmosphere of this cosy, candlelit restaurant hidden away down a characterful *passage*. The traditional cuisine is well prepared and flavoursome; typical dishes are garlic-roasted chicken and mullet in saffron sauce. Lunchtime *plat du jour* and glass of wine €9.50, in the evening *à la carte* from €40. Closed Sun lunch & Mon. M° Etienne-Marcel/Rambuteau/RER Châtelet.

The Marais

Unless otherwise indicated, the listings below are marked on the map on p.114.

Central Marais

Cafés and wine bars

L'Apparemment Café **18 rue des Coutures-St-Gervais, 3e.** A chic but cosy café resembling a series of comfortable sitting rooms, with quiet corners and deep sofas. Locals flock here to play parlour and board games, so you might try to get in a quick game of Scrabble or Trivial Pursuit with your neighbour while waiting for your food. Recommended are the salads, which you compose yourself by ticking off your chosen ingredients and handing your order to the waiter. Popular Sun brunch until 4pm costs €20. Cocktails €9. Mon–Fri noon–2am, Sat 4pm–2am, Sun 12.30pm–midnight. M° St-Sébastien-Froissart.

L'As du Falafel 34 rue des Rosiers, 4e. The sign above the doorway of this falafel shop in the Jewish quarter reads "*Toujours imité, jamais égalé*" ("always copied, but never equalled"), a boast that few would probably challenge, given the quality of the food and the queues outside. Falafels to take away cost only €4, or pay a bit more and sit in the buzzing little dining room. Noon–midnight; closed Fri eve & Sat. M° St-Paul.

Café Martini 11 rue du Pas-de-la-Mule, 4e. **See map on p.110.** Just off place des Vosges, but much more down-to-earth and patronized mostly by locals, this relaxing little café with low wood-beamed ceiling is run by friendly staff and offers low prices and taped jazz in the background. €9 for a huge bowl of salad or a tortilla with chipped potatoes. Cocktails from €6. Happy hour 7–10pm. Daily noon–2am. M° St-Paul/Chemin Vert.

L'Ebouillanté 6 rue des Barres, 4e. A two-floor café that spills onto a picturesque, cobbled street behind the church of St-Gervais in nice weather. You can choose from an extensive choice of drinks, from home-made hot chocolate to iced fruit cocktails. The two-course lunch costs €15, and as well as the usual French dishes you can also get Tunisian *crêpes*. It also does a popular Sunday brunch for €19. Tues–Sun noon–10pm, till 9pm in winter. M° Hôtel-de-Ville.

Le Loir dans la Théière 3 rue des Rosiers, 4e. A characterful, long-established *salon de thé* decorated with antique toys and *Alice in Wonderland* murals. It's a popular spot for meeting friends and lounging about on battered sofas, while feasting on enormous portions of scrummy home-made cakes (around €6) or excellent vegetarian quiches. Sun brunch (€16–22) is particularly busy and queues for a table often stretch out the door. Mon–Fri 11am–7pm, Sat & Sun 10am–7pm. M° St-Paul.

Mariage Frères 30 rue Bourg-Tibourg, 4e. The ultimate tea room, serving over five hundred varieties of tea; a little book accompanies the menu and describes each one. The tea is perfectly brewed and arrives in a huge metal-insulated teapot. The pastries, including excellent fruit tarts and scones with *gelée extra de thé* (tea jelly), go down very nicely, too. The decor is elegant and faintly colonial – rattan chairs and potted palms – while service is assured by handsome white-suited waiters. Reckon on around €15 for tea and pastry. Brunch is also available on weekends, though is a little steeply priced at €25–38. Tues–Sun 3–7pm. M° Hôtel-de-Ville.

Le Petit Fer à Cheval 30 rue Vieille-du-Temple, 4e. A very attractive small bistrot/bar with original fin-de siècle decor, including a marble-topped bar in the shape of a horseshoe (*fer à cheval*). It's a popular drinking spot, with agreeable wine, and you can snack on sandwiches or simple *plats* in the little back room furnished with old wooden métro seats. Mon–Fri 9–2am, Sat & Sun 11–2am; food served noon–midnight. M° St-Paul.

Restaurants

Auberge de Jarente 7 rue Jarente, 4e ☎01.42.77.49.35. This hospitable and friendly Basque restaurant serves up first-class food at moderate prices: *cassoulet*, hare stew, *magret de canard* and *piperade*. Lunch *menu* €14, evening €20. Tues–Sat noon–2.30pm & 7.30–10.30pm; closed Aug. M° St-Paul.

Au Bourguignon du Marais 52 rue François Miron, 4e ☎01.48.87.15.40. A warm, relaxed restaurant and *cave à vins* with attractive contemporary decor and tables outside in summer, serving excellent Burgundian cuisine with carefully selected wines to match. Mains cost €15–25, wine starts at €20. Mon–Fri noon–3pm & 8–11pm; closed two weeks in Aug. M° St-Paul.

Chez Marianne 2 rue des Hospitalières-Saint-Gervais, 4e ☎01.42.72.18.86. A Marais institution, this homely place with cheery red awnings specializes in Middle Eastern and Jewish delicacies at very reasonable prices. A platter of mezzes that might include tabbouleh, aubergine purée, chopped liver and hummus starts at €12, and the wines are inexpensive too. There's seating outside in nice weather, and, unlike many restaurants, it stays open throughout the summer. Daily 11am–midnight. M° St-Paul.

Le Colimaçon 49 rue du Temple, 4e ☎01.48.87.12.01. Delightful, absent-minded owner rushing about only adds to the local charm at this stone-walled, wood-beamed French restaurant set around a spiral staircase (*colimaçon*). The *andouillette à la moutarde* (mustard tripe) is especially good. Two-course *menu* for €22.50. Sun brunch noon–4pm. Tues–Sat 7.30pm–1am, Sun noon–midnight. M° Hôtel-de-Ville/St-Paul.

Le Coude Fou 12 rue du Bourg-Tibourg, 4e **☎01.42.77.15.16.** A popular, relaxed wine bistrot, with wooden beams and brightly painted murals. The menu offers some unusual wines from all over France to accompany traditional and more adventurous dishes, such as *filet de cannette aux kumcoats (duck with kumquats)* and *entrecôte au bleu d'Auvergne* (steak with blue cheese). Lunchtime *formule* €16.90, including a glass of wine; *à la carte* from €30. Booking advisable on weekends. Daily noon–2.45pm & 7.30–midnight. M° Hôtel-de-Ville.

L'Enoteca 25 rue Charles-V, 4e **☎01.42.78.91.44.** A fashionable Italian *bistrot à vins* in an old Marais building. If you take your Italian wine seriously this is the place to come; the list runs to 22 pages and features over 400 varieties, with an ever-changing selection available by the glass. Food doesn't take a back seat either; choose from an array of *antipasti*, fresh pasta or more substantial dishes for around €15 like stuffed courgettes or *cochon de lait* (spit-roasted pork). Two-course lunchtime *menu* for €14 including a glass of wine. Daily noon–2.30pm & 7.30–11.30pm; closed one week in Aug. M° St-Paul.

Piccolo Teatro 6 rue des Ecouffes, 4e **☎01.42.72.17.79.** A good vegetarian restaurant with atmospheric low lighting, stone walls and thick-beamed ceilings. The speciality is *gratins* with poetic-sounding names such as the *douceur et tendresse,* made of spinach, mint, mozzarella and gruyère. The rhubarb crumble comes recommended. Midday *menu* at around €10, evening €15. Best to book on weekends. Tues–Sun noon–3pm & 7–11pm; closed Aug. M° St-Paul.

Le Potager du Marais 22 rue Rambuteau, 4e **☎01.42.74.24.66.** Come early or book in advance for a place at this tiny, good-value vegetarian restaurant, with only 25 covers at a long communal table. The ingredients are all organic and there's plenty for vegans, too. Dishes include goat's cheese with honey, vegetarian shepherd's pie, and ravioli with basil. Mains around €11. Mon–Sat noon–10.30pm. M° Rambuteau.

Le Rouge Gorge 8 rue St-Paul, 4e **☎01.48.04.75.89.** A small, charming *restaurant à vins* with bare stone walls and wood beams, and jazz or classical music playing in the background. It's devoted to exploring a wide range of wines: one week it might be Corsica, the next Spain or the Loire, and the theme is taken up in the frequently changing menu. Mains around €16–18. Wine by the glass starts at €3; if you're taken by a particular vintage you can buy a bottle from the downstairs cellar to take home. Mon–Sat noon–3pm & 7–11pm; closed last fortnight in Aug. M° St-Paul.

Le Temps des Cerises 31 rue de la Cerisaie, 4e **☎01.42.72.08.63.** **See map on p.110.** Formerly part of the old Célestins convent, this time-warp little café, with yellow decor, black-and-white photos and prints of vieux Paris, is a popular lunchtime spot, and no wonder, given the bargain set menu – €13 gets you a hearty main dish such as *côte de veau* with mushroom sauce and homemade chips and a starter or dessert. Expect to share a table, as the tiny dining room fills up with a crowd of habitués, who all seem to be on first-name terms with the patron. Mon–Fri until 8pm; food from 11.30am to 2.30pm only; closed Aug. M° Bastille.

Au Vin des Pyrénées 25 rue Beautreillis, 4e **☎01.42.72.64.94.** A bustling traditional bistrot with a festive atmosphere, decorated with wine bottles and old postcards. It's popular with a youngish, relaxed crowd, who jostle for elbow room around little wooden tables with white-and-red checked tablecloths. The classic French fare ranges from huge, succulent steaks to gigantic salads of melon, ham, lentils, pâté and other goodies; finish off (if you can) with a delicious *moelleux au chocolat* (chocolate fondant gateau). Mains cost €16–18. Mon–Sat noon–3pm & 7.30–11.30pm, Sun brunch noon–4pm. M° St-Paul/Bastille.

Upper Marais

The listings below marked on the map on p.110.

Cafés and wine bars

Le Progrès 1 rue de Bretagne, 3e. Black-leather-jacketed cool types prop up the zinc bar of this hip corner café, with its traditional decor of mustard-coloured walls and mosaic floor. It's especially popular at aperitif time, but also makes a good spot for relaxing with a coffee and newspaper in the morning. M° Filles-du-Calvaire.

Restaurants

404 69 rue des Gravilliers, 3e ⓣ01.42.74.57.81. A very popular trendy Moroccan restaurant, with a pricey menu and a lanterned, dimly lit interior that screams colonialist romance. The standard North African fare here is good enough, but surely it's the Casbah fetish ambience you're paying for. Reckon on €35 exclusive of drinks or go for the bargain €17 lunch *menu*. Their famed weekend Berber Brunch (€21) requires reservations (Sat & Sun noon–4pm). Daily noon–midnight. M° Arts-et-Métiers.

Ambassade d'Auvergne 22 rue de Grenier St-Lazare, 3e ⓣ01.42.72.31.22, ⓦwww.ambassade-auvergne.com. Suited, mustachioed waiters serve scrumptious Auvergnat cuisine that would have made Vercingétorix proud. There's a set menu for €28, but you may well be tempted by some of the house specialities, like the *blanquette d'Agneau* (white Roquefort lamb stew, €19). Among the after-dinner treats are a plate of *fromages*, including the region's brittle, pungent Cantal cheese, as well as divine profiteroles. Reservations recommended. Daily noon–2pm & 7.30–10pm; closed last two weeks in Aug. M° Rambuteau.

Chez Nénesse 17 rue Saintonge, 3e ⓣ01.42.78.46.49. Steak in bilberry sauce and figs stuffed with cream of almonds are two of the unique delights on offer at this welcoming restaurant, along with home-made chips on Thurs lunchtimes. Good-value set lunch for €10. In the evening count on around €35 without wine. Mon–Fri noon–2.30pm & 8–10.30pm; closed Aug. M° Filles-du-Calvaire.

Chez Omar 47 Rue de Bretagne, 3e ⓣ01.42.72.36.26. No reservations are taken at this popular North African couscous restaurant, but it's no hardship to wait for a table at the bar, taking in the handsome old brasserie decor, fashionable crowd and spirited atmosphere. Portions are copious and the couscous light and fluffy. The merguez (spicy sausage) costs €12, or go all out for the royal (€22), though don't expect to have any room afterwards for the sticky cakes passed round on a large platter. No credit cards. Daily except Sun lunch noon–2.30pm & 7–11.30pm. M° Arts-et-Métiers.

Le Taxi Jaune 13 rue Chapon, 3e ⓣ01.42.76.00.40. The decor and name of this perfectly charming café-resto retain the nostalgia of the original 1930s restaurant which ran when Paris sizzled and taxis were still painted yellow. Today, it attracts an urban professional Anglo and French clientele, both gay and straight. Recently reworked by two charming young chefs, the quality of the cuisine has been taken up a notch. Midday two-course *menu* is a bargain €13; in the evening expect to spend at least €25. Mon–Fri 9am–1am (restaurant service noon–3pm & 8–10.30pm). Closed last week in July and first two weeks in Aug. M° Arts-et-Métiers.

The Quartier Latin

Unless otherwise indicated, the listings below are marked on the map on pp.126–127.

Cafés and wine bars

Café des Arts cnr place Contrescarpe and rue Lacépède, 5e. Prettier cups, slightly less pricey – though still very expensive – and a much more authentic atmosphere than its touristy neighbours *Delmas* and *La Contrescarpe*, and the location on this café-packed square is just as good, with a south-facing *terrasse*. Mon–Thurs & Sun 8–2am, Fri & Sat 8–4am. M° Monge.

Café de la Mosquée 39 rue Geoffroy-St-Hilaire, 5e. Drink mint tea and eat sweet cakes beside the courtyard fountain and fig trees of the Paris mosque – a haven of calm. The indoor salon has a beautiful Arabic interior, where delicious tagines and couscous are served for around €15 and up. Sheesha pipes can be had for €6, and there's even a hammam-massage-meal option for €58. Daily 9am–midnight. M° Monge.

Café Notre-Dame cnr quai St-Michel and rue St-Jacques, 5e. This café is fairly ordinary in all ways but one: the view straight across the river to the cathedral. Oh, and Lenin used to drink here. Sun–Thurs 7am–11.30pm, Fri & Sat 5pm–2am. M° St-Michel.

Café de la Nouvelle Mairie 19 rue des Fossés-St-Jacques, 5e. Sleek café-wine bar with a relaxed feel generated by its university clientele (note that it's shut at weekends). Serves good, modern food like lamb curry or linguine, as well as *assiettes* of cheese or *charcuterie* (all around €10). On sunny days or warm nights the outside tables on the picturesque square are delightful. Mon, Wed & Fri 9am–9pm, Tues & Thurs 9am–midnight. M° Cluny-La Sorbonne/RER Luxembourg.

L'Ecritoire 3 place de la Sorbonne, 5e. This classic university café is right beside the Sorbonne, and has outside tables by the fountain. Daily 7am–midnight. M° Cluny-La Sorbonne/RER Luxembourg.

La Fourmi Ailée 8 rue du Fouarre, 5e. Simple, filling fare is served in this former feminist bookshop, now a relaxed *salon de thé*. A high, mural-painted ceiling, a book-lined wall and background jazz contribute to the atmosphere. Around €12 for a *plat*. Daily noon–midnight. M° Maubert-Mutualité.

Les Pipos 2 rue de l'Ecole-Polytechnique, 5e. Old bar in a long-established position opposite the gates of the former *grande école*, with a decor that's heavy on old wood and a local clientele. Serves wines from €5 a glass along with simple plates of Auvergnat *charcuterie*, cheese and the like (€10–15). Mon–Sat 8.30–2am; closed two weeks in Aug. M° Maubert-Mutualité/Cardinal-Lemoine.

Le Reflet 6 rue Champollion, 5e. This artsy cinema café has a strong flavour of the nouvelle vague, with its scruffy black paint scheme, lights rigged up on a gantry and rickety tables packed with intellectual-looking film-goers and chess players. Perfect for a drink either side of a film at one of the arts cinemas on rue Champollion, perhaps accompanied by a steak, quiche or salad from the short list of blackboard specials. Daily 10–2am. M° Cluny-La Sorbonne.

Le Verre à Pied 118bis rue Mouffetard, 5e. Deeply old-fashioned market bar where traders take their morning glass of wine at the bar, or sit down to eat a *plat du jour* for under €10. Some have been doing it so long they've got little plaques on their table, but no-one minds visitors stopping by. Tues–Sat 9am–8.30pm, Sun 9am–3.30pm. M° Monge.

Restaurants

L'Atelier Maître Albert 1 rue Maitre Albert, 5e ☎01.56.81.30.01. Another of chef-entrepreneur Guy Savoy's ventures, this rôtisserie has a decor that's like a contemporary designer's take on a medieval château. It's a fitting backdrop for the speciality of spit-roast meats, though you can also find lighter dishes on the menu such as pan-fried red mullet with penne *gratin*, or a delicious starter of mussels on a bed of celeriac remoulade and lentil jelly. There's a lunch *menu* at €25, but you'll pay double that for dining *à la carte*. Mon–Wed noon–2.30pm & 6.30–11.30pm, Thurs & Fri noon–2.30pm & 6.30pm–1am, Sat 6.30pm–1am, Sun 6.30–11.30pm. M° Maubert-Mutualité.

Au Bistrot de la Sorbonne 4 rue Toullier, 5e ☎01.43.54.41.49. The muralled and pannelled interior seems rather glamorous at first, but this is actually a cosy little restaurant, with comfortable red-velvet banquettes and a relaxed atmosphere. The mostly North African food is comforting rather than exciting: generous couscous and sizzling tagines (€14–20), with evening *menus* from €18.50. Mon–Sat noon–2.30pm & 7pm–midnight. RER Luxembourg.

Brasserie Balzar 49 rue des Ecoles, 5e ☎01.43.54.13.67. This classic, high-ceilinged brasserie is something of an institution, much frequented by the literary

▽ Brasserie Balzar, Quartier Latin

intelligentsia of the Quartier Latin. The decor isn't jaw-droppingly glamorous, but the feel is almost intimidatingly Parisian – you could almost be on a film set – though if you're unlucky, or choose to eat early, the tourist clientele can spoil the Left Bank mood. You can get a steak tartare, a roast chicken or the garnished sauerkraut – garnished with copious amounts of pork and sausage, that is – for around €18, and a glass of kir for €5. Menus from €24, *à la carte* around €40. Daily 8am–11.30pm. M° Maubert-Mutualité.

Le Buisson Ardent 25 rue Jussieu, 5e ⓣ01.43.54.93.02. Generous helpings of inventive, first-class cooking served in a warm-coloured, pleasantly traditional dining room. Lunch *menu* €15, evenings €29. Reservations recommended. Closed Sat lunch & Sun, and two weeks in Aug. M° Jussieu.

Les Cinq Saveurs d'Anada 72 rue du Cardinal-Lemoine, 5e ⓣ01.43.29.58.54. Airy and informal restaurant serving delicious organic, vegetarian food. Salads (€8) are good, or you could try one of the creative meat-substitute dishes (around €14–18), such as tofu soufflé, *confit* of tempeh with ginger, or seitan with celeriac and basil. Tues–Sun noon–2.30pm & 7.30–10.30pm. M° Cardinal-Lemoine.

Au Coin des Gourmets 5 rue Dante, 5e ⓣ01.43.26.12.92. The simple, rather plain setting is nothing to write home about, but this is a standout address for the freshness and homeliness of its southeast Asian food. You might have a tangy, Cambodian tamarind soup with shrimp, then beef with citronella and basil, but there are Laotian and Vietnamese dishes too – you can even try them all on the €35 "Saveurs d'Indochine" menu. Otherwise, evening *menus* at €25. Mon 7–10.30pm, Tues–Sat noon–2.30pm & 7–10.30pm, Sun 7–10pm. M° St-Michel/Maubert-Mutualité.

Coco de Mer 34 bd Saint-Marcel, 5e ⓣ01.47.07.06.64. Off map. Down at the southeastern end of the 5e arrondissement, this Réunionnais restaurant offers (fake) palm trees, happy-island music, a table in a sand pit and some of the best Indian Ocean food in the city. Try the *dos de bourgeois grillée*, a heavenly grilled red snapper cooked in garlic and passion-fruit sauce (€20). Full meals for around €30. Mon 7.30pm–midnight, Tues–Sat noon–3pm & 7.30pm–midnight. M° Saint-Marcel.

Les Degrés de Notre-Dame 10 rue des Grands Degrés, 5e ⓣ01.55.42.88.88. Reliable, substantial and homemade French food – plus a few couscous dishes and tagines – in an old-world bistrot setting, or out on the quaint terrasse. Good-value lunch *menu* at €12.50, otherwise around €25 and up. Mon–Sat 7am–midnight. M° Maubert-Mutualité.

L'Ecurie 58 rue de la Montagne Ste-Geneviève, cnr rue Laplace, 5e ⓣ01.46.33.68.49. Shoe-horned into a former stables on a particularly lovely corner of the Montagne Ste-Geneviève, this family-run restaurant is bustling and very lovable. Outside tables and the cellar below provide a few extra seats, but not many, so book ahead. Expect well-cooked meat dishes served without flourishes – grilled with chips, mostly – for less than €15, and simple starters and desserts for around €5. Mon–Sat noon–3pm & 7pm–midnight, Sun 7pm–midnight. M° Maubert-Mutualité/Cardinal-Lemoine.

Les Fontaines 9 rue Soufflot, 5e ⓣ01.43.26.42.80. The dated brasserie-cum-diner decor looks unpromising from the outside, but the welcome inside this family-run place is warm and genuine, and the cooking is in the same spirit, with honest French meat and fish dishes such as *blanquette de veau* or game in season. Starters around €7, mains €15–18. Mon–Sat noon–3pm & 7.30–11pm. RER Luxembourg.

Le Grenier de Notre-Dame 18 rue de la Bûcherie, 5e ⓣ01.43.29.98.29. There's a distinctly 1970s feel about this restaurant, which serves wholesome and very traditional vegetarian fare, much of it organic, including traditional French dishes made with tofu and unreconstructed classics like cauliflower cheese. It's not the liveliest of venues, but a useful, central vegetarian address nonetheless. *Menu* at €14.50 (€12.50 lunch). Daily noon–2.30pm & 6.30–11.30pm M° Maubert-Mutualité.

Au Jardin des Pâtes 4 rue Lacépède, 5e ⓣ01.43.31.50.71. Delicious homemade pasta made with all manner of freshly ground organic grains, and served with wonderful flourishes and garnishes. The room is stylish, fresh-feeling and airy – almost like a conservatory, and you'll pay no more than €20 for a full meal. There's another branch at 33 bd Arago, 13e (M° Gobelins; closed Sun). Daily noon–2.30pm & 7–11pm. M° Jussieu.

Mavrommatis **42 rue Daubenton, 5e** **☎01.43.31.17.17.** **@www.marommatis.fr.** A highly sophisticated Greek restaurant – forget the food you had on holiday, the cooking here is influenced by French attention to detail. Quite expensive – even the lunchtime *menu* is €20, and mains are all in the €20s – but you are definitely tasting Greek food at its best, and the faintly Classical decor and soft lighting are very serene. Tues–Sat noon–2.30pm & 7.30–10pm. M° Censier-Daubenton.

Perraudin **157 rue St-Jacques, 5e** **☎01.46.33.15.75.** One of the classic bistrots of the Left Bank, featuring solid, homely cooking. The atmosphere is thick with Parisian chatter floating above the brightly lit, packed-in tables. There's a midday *menu* at €18, while in the evening the *menu* costs €28 or you can eat *à la carte* (around €15–25 for a main). No reservations, but you can wait at the bar for a place. Mon–Fri noon–2pm & 7.30–10.15pm; closed Aug. RER Luxembourg.

La Petite Légume **36 rue des Boulangers, 5e** **☎01.40.46.06.85.** This health-food grocery doubles as a vegetarian restaurant and tea room, serving homely, organic *plats* for €8–15, along with fresh-tasting, organic Loire wines. Mon–Sat noon–2.30pm & 7.30–10pm. M° Jussieu.

Le Petit Pontoise **9 rue de Pontoise, 5e** **☎01.43.29.25.20.** This relaxed, young bistrot is as authentically Parisian as you can get this close the river: lace café curtains, little wooden tables, a bar in one corner and specials on the blackboard – perhaps a salad of haricot beans with prawns, lamb steak and duck breast. The wines are good and very reasonably priced, and the puddings outstanding. Expect to pay around €30–40 a head. Daily noon–2.30pm & 7.30–10.30pm. M° Maubert-Mutualité.

Pho 67 **59 rue Galande, 5e** **☎01.45.25.56.69.** A beacon of South Asian authenticity in this desperately touristy area. The Vietnamese proprietors work away in an open kitchen, preparing a good range of inexpensive dishes; go for the famous and filling *pho* soup (€8), made with tender French *entrecôte* or *faux filet* steaks. Daily noon–3pm & 7–11pm. M° Maubert-Mutualité.

Le Pré-Verre **8 rue Thénard, 5e** **☎01.43.54.59.47.** This sleek, modern *bistrot à vins* has a great wine list, as you'd expect, but the food is just as interesting. The blackboard lists are dotted with unusual ingredients and spices – you might find swordfish on a bed of quinoa grain, veal steak with cumin, or roast bananas with mango mousse and an amazing chilli syrup. The evening *menu* is €26.50 – stunning value for the quality – while the lunchtime two-courser costs just €12.50, including a glass of wine and coffee. Tues–Sat noon–2pm & 7.30–10.30pm; closed three weeks in Aug. M° Maubert-Mutualité.

Student restaurants

Students of any age are eligible to apply for tickets for the university restaurants under the direction of CROUS de Paris. They're mostly on the Left Bank, where we've listed some of the more useful addresses, plus one in the Bastille area; you can find a complete list at @www.crous-paris.fr. The tickets have to be obtained from the particular restaurant of your choice; just turn up during opening hours, buy a ticket (bring your student ISIC card as proof of status) and then get your meal. Not all serve evening meals, and most are closed on the weekend and during term time (details are given on the website). Though the food is less than wonderful, it's certainly filling, and you can't complain for the price: meals cost €4.70.

You'll find student restaurants at the following locations: 31 rue Geoffroy Saint-Hilaire, 5e (Mon–Fri 11am–2.30pm; M° Censier-Daubenton/Jussieu); 31 av Georges-Bernanos, 5e (daily 11.30am–2pm & 6.30–8pm; RER Port-Royal); 12 place du Panthéon, 5e (daily 8am–6pm; RER Luxembourg); 5 rue Mazet, 6e (Mon–Fri 11.30am–2pm; M° Odéon); 3 rue Mabillon, 6e (daily 11.30am–2pm & 6–8pm; M° Mabillon); 92 rue d'Assas, 6e (Mon–Fri 11am–2.30pm; RER Port-Royal/M° Notre-Dame-des-Champs); 45 bd Diderot, 12e (Mon–Fri 11.30am–2pm; M° Gare de Lyon/Reuilly-Diderot).

Le Reminet 3 rue des Grands Degrés, 5e ☎01.44.07.04.24. This artful little bistrot-restaurant shows its class through small touches: snowy-white tablecloths and fancy chandeliers liven up the simple dining room, while imaginative sauces grace high-quality traditional French ingredients. Gastronomic *menu* at around €50, but you can get away with two courses *à la carte* for about half that. Mon & Thurs–Sun noon–3pm & 7.30–11pm; closed two weeks in Aug. M° Maubert-Mutualité.

Tashi Delek 4 rue des Fossés-St-Jacques, 5e ☎01.43.26.55.55. Elegantly styled Tibetan restaurant serving Himalayan regional dishes ranging from hearty, warming noodle soups to the addictive, ravioli-like momok and a salty, soupy yak-butter tea. There's a good evening *menu* at €19, but you can eat well for much less. If you prefer a more monastic, Tibetan-style decor, head round the corner and across the street to Kokonor, 206 rue St-Jacques, which serves many of the same specialities. Mon–Sat noon–2.30pm & 7–11pm; closed two weeks in Aug. RER Luxembourg.

St-Germain

The listings below are marked on the map on pp.142–143.

Cafés and wine bars

L'Artisan des Saveurs 72 rue du Cherche-Midi, 6e ☎01.42.22.46.64. This cute, yellow tea salon serves a large menu of elegantly prepared teas to local sophisticates. On Sunday come for the *grasse matinée*, a popular brunch served 11.30am–3.30pm (€19). Mon, Tues & Thurs–Sat noon–6.30pm (till 7pm Sat), Sun 11.30am–3.30pm. M° Vaneau.

L'Assignat 7 rue Guénégaud, 6e. Zinc counter, bar stools, bar football and young regulars from the nearby art school in an untouristy café close to quai des Augustins. Homely *plats du jour* for around €7. Mon–Sat 9am–11pm, food served noon–3pm; closed July. M° Pont-Neuf.

Bar du Marché 75 rue de Seine, 6e. Thrumming café where the *serveurs* are cutely kitted out in flat caps and aprons. Fashionable place for a pre-dinner kir. Admittedly, you pay a little extra for the colours and smells of the rue de Buci market on the doorstep. Daily 7am–2am. M° Mabillon.

Bistrot des Augustins 39 quai de Grands Augustins, 6e. Small, traditional wine bar conveniently located on the riverbank between the Pont Neuf and Place St-Michel. Serves good *charcuterie*, salads and hot *gratins*, all for around €10, and filling *tartines* – perfect with a glass of wine. Daily 9am–11pm. M° St-Michel.

Café Bonaparte cnr rue Bonaparte and place St-Germain, 6e. Less touristy than the nearby *Deux Magots* or *Flore* – that said, a café crème costs €5.50 – and situated at the quieter, sunnier end of the square. Serves a good tarte tatin for €7.50 along with other snacks. Daily 8–2am. M° St-Germain-des-Prés.

Café de la Mairie 8 place St-Sulpice, 6e. A peaceful, pleasant café on the sunny north side of the square, opposite the church of St-Sulpice. Reputedly an old haunt of Henry Miller, now a fashionable place to bask with a coffee or an apéritif. Mon–Sat 7am–2am. M° St-Sulpice.

Café du Musée d'Orsay 1 rue Bellechasse, 7e. The Musée d'Orsay's rooftop café offers one of the city's quirkier views – over the Seine and towards Montmartre – seen through the giant clockface dominating the room. Serves snacks and drinks, with a wonderful outdoor terrace on sunny days. Tues–Sun 11am–5pm. RER Musée-d'Orsay/M° Solférino.

Chez Georges 11 rue des Canettes, 6e. Deeply old-fashioned and atmospherically delapidated old wine bar with its old shop front still in place, though sadly Georges himself is not. Tues–Sat noon–2am; closed Aug. M° Mabillon.

Les Deux Magots 170 bd St-Germain, 6e. Named after its two statues of Chinamen this café on the corner of place St-Germain-des-Prés is the victim of its own reputation as the historic hang-out of Left Bank intellectuals, but it's still great for people-watching. You can get a good breakfast for €18, and an omelette or a fruit tart for around €8. An espresso costs €4.50. Daily 7.30–1am; closed one week in Jan. M° St-Germain-des-Prés.

Les Etages St-Germain 5 rue de Buci, 6e. Bastion of boho trendiness at the edge of the rue de Buci street market, with outside and overhead heaters for winter days. Good for a lunchtime coffee watching the street bustle and, later on, a great spot for people-watching over a glass of beer (€4) or a cocktail (from €7). Daily noon–2am. M° Mabillon.

Le Flore 172 bd St-Germain, 6e. The great rival and immediate neighbour of *Les Deux Magots*, with a trendier and more local clientele. There's a unique traditional hierarchy: tourists on the terrace, beautiful people inside, intellectuals upstairs. Sartre, De Beauvoir, Camus and Marcel Carné used to hang out here – and there's still the odd organized reading or debate. Especially enjoyable for the famous morning hot chocolate, a late-afternoon coffee or an after-dinner drink. Daily 7–1.30am. M° St-Germain-des-Prés.

Ladurée 21 rue Bonaparte, 6e. The latest outpost of Ladurée's tearoom mini-empire has a lovely pale-green muralled conservatory at the back of the shop where elegant locals sip fine teas and eat pink macaroons till they're bursting out of their matching Chanel suits. Mon–Sat 8.30am–7.30pm, Sun 10am–7.30pm. M° St-Germain-des-Prés.

M's Coffee Room 71 rue du Cherche-Midi, 6e. Ideal for a tea break while shopping, or a light *plat du jour* (around €14). M herself, the patronne, is very French, as is the wonderful decor inherited from a turn-of-the-twentieth-century butcher's shop. But the comfy sofas, board games, teas, brownies and apple crumble are distinctly Anglo. Daily noon–7pm. M° Vaneau/Rennes.

La Palette 43 rue de Seine, 6e. This former Beaux Arts student hang-out is now frequented by art dealers and their customers, though it's still very relaxed. The decor is superb, including, of course, a large selection of paint-spattered palettes hanging on the walls. There's a roomy *terrasse* outside, and a short menu of lunchtime specials. Mon–Sat 9–2am. M° Odéon.

Au Petit Suisse 16 rue de Vaugirard, 6e. The perfect retreat from the Jardin du Luxembourg, with everything you'd need from a café: outdoor terrace; in-house tabac; two-hundred-year history; Art Deco interior; menu of sandwiches, salads and decent *plats du jour*; and a mezzanine level that's made for people-watching. Mon–Sat 7am–midnight; Sun 7am–11.30pm. RER Luxembourg/M° Cluny-La Sorbonne.

Le Procope 13 rue de l'Ancienne-Comédie, 6e ⓣ01.40.46.79.00. Opened in 1686 as the first establishment to serve coffee in Paris, this is still a great place to enjoy an afternoon cup and bask in the knowledge that, over the years, Voltaire, Benjamin Franklin, Rousseau, Marat and Robespierre, among others, have done the very same thing. Food is served all day, with a fair range of *menus*, but it's best to leave that to the lunchtime and evening tourist crowds and come for an afternoon coffee. Restaurant daily noon–1am; café service 2.30–6pm only. M° Odéon.

Veggie 38 rue de Verneuil, 7e. You can get organic, vegetarian and very tempting takeaway foods and sandwiches from this health-food shop near the Musée d'Orsay. Mon–Fri 9.30am–3pm & 5–7.30pm. M° Solférino.

Au Vieux Colombier 65 rue de Rennes, 6e. An attractive Art Deco café on the corner of rue du Vieux-Colombier, with a big, curving zinc bar, ice-cream-cone lights and stained-green wooden window frames. Perfect for a coffee break while shopping. Daily 7am–midnight. M° St-Sulpice.

Restaurants

Au 35 35 rue Jacob, 6e ⓣ01.42.60.23.24. This adorably intimate bistrot is filled with Art Deco lamps, mirrors and old posters, but the food's the thing. You might have an exotic, rich *pastilla d'agneau* (lamb in pastry with honey and spices), or a perfectly simple duck breast. Count on around €35 without wine or go for the €22 lunch menu. Mon–Fri noon–2.30pm & 7.30–11pm; Sat 7.30–11pm. M° St-Germain-des-Prés.

Allard 41 rue St-André-des-Arts, 6e ⓣ01.43.26.48.23. Expect the menu at this proudly unreconstructed Parisian restaurant to be meaty and rich rather than sophisticated or imaginative and you'll be very satisfied. The atmosphere is unimpeachably antique: if it wasn't for the almost exclusively international clientele, you could be dining in another century. From around €30. Mon–Sat noon–3pm & 7.30–11pm. M° Odéon.

L'Atlas 11 rue de Buci, 6e ⓣ01.40.51.26.30. Despite a few Art Deco details, the decor at l'Atlas is functional rather than classic, but that's half the charm of this unpretentious market brasserie. Good seafood, and simple, meaty main dishes at around €14 and up. Daily 6.30–1am. M° Mabillon.

Brasserie Lipp 151 bd St-Germain, 6e ①01.45.48.53.91. One of the most celebrated of all the classic Paris brasseries, the haunt of the very successful and very famous, with a wonderful 1900s wood-and-glass interior. There are decent *plats du jour*, including the famous *choucroute* (sauerkraut), for under €20, but gastro-exploring *à la carte* can get expensive. Daily noon–12.45am. M° St-Germain-des-Prés.

Le Christine 1 rue Christine, 6e ①01.40.51.71.64 The Christine is a cut above the usual bistrot. Yes, there are old beams and stone walls, but there are elegant white tablecloths, fresh flowers and artful paintings too. Yes, there's duck leg, rack of lamb and scallops on the list of mains, but the starters include a lentil soup "cappuccino" with foie gras chips, and poached eggs with violet artichokes. *Menus* in the €30s. Daily 6.30pm–midnight. M° St-Germain-des-Prés.

Ferrandaise 8 rue de Vaugirard, 6e ①01.43.26.36.36. The name "Ferrandaise" comes from a rare breed of beef cow from the Auvergne – and it's very much the theme here, with pictures of said cows on the walls and said veal on the menu – along with dishes such as crab ravioli, oven-steamed pikeperch and shoulder of lamb. Rough plaster walls, beams and greenery provide a rustic touch, but don't be fooled: this is an excellent, modern restaurant. Evening *menu* at €32. Tues–Thurs noon–2pm & 7.30–11pm, Fri noon–2pm & 7.30–midnight. Sat 7.30–midnight. M° St-Germain-des-Prés.

Gaya 44 rue du Bac, 6e ①01.45.44.73.73. A wall covered in metal scales hints at the theme at this hyper-designed, upscale mini-restaurant: fish. It's a satellite of the empire of celebrity chef Pierre Gagnaire, so you'll find plenty of his trademark invention: pressé of skate with a bloody mary sauce, carpaccio of wild sea bass with redcurrants, grilled swordfish on a bed of caramel, soya and Asian mushrooms. Relatively low prices for gastro-cuisine – around €80–90 a head with wine. Mon–Fri noon–2.30pm & 7.30–11pm, Sat 7.30pm–midnight. M° St-Germain-des-Prés.

△ Gaya restaurant, 6e

Jacques Cagna 14 rue des Grands-Augustins, 6e ①01.43.26.49.39, ⓦwww.jacques-cagna.com. Classy surroundings for very classy food – beef with Périgord truffles, or pigeon and green Chartreuse pie, for example. You pay for this kind of Michelin-starred, celebrity quality – €100 for the evening *menu*, or a good-value €45 at lunch – and wine can really bump up the bill. Mon & Sat 7.30–10.30pm; Tues–Fri noon–2pm & 7.30–10.30pm. M° Odéon/St-Michel.

La Méditerranée 2 place de l'Odéon, 6e ①01.43.26.02.30. The only thing that isn't decidedly swish about this fish restaurant is the prices – €32 gets you a whole three courses. The menu rings the changes on classic fish-in-sauce dishes – along with a sea bream roasted in honey and ginger, and of course the bouillabaisse. Inside, posh cream and pale blue walls set off deep carpets, and there are lots of little rooms full of soft banquettes, as well as a lovely glazed-in *terrasse*. Daily noon–2.30pm & 7.30–11pm. M° St-Germain-des-Prés.

Le Petit St-Benoît 4 rue St-Benoît, 6e ①01.42.60.27.92. Another of the tobacco-stained St-Germain institutions, all rickety wooden tables and brass train-carriage-style coat racks, this restaurant is packed hugger-mugger with international visitors seeking the authentic Parisian experience. Serves the sort of homely, meaty, unsophisticated comfort food your *grand-mère* would cook: try the *hachis parmentier* – known to lesser mortals as shepherd's pie – or the *boudin noir* (black pudding) with potatoes. Around €30. Mon–Sat noon–2.30pm & 7–10.30pm; closed Aug. M° St-Germain-des-Prés.

Le Petit Vatel 5 rue Lobineau, 6e ①01.43.54.28.49. A tiny, matey, atmospheric place nicely done out with bright yellow walls,

From wine bars to three stars

You don't really feel you've arrived in Paris until you've settled down at a table in a restaurant and raised your glass of sancerre or merlot in anticipation of a fine meal. Paris is after all the place where the restaurant was invented, and there's no shortage of first-rate dining places, ranging from humble bistrots to glittering haute-cuisine establishments, and from handsome Belle époque brasseries to workaday wine bars.

▲ Flo

Brasseries

For an authentic Parisian dining experience you can't beat a **brasserie**. First brought to Paris by Alsatian immigrants fleeing the Franco-Prussian war in 1870, brasseries were originally simple beer taverns (*brasserie* means "brewery"). Although they've since evolved into something more sophisticated, you can still feel the **Alsatian influence**, with good beers on offer as well as white wines such as Riesling and Gewürztraminer, and the famous *choucroute* – which is, at its best, a bowl of steaming sauerkraut stuffed with sausages and hams. Many brasseries retain their beautiful **original decor** of globe lamps, glass cupolas, dark-leather banquettes and brass coat racks. They're usually big – the largest, *La Coupole*, seats literally hundreds – brightly lit and very busy. Lively chatter and the clinking of cutlery fill the air, and waiters in black waistcoats and long white aprons dash up and down the aisles bearing steaming tureens or giant platters of seafood. Alongside the *choucroute*, seafood and traditional meaty dishes such as *foie gras* and *magret de canard* are the order of the day – nothing very adventurous, just satisfying French classics. Most brasseries **stay open late** into the night, when they fill up with excitable post-theatre crowds.

Classic brasseries

La Coupole; see p.340
Flo; see p.345
Gallopin; see p.325
Lipp; see p.336
Thoumieux; see p.339
Vagenende; see p.337
Vaudeville; see p.325
Wepler; see p.346

Bistrots

The traditional Parisian **bistrot** is a tiny, humble restaurant with red-and-white checked tablecloths, serving homely, classic French dishes – often run by a husband-and-wife team with monsieur in the kitchen and madame in the dining room. Tables are usually jammed in close together (getting in and out of your seat can be a good way to get to know your neighbours), and sometimes you're expected to share tables with fellow diners, all making for a convivial, informal dining

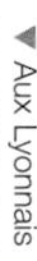

▼ Aux Lyonnais

experience. The **menu** is usually handwritten or chalked up on a blackboard, and passed by the waiter from table to table. It's generally limited to a few choice dishes plus staples like *coq au vin*, *blanquette de veau* or *steak au poivre*. The **wine list**, on the other hand, can be extensive, with a number of wines available by the glass. Alongside the older bistrots, a **new generation** has emerged. Some are run by young chefs keen to experiment with new, more exotic ingredients; others are set up by established gastro-giants wanting to attract livelier, trendier crowds – all part of a lifestyle trend known as *le fooding*. Inaki Aizpitarte, for example, the new young chef at *Le Chateaubriand* in the 11e, spices up classic dishes by adding oriental ingredients: lamb might come with a green tea and coriander sauce, a *filet de boeuf* with pak choy, chocolate mousse with red pepper.

Best traditional bistrots

Au 35; see p.335
Le Bistro des Deux-Théâtres; see p.344
Bistrot Paul Bert; see p.348
Aux Lyonnais; see p.325
Le Petit Pontoise; see p.333
La Régalade; see p.340
L'Os à Moëlle; see p.341

Best inventive bistrots

L'Avant Goût; see p.341
Au Bon Accueil; see p.338
Le Chateaubriand; see p.350
Gaya; see p.336
Mon Vieil Ami; see p.319
Le Pré-Verre; see p.333
Le Villaret; see p.351

Wine bars

Wine bars are convivial, relaxing places for enjoying celebrated wines such as the fruity Beaujolais or flinty Chablis, as well as for exploring little-known, small-production wines – perhaps a red Sancerre or an obscure Corsican vintage. Some wine bars also offer excellent food, as good as any in a quality bistrot, or at the very least they'll have platters of charcuterie, pâté and cheeses. Most wine bars, with one or two exceptions (such as *Juvéniles*; see p.325) concentrate solely on French wines, while some, such as *Le Rouge Gorge* (see p.329), will devote each month to exploring a different wine region.

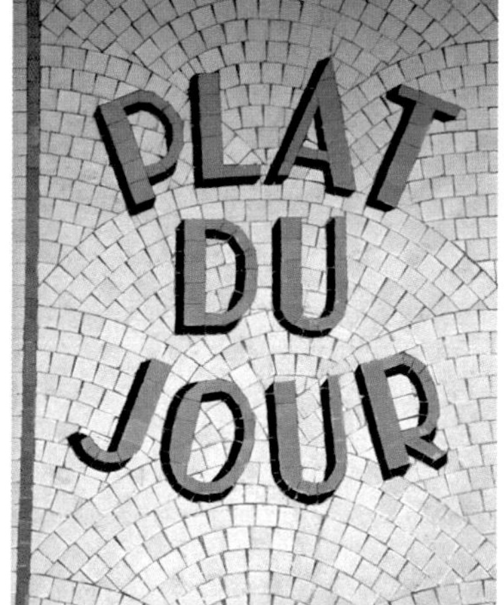

Best wine bars

Taverne Henri IV; see p.318
Le Rubis; see p.323
Juvéniles; see p.325
A la Cloche des Halles; see p.326
Le Baron Rouge; see p.347

Restaurants

A Parisian **restaurant** can be anything from a modest neighbourhood eatery to a sumptuous palace of haute cuisine. An astonishing number of these restaurants stick resolutely to French cuisine, but there's still plenty of variety. Provincial chefs have installed themselves all over the capital, specializing in Basque, Auvergnat, Provençal or Corsican fare, and Mediterranean and even Asian ingredients are creeping onto many menus. While *steak frites* is consistently voted the city's favourite dish, couscous usually follows a close second, and Paris has a great selection of North African restaurants – not to mention Italian, Senegalese, Vietnamese, Chinese and Thai. For many visitors, however, the ultimate dining experience is a meal at a top **haute cuisine restaurant**, whether it's one of the long-standing classics such as *Taillevent,* where diners are treated like royalty and can tuck into a seven-course *menu dégustation* featuring dishes such as Challans duck with cherries and amaretto sauce, or current buzz of the dining scene, triple-Michelin-starred *L'Astrance*, a tiny restaurant seating 26 and serving beautifully presented innovative cuisine.

Best restaurants for:

Regional cuisine
Ambassade d'Auvergne (Auvergnat); see p.330
Auberge Etchegorry (Basque); see p.341
L'Auberge Pyrénées Cévennes (southwestern); see p.349
Casa Olympe (Corsican-influenced); see p.344
Chez Gladines (Basque); see p.342
Le XVIIIème Barathym (Provençal-influenced); see p.343

International cuisine
Le Bambou (Vietnamese); see p.341
Chez Omar (Algerian); see p.330
Au Coin des Gourmets (Southeast Asian); see p.332
Coco de Mer (Indian Ocean); see p.332
Lao Siam (Thai); see p.350
Le Martel (North African); see p.345
Waly Fay (West African); see p.347

Haute cuisine
Alain Ducasse at the Plaza Athénée; see p.322
L'Arpège; see p.338
Astrance; see p.351
Meurice; see p.323
Salon d'Hélène; see p.337
Pierre Gagnaire; see p.322
Taillevent; see p.322

old train and film posters and quirky, colourful cutlery. Good, plain home cooking, including a vegetarian *plat*. The lunch *formule* is just €12, while a three-course meal will cost around €25 a head, including wine. Tues–Sat noon–2.30pm & 7.30–10pm. M° Mabillon.

Le Petit Zinc 11 rue St-Benoit, 6e **Ⓣ01.42.86.61.00.** Excellent traditional dishes, especially seafood, in stunning Art-Nouveau-style premises (actually built thirty years ago). It's not cheap – the dinner *menu* costs €35, and a lavish seafood platter will set you back €90 for two – but the quality is good. Daily noon–2.30pm & 7.30pm–midnight. M° St-Germain-des-Prés.

Polidor 41 rue Monsieur-le-Prince, 6e **Ⓣ01.43.26.95.34.** Eating at Polidor is a classic of Left Bank life. Open since 1845, it's still a bright, easy-going place bustling with aproned, middle-aged waitresses and packed elbow-to-elbow with noisy diners until late in the evening. The food is generally good, solid French classics, with mains like *confit de canard* or guinea fowl with *lardons* for around €12. No bookings; just turn up and wait. Mon–Sat noon–2.30pm & 7–12.30pm, Sun noon–2.30pm & 7–11pm. M° Odéon.

Le Salon d'Hélène 4 rue d'Assas, 6e **Ⓣ01.42.22.00.11.** Underneath celebrity chef Hélène Darroze's gastronomic *Restaurant d'Hélène*, the more relaxed and trendier ground-floor "salon" offers some superbly imaginative, expertly created dishes, many available as tapas portions. She draws on her native Basque cuisine – using sheep's milk cheese, for example – and on Spanish and Asian influences too. Neither the lack of windows nor the hideous tableware should put you off; this is some of the best cooking in Paris, at incredibly low prices for the quality – €35 for three tapas, €45 for four (with two glasses of wine), €88 for the tasting *menu*. Book well in advance. Tues–Sat 12.30–2.15pm & 7.30–10.15pm; closed Aug. M° St-Sulpice/Sèvres-Babylone.

La Tourelle 5 rue Hautefeuille 6e **Ⓣ01.46.33.12.47.** This splendidly medieval little bistrot, named after the stone *échauguette* tower outside, is packed into a low-ceilinged, stone-walled, convivial room. The meaty cuisine is fresh, simple and traditional in the very best sense – they make terrines out of what wasn't finished the day before. Service is particularly considerate – the owner may offer to change your wine if you prefer something in a different style – and the three-course *menu* good value at €19. No bookings are taken, so you'll just have to turn up and wait. Mon–Fri noon–3pm & 7–10.30pm, Sat 7–11.30pm; closed Aug. M° St-Michel.

Vagenende 142 bd St-Germain, 6e **Ⓣ01.43.26.68.18.** This Art Nouveau marvel is registered as a historic monument, all mirrors, marble pillars, chandeliers and dark wood that has been polished for decades to a lustrous glow. Worthwhile if you go for the ambience rather than the food – stick to the straightforward brasserie dishes (mains at €16–26, menu at €24.50) or seafood specials. Daily noon–1am. M° Mabillon.

Ze Kitchen Galerie 4 rue des Grands-Augustins, 6e **Ⓣ01.44.32.00.32.** Halfway between restaurant and trendy art gallery in atmosphere, with zany modern abstracts on the walls and a designer kitchen on open display. The food mixes Asian influences with contemporary Mediterranean cuisine – you might find crayfish tempura with ginger and lemon among the marinated fish starters, gnochetti with squid and nori in the pasta course, and calf's sweetbreads with lemongrass jus as a main. Expect to pay around €50 for three courses, without wine. Mon–Fri noon–2.30pm & 7–11pm, Sat 7.30–11pm. M° St-Michel.

The Eiffel Tower quarter

Unless otherwise stated, the listings below are marked on the map on pp.156–157.

Trocadéro

Cafés

Salon de Porcelain place d'Iéna, 16e **Ⓣ01.47.23.58.03.** The shortage of decent places to eat and drink around Trocadéro makes the café-restaurant of the Musée Guimet a good bet, albeit more for its interesting menu of speciality teas and dishes from all over Asia – dim sum, Thai,

Japanese – than for its basement ambience. *Menus* between €16 and €20. Daily except Tues 10am–6pm. M° Trocadéro.

Restaurants

Aux Marchés du Palais 5 rue de la Manutention, 16e ☎01.47.23.52.80. Simple, traditionally styled bistrot, with sunny tables on the pavement opposite the side wall of the Palais de Tokyo. There's always a good *entrée* and *plat du jour* – you might find a creamy broccoli velouté followed by sturgeon fillet, Charolais steak or prawn risotto. The prices are a little elevated – count on around €35 a head without wine – but then there's nothing half as satisfying anywhere around. Mon–Sat noon–2pm & 7.30–10.30pm. M° Iéna.

Tokyo Eat Palais de Tokyo, 16e ☎01.47.20.00.29. The restaurant inside the Site de Création Contemporaine is a self-consciously cool place to eat, with its futuristic, colourful decor and wealthy, arty clientele. The menu is a mix of modern Mediterranean and fusion dishes – you might choose between lamb fillet, *risotto aux cèpes*, or tuna mince with salsa and mint oil. Starters are priced at around €8–12, mains in the low twenties. The restaurant is open for drinks all day, but the gallery's café is a better bet for a drink and a snack, with a more dressed-down vibe. Tues–Sun noon–1am. M° Iéna/Alma-Marceau.

The 7e

Cafés and wine bars

Café du Marché 38 rue Cler, 7e. Big, busy café-brasserie serving excellent-value meals, with a *plat du jour* for under €10 that's as fresh-tasting as you'd expect, given the position in the middle of the rue Cler market. Outdoor seating, or covered-over terrace in winter. Mon–Sat 7am–midnight. M° La-Tour-Maubourg.

Le Poch'tron 25 rue de Bellechasse, 7e. With a good selection of snacks and wines by the glass, this is a relaxing place to revive yourself after visiting the museums in the arrondissement. Also serves lunch and dinner, with main dishes such as *confit de canard* or pike stew at around €17. Mon–Fri 9am–10.30pm. M° Solférino.

Restaurants

L'Affriolé 17 rue Malar, 7e ☎01.44.18.31.33. Don't be put off by the chilly pseudo-Classical decor; the welcome at this chef-run bistrot is warm and the food superb – traditionally French, but Mediterranean flavours and some brilliant combinations really bring the fresh produce to life. At lunch, two courses with wine costs €19, or there's a €23 *menu* in the evening. Mon–Fri noon–2.45pm & 7–10.30pm; closed Aug. M° Invalides.

L'Ami Jean 27 rue Malar, 7e ☎01.47.05.86.89. Good, hearty French and Basque (*paella*, *pipérade*, *poulet basquaise*) food for around €18 for a main course, or €28 for the *menu*. The ambience is cosy, with lots of dark wood, but gets as robust as the food on rugby nights – the owner is a fan. Tues–Sat noon–2.30pm & 7.30–10.30pm. Closed Aug. M° La-Tour-Maubourg.

L'Arpège 84 rue de Varenne, 7e ☎01.45.05.09.06. Alain Passard is one of France's truly great chefs – and he really pushes boundaries at his restaurant by giving vegetables the spotlight, though you'll also find plenty of lobster, foie gras and duck or pigeon on his menus. He can turn a simple hen's egg into a culinary symphony of textures, tastes and temperatures, and dishes such as grilled turnips with chestnuts or duck with black sesame and orange brandy are just astounding. The lunch menu costs €130, while *à la carte* you'll pay €200–300. The incredible *menu dégustation* costs €340 – two of those and you're well over the annual GDP per capita of some countries. Reserve well in advance and dress up. Mon–Fri noon–2.30pm & 8–11pm. M° Varenne.

Au Babylone 13 rue de Babylone, 7e ☎01.45.48.72.13. The gingham paper tablecloths, old lamps and pictures, and hanging flower baskets give this little restaurant buckets of old-fashioned charm. The *menu* – €19.50 for the set three-courser – is similarly unreconstructed, with good meaty classics such as *andouillette*, *blanquette de veau* and *roti de porc*. Mon–Sat noon–2pm; closed Aug. M° Sèvres-Babylone.

Au Bon Accueil 14 rue de Monttessuy, 7e ☎01.47.05.46.11. Huddled in the shadow of the Eiffel Tower, rue de Monttesuy is something of a gastro-street, and this is one of the most enjoyable restaurants on it. In a relaxed, modern wine-bistrot setting, you might enjoy well-turned-out dishes like a delicate salad of prawns, salmon and lemon verbena, followed by a perfectly cooked veal liver with Jerusalem artichoke purée. Expect to pay €45 with wine. Mon–Fri noon–2.30pm & 7–10.30pm. M° Duroc/Vaneau.

Chez Germaine 30 rue Pierre-Leroux, 7e ⓣ**01.42.73.28.34.** Madame hardly has room to squeeze between the tables, the hatstand and the tiny shelf of wines along the back wall at this charming little family restaurant. On the three-course *menu* (€15) you might have anchovy fillets on potato salad, made with fresh mayonnaise, followed by a meaty pikeperch steak or *tripes à la mode de Caen*. Good-value lunchtime *formule* (€13). Mon–Fri noon–2.30pm & 7–10pm; Sat noon–2.30pm; closed Aug. M° Duroc/Vaneau.

Clos des Gourmets 16 ave Rapp, 7e ⓣ**01.45.51.75.61.** The faintly frumpy classic decor – blue carpet, cream walls, pictures on the walls – belies the friendly welcome at this chef-led restaurant, and the liveliness of the cooking. For €35 (or €29 at weekday lunchtimes) you'll get a spiced velouté of cauliflower with a carpaccio of haddock and nuts, then a roasted Gers chicken with a Corsican jus, finishing with confit fennel in sweet spices and citron sorbet. Tues–Sat noon–2.30pm & 7.30–10.30pm; closed 3 weeks in Aug. RER Pont de l'Alma.

Au Petit Tonneau 20 rue Surcouf, 7e ⓣ**01.47.05.09.01.** Mme Boyer runs this small, friendly, bistrot-style restaurant with panache, cooking delicious traditional French cuisine. Wild mushrooms are a speciality, along with a free-range *coq au vin*. All prices are *à la carte*: under €10 for starters, around €15–20 for mains. Daily noon–3pm & 7–11.30pm. M° Invalides.

Le P'tit Troquet 28 rue de l'Exposition, 7e ⓣ**01.47.05.80.39.** This tiny family restaurant has a discreetly nostalgic feel, with its ornate zinc bar along the back wall topped by an old brass coffeepot. Serves well-judged, traditional, seasonal cuisine to the diplomats of the quartier. On an autumn *menu du marché* (€30) for example, you might find a wild boar terrine or endive tart, followed by *confit* of venison with wild girolles mushrooms or red mullet from Brittany. Mon & Sat 6.30–10.15pm, Tues–Fri noon–2pm & 6.30–10.15pm. M° Ecole Militaire.

Au Pied de Fouet 45 rue de Babylone, 7e ⓣ**01.47.05.12.27.** An atmospheric little place – just four tables and no reservations – where the specials are written up on the mirror. Think home-made *confit* of duck, basil ravioli, or haddock fillet with slivers of cabbage. Under €20 for a full meal. Mon–Fri noon–2.30pm & 7–9pm, Sat noon–2.30pm; closed Sun & Aug. M° St-François-Xavier/Sèvres-Babylone.

Thoumieux 79 rue St-Dominique, 7e ⓣ**01.47.05.49.75.** Cavernous, traditional brasserie replete with mirrors, carved wood, hatstands and bustling, black-and-white-clad waiters. Popular with a smart local clientele for carefully prepared classics, many with a southwestern emphasis, like duck breast, a rich cassoulet or tasty pied de porc. Lunch *menu* at €20 and €30 in the evening, or around €50 *à la carte*. Daily noon–3pm & 7–11pm. M° La-Tour-Maubourg.

La Varangue 27 rue Augereau, 7e ⓣ**01.47.05.51.22.** Also known as Philippe's restaurant, after the proprietor, who presides over the tiny, homely dining room from his minuscule open kitchen. The food ranges from good salads and vegetarian choices – popular with the loyal American clientele – to more traditional mains (around €12) such as *coq au vin* or rabbit in a mustard sauce. Two-course *formule* available for €15.90. Mon–Fri noon–2.30pm & 5.30–9pm (from 6.15pm Wed), Sat & Sun 5.30–9pm. M° Ecole-Militaire.

Montparnasse and southern Paris

Montparnasse and the 14e

Unless otherwise indicated, the listings below are marked on the map on pp.172–173.

Cafés and wine bars

La Closerie des Lilas 171 bd du Montparnasse, 6e. The most ancient Montparnasse café of them all, where the tables are name-plated after celebrated former habitués – Verlaine, Mallarmé, Lenin, Modigliani, Léger, Strindberg… These days it's rather stuffy, incorporating an expensive restaurant in a glass-roofed area, but you can still have a cocktail (€14) or simpler main course (€20) in the older bar-brasserie section, among the gleaming brass rails, tiled floor and dark leather banquettes. Daily noon–1am. RER Port-Royal.

L'Entrepôt 7–9 rue Francis-de-Pressensé, 14e. Arty cinema with a spacious, relaxed café and outside seating in the courtyard. Great Sunday brunch (€22), *plats du jour* for around €13–18, and frequent concerts in the evening. Mon–Sat noon–2am. M° Pernety.

Le Select 99 bd du Montparnasse, 6e. If you want to visit one of the great Montparnasse cafés, as frequented by Picasso, Matisse, Henry Miller and F. Scott Fitzgerald, make it this one. It's the most traditional of them all, the prices aren't over-inflated, and it's on the sunny side of the street. Only the brasserie-style food is disappointing. Daily 7–2am, Fri & Sat till 4am. M° Vavin.

Tea and Tattered Pages 24 rue Mayet, 6e. This secondhand English-language bookshop is rather a long way from anywhere, but inside you can have tea and cakes, speak English and browse through a very good selection of English books. Mon–Sat 11am–7pm; Sun noon–6pm. M° Duroc.

Restaurants

Aquarius 40 rue de Gergovie, 14e
☎01.45.41.36.88. This homely vegetarian restaurant serves wholesome if unspectacular meals to a friendly group of punters. Mobiles hang from the ceiling, the art on the walls is for sale, and there's a tiny kitchen tucked away off the dining room. Main courses such as nut roast, Mexican chilli and lasagne cost around €12, and there's a *menu* at €15 (€11.50 at lunch). Mon–Sat noon–2.30pm & 7.30–11pm; closed three weeks in Aug. M° Pernety/Plaisance.

La Coupole 102 bd du Montparnasse, 14e
☎01.43.20.14.20. The largest and perhaps the most enduringly famous arty-chic Parisian hang-out for dining, dancing and debate. Although now part of the Flo chain of historic brasseries, *La Coupole* remains a genuine institution, buzzing with conversation and clatter from the diners packed in tightly under the high, chandeliered roof. The menu runs from oysters to Welsh rarebit, with plenty of fishy and meaty classics in between; the evening *menu* is priced at €30.50, but you can have two courses for €23.50 at lunchtime and before 6pm and after 10pm. Montparnasse traditions – of a sort – are even kept up with a downstairs nightclub. Daily 8–1am. M° Vavin.

Pavillon Montsouris 20 rue Gazan, 14e
☎01.43.13.29.00. **See map on p.187.** A special treat for summer days. Sit on the terrace or in the elegantly glazed salon overlooking the park, and choose from a menu featuring truffles, foie gras and the divine *pêche blanche rôtie à la glace vanille* (roasted white-flesh peach with vanilla ice cream). Single *menu* at €49. Daily noon–2.30pm & 7.30–10pm; Oct–March closed Sun evening. RER Cité-Universitaire.

Le P'tit Canon 46 rue Raymond Losserand, 14e
☎01.43.21.11.80. A family-run neighbourhood favourite, with a simple decor of fresh flowers and old posters. A loyal, local clientele comes for hearty and well-cooked main dishes like *cassoulet* and *coq au vin*, and a good selection of wines by the glass. Good value at around €10–15 for a main course. Open 7–1am, meals served Mon–Sat noon–3pm & 7.30–10.30pm; closed mid-July to mid-Aug. M° Pernety.

Le Petit Vienne 4 rue Danville, 14e
☎01.40.47.56.81. Relaxed, informal and fresh-feeling restaurant specializing in organic (*biologique*) produce and wines. The prices are a touch elevated – around €20 for mains such as tuna steak with rocket, or pan-fried sea bream – but the set menus are better value, and there's always the inexpensive "*mega salade bio*" and daily pasta dish. Mon–Sat noon–2.30pm & 7.30–10.30pm. M° Denfert-Rochereau.

La Régalade 49 av Jean-Moulin, 14e
☎01.45.45.68.58. Diners at this renowned bistrot are packed cheek-by-jowl onto banquettes and wooden café chairs, and the service can be slow, but that's all part of the joy of this quintessentially old-fashioned place, with its tiled floor and old framed pictures on the walls. Chef Bruno Doucet's dishes sound deceptively simple – beautifully sauced meats, for the most part – but the standard €32 *prix fixe* delivers a memorable meal, and for once the wines aren't marked up with the cooking. Mon 7.30–11.30pm, Tues–Fri noon–2.30pm & 7.30–11.30pm; closed Aug. M° Alésia.

La Rotonde 105 bd du Montparnasse, 6e
☎01.43.26.48.26. One of the grand old Montparnasse establishments, frequented in its time by the full roll call of prewar artists and writers, and of course Lenin and Trotsky. Since those days it has moved well

upmarket, gaining a plush decor of red velvet and brass, and is now best visited for a reliable if pricey French meal, served at almost any time of day or night. Mains cost around €30. Daily 7.15–2am. M° Vavin.

Au Vin des Rues 21 rue Boulard, 14e ☎01.43.22.19.78. This small restaurant and wine bar was once photographer Robert Doisneau's favourite, and it's still charmingly old-fashioned, with tiny tables and rickety wooden chairs. The menu is solid French classics – *andouillette*, *pavé* of salmon, *foie de veau* and so on – and the wines are excellent, specializing in the Beaujolais and Mâconais. Convivial atmosphere, especially on the rowdy accordion and *pot-au-feu* evenings (Thurs). Around €30 a head. Mon–Sat noon–3pm & 7.30–11pm, Sun 7.30–11pm. M° Denfert-Rochereau.

The 15e

The listings below are marked on the map on pp.184–185.

Restaurants

Le Bistrot d'André 232 rue St-Charles, 15e ☎01.45.57.89.14. A reminder of the old Citroën works before the Parc André-Citroën was created, with pictures and models of the classic French car. Homely dishes and great puds. Midday *menu* €13.50, otherwise around €25. Mon–Sat noon–2.30pm & 8–10.30pm. M° Balard.

Le Café du Commerce 51 rue du Commerce, 15e ☎01.45.75.03.27. There aren't quite "a thousand covers", which was the name for this popular brasserie when it opened in 1922, but it's still a buzzing, dramatic place to eat, with the tables set on three storeys of galleries running round a central patio. Honest, high-quality meat is the speciality, with steaks from Limousin cows bought whole, but there's always a fish and vegetarian dish too. Expect to pay €15–20 for a *plat* (€28.90 for the *menu gourmet*). The lunch *menu* is a bargain at €15. Daily noon–3pm & 7pm–midnight. M° Emile-Zola.

L'Os à Moëlle 3 rue Vasco da Gama, 15e ☎01.45.57.27.27. The highlight of chef Thierry Faucher's relaxed bistrot is the €38 *menu*, which brings you six courses showing off the most rewarding side of traditional French cuisine – from Jerusalem artichoke and black truffle soup, via scallops and giant snails to satisfying steaks. There's an inexpensive lunch *menu*, or you could make your way across the road to 181 rue de Lourmel, where *La Cave de l'Os à Moelle* (☎01.45.57.28.88/28) is a no-frills offshoot with two communal tables at which you can enjoy a €20 *menu* of the same exciting food. The ethos is self-service; you help yourself to a steaming pot of stew and cut your own slice of terrine. Reserve well in advance at either. Tues–Sun noon–3pm & 7.30pm–midnight; closed 3 weeks in Aug. M° Lourmel.

The 13e

The listings below are marked on the map on p.187.

Restaurants

Auberge Etchegorry 41 rue Croulebarbe, 13e ☎01.44.08.83.51. Once a *guinguette* on the banks of the Bièvre, now a well-established Basque restaurant, this place has an old-fashioned atmosphere of relaxed conviviality, with hams and garlics hanging from the ceiling next to old copper pans. And the food's good too – lots of duck breast. Expect to pay upwards of €35 a head or go for the €26, €33 or €36 *menus*. Lunch *menu* for €20. Tues–Fri noon–3pm & 7.30–10.30pm; Sat 7.30–10.30pm. M° Gobelins.

L'Avant Goût 37 rue Bobillot, 13e ☎01.45.81.14.06. Small neighbourhood restaurant with a big reputation for excitingly good modern French cuisine – try the richly spicy *pot-au-feu* – and wines to match. Cool, contemporary decor and presentation, with a swish clientele relaxing on bright red leather banquettes. Superb-value lunch *menu* at €14, and evening *menu* at €31. Tues–Sat noon–2.30pm & 7.30–10.45pm; closed three weeks in Aug. M° Place-d'Italie.

Le Bambou 70 rue Baudricourt, 13e ☎01.45.70.91.75. Tiny Asian-quarter restaurant crammed with punters, French and Vietnamese alike, tucking into sublimely fresh-tasting Vietnamese food. Serves giant, powerfully flavoured *pho* soups, packed with beef and noodles (only choose the large version if you really mean it), a full menu of specialities, and the addictive Vietnamese tea and coffee that's made with condensed milk. Last orders at 10.30pm, but you can stay till midnight. Tues–Sun 11.30am–3.30pm & 6.30–10.30pm. M° Tolbiac.

Chez Gladines **30 rue des Cinq-Diamants, 13e ☎01.45.80.70.10.** This tiny, Basque-run corner bistrot is always warm, welcoming and packed with young people. Excellent wines and hearty Basque and southwest dishes – the mashed/fried potato is a must and goes best with *magret de canard*, and there are giant salads for under €9. Less than €20 for a (very) full meal. Mon & Tues noon–3pm & 7pm–midnight; Wed–Sun noon–3pm & 7pm–1am. M° Corvisart.

Chez Paul **22 rue Butte-aux-Cailles, 13e ☎01.45.89.22.11.** A neighbour and rival to *Le Temps des Cerises* (see below), but relatively upmarket. Warm wood is matched with designer cutlery, and the traditional French country food – lots of offal – gets an elegant finish. Such finesse doesn't come cheap: expect to pay around €40. Get there early for an outdoor seat in summer. Daily noon–2.30pm & 7.30pm–midnight. M° Place-d'Italie/Corvisart.

Phuong Hoang **Terrasse des Olympiades, 52 rue du Javelot, 13e ☎01.45.84.75.07.** Take the escalator up from rue Tolbiac to this large, well-known restaurant serving Vietnamese, Thai and Singaporean specialities on a variety of *menus* from €8 and up, all including wine. Not the most stylish of restaurants, but the food is reliable, and the housing-project skyscrapers around the *terrasse* loom overhead like a Modernist architectural fantasy. Daily noon–3pm & 7pm–12.30am. M° Tolbiac.

Le Temps des Cerises **18–20 rue Butte-aux-Cailles, 13e ☎01.45.89.69.48.** Truly welcoming restaurant – it's run as a co-op – with elbow-to-elbow seating and a daily choice of hearty French dishes that ranges from *cassoulet* and black pudding to fillet of ling with artichoke cream. The food can be a bit hit-and-miss, but the atmosphere is perfect. Lunch *menu* at €9.50 and evening *menus* at €14.50 and €22.50 Mon–Fri 11.45am–2.15pm & 7.30–11.45pm; Sat 7.30pm–midnight. M° Place-d'Italie/Corvisart.

Tricotin **Kiosque de Choisy, 15 av de Choisy, 13e ☎01.45.85.51.52 & 01.45.84.74.44.** Tricotin's "kiosque", glazed in like a pair of overgrown fish tanks, is just set back from the broad avenue de Choisy, next to the Chinese-signed McDonald's. Its two restaurants cover much the same ground, and cover it well, but no. 1 (closed Tues) specializes in Thai and grilled dishes, while no. 2 has a longer list of Vietnamese, Cambodian and steamed foods. *Plats complets* cost around €6, but you could multiply dishes and spend around €18. Daily 9am–11.30pm. M° Porte-de-Choisy.

Montmartre and northern Paris

Montmartre

Unless otherwise indicated, the listings are marked on the map on p.194.

Cafés and wine bars

Le Bar du Relais **12 rue Ravignan, 18e.** A quaint building in a beautiful spot just under the Butte, with tables out on the little square where Picasso's Beateau-Lavoir studio used to be. Quiet and atmospheric by day, cool and youthful by night, with an *electronique* playlist. Mon–Thurs 3pm–2am, Fri–Sun noon–2am. M° Abbesses.

Café des Deux Moulins **15 rue Lepic, 18e.** Having seen its heyday of fans on the trawl of Amélie lore (she waited tables here in the film), this diner-style café is back to what it always was: a down-to-earth neighbourhood hang-out, preserved in a bright, charming 1950s interior. Sunday brunch is popular. Mon–Sat 7–2am; Sun 9–2am. M° Blanche.

L'Eté en Pente Douce **23 rue Muller, 18e (cnr rue Paul-Albert) ☎01.42.64.02.67.** An ideal Montmartre lunch or coffee spot, with chairs and tables set out on a terrace alongside the steps leading up to Sacré-Cœur. The food is very good, especially the giant goat's cheese and fig salad; traditional French *plats* cost around €13, but the main reason for coming, summer or winter, is to soak up the pure Montmartre atmosphere. Daily noon–midnight. M° Château-Rouge.

La Fourmi Café **74 rue des Martyrs, 18e.** Trendy, high-ceilinged café-bar full of conscientiously beautiful young Parisians drinking coffee by day and cocktails at night. Snacks and light meals are available at lunchtime. Mon–Thurs 8–2am, Fri & Sat 8–4am, Sun 10–2am. M° Pigalle/Abbesses.

Aux Négociants 27 rue Lambert (cnr rue Custine), 18e ☎01.46.06.15.11. An intimate and friendly *bistrot à vins* with a selection of well-cooked *plats*, homemade *charcuterie* and excellent Loire wines by the glass. It's wise to book if you plan to eat – count on around €25 for a full meal. The clientele is resolutely local, with a smattering of arty-intellectual types. Mon noon–2.30pm, Tues–Fri noon–2.30pm & 7.30–10.30pm; closed Aug. M° Château-Rouge.

Le Progrès 1 rue Yvonne Le Tac, 18e. Generous glazed windows overlook this crossroads at the heart of Abbesses, making this café something of a lighthouse for the young *bobos* (bourgeois-bohemians) of Montmartre. By day a simple, relaxed café serving reasonably priced meals and salads (€12–15), at night it turns into a pub-like venue. The café *Le Carrousel*, opposite, boasts a south-facing terrace for sunny days. Daily 9–2am. M° Abbesses/Anvers.

Le Sancerre 35 rue des Abbesses, 18e. A fashionable hang-out for the young and trendy of all nationalities under the southern slope of Montmartre, with a row of outside tables perfect for watching the world go by. The food can be disappointing, though. Daily 8–2am. M° Abbesses.

Un Zèbre a Montmartre 38 rue Lepic, 18e. Welcoming little bar, with a restaurant somehow crammed in alongside, which serves simple, inexpensive food till late (around 11pm). There's a non-smoking room and a young, friendly and predominantly local clientele. No credit cards. Mon–Sat 9–2am, Sun 10–2am. M° Abbesses.

Restaurants

Le XVIIIème Barathym 2 rue Ramey, 18e ☎01.42.54.61.31. Chef Cid Dugast cooks up appetizing salads, meats and apple-banana *tartes tatins*, all with a distinct Provençale flavour. Music is either jazz, groove or local *chanteuses*, and there is brunch on weekends. You shouldn't pay much more than €20 for a full meal with wine. Lunch menu €12.50. Daily noon–2.30pm and 7pm–2am. M° Jules-Joffrin.

L'Entracte 44 rue d'Orsel, 18e ☎01.46.06.93.41. Tucked down beside the Charles Dullin theatre, this is a taste of old Montmartre, the friendly owner presiding over a tiny room filled with paintings and pot plants accumulated over the last few decades. The food is homely in the proper sense – everything is prepared fresh – and there's a good choice of honest French starters (around €9), from pâté to crudités via marinated mackerel. The list of mains (€17–28) is admirably short, including just a single fish dish, a single *plat du jour*, and a few steaks. Wed–Sat noon–2pm & 7–10pm, Sun noon–2pm. M° Abbesses/Anvers.

Au Grain de Folie 24 rue La Vieuville, 18e ☎01.42.58.15.57. Tiny, simple and colourfully dilapidated vegetarian place. All the food is inexpensive and organic and there's always a vegan option. Tues–Sat 12.30–2.30pm & 7.30–10.30pm, Sun 12.30–2.30pm. M° Abbesses.

L'Homme Tranquille 81 rue des Martyrs, 18e ☎01.42.54.56.28. This genuine, old-fashioned bistrot has been in the same family for three generations. It feels like it, too, with its old posters and atmospherically nicotine-coloured paint. The €26 *menu* includes delicious, imaginative French dishes such as chicken in honey, coriander and lemon. Mon–Sat 7.30–11.30pm; closed Aug. M° Abbesses.

Kokolion 62 rue d'Orsel, 18e ☎01.42.58.24.41. In business for over 35 years, this classic theatre restaurant is owned by a very friendly patron who's done up the walls with headshots of French theatre greats, many of whom have dined at these very candlelit tables. Still frequented by theatregoers, stagehands and leading actors alike, the atmosphere is perfect for a pre-show date at one of the two theatres nearby. Traditional French *menu* for €24. Tues–Sat 7pm–1am, closed Aug. M° Anvers.

Le Mono 40 rue Véron, 18e ☎01.46.06.99.20. Welcoming, family-run Togolese restaurant. Mains (around €10) are mostly grilled fish or meat served with sour, hot sauces – try the delicious *akoboudessi* – a fried African fish in sauce with rice or cassava meal on the side. Starters (€5) include a Scotch Bonnet-rich stuffed crab, and desserts are simple and rewarding – think rum-flambéed bananas. Enjoyable but uninsistent Afro atmosphere, with Afro-print tablecloths, soukous on the stereo and Togolese carvings on the walls. Daily except Wed 7.30–11pm. M° Abbesses.

A la Pomponnette 42 rue Lepic, 18e ☎01.46.06.08.36. A genuine old Montmartre bistrot, with posters, drawings and zinc-top bar. The traditional French food is excellent, with a *menu* at €32; otherwise it will cost you €35–50 *à la carte*. Tues–Thurs noon–2.30pm & 7–11pm, Fri & Sat noon–2.30pm & 7pm–midnight. Mon–Sat 11.30am–1pm & 7–11pm. M° Blanche/Abbesses.

Refuge des Fondus 17 rue des Trois Frères, 18e ⓣ01.42.55.22.65. The €16 *menu* here gets you a hearty fondue – Bourguignonne (meat) or Savoyarde (cheese) – and your personal *biberon*, or baby bottle, full of wine. This idea is unflaggingly popular with a raucous young Parisian crowd, who squeeze onto the banquette tables between the zanily graffitied walls. Daily 7pm–2am. M° Abbesses.

Le Relais Gascon 6 rue des Abbesses, 18e ⓣ01.42.58.58.22. Serving hearty, filling meals all day, this two-storey restaurant (upstairs is cosier but smoky) provides a welcome blast of straightforward Gascon heartiness in this alternately trendy, run-down and touristy part of town. The enormous hot salads cost €10.50, and there are equally tasty *plats* for around €12, plus a good-value lunch *menu* at €14. Daily 10–2am. M° Abbesses.

Le Restaurant 32 rue Véron, 18e ⓣ01.42.23.06.22. Welcoming, reliable corner restaurant whose decor and clientele seem to follow the same fashion for distressed, arty chic. There are a few adventurous flavours, but most of the food is surprisingly homely, and comes in good-sized portions. The two-course *menu* costs just under €20. Mon–Fri 12.30–2.30pm & 7.30pm–midnight, Sat 7.30–11.30pm. M° Abbesses.

Au Virage Lepic 61 rue Lepic, 18e ⓣ01.42.52.46.79. The pink gingham napkins draped over the lamps, the photos of movie stars on the walls and camp 1970s tracks quietly playing on the hi-fi are clues that this isn't quite the classic old bistrot it otherwise appears to be. The warm welcome is old-fashioned, however, as is the cosy atmosphere (tables are very close together) and satisfyingly good *cuisine bourgeoise*, with a two-course *menu* at €18. Daily except Tues 7pm–2am. M° Blanche/Abbesses.

The 9e

The listings below are marked on the map on p.194.

Restaurants

L'Alsaco 10 rue Condorcet, 9e ⓣ01.45.26.44.31. A real Alsatian *winstub* serving the traditional dishes and wines of Alsace with a warm welcome. The two *menus* (at €20 & €32) come with carefully chosen beers and lots of cheese. Mon & Sat 7pm–midnight, Tues–Fri noon–2.15pm & 7pm–midnight; closed mid-July through Aug. M° Poissonnière.

Le Bistro des Deux-Théâtres 18 rue Blanche, 9e ⓣ01.45.26.41.43. Classic luvvie hang-out serving particularly good *cuisine bourgeoise* in a long, plush dining room decorated with actors' photos and usually full of chatty Parisians. The €34 all-in *menu* includes an apéritif, half a bottle of wine and coffee. Daily 11.30am–2.30pm & 7pm–12.30am. M° Trinité.

Casa Olympe 48 rue St-Georges, 9e ⓣ01.42.85.26.01. As a female chef running her own bistrot, Dominique Versini, aka Olympe, finds herself in what is still an unusual position in Paris, but she's more than equal to the challenge. And at under €40, the set *menu* is a bargain for serious cooking like this. Some bold meats are featured – from veal foot to pig's head via spiced pigeon breast – with powerful Corsican sauces and accents. The ambience is classy but not stuffy, with leather banquettes down one wall and a blackboard list of daily specials. Mon–Fri noon–2pm & 8–11pm. Closed Aug. M° St-Georges.

Haynes 3 rue Clauzel, 9e ⓣ01.48.78.40.63. There's a long tradition of black Americans in Paris, ever since jazz and Josephine Baker, and ever since black GIs found themselves more welcome here than at home. This restaurant has been going since the 1940s, serving generous quantities of rich and heavy soul food like honey chicken (€15). Despite the grotto-like decor, the atmosphere is warm, and as there's blues or jazz most nights from around 8pm, you could just stop by here in the evening for a glass of house wine to catch a set. *A la carte* only, at around €35, with wine. Tues–Sat 7pm–midnight. M° St-Georges.

Velly 52 rue Lamartine, 9e ⓣ01.48.78.60.05. Excellent modern French cooking in an intimate bistrot setting with little pretension. You can choose from any of the dishes on the blackboard, which change daily. The sole *menu* costs €23 at lunchtime and €31 in the evening, and there are good wines for around €20. Mon–Fri noon–2.30pm & 7.30–10.45pm, Sat 7.30–11pm; closed three weeks in Aug. M° Notre-Dame-de-Lorette.

The 10e and Goutte d'Or

The listings below are marked on the map on p.204.

Cafés and wine bars

L'Enchotte 11 rue de Chabrol, 10e. A pleasantly ramshackle wine bar opposite the St-Quentin market, with tobacco-stained paintwork and a simple tiled floor. Cheese and *charcuterie* at around €10, as well as more substantial dishes and a menu for €18.50. Mon–Fri noon–2.30pm & 7.30–10.30pm; closed last two weeks of Aug. M° Gare-de-l'Est.

Le Réveil du Dixième 35 rue du Château-d'Eau, 10e. A welcoming, unpretentious wine bar opposite the covered market. Serves inexpensive glasses of wine, *casse-croûte* plates of ham or cheese (€5–10), and honest *plats* like *andouille* or *cuisse de canard*. Mon–Sat 7.15am–9pm. M° Château-d'Eau.

Restaurants

Chez Arthur 25 rue du Faubourg-St-Martin, 10e ⓣ01.42.08.34.33. Low lamps and red walls give this long-established restaurant a cosy boudoir feel. Popular with theatregoers and actors – whose photos deck the walls – especially for post-theatre dining. The cuisine is careful and generously portioned; on the €22 two-course *menu* you might have a leek fondante topped with a poached egg, then a creamily rich dish of prawns *à l'Armoricaine* served with basmati rice. An extra €5 gets you a delicious, hearty pudding. Tues–Fri noon–2.30pm & 7–11.30pm; Mon & Sat 7–11.30pm. M° Strasbourg-St-Denis.

Chez Casimir 6 rue de Belzunce, 10e ⓣ01.48.78.28.80. Thierry Breton, chef-owner of the excellent, French-Breton bistrot *Chez Michel*, two doors down, at no. 10 (ⓣ01.44.53.06.20), runs this little bistrot on the side as a no-frills version. In basic, unrenovated café surroundings you can enjoy inexpensive but well-sourced and well-cooked dishes. You might be brought an entire *terrine de porc*, from which to help yourself, for example, then enjoy succulent wild boar steaks or a rich *coq au vin* – all for €22 at lunch or €29 in the evening. At *Chez Michel*, you'll pay another €10 for cosier decor and a more adventurous, Breton-flavoured *menu*. Mon 7.30–10.30pm, Tues–Fri noon–2pm & 7.30–10.30pm. M° Gare-du-Nord.

Flo 7 cour des Petites-Ecuries, 10e ⓣ01.47.70.13.59. Hidden away down what was once Louis XIV's stableyard, this old-time Alsatian brasserie is so handsome that even the exceptionally slow service and crammed-in clientele can't quite spoil the theatrical experience. You're served (or not served) by old-fashioned waiters in ankle-length aprons. Fish and seafood form the backbone of the menu – look out for the winter specialities of hot oysters in champagne sauce, and salt pork with lentils. It's not cheap or particularly sophisticated, but there's a reasonably priced *menu* at €30.50, or €22.50 at lunchtimes (except Sun). Daily noon–3pm & 7pm–1.30am. M° Château-d'Eau.

Julien 16 rue du Faubourg-St-Denis, 10e ⓣ01.47.70.12.06. Part of the same enterprise as *Flo* (see above), with an even more splendid decor – all globe lamps, hatstands, white linen, brass and polished wood, with frescoes of flowery Art Deco maidens surveying the scene. The cuisine is similar to *Flo*'s, minus the seafood, and with a few seasonal specialities. Again, it's not a place for a cosy, romantic meal, but the surroundings provide a real feeling of spectacle. Daily noon–3pm & 7–1am. M° Strasbourg-St-Denis.

Le Martel 3 rue Martel, 10e ⓣ01.47.70.67.56. Aimed at the trendy loft-living types who have recently moved into the quartier, *Le Martel* has a smart, classic French bistrot decor of zinc bar, polished wood banquettes and dark cream walls, with ultra-low lighting and soft, sometimes trancey music adding stylish touches. The menu is mainly North African, with lots of salads and a few meaty French staples. Couscous is good but pricey, and there's more opportunity for culinary flair with the savoury-sweet *pastilla* or the tagines. Mon–Fri noon–2.30pm & 8–11pm, Sat 11.30pm. M° Château-d'Eau.

Pooja 91 passage Brady, 10e ⓣ01.48.24.00.83, ⓦwww.poojarestaurant.com. Located in a glazed *passage* that is Paris's own slice of the Indian subcontinent, *Pooja* is slightly pricier and sometimes slightly more elaborate than its many neighbours. Lunch *formule* for €12; evening *menu* for around €20. Daily noon–3pm & 7–11pm. M° Strasbourg-St-Denis/Château-d'Eau.

Terminus Nord 23 rue de Dunkerque, 10e ☎01.42.85.05.15. Step off the train and straight into 1920s Paris at this luxurious brasserie. Staff can be brusque and the prices fairly high (at around €40 for a full meal, though there's a fair-value *menu* at €30.50) but the decor is sumptuous – Art Deco lamps, mirrored walls and red leather banquettes under a lofty ceiling – and the food usually pretty good, unless you're eating at a peculiar time of day. Daily 11–1am. M° Gare-du-Nord.

Batignolles

The listings below are marked on the map on p.207.

Cafés and wine bars

L'Endroit 67 place Félix-Lobligeois, 17e. A smartish but youthful neighbourhood café and late-night bar, with a *terrasse* overlooking the attractive square. Daily noon–2am. M° Rome/Brochant.

Restaurants

Bistral 80 rue Lemercier, 17e ☎01.42.63.59.61. *Cuisine d'appellation contrôlée* is the rubric here, or carefully sourced foods. They're imaginatively cooked too – the blackboard menu changes daily but you might find lamb loin with a shrimp crust (delicious) or *andouille* in a pepper butter. Locals love the relaxed, modern bistrot atmosphere, so be sure to book. Mon–Fri noon–2.30pm & 7.30–10.30pm, Sat 7.30–11pm. M° Place-de-Clichy.

Fuxia 69 place du Docteur Félix-Lobligeois, 17e ☎01.42.28.07.79. The food at this urban-styled but unpretentious Italian café-deli chain is excellent value: unfussy, filling and very fresh, with lots of vegetarian choices. Choose from the blackboard list of pasta and salad specials, or go for the giant bruschetta and antipasti platter, served on a wooden board. Daily 9am–midnight. M° Rome/Brochant.

Le Morosophe 83 rue Legendre, 17e ☎01.53.06.82.82. Relaxed contemporary bistrot serving unpretentious, well-cooked seasonal dishes. Lunchtime *menu* at €12, evenings at €20. Mon–Sat noon–2.30pm & 7–11pm. M° Brochant.

Wepler 14 place de Clichy, 18e ☎01.45.22.53.24. Now over a hundred years old, and still a beacon of conviviality amid the hustle of place de Clichy. Its clientele has moved upmarket since it was depicted in Truffaut's *Les 400 Coups*, but as palatial brasseries go *Wepler* has remained unashamedly *populaire*. Serves honest brasserie fare and classic seafood platters (€40–45 *à la carte*). Daily noon–1am, café from 8am. M° Place-de-Clichy.

The Bastille and around

The listings below are marked on the map on pp.212–213.

The Bastille

Cafés and wine bars

L'Armagnac 104 rue de Charonne, 11e. This unpretentious café-bar makes a great spot for a daytime coffee, lunchtime snack or drinks (around €3) well into the night. Mon–Fri 7.30–2am, Sat 10–2am, Sun 10am–midnight. M° Charonne.

Café des Anges 66 rue de la Roquette, 11e. A friendly, scruffy corner café hung with old photos, great for cheap and filling dishes of chips and burgers, salads and quiches and a popular place for evening drinks. Mon–Sat 8–2am. M° Bastille.

Café de l'Industrie 16 rue St-Sabin, 11e. One of the best Bastille cafés, packed out at lunch and every evening. Rugs on the floor around solid old wooden tables, mounted rhinoceros heads, old black-and-white photos on the walls and a young, unpretentious crowd enjoying the comfortable absence of minimalism. *Plats du jour* around €14. Daily 10–2am. M° Bastille.

Pause Café 41 rue de Charonne, cnr rue Keller, 11e. Or maybe "Pose Café" – given its popularity with the quartier's young and fashionable who bag the pavement tables at lunch and aperitif time. *Plats du jour* around €11. Mon–Sat 8–2am, Sun 8.45am–8pm. M° Ledru-Rollin.

△ Pause Café, the Bastille

Restaurants

Le Bistrot du Peintre 116 av Ledru-Rollin, 11e ☎01.47.00.34.39. A charming, traditional bistrot, where small tables are jammed together beneath faded Art Nouveau frescoes and wood panelling. The emphasis is on hearty Auvergne cuisine, with *plats* for around €12. Mon–Sat 7–2am, Sun 10am–8pm. M° Ledru-Rollin.

Bofinger 7 rue de la Bastille, 4e ☎01.42.72.87.82. This popular fin-de-siècle brasserie, with its splendid, perfectly preserved coloured glass coupole, is frequented by Bastille Opera-goers and tourists. Specialities are seafood, and steaming dishes of sauerkraut, set over a burner to keep it hot. Set menu for €30.50. Mon–Fri noon–3pm & 6.30pm–1am, Sat & Sun noon–11pm. M° Bastille.

Chez Paul 13 rue de Charonne, cnr rue de Lappe, 11e ☎01.47.00.34.57. Wonky corner building housing a small restaurant which preserves the faded colours and furnishings of an older Bastille, right down to the black-and-white tiles on the floor. The young customers who pack the place out, however, have a distinctly contemporary style. Food is traditional and affordable, the ambience very congenial. Mains from €13. Booking advised. Daily noon–2.30pm & 7.15pm–12.30am. M° Bastille.

Jacques-Mélac 42 rue Léon-Frot, 11e ☎01.43.70.59.27. Some way off the beaten track (between Père-Lachaise and place Léon-Blum) but a highly respected and very popular *bistrot à vins* set in an oak-beamed former greengrocer's, whose patron even makes his own wine – the solitary vine winds round the front of the shop – and plays host to some renowned fêtes when grapes are harvested. The food, wines and atmosphere are great. Mains around €14, midday *menu* at €14.50. Tues–Sat 9am–4pm & 7.45–11pm; closed Aug. M° Charonne.

Paris-Hanoï 74 rue de Charonne, 11e ☎01.47.00.47.59. A cheap Vietnamese restaurant drawing a youngish, trendy crowd, and busy at lunch and dinner serving soups, noodles and nems. Count on around €13 a head for a full meal. No credit cards. Mon–Sat noon–2.30pm & 7–10.30pm; closed Aug. M° Charonne.

Le Petit Keller 13 rue Keller, 11e ☎01.47.00.12.97. A colourful restaurant, with decorative tiled floor and art exhibitions on the walls, serving very affordable food. The decor may be modern but the food is traditional home-cooking – main dishes like rabbit with prunes, and *terrine de campagne* for starters. *Menu* €19. Tues–Sat noon–2.30pm & 7.30–11pm; closed Sun & Mon. M° Ledru-Rollin/Bastille.

Waly Fay 6 rue Godefroy-Cavaignac, 11e ☎01.40.24.17.79. A West African restaurant with a cosy, stylish atmosphere, the dim lighting, rattan and old, faded photographs creating an intimate, faintly colonial ambience. Smart, young black and white Parisians come here to dine on perfumed, richly spiced stews and other West African delicacies at a moderate cost (mains around €13). Mon–Fri noon–2pm & 7.30–11pm, Sun brunch noon–5pm; closed two weeks in Aug. M° Charonne/Faidherbe-Chaligny.

The Faubourg St-Antoine and around

Cafés and wine bars

Le Baron Rouge 1 rue Théophile-Roussel, cnr place d'Aligre market, 12e. Also known affectionately as *Le Baron Bouge*, this popular *bar à vins* is as close as you'll find to the spit-on-the-floor, saloon stereotype of the old movies. Many shoppers and *commerçants* repair here for a light lunch or aperitif after visiting the place d'Aligre market, especially on Sun. If it's crowded inside you can join the locals on the pavement and stand around the wine barrels lunching on *saucisson*, mussels or Cap Ferrat oysters washed down with a glass of Muscadet; *verres* start at €1.40. All in all, one of those very Paris experiences. Tues–Fri 10am–2pm & 5–10pm, Sat 10am–10pm, Sun 10.30am–3.30pm. M° Ledru-Rollin.

La Ruche à Miel 19 rue d'Aligre, 12e. The mouthwatering array of pistachio, almond, walnut and honey cakes at the entrance to this little Algerian tea shop, on the rue d'Aligre market street, entices in many a passer-by. The best accompaniment to the cakes is mint tea, made with real mint and served in the traditional way. Seating is at low brass tables with comfy benches and pouffes. Around €8 for tea and two cakes. Tues–Sun 9am–7.30pm. M° Ledru-Rollin.

Restaurants

Bistrot Paul Bert 18 rue Paul Bert, 11e ☎01.43.72.24.01. A quintessential Parisian bistrot, with menu chalked up on the board, little wooden tables and white tablecloths, tobacco-stained ceiling, and old posters and paintings on the mustard-coloured walls. A mix of locals and visitors flock here for the cosy, friendly ambience and high-quality simple fare such as poulet rôti as well as more sophisticated dishes such as guineafowl and morel mushrooms. Save room if you can for one of the substantial desserts, such as the perfectly cooked Grand Marnier soufflé. There's a lunch menu at €16 and dinner menu at €32, with a few supplements, and the wine list is reasonably priced, with an excellent selection of familiar and rarer vintages. Reservations advised for dinner. Tues–Sat noon–2pm & 7.30–11pm; closed three weeks in Aug. M° Faidherbe-Chaligny.

L'Encrier 55 rue Traversière, 11e ☎01.44.68.08.16. The simple interior of exposed brick walls and wood beams complements the inexpensive, homely fare served up by pleasant, helpful staff in this little restaurant near the Viaduc des Arts. The food has a slight southwestern influence and might include goose breast in honey or steak and morel mushrooms. Lunchtime *menu* €14, *menus* at €19 and €23 in the evening, and a pichet of wine €3.50. Mon–Fri noon–2.15pm & 7.30–11pm, Sat 7.30–11pm. M° Ledru-Rollin.

Le Mansouria 11 rue Faidherbe-Chaligny, 11e ☎01.43.71.00.16. An excellent and elegant Moroccan restaurant dishing up superb couscous and tagines. *Menu* €30, mains around €17. Noon–2pm & 7.30–11.30pm; closed Sun and lunchtime on Mon & Tues, and a fortnight in Aug. M° Faidherbe-Chaligny.

Le Square Trousseau 1 rue Antoine Vollon, 12e ☎01.43.43.06.00. A handsome belle époque brasserie with a regularly changing menu featuring excellent New French cuisine and a couple of old standbys like *pot-au-feu* and *steak au poivre*. Lunch *menu* for €20, evening €25; *à la carte* you'll pay around €35 excluding wine. You can also eat at midday in their little wine-tasting annex next door, hung with haunches of ham and lined with wine bottles; here you get a *plat du jour* for around €14 and wine by the glass from €3.50. Booking recommended for the restaurant in the evening. Tues–Sat noon–3pm & 8–11.30pm; closed in Aug. M° Ledru-Rollin.

Le Temps au Temps 13 rue Paul Bert, 11e ☎01.43.79.63.40. Booked out every night, this tiny bistrot with barely ten tables attracts a loyal following for its inventive cooking at very affordable prices. Offerings might include Saint-Pierre fish with lentils and mango, or squid ink risotto with clams. Dominating the dining room is a giant gold clock, a tribute to its former incarnation as a clock showroom, though you're unlikely to notice the time passing with such excellent food to attend to. Lunchtime *menu* at €16, evening €30. Wines by the glass from €3.50. Tues–Sat noon–2pm & 8–10.30pm, closed Aug.

The Promenade Plantée and Bercy

Cafés and wine bars

T pour 2 Bercy village, 23 Cour Saint Emilion, 12e. **See map on p.218.** The old stone walls of this coolly converted wine warehouse in Bercy combine with contemporary furnishings to create an attractive and relaxed interior, though the screens showing Fashion TV are a bit distracting. They serve 40 types of teas and 25 different coffees from all over the world, as well as flavoured vodkas and rums, and light snacks, or more substantial fare at lunch and dinner. Evenings hot up with music and often a DJ. Daily 10–2am. M° Cour-Saint-Emilion.

Le Viaduc Café 43 av Daumesnil, 12e ⓣ01.44.74.70.70. In one of the Viaduc des Arts' converted railway arches, with seating outside in nice weather. Makes a good spot for a drink if you've been walking the Promenade Plantée or perusing the nearby galleries. The three-course Sunday jazz brunch (€26) from noon to 4pm is popular, if a bit overpriced. Daily 8–2am (food served till midnight). M° Gare-de-Lyon.

Restaurants

Le Train Bleu Gare de Lyon, 12e ⓣ01.43.43.09.06, ⓦwww.le-train-bleu.com. It would be hard to imagine a better prelude to a journey down to the sunny Côte d'Azur than a meal at *Le Train Bleu*, but a halt at this sumptuous belle époque establishment is a must even if you're not going anywhere. The decor is straight out of a bygone golden era – everything drips with gilt, and chandeliers hang from high ceilings frescoed with scenes from the Paris–Lyon–Marseilles train route; to add to the spectacle, huge windows give onto the arriving and departing trains below. The traditional French cuisine has a hard time living up to all this, but is more than acceptable, if a tad overpriced. Set menu is €48, including half a bottle of wine; à la carte reckon on €70. If you just want a glimpse at the decor you could go for a coffee and petits fours (€8), or take a drink in the comfy bar. Restaurant: daily 11.30am–3pm & 7–11pm. Bar: Mon–Fri 7.30am–11pm, Sat & Sun 9am–11pm. M° Gare-de-Lyon.

Eastern Paris

The Canal St-Martin and place de la République

The listings below are marked on the map on pp.224–225.

Cafés and wine bars

L'Atmosphère 49 rue Lucien-Sampaix, 10e. Lively café-bar with decent evening *plats*, on a pleasant corner beside the Canal St-Martin. Tables on the towpath on sunny days, and occasional live music on Sun, with an alternative flavour. Tues–Fri 11–2am, Sat 5.30pm–2am. M° Gare-de-l'Est.

Chez Prune 36 rue Beaurepaire, 10e ⓣ01.42.41.30.47. Popular with a media and artsy crowd, this is a very friendly and laid-back café with smiley waiting staff and pleasant outdoor seating overlooking the canal. Lunchtime dishes cost around €13; evening snacks like platters of cheese or *charcuterie* are around €9; beer €3. Mon–Sat 8am–2am & Sun 10am–2am. M° Jacques-Bonsergent.

Le Clown Bar 114 rue Amelot, 11e ⓣ01.43.55.87.35. An attractive and popular wine bistrot with a beautifully tiled interior depicting the antics of clowns, appropriately enough, since it's located near the Cirque d'Hiver and attracts a circus clientele come the colder months. *Plats du jour*, such as *sauté de boeuf minute au paprika*, for around €12. No credit cards. Daily except Sun lunch noon–2.30pm & 7pm–midnight, closed mid-Aug. M° Filles-du-Calvaire.

Restaurants

Astier 44 rue Jean-Pierre-Timbaud, 11e ⓣ01.43.57.16.35. Very successful and popular restaurant with simple decor, unstuffy atmosphere, and food renowned for its freshness and refinement. You might start with the rich and intense *fois gras de canard*, followed by roast guineafowl served in a casserole dish. Perhaps the highlight, though, of a meal here is the outstanding selection of perfectly ripe cheeses, passed from table to table on a huge platter, from which you just help yourself. There's a good selection of wine, with bottles starting at €22. Service can be slightly uneven and you may have to ask what the day's specials are. It's wise to book; lunch is often less crowded (€21.50 *menu*) and just as enjoyable. Evening *menu* at €29.50. Daily 12.15–2.15pm & 7.30–10.30pm; closed Aug. M° Parmentier.

L'Auberge Pyrénées Cévennes 106 rue de la Folie Méricourt, 11e ⓣ01.43.57.33.78. Make sure you come hungry to this friendly family-run little place serving hearty portions of country cuisine. Highly recommended are the garlicky *moules marinières* for starters and the superb *cassoulet*, served in its own copper pot. Around €30 a head *à la carte*.

Noon–2pm & 7–11pm, closed Sat lunch and all day Sun. M° République.

Chez Imogène **cnr rue Jean-Pierre-Timbaud and rue du Grand-Prieuré, 11e ☎01.48.07.14.59.** An excellent and friendly little crêperie. The good-value three-course €15 dinner *menu* includes a *kir breton* (cassis with cider instead of white wine or champagne). It's best to book for the evening. Open till 10.30pm; closed all day Sun & lunchtime on Mon. M° Oberkampf.

Ile de Gorée **70 rue Jean-Pierre-Timbaud, 11e ☎01.43.38.97.69.** A small West African place with colourful decor and musicians serenading the tables with guitars. Try the spicy stuffed crab for starters, followed by the filling Colombo Cabri, curried goat stewed with carrots and aubergines. Mains cost around €15. Mon–Sat 7pm–midnight. M° Couronnes.

Au Rendez-Vous de la Marine **14 quai de la Loire, 19e ☎01.42.49.33.40.** **See map on p.228.** Busy, successful old-time restaurant on the east bank of the Bassin de la Villette – but no water view – renowned for its meats and desserts and copious portions all round. A really good meal for €25–30, lunch *menu* for €12. Tables are rather close together, and sociable clientele means that you might make some friends. Booking advised. Tues–Sat noon–2pm & 8–10.30pm. M° Jaurès.

Restaurant de Bourgogne **26 rue des Vinaigriers, 10e ☎01.46.07.07.91.** Homely, old-fashioned, good-value bistrot serving French classics, including snails and frogs' legs. Midday *menu* at €9 and evening *menu* at €16.50. Still has a strong local character despite the changing nature of the area. Book ahead for Sat eve. Mon–Fri noon–2.15pm & 7.30–11pm, Sat 7.30–11pm; closed last week July to third week Aug. M° Jacques-Bonsergent.

Le Sporting **3 rue des Récollets, 10e ☎01.46.07.02.00.** Modern, pan-European dishes like tartare of turbot, pesto ravioli and osso bucco are served to young cosmopolites at this new resto-bar. The food is comforting rather than special, but it's a good, dark spot for dates – be sure to try out their large cocktail menu. Count on €30 without wine. Daily noon–11.30pm. M° Gare-de-l'Est.

Belleville, Oberkampf and Ménilmontant

Unless otherwise indicated, the listings below are marked on the map on pp.224–225.

Cafés and wine bars

Café Chéri **44 bd de la Villette, 19e.** See p.359.

Le Cannibale Café **93 rue Jean-Pierre Timbaud, 11e.** See p.359.

La Caravane **35 rue de la Fontaine-aux-Rois, 11e.** See p.359.

Aux Folies **8 rue de Belleville, 20e.** *Aux Folies* offers a real slice of Belleville life; its outside terrace and long brass bar, with mirrored tiles and red neon lights, are packed day and night with a mixed crowd of North Africans, Chinese, students and artists. Beer €3.50, cocktails €4.50. Daily 6.30–1am. M° Belleville.

La Mère Lachaise **78 bd Ménilmontant, 20e ☎01.47.97.61.60.** The sunny terrace of this trendy bar/restaurant, popular with students and *bobos* (bourgeois-bohemians), makes a good place for a drink after a visit to Père-Lachaise, or check out its cosy interior bar, with retro-chic decor of painted wood and wrought-iron lamps. The restaurant serves classic dishes at affordable prices (best to book on weekends). Mon–Sat 8–2am, Sun 9–1am. M° Père-Lachaise.

Restaurants

Le Baratin **3 rue Jouye-Rouve, 20e ☎01.43.49.39.70.** Friendly, down-to-earth *bistrot à vins* with a good mix of locals of different ages. Fine selection of lesser-known wines, mostly under €30, and whiskies. Midday *menu* €15, around €30 in the evenings. Tues–Fri noon–1am, Sat 8pm–1am; closed first week Jan & three weeks in Aug. M° Pyrénées/Belleville.

Le Châteaubriand **129 av Parmentier, 11e ☎01.43.57.45.95.** Innovative Basque chef and rising star of the Paris dining scene, Inaki Aizpitarte has shaken up this vintage bistrot and turned it into an avant-garde dining room that's booked out every evening. The lunch menu at €14 is fairly straightforward; it's at dinner that Aizpitarte gives his creativity free range and concocts dishes such as mackerel ceviche with pear sorbet, oyster soup with red fruits and beetroot. Reckon on around €40 for dinner, and be sure to book. Tues–Fri noon–2pm & 8–10.30pm, Sat 8–10.30pm. M° Goncourt.

Lao Siam **49 rue de Belleville, 19e ☎01.40.40.09.68.** The surroundings are nothing special, but the excellent Thai and Lao food, popular with locals, makes up for it. Dishes from €8. Best to book in advance.

Mon–Fri noon–3pm & 6–11.30pm, Sat & Sun noon–12.30am. M° Belleville.

Le Villaret 19 rue Ternaux, 11e ⓣ01.43.57.89.76. Unlikely though it may seem, this unassuming-looking place, with simple brick and wood-timbered interior, on a scruffy back-street just off rue Oberkampf, does some of the best creative bistrot cuisine in the capital and draws diners from the other end of Paris. The menu changes daily, but typical dishes are roasted country chicken in Arbois wine sauce and root vegetables in rich stock with foie gras. The exceptional wine list runs to some five hundred vintages (starting from €14). Prices are very reasonable considering the quality; you can get lunchtime *formules* at €21 and €26, or go all out for the €50 five-course *menu dégustation* in the evening; *à la carte* costs €30–50. Mon–Fri 12.15–2pm & 7.30pm–midnight, Sat 7.30pm–1am. M° Parmentier.

Le Zéphyr 1 rue Jourdain, 20e ⓣ01.46.36.65.81. Trendy but relaxed 1930s-style bistrot, with mirrors, frescoes and dark-red leather benches at closely packed tables. You'll pay around €13.50 for lunch, €20 for the evening *menu*, for fine traditional cooking. Service is friendly and boisterous, if sometimes uneven. 10am–11.30pm; closed Sat lunch and all day Sun. M° Jourdain.

Western Paris

Auteuil and Passy

Unless otherwise indicated, the listings below are marked on the map on p.244.

Restaurants

Astrance 4 rue Beethoven, 16e ⓣ01.40.50.84.40. Awarded three Michelin stars in 2007, young chef Pascal Barbot's Astrance produces some of the city's most exciting cuisine. The €150 "surprise" menu allows the chef to give full rein to his creativity, and might include avocado and crab ravioli with almond oil; foie gras and mushroom millefeuille with lemon confit and hazelnut oil; or lemongrass and pepper sorbet. The pleasantly contemporary dining room seats only 26 and bookings are notoriously hard to get; try at least a month in advance. Lunch *menus* €70, €115, €150, evening €110–150. Tues–Fri noon–1.45pm & 8–9.45pm; closed Aug. M° Passy.

La Gare 19 Chaussée de la Muette, 16e ⓣ01.42.15.15.31. This renovated train station is now an elegant restaurant-bar serving, among other things, a popular €18 lunch *menu*. You can sit out on the attractive terrace on sunny days. Daily noon–3pm & 7pm–midnight. Bar open noon–2am. M° Muette.

Le Relais du Parc 59 av Raymond Poincaré, 16e ⓣ01.44.05.66.10. See map on pp.76–77. At this chichi restaurant in a chichi area, celebrated chef Alain Ducasse's menu revolves around lobster, beef, vegetables and fruit in imaginative permutations, such as Canadian roasted lobster tail with peas and potatoes, or thin strips of smoked Spanish beef dressed with fennel, onions and shallots. In the summer meals are served outdoors in a lovely garden. Expect to pay €65 for lunch and €130 for dinner – and a lot more if you explore the wine list. Tues–Sat noon–2.30pm & 7.30–10.30pm. M° Victor Hugo.

La Table Lauriston 129 rue Lauriston, 16e ⓣ01.47.27.00.07. See map on pp.76–77. A slightly older, well-off crowd from the neighbourhood usually dines at this traditional bistrot run by chef-to-the-stars Serge Rabey. Game terrine with chanterelle mushrooms and *poularde fondante au vin jaune* (chicken croquettes with Arbois wine) are indicative of the upscale dishes here, and be sure to taste their famed *Baba au Rhum*. You'll easily spend €40–50 per person, but the *cuisine bourgeoise* is excellent. Mon–Fri noon–2.30pm & 7.15–10pm, Sat 7.30–10.30pm. M° Trocadéro.

20

Bars, clubs and live music

Paris's fame as the quintessential home of decadent, hedonistic **nightlife** has endured literally for centuries. As the first decade of the new millennium wears on, that reputation seems only to grow stronger, fuelled by a vibrant **bar and club scene** – much has been learned from the city's energetic gay community – and a world-leading music programme, from rock and world music to jazz and electro-lounge.

The city's strength in **live music** is partly a reflection of its absorption of immigrant and exile populations. Paris has no rivals in Europe for the variety of world music to be discovered; Algerian, West and Central African, Caribbean and Latin American sounds are represented in force. Hip-hop remains fashionable, both imported and home-grown, though you're unlikely to hear it in the city's bars and clubs, where house and techno still rule, mixed in with good-time Mediterranean, Latin and African flavours. For a relaxed taste of the nightlife of the past, head for one of the old suburban eating-and-drinking venues known as *guinguettes* (see p.411).

Jazz fans are in for a treat, too, with all styles from New Orleans to current experimental to be heard. Then there's French **chanson**, a tradition long associated with Paris, particularly during the war years through cabaret artists like Edith Piaf, Maurice Chevalier and Charles Trenet, and in the 1960s with poet-musicians as diverse as Georges Brassens, Jacques Brel and Serge Gainsbourg. Chanson is currently undergoing something of a revival, with excellent showcase evenings in restaurants and bars.

At the end of the chapter are details of all the **major concert venues**, for big-name events. On June 21 the **Fête de la Musique** sees live bands and free concerts of every kind of music throughout the city (see p.381).

Tickets and information

To find out **what's on** you need to get hold of one of the city's **listings magazines** – see "Basics", p.46 for a rundown. If you want more in-depth coverage, try the *Bons Plans* listings (in French) in the monthly magazine *Nova* (Ⓦwww.novaplanet.com). The best way to find out about the latest club nights is to head to a specialist music shop (see p.405), or pick up flyers – or word-of-mouth tips – in one of the city's trendier shops and cafés.

The easiest place to get **tickets** for concerts, whether rock, jazz or chanson (or indeed classical), is at FNAC, whose main branch is

Music on TV and radio

The private TV channel Canal Plus broadcasts big European concerts, while M6 has some late-night music programmes, as well as numerous video clips during the day. Arte, the fifth channel (after 7pm), shows contemporary opera productions and documentaries on all types of music.

Of the local **radio** stations, Radio Nova (101.5 MHz) plays the best cross section of what's new, from house to hip-hop, and broadcasts updates on the latest and coolest club nights, or soirées. Radio France-Mahgreb (99.5 MHz) does raï; FIP (105.1 MHz) has plenty of jazz; Africa Numéro 1 (107.5 MHz) has African music; Oüi FM (102.3 MHz) is the all-day rock radio; techno and house can be heard on the station Radio FG (98.2 MHz); and Radio Classique carries classical music (101.1 MHz). France-Musiques (91.7 MHz) offers classical, contemporary, jazz, opera and anything really big. Under strict language laws, forty percent of pop music played by any radio station has to be French, and there's a dire Parisian radio station playing nothing but French music, Chante France (90.9 MHz).

in the Forum des Halles, 1–5 rue Pierre-Lescot, 1er (Mon–Sat 10am–7.30pm; Ⓣ08.25.02.00.20, Ⓦwww.fnac.fr; M° Châtelet-Les-Halles). Alternatively, you can use one of the FNAC Musique branches (see p.406), or Virgin Megastore, at 56–60 avenue des Champs-Elysées, 8e (Mon–Sat 10am–midnight, Sun noon–midnight; Ⓣ01.49.53.50.00, Ⓦwww.virginmega.fr; M° Franklin-D. Roosevelt), and at the Carrousel du Louvre, beneath the Louvre, 1er (Sun–Tues 10am–8pm, Wed 10am–9pm, Thurs–Sat 10am–10pm; M° Palais-Royal/Musée-du-Louvre).

Bars

If you're looking for the city's liveliest venues for **night-time drinking**, places that stay open late and maybe have DJs or occasional live music, we've rounded up the best ones here, under "**bars**". Also included are the more vibrant, late-opening **cafés**, Alsatian/German-type **beer cellars**, imported Irish/English **pubs**, American-style **cocktail bars** and the more informal **bar-clubs**. You'll find lower-key and more relaxed cafés listed in the "Cafés and restaurants" chapter (see pp.312–351), while full-on nightclubs, with entry fees and proper sound systems, are reviewed separately under "clubs" (see p.360).

The Champs-Elysées and around

The listings in this section are marked on the map on pp.76–77.

Buddha Bar 8 rue Boissy d'Anglas, 8e Ⓣ01.53.05.90.00, Ⓦwww.buddha-bar.com. This is where the *Buddha Bar* phenomenon all began, and while this particular locale no longer profits from the "it club" status it once enjoyed, it's still well worth a stop, either for drinks at the beautifully designed bar or a meal in the pan-Asian restaurant, presided over by a giant Buddha. Large number of well-priced cocktails, while the restaurant does dishes like Chinese chicken salad and seared sesame tuna – not exactly inventive, but you don't come for the food. Mon–Fri noon–2am, Sat & Sun 4pm–2am. M° Concorde.

Costes Hôtel Costes, 239 rue St-Honoré, 1er. A favourite haunt of fashionistas and film and media stars, this is a decadently romantic place for an apéritif or late-night drinks amid opulent nineteenth-century decor of red velvet, swags and columns, set around an Italianate courtyard draped in ivy and atmospherically lit at night. Don't expect too much deference from the ridiculously good-looking staff. Cocktails around €15. Daily till 2am. M° Concorde/Tuileries.

Impala Lounge 2 rue de Berri, 8e. A trendy, Out-of-Africa-themed bar, with great atmosphere and music – mostly remixed reggae, funk and afro-jazz beats. In the evenings a youngish, intellectual crowd settles in to talk shop. Daily 9–4am. M° George-V.

Pershing Lounge Pershing Hall, 49 rue Pierre Charron, 8e ⊕01.58.36.58.01. The hip, minimalist Pershing Hall Hotel's lounge bar is a delightful retreat from the bustle of the city, with its thirty-metre-high vertical garden, planted with exotic vegetation. It's a bit of a jetsetters' hang-out, with cocktails priced to match. Daily 6pm–2am. M° George-V.

Grands Boulevards and passages

The listings in this section are marked on the map on pp.88–89.

Bar Hemingway Ritz Hôtel, 15 place Vendôme, 1er. Hemingway first came here with F. Scott Fitzgerald in the 1920s at a time when he was too poor to buy his own drinks. Once he'd made his money, he returned here frequently to spend it; with a classic decor of warm wood panelling, stately leather chairs and deferential, suited barmen, it's easy to see why. The walls are now plastered with photos of Hemingway from all stages of his life, great for soaking up his mystique. Sip the famed dry Martinis or choose from a large selection of malt whiskies. There's very little on the drinks list under €20. Daily 6.30pm–2am. M° Tuileries/Opéra.

De La Ville Café 34 bd de la Bonne Nouvelle, 10e. This ex-bordello, with grand staircase, gilded mosaics and marble columns, draws in crowds of hip pre-clubbers, who sling back a mojito or two before moving on to one of the area's clubs. On weekends, well-known DJs spin the disks till the early hours. Daily 11–2am. M° Bonne-Nouvelle.

Kitty O'Shea's 10 rue des Capucines, 2e. A favourite haunt of expats, with excellent Guinness and Smithwicks and reasonably priced down-home meals like Irish stew and fish and chips. Live music on Sun at 9pm. Daily noon–1.30am. M° Opéra.

Sentier

The listings in this section are marked on the map on pp.88–89.

Le Café 62 rue Tiquetonne, 2e. A hip, buzzing café-bar with a popular terrace and cosy interior, full of old travel posters, yellowing maps and African sculptures. Drinks are reasonably priced and the food is pretty good, too; go for one of the lasagne dishes. As it gets quite busy on the weekends, service can lag, but no one seems to mind. Daily noon–2am (Sun till midnight). M° Etienne-Marcel.

Le Café Noir 65 rue Montmartre, 2e. Despite the name, it's the colour red that predominates in this cool little corner café, with papier mâché globes and other bits of eccentric decor. It's great for an aperitif or late-night drinks, when the music and ambience hot up and it's standing room only at the bar. DJ Thurs & Fri. Mon–Fri 8.30–2am, Sat 4pm–2am. M° Les Halles/Sentier.

Le Tambour 41 rue Montmartre, 2e. A colourful local habitués' bar, eccentrically furnished with recycled street signs, old paving stones and the like. A throwback to the old Les Halles market days and still keeping all-night hours. Hearty salads and snacks available, as well as fuller meals, with mains around €13. Daily 24hr (food till 3.30am Tues–Sat, till 1.30am Sun & Mon). M° Sentier.

Villa Keops 56 bd Sebastopol, 3e. Spacious, gay-friendly, modern bar with scruffy, unfinished wood floor and welcoming staff. Burgers, tagines and pasta dishes for around €13. DJs play a varied mix. Happy hour 7–9pm. Sun–Thurs noon–2am, Fri & Sat noon–5am. M° Etienne-Marcel.

Beaubourg and Les Halles

The listings in this section are marked on the map on p.101.

Le Cochon à l'Oreille 15 rue Montmartre, 1er. This classic little wooden café-bar, with its raffia chairs outside and scenes of fruit and veg stalls on ceramic tiles inside, dates from Les Halles' days as a market. The intellectual conversation is accompanied by Coltrane and other bebopping jazz greats. Mon–Sat 6pm–2am. M° Châtelet-Les Halles/Etienne-Marcel.

Le Comptoir 37 rue Berger, 1er ⊕01.40.26.26.66. Jet-set North African bar/restaurant with plush velvet interior and subdued lighting. A young crowd lounges in comfy sofas sipping sweet mint tea and knock-out cocktails (around €10). Happy hour 5–8pm. Sun–Thurs noon–2am, Fri & Sat noon–3am. M° Châtelet-Les-Halles.

Le Fumoir 6 rue de l'Amiral-Coligny, 1er. Animated chatter rises above a mellow jazz soundtrack and the sound of cocktail shakers in this coolly designed bar, popular with a fashionable, thirty-something crowd. You can browse the international press and there's also a restaurant at the back, complete with library. Cocktails around €10. Daily 11–2am. M° Louvre-Rivoli.

Kong 5th floor, 1 rue du Pont Neuf, 1er ⓣ01.40.39.09.00, ⓦwww.kong.fr. The last episode of *Sex in the City* was set in this über-cool, Philippe Starck-fashioned bar/restaurant atop the flagship Kenzo building. Nights here are oh-so-swank, and while the gorgeous *demoiselles* meeting the lift will let you in, you might get ignored by the bartenders – and everyone else – if you can't claim the right pedigree. The decor is new Japan meets old: geisha girls and manga cartoons. Booths eerily beam holograms of heads of models who glare at you as you sip your €12 cocktail. The separate restaurant upstairs is under an impressive glass roof, with views over the Seine. The Asian-influenced food (around €40–60 per head) includes dishes such as chicken in yogurt and wasabi sauce. Happy hour daily 6–8pm. Restaurant daily 10.30–2am, with brunch on Sun; bar 12.30pm–2am. M° Pont-Neuf.

Au Trappiste 4 rue St-Denis, 1er. Over 140 draught beers include Jenlain, France's best-known *bière de garde*, Belgian Blanche Riva and Kriek from the Mort Subite (Sudden Death) brewery – plus very good *moules frites* and various *tartines*. Or, if you've already come on a full stomach, go all out for the giraffe, a table cask bong filled to the brim with three litres of beer. Mon–Thurs noon–2.30am, Fri–Sun noon–4am. M° Châtelet.

The Marais

The listings below are marked on the map on p.110 and p.114.

Andy Wahloo 69 rue des Gravilliers, 3e. This very popular bar decked out in original Pop Art-inspired Arabic decor is fairly quiet during the week but gets packed to the gills at weekends. Yummy mezze appetizers are served until midnight (the €18 *guassâa* is a good large assortment) and the bar serves mojitos and a few original cocktails, including the Wahloo Special (rum, lime, ginger, banana and cinnamon; €9). DJs play a wide range of dance music, Moroccan rock and Algerian raï. Mon–Sat 11–2am, happy hour 5–8pm. M° Arts-et-Métiers.

L'Attirail 9 rue au Maire, 3e. If you feel like a bit of an adventure and a great night out, it's well worth tracking down this intimate little *café concerts* buried away in the upper Marais' Chinatown district. The tiny back room is the venue for an eclectic programme of live music – anything from Balkan gyspy music to jazz rock – lapped up by an enthusiastic and slightly alternative crowd. Music starts around 8 or 9pm. Demi €3.50. Daily 10am till around 2am. M° Arts-et-Métiers.

The Lizard Lounge 18 rue du Bourg-Tibourg, 4e. American-run and popular with young expats, this is a loud and lively, attractive, stone-walled bar on three levels. Choose from a large range of cocktails (around €7). They also do a popular Sunday brunch (noon–4pm; around €16), with €5 Bloody Marys. Daily noon–2am. M° Hôtel-de-Ville/St-Paul.

La Perle 78 rue Vieille du Temple, 3e. This rather ordinary-looking grungy corner bar, with kitsch Seventies decor, is one of the Marais' trendiest hang-outs, packed to the gills most nights with models, photographers and media types, knocking back cheap beer. Daily 6–2am. M° St-Paul.

Le Petit Fer a Cheval 30 rue Vieille-du-Temple, 4e. A very attractive small bar with original fin-de siècle decor, including a marble-topped bar in the shape of a horseshoe (*fer à cheval*). It's a very popular drinking spot, and the little outside terrace is particularly prized. Daily 9–2am. M° St-Paul.

Le Progrès 1 rue de Bretagne, 3e. This traditional café, with zinc bar, raffia chairs and mustard-coloured walls, draws a cool crowd, especially around aperitif time. See also p.329. Mon–Sat 8am–midnight. M° Saint-Sébastien-Froissart/Filles du Calvaire.

Quiet Man 5 rue des Haudriettes 4e. ⓣ01.48.04.02.77, Live traditional Celtic music is played by troubadours nightly downstairs at this tiny Irish pub. Lots of locals, but does pull in its share of the tourist crowd as well. Happy hour 5–8pm, music begins shortly thereafter. Daily 5pm–2am. M° Rambuteau.

Stolly's **16 rue Cloche-Perce, 4e.** Tiny, almost exclusively Anglo bar with very friendly atmosphere and broadcasts of all major sporting events, washed down by pints of Guinness and Kilkenny and a wide selection of spirits and cocktails (€7). Daily 4.30pm–2am, happy hour 5–8pm. M° St-Paul.

Quartier Latin

The listings in this section are marked on the map on pp.126–127.

Le Bateau Ivre **40 rue Descartes, 5e.** Small, dark and ancient, this student bar is just clear of the Mouffetard tourist hotspot, though it attracts a fair number of Anglos in the evenings, especially after about 10pm. If it's packed out, the *Pub River* next door is less appealing but more spacious. Daily 6pm–2am. M° Cardinal-Lemoine.

La Gueuze **19 rue Soufflot, 5e.** Over 150 beers – largely Belgian and French – are in bottles and on draught at this Belgian café-cum-beer hall, with a beery stained-glass theme for decor. Serves half-decent mussels and chips too. Daily noon–2am. RER Luxembourg.

Le Pantalon Bar **7 rue Royer-Collard, 5e.** This archetypal student dive sports weathered mirrors and graffiti-covered walls, and serves very cheap drinks, especially in the pre-evening happy hour – happy two hours, to be precise, starting at 5.30pm. Daily 5.30pm–2am. RER Luxembourg.

Le Piano Vache **8 rue Laplace, 5e.** Venerable bar crammed with students drinking at little tables. Cool music and a laid-back, grungy atmosphere. A *pression* (draft lager) costs €3.50. Mon–Fri noon–2am, Sat & Sun 9pm–2am. M° Cardinal-Lemoine.

Le Violon Dingue **46 rue de la Montagne-Ste-Geneviève, 5e.** Long, dark student pub that's also popular with young travellers. Noisy and friendly, with English-speaking bar staff and cheap drinks. The cellar bar stays open until 4.30am on busy nights. Daily 4pm–2am; happy hour 8–10pm. M° Maubert-Mutualité.

St-Germain

The listings in this section are marked on the map on pp.142–143.

Le 10 **10 rue de l'Odéon, 6e.** Classic Art Deco-era posters line the walls of this small, dark bar, and the theme is continued in the atmospherically vaulted cellar bar, where there's a lot of chatting-up among the studenty clientele. Daily 6pm–2am. M° Odéon.

Bar du Marché **75 rue de Seine, 6e.** This former market café is just as satisfying and just as busy at night as by day. Expect animated conversation rather than banging techno, and kir rather than cocktails. Daily 7–2am. M° Mabillon.

Chez Georges **11 rue des Canettes, 6e.** This superbly tobacco-stained wine bar, with its venerable counter, attracts a young, studenty crowd and stays lively well into the small hours on weekend nights. The cellar bar is rowdier. Tues–Sat noon–2am; closed Aug. M° Mabillon.

Les Etages St-Germain **5 rue de Buci, 6e.** Fashionably distressed café-bar, with a downstairs level open to the street – prime for posing. Upstairs, you can lounge around on dog-eared armchairs, chilling out with a relatively reasonably priced cocktail (around €8). Daily noon–2am. M° Mabillon.

Fubar **5 rue St-Sulpice, 6e.** Good for a late drink on Tues (student night) or Thurs to Sat, when there's anything from R&B to French rock playing, and a young, international crowd drinking well past the last métro. The upstairs room is very cosy, with comfy chairs and deep red walls. Daily 5pm–2am. M° Odéon.

La Mezzanine de l'Alcazar **62 rue Mazarine, 6e.** Both decor and clientele are *très design* at this über-cool cocktail bar, set on a mezzanine level overlooking Conran's *Alcazar* restaurant. Expensive (around €10 for a drink) but exquisite – again, much like the clientele. Most nights start off relaxed and finish with feverish dancing, the harder core moving on to *Le WAGG* club, below. DJs Wed–Sat. Daily 7pm–2am. M° Odéon.

La Rhumerie **166 bd St-Germain, 6e.** Since the 1930s, this café-bar has been enticing publishers, writers and other ne'er-do-wells off the street with the lure of rum and conversation. The Caribbean theme is underplayed (thankfully) and the cocktails pretty basic (punch €5, mojito €8) but it's always brimming over with energy, just as a good rum bar should be. A few token fritters, crab tartines and the like are served during the day. Daily 9–2am. M° St-Germain-des-Prés.

La Taverne de Nesle **32 rue Dauphine, 6e.** Full of local night owls fuelled up by happy-hour cocktails (around €7) and beers at just over

€3 – or more for the speciality French and Belgian brews. Gets busier during student terms, especially at weekends when DJs take to the decks. Happy hour 6–9pm; Mon–Thurs & Sun 6pm–4am, Fri & Sat till 5am. M° Odéon.

Montparnasse and southern Paris

Unless otherwise indicated, the listings in this section are marked on the map on p.187.

L'Entrepôt 7–9 rue Francis-de-Pressensé, 14e. See p.340.

La Folie en Tête 33 rue Butte-aux-Cailles, 13e. Surveying the Butte-aux-Cailles from its prime corner spot, this vibrant, friendly and distinctly lefty café-bar is a classic. The walls are littered with bric-a-brac and musical instruments, the tables and stools with young locals. Gigs seem to have stopped for the time being but there's usually something cool playing on the system – laid-back underground beats, perhaps, or a young singer-songwriter's latest album. Mon–Sat 6pm–2am. M° Place-d'Italie/Corvisart.

Le Merle Moqueur 11 rue Butte-aux-Cailles, 13e. Classic narrow, shop-front-style Butte-aux-Cailles bar, which once saw the Paris debut of Manu Chao. It maintains an alternative edge, though most days serves up 1980s French rock CDs and home-made flavoured rums to young Parisians. If you don't fancy the playlist, you can always try the very similar *Le Diapason*, two doors along, where the sounds can be more varied. Daily 5pm–2am. M° Place-d'Italie/Corvisart.

Le Rosebud 11bis rue Delambre, 14e. See map on pp.172–173. A hushed, faintly exclusive bar just off the boulevard Montparnasse where the clientele keeps up the prewar arty traditions of the area – Sartre and his crew used to drink here. The barmen, who seem to date from the same era as the decor, serve up wonderful, traditional cocktails – think Martinis rather than Sex on the Beach – for around €12. Daily 7pm–2am. M° Vavin.

▽ La Folie en tête, 3e

Montmartre and northern Paris

Unless otherwise indicated, the listings in this section are marked on the map on p.194.

Le Bar du Relais 12 rue Ravignan, 18e. The ancient, ramshackle building has a perfectly picturesque spot on a quiet square on the slopes of the Butte. Cool, youthful and Bohemian-tinged venue, with an electronique playlist. Mon–Thurs 3pm–2am, Fri–Sun noon–2am. M° Abbesses.

Chez Camille 8 rue Ravignan, 18e. *Très chouette* (very cool) is how locals have been describing this little bar for years. In a great location on the slopes of the Butte, the clientele is typical of the location – young and trendy in a well-to-do kind of way. Tues–Sat 9–2am, Sun 9–8pm. M° Abbesses.

L'Entracte 7 rue Biot, 17e. See map on p.207. This pleasantly tatty old café attracts a young, noisy left-leaning crowd in the evenings, including actors from the next-door theatre. Daily 10am–3am. M° Place de Clichy.

La Fourmi Café 74 rue des Martyrs, 18e. The glamourous decor, long bar and high-ceilinged spaciousness draw the discerning *bobos* of Abbesses and the 10e for cocktails, wine and chatter, to the tune of retro-industrial lounge music. Handy launching pad for clubbing in the area. Mon–Thurs 8–2am, Fri & Sat 8–4am, Sun 10–2am. M° Pigalle/Abbesses.

Olympic Café 20 rue Léon, 10e ⓦwww.rueleon.net. In the heart of the poor and peeling Goutte d'Or, this boho café-restaurant pumps out life and energy like a lighthouse. The big Che Guevera banner and faded 1930s Art Deco interior say it all. Meals are served in the evening, but the main draw is the basement venue featuring six gigs a week, from African rock to klezmer, Bulgarian folk and French chanson. Tues–Sun 11–2am. M° Château-Rouge

Au Rendez-Vous des Amis 23 rue Gabrielle, 18e. Halfway up the Butte, this small, ramshackle, smoky and community-spirited hang-out is a magnet for Montmartre locals, especially the young, artsy and alternative-leaning. Daily 8.30–2am. M° Abbesses.

Tribal Café 3 cour des Petits Ecuries, 10e. See map on p.204. Tucked down an atmospheric side street, this North-African Tinged café-bar pulls in the new bohemians of the quarter with loud music, cheap beer and mojitos, outside tables and free couscous on Fri and Sat nights (or free *moules frites* on Wed and Thurs). Daily noon–2am. M° Château-d'Eau.

Un Zèbre à Montmartre 38 rue Lepic, 18e. Trendy but relaxed hang-out for the young of Abbesses, with a laid-back playlist. See p.343. Mon–Sat 9am–2am, Sun 10–2am. M° Abbesses.

The Bastille and around

The listings below are marked on the map on pp.212–213.

Bar des Ferrailleurs 18 rue de Lappe, 11e. Dark and stylishly sinister, with rusting metal decor, an eccentric owner, fun wig-wearing bar staff and a relaxed and friendly crowd. Mon–Fri 5pm–2am, Sat & Sun 3pm–2am. M° Bastille.

Café de l'Industrie 16 rue St-Sabin, 11e. An enduringly popular café, packed out every evening. See p.346. Daily 10–2am. M° Bastille.

Le Fanfaron 6 rue de la Main d'Or, 11e. On a tiny backstreet north of rue du Faubourg Saint Antoine, this little retro bar, with its old film posters and Sixties rock music, has a nostalgic appeal, and the beer is cheap too. Tues–Sat 6pm–2am; closed two weeks in Aug. M° Ledru-Rollin.

Havanita Café 11 rue de Lappe, 11e. Large, comfortable Cuban-style bar/restaurant serving a predictable list of Latino cocktails (around €10) and dishes like *dorado ceviche*; happy hour 5–8pm. Daily 5pm–2am. M° Bastille.

Iguana 15 rue de la Roquette, cnr rue Daval, 11e. A place to be seen in. Decor of trellises, colonial fans and a brushed bronze bar. By day, the clientele studies recherché art reviews over excellent coffee, while things hot up at night with a youngish, high-spirited crowd. DJ on Thurs. Cocktails around €10. Daily 10–2am. M° Bastille.

Le Lèche-Vin 13 rue Daval, 11e. A relaxed, unpretentious little bar with cheap drinks and a rather unusual decor of kitsch religious icons and images (the pics in the toilets on the other hand are far from a pious nature). Gets packed out very quickly in the evenings with a young, cosmopolitan crowd. Daily 6pm–2am. M° Bastille.

SanZSanS 49 rue du Faubourg-St-Antoine, 11e. Gothic get-up of red velvet, oil paintings and chandeliers, popular with a young crowd, especially on Friday and Saturday evenings, when DJs play rare groove and funky/Brazilian house. Drinks are reasonably priced. Tues–Sun 9–5am, Mon 9–3am. M° Bastille.

Eastern Paris

Canal St-Martin

Unless otherwise indicated the listings below are marked on the map on pp.224–225.

L'Abracadabar 123 av Jean-Jaures, 19e ⓦwww.abracadabar.fr. See map on p.228. Tucked away in the far reaches of the 19e, this popular little music bar pulsates with live rock, ragga and techno most evenings, drawing a mixed crowd of students and thirty-somethings. Music usually starts at 9pm and there's sometimes a small entry fee of €2 or €3. Cocktails from €6. Happy hour 6–8.30pm. Daily 6pm–2am, Thurs–Sat till 5am. M° Laumière.

Bar Ourcq 68 quai de la Loire, 19e ⓦwww.barourcq.com. See map on p.228. With its pale-blue facade and large windows looking out onto the canal *quai*, this popular bar really comes into its own in the warmer months when you can sit out on the quayside, or borrow the bar's set of *pétanques*. It also has a cosy interior with sofas and cushions. Drinks are very reasonably priced. DJs on Fri, Sat & Sun. Summer Wed & Thurs 3pm–midnight, Fri & Sat 3pm–2am, Sun 3–10pm; winter Wed–Fri 5–9.30pm, Sat 3pm–2am, Sun 3–9.30pm. M° Laumière.

Favela Chic 16 rue du Faubourg du Temple, 11e ⓦwww.favelachic.com. Touted eclectic music nights and kitsch furnishings bring twenty-somethings of all creeds and persuasions to this Brazilian bar known for its ribald DJ evenings. Table-dancing and dirty hip-grinding are *de rigueur*. Tues–Fri 7.30pm–2am, Sat 7.30pm–4am. M° République.

Le Jemmapes 82 Quai de Jemmapes, 10e. In the summer this neighbourhood resto-bar and *boho* hang-out is well known for letting its patrons cross the road to nip at their drinks along the banks of the canal. The standard French cuisine is good, but the lure here is the hipster atmosphere. Daily 11–2am. M° Jacques-Bonsergent.

Point Ephémère 200 quai de Valmy, 10ᵉ **ⓦwww.pointephemere.org.** A great energetic atmosphere pervades this young creative space for music, dance and visual arts set in a former canal boathouse. The rotating art exhibitions range from the quotidian to the abstract, while the frequent concerts feature cutting-edge rock and electronica bands. There's always interesting multilingual conversation going on around the bar, which serves beer and finger food, and you can even get a decent order of *steak-frites* in the ad-hoc restaurant looking out onto the canal. Daily 1pm–2am (later if there's a concert that night). M° Jaurès/ Louis Blanc.

Belleville and Ménilmontant/ Oberkampf

The listings below are marked on the map on pp.224–225.

Café Charbon 109 rue Oberkampf, 11ᵉ. The place that pioneered the rise of the Oberkampf bar scene in the mid-90s is still going strong and continues to draw in a young, fashionable mixed crowd day and night. Part of its allure is the attractively restored early twentieth-century decor. *Menu* €18; snacks around €5; beer €2.50. Happy hour daily 5-7pm. DJ Thurs, Fri & Sat 10pm–2am. Daily 9–2am. M° St-Maur/Parmentier.

Café Chéri 44 bd de la Villette, 19ᵉ. A cool DJ bar, with scruffy red interior and popular terrace, where local hipsters sit at their laptops or read during the day or drop in for drinks after work and stay long into the night. Drinks are reasonably priced; try one of the fruit cocktails, such as the *plateau* (pineapple, mango, rum and cinnamon), for €6.50. Daily 8am–2am. M° Belleville.

Le Cannibale 93 rue Jean-Pierre Timbaud, 11ᵉ. The sight of a copy of Goya's gory painting *Saturn Devouring his Son* hanging above the bar (and after which the place is named) creates a certain frisson as you walk in the door of this arty café-bar, with fashionably worn and faded old decor. Locals chill out against a soundtrack of electro lounge, or tuck into *blanquette de veau* and other classic dishes in the dining area. There's usually live music (chanson, jazz funk, Cuban) on Sundays at 6pm. Demi €2.60, cocktails €6.50. Daily 8–2am. M° Couronnes.

La Caravane 35 rue de la Fontaine-au-Roi, 11ᵉ. Handsome bar staff serve a Bohemian, arty crowd at this colourful, fun place, with Chinese lanterns, bright-red curtains and mismatched tables and chairs. It's equally popular at lunch, when you can get a plate of pad thai or a quiche and salad for €8. DJ most Fridays and Saturdays. Mon–Fri 11.30–2am, Sat & Sun 4.30pm–2am. M° Goncourt.

Chez Justine 96 rue Oberkampf, 11ᵉ **ⓣ01.43.57.44.03.** During the day a chilled candle-lit bar-restaurant with big wooden tables; after 10pm things hot up with a DJ and the place gets packed out with a young, hip crowd. Draught beer €3. Mon–Sat 8–2am, Sun 10–2am. M° St-Maur/Parmentier.

La Flèche d'Or 102bis rue de Bagnolet, cnr rue des Pyrénées, 20ᵉ ⓣ01.43.72.04.23, ⓦwww.flechedor.fr. A large, lively café attracting the biker, arty, punkish Parisian youth, and a nightly venue for live world music, pop, punk, ska, fusion and chanson. The building itself is the old Bagnolet station on the *petite ceinture* railway that encircled the city until around thirty years ago. Extra €5 or €6 for music. Daily 10–2am. M° Porte-de-Bagnolet/Alexandre-Dumas – a fifteen-minute walk in either case.

Aux Folies 8 rue de Belleville, 20ᵉ. Aux Folies offers a real slice of Belleville life; its outside terrace and 1930s long brass bar, with mirrored tiles and red neon lights, are packed day and night with a mixed crowd of North Africans, Chinese, students and artists. Beer €3.50, cocktails €4.50. Daily 6.30am–1am. M° Belleville.

Lou Pascalou 14 rue des Panoyaux, 20ᵉ. Trendy but friendly place with a zinc bar, this local *boho* hang-out is a great weekend find for the area, especially if you're interested in leaving with your eardrums intact. Be sure to try some of their delicious mint tea – over a ponderous game of chess if you fancy it. Wide range of beers bottled and on tap from €2.50. Daily 9–2am. M° Ménilmontant.

Les Lucioles 102 bd Ménilmontant, 20ᵉ. A relaxed and friendly neighbourhood bar/ restaurant, with an inviting outside terrace in warmer weather, popular with a youngish crowd. Poetry readings on Tues; live music on weekends and party atmosphere. Demi €3; mains €13. Daily 9–2am. M° Père-Lachaise.

Clubs

Paris's **club** scene moves ever further away from big monster-clubs rammed every weekend with techno-heads to fast-changing, esoteric programmes, often put on at smaller venues. Where once deep house and techno ruled, you can now find hip-hop, R&B, electro-lounge, rock and more alternative sounds. The clubs listed below attract some of the trendiest or biggest crowds, but the style of music and the general vibe really depend on who's running the "*soirée*" on a particular night. Some showcase occasional live acts, too.

It's also worth checking the listings for **live music** venues (see opposite), which tend to hold DJ-led sessions after hours, and the **gay and lesbian** club listings (see p.436). Most gay clubs attract huge and very mixed crowds from the trendy end of the nightlife spectrum. Note too that lots of **bars** (see pp.353–359) bring in DJs for weekend nights.

Most clubs **open** between 11pm and midnight, sometimes earlier if they follow on from a gig, but venues rarely warm up before 1am or 2am. It's worth dressing up, especially for trendier clubs, some of which operate very snooty door policies. At least racism, these days, is rare. Most **entry prices** include one free drink (*consommation*), and may vary from night to night. Given the difficulty of finding a **taxi after hours** (see p.28), many Parisian clubbers aim to keep going until the métro starts up at around 5.30am, or even later, moving on to one of the city's famous *after* events.

Club listings

Batofar opposite 11 quai François Mauriac, 13e ⓣ01.56.29.10.33, ⓦwww.batofar.org. See map on p.187. This old lighthouse boat moored at the foot of the Bibliothèque Nationale is a small but very classic address. The programme is mostly electro, house, techno, hip-hop, whatever – with the odd experimental funk night or the like thrown in to mix it up a bit. Tues–Thurs 8pm–2am, Fri 11pm–dawn, Sat 11pm–noon. Entry €8–12. M° Etienne-Marcel.

Le Baron 6 av Marceau, 8e ⓦwww.clublebaron.com. See map on pp.76–77. One of the beacons of the Champs-Elysées nightlife scene, the *Baron* is quite deliberately both expensive and exclusive – you'll have to not only look good but look as if you're in with the right crowd to be allowed the privilege of entry. There's no door charge, but carry a fat wallet for drinks. The result is a small and posey bar-club packed out with well-connected, wealthy and well-dressed Parisians schmoozing, flirting and dancing till dawn. Daily 11.30pm–5am. M° Alma-Marceau.

Le Cab 2 place du Palais-Royal, 1er ⓣ01.58.62.56.25. See map on pp.88–89. Currently one of the most fashionable venues in Paris, somehow dragging the beautiful and designer-clad away from the Champs-Elysées – on weekend nights you'll need to look good to get in. Designer retro-meets-futuristic lounge decor, with a similar music policy. Mon–Sat 11.30pm–5am. Entry €20. M° Palais-Royal.

La Loco 90 bd de Clichy, 18e ⓣ08.36.69.69.28, ⓦwww.laloco.com. See map on p.194. High-tech monster club with three dancefloors, playing mostly house and techno, though you can find all kinds of musical styles on weekday nights and on the two smaller pistes. Not particularly cool, but almost always busy. Tues–Sun 11pm–7am. Entry €12–20. M° Blanche.

Le Nouveau Casino 109 rue Oberkampf, 11e ⓣ01.43.57.57.40, ⓦwww.nouveaucasino.net. See map on pp.224–225. Right behind *Café Charbon* (see p.359) lies this excellent venue. An interesting, experimental line-up of live gigs makes way for a relaxed, dancey crowd later on, with music ranging from electro-pop or house to rock. There's a good sound system and ventilation, but not all that much space. Tues & Wed 9pm–2am, Thurs–Sat midnight–5am. Entry costs range from free up to around €15, depending on who's playing and the time you arrive. M° Parmentier.

Le Redlight 34 rue du Départ, 14e ⓣ01.42.79.94.53, ⓦwww.enfer.fr. See map on pp.172–173. The house is hard rather than happy at this big, serious club, thus pulling in a largely but not exclusively gay crowd. If it all gets too much, the second dancefloor is sometimes – only sometimes – a little more relaxed. Thurs & Sun midnight–6am, Fri & Sat midnight–noon. Entry from €10 (before 1am on certain nights) to €20. M° Montparnasse-Bienvenüe.

Rex Club 5 bd Poissonnière, 2e ⓣ01.42.36.28.83. See map on pp.88–89. The clubbers' club: spacious and serious about its music, which is strictly electronic, notably techno. Attracts big-name DJs. Wed–Sat 11.30pm–5am. Entry €10–13. M° Bonne-Nouvelle.

La Scène Bastille 2bis rue des Taillandiers, 11e ⓣ01.48.06.50.70 (restaurant reservations: ⓣ01.48.06.12.13), ⓦwww.la-scene.com. See map on p.212–213. A club, concert venue and restaurant all rolled into one, in a converted warehouse, snazzily refurbished in plush colours. The eclectic music policy embraces rock, electro and funk, with gay nights on Sun. Mon–Thurs & Sun till 2am, Fri & Sat till 5am. Entry €10–12. M° Bastille.

Le Triptyque 142 rue Montmartre, 2e ⓣ01.40.28.05.55, ⓦwww.letriptyque.com. See map on pp.88–89. *Les physios* (the bouncers) won't turn you away at this unpretentious, grunge-cool club, packed with anyone from local students to lounge lizards. For once, it's all about the music. Themed DJ *soirées* which change nightly – everything from electro to jazz to hip-hop to ska. Open daily till 6am. Entry costs vary, sometimes free, sometimes up to €15. M° Palais de la Bourse.

WAGG 62 rue Mazarine, 6e ⓣ01.55.42.22.00. See map on pp.142–143. Adjoining Terence Conran's flashy *Alcazar* restaurant and bar, the *WAGG* continues the UK theme with the Seventies-themed "Carwash" nights on Fri (free before midnight, €15 after) and UK house on Sat (€12). Fri & Sat midnight–6am. M° Odéon.

Rock and world music

In the last few years Paris clubs and rock venues have begun to concentrate on international sounds, mostly **Latin** and **African** music, or French takes on those sounds, leaving the big rock bands to play the major arenas. Most of the **venues** listed below are primarily concert venues, though some double up as clubs on certain nights, or after hours. A few of them will have live music all week, but the majority host bands on just a couple of nights. Admission prices vary depending on who's playing.

Note that the most interesting **clubs** tend to host gigs earlier on; watch out for the programmes at *Le Nouveau Casino* and *Le Triptyque* in particular (see above). Jazz venues, too (see p.362), often branch into other genres such as world music and folk – *New Morning* is a classic example. We've also listed the really major concert venues separately (see p.365).

Rock and world music venues

Le Bataclan 50 bd Voltaire, 11e ⓣ01.43.14.00.30, ⓦwww.bataclan.fr. Classic pagoda-styled ex-theatre venue (seats 1200) with one of the best and most eclectic line-ups covering anything from international and local dance and rock musicians – Francis Cabrel, Chemical Brothers, Khaled, Stereophonics – to chanson, comedy and techno nights. M° Oberkampf.

Café de la Danse 5 passage Louis-Philippe, 11e ⓣ01.47.00.57.59, ⓦwww.chez.com/cafedeladanse. Rock, pop, world, folk and jazz music played in an intimate and attractive space. Open nights of concerts only. M° Bastille.

La Cigale 120 bd de Rochechouart, 18e ⓣ01.49.25.81.75, ⓦwww.lacigale.fr. Formerly playing host to the likes of Mistinguett and Maurice Chevalier, since 1987 and a Philippe Starck renovation this historic, 1400-seater Pigalle theatre has become a leading venue for cutting-edge rock and indie acts, especially French and other continental European bands. M° Pigalle.

Le Divan du Monde 75 rue des Martyrs, 18e ⓣ01.40.05.06.99, ⓦwww.divandumonde.com. A youthful venue in a café whose regulars once included Toulouse-Lautrec. One of the city's most diverse and exciting programmes, ranging from techno to Congolese rumba, with dancing till dawn on weekend nights. M° Anvers.

Elysée Montmartre 72 bd de Rochechouart, 18e ⓣ08.92.69.23.92, ⓦwww.elyseemontmartre .com. A historic Montmartre nightspot that pulls in a young, excitable crowd with its rock and dance acts – Redman, the Pharcyde, The Hives. Also hosts club nights – the music may be fairly unsophisticated but the single, giant dancefloor under a huge, arching roof guarantees plenty of space, and there's usually a good-time feel. M° Anvers.

La Guinguette Pirate quai François Mauriac, 13e ⓣ01.44.06.96.45, ⓦwww.guinguettepirate.com. Beautiful Chinese barge, moored alongside the quay in front of the Bibliothèque Nationale, hosting relaxed but upbeat world music and folk-rock nights from Tues to Sun. A sound bet for an inexpensive (€5–10), eye-opening night out. M° Quai-de-la-Gare.

Maroquinerie 23 rue Boyer, 20e ⓣ01.40.33.35.05, ⓦwww.lamaroquinerie.fr. The smallish concert venue is the downstairs part of a trendy arts centre. The line-up is rock, folk and jazz, with a particularly good selection of French musicians. M° Gambetta.

Point Ephemère 200 quai de Valmy, 10e ⓣ01.40.34.02.48, ⓦwww.pointephemere.org. Run by an arts collective in a disused warehouse, this superbly dilapidated venue lives up to its reputation as a nexus for alternative and underground performers of all kinds. There are gigs most nights, covering anything from electro to Afro-jazz via folk-rock, as well as dance studios, rehearsal spaces and the like. M° Jaurès.

Le Triptyque 142 rue Montmartre, 2e ⓣ01.40.28.05.55, ⓦwww.letriptyque.com. This smallish but high-profile venue has one of the most intriguing programmes in the city – folk and African acts find space alongside big indie rockers, with DJs from midnight (see also under clubs, p.361). Entry costs vary, sometimes free, sometimes up to €15. M° Palais de la Bourse.

Jazz, blues and chanson

Jazz has long enjoyed an appreciative audience in France, especially since the end of World War II, when the intellectual rigour and agonized musings of bebop struck an immediate chord of sympathy in the existentialist hearts of the après-guerre. Charlie Parker, Dizzy Gillespie, Miles Davis – all were being listened to in the 1950s, when in Britain their names were known only to a tiny coterie of fans.

Gypsy guitarist **Django Reinhardt** and his partner, violinist Stéphane Grappelli, whose work represents the distinctive and undisputed French contribution to the jazz canon, had much to do with the music's popularity. But it was also greatly enhanced by the presence of many front-rank black American musicians, for whom Paris was a haven of freedom and culture after the racial prejudice and philistinism of the States. Among them were the soprano sax player **Sidney Bechet**, who set up in legendary partnership with French clarinettist Claude Luter, and Bud Powell, whose turbulent exile partly inspired the tenor man played by Dexter Gordon (himself a veteran of the Montana club) in the film *Round Midnight*.

Jazz is still alive and well in the city, with a good selection of clubs plying all styles from New Orleans to current experimental. Frequent festivals are also a good source of concerts, particularly in the summer (see "Festivals and Events", pp.380–383). Some names to look out for are saxophonist Didier Malherbe; violinist Didier Lockwood; British-born but long-time Paris resident, guitarist John McLaughlin; pianist Alain Jean Marie; clarinettist Louis Sclavis; and accordionist Richard Galliano, who updates the French *musette* style. All of them can be found playing small gigs, regardless of the size of their reputations. Bistrots and bars are a good place to catch musicians carrying on the tradition of Django

From Johnny to French touch

Ever since the great Serge Gainsbourg blended French chanson (see p.362) with jazz, rock and reggae in the 1960s and 70s, French *auteurs,* or singer-songwriters, have had serious credibility both at home and abroad. Chanson still exerts a powerful influence on contemporary music and still finds enthusiastic audiences – Patrick Bruel's album *Entre-Deux,* for instance, shot to the top of the charts in 2002, with its quirky new angles on old-time classics. Camille and Dominique A, meanwhile, have emerged as two of the more interesting contemporary artists.

France's original soft-rock megastar, **Johnny Halliday**, has enjoyed a somewhat geriatric rebirth in the last decade – though thanks largely to iconic film roles and arena-scale concerts rather than producing exciting new music. Johnny aside, the music of the so-called yé-yé bands, the pale imitations of US rock acts that dominated the 1960s and 70s, has at last died out. The quality and innovation of rock since the 1980s is better represented by the soloists Miossec and Jean-Louis Murat, and the groups Les Rita Mitsouko, Louise Attaque, Mickey 3D, Noir Désir and La Tordue, whose styles combine rock and distinctively Gallic elements.

Since the 1990s, the club scene has produced some hugely successful DJs and artists. Groups such as Air, Daft Punk and St-Germain are known around the world, as are DJs Etienne de Crécy, Laurent Garnier and Dimitri. Internationally, France is perhaps best known for mellow, post-club tracks that mix jazz, world music and 70s retro with electronic sounds to create what's sometimes known as electro-lounge, or **French Touch**.

Big names in **world music** are almost always in town, in particular **zouk** musicians from the French Caribbean, and musicians from **West Africa**. Algerian **raï** continues to flourish, with singers like Faudel, Khaled and Cheb Mami enjoying megastar status. In France, more and more bands have produced their own hybrids. Les Négresses Vertes were perhaps the first group to experiment on this level and be recognized internationally, while the Toulouse-based group Zebda paraded a strong Maghrebi influence – and social conscience. The real international breakthrough, however, came with **Manu Chao**, the former member of Mano Negra, who found huge audiences for his unique combination of Latin American, rap, reggae and rock influences.

The "*marginale*" culture of the *banlieue*, the disaffected, ethnically mixed housing projects of the suburbs, has found explosive expression in **hip-hop**. Pioneers from Marseilles like IAM and MC Solaar have had enormous commercial success, but the Paris *banlieue* continues to be the engine room of hip-hop culture and music, producing a huge number of collectives. Among the biggest names from the Paris region are Less Du Neuf, Lunatic, Mafia K'1 Fry, N.T.M. (now defunct), Secteur Ä and Sniper, while at the political cutting edge are the crews Assassin, Ministère A.M.E.R. and La Rumeur.

Reinhardt – Romane and the Ferré brothers are just some of the musicians doing the rounds – as well as French traditional chansons. **Gigs** aren't usually advertised in the press, but you'll see handmade posters in the venues themselves. In addition to the places below, it's also worth checking out *L'Attirail* (see p.355) and *Café de la Danse* (see p.361) for occasional chanson or jazz concerts.

Mainly jazz

Les 7 Lézards 10 rue des Rosiers, 4e ⓣ01.48.87.08.97, ⓦwww.7lezards.com. A cosy and intimate jazz club, which encourages young, upcoming musicians and attracts more established names, too. Also hosts the odd world music gig, and there's a decent, affordable restaurant (noon–midnight) upstairs. Daily till 2am; concerts at 7pm & 10am. Admission €8–16. M° St-Paul.

Le Baiser Salé 58 rue des Lombards, 1er ⓣ01.42.33.37.71, ⓦwww.lebaisersale.com. A small, crowded upstairs room with live music every night from 10pm – usually jazz, rhythm & blues, fusion, reggae or Brazilian. There are free jam sessions on Mondays, and the downstairs bar is great for just chilling out. Daily 5pm–6am, with most sets starting at 10pm. Admission €13–18. M° Châtelet.

Caveau de la Huchette 5 rue de la Huchette, 5e ⓣ01.43.26.65.05, ⓦwww.caveaudelahuchette.fr. A wonderful slice of old Parisian life in an otherwise touristy area. Both Lionel Hampton and Art Blakey played here. Live jazz, usually trad and big band, to dance to on a floor surrounded by tiers of benches, and a bar decorated with caricatures of the barman drawn on any material to hand. Sun–Wed 9.30pm–2.30am, Thurs–Fri 9.30pm–dawn. Sun–Thurs €11, Fri & Sat €13; drinks from €5.50. M° Saint-Michel.

Au Duc des Lombards 42 rue des Lombards, 1er ⓣ01.42.33.22.88, ⓦwww.ducdeslombards.com. Small, unpretentious bar with performances every night from 9.30pm. This is the place to hear gypsy jazz, as well as jazz piano, blues, ballads and fusion. Sometimes big names. Daily until 3am. Most gigs €23 or €25. M° Châtelet/Les-Halles.

Instants Chavirés 7 rue Richard-Lenoir, Montreuil ⓣ01.42.87.25.91, ⓦwww.instantschavires.com. Avant-garde jazz joint – no comforts – on the eastern edge of the city, close to the Porte de Montreuil. A place where musicians go to hear each other play, its reputation has attracted subsidies from both state and local authorities. Tues–Sat 8.30pm–1am; concerts at 9pm. Admission around €10. M° Robespierre.

Jazz Club Lionel Hampton Hôtel Méridien, 81 bd Gouvion-St-Cyr, 17e ⓣ01.40.68.30.42, ⓦwww.jazzclub-paris.com. Inaugurated by Himself, this is a first-rate jazz venue, with big-name musicians. Daily 7–2am, with concerts at 10.30pm. No entry fee but first drink from €26, refills €13. M° Porte-Maillot.

New Morning 7–9 rue des Petites-Ecuries, 10e ⓣ01.45.23.51.41, ⓦwww.newmorning.com. The decor's somewhat spartan, a bit like an underground garage, but this is the place where the big international names in jazz come to play and it attracts true aficionados. It's often standing room only unless you get here early. Blues and Latin, too. Usually Mon–Sat 8pm–1.30am (concerts start at 9pm). Admission €21. M° Château-d'Eau.

Le Petit Journal 71 bd St-Michel, 5e ⓣ01.43.26.28.59. Small, smoky bar, with good, mainly French, traditional and mainstream sounds. These days rather middle-aged and tourist-prone. Admission with first drink €15–20, subsequent drinks around €5; €45–48 including meal. Mon–Sat 9pm–2am (concerts from 9.15pm); closed Aug. RER Luxembourg.

Le Petit Journal Montparnasse 13 rue du Commandant-Mouchotte, 14e ⓣ01.43.21.56.70, ⓦwww.petitjournal-montparnasse.com. Under the *Hôtel Montparnasse*, and sister establishment to the above, with bigger visiting names, both French and international. Admission with first drink around €18, subsequent drinks from €5.50. There's also the option of dining (three courses and wine, with no extra charge for music €55–85). Mon–Sat 8.30pm–2am (concerts from 10pm). M° Montparnasse-Bienvenüe.

Le Sunset/Le Sunside 60 rue des Lombards, 1er ⓣ01.40.26.46.20, ⓦwww.sunset-sunside.com. Two clubs in one: *Le Sunside* on the ground floor features mostly traditional jazz, whereas the downstairs *Sunset* is a venue for electric and fusion jazz. The *Sunside* concert usually starts at 9pm and the *Sunset* at 10pm, so you can sample a bit of both. Attracts some of the best musicians – the likes of pianist Alain Jean Marie and Turk Mauro. Daily 9pm–2.30am. Admission €20–22. M° Châtelet-Les-Halles.

Mainly chanson

Casino de Paris 16 rue de Clichy, 9e ⓣ01.49.95.99.99, ⓦwww.casinodeparis.fr. This decaying, once-plush casino in one of the seediest streets in Paris is a venue for all sorts of performances – chanson, poetry combined with flamenco guitar, cabaret. Check the listings magazines under "Variétés" and "Chansons". Most performances start at 8.30pm. Tickets from €25 upwards. M° Trinité.

Le Lapin Agile 22 rue des Saules, 18e ⓣ01.46.06.85.87, ⓦwww.au-lapin-agile.com. Old haunt of Apollinaire, Utrillo and other Montmartre artists, some of whose pictures adorn the walls. Cabaret, poetry and chansons. You may be lucky enough to catch singer-composer Arlette Denis, who carries Jacques Brel's flame. Tues–Sun 9pm–2am. €24 including drink, students €17 (except Sat). M° Lamarck-Caulaincourt.

Au Limonaire 18 Cité Bergère, 9e ⓣ01.45.23.33.33, ⓦhttp://limonaire.free.fr. Tiny backstreet venue, perfect for Parisian chanson nights showcasing young singers and zany music/poetry/performance acts. Dinner beforehand – traditional, inexpensive and fairly good – guarantees a seat for the show at 10pm – otherwise you'll be crammed up against the bar, if you can get in at all. M° Grands-Boulevards.

Le Magique 42 rue de Gergovie, 14e ⓣ01.45.42.26.10, ⓦwww.aumagique.com. A bar and "chanson cellar" with traditional French chanson performances by lesser-known stars during the week. Concerts at 9.30pm or 10pm. At weekends the owner takes to the piano. Wed–Sat 8pm–2am. Admission €5, and drinks are very reasonably priced. M° Pernety.

Major concert venues

Events at any of the performance spaces listed below will be well advertised on billboards and posters throughout the city. Tickets can be obtained at the halls themselves, though it's easier to get them through agents like FNAC or Virgin Megastore (see p.398 and p.406).

Olympia 28 bd des Capucines, 9e ⓣ08.92.68.33.68, ⓦwww.olympiahall.com. The classic Paris venue, a renovated old-style music hall hosting top international rock and pop acts, with a good programme of domestic stars as well. M° Madeleine/Opéra.

Palais des Congrès place de la Porte-Maillot, 17e ⓣ01.40.68.00.05, ⓦwww.palaisdescongres-paris.com. Opera, musicals, orchestral music, trade fairs, and middle-of-the-road superstars. M° Porte-Maillot.

Palais Omnisports de Bercy 8 bd de Bercy, 12e ⓣ01.40.02.60.60, ⓦwww.bercy.fr. Opera, cycle racing, Bruce Springsteen, ice hockey, and Citroën launches: a multipurpose stadium, with vertiginous seats – up to 17,000 of them. M° Bercy.

Palais des Sports Porte de Versailles, 15e ⓣ01.48.28.40.10, ⓦwww.palaisdessports.com. Another vast auditorium, ideal for stadium rock and giant French musicals. M° Porte-de-Versailles.

Stade de France St-Denis ⓣ0892.700.900, ⓦwww.stadefrance.fr. One-hundred-thousand capacity stadium, purpose-built for France's hosting of the 1998 Football World Cup and doubling up for use by stadium-rockers. RER B La-Plaine-Stade-de-France/RER D Stade-de-France-St-Denis.

Zenith Parc de la Villette, 211 av Jean-Jaurès, 20e ⓣ01.42.08.60.00, ⓦwww.le-zenith.com/paris. Seating for six thousand in a giant tent designed exclusively for rock and pop concerts, with a good programme including acts like the Arctic Monkeys and Scissor Sisters. Head for the concrete column with a descending red aeroplane. M° Porte-de-Pantin.

21

Film, theatre and dance

Cinema-lovers have a choice of around three hundred **films** showing in any one week. The scene isn't limited to contemporary French movies and Hollywood budget-busters, though there are plenty of these, but takes in classics from all eras and a diverse spread of films from all over the world. In Paris, you can walk into a beautiful old cinema and watch a film that you'd struggle to find on video in another city.

The city also has a vibrant **theatre** scene. Several superstar directors are based here, such as Peter Brook and Ariane Mnouchkine, renowned for their highly innovative, cutting-edge productions. As an obvious stop-off point for touring troupes, Paris is also a great place to catch the pick of the season's festivals. Much space is given over to **dance** and multi-genre stage performances.

As for **cabarets**, with names that conjure up the classic connotations of the sinful city – the *Lido* or the *Moulin Rouge* – they thrive off group bookings for a dinner-and-show formula that is extortionately priced, and retain none of the bawdy atmosphere depicted in Toulouse-Lautrec's sketches or Baz Luhrmann's film. For details, see p.201.

Listings for all films and stage productions are detailed in *Pariscope* (see p.46) and other weeklies, with brief résumés or reviews. Venues with wheelchair access will say "*accessible aux handicapés*". Ushers in theatres and occasionally in independent cinemas expect a small tip from each customer (€1 or so).

Film

Paris remains one of the few cities in the world in which it's possible to get not only serious entertainment but a serious film education from the programmes of regular – never mind specialist – **cinemas**. A few of the more obscure movie houses may have closed in recent years, but plenty of others remain and continue to resist the popcorn-touting clout of the big chains, UGC and Gaumont, by screening classic and contemporary films.

If your French is up to it, you can watch your way through the entire careers of individual directors in the **mini-festivals** held at many independent cinemas, notably the Action chain, the Escurial, the Entrepôt and Le Studio 28. And if you can read French subtitles, you can go and see a Senegalese, Brazilian or

Finnish film that might never be screened in Britain or the US. Even if you have no French at all, it's easy to find **v.o.** (*version originale*) films, both modern and classic. The alternative, to be avoided where possible, is **v.f.** (*version française*), which means the film has been dubbed into French.

The **Quartier Latin**, around the Sorbonne, has a particularly high concentration of arts cinemas showing an almost incredible repertoire of classic films, while the area around the **Gare Montparnasse** is chock-full with big-screen movie-houses offering the latest glossy releases. Some of the **foreign institutes** in the city have occasional screenings, so if your favourite director is a Hungarian, a Swede or a Korean, check what's on at those countries' cultural centres. These will be listed along with other cinema-clubs and museum screenings under "*Séances exceptionnelles*" or "*Ciné-clubs*", and are usually cheaper than ordinary cinemas.

Séances (programmes) start between 1 and 3pm at many places, sometimes as early as 11am, and usually continue through to the early hours. **Tickets** rarely need to be purchased in advance, and they're cheap by European standards. Prices average around €7–10, with the lowest prices at the smaller, independent cinemas. Almost all venues have reductions for students and the unemployed, at least from Monday to Thursday, while some matinée *séances* also carry discounts. For long-termers, UGC, MK2 and Gaumont sell various booklets of tickets and subscriptions, and some independents offer a *carte de fidélité*, giving you a free sixth entry. All Paris's cinemas are non-smoking.

Cinemas

L'Arlequin 76 rue de Rennes, 6e ⓣ01.45.44.28.80. Owned by Jacques Tati in the 1950s, then by the Soviet Union as the Cosmos cinema until 1990, L'Arlequin has now been renovated and is once again *the* cinephile's palace in the Latin Quarter. There are special screenings of classics every Sun at 11am, followed by debates in the café opposite. M° St-Sulpice.

Le Champo 51 rue des Ecoles, 5e ⓣ01.43.54.51.60. Scruffy little cinema at the foot of rue Champollion. Runs themed, *v.o.* programmes over a week or more, featuring the Marx Brothers, perhaps, or Monty Python, or Blaxploitation movies. M° Cluny-La-Sorbonne/Odéon.

L'Entrepôt 7–9 rue Francis-de-Pressensé, 14e ⓣ01.45.40.07.50, ⓦwww.lentrepot.fr. One of the best alternative Paris cinemas, which has been keeping ciné-addicts happy for years with its three screens dedicated to the obscure, the subversive and the brilliant, as well as its bookshop and bar/restaurant. M° Pernety.

L'Escurial Panorama 11 bd de Port-Royal, 13e ⓣ01.47.07.28.04. Combining plush seats, big screen, and more art than commerce in its programming policy, this cinema is likely to be showing a French classic on the small screen and the latest offering from a big-name director – French, Japanese or American – on the panoramic screen (never dubbed). M° Gobelins.

Grand Action 5 rue des Ecoles, 5e ⓣ01.43.29.44.40; Action Ecoles, 23 rue des Ecoles, 5e ⓣ01.43.29.79.89 (both M° Cardinal-Lemoine/Maubert-Mutualité); Action Christine Odéon, 4 rue Christine, 6e ⓣ01.43.29.11.30 (M° Odéon/St-Michel). The Action chain specializes in new prints of old classics and screens contemporary films from around the world. A carnet of ten tickets costs €45.

Le Grand Rex 1 bd Poissonnière, 2e ⓣ01.45.08.93.58, ⓦwww.legrandrex.com. The ultimate 1930s public movie-seeing experience, though you're most likely to be watching a blockbuster and, if foreign, it'll be dubbed. The Big Rex has an Art Deco facade, a ceiling of glowing stars and a kitsch, Hollywood-meets-Baroque cityscape inside its 2750-seater, three-storey Grande Salle. M° Bonne-Nouvelle.

Latina 20 rue du Temple, 4e ⓣ01.42.78.47.86, ⓦwww.lelatina.com. Specializes in Latin American, Portuguese, Italian and Spanish films, usually in *v.o.*, as well as food, art and tango, salsa and flamenco sessions in its restaurant and gallery spaces. M° Hôtel-de-Ville.

Lucernaire Forum 53 rue Notre-Dame-des-Champs, 6e ⓣ01.45.44.57.34. An art complex

Paris on film

Parisians have treated **cinema** as their own private art form ever since the first projection by the **Lumière** brothers' "Cinematograph" at the Parisian *Grand Café du Boulevard des Capucines* in 1895. The 1930s were the golden age of French cinema, as stars of musicals and theatres invaded the cinemas, many of them on liberally censored film vehicles that helped create the French reputation for naughtiness. Meanwhile, more artistically minded *auteurs* were scripting, directing and producing moody, often melodramatic films. The key figure was **Jean Renoir**, son of the Impressionist painter Auguste Renoir. For Parisian scenes, check out his left-wing **Le Crime de Monsieur Lange** (1935), set in a print shop in the then-crumbling Marais. The movement known as Poetic Realism grew up around Renoir and the director Marcel Carné, who made the Canal St-Martin area of Paris famous in **Hôtel du Nord** (1938), a film that starred Arletty, the great populist actress of the 1930s and 40s. Arletty and Poetic Realism reached their apogee in Carné's wonderful **Les Enfants du Paradis** (1945), set in the theatrical world of nineteenth-century Paris, with a script by the poet Jacques Prévert.

After the war, Renoir continued to make great films: his **French CanCan** (1955) is *the* film about the Moulin Rouge and the heyday of Montmartre. Like the vast majority of prewar films, however, even those with Parisian backdrops, it was all shot in the studio. An exception to this system was Claude Autant-Lara's wartime comedy *La Traversée de Paris* (1956), which follows Jean Gabin smuggling black-market goods across the city. From 1959, however, the directors of the **Nouvelle Vague** ("New Wave") dared to take their new, lightweight cameras out onto the streets, abandoning the big studio set-pieces in favour of a fluid, metro-savvy style. Among the seminal works of the movement, **Les Quatre Cents Coups** (1959), by François Truffaut, and **A Bout de Souffle** (1959), by Jean-Luc Godard, both have contemporary Paris as their real star. But perhaps the strongest collaborations between the city and the directors of the Nouvelle Vague are **Paris Vu Par** (*Six in Paris*; 1965), a collection of six shorts by the key figures of the genre; and the quirky **Zazie dans le Métro** (1961), which is only outdone for its Parisian locations by Agnès Varda's **Cléo de 5 à 7** (1962), which depicts two hours in the life of a singer as she moves through the city – mainly around Montparnasse.

Following the success of Claude Berri's *Jean de Florette* (1986), for a long time the French film industry concentrated on glossy "heritage" movies. Few have done Paris any favours, although there have been a couple of recent notable exceptions: Jean-Pierre Jeunet's *Un long dimanche de fiançailles* (2004) re-created the city – including

with three screening rooms, two theatres, an art gallery, bar and restaurant. Shows old arty movies and undubbed current films from around the world. M° Notre-Dame-des-Champs/Vavin.

Max Linder Panorama **24 bd Poissonnière, 9e ⓣ01.44.76.63.00, ⓦwww.maxlinder.com.** Opposite Le Grand Rex, and with almost as big a screen, this Art Deco cinema always shows films in the original and has state-of-the-art sound. M° Bonne-Nouvelle.

MK2 Bibliothèque **128–162 av de France, 13e ⓣ08.92.69.84.84, ⓦwww.mk2.com.** Brand new, and right behind the Bibliothèque Nationale, this is an architecturally cutting-edge cinema with a very cool café and fourteen screens showing a varied range of French films – mostly new, some classic – and *v.o.* foreign movies. M° Bibliothèque/Quai de la Gare.

MK2 Quai de la Seine **14 quai de la Seine, 19e ⓣ08.92.69.84.84, ⓦwww.mk2.com.** On the banks of the Bassin de la Villette. Part of the MK2 chain but distinctive in style – it's covered in famous cinematic quotes and has a varied, art-house repertoire. M° Jaurès/Stalingrad.

La Pagode **57bis rue de Babylone, 7e ⓣ01.45.55.48.48.** The most beautiful of the city's cinemas, built in Japanese style at the turn of the last century to be a rich Parisienne's party place, and recently restored. The wall panels of the Salle Japonaise

the market pavilions of Les Halles – during World War I, while Bernardo Bertolucci's *Innocents*, or *The Dreamers* (2003), was set in the radical Paris of 1968. In complete contrast to the historical spectaculars, the movement known as the **Cinéma du Look** captured a cool, image-conscious version of the city in films such as Léos Carax's *Les Amants du Pont-Neuf* (1991), though its bridge was actually a set in the south of France; Jean-Jacques Beineix's *Diva* (1981), which takes in the Bouffes du Nord theatre (18e); Luc Besson's *Nikita* (1990), with its classic scene in the railway restaurant Le Train Bleu (12e); and Besson's *Subway* (1985), which was filmed largely in the Auber métro station (15e).

As the early energy of the Cinéma du Look petered out in the 1990s, Paris was again depicted in a more meditative and less frenetic style. Krzysztof Kieslowski's *Three Colours: Blue* (1993) featured Juliette Binoche as the perfect melancholy Parisian – and had her swimming in the Pontoise swimming pool (5e). The premise of Cédric Klapisch's *Chacun cherche son chat* (1995) – looking for a cat – was the perfect excuse for a classic exploration of the Bastille quarter in the full, mid-1990s swing of restoration. Far edgier was Mathieu Kassovitz's **La Haine** (1996), an original portrayal of exclusion and racism in the Paris métro and *banlieue*. Kassovitz also had big international hits as an actor in the Jeunet-directed film *Amélie* (2001) – which relaunched Montmartre, especially the area around Abbesses métro, as an international tourist destination – and in Gaspar Noé's utterly shocking *Irréversible* (2002), which follows two bourgeois-Bohemian Parisians as they are drawn into a nightmare underworld.

For American films with classic Paris locations, look no further than: Vincente Minelli's musical *An American in Paris* (1951), featuring Gene Kelly and Leslie Caron dancing on the quais of the Seine – a scene hilariously taken off in Woody Allen's *Everyone Says I Love You* (1996); Billy Wilder's *Love in the Afternoon* (1957); Stanley Donen's musical *Funny Face* (1957) and his comic thriller *Charade* (1963), featuring Cary Grant and Audrey Hepburn; Roman Polanski's nightmarish *Frantic* (1988); Richard Linklater's utterly romantic *Before Sunrise* (1995) and its sequel, *Before Sunset* (2004), both featuring Ethan Hawke and Julie Delpy as transatlantic lovers living out a one-night Parisian fantasy; and Doug Liman's distinctly upmarket thriller, *The Bourne Identity* (2002).

For more information on cinema in France, the English-language **website** Ⓦwww.filmsdefrance.com has excellent listings of French films, searchable by year or by name, as well as directors' and actors' biographies. The best Parisian source of information on films is the Les Halles *videothèque* (see p.370).

auditorium are embroidered in silk; golden dragons and elephants hold up the candelabra; and a battle between warriors rages on the ceiling. Shows a mix of arts films and documentaries, and commercial movies in *v.o.* M° François-Xavier.

Reflet Medicis Le Quartier Latin 3, 5, 7 & 9 rue Champollion, 5e ⓣ01.43.54.42.34. A cluster of inventive little cinemas, tirelessly offering up rare screenings and classics, including frequent retrospective cycles covering great directors, both French and international (always in *v.o*). The small cinema café *Le Reflet*, on the other side of the street, is a little-known cult classic in itself. M° Cluny-La-Sorbonne/Odéon.

▽ Cinéma Reflet Medicis

Le Studio 28 10 rue de Tholozé, 18e ⓣ**01.46.06.36.07.** In its early days, after one of the first showings of Buñuel's *L'Age d'Or*, this was done over by extreme right-wing Catholics who destroyed the screen and the paintings by Dal' and Ernst in the foyer. The cinema still hosts avant-garde premières, followed occasionally by discussions with the director, as well as regular festivals. M° Blanche/Abbesses.

Le Studio des Ursulines 10 rue des Ursulines, 5e ⓣ**08.25.82.61.30.** Screens and sometimes premières avant-garde movies, arts films and documentaries, often followed by in-house debates with the directors and actors. RER Luxembourg.

Cinémathèques and cultural institutions

For the seriously committed film-freak, the best movie venue in Paris is the **Cinémathèque Française**, 51 rue de Bercy, 12e, M° Bercy (ⓣ01.56.26.01.01, ⓦwww.cinemathequefrancaise.com). Along with a dedicated museum of cinema (see p.218), you get a choice of around two dozen different films and shorts every week, many of which would never be shown commercially – and it's all packaged in an incredible building designed by Frank Gehry. Tickets are only €6, or €8 for the Cinéma Bis series of double-handers.

The **Forum des Images**, 2 Grande Galerie, Porte St-Eustache, Forum des Halles, (ⓣ01.44.76.63.00, ⓦwww.forumdesimages.net), is currently closed for restoration but due to open towards the end of 2008. The reopening will be well worth watching out for. Several films (or projected videos) will be screened daily, and there'll be a large and newly accessible library of newsreel footage, film clips, adverts, documentaries, etc.

Cultural institutions and embassies also have their own cinema programmes and screenings. Two with particularly good cinema programmes are the **Pompidou Centre**, place Georges-Pompidou, 4e (M° Rambuteau; ⓣ01.44.78.12.33, ⓦwww.centrepompidou.fr) and the **Institut du Monde Arabe**, 23 quai des Fossés St-Bernard, 5e (M° Jussieu; ⓣ01.40.51.38.14, ⓦwww.imarabe.org).

Film festivals

The **International Festival of Women's Films**, held in mid- or late March, is organized by the Maison des Arts in Créteil, on place Salvador Allende (ⓣ01.49.80.38.98, ⓦwww.filmsdefemmes.com; M° Créteil-Préfecture). At the same time of year (from mid-March to the end of the month) Magic Cinéma (rue du Chemin-Vert, 93000 Bobigny; ⓣ01.41.60.12.34, ⓦwww.magic-cinema.fr) runs the festival **Théâtres au Cinéma**, which takes place in the suburb of Bobigny, to the northeast of the city; it concentrates on the links between literature and cinema. More mainstream films are previewed at the end of March at the **Festival du Film de Paris**, which has recently taken place at the MK2 Quai de la Seine cinema.

During the summer, the Parc de la Villette (M° Porte-de-Pantin) organizes the **Festival du Cinéma en Plein Air** (ⓣ01.40.03.75.75, ⓦwww.villette.com). Films based on changing themes are shown every night (usually from mid-July to the end of August at around 10pm) to an audience of picnickers on the grass. The films are free, but you have to pay if you want to hire a deckchair (€6.50).

Theatre

Certain directors in France do extraordinary things with the medium of **theatre**. Classic texts are shuffled into theatrical moments, where spectacular

Buying theatre tickets

The easiest place to get tickets to see a stage performance in Paris is from one of the FNAC shops or Virgin Megastore (see p.396 and p.404). Alternatively, you can buy tickets through their websites Ⓦwww.fnac.com and Ⓦwww.virginmega.fr. You can either pick up tickets from one of their branches or get them sent to you; FNAC also lets you print them out yourself at home. Another booking service is offered by Ⓦwww.theatreonline.com; you pay for your tickets online and then you're given a reference number which you present to the box office half an hour before the performance to claim your tickets.

Same-day tickets with a fifty-percent discount and a small commission are available from the **half-price ticket kiosks** on place de la Madeleine, 8ᵉ, opposite no. 15, and on the Esplanade de la Gare du Montparnasse, 14ᵉ (Tues–Sat 12.30–8pm, Sun 12.30–4pm), but queues can be very long and the tickets are likely to be for the more commercial plays. Booking well in advance, though, is essential for new productions and all shows by the superstar directors. Prices vary between around €10 and €35. Previews at half price are advertised in *Pariscope*, etc, and there are weekday discounts at some places for students. Most theatres are closed on Sunday and Monday, and during August.

and dazzling sensation takes precedence over speech. Their shows are overwhelming: huge casts, vast sets (sometimes real buildings never before used for theatre), exotic lighting effects, original music scores. It adds up to a unique experience, even if you haven't understood a word. The director *par excellence* of this form is **Ariane Mnouchkine**, whose Théâtre du Soleil is based at the Cartoucherie in Vincennes. **Peter Brook**, the British director based at the Bouffes du Nord theatre, is another great magician of the all-embracing several-day show. Any show by these two should not be missed.

At the same time, bourgeois farces, postwar classics, Shakespeare, Racine and the like are staged with the same range of talent, or lack of it, that you'd find in London or New York. What you'll rarely find are the home-grown, socially concerned and realist dramas of the sort that have in the past kept theatre alive in Britain. Edward Bond plays, often dealing with the nature of power and the oppression of minorities (scarcely performed now in the UK), in translation, are a regular feature on Parisian theatre programmes, and productions of hard-hitting works by playwrights such as Sarah Kane and Mark Ravenhill (who wrote *Shopping and Fucking*) are quite successful – the French equivalents hardly exist.

The great generation of French or Francophone dramatists, which included Anouilh, Genet, Camus, Sartre, Adamov, Ionesco and Cocteau, came to an end with the death of **Samuel Beckett** in 1990 and **Ionesco** in 1994. Their plays, however, are still frequently performed. The Huchette has been playing Ionesco's *La Cantatrice Chauve* every night since October 1952, and the **Comédie Française**, the national theatre for the classics, is as likely to put on Genet's *Les Paravents*, which set off riots on its opening night, as Corneille and Racine.

One of the encouraging things about France and its public authorities is that they take their culture, including the theatre, seriously. Numerous theatres and theatre companies in Paris are subsidized, either wholly or in part, by the government or the Ville de Paris. And the suburbs are not left out, thanks to the ubiquitous **Maisons de la Culture**, which were the brainchild of man of letters André Malraux, de Gaulle's wartime aide, and eventually, in the 1960s, his Minister of Culture. Ironically, however, although they were designed to bring culture to the masses, their productions are often among the most "difficult" and intellectually inaccessible.

Café-théâtre

Although literally a revue, monologue or mini-play performed in a place where you can drink, and sometimes eat, **café-théâtre** is probably less accessible than a Racine tragedy at the Comédie Française. The humour or dirty jokes, wordplay, and allusions to current fads, phobias and politicians can leave even a fluent French-speaker in the dark.

To give it a try, head for one of the main venues concentrated around the Marais. Tickets average around €15, and the spaces are small – though you have a good chance of getting in on the night during the week.

Blancs-Manteaux 15 rue des Blancs-Manteaux, 4e ⓣ01.48.87.15.84, ⓦwww.blancsmanteaux.fr. The programme includes revues, plays, stand-up comedy and chanson evenings. As well as hosting established names, it encourages new talent and has been the launch pad for a number of French stars, such as comédienne Anne Roumanoff. Shows are €16. M° Hôtel-de-Ville/Rambuteau.

Café de la Gare 41 rue du Temple, 4e ⓣ01.42.78.52.51, ⓦwww.cafe-de-la-gare.fr.st. This place retains a reputation for novelty and specializes in stand-up comedy and comic plays. €22. M° Hôtel-de-Ville/Rambuteau.

Point Virgule 7 rue Ste-Croix-de-la-Bretonnerie, 4e ⓣ01.42.78.67.03. With a policy for giving unknown performers a go, this is a place where you can sometimes strike lucky, sometimes not. €17. M° Hôtel-de-Ville/St-Paul.

Another plus is the Parisian theatre's openness to **foreign influence** and foreign work. The troupe at the Théâtre du Soleil is made up of around twenty different nationalities, and foreign artists and directors are frequent visitors. In any month there might be an Italian, Mexican, German or Brazilian production playing in the original language, or offerings by radical groups from Turkey or China, who are denied a venue at home.

The best time of all for theatre lovers to come to Paris is for the **Festival d'Automne** from mid-September to mid-December (see p.382), an international celebration of all the performing arts, which attracts stage directors of the calibre of the American Robert Wilson and Canadian Robert Lepage.

Noteworthy venues

Bouffes du Nord 37bis bd de la Chapelle, 10e ⓣ01.46.07.34.50, ⓦwww.bouffesdunord.com. The ground-breaking theatre director Peter Brook resurrected the derelict Bouffes du Nord in 1974 and has been based there ever since, mounting innovative, unconventional and controversial works, among them his nine-hour *Mahabharata* in 1985, *The Death of Krishna* in 2004, addressing questions of religion and power, and township drama *Sizwe Banzi is Dead* in 2006. The theatre also invites renowned international directors and hosts top-notch chamber music recitals. M° La Chapelle.

Cartoucherie rte du Champ-de-Manœuvre, 12e. This ex-army munitions dump is home to several cutting-edge theatre companies: the Théâtre du Soleil (see above; ⓣ01.43.74.24.08, ⓦwww.theatre-du-soleil.fr); the French-Spanish troupe, Théâtre de l'Epée de Bois (ⓣ01.43.08.39.74, ⓦwww.epeedebois.com); the Théâtre de la Tempête (ⓣ01.43.28.36.36, ⓦwww.la-tempete.fr); the Théâtre du Chaudron (ⓣ01.43.28.97.04); and the Théâtre de l'Aquarium (ⓣ01.43.74.99.61, ⓦwww.theatredelaquarium.com). M° Château-de-Vincennes.

Comédie Française 2 rue de Richelieu, 1er ⓣ01.44.58.15.15, ⓦwww.comedie-francaise.fr. This venerable national theatre is a long-standing venue for the classics – Molière, Racine, Corneille – as well as twentieth-century greats Anouilh, Genet and the like. M° Palais-Royal.

Maison des Arts de Créteil place Salvador-Allende, Créteil ⓣ01.45.13.19.19, ⓦwww.maccreteil.com. As well as hosting the International Festival of Women's Films (see p.381), the Maison des Arts de Créteil also serves as a lively suburban theatre, with a festival in Feb/March of multicultural and cutting-edge performances, known as Festival Exit. M° Créteil-Préfecture.

MC93 1 bd Lénine, Bobigny Ⓣ01.41.60.72.72, Ⓦwww.mc93.com. MC93 succeeds with highly challenging productions, and regularly invites in foreign directors. M° Pablo-Picasso.

Odéon Théâtre de l'Europe 1 place Paul-Claudel, 6e Ⓣ01.44.41.36.36, Ⓦwww.theatre-odeon.fr. This splendid, Neoclassical state-funded theatre puts on contemporary plays by top directors such as Robert Wilson, as well as *version originale* productions by well-known foreign companies. During May 1968, this theatre was occupied by students and became an open parliament with the backing of its directors, Jean-Louis Barrault (of Baptiste fame in *Les Enfants du Paradis*) and Madeleine Renaud, one of the great French stage actresses. Promptly sacked by de Gaulle's Minister for Culture, they formed a new company and moved to the disused Gare d'Orsay. Their final years in the Théâtre du Rond-Point gave Paris its best performances of Beckett. M° Odéon.

Théâtre des Amandiers 7 av Pablo-Picasso, Nanterre Ⓣ01.46.14.70.00, Ⓦwww.nanterre-amandiers.com. Renowned for innovative and avant-garde productions, such as Jonathan Harvey's opera *Wagner Dream*, performed in 2007. RER Nanterre-Préfecture and theatre shuttle bus.

Théâtre des Artistic-Athévains 45bis rue Richard-Lenoir, 11e Ⓣ01.43.56.38.32, Ⓦwww.artistic-athevains.com. Small company heavily involved in community and educational theatre. M° Voltaire.

Théâtre de la Bastille 76 rue de la Roquette, 11e Ⓣ01.43.57.42.14, Ⓦwww.theatre-bastille.com. One of the best places for new work and fringe productions. M° Bastille.

Théâtre de l'Est Parisien 159 av Gambetta, 20e Ⓣ01.43.64.80.80, Ⓦwww.theatre-estparisien.net. Well respected for its experimental work. M° St-Fargeau.

Théâtre de la Huchette 23 rue de la Huchette, 5e Ⓣ01.43.26.38.99. Fifty years on, this intimate little theatre, seating ninety, is still showing Ionesco's *Cantatrice Chauve* (*The Bald Prima Donna*; 7pm) and *La Leçon* (8pm), two classics of the Theatre of the Absurd. Reserve by phone or at the door from 5pm; tickets €19 for one play or €29 for two. M° Saint-Michel.

Théâtre National de Chaillot Palais de Chaillot, place du Trocadéro, 16e Ⓣ01.53.65.30.00, Ⓦwww.theatre-chaillot.fr. Puts on an exciting programme and often hosts foreign productions; Deborah Warner and Robert Lepage are regular visitors. M° Trocadéro.

Théâtre National de la Colline 15 rue Malte-Brun, 20e Ⓣ01.44.62.52.52, Ⓦwww.colline.fr. Known for its modern and cutting-edge productions under director Alain Françon. M° Gambetta.

Théâtre National de Langue Française Parc de la Villette, 211 av Jean-Jaurès, 19e Ⓣ01.40.03.93.95, Ⓦwww.villette.com. Set in an old dining hall once used by the cattle market traders of La Villette, this small theatre, seating 160, specializes in works from French-speaking parts of the world such as Tahiti and Togo. M° Porte de Pantin.

Théâtre de Nesle 8 rue de Nesle, 6e Ⓣ01.46.34.61.04. New French work and reworkings of old texts, as well as English and American in the original. M° Odéon.

Théâtre de l'Opprimé 78 rue du Charolais, 12e Ⓣ01.43.45.81.20, Ⓦwww.theatredelopprime.com. This small theatre puts on mostly contemporary plays, and is inspired by the ideas of Brazilian director Augusto Boal, who believed that theatre can and should change the world. M° Reuilly-Diderot.

Théâtre Paris-Villette Parc de la Villette, 211 av Jean-Jaurès, 19e Ⓣ01.42.02.02.68, Ⓦwww.theatre-paris-villette.com. Showcases contemporary work by young, up-and-coming playwrights and runs a lot of community projects. M° Porte de Pantin.

Dance

The status of **dance** in the capital received a major boost with the inauguration in 2004 of the **Centre National de la Danse**, a long-overdue recognition of the importance of dance in a nation that boasts six hundred dance companies. A huge centre on the scale of the Pompidou, the CND is committed to promoting every possible dance form, from classical to contemporary, and including ethnic traditions. The centre's creation also reflects an increased interest in the capital in dance, especially in contemporary dance, and while Paris itself has few home-grown companies (government subsidies go to regional companies expressly to decentralize the arts) it makes up for this by regularly hosting all the best contemporary practitioners. As well as big international names like Merce Cunningham and William Forsythe, **notable companies** worth looking out for are Régine Chopinot's troupe from La Rochelle, Compagnie Maguy Marin from Rillieux-la-Pape, Jean-Claude Gallotta's from Grenoble, Catherine Diverrès' from Rennes, and Angelin Preljocaj's from Aix-en-Provence. Creative **choreographers** based in Paris include the Californian Carolyn Carlson at La Cartoucherie.

Some of the most **innovative French dance companies** combine different media and genres to create dazzling, unclassifiable spectacles. One such is the Compagnie Montalvo-Hervieu, based in Créteil, just outside Paris and founded in 1988 by Spanish dancer and choreographer José Montalvo, and Dominique Hervieu; their hugely entertaining shows combine every dance genre going: hip-hop, ballet, street swing, break-dancing, all set against a background of giant video images, with which the dancers interact, and accompanied by a soundtrack of music ranging from Vivaldi to Fat Boy Slim.

As for **ballet**, the principal stage is at the restored Opéra Garnier, home to the Ballet de l'Opéra National de Paris, directed by Brigitte Lefèvre. It still bears the influence of Rudolf Nureyev, its charismatic, if controversial, director from 1983 to 1989, and frequently revives his productions, such as *Swan Lake* and *La Bayadère*.

Plenty of space and critical attention are also given to **tap**, **tango**, **folk** and **jazz dancing**, and to visiting traditional dance troupes from all over the world. There are also a dozen or so black African companies in Paris and the fashionable Japanese butoh, as well as several Indian dance troupes, the Ballet Classique Khmer, and many more from exiled cultures.

Major **festivals** combining theatre, dance, mime, classical music and its descendants include the Festival Exit in February/March in Créteil (ⓦwww.maccreteil.com), the Paris Quartier d'Eté from mid-July to mid-August (ⓣ01.44.94.98.00, ⓦwww.quartierdete.com), the Festival Agora at the Pompidou Centre's IRCAM in June (ⓦwww.ircam.fr) and the Festival d'Automne from mid-September to mid-December (ⓣ01.53.45.17.00, ⓦwww.festival-automne.com), where experimental choreographer Trisha Brown usually makes an appearance.

Venues

Centre Mandapa 6 rue Wurtz, 13e ⓣ01.45.89.01.60. Hosts mainly classical Indian dance and also gives lessons. M° Glacière.

Centre National de la Danse 1 rue Victor Hugo, Pantin ⓣ01.41.83.27.27, ⓦwww.cnd.fr. The capital's major new dance centre occupies an impressively large building, ingeniously converted from a disused 1970s monolith into an airy and light high-tech space. Though several of its eleven studios are used for performances, the main emphasis of the centre is to promote dance through training, workshops and exhibitions and to act as a major resource centre for dance professionals (it has a huge archive and multimedia library). M° Hoche/RER Pantin.

Opéra de la Bastille place de la Bastille, 12e ⓣ08.36.69.78.68, ⓦwww.opera-de-paris.fr. Stages some productions by the Ballet de l'Opéra National de Paris, but in general its programme moves away from the classics. M° Bastille.

Opéra de Paris Garnier place de l'Opéra, 9e ⓣ08.36.69.78.68, ⓦwww.opera-de-paris.fr. Main home of the Ballet de l'Opéra National de Paris and the place to see ballet classics. M° Opéra.

Pompidou Centre **rue Beaubourg, 4e ⓣ01.44.78.16.25, ⓦwww.centrepompidou.fr.** The Grande Salle in the basement is used for dance performances by visiting companies. M° Rambuteau/RER Châtelet-Les-Halles.

Regard du Cygne **210 rue de Belleville, 20e ⓣ01.43.58.55.93.** Innovative and exciting new work is performed here. One of the centre's best-known events is its series of Spectacles Sauvages, in which virtually anyone can perform a ten-minute piece to the public. M° Place-des-Fêtes.

Théâtre des Abbesses **31 rue des Abbesses, 18e ⓣ01.42.74.22.77, ⓦwww.theatredelaville-paris.com.** Sister company to the Théâtre de la Ville, hosting Indian and other international dance. M° Abbesses.

Théâtre de la Bastille **76 rue de la Roquette, 11e ⓣ01.43.57.42.14, ⓦwww.theatre-bastille.com.** As well as more traditional theatre, there are also dance and mime performances by young dancers and choreographers. M° Bastille.

Théâtre des Champs-Elysées **15 av Montaigne, 8e ⓣ01.49.52.50.50, ⓦwww.theatrechampselysees.fr.** This prestigious venue occasionally hosts major foreign troupes and stars such as Sylvie Guillem. M° Alma-Marceau.

Théatre de la Cité Internationale **21 bd Jourdan, 14e ⓣ01.43.13.50.50, ⓦwww.theatredelacite.com.** An exciting dance venue that hosts the Presqu'ils de la Danse contemporary dance festival in March and performances from the Festival d'Automne later in the year. RER Cité Universitaire.

Théâtre Musical de Paris **place du Châtelet, 4e ⓣ01.40.28.28.40, ⓦwww.chatelet-theatre.com.** It was here, in 1910, that Diaghilev put on the first season of Russian ballet, assisted by Cocteau. Though mainly used for classical concerts and opera, it also hosts top-notch visiting ballet companies such as the Mariinsky. M° Châtelet.

Théâtre National de Chaillot **Palais de Chaillot, place du Trocadéro, 16e ⓣ01.53.65.30.00, ⓦwww.theatre-chaillot.fr.** Innovative and top-quality dance from France's leading choreographers, as well as regular slots by foreign superstars such as William Forsythe. M° Trocadéro.

Théâtre de la Ville **2 place du Châtelet, 4e ⓣ01.42.74.22.77, ⓦwww.theatredelaville-paris.com.** Specializes in avant-garde dance by top European choreographers, such as Karine Saporta, Anne Teresa de Keersmaeker and Pina Bausch. M° Châtelet.

22

Classical music and opera

Classical music, as you might expect in this Neoclassical city, is alive and well and takes up twice the space of "jazz-pop-folk-rock" in the listings magazines. The **Paris Opéra**, with its two homes – the lavishly decorated Opéra-Garnier and modern Opéra-Bastille – puts on a fine selection of **opera and ballet**, from core repertoire to new commissions. If you're interested in **contemporary music**, check out the Cité de la Musique at La Villette or IRCAM near the Pompidou Centre. Ticket prices for concerts and opera performances are very reasonable, compared with, say, the New York or London venues.

On June 21 the **Fête de la Musique** is a day of music-making throughout the capital; orchestras play in the Palais Royal courtyard, buskers take to the streets and the big music venues stage free concerts.

Classical music

Paris is a stimulating environment for **classical music**, with a choice of ten to twenty concerts every day of the week. Many performances are held in churches, often for free or relatively little. Excellent chamber music can be heard in the fine settings of the Musée du Louvre, Musée d'Orsay and a number of other museums. The main **orchestras** to look out for are the Orchestre de Paris, which has built up a formidable reputation under Christopher Eschenbach, and the Orchestre National de France, which is under the baton of Kurt Masur.

Early music has a dedicated following in Paris. The capital's most respected Baroque ensemble is William Christie's Les Arts Florissants, renowned for their exciting renditions of Rameau's operas and choral works by Lully and Charpentier. The highly regarded Marc Minkowski, another champion of French Baroque music, also conducts regularly in the capital.

Contemporary and experimental computer-based work flourishes, too. Regular concerts are given at IRCAM, a vast laboratory of acoustics and "digital signal processing", generously funded by the state and headed for many years by renowned composer Pierre Boulez, a pupil of Olivier Messiaen, the grand old man of modern French music, who died in 1992.

Although Boulez no longer conducts IRCAM's acclaimed Ensemble Intercontemporain (Ⓦ www.ensembleinter.com), now based at the Cité de la Musique, it still bears its creator's stamp and is committed to performing new work.

The city hosts a good number of **music festivals**, which vary from year to year; the major ones are listed on pp.380–383. For more details, pick up the current year's festival schedule from any of the tourist offices or the Hôtel de Ville, 29 rue du Rivoli, 4e (M° Hôtel-de-Ville).

Two **periodicals** devoted to the music scene are the monthly *Le Monde de la Musique* and *Diapason*. Two free monthlies – *Cadences* and *La Terrasse* – are distributed outside concert venues. A good, general **website** is Ⓦ www.concertclassic.com.

Regular concert venues

While the profile of classical music in Paris is high, the city, rather surprisingly, does not possess a full-scale concert hall of the calibre of the Berlin Philharmonic's, for example. A new project is under way, however, to rectify this lack – French architect Jean Nouvel has been commissioned to design a state-of-the-art **2400-seat auditorium in La Villette**, on the city's northeastern outskirts. Due to open in 2012, it will have "suspended balconies" that will allow sound waves to circulate around and behind them, while the exterior will be topped by an eye-catching fifty-metre-tall white "sail" which will be visible from far around.

Tickets for classical concerts are best bought at the box offices, though for big names you may find overnight queues, and a large number of seats are always booked by subscribers. The price range is very reasonable. The listings magazines and daily newspapers will have details of concerts in the following venues, in the churches and in the suburbs. Look out for posters as well.

Auditoriums and theatres

Cité de la Musique 221 av Jean-Jaurès, 19e Ⓣ 01.44.84.44.84 for the Salle des Concerts, Ⓦ www.cite-musique.fr. Adjustable concert hall with seating for 800–1200 listeners depending on the programme, which can cover anything from traditional Korean music to the contemporary sounds of the Ensemble Intercontemporain. Performances also in the museum amphitheatre with the occasional airing of instruments from the museum. Tickets from €17. M° Jaurès.

Conservatoire National Supérieur de Musique et de Danse de Paris 209 av Jean-Jaurès, 19e Ⓣ 01.40.40.46.46, Ⓦ www.cnsmdp.fr. Debates, masterclasses and free performances from the conservatoire's students. M° Porte-de-Pantin.

IRCAM (Institut de Recherche et Coordination Acoustique/Musique) 1 place Igor Stravinsky, 4e Ⓣ 01.44.78.48.16, Ⓦ www.ircam.fr. IRCAM, the experimental music laboratory set up by Pierre Boulez, now in his 80s, hosts regular concerts on site and also in the main hall (Grande Salle) of the nearby Pompidou Centre and at the Théâtre des Bouffes du Nord. Ticket prices vary. M° Hôtel-de-Ville.

Maison de Radio France 116 av du Président-Kennedy, 16e Ⓣ 01.56.40.15.16, Ⓦ www.radio-france.fr. Radio station France Musique programmes an excellent range of classical music, operas, jazz and world music and sometimes puts on free concerts – just turn up half an hour in advance to claim your *carton d'invitation*. Ticket prices vary. M° Passy.

Salle Gaveau 45 rue de la Boétie, 8e Ⓣ 01.49.53.05.07, Ⓦ www.sallegaveau.com. This atmospheric and intimate concert hall, built in 1907, is a major venue for piano recitals by world-class players, such as Stephen Kovacevich, as well as chamber music recitals and full-scale orchestral works. Ticket prices from €15. M° Saint-Augustin.

Salle Pleyel 252 rue du Faubourg-St-Honoré, 8e Ⓣ 01.45.61.53.00, Ⓦ www.sallepleyel.fr. This venerable concert hall, dating back to 1927, reopened in autumn 2006 after a major and highly acclaimed renovation; accoustics are much improved and the Art Deco reception hall has been restored to full splendour. The Orchestre de Paris (Ⓦ www.orchestredeparis.com), the city's top orchestra, performs here most frequently, along with visiting international performers such as Martha Argerich and Jessye Norman. Tickets start from as little as €10. M° Concorde.

Théâtre des Champs-Elysées 15 av Montaigne, 8e ⓣ01.49.52.50.50, ⓦwww.theatrechampselysees.fr. Two-thousand-seat capacity in this historic theatre built in 1913. Home to the Orchestre National de France under Kurt Masur and the Orchestre Lamoureux, but also hosts international superstar conductors, ballet troupes and operas. Ticket prices from as little as €5 (no view); average-priced tickets are around €30, and you can pay up to €150 or so for star performers such as Cecilia Bartolli. M° Alma-Marceau.

Théâtre Musical de Paris Théâtre du Châtelet, 1 place du Châtelet, 1er ⓣ01.40.28.28.00, ⓦwww.chatelet-theatre.com. A prestigious concert hall with a varied programme of high-profile operas, ballets, concerts and solo recitals. Wide range of tickets from as little as €8. M° Châtelet.

Churches and museums

Archives nationales Hôtel de Soubise, 60 rue des Francs-Bourgeois, 3e ⓣ01.40.20.09.34. Chamber music recitals every Sat, usually at 6pm. Tickets at €5 and €10. M° Rambuteau.

Eglise de la Madeleine place de la Madeleine, 8e ⓣ01.42.50.96.18. Organ recitals and choral concerts. Tickets €20–30. M° Madeleine.

Musée Carnavalet 23 rue de Sévigné, 3e ⓣ01.48.04.85.94. Mainly chamber music from the Baroque period, held in one of the museum's elegant salons. Tickets around €10. M° St-Paul.

Musée du Louvre Palais du Louvre (Pyramid entrance), 1er ⓣ01.40.20.84.00, ⓦwww.louvre.fr. Midday and evening concerts of chamber music in the auditorium. Tickets around €10. M° Louvre-Rivoli/Palais-Royal-Musée-du-Louvre.

Musée National du Moyen Age 6 place Paul Painlevé, 5e ⓣ01.53.73.78.16. Regular concerts of little-known music from the medieval period. Ticket prices vary. M° Cluny-La-Sorbonne.

Musée d'Orsay 1 rue de Bellechasse, 7e ⓣ01.40.49.47.57, ⓦwww.musee-orsay.fr. Varied programme of midday and evening recitals of chamber music in the auditorium. €11–20. M° Solférino/RER Musée d'Orsay.

St-Julien-le-Pauvre 23 quai de Montebello, 5e ⓣ01.42.26.00.00. Mostly chamber music and choral recitals. €13–23. M° St-Michel.

St-Séverin 5 rue des Prêtres St-Séverin, 5e ⓣ01.48.24.16.97. Varied programmes. From €15. M° St-Michel.

Sainte-Chapelle 4 bd du Palais, 1er ⓣ01.42.77.65.65. A fabulous setting for mainly Mozart, Bach and Vivaldi classics. €20–25. M° Cité.

Opera

The Opéra National de Paris has two homes, the original **Palais Garnier** (see p.91), place de l'Opéra, 9e (M° Opéra), and the **Opéra Bastille** (see p.211), 120 rue de Lyon, 12e (M° Bastille), Mitterrand's most extravagant legacy to the city, which opened, with all due pomp, in 1989. It's taken Parisians a while to warm to their new opera house, a rather bloated construction that completely dominates the place de la Bastille. The building hasn't worn particularly well, either; the facade has started to crumble in places and unsightly netting holds bits of it in place. Opinions differ over the acoustics and performers are known to say it's a difficult place to sing in, but the stage is certainly well designed and allows the auditorium uninterrupted views.

The Bastille opera's first years were far from easy; it was beset from the start by politico-musical wranglings resulting in a series of resignations, including that of Daniel Barenboim as musical director, followed soon after by the dismissal of Rudolf Nureyev from the same post. In the late 1990s director Hughes Gall brought a period of stability and put the opera's finances on a sound footing. This healthy state of affairs has allowed his successor, Belgian Gérard Mortier, to be a little more daring, and while the safe-bet *La Traviatas* and *Toscas* continue to be staged, audiences have been treated to more ambitious offerings, too, including a six-hour *Saint François d'Assise* by Messiaen and a sell-out performance of Wagner's *Tristan and Isolde*, directed by Peter Sellars and designed by the video artist Bill Viola.

The restored, lavish **Palais Garnier** is generally used for smaller-scale opera productions and ballets. It may not enjoy the high-tech facilities of the Bastille, and views from some of the side seats can be very poor, but an evening in this glittering palace is unforgettable.

Tickets (€7–160) for operas at both venues can be booked Monday to Saturday 9am to 7pm on ⓣ08.36.69.78.68 at least four weeks in advance, via the Internet (ⓦwww.opera-de-paris.fr) from three months to three days in advance, or at the ticket office (Mon–Sat 11am–6.30pm) within two weeks of the performance – the number of tickets available by this stage, however, is limited and people start queuing at 9am, if not earlier. Unfilled seats are sold at a discount to students five minutes before the curtain goes up. Full programme details are on the website.

The Bastille opera house enjoys a friendly rivalry with the **Théâtre Musical de Paris**, part of the Théâtre du Châtelet, which also puts on large-scale opera productions and pursues an adventurous programming policy, recently staging works by contemporary composers such as Pascal Dusapin and Hans Werner Henze.

Occasional operas and concerts by top soloists are hosted by the **Théâtre des Champs-Elysées** (see p.79), while solo singers are often guests at the **Salle Favart** (**Opéra Comique**, rue Favart ⓣ01.42.44.45.46; M° Richelieu-Drouot), which also puts on daring opera productions, operettas and musicals. Both opera and recitals are sometimes staged at the city's multi purpose performance halls (see p.365).

23

Festivals and events

Paris hosts an impressive roster of **festivals and events**. The city's most colourful jamborees are **Bastille day**, on July 14, and the summer-long beach spectacle that is **Paris Plage**, but throughout the year there's invariably something on. If it's not one of the big *salons*, or exhibitions, it'll be one of the arts events subsidized by the ever-active town hall or culture ministry. The tourist office produces a biannual "Saisons de Paris – Calendrier des Manifestations", which gives details of all the mainstream events; otherwise, check the listings and other Paris magazines (see p.46) like *Pariscope* or look up "Events" on the tourist board's website Ⓦwww.parisinfo.com. Many Parisian quartiers like Belleville, Ménilmontant and Montmartre have *portes ouvertes* (open doors) weeks when artists' studios are open to the public and some festivities are laid on, generally in May and June – keep an eye open for posters and flyers. The following listings give a selection of the most important or entertaining festivals and events in the Paris calendar.

January

La Grande Parade (Jan 1) New Year's Day parade, with floats, dancers and bands, from Porte St-Martin to Madeleine (Ⓦwww.parisparade.com).
Paris Dog Show (early Jan) With three thousand dogs in over three hundred runway shows, Fifi wouldn't want to miss this for the world (Ⓦwww.sc-if.org).

February

Chinese New Year (mid-Feb) Paris's Chinese community brings in the New Year in the heart of Chinatown around avenue d'Ivry in the 13e.
Rétromobile (mid-Feb) Hundreds of classic cars and related memorabilia (Ⓦwww.retromobile.fr).
Salon de l'Agriculture (end of Feb to beginning of March) The biggest agricultural show in the world at the Parc des Expositions, Porte de Versailles (Ⓦwww.salon-agriculture.com).

March

Paris Fashion Week (first week of March) Next to Milan, the fashion event of the year. Technically for fashion professionals only, but surely there's a door left ajar somewhere (Ⓦwww.modeaparis.com).
Banlieues Bleues (early March to early April) International jazz festival in the towns of Seine-Saint-Denis – Blanc-Mesnil, Drancy, Aubervilliers, Pantin, St-Ouen and Bobigny (Ⓦwww.banlieuesbleues.org).
Festival of the Imagination (early March to late April) Performances and exhibitions from traditional peoples and lesser-known cultures from all over the world (Ⓦwww.mcm.asso.fr).
Great Wines Fair (second week of March) Held at the Carrousel du Louvre, this wine festival allows would-be sommeliers to taste vintages for next to nothing (Ⓦwww.idealwine.com).
Poets' Springtime (second Mon of March) Thousands of readings, debates, lectures and workshops on the art of *la poésie* (Ⓣ01.53.80.08.80, Ⓦwww.printempsdespoetes.com).

Festival Exit (end March) International festival of contemporary dance, performance and theatre at Créteil (Ⓦwww.maccreteil.com).
Festival de Films des Femmes (end of March/beginning of April) Major women's film festival out at Créteil (Ⓦwww.filmsdefemmes.com).

April

Poisson d'Avril (April 1) April Fools' Day with spoofs in the media and kids sticking paper fishes on the backs of the unsuspecting.
Foire du Trône (April to May) Centuries-old funfair with an actual freak show located in the Pelouse de Reuilly (Bois de Vincennes, 12^{e}; Ⓦwww.foiredutrone.com).
Marathon International de Paris (mid-April) The Paris Marathon departs from Place de la Concorde and arrives at the Hippodrome de Vincennes 42km later. There's also a half-marathon in March (Ⓦwww.parismarathon.com).
Foire de Paris (end April/beginning of May) Food, wine, house and home fair at the Parc des Expositions, Porte de Versailles (Ⓦwww.foiredeparis.fr).

May

Fête du Travail (May 1) May Day. Everything closes and there are marches and festivities in eastern Paris and around place de la Bastille. Lilies of the valley are sold everywhere.
Jazz in the Parc Floral (May to July) Big jazz names give free concerts in the Parc Floral at the Bois de Vincennes (Ⓦwww.parcfloraldeparis.com).
Internationaux de France de Tennis (last week of May and first week of June) The French Open tennis championships at Roland Garros (Ⓦwww.rolandgarros.org).
Printemps des Rues (end of May) Free street performances in the areas of La Villette, Gambetta, Nation and République (Ⓦwww.leprintempsdesrues.com).
Quinzaine des Réalisateurs (last week in May) Public screenings in the Forum des Images of films from the Cannes alternative film festival (Ⓦwww.quinzaine-realisateurs.com).

June

Festival Agora (early June) Contemporary theatre/dance/music festival organized by IRCAM and the Pompidou Centre (Ⓦwww.ircam.fr).
Foire St-Germain (June to July) Concerts, antique fairs, poetry and exhibitions in the 6e (Ⓦwww.foiresaintgermain.org).
Journées de la Maison Contemporaine (second and third weekend) More than 350 houses designed by modern architects are opened up to the public (Ⓦwww.maisonscontemporaines.com).
Course des Garçons de Café (mid-June) Jacketed waiters and waitresses hightail their trays in an eight-kilometre marathon beginning at the Hôtel-de-Ville (Ⓣ01.42.96.60.75).
Festival de Chopin (mid-June to July) Chopin recitals by candlelight, held in the Orangerie de Bagatelle, in the Bois de Boulogne (Ⓦwww.frederic-chopin.com).
Festival de St-Denis (last two weeks in June) Classical and world music festival with opportunities to hear music in the Gothic St-Denis Basilica (Ⓦwww.festival-saint-denis.fr).
Fête de la Musique (June 21) Live bands and free concerts throughout the city (Ⓦwww.fetedelamusique.culture.fr).
Feux de la Saint-Jean (around June 21) Fireworks for St-Jean's Day at the Parc de la Villette and quai St-Bernard.
Gay Pride (late June) Lesbian and Gay Pride march (Ⓦwww.marche.inter-lgbt.org).
Fête du Cinéma (end of June) A superb opportunity to view a wide range of films from classics to the cutting-edge in French and foreign cinema. Buy one full-price ticket and you can see any number of films during the weekend-long festival for €2 (Ⓦwww.feteducinema.com).

July

La Goutte d'Or en Fête (one week around late June/early July) Music festival of rap, reggae and raï with local and international performers in the Goutte d'Or district, 10e (Ⓦwww.gouttedorenfete.org).
Bastille Day (July 14 and evening before) The 1789 surrender of the Bastille is celebrated in official pomp, with parades of tanks down the Champs-Elysées, firework displays and concerts. On the evening of the 13th, there's dancing in the streets around place de la Bastille to good French bands, and "Bals Pompiers" parties rage inside every fire station in Paris – rue Blanche and rue des Vieux-Colombiers are known to be among the best.

Paris Quartier d'Eté (mid-July to mid-Aug) Cinema, dance, music and theatre events around the city (ⓦwww.quartierdete.com).

Festival de Cinéma en Plein Air (mid July to end Aug) Thousands turn up at dusk every night for free, open-air, classic cinema at the Parc de la Villette (ⓦwww.villette.com or ⓦwww.cinema.arbo.com).

Paris Plage (mid-July to mid-Aug) A popular initiative launched by the mayor, Bertrand Delanoë, in which 3km of the Seine *quais* – from the Pont de Sully to the Tuileries – are closed to traffic and transformed into mini-beaches, complete with imported sand, palm trees, parasols, sun-loungers and beach games. There are free concerts on Fri and Sat evenings. From 2007, there'll also be a beach on the Left Bank, in front of the Bibliothèque Nationale (13e). The Stade de France stadium, meanwhile, is taken over by swimming, sailing, volleyball and other beach-type sports.

Arrivée du Tour de France Cycliste (third or fourth Sun) The Tour de France cyclists cross the finishing line in the avenue des Champs-Elysées (ⓦwww.letour.fr).

August

Cinéma au Clair de Lune (throughout August) Open-air screenings of films shot in Paris on a giant screen that tours the arrondissements (ⓦhttp://clairdelune.forumdesimages.net).

Fête de l'Assomption (Aug 15) A procession from Notre-Dame around the Ile de la Cité.

September

Fête de l'Humanité (second weekend) Sponsored by the French Communist Party and *L'Humanité* newspaper, this annual three-day event just north of Paris at La Courneuve attracts people in their tens of thousands and of every political persuasion. Food and drink (all very cheap), and music and crafts from every corner of the globe, are the predominant features. Each French regional CP has a vast restaurant tent with its specialities; French and foreign bands play on an open-air stage; and the event ends on Sunday night with an impressive firework display. (M° La Courneuve, then bus #177 or special shuttle from RER; ⓦwww.humanite.fr/fete.php3.)

Villette Jazz Festival (mid-Sept) One of the city's best jazz festivals, with music played by legendary greats and local conservatory students, held in the park and Grande Halle at la Villette (ⓦwww.villette.com).

Biennale des Antiquaires (last two weeks) The city's largest antiques show, held at the Carrousel du Louvre with everything from coins to stamps, and art to furniture and jewellery (ⓦwww.biennaledesantiquaires.com).

Festival d'Automne (mid-Sept to late Dec) Major festival of contemporary theatre, music, dance and avant-garde arts. Companies from all over the world descend on the city for three months (ⓦwww.festival-automne.com).

Techno Parade (mid-Sept) One of the highlights of the Rendez-vous Electroniques festival, attracting hundreds of thousands. Floats with sound systems parade from Place de la République to Pelouse de Reuilly, where a big party is held (ⓦwww.technopol.net).

Journées du Patrimoine (third weekend) A France-wide event where normally off-limits buildings – like the Palais de l'Elysée where the President resides – are opened to a curious public. Details in local press and on ⓦwww.jp.culture.fr.

October

Prix de l'Arc de Triomphe (first weekend) Horse flat-racing with high stakes at Longchamp (ⓦwww.prixarcdetriomphe.com).

Fêtes des Vendanges (first or second Sat) The bacchanalian grape harvest festival in the Montmartre vineyard, at the corner of rue des Saules and rue St-Vincent (ⓦwww.fetedesvendangesdemontmartre.com).

Nuit Blanche (first or second Sat) All-night cultural events at unusual venues (ⓦwww.paris.fr).

Foire Internationale d'Art Contemporain (FIAC) (late Oct) Big international contemporary art fair taking place over one week at Paris Expo, Porte de Versailles (ⓦwww.fiacparis.com).

JVC Jazz Festival (mid-Oct) Big-name jazz players play in venues all over the city (ⓦwww.jvc.fr).

Salon du Jeu (mid-Oct) The latest in multimedia and board games (ⓦwww.salondujeu.com).

Salon du Chocolat (Oct–Nov) Chocolatiers come to Paris Expo from all over to show off their skills; there are tastings and even a chocolate fashion parade (ⓦwww.chocoland.com).

November

Les Inrockuptibles (early Nov) "Les Inrocks" features big acts playing at various venues around town – anything from Lily Allen to Joan as Police Woman, by way of lots of French bands (ⓦwww.lesinrocks.com/inrocks/festival).

Paris Photo (mid-Nov) From early works to modern masterpieces, this is actually one of the best events anywhere for seeing some of the world's greatest photography. This month also sees photographic exhibitions held in museums, galleries and cultural centres throughout the city (ⓦwww.parisphoto.fr).

Le Beaujolais Nouveau (third Thurs in Nov) Numerous cafés and wine bars celebrate the new vintage with special menus and events.

December

Patinoire de l'Hôtel de Ville (early Dec to end Feb) Ice-skating rink in front of the town hall, with a smaller rink for younger children. Free entry but you pay €5 to rent ice-skates (ⓦwww.paris.fr).

Noël (Dec 24–25) Christmas eve is a huge affair all across France, and of much more importance than the following day. Both Notre-Dame and Eglise de la Madeleine hold midnight Mass services, though you'll need to arrive early to avoid standing (doors open at 10pm, ceremony begins at 10.30pm).

Le Nouvel An (Dec 31) New Year's Eve means dense crowds of out-of-towners on the Champs-Elysées, fireworks at the Champs de Mars and super-elevated restaurant prices everywhere.

24

Shops and markets

When it comes to **shopping**, Paris is an epicurean wonderland. As if the quality, style and variety weren't stunning enough, the attention to the tiniest detail – a ribbon on a package from the bakery, for instance – makes shopping a delight.

Despite pressures to concentrate consumption in gargantuan underground and multi-storey complexes, Parisians, for the most part, remain fiercely loyal to their small local traders and independently owned shops. Whether you can afford to buy or not, some of the most entertaining and memorable experiences of a trip to Paris are to be had for free just browsing in small shops, their owners proudly displaying their cache of offbeat items, particular passions, one-of-a-kind oddities and mouthwatering treats, carefully created according to instructions handed down from generation to generation.

The most distinctive and unusual shopping possibilities are in the nineteenth-century **arcades**, or *passages*, in the **2e and 9e arrondissements**, many now smartly renovated and harbouring the kind of outlets that make shopping an exciting expedition rather than a chore. On the streets proper, the square kilometre around **place St-Germain-des-Prés** is hard to beat; to the north of the square, the narrow streets are lined with antiques shops and arts and interior design boutiques, while to the south you'll find every designer clothing brand you can think of, Parisian or otherwise.

Les Halles is another well-shopped district and is especially good for high-street fashion. The aristocratic **Marais**, the hip quartier of the **Bastille** and northeastern Paris (**Oberkampf** and the **Canal Saint-Martin**) have filled up with dinky little boutiques, interior design, arty and specialist shops and galleries. For Parisian **haute couture** – Hermès and the like – the traditional bastions are avenue Montaigne, rue François 1er and the upper end of **rue du Faubourg-St-Honoré** in the 8e.

Place de la Madeleine is the place to head for luxury **food** stores, such as Fauchon and Hédiard. For essential foodstuffs, the cheapest supermarket chain is Ed l'Epicier. Other last-minute or convenience shopping is probably best done at FNAC shops (for books and records), the big department stores (for high-quality merchandise) and Monoprix (for basics). **Toy shops**, and shops selling children's clothes and books, are detailed in Chapter 25. Information on **VAT reimbursement** for non-EU citizens is given on p.45.

Markets, too, are a grand spectacle. A cornucopia of food from half the countries of the globe, intoxicating in their colour, shape and smell, assails the senses in even the drabbest parts of town. In Belleville and the Goutte d'Or, North Africa predominates; Southeast Asia in the 13^{e} arrondissement. Though food is perhaps the best offering of the Paris markets, there are also street

Opening hours

Many shops in Paris stay **open all day** from Monday to Saturday. Most tend to close comparatively late – 7 or 8pm as often as not. Some smaller businesses close for up to two hours at lunchtime, somewhere between noon and 3pm. Most shops are closed on Sunday and some on Monday as well, though many food shops, such as boulangeries, will open on Sunday morning, and many shops in the Marais open on Sunday afternoon around 2–7pm.

markets dedicated to secondhand goods (the *marchés aux puces*), clothes and textiles, flowers, birds, books and stamps. See pp.407–409 for a full rundown on Paris's markets.

It is worth being aware that Parisian shopkeepers aren't the most fawning of individuals. But by making an early effort to win them over to your side, your shopping experience can become much more pleasant and successful. A simple "*Excusez-moi de vous déranger, madame* (or *monsieur...*") will go miles towards showing that you are a cultured and considerate shopper who merits assistance. Also, sauntering into a boutique with a designer shopping bag already in tow – evidence that you're not merely window-shopping – has been known to work wonders on the customer service front.

Clothes

Milan, New York and London may have their supporters, but Paris remains the original world capital of **fashion**. As a tourist, there may be no way you can get to see the haute couture shows (see box on p.390) but there's nothing to prevent you trying on fabulously expensive creations – as long as you can brave the intimidatingly chic assistants and the awesome chill of the marble portals. But if it's actual shopping you're interested in, rather than fashion-theatre, Paris is, put simply, a fabulous place to buy clothes. The box on p.386 gives general pointers on the best areas to browse, while the listings offer full contact details and brief reviews for some of the best individual shops in the city.

As long as there's a strong euro, visitors from outside the eurozone will find shopping relatively expensive. That said, the **sales** are officially held twice a year, beginning in mid-January and mid-July and lasting a month. There are reductions of up to forty percent on designer clothes. At the larger stores, the best lines in the best sizes are usually swooped upon within the first couple of days, but if you hold back until the very end of the sales you can scoop up whatever's left at fantastic discounts. Ends of lines and old stock of the couturiers are sold year round in "stock" **discount** shops (see p.391), or out at La Vallée Outlet, inside the frontiers of Disneyland (see p.280).

If you feel overwhelmed by the wealth of opportunities for retail therapy, head for a company like Chic Shopping (Ⓣ06.14.56.23.11, Ⓦwww.chicshoppingparis.com) to do the walking. The small group runs shopping-themed tours in English around different Parisian neighbourhoods. Half- or full-day tours of no more than five people (€125 a head) cover a specific theme – "Unique Boutique", "Cheap and Chic" and "Oh là là Outlets" are some of the most popular – and the experience is meant to be very casual, as though you were out shopping with a group of friends.

Where to shop for clothes in Paris

For designer prêt-à-porter, the **department stores** Galeries Lafayette and Printemps, just behind the Opéra on boulevard Haussmann, have unrivalled selections; if you're looking for a one-stop hit of Paris fashion, this is probably the place to come. Alternatively, the streets around **St-Sulpice** métro, on the Left Bank, are lined with clothing shops of all kinds. You'll find rich pickings if you wander down rues du Vieux Colombier, de Rennes, Madame, de Grenelle and du Cherche-Midi, and the relatively compact size and relaxed, Left-Bank atmosphere make this one of the most appealing of Paris's shopping quarters. The historic Bon Marché department store, on rue de Sèvres, is another good reason to begin your shopping trip in this part of the Left Bank, while rues du Cherche-Midi and de Grenelle are particularly good for shoes, and rue des Saints-Pères is known for its underwear shops.

For couture and seriously expensive designer wear, make for the wealthy, manicured streets around the **Champs-Elysées**, especially avenue François 1er, avenue Montaigne and **rue du Faubourg-St-Honoré**. Younger designers have colonized the lower reaches of the latter street, between rue Cambon and rue des Pyramides – a trend that started with the opening in the mid-90s of the fashion set's favourite, the Hôtel *Costes*, near the corner of rue de Castiglione. In the heart of this area, luxurious **place Vendôme** is the place to come for serious jewellery.

On the eastern side of the city, around the **Marais** and **Bastille**, the clothes, like the residents, are younger, cooler and more relaxed. Chic boutiques line the Marais' main shopping street, **rue des Francs-Bourgeois**, and young, trendy designers and hippie outfits congregate on Bastille streets **rue de Charonne** and **rue Keller**.

At the more alternative and avant-garde end of the spectrum, there's a good concentration of one-off designer boutiques around **Abbesses** métro stop, at the foot of Montmartre – try rues des Martyrs, des Trois Frères, de la Vieuville, Houdon and Durantin. For more streetwise clothing, the **Forum des Halles** and surrounding streets is a good place to browse – though you'll have to sift through a fair few shops selling cheap leather jackets and clubbing gear. **Rue Etienne-Marcel** and pedestrianized **rue Tiquetonne** are good for young, trendy fashion boutiques.

Department stores and hypermarkets

Paris's two largest **department stores**, Printemps and Galeries Lafayette, are right next door to each other near the St-Lazare station, and between them there's not much they don't have. Both stores offer a ten-percent discount for tourists on all red-dot items, which includes almost all the big brands; pick up a tourist discount card in your hotel, at the main tourist office or at the welcome desk at either store. Their main rival is Le Bon Marché, over on the Left Bank.

Bazar de l'Hôtel de Ville (BHV) 52–64 rue de Rivoli, 4e. Only two years younger than the Bon Marché and noted in particular for its DIY department, artists' materials, new menswear department and cheap self-service restaurant overlooking the Seine. For lighter refreshment, hunt out the cosy Bricolo Café in the DIY section (near the rue de Rivoli entrance), done out like an old-fashioned workshop complete with workbenches and lamps. The store is less elegant in appearance than some of its rivals, but the value for money is pretty good. M° Hôtel-de-Ville. Mon–Sat 9.30am–7pm, except Wed & Thurs till 8.30pm.

Le Bon Marché 38 rue de Sèvres, 7e **Ⓦ www.lebonmarche.fr.** The world's oldest department store, founded in 1852 and now run by the luxury goods empire LVMH. It's smaller, calmer and classier than its Right Bank rivals, Galeries Lafayette and Printemps, and has an excellent kids' department and a legendary food hall (see p.398). M° Sèvres-Babylone. Mon–Wed & Fri 9.30am–7pm, Thurs 10am–9pm, Sat 9.30am–8pm.

Galeries Lafayette 40 bd Haussmann, 9e **Ⓦ www.galerieslafayette.com.** The store's forte

▽ Galeries Lafayette department store

is high fashion with two floors given over to the latest creations by leading designers; the third floor is almost entirely dedicated to lingerie, plus there's a large section devoted to clothes for children on the fourth floor. Then there's a host of big names in men's and women's accessories, a huge parfumerie, not to mention a branch of the *Angelina salon de thé*, full of lunching ladies – all under a superb 1900 dome. Just down the road at no. 35 is Lafayette Maison, consisting of five floors of quality kitchenware, linen and furniture. M° Havre-Caumartin. Mon–Sat 9.30am–7.30pm, Thurs till 9pm.

Printemps 64 bd Haussmann, 9e ⓦwww.printemps.com. The main store has an excellent fashion department for women spread over three floors, plus a whole floor devoted to shoes and one to accessories. The sixth-floor brasserie is right underneath the beautiful Art Nouveau glass dome; it's rather overpriced, though, and service is slow, so it's probably best to just go for a drink. Next door is a huge men's store, stocking a wide range of labels; the Paul Smith-designed World Bar on the top floor is a perfect spot for a shopping break. M° Havre-Caumartin. Mon–Sat 9.35am–7pm, Thurs till 10pm.

Tati 4 boulevard Rochechouart, 18e ⓦwww.tati.fr (M° Barbès). Hugely successful budget department store chain with a distinctive pink gingham logo. Sells reliable and utterly cheap clothing, among a host of other items. Branches at Galerie Gaîté Montparnasse, 68 av du Maine, 14e (M° Gaîté); 172 rue du Temple, 3e (M° République); 76 av de Clichy, 17e (M° la Fourche); Centre Comercial d'Italie 2, 30 av d'Italie, 13e (M° Place d'Italie). Mon–Fri 10am–7pm, Sat 9.15am–7pm.

Classic style

agnès b. 2, 3 & 6 rue du Jour, 1er (M° Châtelet-Les-Halles); 6 & 10 rue du Vieux Colombier, 6e (M° St-Sulpice). Born in Versailles, this queen of understatement rebels against heavily styled and elaborate garments, favouring anti-élitist staples for women of all persuasions. While the line has expanded into watches, sunglasses and cosmetics, her clothing remains chic, timeless and, best of all, relatively affordable. (Pronounced "ann-yes bay" in French.) Mon–Sat 10am–7.30pm.

APC 4 rue de Fleurus, 6e (M° St-Placide). Perfect for young, urban basics. Simple cuts and fabrics, but still effortlessly classic in that Parisian way. There's a branch in the Marais at 112 rue Vieille du Temple, 3e (M° St-Paul). Mon, Fri & Sat 11am–7pm, Tues–Thurs 9am–7.30pm. The same gear, but discounted over-stock fare, can be found at Surplus APC, 45 rue Madame, 6e (M° St-Sulpice).

Comptoir des Cotonniers 30 rue de Buci & 58 rue Bonaparte, 6e (M° Mabillon/St-Germain-des-Prés). Utterly reliable little chain stocking comfortable, well-cut women's basics that nod to contemporary fashions without being modish. Trousers, shirts and dresses for around €100. Has around twenty branches in Paris – two handy ones are at 10 rue du Jour (M° Les Halles) and 33 rue des Francs Bourgeois (M° St-Paul). Mon 11am–7pm, Tues–Sat 10am–7.30pm.

Indira 33/68 rue Vaugirard, 6e. Beautiful handmade silk and wool shawls, tunics, kameezes, and trousers in striking colours at this Indian original clothing boutique. Prices aren't bad, generally €60–150; a glimmering, chicken-stitched cotton shirt in burnt umber sells for €90. M° St-Placide. Mon–Sat 11am–1pm & 2.30–7pm.

Isabel Marant 16 rue de Charonne, 11ᵉ. Marant has established an international reputation for her feminine and flattering clothes in quality fabrics such as silk and cashmere. Prices are €90 upwards for skirts, around €250–300 for coats. M° Bastille. Mon–Sat 10.30am–7.30pm.

Kabuki 25 rue Etienne-Marcel, 1ᵉʳ. A one-stop store for all your Prada, Issey Miyake and Calvin Klein needs. M° Etienne-Marcel. Mon–Sat 10.30am–7.30pm.

Patricia Louisor 16 rue Houdon, 18ᵉ. Vibrant and sassy, but springing from a solid base of classic Parisian style. Trousers, skirts and pullovers all come in at around €70–120. M° Abbesses. Daily noon–8pm.

Paul & Joe 62–66 rue des Saints Pères, 7ᵉ (M° Sèvres-Babylone) & 46 rue Etienne Marcel, 2ᵉ (M° Sentier). The clothes here are quintessentially French: quirky but not overly showy, cool but not overly radical, feminine but with an edge – for men and women alike. As long as you've got a slim, French-style figure to match, Paul & Joe will magically transform you into a chic young Parisian. Mon–Sat 10.30am–7.30pm.

Sabbia Rosa 71–73 rue des Saints-Pères, 6ᵉ. Supermodels' knickers – literally, they all shop here – at supermodel prices. Beautiful lingerie creations in silk, fine cotton and Calais lace. An ensemble will cost around €150, and you could pay three times that. M° St-Germain-des-Près. Mon–Sat 10am–7pm.

Sonia/Sonia Rykiel 61 rue des Saints-Pères, 6ᵉ. Sonia Rykiel has been a St-Germain institution almost since her shop opened at 175 bd St-Germain in spring 1968. Since then, her daughter Nathalie has started up this younger, more exciting and less expensive offshoot of the Rykiel brand. M° Sèvres-Babylone. Mon–Sat 10.30am–7pm.

Vanessa Bruno 25 rue St-Sulpice, 6ᵉ. Bright, breezy and effortlessly beautiful women's fashions – trainers/sneakers, dresses and bags – with a hint of updated hippy chic. M° Odéon. Mon–Sat 10.30am–7.30pm.

Vilebrequin 281 rue Saint-Honoré, 8ᵉ ⓦwww.vilebrequin.com. Straight from St Tropez, these fashionably perky men's swimming trunks in bright prints and flowers have style and class, though at €100 a pop they had better. A second shop at 5 rue du Vieux Colombier, 6ᵉ (M° St-Sulpice). M° Tuileries. Mon–Sat 10.30am–7pm.

Zadig & Voltaire 1 & 3 rue du Vieux Colombier, 6ᵉ (M° St-Sulpice). The women's clothes at this small, moderately expensive Parisian chain are pretty and feminine. In style it's not a million miles from agnès b. – and her shop's just opposite too – only with a more wayward flair. Branches at 15 rue du Jour, 1ᵉʳ (M° Les Halles); 9 rue du 29 Juillet, 1ᵉʳ (M° Tuileries); 11 rue Montmartre, 1ᵉʳ (M° Les Halles); 36 rue de Sévigné, 4ᵉ (M° St-Paul). Mon–Sat 10am–7pm.

Trendy and avant-garde

A46 17 rue de la Vieuville, 18ᵉ. Young Turkish designer Tuvana has her own boutique selling glamorous clothing with elegant Oriental and Art Deco touches. Good for exciting, one-off dresses, jackets and skirts, and you can have pieces made to measure – for a price. M° Abbesses. Tues–Sun 11am–7.30pm.

Anne Willi 13 rue Keller, 11ᵉ. Completely original pieces of clothing that respect classic French sartorial design. The works are done in gorgeous, luxurious fabrics and run the gamut from layered casual-chic sets to one-piece geometric studies of the body. Prices from €60 upwards. There are also cute clothes for kids such as wool dresses for €85. M° Ledru-Rollin/Voltaire. Mon 2–8pm, Tues–Sat 11.30am–8pm.

Heaven 83 rue des Martyrs, 18ᵉ. English-bred Lea-Anne Wallis has a wild streak, designing luxurious, sometimes brash sometimes classically elegant clothing for men and women. Her husband, Jean-Christophe Peyrieux, handles the adjacent lighting department. M° Abbesses. Tues–Sat 11am–7.30pm, Sun 2–7.30pm.

S2A 46 rue de l'Arbre Sec, 1ᵉʳ ⓦwww.surface2air.com. Fronting as an art-collective and studio space, this trendy clothing boutique generally sells to the popular nouveau skater look, but has a number of very interesting one-of-a-kind, artsy garments. Also sells books, magazines and the latest can't-do-without accessories, and hosts occasional openings and parties. M° Pont Neuf. Mon–Sat 12.30–7.30pm.

Spree 16 rue de la Vieuville, 18ᵉ. So fashionable it actually looks like an art gallery – and in fact the window section is devoted to changing exhibitions of photographs, paintings or fashion installations.

Following the gallery theme, the hip, feminine clothing collection is led by individual designers such as Vanessa Bruno, Isabel Marant and Christian Wijnants, and there are often a few vintage pieces, too, as well as accessories and even pieces of furniture. Clothing mostly falls in the €100–250 range, but some pieces are priced way higher. M° Abbesses. Mon 2–7pm, Tues–Sat 11am–7.30pm.

Tatiana Lebedev 23 rue Houdon, 18e (M° Abbesses) and 64 rue Vieille du Temple, 3e (M° Hôtel-de-Ville). Tatiana Lebedev's pair of one-woman boutiques have found a secure perch on the trendy designer scene with her innovative use of contemporary fabrics. It's not all high-tech, however, and graceful touches soften the look. Tues–Sat 11am–2pm & 2.30–7pm.

The big designer names

Below is just a selection of the main or most conveniently located outlets of Paris's **top designers**. Nearly all the shops operate normal French boutique **opening hours** of Mon–Sat 10am–7pm.

Cacharel 64 rue Bonaparte, 34 rue Tronchet, 6e. Great interpretation of the waif-chic look with textured and gathered prints in dark, decadent hues. M° St-Germain-des-Prés.

Chanel 42 av Montaigne, 8e. Born in 1883, Gabrielle "Coco" Chanel engendered a way of life that epitomized elegance, class and refined taste. Her most famous signatures are the legendary No. 5 perfume, the black evening dress and the once-omnipresent tweed suit. M° Franklin D. Roosevelt.

Chloé 56 rue du Faubourg-St-Honoré, 8e. Dark, tweed wool trousers, light knit tops and lovely semi-formal prêt-à-porter dresses. M° Concorde.

Christian Lacroix 73 rue du Faubourg-St-Honoré, 8e (M° Miromesnil); 366 rue St-Honoré, 1er (M° Madeleine). Best known for his flamboyant, Zorro-flavoured vests and cloaks, this baroque, theatrical designer now does everything from just-woke-up rumpled trousers to sequined and laméd miniskirts.

Comme des Garçons 54 rue du Faubourg-St-Honoré, 8e. Led by Tokyo-born Rei Kawakubo, this very popular label favours novel tints and youthful, asymmetric cuts that defamiliarize the body. Exceptional lace sweaters. M° Concorde.

Courrèges 40 rue François 1er, 8e. Always forward-looking, André Courrèges is most famous for bringing the miniskirt to high fashion. He also popularized the once-again popular moon girl look, with shimmering thigh-high skirts and shin-high mod boots. M° Franklin-D.-Roosevelt.

Givenchy 3 & 8 avenue Georges V, 8e. Couturier to Jackie Kennedy and Audrey Hepburn, and still producing elegantly cut, chic classics – the men's suits are superb – even though the label is now better known for cosmetics and accessories. M° George V.

Inès de la Fressange 14 av Montaigne, 8e. Though Inès – Chanel's "it" model during the 1980s – has moved on, her boutique now puts out a conservative-ish line that proffers stately, almost matronly, basics. Accompanied well by silk scarves, brooches and walking shoes. M° Alma-Marceau.

Jean-Paul Gaultier 44 av George V, 8e (M° George V) & 6 rue Vivienne, 2e (M° Bourse). The primordial young turk of Paris fashion, whose denim collection is well within reach of those not being chased by paparazzi.

Lagerfeld Gallery 40 rue de Seine, 6e. Though he still designs for Chanel and Fendi, Karl Lagerfeld's life as an intellectual and auteur clearly shows in his own ready-to-wear line, typified by stalwart tailoring, bold colours and comfy-fitting tops and jackets that make a lasting first impression. M° St-Germain-des-Prés.

Lanvin 15–22 rue du Faubourg-St-Honoré, 8e. The designs of this originally Breton mark often incorporate idiosyncratic characteristics like taffeta trench coats, satin capes and removable cuffs and collars. M° Concorde.

Sonia Rykiel women 175 bd St-Germain, 6e; men 194 bd St-Germain, 7e (both M° St-Germain-des-Prés). Branch at 70 rue du Faubourg St-Honoré, 8e (M° Concorde). Unmistakably Parisian designer who threw out her first line when the soixante-huitards threw Europe into social revolution. Her multi-coloured designs – especially those stripey sweaters – are still all the rage, as is Rykiel Woman, her sister shop for women's erotic toys at 6 rue de Grenelle, 6e (M° St-Sulpice).

YSL Rive Gauche 6 & 12 place St-Sulpice, 6e (M° St-Sulpice/Mabillon); 32 & 38 rue du Faubourg Saint Honoré, 8e (M° Concorde). When Yves Saint Laurent retired in 2002, he closed shop on his revered couture line and passed the baton over to Tom Ford, who initially

Haute couture

Paris, the capital of haute couture, is represented nowhere more extravagantly than in the January and July fashion shows. Invitations go out exclusively to the élite of the world's fashion editors and to the two thousand or so clients who don't flinch at price tags between £10,000 and £100,000 for a dress. The world's paparazzi descend on the city to stalk the top hotels and designer restaurants for shots of famous bodies cloaked in famous names, and pages are devoted to outrageous catwalk outfits in newspapers and magazines around the world. Couture, everyone who is anyone agrees, is the ultimate arbiter of taste.

The truth, of course, is that the catwalks and the clientele are there to promote mass-produced and mass-consumed luxury goods – from prêt-à-porter lines to handbags and perfumes. When Paris's greatest designer, Yves Saint-Laurent, retired in 2002 it was said to be because he was disillusioned with big-business realities and the loss of the client-couturier relationship. He was reportedly equally disenchanted with the theatrical excesses of the younger generation. Certainly the trend in Paris over the last few years has been for ever more lavish shows, sometimes staged in unconventional places such as stadiums and even train stations, as well as in the dedicated space under the Louvre's Pyramide Inversée, of *Da Vinci Code* fame. Enfants terribles John Galliano and Alexander McQueen are known in particular for wild extravaganzas. In 2007 Galliano set his spring collection in an old market hall and made the interior look like an old mansion; he dressed his models in the guise of actors in a family drama, and had cages of pigs and chickens on stage, as well as two labrador dogs wandering about. Whatever you think about the theatricality of the shows, or the glaring gap between the high street and the catwalk, Paris makes other fashion events look decidedly dull. Milan is too much of a commercial affair, while New York's shows have, understandably, been more subdued in the last few years, and London designers can barely scrape enough money together to hire models (these days, les girls command about forty percent of the budget). London may have produced some of the trend-setting designers of tomorrow – Galliano, McQueen, Stella McCartney, Julien McDonald – but Paris is still where they all head for.

designed this prêt-à-porter spin-off. Now run by ex-Prada man Stefano Pilati, the line has been modernized once again, with beige tulip skirts and colourful polka-dot jackets for women. Classic monochrome chic remains the staple for men.

Discount

A number of dedicated "stock" shops (short for *déstockage*) sell end-of-line and last year's models at thirty- to fifty-percent **reductions**. Before you get too excited, however, remember that thirty percent off €750 still leaves a hefty bill – not that all items are this expensive. The best times of year to join the scrums are after the new collections have come out in January and October.

Cacharel Stock 114 rue d'Alésia, 14e. One of a cluster of factory shops on this stretch of rue d'Alésia, with a good range of Cacharel clothes from last season at 40–50 percent discounts. Lots of suits for men and women. M° Alésia. Mon–Sat 10am–7pm.

La Clef des Marques 124 bd Raspail, 6e. Huge store with a wide choice of inexpensive brand-name clothes for men and women – also lots of lingerie and children's clothes. M° Vavin. Mon 12.30–7pm, Tues–Sat 10.30am–7pm.

Défilé de Marques 171 rue de Grenelle, 7e. Dépôt-vente shop selling a wide choice of designer clothes for women – as returned unsold from the big-name boutiques. Labels from Prada to Paco Rabanne discounted for around €200–300. M° La Tour-Maubourg. Tues–Sat 10am–2pm & 3–7.30pm.

Le Mouton à Cinq Pattes 138 bd St-Germain, 6e. Names such as Helmut Lang and Gaultier can be found among the racks of smart but discounted end-of-line and last-season's clothes for men and women, though often enough the labels are cut out so you'll have to trust your judgement. M° Odéon/Mabillon. Mon–Sat 10.30am–7.30pm. There's a branch for women's clothes at 8 rue St-Placide, 6e, and a general branch at 18 rue St-Placide (both Mon–Sat 10am–7pm; M° Sèvres-Babylone).

Passé Devant 62 rue d'Orsel, 18e. Big-name labels such as Yamamoto, Donna Karan, Miu Miu and D&G hang alongside smaller designers' work, most of it ex-sale-or-return stock at heavily discounted prices. The €75 Diesel jeans here are a steal. M° Abbesses. Tues–Sat 10.30am–7pm

SR Store 64 and 110–112 rue d'Alésia, 14e. Two boutiques dedicated to selling off last year's Sonia Rykiel clothing at 50 percent discounts. No. 110 stocks the classic Sonia Rykiel collection, while no. 64 has the lower-priced, more relaxed "Sonia" range. M° Alésia. Wed–Sun 10.30am–7pm.

La Vallée 3 Cours de la Garonne, 77700 Serris ⓦwww.lavalleevillage.com. Though thirty minutes outside Paris, just next to Disneyland, this American-style outlet centre may be worth a gander if large-scale discount shopping is your thing. Dozens of men's and women's clothing designers – as well as handbags, shoes, luggage, lingerie, jewellery and accessories – at prices starting 30 percent off retail. RER Val d'Europe – Serris-Montévrain. Mon–Sat 10am–7pm, Sun 11am–7pm. See under Disneyland Paris (p.280) for more details.

Secondhand and rétro

Rétro consists mostly of unsold factory stock from the 1950s and 1960s, though some shops specialize in expensive high-fashion articles from as far back as the 1920s. These vintage shops generally differ from *dépôts-vente*, stores selling secondhand designer gear for hundreds of euros off retail. Plain **secondhand** stuff is referred to as *fripe* – not especially interesting compared with London or New York, and dominated by the US combat-jacket style. A great place to look is the Porte de Montreuil flea market (see p.407).

Alternatives 18 rue du Roi-de-Sicile, 4e. Vintage meets designer at this fantastic stop where you can perfect *le look parisien* both with fashionable marks and lesser-known brands. The clothes here are often straight off the bodies of runway models. M° St-Paul. Tues–Sat 1–7pm.

Dépôt-vente du 17e 109 rue de Courcelles, 17e. Big, chic shop whose speciality is designer ready-to-wear brands like Armani, Dior and Rykiel. Recent sightings included a quilted frockcoat in silk from Dior (€330) and a Burberry men's tartan overcoat (€210). M° Courcelles. Mon 2–7pm, Tues–Sat 10.30am–7pm.

Ding Dong Bazaar 24 rue Mouffetard, 5e. Run by the eccentric Madame Samira, this tiny store on the corner takes you back with attractive oddments of clothes, table accessories and paste jewellery dating from the prewar years. M° Place Monge. Mon & Wed–Sat noon–2pm & 4–8pm.

Kiliwatch 64 rue Tiquetonne, 2e. No problems coming up with an original clubbing outfit here: a clubbers' mecca, where rails of new cheap 'n' chic youth streetwear and a slew of trainers/sneakers meet the best range of unusual secondhand clothes and accessories in Paris. Resale here includes army surplus, lumberjack bomber jacket and retro athletic looks, all abundantly stocked. The place in Paris to buy jeans for men, with no fewer than fifteen brands stocked and well displayed. M° Etienne-Marcel. Mon 2–7pm, Tues–Sun 10am–7pm.

Moda di Andréa 79 rue de la Victoire, 9e. Sounds too good to be true, but this diamond in the rough sells all the big names in footwear – Prada, Miu Miu, Jil Sander and YSL – for up to half what you'll pay in most other shops. M° Trinité/Chaussée d'Antin. Mon–Sat 10.30am–7.30pm.

L'Occaserie 30 rue de la Pompe, 16e ⓦwww.occaserie.com. Specialists in secondhand haute couture – Dior, Prada, Cartier and the like. "Secondhand" doesn't mean cheap though: Chanel suits are around €720, Louis Vuitton handbags €300. M° Muette/Passy. Tues–Sat 11am–7pm. Several smaller boutiques nearby: 16 & 21 rue de l'Annonciation, 14 rue Jean Bologne and 19 rue de la Pompe (all M° Muette/Passy).

Réciproque 89, 92, 93–97, 101 & 123 rue de la Pompe, 16e ⓦwww.reciproque.fr. A similar series of shops to L'Occaserie's, this one is slightly more chichi and better for couture labels, with expensive finds like Christian Lacroix, Moschino and Manolo Blahnik. Women's design at no. 93–95; accessories and coats for men at no. 101; more accessories and coats for women at no. 123. M° Pompe. Tues–Sat 11am–7pm.

Shoes

The French on the whole tend to have smaller, narrower feet, so women (and men) in need of wider sizes may find themselves out of luck in this department. In addition to the shops mentioned below, just walk down rue Grenelle and rue du Cherche-Midi in the 6e, or rue du Meslay in the 3e, for a great choice of shoe places.

Autour du Monde 8 rue des Francs Bourgeois, 4e. Stocks cute canvas pumps (€24) by Bensimon in colours such as lime-green, orange and pink, but you can't beat the classic white. M° St-Paul. Mon–Sat 11–7.30pm, Sun 2–7pm.

Eighty Four 84 rue Saint-Honoré, 8e ⓦ www.84shoes.com. All of your favourite footers including Zanotti, Michael Kors and Pedro Garcia, any of whose creations you can try on upstairs in opulent red velvet under a decadent crystal chandelier. An impressive 150 styles of shoes and boots in all, from €300 to €800. M° Franklin-D.-Roosevelt. Mon–Sat 10am–7pm.

Freelance 30 rue du Four, 6e. From leather to feathers, this very popular free-spirited shoe shop attracts the young and extremely funky. €200 and up. M° Mabillon. Mon–Sat 10am–7pm.

Iris 28 rue de Grenelle, 7e. Iris is well known in Paris for stocking the best selection of the most desirable brands, including Chloé, Marc Jacobs and Allessandro dell'Acqua. M° Rue-du-Bac. Mon–Sat 10am–7pm.

Repetto 22 rue de la Paix, 2e. This long-established supplier of ballet shoes has branched out to produce attractive ballerina pumps in assorted colours, much coveted by the fashion crowd, from €120. M° Opéra. Mon–Sat 9.30am–7.30pm.

Shinzo 30 rue Etienne Marcel, 1er. Limited and collectors' editions of all major trainer/sneaker brands at good prices. M° Etienne-Marcel. Mon–Sat 10.30am–7.30pm.

Swingtap 21 rue Keller, 11e ⓦ www.swingtap.com. The hoofers' mecca: tap shoes, CDs to dance along to, and details on tap-dancing classes and shows around town. M° Ledru-Rollin. Tues–Sat 2–7pm.

Hats

Anthony Peto 56 rue Tiquetonne, 2e. This largely men's *chapelier* is loaded with fedoras, top hats, panamas and fezzes done in wool and cotton plaid, tweed, velour and fur. Run by friendly, helpful staff. Most of the fancier hats run at around €100. M° Etienne-Marcel. Mon–Sat 11am–7pm.

Jacques Le Corre 193 rue Saint-Honoré, 1er. Creative, original hats, footwear and handbags. The stylish, unisex hats here come in interesting colours and shapes; Jacques is famed for his classic cotton *cloche*, perfecting the vagrant-chic look. M° Tuileries. Mon–Sat 11am–7pm.

Marie Mercié 23 rue St-Sulpice, 6e. This grande dame of *chapellerie* sells a glamorous collection of plaid, felt and fur hats for all occasions, €180 and up. M° Etienne-Marcel. Mon–Sat 11am–7pm.

Accessories and jewellery

Biberon & Fils 334 rue Saint-Honoré, 1er. An unexpected find on one of the city's most exclusive shopping streets, this bargain shop sells very stylish French-made leather handbags in citrus colours and classic shades (€60–80). M° Pyramides/Tuileries. Mon–Sat 10.30am–6.30pm.

Cécile et Jeanne 49 av Daumesnil, 12e. Innovative jewellery design from local artisans in one of the Viaduc des Arts showrooms. Many pieces under €100. M° Gare-de-Lyon. Mon–Fri 10am–7pm, Sat & Sun 2–7pm.

Décalage 33 rue des Francs-Bourgeois, 4e. Beautiful handcrafted jewellery – in classic and contemporary designs. Prices are reasonable; earrings, for example, start at €50. M° St-Paul. Tues–Sat 11am–7pm, Sun & Mon 2–7pm.

Galerie Hélène Porée 1 rue de l'Odéon, 6e ⓦ www.galerie-helene-poree.fr. Original jewellery from a number of artisan jewellers, as well as ceramics. Prices range from €200 to several thousand euros. M° Odéon. Tues–Sat 11am–7pm.

Harpo 19 rue Turbigo, 2e ⓦ www.harpo-paris.com. Specializing in turquoise Native American-style jewellery, this popular shop sells necklaces, bracelets, rings, clasps, bolas and headgear in every imaginable shape and size, much of it for under €100. M° Etienne-Marcel. Mon–Fri 9am–7pm, Sat noon–7pm.

Hermès 24 rue du Faubourg-St-Honoré, 8e. Luxury clothing and accessory store. Come here for the ultimate silk scarf – at a price. M° Concorde. Mon–Sat 10am–6.30pm.

Hervé Chapelier 1 rue du Vieux-Colombier, 6e www.herve-chapelier.com. Often imitated, rarely matched, these classic bags are striped in two-tone to never go out of fashion. Priced affordably from €20 to €150. M° St-Sulpice. Mon–Sat 10am–7pm.

Jamin-Puech 61 rue d'Hauteville, 10e www.jamin-puech.com. An exquisite range of beautifully crafted bags (around €200) in brightly coloured leather, crepe silk and other luxury fabrics. M° Poissonière. Tues–Sat 10.30am–7pm. There's also a branch at 68 rue Vieille du Temple, 4e (Tues noon–7pm, Wed–Sat 11am–7pm; M° Hôtel-de-Ville).

Peggy Huyn Kinh 9–11 rue Coëtlogon, 6e. Chichi bags in supple leather, lizard and alligator-skin. All shapes and sizes, the beasts start at €250. M° St-Sulpice. Mon–Sat 11am–7pm.

Tati Or 24 bd Rouchechouart, 18e www.tati.fr. The well-known budget clothing chain, Tati, also sells cheap gold jewellery. M° Barbès. Mon–Sat 10am–7pm.

Maternity

Paris is an excellent place to shop for maternity wear. Streets to check out include rue Guichard in the 16e and boulevard Raspail in the 7e, each with no fewer than five different boutiques for expecting mums.

1 et 1 font 3 9 rue Guichard, 16e www.1et1font3.com. Small, blissful shop with a stylish selection of maternity wear, both casual and semi-formal. Most pieces cost around €100. M° Victor-Hugo. Mon–Sat 10.30am–7pm.

En Attendant Bébé 2 rue Guichard, 16e www.enattendantbebe.fr. Fairly sophisticated place selling relaxed but stylish maternity clothes under the logo "nine months that look like me". Many items under €100. M° La Muette Mon 2–7pm, Tues–Sat 10.30am–7.30pm.

Perfumes

Annick Goutal 12 place Saint-Sulpice, 6e. Though Goutal has passed on, the business is still in the family, continuing to produce her exquisite perfumes, all made from natural essences. Many of Goutal's perfumes were inspired by people she knew or places that were special to her. Her best-selling fragrance is Eau d'Hadrien, a heady blend of citrus fruits and cypress. There's also a range for men, including Eau de Monsieur, a delicious lemony amber scent. This is the best branch, but there are many other outlets too. M° Saint-Sulpice. Mon–Sat 10am–7pm.

Editions de Parfums Frédéric Malle 37 rue de Grenelle, 7e www.editionsdeparfums.com. All the perfumes at this deliciously serious boutique have been created by "authors", which means professional parfumeurs working under their own name through this "publishing house". A 50ml bottle costs upwards of €50, or you could spend a fortune having a perfume individually designed for you. M° Rue-du-Bac. Mon Sat 11am–7pm; closed two weeks in Aug.

Séphora 70 av des Champs-Elysées, 8e www.sephora.com. A huge perfume and cosmetics emporium, stocking every conceivable brand. There are lots of testers, and you can get free make-overs and beauty consultations. M° Franklin-D. Roosevelt. Mon–Sat 10am–midnight, Sun 11am–midnight. Also branches at Forum des Halles, level 3, 1er (M° Châtelet-Les-Halles); 1 rue Pierre Lescot, 1er (M° Châtelet-Les-Halles); and 30 av d'Italie, 13e (M° Place-d'Italie); all Mon–Sat 10am–7.30pm.

Art and design

The commercial **art galleries** are concentrated in the 8e, especially in and around avenue Matignon; in the upper Marais; on rue Quincampoix, near the Pompidou Centre; around the Bastille; and in St-Germain. A new crop of next-generation conceptual art galleries is located in rue Louise-Weiss in the 13e, just west of the new Bibliothèque Nationale de France-Mitterrand.

There are literally hundreds of galleries, and for an idea of who is being exhibited where, look up details in *Pariscope* under "Expositions", or *L'Officiel des Spectacles* under "Galeries". Entry to commercial galleries is free to all.

Artists' materials

Comptoir des Ecritures 35 rue Quincampoix, 4e ⓦwww.comptoirdesecritures.com. A delightful shop entirely devoted to the art of calligraphy, with an extensive collection of paper, pens, brushes and inks. Also runs lessons and mounts exhibitions. M° Rambuteau. Tues–Sat 11am–7pm.

Dubois 20 rue Soufflot, 5e ⓦwww.dubois-paris.com. In the same great apothecary-style building since the mid-1800s, the Dubois family still offers an excellent selection of art supplies and paints alongside very knowledgeable service. RER Luxembourg. Mon 10am–12.30pm & 2–7pm, Tues–Sat 9.30am–7pm.

Papier Plus 9 rue du Pont-Loius-Philippe, 4e ⓦwww.papierplus.com. Fine-quality, colourful stationery, including notebooks, travel journals, photo albums and artists' portfolios. M° St-Paul. Mon–Sat noon–7pm.

Paris American Art 2 & 4 rue Bonaparte, 6e. Local art suppliers for the Beaux-Arts students residing around the corner. M° St-Germain-des-Prés. Tues–Sat 10am–1pm & 2.30–6.30pm.

Sennelier 3 quai Voltaire, 7e. Upmarket art supplies, with some beautiful and reasonably priced sketch books. M° St-Germain-des-Prés. Mon 2–6.30pm, Tues–Sat 10am–12.45pm & 2–6.30pm.

Design

A small selection of places where contemporary and the best of twentieth-century **design** can be seen is listed below. Also worth checking out are the shops of the art and design museums, and the streets around the Bastille, with a high concentration of shops specializing in particular periods.

Colette 213 rue Saint-Honoré, 1er ⓦwww.colette.fr. This cutting-edge concept store, combining high fashion and design, complete with photo gallery and exhibition space, has become something of a tourist attraction. When you've finished sizing up the Pucci underwear, Stella McCartney womenswear and Sonia Rykiel handbags, you could head for the cool Water Bar, with its 80 different kinds of H_2O – agonize between the Brazilian Petropolis Paulista, the Corsican Orezza and the limited-edition Evian. M° Tuileries. Mon–Sat 11am–7pm.

CSAO (Compagnie du Sénégal et de l'Afrique de l'Ouest) 1 & 3 rue Elzévir, 3e ⓦwww.csao.fr. Fairly traded crafts and artwork from West Africa, including quilts, cushion covers and Malian cotton scarves in rich, earthy tones, and painted glass from Senegal. Run in concert with the African-music bar-resto, Jokko, next door. M° St-Paul. Mon–Sat 11am–7pm, Sun 2–7pm.

Fiesta Galerie 45 rue Vieille-du-Temple, 4e. A big selection of twentieth-century kitsch and retro objects. M° Hôtel-de-Ville. Tues–Sat noon–7pm, Sun & Mon 2–7pm.

Galerie Documents 53 rue de Seine, 6e. The place to come for vintage posters – all well displayed in this upscale gallery. There are lots of prints and souvenirs to buy for around €30–100, but the original, collectors' film posters are priced at anything from €200 all the way to €30,000. M° Odéon. Mon 2.30–7pm, Tues–Sat 10.30am–7pm.

Galerie Maeght 42 rue du Bac, 7e. Celebrated gallery that makes its own beautifully printed art books, as well as posters and exquisitely made postcards. M° Rue-du-Bac. Mon 10am–6pm, Tues–Sat 9.30am–7pm.

Galerie Patrick Séguin 34 rue de Charonne, 11e ⓦwww.patrickseguin.com. A fine collection of furniture and objects from the 1950s, including pieces by Le Corbusier and Jean Prouvé, though not everything is for sale. There's another showroom nearby in rue des Taillandiers. M° Bastille. Tues–Sat noon–7pm.

Louvre des Antiquaires 2 place du Palais-Royal, 1er ⓦwww.louvre-antiquaires.com. An enormous antiques and furniture hypermarket where you can pick up anything from a Mycenaean seal ring to an Art Nouveau vase – for a price. M° Palais-Royal-Musée-du-Louvre. Tues–Sun 11am–7pm; closed Sun in July and Aug.

Lulu Berlu 27 rue Oberkampf, 11e ⓦwww.luluberlu.com. Crammed with twentieth-century toys and curios, most with their original packaging. M° Oberkampf. Mon–Sat 11.30am–7.30pm.

M & B 43 rue du Faubourg Saint-Antoine, 11e. Though you sure won't find the next Jackson Pollock here, you will find over ten thousand original oil paintings, from as little as €40. M° Oberkampf. Mon–Sat 10am–8pm, Sun 2–10pm.

Résonances 9 cour St-Emilion, 12e ⓦ **www.resonances.fr.** Stylish kitchen and bathroom accessories, with an emphasis on French design. Covetable items include elegant wine decanters and a white porcelain hot-chocolate maker. M° Cour St-Emilion. Daily 11am–9pm.

Le Viaduc des Arts 9–129 av Daumesnil, 12e. Practically the entire north side of the street is dedicated to an extremely high standard of skilled workmanship and craft. Each arch of this old railway viaduct houses a shop front and workspace for the artists within, who produce contemporary metalwork, ceramics, tapestry, sculpture and much more. M° Bastille/Gare de Lyon. Most shops open Mon–Sat 10.30am–7.30pm. See also p.385.

Books

The most atmospheric areas for **book** shopping are the Seine *quais*, with their rows of new and secondhand bookstalls perched against the river parapet, and the narrow streets of the Quartier Latin.

English language

English-language bookshops function as home-away-from-home for expats, often with readings from visiting writers, and sometimes handy notice boards for flat-shares, language lessons and work. The Australian Bookshop and Abbey's in particular operate as cultural ambassadors for Australia and Canada respectively, with a large range of the national literature available in French translation.

Abbey Bookshop 29 rue de la Parcheminerie, 5e. A Canadian bookshop round the corner from Shakespeare & Co (see p.398), with lots of secondhand British and North American fiction; good social science sections; knowledgeable and helpful staff – and free coffee. M° St-Michel. Mon–Sat 10am–7pm.

Brentano's 37 av de l'Opéra, 2e ⓦ **www.brentanos.fr.** English and American books. Good section for kids, with storytelling on Wed afternoons and Sat mornings. M° Opéra/RER Auber. Mon–Sat 10am–7pm.

Galignani 224 rue de Rivoli, 1er. Claims to be the first English bookshop established on the Continent way back in 1802. Stocks a good range, including fine art and children's books. M° Concorde. Mon–Sat 10am–7pm.

Red Wheelbarrow 22 rue Saint Paul, 4e ⓦ **www.theredwheelbarrow.com.** A small, friendly, Canadian-run bookshop, stocking a good selection of general fiction, history and children's books, as well as books set in Paris in English. Check the website for occasional readings and musical soirées. M° Saint Paul. Mon 10am–6pm, Tues–Sat 10am–7pm, Sun 2–6pm.

San Francisco Bookshop 17 rue Monsieur le Prince, 6e. American-run secondhand bookshop with a selection of contemporary literature that would be impressive anywhere. Quite a collection of books on jazz, and sections for everything from gay and lesbian to Latin American studies. Well organized and calm – not a social hang-out. M° Odéon. Mon–Sat 11am–9pm, Sun 2–7.30pm.

Shakespeare & Co 37 rue de la Bûcherie, 5e ⓦ **www.shakespeareco.org.** A cosy and very famous literary haunt (see p.129). Has the biggest selection of secondhand English books in town and every Monday at 8pm there are readings in the library upstairs (where you can sit and read for as long as you like at other times). M° Maubert-Mutualité. Daily noon–midnight.

Tea and Tattered Pages 24 rue Mayet, 6e. Secondhand bookshop with more than 15,000 titles in English, mostly tatty fiction. You can munch on cheesecake, bagels and the like in the small attached *salon de thé*. M° Duroc. Mon–Sat 11am–7pm, Sun noon–6pm.

Village Voice 6 rue Princesse, 6e ⓦ **www.villagevoicebookshop.com.** A welcoming re-creation of a neighbourhood bookstore, with a good, two-floor selection of contemporary fiction and non-fiction, and a decent list of British and American poetry and classics. Also runs frequent readings and author signings. M° Mabillon. Mon 2.30–7pm, Tues–Sat 10am–7.30pm, Sun 1–6pm.

W. H. Smith 248 rue de Rivoli, 1er. Parisian outlet of the British chain. Wide range of new books, newspapers and magazines. M° Concorde. Mon–Sat 9am–7.30pm, Sun 1–7.30pm.

General French

For **general French titles**, the biggest and most convenient shop has to be the FNAC in the Forum des Halles, but it'd be a pity to miss out on the slightly chaotic Left Bank experience at Gibert Jeune.

L'Arbre du Voyageur 55 rue Mouffetard, 5e. A veritable institution in the Latin Quarter, this great old bookshop has thousands of French prose, poetry and social science titles. M° Place-Monge. Mon 1.30–7pm, Tues–Fri 9.30am–7.30pm, Sat 10am–8pm Sun 10.30am–7.30pm.

FNAC Forum des Halles, niveau 2, Porte Pierre-Lescot, 1er (M°/RER Châtelet-Les-Halles). Other branches include 136 rue de Rennes, 6e (M° Saint-Placide); 26 av des Ternes, 17e (M° Ternes); and 4 place de la Bastille 12e (M° Bastille); ⓦ www.fnac.com. FNAC is France's leading retail chain for books, CDs and electronic equipment – as well as for concert and sports event tickets. The shops are mostly huge in scale and offer supermarket-style discounting, but the range of books and music extends into the higher brow. Lots of *bandes dessinées*, guidebooks and maps, among everything else. Mon–Sat 10am–8pm.

Gallimard 15 bd Raspail, 7e. Most French publishers operate their own flagship bookshops, and Gallimard's boulevard Raspail store is one of the greats. M° Sèvres-Babylone. Daily 10am–7pm.

Gibert Jeune 10 place St-Michel & 27 Quai St-Michel, 5e. The biggest of the Quartier Latin student/academic bookshops with a vast selection of French books, this is a real institution. There's a fair English-language and discounted selection at Gibert Joseph, 26 bd St-Michel, 5e. M° St-Michel for all branches. Mon–Sat 9.30am–7.30pm.

Art and architecture

Artcurial 7 Rond-Point des Champs Elysées, 8e ⓦ www.artcurial.com. The best art bookshop in Paris, set in an elegant town house. Sells French and foreign editions, and there's also a gallery, which puts on interesting exhibitions, and an attractive café. M° Franklin-D.-Roosevelt. Mon–Sat 10.30am–7pm; closed two weeks in Aug.

La Hune 170 bd St-Germain, 6e. A good general French range, but the main selling point – apart from its fifty-year history as a Left Bank arts institution – is the art, design, fashion and photography "image" collection on the first floor. M° St-Germain-des-Prés. Mon–Sat 10am–11.45pm, Sun 11am–7.45pm.

Librairie des Archives 83 rue du Temple, 3e ⓦ www.librairiedesarchives.com. Extensive selection of fine and decorative arts and fashion, and a large number of out-of-print books as well. M° Rambuteau/Hôtel-de-Ville. Tues–Sat noon–7pm.

Librairie de l'Ecole Supérieure des Beaux-Arts 17 quai Malaquais, 6e. The bookshop of the national Fine Arts school: own publications, posters, reproductions, postcards, etc. M° St-Germain-des-Prés. Mon–Sat 1–7pm, during exhibitions only.

Librairie le Moniteur 7 place de l'Odéon, 6e. Entirely dedicated to architecture, contemporary and historical, with books in English as well as French. There's even an in-house magazine devoted to public building projects. M° Odéon. Mon–Sat 10am–7pm.

Librairie du Musée d'Art Moderne de la Ville de Paris Palais de Tokyo, 11 av du Président-Wilson, 16e. Specialist publications on modern art, including foreign works. M° Iéna. Tues–Fri 10am–5.30pm, Sat & Sun 10am–6.30pm.

Librairie du Musée des Arts Décoratifs 107 rue de Rivoli, 1er. Design, posters, architecture, graphics, etc. M° Palais-Royal. Daily 10am–7pm.

Taschen 2 rue de Buci, 6e. The Paris home of this renowned publisher of art, photo and architecture books. M° Mabillon. Daily 11am–8pm, stays open until midnight Fri & Sat evenings for late-night browsing.

Film and photography

La Chambre Claire 14 rue St-Sulpice, 6e. Photography specialist, selling art-house titles, style guides and instruction manuals, with a good number of English-text titles. Sells photographs too. M° Odéon. Tues–Sat 10am–7pm.

Ciné Reflet **14 rue Monsieur le Prince, 6e.** This specialized and rather serious little shop has an excellent collection of books on cinema, many but not all in French, as well as pieces of film memorabilia. M° Odéon. Mon–Sat 1–8pm.

Comics (Bandes dessinées)

Album **6–8 rue Dante, 5e (M° Maubert-Mutualité) & 60 rue Monsieur-le-Prince, 6e (M° Odéon); ⓦ www.album.fr.** Serious collection of French BDs, some of them rare editions with original artwork. This block of rue Dante houses no fewer than five separate comic-book shops. Mon–Sat 10am–8pm.

Boulinier **20 bd St-Michel, 6e.** Renowned for its selection of secondhand videos and comics, including many that are difficult to obtain. Good collection of secondhand CDs as well, and many books under €1. M° St-Michel. Tues–Thurs 10am–11pm, Mon, Fri & Sat 10am–midnight, Sun 2pm–midnight.

Editions Déesse **8 rue Cochin, 5e.** Specializes in older, rarer comics. The well-informed owner speaks excellent English and should be able to help you locate whatever you need. M° Maubert-Mutualité. Mon 2.30–7pm, Tues–Fri 11am–1pm & 2.30–7pm, Sun 11am–7pm.

Manga Loisirs **134 rue de Tolbiac, 13e.** Small japanimation boutique that sells largely figurines, models and other related goodies but some books too. M° Tolbiac. Mon–Sat 10am–7pm, Sun 2–7pm.

Thé-Troc **52 rue Jean-Pierre-Timbaud, 11e.** The friendly owner publishes The *Fabulous Furry Freak Brothers* in French and English (he is a friend of the author of the famous Seventies comics, who lives nearby). There are other comic books and memorabilia on sale, too, as well as a wide selection of teas and teapots, secondhand records, jewellery and assorted junk. The attached *salon de thé* (until 7pm) is comfy, colourful and restful, with board games. M° Parmentier. Mon–Fri 9.30am–8pm, Sat 11am–8pm.

Cookery

Librairie Gourmande **90 rue Montmartre, 2e ⓦ www.librairie-gourmande.fr.** The very last word in books about cooking. M° Sentier/Etienne-Marcel. Mon–Sat 10am–7pm.

Performing arts

Librairie Coup de Théâtre **19 bd Raspail, 6e ⓦ www.bonaparte-spectacles.com.** Exhaustive stock of books on ballet, theatre, opera, puppets, music hall, *chansonniers* and the like, and some prints. M° Rue-du-Bac/Sèvres-Babylone. Tues–Sat 10am–7pm.

Gay and lesbian

Les Mots à la Bouche **6 rue Ste-Croix-de-la-Bretonnerie, 4e.** Selling mainly gay-interest books, guides and magazines, plus some lesbian titles. There's a section with English-language literature, and the staff speak good English. A handy place for contacts, with a good notice board and a stack of free listings magazines. M° Hôtel-de-Ville. Mon–Sat 11am–11pm, Sun 2–8pm.

Travel

Institut Géographique National (IGN) **107 rue La-Boétie, 8e ⓦ www.ign.fr.** The official (and best) source for maps of France, and indeed the entire world, plus guidebooks, satellite photos, old maps of Paris and raised relief maps of the mountainous regions of France. M° St-Philippe-Roule. Mon–Fri 9.30am–7pm, Sat 11am–12.30pm & 2–6.30pm.

Librairie Ulysse **26 rue St-Louis-en-l'Ile, 4e.** A tiny bookshop, piled from floor to ceiling with new and secondhand travel books and run by a friendly English-speaking owner. M° Pont-Marie/Sully-Morland. Mon noon–6.30pm, Tues–Fri 11am–7pm, Sat 11am–6.30pm.

Food and drink

Paris has resisted the march of mega-stores with admirable resilience. Almost every quartier still has its *charcuterie*, *boulangerie* and weekly market, while some streets, such as rue Cler, in the 7e, and rue des Martyrs, in the 9e, are literally lined with grocers', butchers' shops delicatessens, pâtisseries, cheese shops, and wine-merchants.

Gourmet food shops

Any list of food shops in Paris has to have at its head three palaces:

Fauchon 24–30 place de la Madeleine, 8e ⓦwww.fauchon.fr. An amazing range of extravagantly beautiful groceries, exotic fruit and vegetables, charcuterie, wines both French and foreign – almost anything you can think of, all at exorbitant prices. The quality is assured by blind testing, which all suppliers have to submit to. Just the place for presents of tea, jam, truffles, chocolates, exotic vinegars, mustards and so forth. There's a traiteur that stays open a little later, until 8.30pm, and a restaurant was about to open at the time of writing. M° Madeleine. Mon–Sat 9am–8pm.

La Grande Epicerie 38 rue de Sèvres, 7e. This edible offshoot of the famous Bon Marché department store may not be quite as nakedly epicurean as Fauchon and Hédiard, but it's a fabulous emporium of fresh and packed foods. Popular among choosy Parisians, moneyed expats (for its country-specific favourites) and gastro-tourists alike. M° Sèvres-Babylone. Mon–Sat 8.30am–9pm.

Hédiard 21 place de la Madeleine, 8e ⓦwww.hediard.fr. Since the 1850s, the aristocrat's grocer, with sales staff as deferential as servants, as long as you don't try to reach for items for yourself. Superlative quality in their coffees, spices and confitures. You can also eat at the restaurant upstairs. Among the other, smaller branches are those at 31 av Georges V, 8e (M° Georges-V); 106 bd de Courcelles, 17e (M° Courcelles); and 118 rue Monge, 5e (M° Place Monge). M° Madeleine. Mon–Sat 8am–10pm.

Buying food at these places is an aesthetic experience, a feast for the eyes quite as much as the palate.

Our listings, below, are for **specialist food shops**, many of which are veritable palaces of gluttony and fairly expensive, while **street markets** are detailed in a separate section at the end of this chapter. **Food halls** to equal that of Harrods are to be found at Fauchon and Hédiard, on place de la Madeleine, and the Grande Epicerie, in the Bon Marché department store – each with exhibits to rival the best of the capital's museums. In addition, there are one-product specialists for whom gourmets will cross the city: Poilâne's or Ganachaud's for bread, Barthélémy for cheese, La Maison de l'Escargot for snails.

As for buying food with a view to economic eating, you will be best off shopping at the street markets or supermarkets – though save your bread-buying at least for the local boulangerie and let yourself be tempted once in a while by the apple *chaussons*, *pains aux raisins*, *pains au chocolat*, *tartes aux fraises* and countless other goodies found in the city's pâtisseries. Useful **supermarkets** with branches throughout Paris are Franprix, Monoprix and Ed l'Epicier; the latter is particularly cheap.

Bread

La Fournée d'Augustine 96 Rue Raymond-Losserand, 14e. You'd have to be a bread fanatic to come down to Pernety just for a baguette, but then lots of Parisians apparently are; the presidential Elysée palace, of course, just has it delivered. Youthful baker Pierre Thilloux was the winner of the official 2004 Grand Prix de la Baguette, and he makes a mean Madeleine cake, too. M° Pernety. Mon–Sat 8am–7.30pm.

Ganachaud 226 rue des Pyrénées, 20e. Although father Ganachaud has left the business, his three daughters continue his recipes, and the bread is still out of this world. The cakes, especially the almond pastries, are also well worth sampling. M° Gambetta. Tues–Sat 7.30am–8pm.

Poilâne 8 rue du Cherche-Midi, 6e ⓦwww.poilane.fr. The source of the famous "Pain Poilâne" – a bread baked using traditional methods (albeit ramped up on an industrial scale) as conceived by the late, legendary Monsieur Poilâne himself. A second branch at

49 bd Grenelle, 15e (M° Duplex) operates the same hours plus Sun 7.15am–8.15pm. M° Sèvres-Babylone. Mon–Sat 7.15am–8.15pm.
Poujauran 20 rue Jean-Nicot, 7e. Poujauran was a pioneer in the revival of traditional breads; he recently sold this shop, but the quality of the baguettes is still good, the pâtisseries wonderful, and the decor exquisite, with its original belle-époque painted glass panels and tiles. M° Latour-Maubourg. Tues–Sat 8am–8.30pm.

Charcuterie

Le Comptoir de la Gastronomie 34 rue Montmartre, 1er. The walls of this lovely old-fashioned shop are stacked high with wine bottles, foie gras, saucisses, preserves and hams. There's also a fine little restaurant attached, ideal for a lunchtime snack. M° Les Halles/Etienne Marcel.
Aux Ducs de Gascogne 111 rue St-Antoine, 4e (M° St-Paul) & 54 av Victor Hugo, 16e (M° Kléber). Excellent range of high-quality *charcuterie*, as well as enticing – and expensive – deli goods ranging from little salads to caviar. Mon–Sat 10am–8pm.
Flo Prestige 42 place du Marché-St-Honoré, 1er. All sorts of super delicacies, plus wines, champagne and exquisite ready-made dishes. M° Pyramides. Daily 8am–11pm.
Labeyrie 6 rue Montmartre, 1er. Specialist in products from the Landes region, pâtés in particular: Bayonne hams, goose and duck pâtés, conserves, etc. M° Châtelet-Les-Halles. Tues–Fri 11am–2pm & 3–7pm.
Maison de la Truffe 19 place de la Madeleine, 8e ⓦwww.maison-de-la-truffe.fr. Truffles, of course, both noires, from France, and blanches, from Italy – either way a mere €1464 per 400g. Also sells roe, foie gras and similar haute delicacies. You can try before you buy at the attached restaurant, but bring a second credit card for backup. M° Madeleine. Mon–Sat 9.30am–9pm.
Sacha Finkelsztajn 27 rue des Rosiers, 4e. Marvellous Jewish deli for takeaway snacks and goodies: gorgeous East European breads, apple strudel, gefilte fish, aubergine purée, tarama, blinis and borscht. M° St-Paul. Wed–Mon 10am–2pm & 3–7pm; closed Aug.

Cheese

Barthélémy 51 rue de Grenelle, 7e ⓣ01.45.48.56.75. Purveyors of carefully ripened and meticulously stored seasonal cheeses to the rich and powerful. Can arrange home delivery. M° Bac. Tues–Sat 8.30am–1pm & 4–7.15pm; closed Aug.
La Fromagerie 31 64 rue du Seine, 6e. A decent selection of cheeses at this corner shop, including Livarot, Pont L'Evêgne and Artisanale Roquefort Carlés. The helpful staff are happy to give you a taste of anything you see that tickles your fancy. M° Tuileries. Tues–Thurs 10am–3pm & 5–8.30pm, Fri & Sat 10am–8pm, Sun 10am–1.30pm.
Fromagerie Alléosse 13 rue Poncelet, 17e. A connoisseur's selection of high-quality cheeses, including Brie from Champagne, creamy Billat-Savarin, nutty-flavoured Mont d'Or and an enormous variety of goat's cheeses. M° Ternes. Mon–Thurs 9am–1pm & 4–7pm, Fri & Sat 9am–7pm, Sun 9am–1pm.
La Maison du Fromage 118 rue Mouffetard, 5e. Offers a wonderful selection, beautifully displayed. Specializes in goat's, sheep's and mountain cheeses. M° Censier-Daubenton. Tues–Sat 9am–1pm & 4–7.30pm, Sun 9am–1pm. Another branch at 62 rue de Sèvres, 6e (M° Sèvres-Babylone).

Chocolates and pâtisseries

La Bague de Kenza 106 rue St Maur, 11e. It's very hard to walk by without pausing at the window of this Algerian patisserie chock-full of mounds of enticing cakes made of dates, orange, pistachio, figs, almonds and other tasty ingredients. There's also a little *salon de thé* attached. M° Saint-Maur. Mon–Sat 10am–8pm.
Cacao et Chocolat 29 rue de Buci, 6e. The aroma alone makes it worth stopping in at this chocolate shop, which crafts confections of cacao from around the world and offers its own version of liquid chocolate in the small salon area. M° Mabillon. Also at 63 rue Saint-Louis-en-l'Isle, 4e (M° Pont-Marie). Both open daily 10.30am–7.30pm.
Debauve and Gallais 30 rue des Saints-Pères, 7e. A beautiful shop specializing in chocolate and elaborate sweets that's been around since chocolate was taken as a medicine – and an aphrodisiac. M° St-Germain-des-Prés/Sèvres-Babylone. Mon–Sat 9.30am–7pm.
Joséphine Vannier 4 rue Pas de la Mule, 4e. This marvellous chocolatier sells

chocolate shaped into accordions, violins, books, Eiffel Towers and Arcs de Triomphe – exquisite creations, almost too beautiful to eat. Prices are reasonable, too, from around €16. M° Bastille. Tues–Sat 11am–1pm & 2–7pm.

Ladurée 16 rue Royale, 8e. Justly famous for their melt-in-your-mouth macaroons which are crispy, gooey, and worth every cent. Slightly more substantial fare in the chic *salon de thé*. M° Madeleine. Mon–Sat 8.30am–7pm.

Pâtisserie Stohrer 51 rue Montorgueil, 2e. Bread, pâtisseries, chocolate and charcuterie baked here since 1730. Discover what *pain aux raisins* should really taste like. M° Sentier. Daily 7.30am–8pm; closed first two weeks Aug.

Herbs, spices and oils

G. Détou 58 rue Tiquetonne, 2e. Friendly épicerie that gets packed to the gills on Saturdays. Kilos of spices, nuts and chocolate, plus the usual *confit* and foie gras. M° Etienne-Marcel. Mon–Sat 8.30am–6.30pm.

Izraël 30 rue François-Miron, 4e. A cosmopolitan emporium of goodies from all round the globe: vinegars, oils, spices and mustards. M° St-Paul. Tues–Fri 9.30am–1pm & 2.30–7pm, Sat 9.30am–7pm.

Maille 6 place de la Madeleine, 8e. Founded in 1747, Maille is best known for its Dijon mustard, but it also makes 28 other varieties, all available here, plus all kinds of flavoured vinegars and hand-painted mustard pots. M° Madeleine. Mon–Sat 10am–7pm.

Asian and health food

Diététique D J Fayer 45 rue St-Paul, 4e. Tiny shop, one of the city's oldest specialists, selling dietary, macrobiotic and vegetarian products. M° St-Paul. Mon–Sat 9.30am–7pm.

Naturalia 332 rue Lecourbe, 15e. Feel you need a vitamin boost? Or, after too many rich meals, some rice cakes and seaweed? This massive health-food centre has 24 branches all over the city, including one at 52 rue St-Antoine, 4e (M° St-Paul/Bastille). M° Lourmel. Mon–Sat 10am–7.30pm.

Rendez-Vous de la Nature 96 rue Mouffetard, 5e. One of the city's largest and most comprehensive health-food stores, with everything from organic produce to herbal teas. M° Censier-Daubenton. Tues–Sat 9.30am–7.30pm, Sun 9.30am–1pm.

Tang Frères 168 av de Choisy (M° Place d'Italie) & 44 av d'Ivry, 13e (M° Porte de Choisy). The original and classic "Chinese" supermarket – though the Tang brothers actually came from Laos originally, and their shop sells southeast Asian goods as much as, if not more than, Chinese. At 192 av de Choisy there's a deli-restaurant, Tang Gourmet, which does fast business in lunchtime noodles. Tues–Sun 9am–7.30pm, Sun 9.30am–1pm.

Honey

Les Abeilles 21 rue Butte-aux-Cailles, 13e. Honey from all over France and further afield, sold by an experienced beekeeper. Around €5 for a 250g pot. M° Corvisart/Place-d'Italie. Tues–Sat 11am–7pm.

Les Rûchers du Roy 37 rue du Roi de Sicile, 4e. Well-priced and original flavoured honeys, honey jams, honey sweets and some interesting apitherapy products meant to cure digestive and cardiovascular ailments. M° St-Paul. Tues–Sun 2–8pm.

Kitchen equipment

Rue Montmartre, just north of Les Halles, is a great place to start looking for **kitchenware**, with no fewer than three superb locales for price-comparison shopping. Also try the kitchen section at BHV (see p.386) for a great selection of cookware, especially the colourful Le Creuset dishes so coveted by gourmands abroad. Lafayette Maison (see p.386) also stocks a dazzling range, including Sabatier knives and Sabre cutlery.

A. Simon 48–52 rue Montmartre, 2e ⓦ www.simon-a.com. A huge collection of anything and everything for the kitchen, including a wide range of cast-iron and copper cookware, and glassware. M° Etienne-Marcel. Mon 1.50–6.30pm, Tues–Sat 9.30am–6.30pm.

La Bovida 36 rue Montmartre, 1er. Not quite as massive a culinary offering as its competitor down the street, but still a lot of good kitchen gear on these three floors, including some nice dishware, all neatly laid out. It stocks an especially large selection of kitchen knives, four sizes of tarte tatin tin and six different-sized whisks. M° Etienne-Marcel. Mon–Sat 10am–6.30pm.

E Dehillerin 18–20 rue Coquillière, 1er ⓦwww.e-dehillerin.fr. This nineteenth-century institution, in business since 1820, is laid out like a traditional ironmonger's: narrow aisles, no fancy displays, prices buried in catalogues, but good-quality stock of knives, slicers, peelers, presses and assorted cookware, many of restaura-teur quality at reasonable prices. A great selection of very durable copper and pewter pans. M° Châtelet-Les-Halles. Mon 9am–12.30pm & 2–6pm, Tues–Sat 9am–6pm.

MORA 13 rue Montmartre, 1er. An exhaustive collection of tools of the trade for the top professionals. Excellent for bakeware and cake decorations. M° Châtelet-Les-Halles. Mon–Fri 9am–6pm, Sat 8.30am–5.30pm.

La Vaissellerie 80 bd Haussmann, 8e. Simple, inexpensive French crockery, mostly in white, but they also stock the cheerful bright-yellow Chocolat Menier and Banania ranges. M° Havre-Caumartin. Also branches at 85 rue de Rennes, 6e (M° Rennes); 79 rue St-Lazare, 9e (M° Trinité); 332 rue St-Honoré, 1er (M° Pyramides); and 92 rue St-Antoine, 4e (M° St-Paul). Mon–Sat 9.30am–7pm.

Salmon, caviar and other seafood

Caviar Kaspia 17 place de la Madeleine, 8e ⓦwww.caviarkaspia.com. Blinis, smoked salmon and Beluga caviar. M° Madeleine. Mon 10am–midnight, Tues–Sat 10am–1am.

Comptoir du Saumon 60 rue François-Miron, 4e and several other addresses. Salmon especially, but eels, trout and all things fishy as well. Plus a delightful little restaurant in which to taste the fare. M° St-Paul. Mon–Sat 10am–10.30pm, Sun 11am–8pm.

Petrossian 18 bd de Latour-Maubourg, 7e ⓦwww.petrossian.fr. Not just gilt-edged fish eggs, but other Russian and French delicacies, too. You can try delights such as smoked salmon sorbet at the restaurant next door. M° Latour-Maubourg. Mon–Sat 9.30am–8pm.

Snails

La Maison de l'Escargot 79 rue Fondary, 15e. As the name suggests, this place specializes in snails: they even sauce them and re-shell them while you wait. M° Dupleix. Tues–Sat 9.30am–7pm; closed mid-July to Sept.

Tea and coffee

Mariage Frères 30 rue du Bourg-Tibourg, 4e. Hundreds of teas, neatly packed in tins, line the floor-to-ceiling shelves of this 100-year-old tea emporium. There's also a classy *salon de thé* (see p.328) on the ground floor. M° Hôtel-de-Ville. Daily 10.30am–7.30pm.

Verlet 256 rue St-Honoré, 1er. An old-fashioned *torréfacteur* (coffee merchant), one of the best-known in Paris, selling both familiar and less common varieties of coffee and tea from around the world. There's also a tea room, perfect for a pick-me-up. M° Palais-Royal-Musée-du-Louvre. Mon–Sat 9am–7pm.

Wine and beer

Le Baron Rouge 1 rue Théophile-Roussel, 12e. A good selection of dependable lower-range French wines; €1.30–3.20 for a small tasting glass at the bar. Very drinkable Merlot at around €3 a litre, if you bring your own containers. M° Ledru-Rollin. Tues–Fri 10am–2pm & 5–10pm, Sat 10am–10pm, Sun 10.30am–3.30pm.

Bieres Spéciales 77 rue Saint-Maur, 11e. Sells a wide range of European and Asian beers at fairly good prices. M° St-Maur. Mon–Sat 10.30am–2pm & 4–9pm.

Les Caves Augé 116 bd Haussmann, 8e. This old-fashioned, wood-panelled shop is the oldest *cave* in Paris, dating back to 1850, and sells around six thousand French and foreign wines made from organic grapes. M° St-Augustin. Mon 1–7.30pm, Tues–Sat 9am–7.30pm.

Caves Michel Renaud 12 place de la Nation, 12e. Established in 1890 and purveying superb-value French and Spanish wines, champagnes and Armagnac. You can also buy a bottle of Green Muse, a special unsweetened absinthe from southwestern France. M° Nation. Mon 3–8.30pm, Tues–Sat 9.30am–1pm & 2.30–8.30pm, Sun 10am–1pm.

Les Caves St-Antoine 95 rue St-Antoine, 4e. A small, amicable outfit, selling almost exclusively French wines. M° St-Paul. Tues–Fri 9am–1pm & 3–8pm, Sat 9am–8pm, Sun 9am–1pm.

La Crèmerie 9 rue des Quatre-Vents, 6e. Excellent wine shop set behind an attractive old dairy shop front. The Miard family, who run it, can recommend some fine lesser-known wines, especially from the Loire and Burgundy. Like an Italian *enoteca*, they offer wines by the glass, with plates of hams and cheeses (€6–11) to aid tasting. M° Odéon. Tues–Sat 10.30am–10pm; closed Aug.

Lavinia 3–5 bd de la Madeleine, 8e. The largest wine and spirits store in Europe. The modern interior displays thousands of bottles of wines from over 43 countries, and the wine cellar holds some of the rarest bottles in the world. Attached wine library and bar/restaurant allow you to read up, then drink up. M° Madeleine. Mon–Fri 10am–8pm, Sat 9am–8pm.

Nicolas 31 place de la Madeleine, 8e. A reliable merchant, with dozens of shops across the city, stocking a good general selection. On the top floor there's a wine bar where you can taste what looks good (noon–3pm). M° Madeleine. Mon–Sat 9.30am–8pm.

Le Repaire de Bacchus 112 rue Mouffetard, 5e. A good chain to look out for, with more than thirty branches all over Paris, one in nearly every arrondissement. Sells many lesser-known and cheaper wines. M° Censier-Daubenton. Mon 3.30–8.30pm, Tues–Sat 10am–8.30pm, Sun 9am–1.30pm.

De Vinis Illustribus 48 rue de la Montagne Sainte Geneviève, 5e. International wine dealer and connoisseur extra-ordinaire Lionel Michelin set up shop ten years ago in this ancient wine cellar where Hemingway used to come to buy his wine. He still specializes in very old and very rare vintages (the 1969 Romanee Conti at €4900 is one of his finest), but is just as happy selling you an €8 bottle of 2002 Coteaux du Languedoc and orating eloquently on its tannins. M° Maubert-Mutualité. Tues–Sat 11am–8pm.

A miscellany

Abdon 6 bd Beaumarchais, 11e. New and secondhand photographic equipment. If they don't have what you're looking for, try the half-dozen other camera shops on the same street. M° Chemin-Vert. Tues–Sat 9.30am–12.30pm & 1.30–6.30pm.

Archives de la Presse 51 rue des Archives, 3e. A fascinating shop for a browse, trading in old French newspapers and magazines. The window always has a display of outdated newspapers corresponding to the current month, and there are piles upon piles of old magazines inside, with vintage *Vogues* giving a good insight into the changing fashion scene. M° Rambuteau. Mon–Sat 10.30am–7pm.

L'Artisanat Monastique 68bis av Denfert-Rochereau, 14e. An unusual address in an odd location – the vaulted basement of a hospice run by nuns. All the products on sale are handmade by French monks or nuns, and run the gamut from religious kitsch to beautifully old-fashioned clothes for young children, and from fine beeswax cleaning products to herb unguents and Chartreuse liqueurs. M° Denfert-Rochereau/RER Port Royal. Mon–Fri noon–6.30pm, Sat 2–7pm.

Attica 106 bd Richard Lenoir, 11e www.attica.fr. All the books, CD-ROMS, dictionaries, videos and audio cassettes one could possibly need to learn any number of the two hundred languages represented at this language-learning mecca. Online ordering enables you to hit the books before hitting the road. M° Oberkampf. Tues–Sat 10am–7pm.

Boîte à Musique Anna Joliet Jardin du Palais Royal, 9 rue de Beaujolais, 1er. A delightful, minuscule boutique selling every style of music box, from inexpensive self-winding toy models to grand cabinets costing thousands of euros. Parisians have long loved mechanical instruments, and many of these play old favourites such as *La Vie en Rose* and *Chim-Chimney*. Prices begin at around €10 and quickly go up from there. M° Palais-Royal-Musée-du-Louvre. Mon–Sat 10am–7pm.

De Bouche à Oreille 26 rue du Roi de Sicile, 4e. Attractive *objets* for the home, such as Baroque-style candelabras, lamps, embroidered teacloths (€29), glass carafes (€39) and reproductions of Robert de Vaugandy's globe (1745) – just the thing for the study. M° St-Paul. Tues–Sat 11.30am–7pm.

Ciné-Images 68 rue de Babylone, 7e www.cine-images.com. Suitably located right opposite the famous Pagode cinema, this classy shop sells original and mainly French film posters. Prices range from €30 for something small and recent to €15,000 for the historic advert for the Lumière brothers' *L'Arroseur Arrosé*. M° Sèvres-Babylone. Tues–Fri 10am–1pm & 2–7pm, Sat 2–7pm.

Le Laguiole du Marais 6 rue du Pas de la Mule, 3e. Tiny shop selling a large range of the celebrated knives from Laguiole in the Massif Central. M° Chemin-Vert. Mon–Sat 10am–12.30pm & 1.30–7pm, Sun 2–7pm.

La Maison du Collectionneur 137 av Emile-Zola, 15e. Old books, hats, newspapers of the wartime liberation, and assorted junk. M° Emile-Zola. Tues–Sat 11am–7pm.

Marché St-Pierre 2 rue Charles-Nodier, 18e. Five floors of inexpensive fabrics. Well worth a visit even if you're not buying. M° Anvers. Mon–Sat 10am–6.30pm.

Pierre Frey 1 & 2 rue de Fürstenberg, 6e. Stocks a huge range of stunning fabrics for furnishings and curtains. If you don't find what you're after here, try the handful of rival shops in the same street. M° Mabillon/St-Germain-des-Prés. Tues–Sat 10am–6.30pm.

Le Pot à Tabac 28 rue de la Pépinière, 8e. Classy selection of pipes, cigars, tobacco and thermidors, plus an enormous choice of international cigarettes. M° St-Augustin. Daily 7.30am–7.30pm.

Trousselier 73 bd Haussmann, 8e ⓦwww.trousselier.com. Described in French *Vogue* as the artificial flower shop. Every conceivable species of flora fashioned from manmade fibre, from a simple basket of roses for €9 to more decadent and pricey arrangements. Also does a good selection of tableware, such as very French-looking espresso cups (€25), and attractive picnic hampers (€35). M° St-Augustin. Mon–Sat 10.30am–7pm.

Music

Records, cassettes and **CDs** are not particularly cheap in Paris, but there are plenty of secondhand bargains, and you may come across selections that are novel enough to tempt you. Brazilian, Caribbean, Antillais, African and Arab albums that would be **specialist rarities** in London or the States, as well as every kind of jazz, abound in Paris. **Rue Keller** and **rue des Taillandiers**, in the 11e (M° Bastille), have a wide range of offbeat record shops selling current trends. Secondhand traders offer up scratchy treats – anything from the Red Army choir singing the Marseillaise to African drummers on skins made from spider ovaries. The **flea markets** (St-Ouen especially), and the *bouquinistes* along the Seine, are good places to look for old records.

In the **classical** department, the choice of interpretations is generous and multinational. For all new and mainstream records, FNAC Musique (see p.406) usually has the best prices.

Also listed below are a couple of bookshops selling **sheet music**, **scores** and **music literature**, and some that sell instruments. Victor-Massé, Douai, Houdon, boulevard Clichy and other streets in the **Pigalle** area are full of **instrument and sound-system shops**. Guitarists especially will enjoy a look in at 16 rue V-Massé, 9e – afternoons only – where François Guidon builds jazz guitars for the greats and amateurs. For instruments and scores, head for Paul Beuscher, at the Bastille, which has amazing sales in spring.

Afric' Music 3 rue des Plantes, 14e. A small shop with an original selection of African, Caribbean and reggae discs. M° Mouton-Duvernet. Mon–Sat 10am–7pm.

Analog collector 13 rue Charles V, 4e. ⓦwww.analog-collector.com. Stocks a fine collection of classical music and jazz on vinyl. M° St-Paul. Mon Fri 1–7pm.

Arts Sonores 8 rue des Taillandiers, 11e. Sells secondhand vinyl and is particularly strong on French chanson. M° Bastille. Tues–Sat 1.30–7.30pm.

Camara 45 rue Marcadet, 18e. Paris's best selection of West African music on cassette and video. M° Marcadet-Poissonnière. Mon–Sat noon–8pm.

La Chaumière 5 rue de Vaugirard, 6e ⓦ www.chaumiereonline.com. Friendly staff here advise on a wide selection of classical music and some jazz, with more than fifteen thousand CD recordings to choose from, many discounted. M° Odéon/RER Luxembourg. Mon–Fri 11am–8pm, Sat 10am–8pm, Sun 2–8pm.

Crocodisc 40–42 rue des Ecoles, 5e. Folk, Oriental, Afro-Antillais, raï, funk, reggae, salsa, hip-hop, soul, country. New and secondhand, at some of the best prices in town. M° Maubert-Mutualité. Tues–Sat 11am–7pm; closed Aug.

Crocojazz 64 rue de la Montagne-Ste-Geneviève, 5e. Mainly new imports of jazz and blues, but a big grab-bag of inexpensive used titles for around €7. M° Maubert-Mutualité. Tues–Sat 11am–7pm.

Disc' Inter 2 rue des Rasselins, 20e. Wide-ranging stock of Afro-Caribbean music on CD, cassette, video and vinyl. M° Porte-de-Montreuil. Mon–Sat 10am–7pm.

FNAC Musique 4 place de la Bastille, 12e, next to the opera house ⓦ www.fnac.fr. Extremely stylish shop in black, grey and chrome with computerized catalogues, every variety of music, books, and a concert-booking agency. M° Bastille. Mon–Sat 10am–8pm, Wed & Fri till 10pm. The other FNAC shops (see under "Bookshops") also sell music and hi-fi. Try FNAC-Etoile, at 26 av des Ternes, 17e (M° Ternes), Mon–Sat 10am–7pm, for jazz.

Hamm 17–21 rue Monge, 5e. The biggest general music shop in Paris, selling instruments new and old, sheet music, scores, manuals, librettos, etc. M° Place Monge. Tues–Sat 10.30am–1pm & 2–7pm.

Jussieu Music 16–19 rue Linné, 5e ⓦ www.jussieumusic.com. A hundred thousand or so new and used CDs and DVDs ranging from rock and hip-hop to jazz, classical and world. M° Jussieu. Mon–Sat 11.30am–7.30pm.

Librairie Musicale de Paris 68bis rue Réaumur, 3e. Huge selection of books on music and of music, from Baroque oratorios to heavy metal. M° Réaumur-Sébastopol. Tues–Sat 10.15am–7pm.

Maison Sauviat 124 bd de la Chapelle, 18e. Wonderful shop that's been going strong since the 1920s. Now specializing in North and West African and Middle Eastern music. M° Barbès-Rochechouart. Mon–Sat 9.45am–6.45pm.

Moby Disques 28 rue Monge, 5e. Passionate jazz fans will like this small shop; jazz on vinyl – many collectors' items and Japanese imports – bought, sold and exchanged at reasonable prices. M° Cardinal-Lemoine. Mon–Sat 1.30–6pm.

Paris Jazz Corner 5 & 7 rue Navarre, 5e. Worth it just for the dustily dedicated atmosphere of the shop, which faces the Arènes de Lutèce. Great collection of jazz and blues, with lots of secondhand vinyl. M° Monge. Tues–Sat noon–8pm.

Paul Beuscher 15–27 bd Beaumarchais, 4e ⓦ www.paul-beuscher.com. A music department store that's been going strong for more than a hundred years. Instruments, scores, books, recording equipment, etc. M° Bastille. Mon 2–7pm, Tues–Sat 10.15am–7pm.

Virgin Megastore 52 av des Champs-Elysées, 8e (M° Franklin-D.-Roosevelt); Carrousel du Louvre, under the Louvre, 1er (M° Palais-Royal-Musée-du-Louvre); and 5 bd Montmartre, 2e (M° Grands-Boulevards). This is one of the biggest music stores in the country, and is a great place to get acquainted with French music, as you can listen to much of the music through digital listening-posts. Also houses a concert-booking agency. Mon 10am–9pm, Tues 10am–8pm, Wed–Sun 10am–10pm.

Voltage 23 rue Roi de Sicile, 4e. An extensive collection of good-condition vinyl – mostly heavy metal and thrash rock. M° St-Paul Mon–Sat 10am–7pm.

Sport

Bicloune 7 rue Froment, 11e ⓦ www.bicloune.fr. A bike shop with some bizarre models on show. Repairs carried out. M° Bréguet-Sabin. Tues–Fri 1–6pm, Thurs till 8pm, Sat 9am–6pm.

Décathlon 26 av de Wagram, 17e. A brilliant selection of sports gear and swimming costumes. M° Charles-de-Gaulle-Etoile. Mon–Sat 10am–8pm.

La Haute Route 33 bd Henri-IV, 4e ⓦ www.lahauteroute.com. Mainly skiing and mountaineering equipment: to rent or to buy – new and secondhand. M° Bastille.

Tues–Sat 10am–1pm & 2–7pm, Dec–May also Mon 2–7pm.

Marathon 26 rue Léon Jost, 17e. Specialists in running shoes. The shop is owned by an experienced marathon runner. M° Courcelles. Tues–Sat 10am–7pm.

Nomades 37 bd Bourdon, 4e ⓦwww.nomadeshop.com. The place to buy and rent rollerblades and equipment, with its own bar out back where you can find out about the scene. See also "Rollerblading", p.417. M° Bastille. Tues–Fri 11.30am–7.30pm, Sat 10am–7pm, Sun noon–7pm.

Au Vieux Campeur 48 rue des Ecoles, 5e ⓦwww.au-vieux-campeur.fr. This giant outdoor activities group has colonized an entire couple of blocks immediately north of rue des Ecoles and east of rue St-Jacques with a dozen well-stocked shops – there's even a small climbing wall. You'll be directed to the right branch for maps, guides, boots, climbing, hiking, camping and ski gear, tents, sleeping bags and so on. M° Maubert-Mutualité. Mon–Fri 11am–7.30pm, Thurs till 9pm, Sat 9.30am–7.30pm.

Markets

Several of the **markets** listed below are described in the text of the Guide. These, however, are the details – and the highlights. The map on pp.406–407 shows their locations.

Books, stamps and art

As well as the specialized **book markets** listed below, you should of course remember the wide array of books and all forms of printed material on sale from the **bouquinistes**, who hook their green padlocked boxes onto the riverside quais of the Left Bank.

Marché du Livre Ancien et d'Occasion Pavillon Baltard, Parc Georges-Brassens, rue Brancion, 15e. Secondhand and antiquarian books. M° Porte-de-Vanves. Sat & Sun 9am–1pm.

Marché aux Timbres junction of avs Marigny & Gabriel, on the north side of place Clemenceau in the 8e. *The* stamp market in Paris. M° Champs-Elysées-Clemenceau. Thurs, Sat, Sun & hols 10am–7pm.

Clothes and flea markets

Paris has three main **flea markets** (*marchés aux puces*) of ancient descent gathered about the old gates of the city. No longer the haunts of the flamboyant gypsies and petty crooks of literary tradition, they are nonetheless good entertainment, and if you go early enough you might just find something special. Some of the food markets have spawned secondhand clothes and junk stalls, notably the place d'Aligre, in the 12e, and the place des Fêtes, in the 20e.

Porte de Montreuil av de Porte de Montreuil, 20e. Cheap new clothes have begun to dominate what was the best of Paris's flea markets for secondhand clothes – still cheapest on Mon when leftovers from the weekend are sold off. Also old furniture, household goods and assorted junk. M° Porte-de-Montreuil. Sat, Sun & Mon 7.30am–5pm.

Porte de Vanves av Georges-Lafenestre/av Marc-Sangnier, 14e. The best choice for bric-a-brac and little Parisian knick-knacks. Professionals deal alongside weekend amateurs. M° Porte-de-Vanves. Sat & Sun 7am–1.30pm.

St-Ouen/Porte de Clignancourt 18e. The biggest and most touristy flea market, with nearly a thousand stalls selling new and secondhand clothes, shoes, records, books and junk of all sorts. The majority of the covered market, however, is now given over to expensive antiques. For a full description, see p.208. M° Porte-de-Clignancourt. Mon, Sat & Sun 7.30am–7pm.

Flower markets

Paris used to have innumerable **flower markets** around the streets, but today only the three listed below remain. Throughout the week, however,

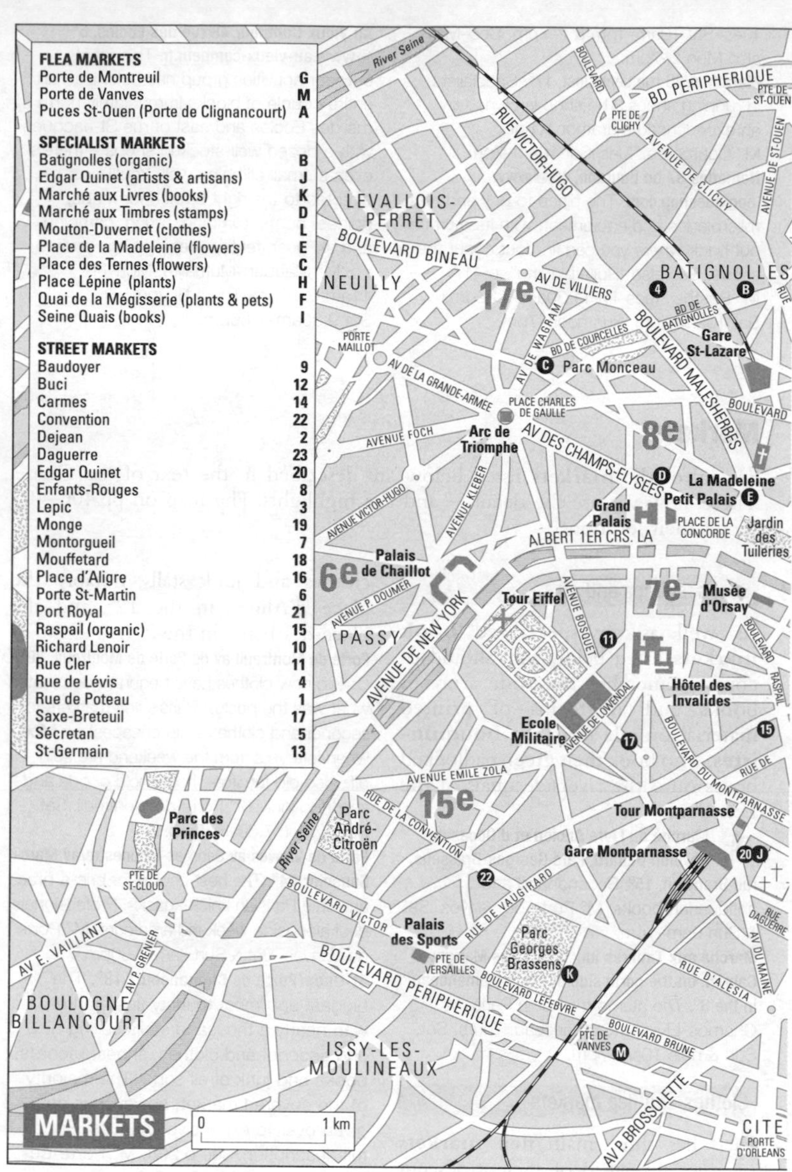

there's also the heavy concentration of plant and pet shops along the quai de la Mégisserie, between Pont-Neuf and Pont-au-Change.

Place Lépine Ile de la Cité, 1er. On Sun, the flower market is augmented with birds and pets. M° Cité. Daily 8am–7pm.

Place de la Madeleine 8e. Flowers and plants. M° Madeleine. Tues–Sun 8am–7.30pm.

Place des Ternes 8e. Flowers and plants. M° Ternes. Tues–Sun 8am–7.30pm.

Food markets

The street **food markets** provide one of the capital's more exacting tests of willpower. At the top end of the scale, there are the lavish arrays in rue de Lévis in the 17e and rue Cler in the 7e, both of which are more market street than street market, with their stalls mostly metamorphosed into permanent shops. The real **street markets** include a tempting scattering

△ Puces St-Ouen

in the Left Bank – especially place Maubert and place Monge – along with bigger ones at Montparnasse, in boulevard Edgar-Quinet, and opposite Val-de-Grâce in boulevard Port-Royal. The largest is in rue de la Convention, in the 15e. A small selection is given below; a full list of food markets can be found at the Mairie's website, ⓦ www.paris.fr, under "Les marchés Parisiens", "marchés alimentaires". For a different feel and more exotic **foreign produce**, take a look at the Mediterranean/Oriental displays in boulevard de Belleville, rue Dejean and rue d'Aligre. Markets are traditionally **morning** affairs, usually starting between 7am and 8am and tailing off sometime between 1pm and 2.30pm. However, in a break with Parisian tradition a few afternoon-only markets have recently opened, and so far they have been very well received by sleepers-in-late and others.

Aguesseau place de la Madeleine, 8e. M° Madeleine. Tues & Fri.

Alésia rue de la Glacière and rue de la Santé, 13e. M° Glacière. Wed & Sat.

Alibert rue Alibert by the Hôpital St-Louis, 10e. M° Goncourt. Sun 7am–3pm.

Auguste-Blanqui bd Blanqui between place d'Italie and rue Barrault, 13e. M° Corvisart. Fri & Sun.

Batignolles rue de Turin and rue des Batignolles, 8e. Organic produce. M° Rome. Sat 8.30am–1pm.

Baudoyer place Baudoyer, 4^{e}. M° Hôtel-de-Ville. Wed 3–8.30pm & Sat 7am–3pm.

Belleville bd de Belleville, 11e. M° Belleville. Tues & Fri.

Bercy place Lachambaudie, 12e. M° Cour St-Emillon. Wed & Sun.

Boulevard de Grenelle rue Lourmel, 15e. M° La-Motte-Picquet. Wed & Sun.

Brancusi place Brancusi, 14e. Specialist organic market. M° Gaîté. Sat 9am–3pm.

Charonne rue de Charonne & rue Dumas, 11e. M° Alexandre Dumas. Wed & Sat.

Convention rue de la Convention, 15e. M° Convention. Tues, Thurs & Sun.

Cours de Vincennes bd Picpus and rue Arnold Netter, 12e. M° Nation. Wed & Sat. Château-Rouge. Tues–Sun.

Dejean place du Château-Rouge, 18e. African foods. M° Château-Rouge. Tues–Sun.

Edgar-Quinet bd Edgar-Quinet, 14e. M° Edgar-Quinet. Wed & Sat. Flea market Sun 9am–7.30pm.

Enfants-Rouges 39 rue de Bretagne, 3e. M° Filles-du-Calvaire. Tues–Sat 8am–1pm & 4–7.30pm, Sun 9am–1pm.

Ledru-Rollin av Ledru-Rollin between rue de Lyon and rue de Bercy, 12e. M° Gare de Lyon. Thurs & Sat.

Maubert place Maubert, 5e. M° Maubert-Mutualité. Tues & Thurs 7am–2.30pm, Sat 7am–3pm.

Monge place Monge, 5e. M° Monge. Wed & Fri 7am–2.30pm, Sun 7am–3pm.

Montorgueil rue Montorgueil & rue Montmartre, 1er. M° Châtelet-Les-Halles/Sentier. Tues–Sat 8am–1pm & 4–7pm, Sun 9am–1pm.

Mouffetard rue Mouffetard, 5e. M° Censier-Daubenton. Tues–Sun.

Père-Lachaise bd de Menilmontant, between rue des Panoyaux and rue des Cendriers, 11e. M° Menilmontant. Tues & Fri.

Place d'Aligre 12e. M° Ledru-Rollin. Tues–Sun until 1pm.

Popincourt bd Richard-Lenoir between rue Oberkampf and rue Jean-Pierre Timbaud, 11e. M° Oberkampf. Tues & Fri.

Port-Royal bd de Port-Royal, near Val-de-Grâce, 5e. RER Port-Royal. Tues, Thurs & Sat.

Raspail bd Raspail, between rue du Cherche-Midi & rue de Rennes, 6e. Great organic market on Sun with herbal remedies as well as produce. M° Rennes. Tues & Fri.

Richard Lenoir bd Richard Lenoir, 11e. M° Bastille. Thurs & Sun.

Rue Cler 7e. M° Ecole-Militaire. Tues–Sun 8.30am–noon.

St-Germain rue Mabillon, 6e M° Mabillon. Tues–Fri 8am–1pm & 4–8pm, Sat 8am–1.30pm & 3.30–8pm, Sun 8am–1.30pm.

St-Honoré place du Marché Saint Honoré, 1er. M° Pyramides. Wed 3–8.30pm, Sat 7am–3pm.

St-Martin 31–33 rue du Château-d'Eau, 10e. Covered market. M° Château-d'Eau. Tues–Fri 9am–1pm & 4–7.30pm, Sat 9am–7.30pm, Sun 9am–1.30pm.

St-Quentin 85 bis bd Magenta, 10e. M° Gare-de-l'Est. Tues–Fri 9am–1pm & 4–7.30pm, Sat 9am–1pm & 3.30–7.30pm, Sun 8.30am–1.30pm.

Saxe-Breteuil av de Saxe, 7e. M° Ségur. Thurs & Sat.

25

Activities and sports

If you've had enough of following crowds through museums or wandering through the city in the blazing sun or pouring rain, then it may just be time to do what the Parisians do. There are saunas to soak in, ice skating rinks to fall on, vintage wines to taste, dancehalls to tango in, libraries to peruse and swimming pools to dive into. You can rent a bike, go on a boat trip or view the city from a balloon. If you're feeling especially bold, try your hand at learning the tricks of the gourmet chef at a cookery school or toss a few rounds of boules and bring home the souvenir of a new skill.

Pariscope has useful **listings** of **sports** facilities, pools, hammams and so on (under "Sport et bien-être"). **Information** on municipal facilities is available from the town hall, the Mairie de Paris; you can pick up their free 500-page tome *Parisports* at the Hôtel de Ville and at any individual arrondissement's Mairie. Alternatively, call ⓣ08.20.00.75.75, or check the comprehensive website ⓦwww.paris.fr.

For details of current **sporting events**, try the daily sports paper *L'Equipe*. A major venue for all sports, including athletics, cycling, show jumping, ice hockey, ballroom dancing, judo and motorcross, is the Palais Omnisport Paris-Bercy (POPB), 8 bd Bercy, 12^{e} (ⓣ01.40.02.60.60, ⓦwww.bercy.fr; M° Bercy). The highlight of the calendar is, of course, the triumphal arrival of cycling's Tour de France in July.

Boat trips and balloon rides

Seeing Paris by **boat** is one of the city's most popular and durable tourist experiences – and a lot of fun. Seeing it **from the air** is even better.

Bateaux-Mouches

Many a romantic evening walk along the *quais* has been rudely interrupted by the sudden appearance of a bulging **Bateau-Mouche**, with its dazzling floodlights and blaring commentaries. One way of avoiding the ugly sight of these hulking hulls is to get on one yourself. You may not be able to escape the trite narration, but the rides certainly give a glamorous close-up view of the classic buildings along the Seine.

Bateaux-Mouches **boat trips** start from the Embarcadère du Pont de l'Alma, on the Right Bank in the 8e (information ⓣ01.40.76.99.99, ⓦwww.bateaux-mouches.fr; reservations ⓣ01.42.25.96.10; M° Alma-Marceau). The rides, which usually last an hour, run roughly hourly to every half hour, depending on the season. Summer departures are 10am–10.30pm, winter 10.15am–9.30pm. Tickets cost €8, or €4 for under-12s and over-60s. You're probably best off avoiding the overpriced lunch and dinner trips, for which "correct" dress is mandatory (€50 for lunch, from €95 for dinner).

The main **competitors** to the Bateaux-Mouches are: Bateaux Parisiens Notre-Dame, Quai de Montebello, 5e (Ⓣ01.43.26.92.55; M° St-Michel); Bateaux Parisiens Tour Eiffel, Port de la Bourdonnais, 7e (Ⓣ01.44.11.33.44; M° Trocadéro); Bateaux-Vedettes de Paris, Port de Suffren, 7e (Ⓣ01.47.05.71.29; M° Bir-Hakeim); and Bateaux-Vedettes du Pont Neuf, Square du Vert-Galant, 1er (Ⓣ01.46.33.98.38; M° Pont-Neuf). They're all much the same, and can be found detailed in *Pariscope* under "Croisières" in the "Visites-Promenades" section and in *L'Officiel des Spectacles* under "Promenades" in the "A Travers Paris" section.

An alternative way of riding on the Seine – one in which you are mercifully spared the commentary – is the **Batobus** (Ⓣ01.44.11.33.99, Ⓦwww.batobus.com), a river transport system operating nearly all year round. See "Basics" (p.29) for more details.

Canal trips

Less overtly touristy than the Bateaux-Mouches and their clones are the **canal-boat trips**. Canauxrama (reservations Ⓣ01.42.39.15.00, Ⓦwww.canauxrama.com) chugs up and down between the Port de l'Arsenal (opposite 50 bd de la Bastille, 12e; M° Bastille) and the Bassin de la Villette (13 quai de la Loire, 19e; M° Jaurès) on the Canal St-Martin. There are daily departures at 9.45am and 2.45pm from La Villette (in summer only) and at 9.45am and 2.30pm from the Port de l'Arsenal. At the Bastille end is a long, spooky tunnel from which you don't surface till the 10e arrondissement. The ride lasts around two and a half hours – not bad for €15 (students €11, under-12s €8, under-6s free; no reductions weekends or holiday afternoons).

A more stylish vessel for exploring the canal is the **catamaran** of Paris-Canal, with trips between the Musée d'Orsay (quai Anatole-France by the Pont Solférino, 7e; M° Solférino) and the Parc de la Villette (La Folie des Visites Guidées, on the canal by the bridge between the Grande Salle and the Cité des Sciences, 19e; M° Porte-de-Pantin), which also last two and a half hours. The catamaran departs from the Musée d'Orsay at 9.30am; daily mid-March to mid-November, Sunday only other months. Parc de la Villette departures are at 2.30pm. Trips cost €16, 12–25s and over-60s €13 (except Sun and holiday afternoons), 4–11s €9; reservations Ⓣ01.42.40.96.97.

Paris by balloon

After Paris from the water, the next step up is Paris from the air. You can opt to go up in a **hot-air balloon** with France Montgolfières (Ⓣ08.10.60.01.53, Ⓦwww.franceballoons.com). Cost is approximately €185–250, depending on the length of the trip and whether it's midweek or a weekend. A much cheaper option (€10), and nearly as panoramic, is Eutelsat's tethered balloon – the world's largest – in the Parc André Citroën (see p.183). Opened in 2002, the thirty-passenger balloon ascends daily to geostationary orbit at an altitude of 150m above Paris.

Tea dances and guinguette

For many years, a less obvious but very Parisian way to fill the afternoon hours was at a **bal musette** – a traditional knees-up, usually to the tune of an

Great views of the city

Few cities present such a uniform skyscape as Paris. Looking down on the ranks of seven-storey apartment buildings from above, it's easy to imagine the city as a lead-roofed plateau split by the leafy canyons of the boulevards and avenues. Spires, towers and parks – not to mention multi-coloured art museums and glass pyramids – stand out all the more against the solemn grey backdrop. Fortunately, many of Paris's tall buildings provide access to wonderful **rooftop views**. Here are some of the best vistas in town:

Arc de Triomphe (see p.75): look out on an ocean of traffic and enjoy impressive vistas of the Voie Triomphale.

Centre Pompidou (see p.100): a stunning backdrop to modern art.

Grande Arche de la Défense (see p.251): take the long view.

Eiffel Tower (see p.155): the classic, best at night.

Institut du Monde Arabe (see p.138): sip mint tea on the rooftop overlooking the Seine.

Musée d'Orsay (see p.151): look through the old station clock towards Montmartre.

Notre-Dame (see p.52): perch among the gargoyles.

Parc André-Citroën (see p.183): a tethered balloon rises 150m above this quirky park.

Parc de Belleville (see p.235): watch the sun set over the city.

Sacré-Coeur (see p.193): this puffball dome soars over Montmartre.

Tour Montparnasse (see p.171): stand eye to eye with the Eiffel Tower.

accordion (*musette*) band. The dancehalls where they took place were the between-the-wars solution in the down-and-out parts of the city to depression, the dole and the demise of the Popular Front. The nearest equivalent these days is the **tea dance**, or *thé dansant* – a much more genteel or camp experience. One of the best known is that held at the former *guinguette*, *Balajo*, every Sunday afternoon (see p.214). Other tea dances are often held by different promoters on a monthly or occasional basis; check the listings in magazines like *Nova*. Absolutely free and more casual are the open-air dances held on Sunday afternoons throughout the summer at the **Kiosque de Musique** at the Parc de la Villette. The music is live, loud and international and the atmosphere is particularly conducive to kicking off your shoes and dancing on the grass. See p.227 for details of the park.

For the ultimate Parisian retro experience, head for a traditional riverbank **guinguette**. You can usually eat good, homely French food, but the real draw is the orchestra. Families, older couples and trendy young things from the city sway with varying degrees of skill to foxtrots, tangos and lots of well-loved accordion numbers – especially good for a Sunday afternoon.

Chalet du Lac facing the lac de St-Mandé, Bois de Vincennes, 11e ⓣ01.43.28.09.89, ⓦwww.chaletdulac.fr. Afternoon dancing on Thurs, Fri and Sat, but it's best to save yourself for the elegant Sunday Grand Bal (3–8.30pm; €12.50), when a live band helps smooth out your footwork. The restaurant serves good brasserie classics. M° St-Mandé-Tourelles.

Chez Gégène 162bis quai de Polangis, Joinville-le-Pont ⓣ01.48.83.29.43, ⓦwww.chez-gegene.fr. Just the other side of the Bois de Vincennes, this is a genuine *guinguette* established in the 1900s, though the band mixes in pop anthems with the accordion classics. There's a decent restaurant, but the time to come is on Sat nights (April–Dec 8pm–2am) and Sun afternoons

(3–7pm), when a live band plays ballroom classics and traditional French numbers. Admission €6 for non-diners. Open April–Oct. RER Joinville-le-Pont.

Divan du Monde 75 rue des Martyrs, 18e ⓣ01.40.05.06.99, ⓦwww.divandumonde.com. A venue to keep an eye on, with occasional afternoon events such as gay tea dances or the monthly kids' ball. M° Pigalle.

Guinguette de l'Ile du Martin-Pêcheur 41 quai Victor-Hugo, Champigny-sur-Marne ⓣ01.49.83.03.02, ⓦwww.guinguette.fr. Traditional and charming *guinguette* situated on an island in the River Marne. You don't have to dine – or pay – to dance. Dancing mid-March to Dec (mostly Thurs–Sat 7.30pm–2am, Sun noon–6pm, but check website). RER A2 to Champigny-sur-Marne.

Le Tango 13 rue au Maire, 3e ⓣ01.42.72.17.78. Tea dances, mostly gay- and lesbian-oriented, take place most Sun afternoons from 5pm or 6pm as well as Fri and Sat evenings at 10.30pm, with entry price around €5–7. M° Arts-et-Métiers.

Libraries

The city's **libraries** naturally provide the perfect environment for a quiet moment with a book or a newspaper, and some have beautiful interiors. For English-language books, the collection of the American library is unrivalled. Paris also has a library of films, the **vidéothèque** (see listing below), where getting out a movie and watching it on the spot is as easy as taking out a book. Some of the collections below require non-residents without a library card to buy day passes (around €3).You can find information on the city's 64 municipal libraries organized by arrondissement at ⓦwww.paris-bibliotheques.org.

American Library In Paris 10 rue du Général-Camou, 7e ⓣ01.53.59.12.60, ⓦwww.americanlibraryinparis.org. Hundreds of American magazines and newspapers and a vast range of 90,000 books, plus readings, children's story hours and other events. Day pass €12, week €15, annual €100. Free Internet access in 30-minute increments. Tues–Sat 10am–7pm. M° Ecole-Militaire.

Bibliothèque des Femmes Marguerite Durand 79 rue Nationale, 13e. A feminist library with books, journals, photos, posters and original manuscripts and letters. Tues–Sat 2–6pm. M° Nationale/Tolbiac.

BIFI Cinémathèque Francaise 51 rue de Bercy, 12e ⓦwww.bifi.fr. The Bibliothèque du Film encompasses magazines, books, stills, posters, videos and DVDs. €3.50 day pass. Mon–Fri 10am–7pm. M° Ledru-Rollin.

Bibliothèque Forney Hôtel de Sens, 1 rue du Figuier, 4e. Medieval building filled with volumes on fine and applied arts. Tues–Sat 1.30–7pm. M° Pont-Marie.

Bibliothèque Historique de la Ville de Paris Hôtel Lamoignon, 24 rue Pavée, 4e. Sixteenth-century mansion housing centuries of texts and picture books on the city. Mon–Fri 1–6pm, Sat 9.30am–6pm. M° St-Paul.

Bibliothèque Mazarine Institut de France, 23 quai de Conti, 6e ⓣ01.44.41.44.06, ⓦwww.bibliotheque-mazarine.fr. History of France and of religion. The setting, in a magnificent seventeenth-century building, with fine views across the Seine to the Louvre, is the real lure here. Some identification is required. Mon–Fri 10am–6pm. M° St-Michel.

Bibliothèque Nationale François Mitterrand quai François-Mauriac, 13e ⓦwww.bnf.fr. The elephantine new national library, with two levels, one for the public, the other for accredited researchers. Hosts a large number of exhibitions and presentations. For a fuller description, see p.96. €3.30 day pass. Tues–Sat 10am–7pm, Sun 1–7pm. Closed second two weeks in September. M° Quai-de-la-Gare/Bibliothèque-François Mitterrand.

Bibliothèque Ste-Geneviève 10 place du Panthéon, 5e. Reference library with beautiful murals in the foyer and a gorgeous reading room built around an iron skeleton. You need to be keen to get in: you have to register, bringing identification and a photo. Mon–Sat 10am–10pm. RER Luxembourg.

BPI Centre Georges Pompidou, 3e ⓦwww.bpi.fr. The vast Bibliothèque Publique d'Information collection includes the foreign press, videos and a language lab to brush up on your French. Free. Mon & Wed–Fri noon–10pm, Sat, Sun & public hols 11am–10pm; closed Tues & May 1. M° Rambuteau.

Vidéothèque **Forum des Images, 2 Grande Galerie, Porte St-Eustache, Forum des Halles, 1er ⓣ01.44.76.62.00, ⓦwww.forumdesimages .net.** For a small entry fee, you can watch any of the four films screened each day and, in the Salle Pierre Emmanuel, make your own selection from thousands of film clips, newsreel footage, commercials, documentaries, soaps and the like, from 1896 to the present day. All the material is connected to Paris in some way, and you can make your choice – on your individual screen and keyboard – via a Paris place name, actor, director, date, and so on. The Forum des Images is fresh from a major revamp in autumn 2007, with more space and a new café. Tues 1–10pm, Wed–Sun 1–9pm. RER Châtelet-Les-Halles/M° Châtelet.

Cookery and wine courses

Paris is, of course, the perfect place to try to get to grips with French gastronomy and wines. There are a large number of places offering **courses** to extend your knowledge, a handful of which are listed below.

Cordon Bleu 8 rue Léon-Delhomme, 15e ⓣ01.53.68.22.50, ⓦwww.cordonbleu.net. International chain of cooking schools offers cookery demonstrations followed by tastings (morning or afternoon sessions, some in English; 48-hr advance booking; €45), or day-long hands-on sessions (again some in English, two weeks' advance booking required; €142). M° Vaugirard/Convention.

Ecoles Grégoire Ferrandi 28 rue de l'Abbé-Grégoire, 6e ⓣ01.49.54.28.03, ⓦwww.egf.ccip .fr. Antoine Schaefers runs friendly sessions for amateurs on Wednesday evenings 6.30–10.30pm. Along with a dozen-odd Parisians, you help prepare a demonstration three-course meal, then sit down to eat and discuss it. You'll need good French, however, as there's no translation. €70 for the evening; longer courses also available. M° St-Placide/Montparnasse-Bienvenüe.

Promenades Gourmandes 187 rue du Temple, 3e ⓣ01.48.04.56.84, ⓦwww .promenadesgourmandes.com. At the other end of the scale from the Cordon Bleu school is this one-woman show, run by Paulle Caillat, who speaks flawless English. You take a trip to the market then back to the kitchen for a three-course demonstration, with lots of hands-on work. This level of personal attention doesn't come cheap: the full day costs €360. M° Temple.

Gyms, fitness clubs and dance classes

The body beautiful is big business in Paris. You'll find any number of aerobics classes, dance workouts and anti-stress fitness programmes offered, along with yoga, t'ai chi and martial arts. For shops selling sports gear and equipment, see p.404. Many **fitness clubs** organize their activities in courses or require a minimum month's or year's subscription (big gym chains like Garden Gym and Gymnase Club are financially prohibitive), but if your last meal has left you feeling the need to shed a few kilos, here are some options.

Aquaboulevard 4 rue Louis-Armand, 15e ⓣ01.40.60.10.00, ⓦwww.aquaboulevard.com. The biggest in town, with a state-of-the-art fitness centre containing 250 weight-training machines and offering 120 fitness lessons, squash and tennis courts, a climbing wall, golf tees, aquatic diversions, hammams, dancefloors, shops and restaurants. To gain access to the full range of facilities, most importantly the gym, you're supposed to be accompanied by a member, but exceptions are sometimes made. €20 for a day pass. M° Balard/Porte-de-Versailles/RER Bd-Victor.

Centre de Danse du Marais 41 rue du Temple, 4e ⓣ01.42.72.15.42, ⓦwww.parisdanse.com. Try out rock'n'roll, folkloric dance classes from the East, tap dancing, modern dance, physical expression or flamenco. You'll find a board advertising all the workshops in the alleyway. Each 90-minute session costs €18, though you must become a member for insurance purposes (€11). Daily 9am–9pm. M° Hôtel-de-Ville.

Centre de Yoga Sivananda 123 bd de Sébastopol, 2e ⓣ01.40.26.77.49, ⓦwww.sivananda.org/paris. A first trial lesson is free, and while speaking French helps, it's not essential. M° Strasbourg-St-Denis.

Club Quartier Latin 19 rue de Pontoise, 5e ⓣ01.55.42.77.88, ⓦwww.clubquartierlatin.com. Dance, gym, swimming and squash; €19 day pass for the pool and gym. Mon–Fri 9am–11.45pm, Sat & Sun 9.30am–7pm. M° Maubert-Mutualité.

Espace Vit'Halles place Beaubourg, 48 rue Rambuteau, 3e ⓣ01.42.77.21.71, ⓦwww.vithalles.fr. One of the flashiest fitness clubs in the city, with endless classes of every kind, weight rooms, various gyms, a sauna and hammam, and everything else you'd expect. Quite popular among Americans. For €20, the day pass gives access to all of the above. Mon–Fri 8am–10.30pm, Sat 10am–7pm, Sun 10am–6pm. M° Rambuteau.

Swimming pools

For €2.60, you can go swimming in most of Paris's excellent **municipal pools.** If you plan to go swimming a lot, the carnet of ten tickets (each good for one entrance) works out to be even cheaper. **Privately run pools**, whether owned by the city or not, are usually more expensive.

Municipal pools

At weekends, the **opening hours** of most municipal pools are something like Saturday 7am–6pm, Sunday 8am–6pm. On weekdays during school hours, opening hours in municipally owned pools (whether publicly or privately run), are complicated. A general rule is that on weekdays during school terms they open for an hour in the early morning and at lunch, then close for the morning and afternoon school sessions, then reopen in the later afternoon until about 6–8pm. All the opening hours can be found at ⓦwww.paris.fr – click on *Sport*, then *Piscines*.

It's best to ring in advance, check the Mairie's website (ⓦwww.paris.fr) or choose a pool nearby and consult their timetable. Many are closed on Monday in school terms. The following are among the best.

Les Amiraux 6 rue Hermann-Lachapelle, 18e ⓣ01.46.06 46.47. Handsome 1920s pool – as featured in the film *Amelie* – surrounded by tiers of changing cabins. M° Simplon.

Armand-Massard 66 bd Montparnasse, 15e ⓣ01.45.38.65.19. Three underground pools – 33-metre, 25-metre and a 12.5-metre kiddies' pool – with lots of space to lounge about in between. M° Vavin.

Butte aux Cailles 5 place Paul-Verlaine, 13e ⓣ01.45.89.60.05. Housed in a spruced-up 1920s brick building with an Art Deco ceiling, this is one of the most pleasant swims in the city. There's a children's pool inside, and in summer a 25-metre heated outside pool. M° Place-d'Italie.

Château-Landon 31 rue du Château-Landon, 10e ⓣ01.55.26.90.35. Two pools, including one for children. M° Louis-Blanc.

Henry-de-Montherlant 32 bd Lannes, 16e ⓣ01.40.72.28.30. Two pools, one 25-metre and one 15-metre, plus a terrace for sunbathing, a solarium – and the Bois de Boulogne close by. M° Porte-Dauphine.

Jean Taris 16 rue Thouin, 5e ⓣ01.55.42.81.90. A 25-metre unchlorinated pool in the centre of the Latin Quarter and a student favourite. There's a small pool for children and swim groups for those with disabilities. M° Cardinal-Lemoine.

Pailleron 32 rue Edouard Pailleron, 5e ☎01.40.40.27.70. Completely refurbished in 2004, this is one of the coolest pools in the city – a 1930s Art Deco marvel surrounded by tiers of changing rooms and arched over by a gantrywork roof. During school holidays it's open late (Mon–Thurs 8am–10.30pm, Fri & Sat 9am–midnight, Sun 9am–6pm). M° Bolivar.

Privately run pools

Aquaboulevard 4 rue Louis-Armand, 15e ☎01.40.60.10.00, ⓦwww.aquaboulevard.com. The pool has wave machines and some incredible water slides, and there are Jacuzzis and a grassy outdoor sunning area. €25 (€10 for children aged 3–11). M° Balard/Porte-de-Versailles/RER Bd-Victor.

Georges-Vallerey Tourelles 148 av Gambetta, 20e ☎01.40.31.15.20. Two pools – one 37-metre – and a solarium. €2.60. M° Porte-des-Lilas.

Les Halles Suzanne Berlioux 10 place de la Rotonde, niveau 3, Porte du Jour, Forum des Halles, 1er ☎01.42.36.98.44. Very centrally located, this 50-metre pool with vaulted concrete ceiling sports a glass wall looking through to a tropical garden. €3.80. RER Châtelet-Les-Halles/M° Châtelet.

Pontoise-Quartier Latin 19 rue de Pontoise, 5e ☎01.55.42.77.88. Art Deco architecture, beautiful blue mosaic interior and a 33-metre pool. Juliette Binoche memorably swam here in the Kieslowski film *Three Colours: Blue.* On weekdays outside school terms, features weekday night sessions until 11.45pm. Pool €3.70. There are squash courts too – see Club Quartier Latin on p.415. M° Maubert-Mutualité.

Roger-Le Gall 34 bd Carnot, 12e ☎01.44.73.81.12. Most of the extras are reserved for club members, but anyone can swim in the 50-metre pool (open in summer; covered in winter), though it's a bit of a hike from the centre. €2.60, or €5 after 5pm. M° Porte-de-Vincennes.

Hammams

Hammams, or Turkish baths, are one of the unexpected delights of Paris. Much more luxurious than the standard Swedish sauna, these are places to linger and chat, and you can usually pay extra for a massage and a *gommage* – a rubdown with a rubber glove – followed by mint tea to recover. Don't let modesty get the better of you – all are quite restrained in terms of nudity and the staff are consummate professionals. You're provided with a strip of linen, but swimsuits are almost always required for mixed men-and-women sessions.

Les Bains du Marais 31–33 rue des Blancs-Manteaux, 4e ☎01.44.61.02.02, ⓦwww.lesbainsdumarais.com. As much a posh health club as a hammam, with a rather chichi clientele and glorious interior. Offers facials, massage and haircuts, and you can lounge about in a robe with mint tea and a newspaper. Sauna and steam room entry costs €35, massage/*gommage* is €35 extra. There are exclusive sessions for women (Mon 11am–8pm; Tues 11am–11pm; Wed 10am–7pm) and men (Thurs 11am–11pm; Fri 10am–8pm), as well as mixed sessions (Wed 7–11pm; Sat 10am–8pm; Sun 11am–11pm) for which you have to bring a swimsuit. M° Rambuteau/St-Paul.

Hammam Med 43–45 rue Petit, 19e ☎01.42.02.31.05, ⓦwww.hammam-medina.com. A bit far away from the centre, but it's one of the nicer hammams in the city, offering great mud treatments. Women: Mon–Fri 11am–10pm & Sun 9am–7pm; mixed (bring a swimsuit): Sat 10am–9pm. €39 hammam and *gommage*; €55 with massage. M° Laumière.

Hammam de la Mosquée 39 rue Geoffroy-St-Hilaire, 5e ☎01.43.31.38.20. One of the most atmospheric baths in the city, with its vaulted cooling-off room and marble-lined steam chamber. It's not intimidating – this is a proper public baths, where people come to wash as well as relax. It's very good value at €15, though towels are extra, and you can also have a reasonably priced massage and *gommage*. After your bath you can enjoy mint tea and honey cakes around a fountain in the little courtyard café. Times may change, so check first, but generally women: Mon, Wed, Thurs & Sat 10am–9pm, Fri 2–9pm; men: Tues 2–9pm, Sun 10am–9pm. M° Censier-Daubenton.

Participatory sports

Ice skating, skateboarding, jogging, billiards, boules – it's all here to be enjoyed. Cycling and rollerblading, or in-line skating, are especially popular. Soccer-players may be able to shoulder their way into a pick-up game in the Jardin des Tuileries. One sport that is not really worth trying in Paris is horse riding (*équitation*). You need to have all the gear with you and a licence, the Carte Nationale de Cavalier, before you can mount. For shops selling sports gear and equipment, see p.404.

Rollerblading and skateboarding

Rollerblading has become so popular in Paris that it takes over entire streets most Friday nights from 9.30pm, when expert skaters – up to 25,000 on fine evenings – meet on the esplanade of the Gare Montparnasse in the 14e (M° Montparnasse) for a demanding **three-hour circuit** of the city; check out Ⓦwww.pari-roller.com for details. A more sedate outing – and a better choice for families – takes place on Sundays, departing at 2.30pm from the Place de la Bastille and returning at 5.30pm (Ⓦwww.rollers-coquillages.org).

The best places to find more **information** and **hire blades** (around €7 for a half day) are: Vertical Line, 4 rue de la Bastille, 4e (Ⓣ01.42.74.70.00, Ⓦwww.vertical-line.com; M° Bastille); and Nomades, 37 bd Bourdon, 4e (Ⓣ01.44.54.07.44, Ⓦwww.nomadeshop.com; M° Bastille); both hold their own roller events. The main outdoor **rollerblading and skateboarding arenas** are on the concourses of the Palais Omnisport, Bercy (M° Bercy) and the Palais de Chaillot (M° Trocadéro). The flat areas just beside the place de la Bastille and place du Palais-Royal are also very popular, as well as the central quays of the Seine on Sundays (see Cycling, p.419).

Ice skating

In winter, a big **outdoor rink** is set up on place de l'Hôtel de Ville, 3e (Dec–March Mon–Thurs noon–10pm, Fri noon–midnight, Sat 9am–midnight, Sun 9am–10pm; M° Hôtel de Ville); you can hire skates (*patins*) for around €5 (bring your passport) and there's a small section cordoned off for children under 6. In past years a small rink has actually been set up on the Eiffel Tower, but the prospect of this being repeated in the future seems doubtful. You can check at Ⓦwww.tour-eiffel.fr.

You can get on the ice year-round at the **Patinoire de Bercy**, at the Palais Omnisports, 8 bd de Bercy, 12e Ⓣ01.40.02.60.60 (Wed 3–6pm, Fri 9.30am–12.30am, Sat 3–6pm & 9.30pm–12.30am, Sun 10am–noon & 3–6pm; M° Bercy). The **Patinoire Pailleron**, 32 rue Edouard Pailleron, 19e Ⓣ01.40.40.27.70 (school holidays: Mon–Thurs noon–10pm, Fri–Sat noon–midnight, Sun 10am–6pm; times vary during term) is big and newly refurbished. From early December to February, two further seasonal rinks can be found on Place Raoul Dautry, 15e (M° Montparnasse-Bienvenüe), and outside the Bibiliothèque Nationale-François Mitterrand (M° Bibiliothèque François Mitterrand/ Quai de la Gare). Entrance is free, though skate hire is €5.

△ Ice skating at the Hôtel de Ville

Jogging – and the Marathon

For running or **jogging**, the Jardin du Luxembourg, Tuileries and Champs de Mars are particularly popular with Parisians; all provide decent, varied runs, and are more or less flat. If you want to run hills, head for the Parc des Buttes-Chaumont in the 19^{e} or Parc Montsouris in the 14^{e} for plenty of suitably punishing gradients. If you have easy access to them, try the Bois de Boulogne and the Bois de Vincennes, which are the largest open spaces, though both are cut through by a number of roads.

The **Paris Marathon** is held in early April over a route from place de la Concorde to Vincennes. If you want to join in, check out Ⓦwww.parismarathon.com, where you can register to run. A half-marathon is held in early March, and "Les 20km de Paris" takes place in mid-October, beginning and ending at the Eiffel Tower (Ⓦwww.20kmparis.com).

Cycling

Since 1996 the Mairie de Paris has made great efforts to introduce dedicated **cycle lanes** in the city, which now add up to some 250km. You can pick up a free leaflet, *Paris à Vélo*, outlining the routes, from town halls, the tourist office, or bike rental outlets (see below). You can also download it from the web at Ⓦwww.paris.fr – click on the "Sport" link. If you prefer cycling in a more natural environment, note that the Bois de Boulogne and the Bois de Vincennes have extensive bike tracks. "**Paris Breathes**", a town-hall-sponsored scheme, closes off the following roads on Sundays and public holidays year-round, making them popular places for cyclists and rollerbladers to meet up: the right bank of the Seine in the 8ᵉ and 12ᵉ arrondissements, along voie Georges Pompidou (9am–5pm); the left bank from quai Anatole France to quai Branly, in the 7ᵉ (9am–5pm); around rue Mouffetard, rue Descartes and rue de l'Ecole Polytechnique in the 5ᵉ (10am–6pm); on quai Valmy and quai de Jemmapes, in the 10ᵉ (10am–6pm; 10am–8pm in summer). Additionally, the Sentier (2ᵉ) and the Butte Montmartre (18ᵉ) have recently been closed to traffic all year round on Sundays and public holidays (10am–6pm).

The newest way to **rent a bike** in Paris is to get hold of one of the town hall's twenty thousand **Vélib'** machines. These three-gear, unisex municipal bikes can be picked up from any one of the 1450 stations (found every 300m or so across Paris), and can be deposited at any other. It sounds ideal, but time will tell whether or not availability becomes a problem. To get hold of a bike, you have to first buy a subscription card from one of the bigger bike stations (or alternatively online at Ⓦhttp://velib.paris.fr, at any arrondissement's Mairie, or at any of the small shops and boulangeries, etc that display the Vélib' logo). This **carte Vélib'** can be valid for one day (€1), seven days (€5) or one year (€29). Once you've got a card, you put it into the *borne*, the pillar-shaped automatic vending machine at every bike station, then type in how long you want to rent a bike for and pay the total amount displayed. The first half-hour of any bike rental in that period is free; after that you have to pay a €1 supplement for the second half-hour, €2 for the third, and €4 per half hour thereafter. Once your card is paid-up, you simply press it against the reader by the bike you want – which is then released automatically.

Beyond Vélib', several outlets detailed below **rent bikes**, by the hour, day, weekend or week. Prices depend on the type of bike, but are usually about €15–20 a day, or upwards of €50 for a week; you have to leave a variable *caution* (deposit) or your credit-card details. If you want a bike for Sunday, when all of Paris takes to the *quais*, you'll need to book in advance. Some companies also offer **bike tours**.

Bois de Boulogne at the roundabout near the Jardin d'Acclimatation, for rides through the wood. €6 for a 3-hour rental; bring your passport. M° Les-Sablons.

Bois de Vincennes Bikes for the several trails here can be rented from Paris Cycles just at the western entrance to the park at Porte Dorée. €6 for a 3-hour rental. M° Porte-Dorée.

Fat Tire Bike Tours 24 rue Edgar Faure, 15ᵉ Ⓣ01.56.58.10.54, Ⓦwww.fattirebiketoursparis.com. Bike rental and four-hour guided bicycle trips in English, with a choice of day (€24) and night (€28) tours. Groups meet and leave from the base of the Eiffel Tower, mid-Feb to beginning of Jan only. Good exercise and cheerful camaraderie of all ages for those looking to cruise the streets of Paris, but don't want to go it alone. Reservations required. Daily 9am–7pm. M° Dupleix.

Paris à Vélo C'est Sympa/Vélo Bastille 22 rue Alphonse Baudin, 11e ⓣ01.48.87.60.01, ⓦwww.parisvelosympa.com. One of the least expensive (from €25 for the weekend) and most helpful for bike rental. Their excellent three-hour tours of Paris – including one at night and another at dawn – all cost €34, under-26s €28. Daily 9.30am–5.30pm (weekends till 6pm), closed every day 1–2pm. M° Richard Lenoir.

Paris-Vélo 2 rue du Fer-à-Moulin, 5e ⓣ01.43.37.59.22, ⓦwww.paris-velo-rent-a-bike.fr Offers 21-speed and mountain bikes. €14 per day, €64 per week. Mon–Sat 10am–7pm, Sun 10am–2pm & 5–7pm. M° Censier-Daubenton.

Billiards and pool

Unlike bowling, **billiards** (*billard*) is an original and ancient French game played with three balls and no pockets. If you want to watch or try your hand (for around €10 per hour, plus around €15 deposit), head for one of the following:

Académie de Billard Clichy-Montmartre 84 rue de Clichy, 9e ⓣ01.48.78.32.85, ⓦwww.academie-billard.com The classiest billiard hall in Europe, where the players look as if they've stepped out of a *Men in Vogue* ad, the decor is all ancient gilded mirrors, high ceilings and panelled walls, and staff in bow ties deliver drinks to your table. Pool and snooker tables are also available. €12 per hour. Daily 11am–6am. M° Place-de-Clichy.

Blue-Billard 111 rue St-Maur, 11e ⓣ01.43.55.87.21. Cocktails, chess and backgammon as well as billiards, in an arty-intellectual café-bar close to Belleville. If you arrive between 2pm and 4pm, you can have the *plat du jour* and an hour's billiards for €8.50. €12 per hour. Daily 11am–2am; weekends until 4am. M° Parmentier.

Salle de Billard des Halles niveau -2, 14 rue Porte-du-Jour, Forum des Halles, 1er. Two French billiard tables among the half-dozen pool tables. Daily 1-9pm (noon-10pm in winter). RER Châtelet-Les-Halles.

Boules

The classic French game involving balls, **boules** (or *pétanque)*, is best performed or watched at the Arènes de Lutèce (see p.138) and the Bois de Vincennes (see p.219). The principle is the same as British bowls but the terrain is always rough – usually gravel or sand and never grass – and the area much smaller. The metal ball is usually thrown upwards from a distance of about 10m, with a strong backspin that stuns it in order to stop it skidding away from the wooden marker (*cochonnet*). It's very male-dominated, and socially the equivalent of darts or perhaps pool; there are café or neighbourhood teams and endless championships. On balmy summer evenings it's a common sight in many of the city's parks and gardens.

Tennis, squash and table tennis

One of the nicest places to play **tennis** is on one of the six asphalt courts at the Jardins du Luxembourg (daily 8am–9pm; €6.50 per hour, cheaper before 11am; M° Notre-Dame-des-Champs). You can book any of the city's forty or so municipal courts online at ⓦwww.tennis.paris.fr. In practice, it's often OK to just turn up with your kit and wait on the spot – usually no more than an hour – though as a rule school holidays are generally less busy. Most city courts are in quite good shape; private clubs demand steep membership fees.

There are several dedicated **squash** centres, including Squash Montmartre, 14 rue Achille-Martinet, 18e ⓣ01.42.55.38.30 (Mon–Fri 10am–11pm, Sat & Sun 10am–7pm; M° Lamarck-Caulaincourt), which charges €10 for half an hour. Alternatively, the Club Quartier Latin (see p.415) has squash courts for €26 for one hour.

The Mairie provides outdoor **table-tennis** tables in many of the smaller parks and outdoor spaces in Paris. It's up to you to bring a racket and balls. Some good locations include: Jardin Marco-Polo (6e), Square de la Trinité

(9e), Parc Floral (12e), Parc Georges-Brassens (15e), Jardin des Batignolles (17e) and Place des Abbesses (18e).

Rock climbing

While you might not be able to scale Notre Dame (at least not in broad daylight) you'll be pleased to know that Paris lays claim to one of the world's largest **indoor climbing** arenas. Mur-Mur Pantin, 55 rue Cartier Bresson, Pantin (Mon–Fri noon–11pm, Sat & Sun 9.30am–6.30pm; ⓣ01.48.46.11.00, ⓦwww.murmur.fr; M° Aubervilliers/RER Pantin), offers some 13,000 square metres of wall space, as well as a special section for honing your ice-climbing skills. Admission costs €13, or €7 Mon–Fri noon–2pm.

Spectator sports

Paris St-Germain (PSG) is one of France's richest and most powerful **football** teams – and it's the only major-league club in the city. Formerly owned by the French cable station Canal-Plus, and recently taken over by a trio of investment banks, it hardly enjoys a local following. The capital's teams retain a special status, too, in the **rugby**, **cycling** and **tennis** worlds. **Horse racing** is as serious a pursuit as in Britain, Australia or North America.

Football and rugby

The Parc des Princes, 24 rue du Commandant-Guilbaud, 16^{e} (M° Porte-de-St-Cloud) is the capital's main stadium for both **rugby union** and domestic **football** events (*le foot*), and home ground to the first-division Paris football team PSG (Paris St-Germain) and the rugby team, Le Racing. The next-door Stade Jean-Bouin, home to the Stade Français rugby club, hosts most of their home matches-with high, profile clashes being hosted in the bigger stadium next door. PSG tickets are sold exactly two weeks before any match (and usually sell out within a week); to buy them, you can call in at the club shop, 27 av des Champs-Elysées, 8e, or contact the club directly on ⓣ3275 (premium rate) or ⓦwww.psg.fr. Prices range from €15–115. The **Stade de France**, on rue Francis de Pressensé in St-Denis (ⓣ08.92.70.09.00, ⓦwww.stadefrance.com; RER Stade-de-France-St-Denis), specially built to host the 1998 World Cup, is now the venue for international football matches and rugby Six Nations' Cup matches.

Cycling

The sport the French are truly mad about is **cycling**, and the biggest event of the French sporting year is the grand finale of the **Tour de France**, which ends in a sweep along the Champs-Elysées in the third week of July with the French president himself presenting the *maillot jaune* (the winner's yellow jersey).

It was, after all, in Paris's Palais Royal gardens in 1791 that the precursor of the modern bicycle, the *célérifère*, was presented, and seventy years later that the Parisian father-and-son team of Pierre and Ernest Michaux constructed the *vélocipède* (hence the modern French term *vélo* for bicycle), the first really efficient bicycle. The French can also legitimately claim the sport of cycle racing as their own, with the first event, a 1200-metre sprint, held in Paris's Parc St Cloud in 1868 – sadly for national pride, however, the first champion was an Englishman.

The Tour de France was inaugurated in 1903; France, though, hasn't had a victory since Bernard Hinault in 1985. The last day of the 4000-odd-kilometre, three-week race often features some thrilling sprinting, but the overall winner of the Tour has usually long since been determined. Only very rarely does Paris witness memorable scenes such as those of 1989, when American Greg Lemond snatched the coveted *maillot jaune* on the final day. Drug scandals have dogged the race since its beginning, culminating in 2006 when American rider Floyd Landis was stripped of the title after testing positive for excess testosterone.

Other classic long-distance bike races that begin or end in Paris include the 600-kilometre **Bordeaux-Paris**, the world's longest single-stage race, first held in 1891; the **Paris-Roubaix**, instigated in 1896, which is reputed to be the most exacting one-day race in the world; the **Paris-Brussels** held since 1893; and the rugged six-day **Paris-Nice** event, covering more than 1100km.

The Palais Omnisports Paris-Bercy (see below) holds cycling events including time trials.

Tennis

The French equivalent of Britain's Wimbledon complex, **Roland-Garros**, lies between the Parc des Princes and the Bois de Boulogne, with the excellent address of 2 av Gordon-Bennett, 16e (Ⓣ01.47.43.48.00; Ⓦwww.frenchopen.org; M° Porte-d'Auteuil). The **French Tennis Open**, one of the four major events which together comprise the Grand Slam, takes place in the last week of May and first week of June. Tickets need to be reserved months in advance using the postal booking system (check the website above for details), and tennis club members are heavily favoured. However, you can sometimes pick up tickets for unseeded matches online at Ⓦwww.ticketnet.fr, or at Roland Garros itself on the day of the tournament – if you're lucky.

Athletics and other sports

The **Palais Omnisports Paris-Bercy** (POPB) at 8 bd Bercy, 12e (Ⓣ01.40.02.60.60, Ⓦwww.bercy.com; M° Bercy) hosts all manner of sporting events – athletics, cycling, handball, dressage and show-jumping, ice hockey, ballroom dancing, judo and motocross – as well as stadium rockers like Iron Maiden and Lord of the Dance. Keep an eye on the sports pages of the newspapers (except *Le Monde*, which has no sports coverage at all), and you might find something that interests you. The complex holds 17,000 people, so you've a fair chance of getting a ticket at the door, championships excepted. Otherwise, tickets are sold through the usual outlets: FNAC and Virgin Megastore (see p.404), and online at Ⓦwww.ticketnet.fr.

Horse racing

The **biggest races** are the Grand Prix de l'Arc de Triomphe and the Prix de la République, held on the first and last Sundays in October respectively at Auteuil and Longchamp. Auteuil in May also hosts the Great Paris Steeplechase, the poshest of all French equestrian competitions. The week starting the last Sunday in June sees nine big racing events, at Auteuil, Longchamp, St-Cloud and Chantilly (see p.269). If you want to try your luck with **betting**, any bar or café with the letters PMU will take your money on a three-horse bet, known as *le tiercé*.

St-Cloud Champ de Courses is in the Parc de St-Cloud off Allée de Chamillard. Auteuil is off the route d'Auteuil (M° Porte-d'Auteuil), and Longchamp off the route des Tribunes (M° Porte-Maillot and then bus 244, or free shuttle buses on major race days), both in the Bois de Boulogne. *L'Humanité* and *Paris-Turf* carry details, and admission charges are €4–8, depending on the day.

Trotting races, with the jockeys in chariots, run from August to September on the Route de la Ferme in the Bois de Vincennes.

26

Kids' Paris

The French are extremely welcoming to **children** on the whole, and Paris's vibrant atmosphere, with its street performers and musicians, lively pavement cafés and brightly lit carousels, is certainly family-friendly. The obvious pull of Disneyland aside (covered in Chapter 17), there are plenty of other attractions and activities to keep kids happy, from circuses to rollerblading. As you'd expect, **museum**-hopping with youngsters in Paris can be as tedious as in any other big city, but remember that while the Louvre and Musée d'Orsay cater to more acquired tastes, the Musée des Arts et Métiers, the Pompidou Centre, Parc de la Villette and some of the other attractions listed below will interest children and adults alike. Travelling with a child also provides the perfect excuse to enjoy some of the simpler pleasures of city life – the playgrounds, ice-cream cones, toy shops and pastries that Paris seems to offer in endless abundance.

In terms of **practicalities**, many cafés, bars or restaurants offer *menus enfants* (special children's set menus) or are often willing to cook simpler food on request, and hotels tack only a small supplement for an additional bed or cot on to the regular room rate. You should have no difficulty finding disposable nappies/diapers, baby foods and milk powders (see box, p.426) for infants. Throughout the city the RATP (Paris Transport) charges half-fares for 4–10s; under-4s travel free on **public transport**.

The most useful sources of information for current **shows**, **exhibitions** and **events** are the special sections in the listings magazines: "Enfants" in *Pariscope* and "Pour les jeunes" in *L'Officiel des Spectacles*. The best place for details of **organized activities**, whether sports, courses or local youth clubs, is the Centre d'Information et de Documentation de la Jeunesse (CIDJ), 101 quai Branly, 15^e^; ⓣ01.43.06.15.38, ⓦwww.cidj.com (Mon–Fri 9.30am–6pm & Sat 9.30am–1pm; M° Bir-Hakeim). The Mairie of Paris provides information about sports and special events at the Kiosque Paris-Jeunes, 25 bd Bourdon, 4^e^ ⓣ01.42.76.22.60 (Mon–Fri 10am–7pm; M° Bastille). The bimonthly *Paris Mômes – môme* is the French word for "kid" – provides the lowdown on current **festivals**, **concerts**, **films** and other activities for children up to age 12; it's available for free from the tourist office. The tourist office also publishes a free booklet in French, *Paris-Ile-de-France avec des Yeux d'Enfants*, with lots of ideas and contacts, or you can look up the children's section on its website ⓦwww.paris-info.com. Also, be sure to check out the festivals list on pp.380–383, as there are a number of annual events perfect for children, including Paris Plage, Bastille Day, the Tour de France and the Course des Garçons de Café.

It's worth remembering that **Wednesday afternoons**, when primary school children have free time, and **Saturdays** are the peak times for children's activities

Babysitting

Reliable **babysitting agencies** include Baby Sitting Services, 4 rue Nationale, Boulogne Billancourt 92100 (ⓣ01.46.21.33.16, ⓦwww.babysittingservices.com; from €6.80 per hour – minimum of three consecutive hours – plus €10.90 fees). Otherwise, try individual notices at the American Church, 65 quai d'Orsay, 6e (M° Invalides; ⓦwww.acparis.org), the Alliance Française, 101 bd Raspail, 6e (M° St-Placide; ⓦwww.alliancefr.org), or CIDJ, 101 quai Branly, 15e (M° Bir-Hakeim; ⓣ01.44.49.12.00, ⓦwww.cidj.com).

and entertainment; Wednesdays continue to be child-centred even during the school holidays.

Parks, gardens and zoos

Younger kids in particular are well catered for by the **parks and gardens** within the city. The most standard forms of entertainment are puppet shows and **Guignol**, the French equivalent of Punch and Judy; these usually last about 45 minutes, cost around €2.50 and are most common on Wednesday, Saturday and Sunday afternoons. Children under about 8 seem to appreciate these shows most, with the puppeteers eliciting an enthusiastic verbal response from them; even though it's all in French, the excitement is contagious and the stories are easy enough to follow.

Although there aren't, on the whole, any open spaces for spontaneous games of football, baseball or cricket, most parks have an enclosed playground with swings, climbing frames and a sand pit, while there's usually a netted enclosure where older children play casual **ballgames**. Otherwise, French sport tends to be thoroughly organized (see Chapter 25, "Activities and sports").

The real star attractions for young children have to be the **Jardin d'Acclimatation** and the **Parc de la Villette**, though you can also let your kids off the leash at the **Jardin des Plantes**, 57 rue Cuvier, 5e (M° Jussieu/ Monge). Open from 7.30/8am until dusk, it contains a small **zoo**, the **Ménagerie** (June–Sept Mon–Sat 9am–6pm, Sun till 6.30pm; Oct–May Mon–Sat 9am–5pm, Sun till 6.30pm; €7/€5, under-4s free), a **playground**, hothouses and plenty of greenery; for more details see p.137. Paris's top zoo, at the Bois de Vincennes, is currently undergoing renovation (see p.220).

The Jardin d'Acclimatation

In the Bois de Boulogne, by Porte des Sablons (M° Les Sablons/Porte-Maillot), ⓣ01.40.67.90.82, ⓦwww.jardindacclimatation.fr. Adults and children €2.70, under-3s free; rides €2.50, or buy a carnet of 15 tickets for €30. Daily: May–Sept 10am–7pm; Oct–April 10am–6pm, with special attractions Wed, Sat, Sun & all week during school hols, including a little train to take you there from M° Porte-Maillot (behind L'Orée du Bois restaurant; every 15min, 11am–6pm; €5.20 return, includes admission).

The Jardin d'Acclimatation is a cross between a funfair, zoo and amusement park, with temptations ranging from bumper cars, go-karts, pony and camel rides, sea lions, birds, bears and monkeys, to a magical mini-canal ride (*"la rivière enchantée"*), distorting mirrors, a huge trampoline, scaled-down farm buildings, a puppet theatre and a golf driving range sure to occupy most fathers, if not their sons as well. Astérix and friends may be explaining life in their Gaulish village, or Babar the world of the elephants in the created-for-children Musée en Herbe

(Ⓦ www.musee-en-herbe.com; Mon–Fri & Sun 10am–6pm, Sat 2–6pm).

The museum also has a permanent interactive exhibition aimed at 4- to 12-year-olds, introducing them to the history of European art. There'll be game sheets (also available in English), workshops and demonstrations of traditional crafts. Children can further develop their curiosity and imagination at the high-tech Explor @dome, designed to help children discover science, the five human senses and art through interactive computer-based exhibits and the usual array of hands-on activities. Children who are after more passive participation can just watch and listen at the Théâtre du Jardin pour l'Enfance et la Jeunesse, which puts on musicals, ballets and poetry readings, or they could watch a performance by the Cirque Phenix Jr, the park's own circus (see p.430 for performance times).

△ The Jardin d'Acclimatation

Paris with babies

You will have little problem in getting hold of **essentials for babies**. Familiar brands of baby food are available in the supermarkets, as well as disposable nappies/diapers (*couches à jeter*), etc. After hours, you can get most goods from late-night pharmacies, though they are slightly more expensive.

Getting around with a pushchair poses the same problems as in most big cities. The métro is especially bad, with its constant flights of stairs (and few escalators), difficult turnstiles and very stiff doors. Some stations, however, have a disabled access door; you'll need to ask at the ticket desk for them to open it and you'll be expected to pass your ticket through the turnstile first.

Unfortunately, many of the lawns in Parisian **parks** are out of bounds ("*pelouse interdite*"), so sprawling on the grass with toddlers and napping babies is often out of the question. That said, more and more parks are now opening the odd grassy area to the public. Just be sure to spot others indulging before you do.

Finding a place to **change and nurse** a baby is especially challenging. While most of the major museums and some department stores have areas within the women's toilets equipped with a shelf and sink for changing a baby, most restaurants do not. Breastfeeding in public, though not especially common among French women, is, for the most part, tolerated if done discreetly.

For emergency medical care, see under "Health" p.33.

Outside the Jardin, in the Bois de Boulogne, older children can amuse themselves with mini-golf and bowling, or boating on the Lac Inférieur. By the entrance to the Jardin there's bike rental (bring your passport) for roaming the wood's 14km of cycle trails, and the park offers babysitting services in the summer. See p.248 for more on the Bois de Boulogne.

Parc de la Villette

In the 19e between avs Jean-Jaurès and Corentin-Cariou ⓣ01.40.03.75.75, ⓦwww.villette.com. Daily 6–1am; entry to park free. M° Porte-de-Pantin/Porte-de-la-Villette.

As well as the Cité des Sciences, various satellite attractions (see p.227), and wide-open spaces to run around or picnic in, the Parc de la Villette has a series of ten themed gardens, some specially designed for kids. All are linked by a walkway called the Promenade des Jardins, indicated on the park's free map.

Polished steel monoliths hidden amongst the trees and scrub cast strange reflections in the Jardin des Miroirs, while the Jardin des Brouillards has jets and curtains of water at different heights and angles. Formalized shapes of dunes and sails, windmills and inflated mattresses make up the Jardin des Vents et des Dunes (under-12s only and their accompanying adults). Strange music creates a fairy-tale or horror-story ambience in the imaginary forests of the Jardin des Frayeurs Enfantines. The Jardin des Voltiges has an obstacle course with trampolines and rigging. Small bronze figures lead you through the vines and other climbing plants of the Jardin de la Treille; and the Jardin des Bambous is filled with the sound of running water. On the north side of the canal de l'Ourcq is the extremely popular eighty-metre-long Dragon Slide. Some of the park's "follies" have activities for kids: video editing in the Folie Vidéo and a game-filled crèche for 2- to 5-year-olds in the Petite Folie, both on the south bank of the canal de l'Ourcq. There are also arts activities for 7- to 10-year-olds in the Folie des Arts Plastiques, by the northeast corner of the Grande Halle (details on ⓣ01.40.03.75.03 or see website). Additionally, guided tours are given of the park grounds every first Sat of the month from April until Oct (ⓣ01.40.03.75.75).

Parc Floral

In the Bois de Vincennes, on route du Champ de Manœuvre (M° Château-de-Vincennes, then bus #112 or a ten-minute walk past the Château de Vincennes), ⓣ01.49.57.24.84, ⓦwww.parcfloral.com. April to mid-Sept 9.30am–8pm; mid-Sept to mid-Oct 9.30am–7pm; mid-Oct to March 9.30am–5/6pm; admission €1, children

aged 7–16 €0.50 plus supplements for some activities, under-7s free.
There's always fun and games to be had at the Parc Floral, in the Bois de Vincennes. The excellent playground has slides, swings, ping-pong and pedal carts (from 2pm), mini-golf modelled on Paris monuments (from 2pm), an electric car circuit, and a little train touring all the gardens (April–Oct daily 1–5pm). Tickets for the paying activities are sold at the playground between 2pm and 5.30pm weekdays and until 7pm on weekends; activities stop fifteen minutes afterwards. Note that many of these activities are available from March/April to August only and on Wed and weekends only in Sept and Oct. On Wed at 2.30pm (May–Sept) there are free performances by clowns, puppets and magicians. Also in the park is a children's theatre, the Théâtre Astral (☎01.43.71.31.10), which has mime, clowns or other not-too-verbal shows for small children aged 3 to 8, for which you're best off calling ahead and making reservations as they're quite popular with school groups (Wed & Sun 3pm, school hols Mon–Fri & Sun 3pm; €6; ☎01.43.71.31.10). There is also a series of pavilions with child-friendly educational exhibitions (free entry), which look at nature in Paris; the best is the butterfly garden (mid-May to mid-Oct Mon–Fri 1.30–5.15pm, Sat & Sun 1.30–6pm).

Other parks, squares and public gardens

All of these assorted open spaces can offer play areas, puppets or, at the very least, a bit of room to run around in, and are open from 7.30am or 8am till dusk. Guignol and puppet shows take place on Wed and weekend afternoons (more frequently in the summer holidays) and cost around €3.

Arènes de Lutèce rue des Arènes, 5e. This great public park, built on what used to be a Roman theatre, has a fountain, sand pit and jungle gyms. M° Place Monge.

Buttes-Chaumont 19e ☎01.42.40.88.66. Built on a former quarry, these grassy slopes are perfect for rolling down and offer great views. Unusually for Paris there are no "keep off the grass" signs. You'll also find a lake, a waterfall and Guignol shows (see p.424). M° Buttes-Chaumont/Botzaris.

Champs-de-Mars 7e ☎01.48.56.01.44. Puppet shows Wed, Sat & Sun at 3.15pm & 4.15pm. M° Ecole-Militaire.

Jardin du Luxembourg 6e ☎01.43.26.46.47. A large playground, pony rides, toy boat rental (Wed & Sun), bicycle track, rollerblading rink, and puppets (see p.145). A 45-minute marionette show takes place Wed & Sat at 3.30pm, Sun at 11am & 3.30pm. M° St-Placide/Notre-Dame-des-Champs/RER Luxembourg.

Food for kids

Restaurants in Paris are usually good at providing small portions or allowing children to share dishes. *Dame Tartine*, 2 rue Brisemiche, 4e (daily noon–11.30pm; M° Rambuteau/Hôtel-de-Ville), is family-friendly, relaxed and affordable, in a great spot overlooking the Stravinsky Fountain, right beside the Pompidou Centre. Children can share things from the menu like the delicious open toasted sandwiches, or there's a reasonably priced special kids' menu. Another good choice is *Spicy Restaurant*, 8 av Franklin D. Roosevelt, 4e (daily noon–midnight; ☎01.56.59.62.59, Ⓦwww.spicyrestaurant.com; M° Franklin-D. Roosevelt), where Sunday family brunches (with plenty of non-spicy options) have a clown and cartoons on standby (€28 adults, €15 children). Several other eating places listed in our "Cafés and restaurants" section (see pp.312–351) offer a *menu enfant*, including *Chez Imogène* (see p.350). One thing to remember when ordering a steak, hamburger, etc, is that the French will serve it rare unless you ask for it "*bien cuit*".

Branches of *McDonald's* and *Quick Hamburger* can be found all over the city; slightly healthier and very reasonably priced is the family-friendly, French-style "*fast foude*" chain, *Hippopotamus* (branches throughout the centre of the city, including 1 bd des Capucines, 2e ☎01.47.42.75.70; M° Opéra; daily 11–5am; €7.90 *menu enfant*); they offer toys, games and colouring books to boot.

Jardins du Ranelagh av Ingres, 16e. Marionettes, cycle track, rollerblading rink and playground. M° Muette.

Jardins du Trocadéro place du Trocadéro, 16e. Rollerblading, skateboarding and aquarium. M° Trocadéro.

Jardin des Tuileries place de la Concorde/rue de Rivoli, 1er. Pony rides, period merry-go-round, marionettes, trampolines, toy sailing boats (Wed & Sun) and funfair in July. See p.84. M° Place-de-la-Concorde/Palais-Royal-Musée-du-Louvre.

Parc Georges-Brassens rue des Morillons, 15e ☎01.48.42.51.80. Climbing rocks, puppets, artificial river, playground and scented herb gardens (see p.186). Access the park at the entrance across from 86 rue Brancion. M° Convention/Porte-de-Vanves.

Parc Monceau bd de Courcelles, 17e ☎01.42.67.04.63. Rollerblading rink (see p.81). M° Monceau.

Parc Montsouris bd Jourdan, 14e. Puppet shows by the lake (Wed & Sat 3.30pm & 4.30pm, Sun 11.30am, 3.30pm, 4.30pm & 5.30pm), and a number of playgrounds (see p.181). M° Glacière/RER Cité-Universitaire.

Place de la Bastille 11e ☎08.20.00.39.75. In Dec, the square becomes a Christmas fantasyland, with a giant trampoline, carousels, a North Pole market and ready-to-listen French Santas. M° Bastille.

Place des Vosges Marais, 4e. The oldest square in Paris has a popular sandpit and plenty of space to run around (see p.111). M° Bastille.

Funfairs

Three big **funfairs** (*fêtes foraines*) are held in Paris each year. The season kicks off in late March with the Fête du Trône in the Bois de Vincennes (running until late May), followed by the funfair in the Tuileries gardens in mid-June to late August, with more than forty rides, including a giant Ferris wheel, and ending up with the Fête à Neu Neu, held near the Bois de Boulogne from early September to the beginning of October. Look up "Fêtes Populaires" under "Agendas" in *Pariscope* for details if you're in town at these times. Very occasionally, rue de Rivoli around M° St-Paul hosts a mini-fairground.

There's usually a **merry-go-round** at the Forum des Halles and beneath Tour St-Jacques at Châtelet, with carousels for smaller children on place de la République, at the Rond-Point des Champs-Elysées by avenue Matignon, at place de la Nation, and at the base of the Montmartre funicular in place St-Pierre.

Swimming, rollerblading and other family activities

One of the most fun things a child can do in Paris – and as enjoyable for the minders – is to have a wet and wild day at **Aquaboulevard**, a giant leisure complex with a landscaped wave pool, slides and a grassy outdoor park. In addition, many municipal **swimming pools** in Paris have dedicated children's pools. See "Activities and sports", p.415 for more details.

Cycling and **rollerblading** are other fun undertakings for the whole family. Sunday is now the favoured day to be en famille on wheels in Paris, when the central *quais* of the Seine and the Canal St-Martin are closed to traffic. One of the most thrilling wheelie experiences is the **mass rollerblading** that takes place on Friday nights and Sunday afternoons (the Sunday outings are more family affairs and the pace tends to be a bit slower). See p.417 for more details and a list of bike and rollerblade hire places. Paris à Vélo C'est Sympa (see p.420) has a good range of kid-sized bikes as well as baby carriers and tandems, and they also offer bicycle tours of Paris.

Boules and **billiards** are both popular in Paris and might amuse your teenagers (see p.420).

There is also a funfair museum, the privately owned **Musée des Arts Forains**, on the edge of the Parc de Bercy at 53 av des Terroirs de France, 12e. Located within one of the old Bercy wine warehouses, the museum has working merry-go-rounds as well as fascinating relics from nineteenth-century fairs. Visits, which consist of an hour-and-a-half guided tour and cost €12 (children €4), are by arrangement only on ⓣ01.43.40.16.15; M° Bercy then bus #24.

Theme parks

Disneyland Paris (see Chapter 17) has put all Paris's other fantasy worlds and **theme parks** into the shade. And unfortunately it's the only one with direct transport links. But, if you're prepared to make the effort, **Parc Astérix** is better mind-fodder, less crowded and cheaper than Disney.

Parc Astérix

In Plailly, 38km north of Paris off the A1 autoroute ⓣ08.26.30.10.40, ⓦwww.parcasterix.fr. The easiest way to get here is to get the shuttle bus from the Louvre, which leaves at 8.45am, and goes direct to the park (€54, under-12s €38, includes entry to park). Alternatively, take the half-hourly shuttle bus (9.30am–1.30pm & 4.30–6/7pm) from RER Roissy-Charles de Gaulle (line B). Park open April–June Mon–Fri 10am–6pm, Sat & Sun 9.30am–7pm; July & Aug daily 9.30am–7pm; Sept & Oct Wed, Sat & Sun only 10am–6pm. Also closed for several days in May and June – it's best to check the website (in English and French) or phone ahead. Admission is €35, 3–11s €25, under-3s free; at most RER and métro stations you can buy an inclusive transport (including shuttle bus) and admission fee ticket for €41.60 and under-12s €27. Parking is €5. Interesting historical-themed sections like Ancient Greece, Roman Empire, Gallic Village, the Middle Ages and Old Paris are sure to spark curiosity in your children. A Via Antiqua shopping street, with buildings from every country in the Roman Empire, leads to a Roman town where gladiators play comic battles and dodgem chariots line up for races. There's a legionnaries' camp where incompetent soldiers attempt to keep watch, and a wave-manipulated lake which you cross on galleys and longships. In the Gaulish village, Panoramix mixes his potions, Obélix slavers over boars, Astérix plots further sorties against the occupiers, and the dreadful bard is exiled up a tree. In another area, street scenes of Paris show the city changing from Roman Lutetia to the present-day capital. All sorts of rides are on offer (with long queues for the best ones). Favourites include the Trace du Hourra, a bobsled that descends very fast from high above, and the Transdemonium, a new ghost train. Dolphins and sea lions perform tricks for the crowds; there are parades and jugglers; restaurants for every budget; and most of the actors speak English (even if they occasionally get confused with the variations on the names).

Circuses, theatre and music

Language being less of a barrier for smaller children, the younger your kids, the more likely they are to appreciate Paris's many special **theatre** shows and **films**. There's also **mime** and the **circus**, which need no translation.

Circus (Cirque)

Circuses, unlike funfairs, are taken seriously in France. They come under the heading of culture as performance art (and there are no qualms about performing animals). Some circuses have permanent venues, of which the most beautiful in Paris is the nineteenth-century Cirque d'Hiver

Bouglione (see below). You'll find details of the seasonal ones under "Cirques" in the "Pour les Jeunes" section of *L'Officiel des Spectacles* and under the same heading in the "Enfants" section of *Pariscope*, and there may well be visiting circuses from Warsaw or Moscow.

Cirque Diana Moreno Bormann 112 rue de la Haie Coq, 19e ⓣ01.48.39.04.47, ⓦwww.cirque-diana-moreno.com. A traditional circus, with lion tamers, elephants, zebras, acrobats, jugglers, trapeze artists – the lot. Performances on Wed, Sat and Sun at 3pm throughout the year. From €10, children under 4 free. Bus #65 (direction Mairie d'Aubervilliers).

Cirque d'Hiver Bouglione 110 rue Amelot, 11e ⓣ01.47.00.28.81, ⓦwww.cirquedhiver.com. Strolling players and fairy lights beneath the dome welcome circus-goers from Oct to Jan (and TV and fashion shows the rest of the year). The Christmas shows are extremely popular. Shows Wed 2pm, Sat & Sun 2pm & 5pm. Tickets €18–37. M° Filles-du-Calvaire.

Cirque de Paris Parc des Chantereines, 115 bd Charles-de-Gaulle, Villeneuve-La Garenne ⓣ01.47.99.40.40, ⓦwww.journeeocirque.com. This dream day out allows you to spend an entire day at the circus (Oct–June Wed, Sun & school hols 10am–5pm; from €36.50, under-12s from €29, including show and lunch). In the morning you are initiated into the arts of juggling, walking the tightrope, clowning and make-up. You have lunch in the ring with your artist tutors, then join the spectators for the show, after which, if you're lucky, you might be taken round to meet the animals. You can, if you prefer, just attend the show at 3pm (from €11, under-12s from €7), but you'd better not let the kids know what they missed. RER Gennevilliers/St-Denis.

Cirque Phenix Jr Jardin d'Acclimatation in the Bois de Boulogne, by Porte des Sablons ⓣ01.40.67.90.82, ⓦwww.cirquephenix.com. This circus includes very few animals and is generally geared towards slightly older children and their parents. The shows here mix traditional circus acrobatics with poetry, comedy and magic (Wed, Sat & Sun 2.30pm & 4pm; from €17.50 including park entrance). M° Les Sablons/Porte-Maillot.

Theatre and magic

The "Spectacles" section under "Enfants" in *Pariscope* lists details of magic, mime, dance and music shows. Several **theatres**, apart from the ones in the Parc Floral and the Jardin d'Acclimatation, specialize in shows for children, and a few occasionally have shows in English.

Au Bec Fin, 6 rue Thérèse, 1er (ⓣ01.42.96.29.35; M° Pyramides), Blancs-Manteaux, 15 rue des Blancs-Manteaux, 4e (ⓣ01.48.87.15.84, ⓦwww.blancsmanteaux.fr; M° Hôtel-de-Ville) and Point Virgule, 7 rue Sainte-Croix-de-la-Bretonnerie, 4e (ⓣ01.42.78.67.03; M° Hôtel-de-Ville) in the Marais have excellent reputations for occasional programming for kids, while the Théâtre des Jeunes Spectateurs in Montreuil, 26 place Jean-Jaurès (ⓣ01.48.70.48.91, ⓦwww.cdnm-theatre-montreuil.com; M° Mairie-de-Montreuil) specializes in children's theatre.

The **magicians' venue**, Le Double-Fond, 1 place du marché Ste-Catherine, 4e (ⓣ01.42.71.40.20, ⓦwww.doublefond.com), has a special children's magic show every Saturday at 2.30pm and Wednesdays and Sundays at 4.30pm, though it's pricey at €9 for a child or adult, and there's a lot of chat in French along with the sleight of hand. If your kids are really into magic they should visit the **Musée de la Curiosité** (see p.123), where a magician performs throughout the day.

Cinema

There are many **cinemas** showing cartoons and children's films, but if they're foreign they are inevitably dubbed into French. Listings of the main Parisian cinemas are given in Chapter 21. The pleasure of an Omnimax projection at La Géode in La Villette or Dôme-Imax at La Défense, however, is greatly enhanced by not understanding the commentary. The Cinaxe projection at La Villette simulates motion to accompany high-definition film (see p.232). Films at the Louis-Lumière cinema (also in the Cité des Sciences – see p.231) may be less accessible, but you can ask at the enquiry desk for advice.

Music

Depending on the type of establishment, most **music events** welcome children of all ages. The Théâtre Musical de Paris, 1 place du Châtelet, 1er (Ⓣ01.42.56.90.10, Ⓦwww.chatelet-theatre.com) runs singing workshops on Sunday mornings for children up to 14 years old. While your kids are warming up their vocal cords, you can attend one of the theatre's classical music concerts. Programmes are Sundays at 11am from October to May and reservations are a must (kids free, adults €23). If you're around in late July, you may well want to venture out of town to **Rockyssimômes**, a summer music festival that has been called the Woodstock for 3–12-year-olds. Except for the paucity of barbiturates and the overabundance of babysitters, it's very much the same thing: ten thousand kids with face paint running happily amuck for hours listening to unique and innovative music. The bands range from African folk groups to rock ensembles dedicated to children's performance, and there's even an open-mike area for budding stars. The festival takes place in Sablé-sur-Sarthe, just over an hour by TGV from Paris (Ⓣ02.43.95.49.96, Ⓦwww.sable-sur-sarthe.com).

Museums and sights

The best treat for children of every age from 3 upwards is the **Cité des Enfants** within the Cité des Sciences, and the **Cité des Sciences** museum itself, in the Parc de la Villette. All the other museums, despite entertaining collections and special activities and workshops for children, pale into insignificance. So beware that, if you visit the Cité on your first day, your offspring may decide that's where they want to stay.

Other monuments and museums likely to appeal are the gargoyles of **Notre-Dame**, the tropical fish- and crocodile-filled **aquarium** at the new Cité nationale de l'histoire de l'immigration (see p.221), the inventions at the **Musée des Arts et Métiers** (p.120) and the **Grande Galerie de l'Evolution** (see p.137), which also has a children's discovery room on the first floor with child-level microscopes, glass cases with live caterpillars and moths and a burrow of Mongolian rodents. The **Musée de la Poupée** (see p.105) should please children who like dolls; and the bizarre nature of the **Musée de la Curiosité** (see p.123) should appeal to most kids. The **Pompidou Centre** (p.100) has a special children's gallery with fun exhibits designed to appeal to children; workshops are also held most Wednesday and Saturday afternoons for children aged 6 to 12 or sometimes for the whole family. The collections of cutting-edge furniture and gadgets at the **Musée de l'Art Moderne** (p.103) may well appeal to some teenagers, as might trying to distinguish imitations from originals at the **Musée du Contrefaçon** (p.250). Excursions to the **catacombs** (see p.179) or even the **sewers** (see p.160) will also delight most children.

If outer space is the kids' prime interest, then bear in mind the two **planetariums**, in the Palais de la Découverte (see p.80) and the Cité des Sciences (see p.231).

Certain museums have **children's workshops**. For a current programme, look under "Animations" in the "Pour les Jeunes" section of *L'Officiel des Spectacles*. The **Musée d'Art Moderne de la Ville de Paris** has special exhibitions and workshops in its children's section (Wed & Sat; entrance 14 av de New-York. See p.168). The **Musée d'Orsay** (see p.151) provides English worksheets for children that help them explore the transformation of the building from a train station into a museum. Other museums with sessions for kids include the **Musée Carnavalet** (see p.113), **Musée de la Mode et du Textile** (see p.73), **Musée des Arts Décoratifs** (see p.73), **Institut du Monde Arabe** (see p.138), the **Louvre** (see p.58) and the **Petit Palais** (see p.79).

Full details of all the state museums' activities for children, which are included in the admission charge, are published in *Objectif Musée*, a booklet available from the museums or from the Direction des Musées de France (34 quai du Louvre, 1er; M° Louvre-Rivoli; closed Tues).

Two fun ways for children to find out about Paris itself and its history are the **Paris-Story** (see p.91), an enjoyable, if highly romanticized, 45-minute, widescreen film on the history of Paris, and the Musée Grévin (see p.90), with its mock-ups of key events in French history, especially the more grisly ones.

Cité des Enfants

Cité des Sciences, Parc de la Villette, 30 av Corentin-Cariou, 19e Ⓦwww.cite-sciences.fr. (M° Porte-de-la-Villette); see pp.227–231 for detailed information on La Villette and the Cité des Sciences. The Cité des Enfants (90min sessions; Tues, Thurs & Fri 9.30am, 11.30am, 1.30pm & 3.30pm; Wed, Sat, Sun & public hols 10.30am, 12.30pm, 2.30pm & 4.30pm; €6; advance reservations at the Cité des Sciences ticket office on Ⓣ08.92.69.70.72 are advised, to avoid disappointment), the Cité des Science's special section for children, divided between 3–5s and 5–12s, is totally engaging. The kids can touch and smell and feel inside things, play about with water, construct buildings on a miniature construction site (complete with cranes, hard hats and barrows), experiment with sound and light, manipulate robots, race their own shadows, and superimpose their image on a landscape. They can listen to different languages by inserting telephones into the appropriate country on a globe, and put together their own television news. Everything, including the butterfly park, is on an appropriate scale, and the whole area is beautifully organized and managed. If you haven't got a child, it's worth borrowing one to get in here.

The rest of the museum is also pretty good for kids, particularly the planetarium, the various film shows, the Argonaute submarine, children's médiathèque (Tues noon–7.45pm, Wed–Sun noon–6.45pm; free) and the frequent temporary exhibitions designed for the young. In the Parc de la Villette, there's lots of wide-open green space and a number of themed gardens (see p.426).

The catacombs and the sewers

Catacombs 1 place Denfert-Rochereau, 14e. Tues–Sun 10am–5pm; €7/€3.50; M° Denfert-Rochereau.

Sewers place de la Résistance, on the corner of quai d'Orsay and the Pont de l'Alma, 7e. May–Sept Mon–Wed, Sat & Sun 11am–5pm; Oct–April same days 11am–4pm; closed the last three weeks in Jan; €4/€3.20; M° Alma-Marceau.

Older children will probably relish the creepiness of the catacombs, stacked with millions of bones from the city's old charnel houses and cemeteries (see p.179 for more).

The archetypal pre-teen fixation, on the other hand, can be indulged in the sewers – *les égouts*. Five hundred metres down, they are dank, damp, dripping, claustrophobic and filled with echoes: just the sort of place kids love. Entered through a large, square manhole, it's a really fascinating way to explore the city. For further details, see p.160.

Shops

The fact that Paris is filled with beautiful, enticing, delicious and expensive things all artfully displayed is not lost on most modern youngsters. Toys, gadgets and clothing are all bright, colourful and very appealing, while the sheer amount of ice cream, chocolate, biscuits and sweets of all shapes and sizes is almost overwhelming. The only goodies you are safe from are high-tech toys, of which France seems to offer a particularly poor range. Below is a small selection of **shops** to seek out, be dragged into or to avoid at all costs.

Books

The following stock a good selection of English books.

Brentano's 37 av de l'Opéra, 2e ⓦwww.brentanos.fr. Children's section in the basement. Organizes occasional storytelling sessions, singing and crafts on Wednesday afternoons and Saturday mornings. Check on the website for details. Mon–Sat 10am–7pm. M° Opéra.

Chantelivre 13 rue de Sèvres, 6e. A huge selection of everything to do with and for children, including good picture books for the younger ones, an English section, and a play area. Mon 1–6.50pm, Tues–Sat 10am–6.50pm; closed mid-Aug. M° Sèvres-Babylone.

Galignani 224 rue de Rivoli, 1er. This long-established English bookshop stocks a decent range of children's books. Mon–Sat 10am–7pm. M° Tuileries.

Shakespeare & Co 37 rue de la Bûcherie, 5e ⓦwww.shakespeareco.org. Upstairs there's a comfy children's classics area. Daily noon–midnight. M° Maubert-Mutualité.

W H Smith 248 rue de Rivoli, 1er. The first floor of this British bookseller has a very good children's section. Mon–Sat 9am–7.30pm, Sun 1–7.30pm. M° Concorde.

Toys and games

In addition to the shops below, be sure to check out the superb selection of toys at the Le Bon Marché department store.

Le Bonhomme de Bois 141 rue d'Alésia, 14e ⓦwww.bonhommedebois.com. Perfect little shop with classic wooden cars and dolls, and plush, colourful, floppy-eared stuffed animals. Mon–Sat 10am–7.30pm. M° Alésia.

Celis 72 rue Vieille du Temple, 4e. A tiny shop selling colourful knitted hats, mittens, sweaters and, most appealing of all, knitted finger puppets – you can buy a whole set of Little Red Riding Hood characters. Wed–Sat 11.30am–7pm, Sun, Mon & Tues 2–7pm. M° St Sébastien-Froissart.

Le Ciel Est à Tout le Monde 10 rue Gay-Lussac, 5e (RER Luxembourg); 7 av Trudaine, 9e (M° Anvers); ⓦwww.lecielestatoutlemonde.com. The best kite shop in Europe also sells frisbees, boomerangs, etc, and, next door, books, slippers, mobiles and traditional wooden toys. Mon 1–7pm, Tues–Sat 10.30am–7pm.

Cité des Sciences (see p.231). The museum shop has a wonderful selection of books, models, games, scientific instruments and toys covering a wide price range.

Au Cotillon Moderne 13 bd Voltaire, 11e. Celluloid and supple plastic masks of animals and fictional and political characters, plus trinkets, festoons and other party paraphernalia. Mon–Sat 10am–7pm; closed Aug. M° Oberkampf.

Les Cousins d'Alice 36 rue Daguerre, 14e. Alice in Wonderland decorations, toys, games, puzzles and mobiles, plus a general range of books and records. Tues–Sat 10am–1pm & 3–5pm, Sun 11am–1pm; closed Mon & Aug. M° Gaîté/Edgar-Quinet.

Galeries Lafayette 40 bd Haussmann, 9e ⓦwww.galerieslafayette.com. Lego sets, dolls, stuffed animals, building toys, and all sorts of little shiny things that kids just love. Mon–Sat 9.30am–7.30pm, Thurs till 9pm. M° Havre-Caumartin.

JouéClub Passage des Princes, 2e. This toy emporium is the largest in Paris and takes up the whole of the renovated passage des Princes. This is the place to buy French Trivial Pursuit or two-thousand-piece jigsaws of French paintings such as Renoir's *Moulin de la Galette*. Mon–Sat 10am–8pm. M° Richelieu-Drouot.

Mayette Magie Moderne 8 rue des Carmes, 5e ⓦwww.mayette.com. The oldest French magic shop, founded in 1808. There's usually someone here who speaks English. Mon–Sat 1.30–8pm. M° Maubert-Mutualité.

Le Monde En Marche 34 rue Dauphine, 6e ⓦ www.le-monde-en-marche.com. Small, friendly toy shop with a nice selection of wooden toys (some hand-crafted in France) for toddlers; marionettes, dolls' house furniture and games for primary school-aged children. Mon–Sat 10.30am–7.30pm. M° Odéon.

Au Nain Bleu 5 blvd Malesherbes, 8e ⓦ www.aunainbleu.com. Around since the 1830s, this shop is expert at delighting children with wooden toys, dolls, and faux china tea sets galore. Mon–Sat 10am–6.30pm; closed Mon in Aug. M° St-Augustin.

Pains d'Epices 29 passage Jouffroy, 9e ⓦ www.paindepices.fr. Fabulous dolls' house necessities from furniture to wine glasses, and puppets. Mon 12.30–7pm, Tues–Sat 10am–7pm, Thurs till 9pm. M° Grands-Boulevards.

Puzzles Michèle Wilson 116 rue du Château, 14e ⓦ www.pmw.fr. Puzzles galore, with workshop on the premises. Tues–Fri 10am–8pm, Sat 10am–7pm. M° Pernéty.

Si Tu Veux 68 galerie Vivienne, 2e. Well-made traditional toys plus do-it-yourself and ready-made costumes. Mon–Sat 10.30am–7pm. M° Bourse.

Clothes

Besides the specialist shops listed here, most of the big department and discount stores have children's sections (see Chapter 24). Of the latter, Tati is the cheapest place to go, while Monoprix has decent prices and matching quality.

ABC Carnaval et Fêtes 22 av Ledru-Rollin, 12e. Need something a little different? Fancy dress galore, gimmicks, masks, accessories and stage make-up, all for hire or purchase. Tues–Sat 10am–7pm. M° Gare-de-Lyon.

agnès b. 2 rue du Jour, 1er. Very fashionable and desirable clothes, as you'd expect from this chic Parisian designer. Just opposite is Le Petit B for babies, selling lots of very French-looking outfits in navy blue and white. Mon–Sat 10am–7pm. M°/RER Châtelet-Les-Halles.

Baby Dior 26 av Montaigne, 8e. Unaffordable, but entertaining – especially the prices. Mon–Sat 10am–6.30pm. M° Franklin-D.-Roosevelt.

Bonpoint 50 rue Etienne-Marcel, 2e ⓦ www.bonpoint.fr. Over-designed but gorgeous traditional couture outfits for the 0- to-6-year-old going on 24. Most items €50–100. A half-dozen other branches around the city. Mon–Sat 10am–7pm. M° Etienne-Marcel.

Menkes 12 rue de Rambuteau, 3e. A vibrant selection of Spanish flamenco outfits, sombreros, fans and footwear for boys and girls. Classes also on offer. Tues–Sat 10am–12.30pm & 2–7pm. M° Rambuteau.

Du Pareil au Même 122 rue du Faubourg-St-Antoine, 12e ⓦ www.dpam.fr. Beautiful kids' clothing at very good prices. Gorgeous floral dresses, cute jogging suits and bright-coloured basics. Branches all over Paris. Mon–Sat 10am–7pm. M° Ledru-Rollin.

Petit Bateau 116 av des Champs-Elysées, 8e ⓦ www.petit-bateau.fr. Stylish and comfortable cotton T-shirts, vests and pyjamas. Dozens of branches all over France. Mon–Sat 10am–7.30pm. M° Charles-de-Gaulles-Etoile.

Pom d'Api 13 rue du Jour, 1er. The most colourful, imaginative and well-made shoes for kids in Paris (up to size 40/UK 7, and from €40), plus exquisite chairs in the shape of swans and dogs for the little ones to sit on while they have their feet measured up. Mon–Sat 10.30am–7pm. M°/RER Châtelet-Les-Halles. Also at 28 rue du Four, 6e (M° St-Germain-des-Prés; Mon–Sat 10am–7pm).

Au Vieux Campeur 48 rue des Ecoles, 5e ⓦ www.au-vieux-campeur.fr. The best camping and sporting equipment range in Paris, spread over several shops in the quartier. The special attraction for kids is a climbing wall. Mon–Wed & Fri 11am–7.30pm, Thurs 11am–9pm, Sat 10am–7.30pm. M° Cluny-La-Sorbonne.

27

Gay and lesbian Paris

Paris is one of the world's great cities in which to be **gay**, with numerous bars, clubs, restaurants, saunas and shops catering for a gay clientele. The focal point of the gay scene is the **Marais**, whose central street, rue Ste-Croix-de-la-Bretonnerie, has visibly gay-oriented businesses at almost every other address. **Lesbians** are less well served commercially, but there are networks of feminist groups and specific publications that cater to the lesbian community.

In general, the French consider sexuality to be a private matter, whether gay or straight. No-one seems any more bothered by the sexuality of Paris's gay mayor, Bertrand Delanoë, than they are by the sexual antics of straight politicians. Casual, unthinking homophobia may be commonplace in straight society – *pédé*, the slang term for queer, is short for *pédéraste*, for example – but in practice most Parisians are not intolerant. Homophobic violence, certainly, has always been very uncommon.

Legally, homosexuality was decriminalized over twenty years ago, and sexual majority is now fixed at sixteen. (Full legal majority is at eighteen, however, so if you've got a seventeen-year-old boyfriend you're technically supposed to get his parents' permission for your relationship, or risk being charged with *détournement de mineurs*. Luckily, the risk of prosecution is pretty small.) The **PACS** law, from Pacte Civil de Solidarité, allows couples over 18 of the same or different sex to sign a civil pact (*se pacser*), acknowledging their unity.

The high spots on the calendar are the huge annual **Marche des Fiertés LGBT**, or gay pride march, which normally takes place on the last Saturday in June, and the **Bastille Day Ball** (July 13, 10pm–dawn), a wild open-air dance on the quai de la Tournelle, 5e (M° Pont-Marie), which is free for all to join in. Gais Musette (ⓦwww.gaismusette.com), an association dedicated to "*danse à deux*", organizes the **Carnaval Interlope** in mid-February every year; not every one of the thousand revellers comes in disguise, or indeed dances *à deux*, but it's one of the best nights of the year.

Information and contacts

The gay and lesbian community is well catered for by rights and support organizations and an active **media**. Listed on the following page are a handful of the most useful contacts.

Useful contacts and organizations

Centre Gai et Lesbien de Paris 3 rue Keller, 11e ⓣ01.43.57.21.47, ⓦwww.cglparis.org. Fights for political rights and acts as a first port of call for information and advice – legal, social, psychological and medical. Also has a good library and puts on small exhibitions. Open Mon–Sat 4–8pm. M° Bastille/Ledru-Rollin/Voltaire.

Inter-LGBT 127 rue Amelot, 11e ⓣ01.53.01.47.01, ⓦwww.inter-lgbt.org. Actively fights for gay rights and organizes the annual pride march. M° St-Sébastien-Froissart.

MAG 106 rue de Montreuil, 11e ⓣ01.43.73.31.63, ⓦwww.mag-paris.org. The Mouvement d'Affirmation des Jeunes Gais et Lesbiennes, a group aimed at young people that organizes a drop-in welcome service as well as occasional tea dances, picnics, and cinema and theatre nights.

Maison des Femmes 163 rue de Charenton, 12e ⓣ01.43.43.41.13, ⓦhttp://maisondesfemmes.free.fr. The main women's centre in Paris and home to a number of lesbian groups, who organize workshops and meetings. Frequent gay/straight lunches and parties, too. Mon–Wed 9am–7pm, Thurs & Fri 9am–5pm. M° Reuilly-Diderot.

Paris Gai Village ⓦwww.parisgaivillage.com. Voluntary association that acts as an alternative tourist office, with guided walks and museum visits ("gay Louvre", for example) and a one-hour welcome-to-gay-Paris service.

Pharmacie du Village 26 rue du Temple, 4e ⓣ01.42.72.60.71. Gay-run pharmacy. Open Mon–Sat 8.30am–9.30pm, Sun 9am–8pm. M° Hôtel-de-Ville.

SOS Homophobie ⓣ01.48.06.42.41, ⓦwww.sos-homophobie.org. First-stop helpline for victims of homophobia. Open Mon & Fri 6–10pm, Tues–Thurs 8–10pm, Sat 2–4pm, Sun 8–10pm.

The media and websites

2X ⓦwww.2xparis.fr. "Deux Fois" aka "Two Weeks" is the premier free gay paper for cultural and nightlife listings, small ads, lonely hearts, services, etc. Comes out every other Thurs.

Citegay ⓦhttp://citegay.fr. One of the best websites, with lots of links, features and contacts.

Lesbia ⓦwww.lesbiamag.com. France's leading lesbian monthly.

Les Mots à la Bouche 6 rue Ste-Croix-de-la-Bretonnerie, 4e ⓣ01.42.78.88.30, ⓦwww.motsbouche.com. The main gay and lesbian bookshop, with exhibition space and meeting rooms; a selection of literature in English, too. Lots of free listings maps and club flyers to pick up, and one of the helpful assistants usually speaks English. Mon–Sat 11am–11pm, Sun 1–9pm. M° Hôtel-de-Ville.

Paris Gay ⓦwww.paris-gay.com. Major portal for gay tourists visiting Paris. The online Guide Gay has lots of reviews of bars, restaurants, clubs, saunas etc, though the English translations tend to be rather brief.

Têtu ⓦwww.tetu.com. The glossiest and most readable of France's gay monthlies – the name means "headstrong". The pull-out section, "Agenda", is full of contact details, addresses and reviews, though it's not restricted to Paris.

Nightlife

In terms of **nightlife**, the key centre is the "gay village" of the Marais. It's not just *Le Central* and the *Open Café* any more – there's a huge range of **bars** – the selection below only scratches the surface. **Lesbians** don't enjoy a similarly wide selection, but there are a few great women-only addresses, and women are welcome in some of the predominantly male clubs. Sadly, the legendary lesbian club, *Le Pulp*, had closed down and was looking for a new venue at the time of writing.

The reputation of wild hedonism in gay **clubs** has spread beyond the gay community and attracted heterosexuals in search of a good time. Consequently, straights are welcome in some gay establishments, especially when in gay company. In fact, some gay clubs have all but abandoned a gay policy – the legendary *Le Queen*, for instance, is gay only on weekends and Wednesdays now – while many of the more mainstream clubs have started doing gay *soirées*.

Big nights out are less **drug**-fuelled than they were a few years ago, but ecstasy, cocaine and amphetamines (*ecstasy*; *cocaïne* or *coke*; *amphés* or *speed*) are still an integral part of the scene, and largely sold through contacts – often inside clubs. Similar laws and risks apply in Paris as in most Western countries.

Mainly women – bars

3W-Kafé 8 rue des Ecouffes, 4e ☎01.48.87.39.26. The ex-*Scandaleuses* has had a designer makeover, turning itself into a swish lipstick-lesbian lounge-café. Sophisticated professionals earlier on, but it warms up considerably at weekends, when the cellar bar gets moving. Daily 5.30pm–2am. M° Hôtel-de-Ville.

Le Nix Café 30 rue du Roi de Sicile, 3e ☎01.42.78.49.36. Small, laid-back bar with a good programme of DJ *soirées*, massage sessions and so on. Draws a friendly, fairly cool crowd of lesbians, straights and gay guys. At weekends, a surprisingly large number of people squeeze in, spilling down the stairs into the cellar bar later on. Daily 5pm–2am. M° St-Paul.

L'Unity Bar 176 rue St-Martin, 3e. Predominantly butch bar with a pool table and an almost exclusively lesbian clientele. Daily 4pm–2am. M° Rambuteau.

Mainly men – bars

Amnesia Café 42 rue Vieille-du-Temple, 4e ☎01.42.72.16.94. Pleasantly trashy gay bar with a relaxed, largely Parisian clientele lounging around on sofas. Later on, the tiny dancefloor in the basement pulls in happy good-timers with a noisy, camp playlist. Daily 11am–2am. M° St-Paul.

Banana Café 13 rue de la Ferronnerie, 1er ☎01.42.33.35.31. Somewhat away from the main scene, right beside Les Halles, but a historic gay address, and still a friendly place to come. By day it's a fairly ordinary café, albeit with a furiously camp tropical decor and a nice *terrasse*; at night it gets more hedonistic and trendy. Daily 6pm–5am. M° Châtelet.

Café Cox 15 rue des Archives, 3e ☎01.42.72.08.00. Muscular, shaved-head body-beautiful clientele up for a seriously good time. Friendly – if your face fits – and has DJs on weekend nights. Daily noon–2am. M° Hôtel-de-Ville.

Le Carré 18 rue du Temple, 4e ☎01.44.59.38.57. Stylish, designer café with good food, comfortable chairs, cool lighting, an excellent *terrasse* on the street, and occasional video projects or fashion shows on the side. Mostly full of sophisticated, good-looking Parisians, but occasional clued-up tourists finds their way here too. Daily 10am–4am. M° Hôtel-de-Ville.

Le Duplex 25 rue Michel-le-Comte, 3e ☎01.42.72.80.86. Popular with intellectual or media types for its relatively relaxed and chatty atmosphere. Friendly rather than cruisy – the barmen know all the regulars by name. Sun–Thurs 8pm–2am, Fri & Sat 8pm–4am. M° Rambuteau.

Le Mixer 23 rue Ste-Croix de la Bretonnerie, 4e ☎01.42.78.26.20. Popular and crowded Marais bar with a high-tech decor and a mezzanine level looking down on the bar area. Some say the name comes from the DJ on his podium, raising the pulse of the crowd with a techno and house soundtrack, others from the clientele, which is – unusually for Paris – a genuine mix of gay, straight, black, white, whatever. Daily 5pm–2am. M° Hôtel-de-Ville.

▽ Le Mixer

L'Open Café 17 rue des Archives, 3e ⓣ**01.48.87.80.25.** The first gay café-bar to have tables out on the pavement, and they're still there, with overhead heaters in winter. *L'Open* is *the* most famous gay bar in Paris and, as such, it's expensive and quite touristy, but still fairly cool. Tues–Sun 5pm–2am. M° Arts-et-Métiers.

La Petite Vertu 15 rue des Vertus, 3e ⓣ**01.48.04.77.09.** Welcoming, inventive Marais address pulling in gay, lesbian and straight punters alike. Frequent special events, and special "tourist welcome" sessions on Sat from 6pm. Tues–Sun 5pm–2am. M° Arts-et-Métiers.

Le Raidd 23 rue du Temple, 4e. All-new, and instantly one of the city's premier gay bars, famous for its beautiful staff, topless waiters and go-go boys' shower shows... Daily 5pm–2am. M° Hôtel-de-Ville.

Clubs

Le Folie's Pigalle 11 place Pigalle, 9e ⓣ**01.48.78.25.26.** You really have to find out what's on when to get the best out of this former cabaret turned nightclub. There are frequent early-morning *after* events, which can be superbly trashy, and big, if occasional, themed gay events. Mon–Thurs midnight–6am, Fri & Sat midnight–noon, Sun 6pm–6am. €20. M° Pigalle.

L'Insolite 33 rue des Petits-Champs, 1er ⓣ**01.40.20.98.59.** Dinky little basement club pulling in a chatty, international mixed crowd, from beautifully dressed PR execs to guys in vests. A classic venue with a lively, packed-out dancefloor and a retro playlist. Busy right through the week. Daily 11pm–5am. €15–20. M° Pyramides.

Le Queen 102 Champs-Elysées, 8e ⓣ**01.53.89.08.89,** ⓦ**www.queen.fr.** Too successful to remain purely gay, and the decor hasn't really changed since its early 1990s heyday, but still runs gay R&B nights on Wed, and massive, loved-up and very gay house events on Saturday and Sunday. Daily midnight–6am. €10–20. M° George-V.

Le Redlight 34 rue du Départ, 14e ⓣ**01.42.79.94.53.** Huge club with a serious sound system and two dancefloors. The industrial decor fits the largely deep house music policy, though Fri are more mixed, both in terms of music policy (garage, R&B) and sexual orientation (straights from the suburbs too). Thurs & Sun midnight–6am, Fri & Sat midnight–noon. €20. M° Montparnasse-Bienvenüe.

La Scène Bastille 2bis rue des Taillandiers, 11e ⓣ**01.48.06.50.70,** ⓦ**www.la-scene.com.** Restaurant, live venue and nightclub combined. After the gigs and the dining are over, at around midnight, Fri often feature largely gay, house sessions such as Pearl or Man Machine, while there's usually a tea dance on Sunday from 6pm. €12–20. M° Bastille/Ledru-Rollin.

Le Tango 13 rue au-Maire, 3e ⓣ**01.42.72.17.78.** Gay and lesbian club with a traditional Sunday-afternoon *bal* from 6pm, featuring proper slow dances as well as tangos and camp 1970s and 1980s disco classics. Turns into a full-on club later on, and on Fri and Sat nights. Fri & Sat 10.30pm–dawn, Sun 5pm–5am. €6.50. M° Arts-et-Métiers.

Hotels and restaurants

Although gays and lesbians aren't likely to come across any antisocial behaviour in **hotels** and **restaurants**, there is a choice of gay-oriented places to stay and eat in should you wish. You don't need to look any further than the Marais; hotels and restaurants are plentiful, and, even if they aren't exclusively gay, the location can almost guarantee a gay-friendly atmosphere.

Hotels

Hôtel Beaumarchais 3 rue Oberkampf, 11e ⓣ**01.53.36.86.86,** ⓦ**www.hotelbeaumarchais.com.** M° Filles-du-Calvaire/Oberkampf. See p.307.

Hôtel Central Marais 33 rue Vieille-du-Temple, 4e ⓣ**01.48.87.56.08,** ⓦ**www.hotelcentralmarais.com.** M° Hôtel-de-Ville. See p.299.

Restaurants

B4 Le Resto 6–8 rue Ste-Croix de la Bretonnerie, 4e ⓣ**01.42.72.16.19.** Stylish, up-front café-restaurant with a chic modern decor and a stylish up-front clientele. At lunch and dinner there's delicious modern Mediterranean cuisine. Count on around €30–40 *à la carte*. Daily noon–2.30pm & 7.30–11.30pm. M° Hôtel-de-Ville.

La Coupe Gorge 2 rue de la Coutellerie, 4e ⓣ01.48.04.79.24. Traditional in cuisine and decor, with its old-style zinc bar counter, rustic upstairs room and great dishes such as *magret de canard*. Set menu at €16. Mon–Fri noon–2.30pm & 7.30pm–midnight, Sat & Sun 7.30pm–midnight; closed Aug. M° Hôtel-de-Ville.

Le Loup Blanc 42 rue Tiquetonne, 2e ⓣ01.40.13.08.35. Bustling, trendy restaurant with changing artwork on the walls. Attracts a fun, camp crowd, and serves great *assiettes* of grilled and marinated meats and fish (€10–15), with a selection of delicious sauces on the side. Daily 7.30pm–midnight, Sun brunch 11am–4.30pm. M° Etienne Marcel.

Le Petit Prince 12 rue de Lanneau, 5e ⓣ01.43.54.77.26. The location – deliciously hidden away on a Latin Quarter backstreet – makes it feel like a secret, but this friendly restaurant is well-known on both the gay and tourist scenes. The food fits the decor: cosy, unpretentious, old-fashioned and deeply French. Menus from €18. Daily 7.30pm–midnight. M° Cluny–La Sorbonne.

Gyms, saunas and sex clubs

Paris's proud history as the erotic capital of Europe is reflected in the modern-day plethora of gay **saunas**, **gyms** and full-on **sex clubs**. A handful of stand-out venues are listed here – good first ports of call if you plan to explore the scene in more depth.

Venues

Le Depôt 10 rue aux Ours, 3e ⓦwww.ledepot.com. A Parisian institution, this is allegedly "Europe's biggest backroom", spread over a maze of different rooms and levels, with a pumping dancefloor. It's usually packed – you'll have to queue for a cubicle, though it's not obligatory. Daily 2pm–8am. €8.50–12.50. M° Etienne-Marcel/Rambuteau.

IDM 4 rue du Faubourg-Montmartre, 9e. This gay gym and sauna has been well established for some thirty years, and it's still going strong with its beautiful, posey clientele, restaurant, basement backroom, "toy" rooms and, lest it be forgotten, its well equipped gym. Daily noon–1am, Sun 6–2am. €10–18. M° Grands Boulevards.

Le Next 87 rue St-Honoré, 1er ⓦwww.lenext.fr. Refurbished sex club with a funky red-and-black decor, dancefloor, private cabins and video backroom. Mon–Fri & Sun noon–5am, Sat noon–6am. €6. M° Louvre-Rivoli.

Univers Gym 20–22 rue des Bons-Enfants, 1er ⓦwww.univers.net. Much more than just a gym, this is a sauna, café and tanning centre, with personal trainers and hairdressers on hand – and a very beautiful clientele. Very flash and very sociable, with frequent party events. Mon–Sat noon–2am, Sun 6–2am. €7–17.50. M° Palais-Royal/Les-Halles.

Contexts

Contexts

A brief history of Paris

The following is a potted history of Paris, featuring mud and marshes, riots and revolutions, palaces and city planning – and, of course, the Parisians.

From mud to the Parisii

Early humans – and for many millenia their Neanderthal cousins alongside them – first lived in the Paris region some 600,000 years ago, when deer, boars, bears and aurochs roamed the banks of a half-kilometre-wide river. The waters slowly shifted southward before settling in the current bed of the Seine in around 30,000 BC (leaving behind today's Marais or "marsh"). The discovery of 14,000-year-old reindeer-hunter campsites at Pincevent, Verberie and Etiolles, in the Paris basin, suggests that modern humans arrived relatively recently.

The most significant evidence of early human activity was discovered in 1991, when excavations at Bercy, beside the river in the east of the modern city, unearthed several dugout canoes (now on display in the Musée Carnavalet) dating back to around 4500 BC. They had been preserved by the marshy, muddy ground. Mud and water were clearly still major features of the area when the **Gauls** or **Celts** began to settle, probably in the third century BC, as the Roman rendition of their name for the city, **Lutetia** or Lucotetia, is drawn from *luco*, a Celtic root word for "marshland".

The local Quarisii or **Parisii** tribe built an oppidum or Iron-Age fort on the eastern part of what is now the Ile de la Cité. The island was originally part of a miniature archipelago of five islets, with two further islets lying to its east (these became the modern Ile St-Louis; another, easternmost island was only joined to the Right Bank at boulevard Morland in 1843). The fort of the Parisii commanded a perfect site: defensible and astride the most practicable north–south crossing point of an eminently navigable river.

Roman Paris

When Julius Caesar's conquering armies arrived in 52 BC, they found a thriving and populous settlement – the Parisii had managed to send a contingent of some eight thousand men to stiffen the Gallic chieftain Vercingétorix's doomed resistance to the invaders. Romanized Lutetia prospered, thanks to its commanding position on the Seine trade route, the river's *nautes*, or boatmen – remembered in the carved pillar now in the Musée du Moyen Age (see p.130) – occupying an important position in civic society. And yet the town was fairly insignificant by **Roman** or even Gaulish standards, with a population no larger than the Parisii's original eight-thousand-strong warband – other Gallo-Roman cities, by contrast, had populations of twenty to thirty thousand. The Romans established their basilica on the Ile de la Cité, but the town lay almost entirely on the Left Bank, on the slopes of the Montagne Ste-Geneviève. Though no monuments of their presence remain today, except the baths by the Hôtel de Cluny and the amphitheatre in rue Monge, their street plan, still visible in the north–south axes of rue St-Martin and rue St-Jacques, determined the future growth of the city.

Although Roman rule in Gaul disintegrated under the impact of **Germanic invasions** around 275 AD, at about the same time St Denis (see box, p.261) established **Christianity** in the Paris region. Lutetia itself, or "Paris", as it was beginning to be called, held out for almost two hundred years. The Emperor Julian was headquartered in the city for three years from 358, during his campaign against the German and Frankish tribes – the latter so-called after the Latin word for "ferocious" – making Paris the de facto capital of the Western Empire. Julian found the climate agreeable, with mild winters and soft breezes carrying the warmth of the ocean, and noted that the water of the Seine was "very clear to the eye".

Franks and Capetians

The marauding bands of **Attila the Hun** were repulsed in 451, supposedly thanks to the prayerful intervention of Geneviève, who became the city's patron saint. (Popular legend has it that Attila had massacred eleven thousand virgins in Cologne, on his way to Paris, and that there weren't enough virgins in the city to make it worth his while.) In any case, the city finally fell to **Clovis the Frank** in 486, the leader of a group of Germanic tribes who traced their ancestors back to Merowech, the son of a legendary sea monster – hence the name of the **Merovingian** dynasty Clovis founded. (This sea-monster story has, if anything, more respectable historical roots than the conspiratorial theory that the Merovingians were the descendants of Jesus and Mary Magdalene.) It was the first but by no means the last time the city would fall to German troops.

Clovis's own conversion to Christianity hastened the Christianization of the whole country. In 511 Clovis's son Childebert commissioned the cathedral of St-Etienne, whose foundations can be seen in the *crypte archéologique* under the square in front of Notre-Dame. He also imported the relics of St Vincent to a shrine on the Left Bank. The site slowly grew to become the great monastery at St-Germain-des-Prés, while St-Denis, to the north of the city, became the burial site of the Merovingians from Dagobert I onwards, in the early seventh century.

The endlessly warring, fratricidally minded Merovingians were gradually supplanted by the hereditary Mayors of the Palace, the process finally confirmed by the coronation of Pépin III, "the Short", in St-Denis, in 754. Pépin's heir, Carolus Magnus or "**Charlemagne**", who gave his name to the new Carolingian dynasty, conquered half of Europe and sparked a mini-Renaissance in the early ninth century. Unfortunately for Paris, he chose to live far from the city. Paris's fortunes further plummeted after the break-up of Charlemagne's empire, being repeatedly sacked and pillaged by the **Vikings** from the mid-840s onwards. Finally, in the 880s, **Eudes**, the Comte de Paris, built strong fortifications on the Ile de la Cité, and the Vikings were definitively repulsed. Yet Paris lay largely in ruins, a provincial backwater without power, influence or even a significant population. Only the Right Bank, which lacked the wealthy monasteries of the main city, had escaped the Vikings' depredations. It was to emerge as the heart of a reborn city.

The medieval heyday

In 987, Eudes' descendant Hugues Capet was crowned king, but the early rulers of the new **Capetian dynasty** rarely chose to live in Paris, despite the association of the monarchy with the city. Regrowth, therefore, was slow, and by 1100, the city's population was only around three thousand. One hundred years later, however, Paris had become the largest city in the Christian world (which it would remain until overtaken by London in the eighteeth century), as well as its intellectual and cultural hub. By the **1320s**, the city's population had swollen again to around a quarter of a million. This unparalleled success rested on the city's valuable river-borne trade and the associated expansion of the **merchant classes**, coupled with thriving **agriculture** in the wider Paris region. Vines and cereals grew to the south, while swathes of rich woodland lay to the east and west, and in the north, between the city and the hill of Montmartre. The economic boom was matched by the growth of the city's university, and protected by the novelty of a relatively strong – and largely Paris-based – monarchy, which gradually brought the surrounding regions under its overlordship. Between them, Louis VI, Louis VII and Philippe-Auguste ruled with confidence for almost all the twelfth century.

The city's commercial activity naturally centred around the place where the goods were landed. This was the place de Grève on the Right Bank, where the Hôtel de Ville now stands. Originally marshy ground, it was gradually drained to accommodate the business quarter. The Left Bank's intellectual associations are similarly ancient, dating from the growth of schools and student accommodation around the two great monasteries of Ste-Geneviève and St-Germain-des-Prés. Europe's pre-eminent scholar, Pierre Abélard – famously the lover of Héloïse and the victim of violent castration – taught in Paris in the early twelfth century, and in 1215 a papal licence allowed the official formation of what gradually became the renowned University of Paris, eventually to be known as the **Sorbonne**, after Robert de Sorbon, founder of a college for poor scholars in 1257. By 1300 there were around three thousand students on the Left Bank of the city, protected by ecclesiastical rather than city law. At this time, the Latin used both inside and outside the schools gave the student district its name of the "Latin Quarter".

To protect his burgeoning city, **Philippe-Auguste** (1180–1223) built the **Louvre fortress** whose excavated remains are now on display beneath the Louvre museum. He also constructed a vast **city wall**, which swung north and east to encompass the Marais, and south to enclose the Montagne Ste-Geneviève – a line roughly traced by the inner ring of modern Paris's 1er–6e arrondissments (though the abbey at St-Germain-des-Prés remained *extra muros*). European contemporaries saw the fortifications as a wonder of the world (even if by Rabelais' time "a cow's fart" would have brought down the walls on the Left Bank), a vital guarantee of the city's security and a convincing proof of the monarchy's long-term ambitions to construct an imperial capital. Famously appalled by the stench of the city's mud as a young man, Philippe-Auguste even began to pave some of the city's streets, though most remained filthy, hopelessly rutted and crowded with people and animals – Louis VI's heir had even been killed when dehorsed by a runaway pig in 1131.

The administration of the city remained in the hands of the monarchy until 1260, when **Louis IX** (St Louis) ceded a measure of responsibility to the *échevins* or leaders of the Paris watermen's guild, whose power was based on their monopoly control of all river traffic and taxes thereon. The city's government, when it has been allowed one, has been conducted ever since from the place de Grève/place de l'Hôtel-de-Ville.

A city adrift

From the **mid-fourteenth** to **mid-fifteenth centuries** Paris shared the same unhappy fate as the rest of France, embroiled in the long and destructive **Hundred Years' War**, which pitted the French and English nobility against each other in a power struggle whose results were misery for the French peasant classes, and penury for Paris. A break in the Capetian line led to the accession of Philippe VI, the first of the **Valois dynasty**, but the legitimacy of his claim on the throne was contested by Edward III of England. Harried by war, the Valois monarchs spent much of their troubled reigns outside their capital, whose loyalty was often questionable. Infuriated by the lack of political representation for merchant classes, the city mayor, or Prévôt des Marchands, **Etienne Marcel**, even let the enemy into Paris in 1357.

Charles V, who ruled from 1364, tried to emulate Philippe-Auguste by constructing a new Louvre and a new city wall that increased Paris's area by more than half again (roughly incorporating what are now the modern 9e–11e arrondissements, on the Right Bank), but the population within his walls was plummeting due to disease and a harsh climate in Europe generally, as well as warfare and political instability. The **Black Death**, which arrived in the summer of 1348, killed some eight hundred Parisians a day, and over the next 140 years one year in four was a plague year. Amid the chaos, the scapegoat knights of the wealthy Templar order were burnt at the stake on the tip of the Ile de la Cité in 1314, to be followed to their deaths by hundreds of **Jews** – falsely accused of poisoning the city's wells – who were definitively expelled from the kingdom in 1394. Paris had lost two of its most economically productive minorities. Harvests repeatedly failed – icebergs even floated on the Seine in 1407 – and politically, things were no better. Taxes were ruinous, trade almost impossible and government insecure.

In 1422 the Duke of Bedford based his overlordship of northern France in Paris. **Joan of Arc** made an unsuccessful attempt to drive the English out in 1429, but was wounded in the process at the Porte St-Honoré, and the following year the English king, Henry VI, had the cheek to have himself crowned king of France in Notre-Dame. Meanwhile, the Valois kings fled the city altogether for a life of pleasure-seeking irrelevance in the gentle Loire Valley, a few days' ride to the southwest.

Renaissance and civil war

In the course of the hundred years leading up to the mid-fifteenth century, Paris's population more than halved. It was only when the English were expelled – from Paris in 1437 and from France in 1453 – that the economy had the chance to recover from decades of devastation. Even so, it was many more years before the Valois monarchs felt able to quit their châteaux and hunting grounds in the Loire and return to the city. Finally, in 1528, **François I** decided to bring back the royal court to Paris aiming, like Philippe-Auguste before him, to establish a new Rome. Work began on reconstructing the Louvre and building the Tuileries palace for **Catherine de Médicis**, and on transforming Fontainebleau and other country residences into sumptuous Renaissance palaces. An economic boom brought peasants in from the countryside in their thousands, and the city's population surpassed its medieval peak by the 1560s. Centralized planning coughed into life to cope with the influx; royal edicts banned overhanging eaves on houses, and a number of gates were removed from Charles V's walls to improve street congestion. But Paris remained, as Henri II put it, a city of "mire, muck and filth".

In the second half of the century, war interrupted the early efforts at civic improvement – this time **civil war** between Catholics and Protestants. Paris, which swung fanatically behind the Catholic cause – calls for the establishment of a new Jerusalem quickly replaced the old Roman ideals – was the scene of one of the worst atrocities ever committed against French Protestants. Some three thousand of them were gathered in Paris for the wedding of Henri III's daughter, Marguerite, to Henri, the Protestant king of Navarre. On August 25, 1572, **St Bartholomew's Day**, as many as two thousand Protestants were massacred at the instigation of the noble "ultra-Catholic" Guise family. When, through this marriage, Henri of Navarre became heir to the French throne in 1584, the Guises drove his father-in-law, Henri III, out of Paris. Forced into alliance, the two Henris laid siege to the city in May 1590 – Henri III claiming to love the city more than he loved his own wife (which, given he was a notorious philanderer among both men and women, was almost certainly true). Parisians were quickly reduced – and it wasn't to be for the last time – to eating donkeys, dogs and rats. Five years later, after Henri III had been assassinated and some forty thousand Parisians had died of disease or starvation, Henri of Navarre entered the city as king **Henri IV**. "Paris is worth a Mass", he is reputed to have said, to justify renouncing his Protestantism in order to soothe Catholic sensibilities.

The Paris he inherited was not a very salubrious place. It was overcrowded. No domestic building had been permitted beyond the limits of Philippe-Auguste's twelfth-century walls because of the guilds' resentment of the unfair advantage enjoyed by craftsmen living outside the jurisdiction of the city's tax regulations. The swollen population had caused an acute housing shortage and a terrible strain on the rudimentary water supply and drainage system. It is said that the first workmen who went to clean out the city's cesspools in 1633 fell dead from the fumes. It took seven months to clean out 6420 cartloads of filth that had been accumulating for two centuries. The overflow ran into the Seine, whence Parisians drew their drinking water.

Planning and expansion

The first systematic attempts at **planning** were introduced by Henri IV at the beginning of the **seventeenth century**: regulating street lines and uniformity of facade, and laying out the first geometric squares. The splendidly harmonious place Royale (later renamed the place des Vosges) and place Dauphine date from this period, but most emblematic of all the new construction work was the **Pont Neuf**, the first of the Paris bridges not to be cluttered with medieval houses. Paris's "biographer" Colin Jones has called it "the Eiffel Tower of the Ancien Régime", a potent symbol of Paris's renewal and architectural daring. After Henri IV was assassinated in 1610 – while caught in his carriage in a seventeenth-century traffic jam on rue de la Ferronnerie – his widow built the **Palais de Luxembourg**, the first secular step in the city's colonization of the western Left Bank – though the construction of new churches and monasteries easily kept pace.

The tradition of grandiose public building initiated by Henri IV (aided by his energetic minister, the Duc de Sully) was to continue to the Revolution and beyond; it was a tradition that perfectly symbolized the bureaucratic, centralized power of the newly self-confident state concentrated in the person of its absolute monarch. The process reached its apogee in the seventeenth century under **Louis XIV**, whose director of the new Académie d'Architecture, François Blondel, told the king that he would "fill [his] territories with so many magnificent buildings that the whole world will look on in wonder". Under the unifying design principles of grace and **Classicism**, the places Vendôme and Victoire were built, along with the Porte St-Martin and St-Denis gateways, the sublime Cour Carrée of the Louvre, and the Italianate Baroque domes at Val-de-Grâce in the Quartier Latin, St-Paul, in the Marais, the Sorbonne, Les Invalides, the Salpêtrière hospital, and the Collège des Quatre-Nations, opposite the Louvre.

In 1671, however, Louis repaired with his entire court to a new and suitably vast palace at **Versailles**, declaring it was "the spot where I can most be myself". The move marked the end of the royal campaign "to make of Paris what Augustus made of Rome" (and in fact, the monarchy didn't return until Louis' grandson, Louis XVI, was brought back at pike-point in 1789). Louis XIV's most significant architectural legacy to his capital was perhaps the demolition of Charles X's old fortifications to make way for the new boulevards – which took their name from the *bulwarks*, or giant earthen ramparts, that they replaced – and the creation of long, tree-lined avenues such as the Champs-Elysées, which was laid out in 1667 by the landscape designer Le Nôtre. **Avenues** and **boulevards** were to become the defining feature of Paris's unique cityscape.

Grandiose building projects were commissioned as often without royal patronage as with it. The aristocratic *hôtels*, or private mansions, of the **Marais** were largely erected during the seventeenth century, to be superseded early in the **eighteenth century** by the **Faubourg St-Germain** as the fashionable quarter of the rich and powerful. Despite the absence of the court, Paris only grew in size, wealth and prestige, until the writer Marivaux could claim, with some truth, in 1734 that "Paris is the world, and the rest of the earth nothing but its suburbs". By the 1770s and 1780s, conversational *salons*, Masonic lodges, coffee-houses or "cafés" and newspapers had opened by the hundreds to serve the needs of the burgeoning **bourgeoisie**, while the Palais Royal became the hub of fashionably decadent Europe – a gambling den, brothel, mall and society venue combined.

Obscured by all the glitter, however, were the **poor living conditions** of the ordinary citizens. The centre of the city remained a densely packed and unsanitary warren of medieval lanes and tenements. And it was only in the years immediately preceding the 1789 Revolution that any attempt was made to clean it up. The buildings crowding the bridges were dismantled as late as 1786. Pavements were introduced for the first time and attempts were made to improve the drainage. A further source of pestilential infection was removed with the emptying of the overcrowded cemeteries into the catacombs. One grave-digger alone claimed to have buried more than ninety thousand people in thirty years, stacked "like slices of bacon" in the charnel house of the Innocents, which had been receiving the dead of 22 parishes for eight hundred years.

In 1786 Paris received its penultimate ring of fortifications, the so-called **wall of the Fermiers Généraux**, which roughly followed the line of modern Paris's inner and outer ring of arrondissements. The wall had 57 *barrières* or toll gates (one of which survives in the middle of place Stalingrad), where a tax was levied on all goods entering the city. At its outer edge, beyond the customs tolls, new houses of entertainment sprang up, encouraging a long tradition of

Parisians crossing the boundaries of the city proper in search of drink, dancing and other kinds of transgression. It was a tradition that would culminate – and largely die – with the early twentieth-century artistic boom towns of Montmartre and Montparnasse.

Revolution

One of the leading causes of the **Revolution of 1789** was a crisis in finance. France had been involved in a number of costly wars in the mid-eighteenth century, leaving the government desperately short of money. The only way to substantially increase revenue was to tax the privileged classes, the clergy and nobility, traditionally exempt from taxation. They naturally resisted this perceived attack on their status. Louis XVI, though wielding absolute power, couldn't simply impose his will in this matter, for fear of being charged with despotism. Louis' response to the stalemate was to recall the **Estates General** for the first time since 1614 to try and secure assent to fiscal reform. The Estates General was made up of representatives of the country's three "estates", or orders: the clergy (the First Estate), the nobility (the Second) and the rest of the population – the vast majority – namely the middle classes and the peasantry, known as the Third Estate. The Estates duly met in May 1789 and each of the three orders presented its grievances to the Crown; what the government hadn't expected was such a long list of complaints from the Third Estate, mainly represented by outspoken members of the bourgeoisie, increasingly resentful at not having political power commensurate with their social position and wealth. Tension arose, too, over voting procedures – whether voting should be by order (in which case the privileged orders would dominate) or by head (in which case the Third Estate would have a majority). Under popular pressure, Louis XVI seemed to give way to a vote by head, but at the same time he began posting troops around Versailles and Paris, as though already regretting what he had done and preparing for a coup to reverse his actions. The fear of attack by royal troops propelled the Parisian people from the sidelines into the heart of the action. The electoral assembly that had made the final selection for the Parisian deputies for the Estates General entered the Hôtel de Ville and declared itself the municipal government or **Commune**. It set up a bourgeois militia, later to become known as the National Guard; the militia prepared to defend Paris against attack and tried to keep order in a by-now agitated city. It joined in, however, when a band of ordinary Parisians stormed the **Bastille** prison on July 14 looking for weapons with which to arm themselves. As a symbol of victory over the oppressive forces of the monarchy, the capture of the Bastille acquired huge significance.

Although the effects of the Revolution were felt all over France and indeed Europe, it was in Paris that the most profound changes took place. Being as it were on the spot, the ordinary people of Paris, known as the **sans-culottes**, literally "the people without breeches" – a form of dress associated with aristocrats and the rich – became major players in the unfolding drama. They formed the revolutionary shock troops, the driving force at the crucial stages of the Revolution. Where the bourgeois deputies were concerned principally with political reform, the *sans-culottes* expressed their demands in economic terms: price controls, regulation of the city's food supplies, and so on. By their practice of taking to the streets, they also established a long tradition of revolutionary action.

While the king had been gathering troops at Versailles, the members of the Third Estate had proclaimed themselves the **National Assembly** and invited the clergy and nobility to join them (many members of the lower clergy and some nobles did). A majority of the assembly would probably have been content with constitutional reforms that checked monarchical power on the English model, but their power depended largely on their ability to wield the threat of a Parisian popular explosion.

The king bowed to pressure and legalized the National Assembly, which in August 1789 passed the **Declaration of the Rights of Man**, sweeping away the feudal privileges of the old order. Rumours were rife of counter-revolutionary intrigues at the court in **Versailles**, and in October a group of Parisians marched on Versailles and forced the king to return to Paris with them; they installed him in the Tuileries, where he was basically kept prisoner. In 1791 he attempted to flee abroad, but was stopped at Varennes and humiliatingly brought back to Paris.

Unlike the king, many nobles had managed to leave the country and had started stirring up foreign governments against the Revolution. Some members of the National Assembly wanted war as a means of spreading the Revolution abroad and of rallying the nation to its cause. Following an initiative by the **Girondin** faction (a group of deputies from the Gironde region around Bordeaux), the Assembly decided to fight to protect the Revolution. War was declared on Austria in 1792 and the **French Revolutionary Wars** began. Things went badly at first and radicalized many who had previously been moderate. Clamours for a republic and the overthrow of the king grew. The National Assembly was divided, and it was the Parisian people who took matters into their own hands – in August 1792 the *sans-culottes* marched on the Hôtel de Ville, set up an **insurrectionary Commune** and imprisoned the king. Under pressure from the Commune, the Assembly agreed to disband and order elections for a new **Convention** to draw up a new, republican, constitution. Parisian popular militants undoubtedly played a significant part in establishing the republic, but they were also responsible for one of the Revolution's worst atrocities: the 1792 September **massacres**, in which some 1200 inmates of Paris's prisons (the Conciergerie, La Force, etc) were brutally murdered; as well as common criminals, these included recalcitrant priests and political prisoners, and the Princesse de Lamballe, Marie-Antoinette's close friend.

Later that month the Convention held its first meeting and immediately abolished the monarchy, set up a republic and proceeded to try the king for treason. Louis was convicted and guillotined on place de la Révolution (now place de la Concorde) in January 1793. The effect was to reinforce royalist resistance at home and abroad, and a wider war coalition was formed against France.

The Convention itself was wracked with infighting – the two main factions were the Girondins and the more radical **Jacobins**. Gradually the moderate Girondin faction lost out and was purged in June 1793. The Convention set up a war dictatorship and operated through various bodies, including the Committee of Public Safety, headed by the chillingly ruthless Maximilien **Robespierre**. Justifying its actions on the grounds of national emergency, the Committee of Public Safety began the extermination of "enemies of the people", a period known as the *Grande Terreur*. Among the first casualties was **Marie-Antoinette**, who went with calm dignity to the guillotine in October 1793. Over the next few months some further 2600 individuals were executed, including many of the more moderate revolutionaries such as **Danton** whose last words as he went to his death were typical of his proud spirit: "Above all, don't forget to show my head to the people; it's well worth having a look at."

Guillotined along with him was the romantic idealist Camille Desmoulins, who had stood on a café table in the Palais Royal on July 12, 1789, and called the people to arms. **The Terror** finally ended in July 1794 when Robespierre, now widely perceived as a tyrant, was himself arrested by members of the Convention, fearing that the Terror would be turned against them, and suffered the fate he had meted out to so many.

After the end of the Terror there was a return to more temperate policies and power was put into the hands of a five-man **Directory**, characterized by weakness and corruption. A period of instability followed as conflict between royalists and revolutionaries rumbled on. The political class began to look for a strong leader who could rewrite the constitution giving more power to the executive. This leader emerged in the form of General **Napoleon Bonaparte**. Napoleon had already distinguished himself on the battlefield in Italy and Austria and had put down a Royalist insurrection in Paris in October 1795 with the minimum of fuss. In November 1799 he overthrew the Directory in a **coup d'état**. He appointed himself first consul for life in 1802 and **emperor** in 1804.

Napoleon

Although Napoleon took France into numerous costly **wars**, culminating in the disastrous Russian campaign, in which much of the Grande Armée was annihilated, the period of his rule was one of relative prosperity and stability. He upheld the fundamental reforms of the Revolution, and drew up a new set of laws, central to which were equal rights and equal treatment of all citizens (though not women, still classed as minors); the Code Civil, or Code Napoléon, long outlasted Napoleon's empire and has been a major influence on legal systems in many other countries. Napoleon did much to improve **education**

△ The fall of the Republic – Jacques-Louis David's Coronation of the Emperor and Empress

and spent more money on this than anything else – he established lycées, the baccalauréat and the Ecole Normale Supérieure, all of which still endure.

Other long-lasting reforms included the creation of a very efficient and very **centralized bureaucracy** that put Paris in firm control of the rest of the country – even more so than under Louis XIV. Napoleon replaced the power of local institutions by a corps of préfets answerable to himself, made judges into state functionaries, redesigned the tax system and created the Banque de France.

Napoleon wanted to make Paris the most beautiful city in Europe, the "capital of capitals" and concentrated the majority of his **public works** and grandiose building schemes here. He lined the Seine with two and a half miles of stone *quais* to prevent flooding, spanned the river with three bridges and created canals and reservoirs, providing Paris with its modern water supply. He built the Arcs de Triomphe and Carrousel and a further extension for the Louvre. He drew up plans for a temple to the Grande Armée, which later became the church of the Madeleine, and remodelled the facade of the Palais-Bourbon, opposite, in matching Roman style. He laid out the long and straight rue de Rivoli and rue de la Paix and devised new street-numbering (still in place) – odd on one side, even on the other; where streets ran parallel to the Seine, the numbering followed the flow of the river; in other streets, numbering started at the end nearest the river.

Napoleon's enormous energy on the home front was more than matched by his endeavours in the field. In the early 1800s he brought home a string of dazzling **military victories** and by 1809 his conquered territory stretched from southern Italy to the Baltic, an empire much greater than that achieved by Louis XIV or Charlemagne. Napoleon, however, overreached himself with his **invasion of Russia** in 1812. It was a colossal disaster. The Russians simply retreated, drawing the French army deeper and deeper into Russia. When the French finally reached Moscow they found it had already been burned and deserted; Napoleon was forced to retreat and on the way back tens of thousands of his troops perished from the bitter cold of the Russian winter. Out of four hundred thousand men (half of whom were conscripts from Napoleon's empire) barely twenty thousand made it back home. After further defeats by a coalition of European powers and the entry of an army of Russians, Prussians and Austrians into Paris in March 1814 (the first time Paris had experienced foreign invasion since the English entered the city in 1429), Napoleon was forced to abdicate and **Louis XVIII**, brother of the decapitated Louis XVI, was installed as king. In a last desperate attempt to regain power, Napoleon escaped from exile on the Italian island of Elba and reorganized his armies, only to meet final defeat at **Waterloo** on June 18, 1815. Louis XVIII was restored to power.

Restoration – and back to the barricades

For the rest of the **nineteenth century** after Napoleon's demise, France was left to fight out the contradictions and unfinished business left behind by the Revolution of 1789. Aside from the actual conflicts on the streets of the capital, there was a tussle between the class that had risen to wealth and power as a direct result of the destruction of the monarchy and the survivors of the old order, who sought to make a comeback in the 1820s under the **restored monarchy** of Louis XVIII and Charles X. This conflict was finally resolved in favour of the new bourgeoisie. When Charles X refused to accept the result of the 1830 National Assembly elections, **Adolphe Thiers** – who was to become the veteran conservative politician of the nineteenth century – led the opposition in revolt. Barricades were erected in Paris and there followed three days of bitter street fighting, known as **les trois glorieuses**, in which 1800 people were killed (they are commemorated by the column on place de la Bastille). The outcome of this **July Revolution** was parliament's election of **Louis-Philippe** in August 1830 as constitutional monarch, or *le roi bourgeois*, and the introduction of a few liberalizing reforms, most either cosmetic or serving merely to consolidate the power of the wealthiest stratum of the population.

As the demands of the disenfranchised poor continued to go unheeded, so their radicalism increased, exacerbated by **deteriorating living and working conditions** in the large towns, especially Paris, as the Industrial Revolution got under way. There were, for example, twenty thousand deaths from cholera in Paris in 1832, and 65 percent of the population in 1848 were too poor to be liable for tax. Eruptions of discontent invariably occurred in the capital, with insurrections in 1832 and 1834. When Thiers ringed Paris and its suburbs with a defensive wall (thus defining the limits of the modern city), his efforts soon appeared misdirected. In 1848, the lid blew off the pot. Barricades went up in February, and the **Second Republic** was quickly proclaimed. It looked for a time as if working-class demands might be at least partly met, but in the face of agitation in the streets, the more conservative Republicans lost their nerve, and the nation showed its feelings by returning a spanking reactionary majority in the April elections.

Revolution appeared the only alternative for Paris's radical poor. On June 23, 1848, working-class Paris – Poissonnière, Temple, St-Antoine, the Marais, Quartier Latin, Montmartre – rose in revolt. In what became known as the **1848 Revolution**, men, women and children fought side by side against fifty thousand troops. In three days of fighting, nine hundred soldiers were killed. No-one knows how many of the *insurgés* – the insurgents – died. Fifteen thousand people were arrested and four thousand sentenced to prison terms. **Louis Napoléon Bonaparte**, the nephew of Napoleon I, was elected President in November 1848, but within three years he brought the tottering republic to an end by announcing a coup d'état. Twelve months later, he had himself crowned Emperor **Napoléon III**.

Haussmann

There followed a period of foreign acquisitions on every continent and of laissez-faire capitalism at home, both of which greatly increased the **economic wealth** of France, then lagging far behind Britain in the industrialization stakes. Foreign trade trebled, a huge expansion of the rail network was carried out, investment banks were set up, and so forth. The rewards, however, were very unevenly distributed, and the regime relied unashamedly on repressive measures – press censorship, police harassment and the forcible suppression of strikes – to hold the underdogs in check.

During the nearly twenty years of the **Second Empire**, the city suffered the greatest ever shock to its system. **Baron Haussmann**, appointed Prefect of the Seine department with responsibility for Paris by Napoléon III, undertook the total **transformation of the city**. In love with the straight line and grand vista, he drove 135km of broad new streets through the cramped quarters of the medieval city, linking the interior and exterior boulevards, and creating long, straight north–south and east–west cross-routes – the last being one of the main factors behind the relentless severity of the bitter winds that can plague Paris on winter days. Haussmann's taste dictated the uniform grey stone facades, mansard roofs and six to seven storeys that are still the architectural hallmark of the Paris street today. In fact, such was the logic of his planning that construction of his projected streets continued long after his death, boulevard Haussmann itself being completed only in 1927.

In 1859, all the land up to Thiers' wall of 1840 was incorporated into the city of Paris. A contemporary journalist railed "they have sewn rags onto the dress of a queen", but it was a brave and possibly brilliant decision – and a move that subsequent governments have consistently failed to emulate, leaving Paris's future suburbs to swell energetically but chaotically, then wallow in unregulated and unadorned semi-squalor. Between 1860 and the outbreak of World War I, the population of Paris "beyond the walls", or the **banlieue** as it became known, tripled in size, becoming the home of 1.5 million almost-Parisians. (The city proper had been surpassed in population by London in the eighteenth century; after 1900 it was overtaken by New York too, with Berlin, Vienna and St Petersburg catching up fast.)

Despite the scale of Haussmann's demolitions and redevelopments, **the poor** within the city were largely left to fend for themselves. Some 350,000 Parisians were displaced. The prosperous classes moved into the new western arrondissements, abandoning the decaying older properties. These were divided and subdivided into ever-smaller units as landlords sought to maximize their rents. Sanitation was nonexistent. Water standpipes were available only in the street. Migrant workers from the provinces, sucked into the city to supply the vast labour requirements, crammed into the old villages of Belleville and Ménilmontant. Many, too poor to buy furniture, lived in barely furnished digs or *demi-lits*, where the same bed was shared by several tenants on a shift basis. Cholera and TB were rife. Until 1870 refuse was thrown into the streets at night to be collected the following morning. When in 1884 the Prefect of the day required landlords to provide proper containers, they retorted by calling the containers by his name, Poubelle – and the name has stuck as the French word for "dustbin".

Haussmann's scheme was at least in part designed to keep the workers under control. Barracks were located at strategic points like the place du Château-d'Eau, now République, controlling the turbulent eastern districts, and the broad boulevards were intended to facilitate cavalry manoeuvres and artillery fire, with angled intersections that would allow troops to outflank any barricades that discontented citizens might erect.

The siege and the Commune

In September 1870, Napoléon III surrendered to Bismarck at the border town of Sedan, less than two months after France had declared war on the well-prepared and superior forces of the **Prussian** state. The humiliation was enough for a Republican government to be instantly proclaimed in Paris. The Prussians advanced and by September 19 were laying **siege** to the capital. Minister of the Interior Léon Gambetta was flown out by hot-air balloon to rally the provincial troops but further balloon messengers ended up in Norway or the Atlantic. The few attempts at military sorties from Paris turned into yet more blundering failures. Meanwhile, the city's restaurants were forced to change menus to fried dog, roast rat or peculiar delicacies from the zoos, and death from disease or starvation became an ever more common fate.

The government's half-hearted defence of the city – more afraid of revolution within than of the Prussians – angered Parisians, who clamoured for the creation of a 1789-style Commune. The Prussians, meanwhile, were demanding a proper government to negotiate with. In January 1871, those in power agreed to hold elections for a new National Assembly with the authority to surrender officially to the Prussians. A large monarchist majority, with the conservative Adolphe Thiers at its head, was returned, and on March 1, Prussian troops marched down the Champs-Elysées and garrisoned the city for three days while the populace remained behind closed doors in silent protest. On March 18, amid growing resentment from all classes of Parisians, Thiers' attempt to take possession of the National Guard's artillery in Montmartre (see p.197) set the barrel alight. The **Commune** was proclaimed from the Hôtel de Ville and Paris was promptly subjected to a second siege by Thiers' government, which had fled to Versailles, followed by the remaining Parisian bourgeoisie.

The Commune lasted 72 days – a festival of the oppressed, Lenin called it. Socialist in inspiration, it had no time to implement lasting reforms. Wholly occupied with defence against Thiers' army, it succumbed finally on May 28, 1871, after a week of street-by-street warfare – the so-called *semaine sanglante*, or "Bloody Week" – in which some 25,000 men, women and children were killed, including thousands in random revenge shootings by government troops. Among the non-human casualties were several of the city's landmark buildings, including the Tuileries palace, Hôtel de Ville, Cours des Comptes (where the Musée d'Orsay now stands) and a large chunk of the rue Royale.

Belle époque

Physical **recovery** was remarkably quick. Within six or seven years few signs of the fighting remained. Visitors remarked admiringly on the teeming streets, the expensive shops and energetic nightlife. Charles Garnier's Opéra was opened in 1875. Aptly described as the "triumph of moulded pastry", it was a suitable image of the frivolity and materialism of what the British called the "naughty" Eighties and Nineties, and the French called the **belle époque**, or "Age of Beauty". In 1889 the **Eiffel Tower** stole the show at the great Exposition. For the 1900 repeat, the Métropolitain or "**métro**" was unveiled.

The years up to World War I were marked by the unstable but thoroughly conservative governments of the **Third Republic**. On the extreme right, fascism began to make its ugly appearance with Maurras' proto-Brownshirt organization, the Camelots du Roi. Despite – or maybe in some way because of – the political tensions, Paris emerged as the supremely inspiring environment for artists and writers – the so-called Bohemians – both French and foreign. It was a constellation of talents such as Western culture has rarely seen. **Impressionism**, **Fauvism** and **Cubism** were all born in Paris in this period, while French **poets** like Apollinaire, Laforgue, Max Jacob, Blaise Cendrars and André Breton were preparing the way for Surrealism, concrete poetry and Symbolism. **Cinema**, too, first saw the light in Paris, with the jerky documentaries of the Lumière brothers and George Méliès' fantastical features both appearing in the mid-1890s.

War, depression and occupation

As a city, Paris escaped **World War I** relatively lightly, with only a brief Zeppelin bombardment in 1916, and heavy shelling from the Germans' monstrous, long-range "Big Bertha" cannon mercifully restricted to the early part of 1918. The human cost was rather higher: one in ten Parisian conscripts failed to return. But Paris remained the world's art – and party – capital after the war, with an injection of foreign blood and a shift of venue from Montmartre to Montparnasse. Indeed, the **années folles** (or "mad years") of the 1920s were among Paris's most decadent and scintillating, consolidating a long-standing international reputation for hedonistic, often erotic, abandon that has sustained its tourism industry for the best part of a century. Meanwhile, work on the dismantling of Thiers' outmoded fortifications progressed with aching slowness from 1919 until 1932 – after which the cleared space languished as a wilderness of shantytowns, or *bidonvilles*, until the construction of the *boulevard périphérique* ring road in the 1960s.

As **Depression** deepened in the 1930s and Nazi power across the Rhine became more menacing, however, the mood changed. Politicized thuggery grew rife in Paris, culminating in a pitched battle outside the Chamber of Deputies in February 1934. Socialist leader **Léon Blum** was only saved from being lynched by a funeral cortege through the intervention of some building workers who happened to notice what was going on in the street below. The Left, including the Communists, united behind the banner of the Popular Front, winning the **1936 elections** with a handsome majority. A wave of strikes and factory sit-ins followed. Frightened by the apparently revolutionary situation, the major employers signed the Matignon Agreement with Blum – now Prime Minister – which provided for wage increases, nationalization of the armaments industry and partial nationalization of the Bank of France, a forty-hour week, paid annual leave and collective bargaining on wages. These reforms were pushed through Parliament, but when Blum tried to introduce exchange controls to check the flight of capital the Senate threw the proposal out and he resigned. The Left returned to opposition, where it remained, with the exception of coalition governments, until 1981.

During the **occupation** of Paris in **World War II**, the Germans found some sections of Parisian society, as well as the minions of the Vichy government, only too happy to hobnob with them. For four years the city suffered fascist rule with curfews, German garrisons and a Gestapo HQ. Parisian Jews were forced to wear the star of David and in 1942 were rounded up – by other Frenchmen – and shipped off to Auschwitz (see p.182).

The **Resistance** was very active in the city, gathering people of all political persuasions into its ranks, but with Communists and Socialists, especially of East European Jewish origin, well to the fore. The job of torturing them when they fell into Nazi hands – often as a result of betrayals – was left to their fellow citizens in the fascist militia. Those who were condemned to death – rather than the concentration camps – were shot against the wall below the old fort of Mont Valérien above St-Cloud.

As Allied forces drew near to the city in 1944, the FFI (armed Resistance units), called their troops onto the streets. Alarmed at the prospect of the Left seizing power in his absence, the free French leader, **Général de Gaulle**, urged the Allies to let him press on towards the capital. To their credit, the Paris police also joined in the uprising, holding their Ile de la Cité HQ for three days against German attacks. On August 23, Hitler famously gave orders that Paris should be physically destroyed, but the city's commander, Von Cholitz, delayed just long enough. **Liberation** arrived on August 25 in the shape of General Leclerc's tanks, motoring up the Champs-Elysées to the roar of a vast crowd.

Postwar Paris

Postwar Paris has remained no stranger to political battles in its streets. Violent demonstrations accompanied the Communist withdrawal from the coalition government in 1947. In the Fifties the Left took to the streets again in protest against the colonial wars in Indochina and Algeria. And, in 1961, in one of the most shameful episodes in modern French history, some two hundred Algerians were killed by the police during a civil rights demonstration.

This "**secret massacre**", which remained covered by a veil of total official silence until the 1990s, took place during the **Algerian war**. It began with a peaceful demonstration against a curfew on North Africans imposed by **de Gaulle**'s government in an attempt to inhibit FLN (National Liberation Front) resistance activity in the French capital. Whether the police were acting on higher orders or merely on the authority of their own commanders is not clear. What *is* clear from hundreds of eyewitness accounts, including some from horrified policemen, is that the police went berserk. They opened fire, clubbed people and threw them in the Seine to drown. Several dozen Algerians were killed in the courtyard of the police HQ on the Ile de la Cité. For weeks afterwards, corpses were recovered from the Seine, but the French media remained silent, in part through censorship, in part perhaps unable to comprehend that such events had happened in their own capital. Maurice Papon, the police chief at the time, was subsequently decorated by de Gaulle. He later came under scrutiny for his role in deporting Jews to camps in Germany during World War II and was later sentenced to ten years in prison "for complicity in crimes against humanity".

In the extraordinary month of **May 1968**, a radical, libertarian, leftist movement gathered momentum in the Paris universities. Students began by occupying university buildings in protest against old-fashioned and hierarchical university structures (see p.132), but the extreme reaction of the police and government helped the movement to spread until it represented a mass revolt against institutional stagnation that ended up with the occupation of hundreds of factories across the country and a general strike by nine million workers.

Yet this was no revolution. The vicious battles with the paramilitary CRS police on the streets of Paris shook large sectors of the population – France's silent majority – to the core. Right-wing and "nationalist" demonstrations – orchestrated by de Gaulle – left public opinion craving stability and peace, and a great many workers were satisfied with a new system for wage agreements. Elections called in June returned the Right to power, the occupied buildings emptied and the barricades in the Latin Quarter came down. For those who thought they were experiencing The Revolution, the defeat was catastrophic.

But French institutions and French society had changed – de Gaulle didn't survive a referendum in 1969. His successor, **Georges Pompidou**, only survived long enough to begin the construction of the giant Les Halles development, and the expressways along the *quais* of the Seine. In 1974, he was succeeded by the conservative **Valéry Giscard d'Estaing**, who appointed one Jacques Chirac as his prime minister. In 1976, Chirac resigned, but made a speedy recovery as Mayor of Paris less than a year later.

Mitterrand's presidency

When **François Mitterrand** became president in 1981, thus inaugurating the first Socialist government for 23 years, there was a mood of euphoria on the Left. Even in conservative Paris, hopes and expectations were initially high. By 1984, however, the flight of capital, inflation and budget deficits had forced a complete volte-face, and the Right won parliamentary elections in 1986, with **Chirac** as the new prime minister – while continuing as Paris's mayor. This was France's first period of "cohabitation": the head of state and head of government belonging to opposite sides of the political fence.

While Mitterrand won a second mandate in 1988, Paris remained in the grip of the Right – indeed, the town halls of all twenty of the city's arrondissements stayed under right-wing control through much of the 1980s. Many Parisians were becoming increasingly discontented. Tent cities were erected by homeless Africans in the 13ᵉ arrondissement and in the Bois de Vincennes to protest against discrimination in housing allocation. After waves of strikes and scandals and the suicide of Prime Minister Pierre Bérégovoy, Mitterrand tottered on to the end of his presidential term, looking less and less like the nation's favourite uncle. By the end of his presidency, allegations of **corruption** against mayors, members of parliament, ministers and leading figures in industry were becoming an almost weekly occurrence.

The Chirac era

Paris's own mayor, **Jacques Chirac**, was one of many mayors implicated in corruption scandals (see opposite). It didn't stop him winning the election as **president** and taking office in May 1995 – in fact, much of the dodgy dealings seemed aimed precisely at achieving that result. Corruption was just one of the issues that would dog Chicac all the way through his presidency. The others were economic stagnation and the various controversies swirling around Islam, immigration and the disaffected suburbs. It wasn't long before they reared their heads.

In the summer of 1995, **bombs** planted by an extremist Algerian Islamic group exploded across Paris, killing eight people and injuring over a hundred. The home affairs minister, Charles Pasqua, stepped up **anti-immigration measures.** In March 1996 three hundred Malian immigrants, many of them failed asylum-seekers, sought refuge in the Paris church of St-Ambroise, in the 11ᵉ arrondissement. When they were forcibly evicted by riot police, frustration at discrimination, assault, abuse and economic deprivation erupted into running battles in the streets, and several young men died at the hands of the police. It was the first such protest of Chirac's presidency, but far from the last. For many blacks or Arabs seeking work, particularly young men, the ring road dividing the city from its suburbs might as well have been a wall of steel, and unemployment in some suburbs ran as high as fifty percent.

Even in the wealthy heart of Paris itself, the economy was sluggish. The solutions proposed by Prime Minister Alain Juppé, however, met even fiercer resistance than immigration measures. **Economic reform** – including cuts to the state's social spending, relaxation of labour laws and trade liberalization – was seen by many as a threat to the founding values of the French republic itself, and over the course of three weeks in late 1995, some five million people

Skeletons in the presidential cupboard

Jacques Chirac's years in power were marked by endless **corruption scandals** involving his subordinates and political enemies alike. No sooner did one case come to trial than another emerged. Early in his presidency, it was revealed that his Prime Minister and right-hand man, Alain Juppé, was renting a luxury flat in Paris at below-market rates. Then, in 1998, the then-Mayor of Paris, Jean Tiberi, was implicated in a scandal involving subsidized real-estate and salaries for fake jobs for party members. This reflected badly on Chirac, recalling the string of **town hall scandals** that had taken place while he was Mayor of Paris, including accusations that contracts were awarded in return for kickbacks to political parties. As if this wasn't bad enough, Chirac himself was also accused of using cash from illegal sources to pay for luxury holidays for himself, his family and friends between 1992 and 1995. In 2003, moreover, it was revealed that in eight years in office as Mayor of Paris he and his wife had run up grocery bills of €2.2 million – over half of which had been reimbursed in cash.

Chirac has long used his **presidential immunity** to avoid having to face questions from investigating magistrates, but the judiciary seems to inch ever closer towards him. What will happen in his retirement is as yet uncertain, although an ominous note was sounded in 2004 when Alain Juppé was convicted of involvement in the town-hall fake jobs scam. Some argued this should have caused him to be banned from office for ten years, but after legal challenges Juppé made a dramatic comeback – in 2007, he was nominated as number two in the cabinet of new Prime Minister François Fillon.

If Alain Juppé can survive conviction, the master operator himself can surely wriggle out of any legal difficulties. In September 2006, critics accused him of taking out insurance after he appointed his former legal adviser, Laurent de Mesle, as Paris's chief public prosecutor. Rumours also swirled around a supposed deal with Nicolas Sarkozy, who was alleged to have proposed a ten-year statutory limit on crimes coming to court in return for Chirac's backing. Sarkozy vehemently denied the charges. At the time of writing, investigating magistrates were said to have linked him to a multi-million euro **bank account in Japan**. The vultures, it seems, are circling over Chirac's political corpse.

took to the streets. There were typical scenes of **Parisian revolt**: burning tyres and railway sleepers; flying tear-gas canisters, paving stones and petrol bombs; and bands playing for free in place de la République. Public transport was almost entirely shut down, and people walked, cycled, rollerbladed and hitched to work. Many commented on the feeling of public elation and the sense of solidarity on the streets. They felt truly Parisian. Over the course of his presidency, Chirac would face similar protests again and again, ultimately frustrating every attempt to alter the course of the French economy.

Election earthquakes

When France won the **World Cup** in July 1998, change seemed to be in the air. The victory at the new Stade de France, with a multi-ethnic team in the ethnically mixed Paris suburb of St-Denis, prompted a wave of popular patriotism. For once, support for "les bleus" seemed to override all other colour distinctions, and some even thought that Parisians might start being interested in football. Both notions would soon be proved ephemeral.

A far deeper change took place with far less fuss, when the unassuming Socialist candidate, **Bertrand Delanoë**, was elected Mayor of Paris in March 2001. The fact that this was the first time the Left had won control of the capital since the bloody uprising of the Paris Commune in 1871 was far more of a shock to most Parisians than the fact that he was openly gay – in Paris, a politician's private life has almost always been seen as exactly that. His brief was to end town-hall corruption, tackle crime and traffic congestion and instil new pride and energy into the city.

France's second cataclysm of the new millennium – not counting the **introduction of the euro** on January 1, 2002, which went smoothly – was the presidential election of spring 2002 and shocking success of far-Right candidate **Jean-Marie Le Pen**. Against all predictions, he beat Socialist candidate Lionel Jospin in the first round and went head to head with Chirac for President. On May 1, some 800,000 people packed the boulevards of Paris in the biggest **demonstration** the capital had seen since the student protests of 1968. Two weeks later, in the run-off, Chirac duly swept the board, winning 82 percent – 90 percent in Paris – of the vote: by far the biggest majority ever won by a French president.

The drama wasn't over yet though. During Paris's Bastille Day parade on July 14, a neo-Nazi sympathizer attempted to **assassinate** President Chirac. The incident drew attention to the bitterness felt by the far Right at having failed to gain any seats in parliament despite winning 13 percent of the vote – in effect six million voters had been disenfranchised. For the regions, Paris felt more remote than ever.

Heatwaves

With his eighty-percent mandate behind him, Chirac and his newly reformed party, now called the UMP, decided to take on the public sector. First to go under the knife were the state's generous pensions and unemployment benefits. Next would come worker-friendly hiring and firing rights, and finally the world-leading health service. The government of Prime Minister Jean-Pierre Raffarin insisted that there simply wasn't enough money in the pot, but much of France saw the programme as getting their most sacred cow ready to be sent off to slaughter. On May 13, two million workers went out on strike. Two weeks later, half a million protested on the streets of Paris.

The government found itself in equally hot water internationally, thanks to Chirac's declaration in March 2003 that he would veto any UN resolution that contained an ultimatum leading to **war in Iraq**. On either side of the Atlantic, the cherished Franco-American relationship suffered its worst spat ever. In Paris, American tourist numbers plummeted, and the nation indulged itself in an orgy of anti-Americanism.

Some French commentators argued that the presence of the country's almost five million-strong Muslim population, the largest in Western Europe, had influenced the French government's position – though Muslim feelings didn't seem to prevent French MPs voting to **ban Islamic headscarves**, first on ID photos and then, in August 2004, in all schools. The move was trumpeted as a defence of the French state's cherished *laïcité* or secularism, an ideal with its roots firmly anchored in the Revolution. More sceptical commentators saw the law as pandering to the ever-present elements of racism and xenophobia in French national politics.

The **summer of 2003** was just as heated in reality as politically. Parisian temperatures in the first half of August were the hottest ever recorded, regularly topping 40°C (104°F) – more than 10°C above the average maximum for the time of year. In France, some fifteen thousand deaths were attributed to the astonishing **heatwave**, and **climate change** finally forced its way onto the mainstream agenda.

"Sarko"

In 2004, a new political force emerged in the shape of the energetic finance minister **Nicolas Sarkozy** – a kind of Margaret Thatcher meets J.F.K. He set out a fresh programme of privatizations and public-sector parsimony and manoeuvred himself into position as leader of a re-energized UMP. A check to the causes of "Sarko" and the UMP came in early 2005, after stories of yet more official corruption broke, this time focusing on government ministers lying about their living arrangements in order to claim absurdly generous state property subsidies. Meanwhile, the economic reform programme quietly motored on; laws were tabled to modify the cherished 35-hour week, allowing employees to sign up for an additional 13 hours (the EU maximum) if they chose. Yet again, waves of passionate strikers flooded the city streets, while buses, métro trains and planes sat motionless all over the city.

Unfortunately for Paris, the largest strikes and demonstrations coincided with the arrival of the International Olympic Committee in Paris to assess the city's bid for the **2012 Olympic Games**. Union organizers handed out "Paris 2012" T-shirts in an attempt to mitigate the PR disaster, and pledged a "ceasefire" in industrial action if the games did indeed come to Paris. The IOC were not convinced.

Riot and rebellion in 2005

A fresh wave of **civil unrest** swept France's urban areas in November 2005. This time, the cause was the accidental deaths of two teenagers who believed police were chasing them and sheltered in an electricity substation in Clichy-sous-Bois, a run-down area in the Paris *banlieue*. They were electrocuted. Local anger led to numerous **car-burnings** and confrontations with police, and unrest quickly spread to other Parisian suburbs and then beyond. Night after night, youths across France torched cars, buses, schools, and police and power stations – anything associated with the state. The notorious, hardline response of "Sarko", as the Interior Minister was now dubbed, was to call the rioters *une racaille* ("a rabble") and to demand the neighbourhoods were cleaned with power-hoses. After three weeks, the *banlieue* seemed to have burned itself out. Some nine thousand vehicles had gone up in smoke and almost 2900 people had been arrested. Right-wingers opportunistically tried to blame Muslim radicals but this idea was quickly and comprehensively discredited. Young people who actually lived in the *cités* saw the main causes as anger at **racism** and exclusion from society, including exclusion from employment. In many of the worst-affected areas – home to communities of largely African or North-African origin – youth unemployment was (and still is) as high as fifty percent – double the already high average among young people.

In the wake of the rioting, Sarkozy's main political rival, the newly appointed Prime Minister **Dominique de Villepin**, launched a fresh attempt to tackle France's stagnant growth and stubborn budget deficit. He proposed giving small companies the right to dismiss new employees – those with under two years' service – without having to give cause. Labour-market flexibility was the goal. Some young people might have benefited, but from a historical perspective this looked like an attack by neoliberal or "Anglo-Saxon" capitalism on France's cherished and hard-won labour rights. On October 5, 2005, a million workers across the country marched against the new labour law. In 2006, the laws were to be extended to all companies employing workers under the age of 26, as part of the *Contrat première embauche* (**CPE**), or first employment contract. The law was supposed to encourage firms to hire young people. Students and the young, however, saw it differently: why should they, uniquely, be denied the rights their elders took for granted?

In March, students in Paris **occupied the Sorbonne**, in conscious imitation of May 1968. Once again, they were brutally driven out by riot police. And just as in 1968, people protested across France in their millions – only this time in the hope not that France would radically change, but that everything would stay the same. A notorious survey at this time concluded that the most desired job among young people in France was not that of film director or political activist, but of civil servant. *Casseurs*, or hooligans, blended in and sometimes clashed with the protestors – who seemed determined not to back down. On April 10, Dominique Villepin withdrew the law.

A new Napoleon?

As Chirac's presidency limped to its end, the French began to look for a new leader. To many, the idea of an economic hard-man who could break down the strikers seemed increasingly attractive. In the **presidential elections of 2007**, they rejected the consensus-seeking charms of the centrist Socialist candidate, **Ségolène Royal**, and plumped for change. They went for a confrontational right-winger who had promised to take the French state by the scruff of its neck – a man who, the night before the election, had himself filmed parading around on a white horse in conscious emulation of Napoleon. On May 16, 2007, Nicolas Sarkozy became President of France, and appointed a surprisingly conciliatory cabinet. Half of his ministers were women, including Rachida Dati, whose parents were North African; his foreign minister, meanwhile, was dashing left-winger and co-founder of Médecins sans Frontières, Bernard Kouchner. Early polls revealed Sarkozy to be the most popular new president since de Charles de Gaulle. Real reform, however, still lay ahead.

Delanoë and the new Paris

Sarkozy may be much-hyped as a national reformer, but for the city of Paris, effective reform has been under way for years. In 2002, **Mayor Bertrand Delanoë** launched Paris's new image with two high-profile events. He boldly ordered a three-kilometre length of the riverbank roads to be turned into a public beach between July 21 and August 18. The scene was complete right down to palm trees, deckchairs and 150 tonnes of sand – the only thing missing was the chance to take a dip in the river. Over half a million people visited on the first day, and **Paris Plage** ("Paris beach") is now an established part of the city's calendar. The next landmark event was October's **Nuit Blanche** ("sleepless night"), in which hundreds of museums, bars, restaurants and public buildings remained open for a city-wide all-night party of live music and performance art. The event was an enormous success for everyone except Delanoë himself; while attending the town hall's own champagne party, he was stabbed in the stomach by a man in the crowd, putting him in Paris's Pitié-Salpetrière hospital for a week.

Less glamorous but more far-reaching policies have already changed the face of Paris. During the summer of 2001, Delanöe shut off the riverside *quais* to traffic, causing apoplexy among Paris's fiercely independent car-users. Since then, **bus and cycle lanes** have been installed throughout the city, against fierce conservative opposition – the planning commission even judged the lane separators as "unaesthetic". Buses now run longer and more frequently, while all-new **tramway lines** now connect the suburbs to each other and will eventually encircle the entire city. The Batobus ferries, meanwhile, are to transform themselves into part of a fully integrated **métro fluvial** service. When you're cycling happily through green space on a once-choked boulevard, it's easy to sense the impact of the traffic policies. Statistics back up the feeling: car miles are down 15 percent since 2001, and bike trips are on the up.

Cars and Gauloises – slaying giants

If there are two items close to any Parisian's heart, they are the car and the cigarette. All that is set to change. One plan for Paris's future envisages **banning cars** from the historic centre for all except residents. Designed by Green Party official Denis Baupin, the proposed scheme would cut the centre's speed limit to 30kph in its first phase. Phase two – to exclude cars from the centre on Sundays and expand pedestrianization around Les Halles – would prove harder to push through. The final phase – prohibiting outsiders' vehicles from the first four arrondissements altogether, and restricting the express routes along the north bank to cyclists and pedestrians – may be too much for Paris's rarely phlegmatic motorists to swallow.

The other ban, on **smoking in public places**, is a done deal. Since 1991, smoking in bars and restaurants has been theoretically illegal, outside designated zones, at least. All but a tiny minority of Parisian owners simply sidestepped the law by declaring their entire establishment a smoking zone. A new law will come into place from February 1, 2008, however. Smoking will be completely banned in all bars, restaurants and nightclubs, and "cigarette police" will monitor the scheme and hand out €68 fines.

The living city

Transport and smoking may be high-profile, symbolic issues, but the biggest problem Paris faces in the twenty-first century is the relationship of its centre to its **suburbs**. The city's gentrification has always progressed at the expense of its hinterland. The French government has long lavished money on central Paris, endlessly adorning the jewel in its crown with grand buildings, cutting-edge infrastructure and endless cultural institutions and events. Meanwhile, the *banlieue*, or suburbs, have festered as they have grown.

In 1860, outlying villages such as Belleville and Montmartre were absorbed into the city when an outer ring of arrondissements was created. Since then, the population of Paris has swollen to around ten million, and yet the **official boundaries** have stayed the same – the *périphérique* ring-road now providing a powerful visible symbol of the divide. Beyond it, the three administrative *départements* of the "Petite Couronne", the suburban districts encircling Paris, now incorporate some four million people – twice as many as Paris proper. Yet the city government has no remit to be concerned with them or their affairs. **The poor**, including large numbers of immigrants and their families, are effectively excluded from the city centre. The high-paying, white-collar jobs of the shopping, banking and governmental districts just don't seem to be available to black youths from the "9–3"– as the depressed *département* of Seine Saint-Denis, officially numbered 93, is known.

While the troubled *cités*, the housing projects of the *banlieue*, simmer with discontent, the desirable newtowns to the south and west of the city are sucking away Paris's lifeblood: its **population**. There are now 2.1 million people living "intra-muros", or in Paris proper, down from 2.8 million in the late 1950s – although a million more "greater Parisians" travel in to work every weekday. In the city, a majority of residents live in one-person households, while retirees make up fifteen percent of the population, and less than five percent of residents hold traditionally working-class jobs – and half of these are foreigners. What cultural future can there be for a city without a real resident population?

Intent on preventing the "museumification" of Paris, the Mairie has started to buy up private apartment buildings in central Paris, to be rented out as **social housing**. However, at a rate of some 3500 apartments a year, it's unlikely that this can turn around Paris's major trend of falling population. Parisians, who have long been inclined to judge a city's success by its gastronomic activity, are regularly alarmed by the publication of horrifying statistics such as the fact that the city has lost roughly a quarter of its small food stores and butcher's shops in the last decade, and that there is scarcely a single bakery in the vicinity of the Champs-Elysées. They may be comforted to learn, however, that a city with "only" 159 cheese shops, and "just" one grocery for every thirty people is not yet facing a crisis.

Books

In the selected listing of books below, publishers are detailed in the form of British publisher/American publisher. Where books are published in one country only, UK or US follows the publisher's name. The abbreviation "o/p" means "out of print", while the book symbol marks titles that are particularly recommended.

Guides

David Hampshire *Living and Working in France* (Survival Books Limited). With over 500 pages, this accurate and comprehensive guide takes you beyond our advice in "Basics" and deep into the bureaucratic niceties of expat life in France. Usually updated every couple of years. Includes advice on buying property.

Miroslav Sasek *This is Paris* (Universe). A kind of illustrated child's travel guide, with enticing facts about the city and beautiful, quirky watercolours and drawings. First published in 1959, but still a brilliant companion (or preparation) for a trip with children.

Various authors *Time Out Paris Eating and Drinking* (Time Out Guides). With over 800 reviews, this is the most comprehensive English-language guide to Paris's bars and restaurants, though some accounts can suffer from either a jaded expat's-eye view or "latest-thing" fever.

History and politics

The Letters of Abélard and Héloise (Penguin). The letters exchanged between these two medieval lovers, who were tragically separated after an illicit affair and spent the rest of their lives in religious orders, make for fascinating reading. Héloise's frankness about her passionate feelings for Abélard is especially striking, as are her dignity and gradual acceptance of their changed relationship.

Anthony Beevor & Artemis Cooper *Paris After the Liberation: 1944–1949* (Penguin). Gripping account of a crucial era in Parisian history, featuring de Gaulle, the Communists, the St-Germain scene and Dior's New Look. Five strange, intense years that set the tone for the next fifty.

Robert Cole *A Traveller's History of Paris* (Windrush Press/Interlink). This brief history of the city from the first Celtic settlement to the present day is an ideal starting point for anyone wishing to delve into the historical archives.

Vincent Cronin *Napoleon* (HarperCollins). A highly engaging biography of Napoleon that attempts to uncover the man behind the myth. Cronin dispels the common notion that Napoleon was little more than an overambitious egoist and draws a much more likeable and complex character, to some extent a victim of events beyond his control.

Norman Hampson *A Social History of the French Revolution* (Routledge). An analysis that concentrates on the personalities involved. Its particular interest lies in the attention it gives to the *sans-culottes*, the ordinary poor of Paris.

Christopher Hibbert *The French Revolution* (Penguin). Good, concise popular history of the period. The description of events is vivid, but it's not so good on the intellectual background and the meaning of the Revolution.

Alistair Horne *The Fall of Paris* (Pan) and *Seven Ages of Paris* (Pan/Vintage). Highly regarded historian Alistair Horne's *The Fall of Paris* is a very readable and humane account of the extraordinary period of the Prussian siege of Paris in 1870 and the ensuing struggles of the Commune. His *Seven Ages of Paris* is a compelling (if rather old-fashionedly fruity) account of significant episodes in the city's history.

Andrew Hussey *Paris, The Secret History* (Penguin). An entertaining book that delves into some fascinating and little-known aspects of Paris's history, including occultism, freemasonry and the seedy underside of the city. Hussey is concerned above all with ordinary Parisians and shows how in large part the history of Paris is shaped by its citizens' suffering and frequent clashes with authority.

Colin Jones *Paris: Biography of a City* (Allen Lane/Viking). Jones focuses tightly on the actual life and growth of the city, from the Neolithic past to the future. Five hundred pages flow by easily, punctuated by thoughtful but accessible "boxes" on characters, streets and buildings whose lives were especially bound up with Paris's, from the Roman *arènes* to Zazie's métro. The best single book on the city's history.

Peter Lennon *Foreign Correspondent: Paris in the Sixties* (Picador/MacMillan). Irish journalist Peter Lennon went to Paris in the early 1960s unable to speak a word of French. He became a close friend of Samuel Beckett and was a witness to the May 1968 events.

Philip Mansel *Paris Between Empires* (Orion/Phoenix). Serious but gripping tale of an often-ignored patch of Paris's history: the turbulent years of revolutions and restorations that followed in the wake of Napoleon. Brilliantly conjures up the events of the streets and the *salons*.

Karl Marx *Surveys from Exile* (Penguin/Random House); *On the Paris Commune* (Monthly Review Press). *Surveys* includes Marx's speeches and articles at the time of the 1848 Revolution and after, including an analysis, riddled with jokes, of Napoléon III's rise to power. *Paris Commune* – more rousing prose – has a history of the Commune by Engels.

Lucy Moore *Liberty: The Lives and Times of Six Women in Revolutionary France* (HarperCollins). This utterly engaging book follows the lives of six influential women through the Revolution. Moore conjures up the fervid atmosphere of the times superbly, taking in everything from sexual scandal to revolutionary radicalism. The book has a serious edge to it, too, exploring how the ideals of liberty and equality were betrayed – for women, at least.

Orest A. Ranum *Paris in the Age of Absolutism* (Pennsylvania State UP). A truly great work of city biography, revealing how and why seventeenth-century Paris rose from medieval obscurity to become the foremost city in Europe under Louis XIV.

Duc de Saint-Simon *Memoirs* (Athena). Written by an insider, this compelling memoir of life at Versailles under Louis XIV is packed with fascinating, gossipy anecdotes.

Ruth Scurr *Fatal Purity: Robespierre and the French Revolution* (Chatto & Windus). Scurr's highly readable biography adeptly illuminates the connections between Robespierre's complex, intriguing personality and the course of the Revolution from its beginnings right up to its bloody finale.

Madame de Sévigné *Selected Letters* (Penguin). The letters of Madame de Sévigné, a noblewoman who moved in the highest circles, were written – mostly to her beloved daughter – at the time of Louis XIV and are full of witty observations on court life, frank opinions on the latest Racine or Corneille play, political commentary, as well as plenty of entertaining gossip and trivia. Among other pieces of brilliant journalism is a vivid account of the trial of Nicolas Fouquet, the finance minister who was imprisoned for corruption.

Robert Tombs *The Paris Commune 1871* (Longman). An academic historian weighs up the origins, events and consequences of the Commune. Serious-minded – lots of facts, figures and sociological analysis – but concise, generally accessible and occasionally stirring.

Theodore Zeldin *A History of French Passions, 1848–1945.* A subtle, humanistic attempt to understand France through its history, culture and people, tackled by themes, such as intellect and taste. Big both in size and ambition, but very readable nonetheless.

Culture and society

John Ardagh *France in the New Century: Portrait of a Changing Society* (Penguin). Probably the most useful book if you want to get to grips with French culture, society and recent political history (it was published in 2000). There's material on food, film, education and holidays as well as the drier political-historical stuff, and there's a fair amount on the relationship between Paris, its suburbs and the rest of France.

Marc Augé *In the Metro* (University of Minnesota Press US). A philosophically minded anthropologist descends deep into metro culture and his own memories of life in Paris. A brief, brilliant and utterly Barthian essay (see below).

Roland Barthes *Mythologies* (Vintage). A classic and brilliant intellectual rhapsody on how the ideas, prejudices and contradictions of French thought and behaviour manifest themselves in food, wine, the Citroën DS, travel guides and other cultural offerings. Barthes' piece on the Eiffel Tower doesn't appear, but it's included in the *Selected Writings* (Vintage), published in the US as *A Barthes Reader* (ed Susan Sontag; Hill and Wang).

Simone de Beauvoir *The Second Sex* (Vintage). One of the prime texts of Western feminism, written in 1949, covering women's inferior status in history, literature, mythology, psychoanalysis, philosophy and everyday life.

Walter Benjamin *The Arcades Project* (Harvard University Press/ Belknap Press). An all-encompassing portrait of Paris covering 1830–70, in which the *passages* are used as a lens through which to view Parisian society. Never completed, Benjamin's magnum opus is a kaleidoscopic assemblage of essays, notes and quotations, gathered under such headings as "Baudelaire", "Prostitution", "Mirrors" and "Idleness".

James Campbell *Paris Interzone* (Vintage/Secker and Warburg). The feuds, passions and destructive lifestyles of Left Bank writers in 1946–60 are evoked here. The cast includes Richard Wright, James Baldwin, Samuel Beckett, Boris Vian, Alexander Trocchi, Eugène Ionesco, Sartre, de Beauvoir, Nabokov and Allen Ginsberg.

Rupert Christiansen *Paris Babylon: Grandeur, Decadence and Revolution 1869–1875* (Pimlico UK). Written with verve and dash – some of it slap – Christiansen's account of Paris at the time of the Siege and the Commune is exuberant, original and captivating. Worth reading for its evocative and insightfully chosen contemporary quotations alone – it begins with a delightful 1869 guidebook to "Paris Partout!".

Richard Cobb *Paris and Elsewhere* (John Murray/New York Review of Books). Selected writings on postwar Paris by the acclaimed historian of the Revolution, with a personal and meditative tone.

Jessica Duchen *Gabriel Fauré* (Phaidon). An illuminating biography of this composer of highly refined and beautiful music. Duchen places Fauré's life and works in context and explores his relationship with figures such as Proust, Verlaine, Liszt and Saint-Saëns. The result is a vivid picture of the creative melting pot of fin-de-siècle Paris.

Noel Riley Fitch *Sylvia Beach and the Lost Generation: A History of Literary Paris in the Twenties and Thirties* (Penguin/W.W. Norton and Co). Founder of the original Shakespeare & Co. bookstore and publisher of James Joyce's *Ulysses*, Beach was the lightning rod of literary Paris, and a torch-bearer for literary lesbianism.

Adam Gopnik *Paris to the Moon* (Vintage/Random House). Intimate and acutely observed essays from the Paris correspondent of the *New Yorker* on society, politics, family life and shopping. Probably the most thoughtful and enjoyable book by an expat in Paris.

Gisèle Halimi *Milk for the Orange Tree* (Quartet Books). Born in Tunisia, daughter of an Orthodox Jewish family; ran away to Paris to become a lawyer; defender of women's rights, Algerian FLN fighters and all unpopular causes. A gutsy autobiographical story.

Tahar Ben Jelloun *Racism Explained to my Daughter* (New Press). An honest and straightforward account of the racial tensions in France as seen through the eyes of its Moroccan-born author.

Ian Littlewood *A Literary Companion to Paris* (Penguin/HarperCollins). A thorough account of which literary figures went where, and what they had to say about it.

François Maspero *Roissy Express* (Verso o/p); photographs Anaïk Frantz. A "travel book" along the RER line B from Roissy to St-Rémy-les-Chevreuse (excluding the Paris stops). Brilliant insights into the life of the Paris suburbs, and fascinating digressions into French history and politics.

Barry Miles *The Beat Hotel: Ginsberg, Burroughs, and Corso in Paris, 1958–1963* (Atlantic Books UK). Follows the self-indulgent exploits of the residents of The Beat Hotel at 9 rue Gît-le-Coeur, on the Left Bank – notably William Burroughs and Allen Ginsberg.

Edith Piaf *My Life* (Penguin/Dufour Editions). The dramatic story of the "little sparrow", from her harsh upbringing in Ménilmontant, through the war years and on to her relationship in America with the boxer Marcel Cerdan. Told pretty much in her words.

Andrea Kupfer Schneider *Creating the Musée d'Orsay: The Politics of Culture in France* (Penn State UP). Interesting and sometimes amusing account of the struggles involved in transforming the Gare d'Orsay into one of Paris's most visited museums.

Tad Szulc *Chopin in Paris: The Life and Times of the Romantic Composer* (Da Capo Press/Scribner). Not much on music, but explores Chopin's relationship with his friends – Balzac, Hugo, Liszt among them – and his lover, George Sand, and their shared life in Paris.

Judith Thurman *Colette: Secrets of the Flesh* (Bloomsbury/Ballantine Books). An intelligent and entertaining biography of Colette (1873–1954), highly successful novelist, vaudeville artist, libertine and flamboyant bon viveur.

Edmund White *The Flâneur* (Bloomsbury). An American expat novelist muses over Parisian themes and places as diverse as the Moreau museum, gay cruising and the history of immigration, as well as the art of being a good *flâneur* – a loiterer or stroller.

William Wiser *The Twilight Years: Paris in the 1930s* (Carroll and Graf). Breathless account of the crazy decade before the war, all jazz nights, scandals and the social lives of expat poets and painters.

Theodore Zeldin *The French* (Harvill Press/Kodansha). A wise and original book that attempts to describe a country through the thoughts and feelings of its people. Draws on the author's conversations with a fascinating range of French people, about money, sex, phobias, parents and everything else.

Art, architecture and photography

Brassaï *Le Paris Secret des Années 30* (Gallimard). Extraordinary photos of the capital's nightlife in the 1930s – brothels, music halls, street cleaners, transvestites and the underworld – each one a work of art. Henry Miller accompanied Brassaï on many of his nocturnal expeditions, a friendship captured in his book *Henry Miller: the Paris Years*.

Henri Cartier-Bresson *A Propos de Paris* (Bulfinch Press). Some of the greatest photos ever taken: a brilliant blend of the ordinary and the surreal, of photojournalism and art photography.

André Chastel *French Art* (Flammarion). The great French art historian tries to define what is distinctively French about French art in this insightful and superbly illustrated three-volume work.

Robert Doisneau *Three Seconds of Eternity* (Te Neues). The famous *Kiss in front of the Hôtel de Ville* takes the front cover, but there's more to Doisneau than this. A collection chosen by the man himself of photographs taken in France, but mainly Paris, in the 1940s and 1950s. Beautifully nostalgic.

Dan Franck *The Bohemians – the Birth of Modern Art: Paris 1900–1930* (Weidenfeld and Nicolson UK). Anecdotes and encounters from within the Bohemian demi-monde that gave birth to modern art. Encompasses the Montmartre years, when Picasso hung out with Apollinaire, and the Montparnasse era of André Derain, Man Ray and the Surrealists.

Matthew Gale *Dada and Surrealism* (Phaidon Press). Part of Phaidon's acclaimed Art and Ideas series, this stimulating account makes sense of these two revolutionary (and sometimes baffling) art movements. The author looks at works by a wide range of artists, including Duchamp, Ernst, Magritte and Dali – all amply illustrated with quality colour photographs.

Anne Higonnet *Berthe Morisot* (University of California Press). A touching and sensitive portrait of one of the lesser-known pioneers of Impressionism. Higonnet delivers fascinating insights into the life of this shy yet quietly determined woman, who forged life-long friendships with leading artists such as Renoir, Manet and Degas, and who succeeded in combining a career with a family life at a time when society placed severe restraints on women.

Michel Poisson *The Monuments of Paris* (I.B. Tauris). Arrondissement by arrondissement survey of Paris's chief buildings, with attractive line drawings and brief notes. Short on contemporary architecture but otherwise fairly comprehensive.

John Richardson *The Life of Picasso: Vol 1 1881–1906, Vol 2 1907–1917, Vol 3 1917–1932* (Pimlico/Random House). No twentieth-century artist has ever been subjected to scrutiny as close as that which Picasso receives in Richardson's exhaustive and brilliantly illustrated biography. Volume 4 is in the pipeline.

Vivian Russell *Monet's Garden* (Frances Lincoln). An exceptional book illustrated with sumptuous colour photographs by the author and reproductions of Monet's paintings. Superb opening chapter on Monet as "poet of nature", plus a detailed description of the garden.

Gertrude Stein *The Autobiography of Alice B. Toklas* (Penguin/Vintage). The most accessible of Stein's works, written from the point of view of her long-time lover, is an amusing account of the artistic and literary scene of Paris in the 1910s and 1920s.

Anthony Sutcliffe *Paris – An Architectural History* (Yale UP). Excellent overview of Paris's changing cityscape, as dictated by fashion, social structure and political power.

Heinfried Wischermann *Paris: an Architectural Guide* (Arsenale US). User-friendly guide to over two hundred Parisian landmark buildings. Each comes with a small black-and-white photo and a brief, pithy description.

Cookery

Alain Ducasse *Flavors of France* (Artisan US) and *L'Atelier of Alain Ducasse: The Artistry of a Master Chef and his Protégés* (John Wiley & Sons). The charismatic culinary entrepreneur offers a tour of the gastronomy of France and some of the secrets of his successful kitchen, combining breezy prose with inspirational photos.

Nicolle Meyer & Amanda Smith *Paris in a Basket (Könemann)*. Would be little more than a glossy coffee-table book if it didn't capture the sights, smells, anecdotes and recipes of Paris's open-air markets with so much aplomb.

Patricia Wells *The Paris Cookbook* (Kyle Cathie Ltd/HarperCollins). Long-time resident of the capital and *the* Anglophone writer on French food, American journalist Patricia Wells takes her inspiration for these sophisticated recipes from her favourite Parisian restaurants, shops and markets.

Fiction and travel writing

In English

Helen Constantine (translator) *Paris Tales* (OUP). Twenty-two (very) short stories and essays, each chosen for their evocation of a particular place in Paris. From Balzac in the Palais Royal and Colette in Montmartre cemetery, to Perec on the Champs-Elysées and Jacques Réda on the rue du Commerce. An ideal travel or bedside companion.

Charles Dickens *A Tale of Two Cities* (Penguin/Vintage). Paris and London during the 1789 Revolution and before. The plot is pure, breathtaking Hollywood, but the streets and the social backdrop are very much for real.

Julien Green *Paris* (Marion Boyars). Born in Paris in 1900, Green became one of the city's defining writers. This bilingual edition presents twenty-odd short, meditative and highly personal essays on different aspects and quarters of Paris, from Notre Dame and the 16e to "stairways and steps" and the lost cries of the city's hawkers. Proust meets travel-writing.

Ernest Hemingway *A Moveable Feast* (Arrow/Scribner). Hemingway's memoirs of his life as a young man in Paris in the 1920s. Includes fascinating accounts of meetings with literary celebrities Ezra Pound, F. Scott Fitzgerald and Gertrude Stein, among others.

J.K. Huysmans *Parisian Sketches* (Dedalus European Classics). Published in 1880, Huysmans' fantastical, intense prose pieces on contemporary Paris drip with decadence, and cruelly acute observation. Rhapsodies on "Landscapes" and "Parisian characters" are matched by an exhilaratingly vivid account of the Folies-Bergères. If Manet was a novelist, he might have produced this.

Jack Kerouac *Satori in Paris* (Flamingo/Grove Press)... and in Brittany, too. Uniquely inconsequential Kerouac experiences, on a ten-day pilgrimage to trace his French roots.

Henry Miller *Tropic of Cancer* (Flamingo/Grove Press); *Quiet Days in Clichy* (New Eng Lib/Grove Press). Again 1930s Paris, though from a more focused angle – sex, essentially. Erratic, wild, self-obsessed writing, but with definite flights of genius.

Anaïs Nin *Delta of Venus* (Penguin/Harvest). Written in the early 1940s for a dollar a page, these short stories make up what is probably the most inventive, literate and sexy exotica ever written.

George Orwell *Down and Out in Paris and London* (Penguin/Harvest). Documentary account of breadline living in the 1930s – Orwell at his best.

Jean Rhys *Quartet* (Penguin/Norton). A beautiful and evocative story of a lonely young woman's existence on the fringes of 1920s Montparnasse society.

Sarah Turnbull *Almost French: A New Life in Paris* (Nicholas Brealey/Gotham Books). Funny but mostly painful account of a young Australienne falling in love, moving to Paris and desperately failing to fit in. Acute observation lifts it above chick-lit travel status. A must for would-be expats.

French (in translation)

Paul Auster (ed) *The Random House Book of Twentieth Century French Poetry* (Random House). Bilingual anthology containing the major French poets of the twentieth century, most of whom were based in Paris: includes Apollinaire, Cendrars, Aragon, Eluard and Prévert.

Honoré de Balzac *The Père Goriot* (Oxford Paperbacks). Biting exposé of cruelty and selfishness in the contrasting worlds of the fashionable faubourg St-Germain and a down-at-heel but genteel boarding house in the Quartier Latin. Like Dickens, but with a tougher heart. Balzac's equally brilliant *Wild Ass's Skin* (Penguin) is a strange moralistic tale of an ambitious young man's fall from grace in early nineteenth-century Paris.

André Breton *Nadja* (Penguin/Grove Press). First published in 1928, *Nadja* is widely considered the most important and influential novel to spring from the Surrealist movement. Largely autobiographical, it portrays the complex relationship between the narrator and a young woman in Paris.

Louis-Ferdinand Céline *Death on Credit* (Calder/Riverrun Press). Céline's disturbing and powerful semi-autobiographical novel is a landmark in twentieth-century French literature. In it he recounts the delirium of the world as seen through the eyes of an adolescent in working-class Paris at the beginning of the twentieth century. Much of the action takes place in the passage Choiseul, and its claustrophobic atmosphere is vividly evoked.

Blaise Cendrars *To the End of the World* (Peter Owen/Dufour Editions). An outrageous bawdy tale of a randy septuagenarian Parisian actress, having an affair with a deserter from the Foreign Legion.

Colette *Chéri* (Vintage/Secker and Warburg). Considered Colette's finest novel, *Chéri* brilliantly evokes the world of a demi-monde Parisian courtesan who has a doomed love affair with a man at least half her age.

Didier Daeninckx *Murder in Memoriam* (Serpent's Tail). A thriller involving two murders: one of a Frenchman during the massacre of the Algerians in Paris in 1961, the other of his son twenty years later. The investigation by an honest detective lays bare dirty tricks, corruption, racism and the cover-up of the massacre.

Agnès Desarthe *Good Intentions* (Flamingo UK). Desarthe's unsettling novella describes with black humour a young woman's attempts to deal with difficult neighbours in a Belleville apartment block. Came out in France around the same time as the feel-good film *Amélie* and couldn't be a better antidote.

Alexandre Dumas *The Count of Monte Cristo* (Penguin). One hell of a good yarn, with Paris and Marseilles locations.

Gustave Flaubert *Sentimental Education* (Penguin). A lively, detailed 1869 reconstruction of the life, manners, characters and politics of Parisians in the 1840s, including the 1848 Revolution.

Alan Furst *Red Gold* (Harper Collins/Random House). Once-celebrated film producer Jean Casson struggles by in Occupation Paris, and is reluctantly drawn into the less-than-heroic world of the Resistance. A tautly written, gritty historical thriller shot through with a love and intimate knowledge of Paris. Moody rather than actually thrilling.

Faïza Guène *Just Like Tomorrow* (Chatto and Windus/Harvest). A simple, touching tale of a shy, fifteen-year-old Muslim girl in the Paris housing projects trying to make good. Published in the US with a literal translation of the original French title: *Kiffe Kiffe Tomorrow*.

Victor Hugo *Les Misérables* (Penguin). A long but eminently readable novel by the master. Set among the Parisian poor and low-life in the first half of the nineteenth century, it's probably the greatest treatment of Paris in fiction – unless that title goes to Hugo's haunting (and shorter) *Notre Dame de Paris* (Penguin/Modern Library), a novel better known in English as *The Hunchback of Notre Dame*.

François Maspero *Cat's Grin* (Penguin). Moving and revealing semi-autobiographical novel about a young teenager living in Paris during World War II, with an adored elder brother in the Resistance. His parents are taken to concentration camps as Paris is liberated.

Guy de Maupassant *Bel-Ami* (Penguin/Hatier). Maupassant's chef-d'oeuvre is a brilliant and utterly sensual account of corrupt Parisian high society during the belle époque. Traces the rake's progress of the fascinating journalist and seducer, Georges Duroy.

Daniel Pennac *Monsieur Malaussène* (Harvill Press/Kiepenheuer & Witsch). The last in the "Belleville Quintet" of quasi-detective novels set in the working-class east of Paris is possibly the most disturbing, centred on a series of macabre killings. Witty, experimental and chaotic, somewhat in the mode of Thomas Pynchon. Pennac's novels have a cult following in France.

Georges Perec *Life: A User's Manual* (Vintage/David R. Godine). An extraordinary literary jigsaw puzzle of life, past and present, human, animal and mineral, extracted from the residents of an imaginary apartment block in the 17e arrondissement of Paris.

Marcel Proust *Remembrance of Things Past* (Penguin/Modern Library). Proust's 3000-page novel, much of it set in Paris, is one of the twentieth century's greatest works of fiction. Its fascination with memory, love and loss, and its stylistic innovation have had a huge influence on the modern novel.

Jacques Réda *The Ruins of Paris* (Reaktion Books). Impressionistic, meditative wanderings around the city written by a Parisian poet in the late 1970s. Either brilliantly avant-garde or deeply pretentious, depending on how well you can stomach Réda's self-conscious prose.

Jean-Paul Sartre *The Age of Reason* (Penguin/Vintage). The first in Sartre's *Roads to Freedom* trilogy is probably his most accessible work – if hardly a spanking good read. A philosophy teacher in wartime Paris's Montparnasse quartier struggles to find both the money for his girlfriend's abortion and the answers to his obsession with freedom.

Georges Simenon *Maigret at the Crossroads* (Penguin/New York Review of Books) – or any other of the Maigret crime thrillers. The Montmartre and seedy criminal locations are unbeatable. If you don't like crime fiction you should go for *The Little Saint*, the story of a little boy growing up in the rue Mouffetard when it was a down-at-heel market street.

Emile Zola *Nana* (Penguin). The rise and fall of a

courtesan in the decadent times of the Second Empire. Not bad on sex, but confused on sexual politics. A great story, nevertheless, which brings mid-nineteenth-century Paris alive, direct, to present-day senses. Paris is also the setting for Zola's *L'Assommoir*, *L'Argent*, *Thérèse Raquin* and *The Debacle* (all Penguin) – the background for the last is the Franco-Prussian war and its aftermath, the Paris Commune.

Language

Language

Language

There's probably nowhere harder to speak or learn French than Paris. Like people from most capital cities, many Parisians speak a kind of hurried slang. Worse still, many speak fairly good English – which they may assume is better than your French. Generations of keen visitors have been offended by being replied to in English after they've carefully enunciated a well-honed question or menu order. Then there are the complex codes of politeness and formality – knowing when to add Madame/Monsieur is only the start of it. Despite this, the essentials are not difficult to master and can make all the difference. Even just saying "Bonjour Madame/Monsieur" and then gesticulating will usually get you a smile and helpful service, even if your efforts to speak French come to nothing.

French pronunciation

One easy rule to remember is that consonants at the end of words are usually silent. *Pas plus tard* (not later) is thus pronounced "pa-plu-tarr". But when the following word begins with a vowel, you run the two together: *pas après* (not after) becomes "pazapray".

Vowels are the hardest sounds to get right. Roughly:

a	as in hat	**o**	as in hot
e	as in get	**o/au**	as in over
é	between get and gate	**ou**	as in food
è	like the ai in pair	**u**	as in a pursed-lip, clipped version of toot
eu	like the u in hurt		
i	as in machine		

More awkward are the combinations in/im, en/em, on/om, un/um at the end of words, or followed by consonants other than n or m. Again, roughly:

in/im	like the "an" in anxious	**on/om**	like "on" said by someone with a heavy cold
an/am, en/em	like "on" said with a nasal accent	**un/um**	like the "u" in understand

Consonants are much as in English, except that ch is always sh, h is silent, th is the same as t, ll is sometimes pronounced like the y in "yes" when preceded by the letter "i" as in "fille" and "tilleul", w is v, and r is growled (or rolled).

Learning materials

Rough Guide French Phrasebook (Rough Guides). Mini dictionary-style phrasebook with both English–French and French–English sections, along with cultural tips for tricky situations and a menu reader.

Mini French Dictionary (Harrap/Prentice Hall). French–English and English–French, plus a brief grammar and pronunciation guide.

Breakthrough French and Further Breakthrough French (Pan; book and two cassettes). Excellent teach-yourself course.

A Comprehensive French Grammar Byrne & Churchill (Blackwell). Easy-to-follow reference grammar.

Pardon my French! Pocket French Slang Dictionary (Harrap). A bit large to carry, but the key to understanding everyday French.

A Vous La France; Franc Extra; Franc Parler (BBC Publications; each has a book and two cassettes). BBC radio courses, running from beginners' to fairly advanced language.

ⓦ **www.bbc.co.uk/education/languages/french** has a number of online courses ranging from beginner level to more advanced. French Steps is a self-contained language course for beginners and gives you basic vocabulary for conversing in everyday situations; Talk French is also for beginners and ties in with a book and TV series; while French Experience, slightly more advanced, also ties in with a TV series on the BBC learning zone and consists of a series of multimedia activities.

Words and phrases

Basics

oui	yes
non	no
s'il vous plaît	please
merci	thank you
pardon/excusez-moi	excuse me
pardon, Madame/ Monsieur	sorry
bonjour	hello
allô	hello (phone)
au revoir	goodbye
bonjour	good morning/ afternoon
bonsoir	good evening
bonne nuit	good night
d'accord	OK/agreed
Je comprends	I understand
Je ne comprends pas	I don't understand
Laissez-moi tranquille	Leave me alone
Aidez-moi, s'il vous plait	Please help me
au secours!	help!

Key words and phrases

French nouns are divided into masculine and feminine. This causes difficulties with adjectives, whose endings have to change to suit the gender of the nouns they qualify. If you know some grammar, you will know what to do. If not, stick to the masculine form, which is the simplest – it's what we have done in this glossary below.

aujourd'hui	today
hier	yesterday
demain	tomorrow
le matin	in the morning
l'après-midi	in the afternoon
le soir	in the evening
maintenant	now
plus tard	later
à une heure	at one o'clock
à trois heures	at three o'clock
à dix heures et demi	at ten-thirty
à midi	at midday
un homme	man
une femme	woman
ici	here
là	there
ceci	this one
cela	that one

ouvert	open
fermé	closed
grand	big
petit	small
plus	more
moins	less
un peu	a little
beaucoup	a lot
la moitié	half
bon marché/ pas cher	cheap
cher	expensive
bon	good
mauvais	bad
chaud	hot
froid	cold
avec	with
sans	without

Talking to people

When addressing people you should always use Monsieur for a man, Madame for a woman, Mademoiselle for a girl. Plain "bonjour" by itself is not enough. This isn't as formal as it seems, and it has its uses when you've forgotten someone's name or want to attract somcone's attention. "Bonjour" can be used well into the afternoon, and people may start saying "bonsoir" surprisingly early in the evening, or as a way of saying goodbye.

Comment allez-vous?/Ça va?	How are you?
Très bien, merci	Fine, thanks
Je ne sais pas	I don't know
Ah bon!	I see!
Vous parlez anglais?	Do you speak English?
Comment dit-on ...en français?	How do you say... in French?
Comment vous appelez-vous?	What's your name?
Je m'appelle . . .	My name is . . .
Je suis anglais(e)/	I'm English/

irlandais(e)/	Irish/
écossais(e)/	Scottish/
gallois(e)/	Welsh/
américain(e)/	American/
australien(ne)/	Australian/
canadien(ne)/	Canadian/
néo-zélandais(e)	a New Zealander
S'il vous plaît, parlez moins vite	Can you speak slower?
Allons-y	Let's go
A demain	See you tomorrow
A bientôt	See you soon

Questions and requests

The simplest way of asking a question is to start with "s'il vous plaît" (please), then name the thing you want in an interrogative tone of voice. For example:

S'il vous plaît, la boulangerie?	Where is there a bakery?
S'il vous plaît, pour aller à la Tour Eiffel?	Which way is it to the Eiffel Tower?

S'il vous plaît, une chambre pour deux We'd like a room for two

S'il vous plaît, un kilo d'oranges Can I have a kilo of oranges?

où? where?

comment? how?

combien? how many?

c'est combien? how much is it?

quand? when?

pourquoi? why?

à quelle heure? at what time?

quel est? what is/which is?

Getting around and directions

métro metro/subway station

Où est le métro le plus proche? Where is the nearest metro?

bus bus

car bus (coach)

gare routière bus station

arrêt bus stop

voiture car

train/taxi/ferry train/taxi/ferry

bâteau boat

avion plane

gare railway station

quai platform

Il part à quelle heure? What time does it leave?

Il arrive à quelle heure? What time does it arrive?

un billet pour . . . a ticket to . . .

aller simple single ticket

aller retour return ticket

compostez votre billet validate your ticket

valable pour valid for

vente de billets ticket office

combien de kilomètres? how many kilometres?

combien d'heures? how many hours?

à pied on foot

Vous allez où? Where are you going?

Je vais à . . . I'm going to . . .

Je voudrais descendre à . . . I want to get off at…

la route pour . . . the road to . . .

près/pas loin near

loin far

à gauche left

à droite right

tout droit straight on

de l'autre côté de on the other side of

à l'angle de on the corner of

à côté de next to

derrière behind

devant in front of

avant before

après after

sous under

traverser to cross

pont bridge

garer la voiture to park the car

un parking car park

défense de stationner/stationnement interdit no parking

poste d'essence petrol station

Accommodation

une chambre pour une personne/deux personnes a room for one/two people

avec un grand lit with a double bed

une chambre avec douche a room with a shower

une chambre avec salle de bain a room with a bath

pour une/deux/trois nuit(s) for one/two/three nights

Je peux la voir? Can I see it?

une chambre sur la cour a room in the courtyard

une chambre sur la rue a room over the street

premier étage first floor

deuxième étage second floor

avec vue with a view

clef key

repasser to iron

faire la lessive do laundry

draps sheets

couvertures blankets

calme	quiet
bruyant	noisy
eau chaude	hot water
eau froide	cold water
Est-ce que le petit déjeuner est compris?	Is breakfast included?
Je voudrais prendre le petit déjeuner	I would like breakfast
Je ne veux pas le petit déjeuner	I don't want breakfast
un camping/terrain de camping	campsite
auberge de jeunesse	youth hostel

Months, days, dates and numbers

janvier	January
février	February
mars	March
avril	April
mai	May
juin	June
juillet	July
août	August
septembre	September
octobre	October
novembre	November
décembre	December
lundi	Monday
mardi	Tuesday
mercredi	Wednesday
jeudi	Thursday
vendredi	Friday
samedi	Saturday
dimanche	Sunday
le premier août	August 1
le deux mars	March 2
le quatorze juillet	July 14
le vingt-trois novembre, deux mille quatre	November 23, 2004

Numbers

un	1
deux	2
trois	3
quatre	4
cinq	5
six	6
sept	7
huit	8
neuf	9
dix	10
onze	11
douze	12
treize	13
quatorze	14
quinze	15
seize	16
dix-sept	17
dix-huit	18
dix-neuf	19
vingt	20
vingt-et-un	21
vingt-deux	22
trente	30
quarante	40
cinquante	50
soixante	60
soixante-dix	70
soixante-quinze	75
quatre-vingts	80
quatre-vingt-dix	90
quatre-vingt-quinze	95
cent	100
cent un	101
deux cents	200
mille	1000
deux mille	2000
un million	1,000,000

Food and drink terms

Basic words and phrases

déjeuner	lunch
dîner	dinner
menu	set menu
carte	menu
à la carte	individually priced dishes
entrées	starters
les plats	main courses
une carafe d'eau/ de vin	a carafe of tap water/ wine
eau minérale	mineral water
eau gazeuse	fizzy water
eau plate	still water
carte des vins	wine list
un quart/demi de rouge/blanc	a quarter/half-litre of red/white house wine
un (verre de) rouge/blanc	a glass of red/white wine
Je voudrais réserver une table	I'd like to reserve a table
pour deux personnes, à vingt heures et demie	for two people, at eight thirty
Je prendrai le menu à quinze euros	I'm having the €15 menu
Monsieur/madame!	Waiter! (never say "garçon")
l'addition, s'il vous plaît	the bill, please
une pression	a glass of beer
un café	coffee (espresso)
un crème	white coffee
un café au lait	big bowl of milky breakfast coffee
un cappuccino	cappuccino

Cooking terms

Chauffé	Heated
Cuit	Cooked
Cru	Raw
Emballé	Wrapped
à emporter	Takeaway
Fumé	Smoked
Salé	Salted/savoury
Sucré	Sweet

Essentials

Pain	Bread
Beurre	Butter
Oeufs	Eggs
Lait	Milk
Huile	Oil
Poivre	Pepper
Sel	Salt
Sucre	Sugar
Vinaigre	Vinegar
Bouteille	Bottle
Verre	Glass
Fourchette	Fork
Couteau	Knife
Cuillère	Spoon
Bio	Organic

Snacks

Crêpe	Pancake (sweet)
au sucre	with sugar
au citron	with lemon
au miel	with honey
à la confiture	with jam
aux œufs	with eggs

à la crème de marrons	with chestnut purée
Galette	Buckwheat (savoury) pancake
Un sandwich/ une baguette	A sandwich . . .
jambon	with ham
fromage	with cheese
saucisson	with sausage
rillettes	with coarse pâté
pâté (de campagne)	with pâté (country-style)
croque-monsieur	Grilled cheese & ham sandwich
croque-madame	Croque-monsieur with an egg on top
panini	Flat toasted Italian sandwich
Oeufs	Eggs
au plat	fried
à la coque	boiled
durs	hard-boiled
brouillés	scrambled
Omelette	Omelette
nature	plain
aux fines herbes	with herbs
au fromage	with cheese
Salade de	Salad of
tomates	tomatoes
betteraves	beetroot
concombres	cucumber
carottes rapées	grated carrots

Other fillings/salads

Andouillette	Tripe sausage
Boudin	Meat sausage
Cœurs de palmiers	Palm hearts
Fonds d'artichauts	Artichoke hearts
Hareng	Herring
Langue	Tongue
Poulet	Chicken
Thon	Tuna

Soups (soupes)

Bisque	Shellfish soup
Bouillabaisse	Marseillais fish soup
Bouillon	Broth or stock
Bourride	Thick fish soup
Consommé	Clear soup
Pistou	Parmesan, basil & garlic paste added to soup
Potage	Thick vegetable soup
Potée	Hearty meat soup, usually containing pork, cabbage and potatoes
Rouille	Red pepper, garlic & saffron mayonnaise with fish soup
Velouté	Thick soup, usually made with fish or poultry

Starters (hors d'œuvrs)

Assiette anglaise	Plate of cold meats
Crudités	Raw vegetables with dressings
Hors d'œuvres variés	Combination of the above

Fish (poisson), seafood (fruits de mer) and shellfish (crustacés or coquillages)

Anchois	Anchovies
Anguilles	Eels
Bar	Sea bass
Barbue	Brill
Bigorneau	Periwinkle
Brème	Bream

Brochet	Pike
Cabillaud	Cod
Calmar	Squid
Carrelet	Plaice
Claire	Type of oyster
Colin	Hake
Congre	Conger eel
Coques	Cockles
Coquilles St-Jacques	Scallops
Crabe	Crab
Crevettes grises	Shrimps
Crevettes roses	Prawns
Daurade	Sea bream
Eperlan	Smelt or whitebait
Escargots	Snails
Flétan	Halibut
Friture	Whitebait
Gambas	King prawns
Hareng	Herring
Homard	Lobster
Huîtres	Oysters
Langouste	Spiny lobster
Langoustines	Saltwater crayfish (scampi)
Limande	Lemon sole
Lotte de mer	Monkfish
Loup de mer	Sea bass
Louvine, loubine	Similar to sea bass
Maquereau	Mackerel
Merlan	Whiting
Morue	Dried, salted cod
Moules (marinière)	Mussels (with shallots in white-wine sauce)
Oursin	Sea urchin
Palourdes	Clams
Praires	Small clams
Raie	Skate
Rouget	Red mullet
Sandre	Pike-perch
Saumon	Salmon
Seiche	Squid
Sole	Sole
Thon	Tuna
Truite	Trout
Turbot	Turbot

Fish: dishes and related terms

Aïoli	Garlic mayonnaise served with salt cod and other fish
Béarnaise	Sauce made with egg yolks, white wine, shallots & vinegar
Beignets	Fritters
Darne	Fillet or steak
La douzaine	A dozen
Frit	Fried
Fumé	Smoked
Fumet	Fish stock
Gigot de mer	Large fish baked whole
Grillé	Grilled
Hollandaise	Butter & vinegar sauce
A la meunière	In a butter, lemon & parsley sauce
Mousse/mousseline	Mousse
Quenelles	Light dumplings

Meat (viande) and poultry (volaille)

Agneau (de pré-salé)	Lamb (grazed on salt marshes)
Andouille, andouillette	Tripe sausage
	Bavette beef flank steak
Bœuf	Beef
Bifteck	Steak
Boudin blanc	Sausage of white meats
Boudin noir	Black pudding
Caille	Quail
Canard	Duck
Caneton	Duckling
Contrefilet	Sirloin roast
Coquelet	Cockerel
Dinde	Turkey
Entrecôte	Ribsteak
Faux filet	Sirloin steak

Foie	Liver
Foie gras	Fattened (duck/goose) liver
Gigot (d'agneau)	Leg (of lamb)
Grillade	Grilled meat
Hachis	Chopped meat or mince hamburger
Langue	Tongue
Lapin, lapereau	Rabbit, young rabbit
Lard, lardons	Bacon, diced bacon
Lièvre	Hare
Merguez	Spicy, red sausage
Mouton	Mutton
Museau de veau	Calf's muzzle
Oie	Goose
Onglet	Cut of beef
Os	Bone
Porc	Pork
Poulet	Chicken
Poussin	Baby chicken
Ris	Sweetbreads
Rognons	Kidneys
Rognons blancs	Testicles
Sanglier	Wild boar
Tête de veau	Calf's head (in jelly)
Tournedos	Thick slices of fillet
Tripes	Tripe
Veau	Veal
Venaison	Venison

Meat and poultry: dishes and related terms

Aile	Wing
Blanquette de veau	Veal in cream & mushroom sauce
Bœuf bourguignon	Beef stew with red wine, onions & mushrooms
Canard à l'orange	Roast duck with an orange-and-wine sauce
Carré	Best end of neck, chop or cutlet
Cassoulet	A casserole of beans & meat
Choucroute garnie	Sauerkraut served with sausages or cured ham
Civet	Game stew
Confit	Meat preserve
Coq au vin	Chicken with wine, onions & mushrooms, cooked till it falls off the bone
Côte	Chop, cutlet or rib
Cou	Neck
Cuisse	Thigh or leg
Daube, estouffade, hochepot, navarin and ragoût	All are types of stew
En croûte	In pastry
Epaule	Shoulder
Farci	Stuffed
Au feu de bois	Cooked over wood fire
Au four	Baked
Garni	With vegetables
Gésier	Gizzard
Grillé	Grilled
Magret de canard	Duck breast
Marmite	Casserole
Médaillon	Round piece
Mijoté	Stewed
Museau	Muzzle
Pavé	Thick slice
Rôti	Roast
Sauté	Lightly cooked in butter
Steak au poivre(vert/rouge)	Steak in a black (green/red) peppercorn sauce
Steak tartare	Raw chopped beef, topped with a raw egg yolk

For steaks

Bleu	Almost raw
Saignant	Rare
A point	Medium
Bien cuit	Well done
Très bien cuit	Very well cooked
Brochette	Kebab

Garnishes and sauces

Beurre blanc	Sauce of white wine & shallots, with butter
Chasseur	White wine, mushrooms & shallots
Diable	Strong mustard seasoning
Forestière	With bacon & mushroom
Fricassée	Rich, creamy sauce
Mornay	Cheese sauce
Pays d'Auge	Cream & cider
Piquante	Gherkins or capers, vinegar & shallots
Provençale	Tomatoes, garlic, olive oil & herbs

Vegetables (légumes), herbs (herbes) and spices (épices)

Ail	Garlic
Algue	Seaweed
Anis	Aniseed
Artichaut	Artichoke
Asperges	Asparagus
Avocat	Avocado
Basilic	Basil
Betterave	Beetroot
Carotte	Carrot
Céleri	Celery
Champignons, cèpes, chanterelles	Mushrooms of various kinds
Chou (rouge)	(Red) cabbage
Chou-fleur	Cauliflower
Ciboulette	Chives
Concombre	Cucumber
Cornichon	Gherkin
Echalotes	Shallots
Endive	Chicory
Épinards	Spinach
Estragon	Tarragon
Fenouil	Fennel
Flageolets	White beans
Gingembre	Ginger
Haricots	Beans
verts	string (French)
rouges	kidney
beurres	butter
Laurier	Bay leaf
Lentilles	Lentils
Maïs	Corn
Menthe	Mint
Moutarde	Mustard
Oignon	Onion
Pâtes	Pasta
Persil	Parsley
Petits pois	Peas
Piment	Pimento
Pois chiche	Chickpeas
Pois mange-tout	Snow peas
Pignons	Pine nuts
Poireau	Leek
Poivron (vert, rouge)	Sweet pepper (green, red)
Pommes (de terre)	Potatoes
Primeurs	Spring vegetables
Radis	Radishes
Riz	Rice
Safran	Saffron
Salade verte	Green salad
Sarrasin	Buckwheat
Tomate	Tomato
Truffes	Truffles

Vegetables: dishes and related terms

Beignet	Fritter
Farci	Stuffed
Gratiné/au gratin/ gratin de	Browned with cheese or butter
Jardinière	With mixed diced vegetables
Forestière	With mushrooms
A la parisienne	Sautéed in butter (potatoes); with white wine sauce & shallots

Parmentier	With potatoes
Sauté	Lightly fried in butter
A la vapeur	Steamed

Fruits (fruits) and nuts (noix)

Abricot	Apricot
Amandes	Almonds
Ananas	Pineapple
Banane	Banana
Brugnon, nectarine	Nectarine
Cacahouète	Peanut
Cassis	Blackcurrants
Cerises	Cherries
Citron	Lemon
Citron vert	Lime
Figues	Figs
Fraises (des bois)	Strawberries (wild)
Framboises	Raspberries
Fruit de la passion	Passion fruit
Groseilles	Redcurrants & gooseberries
Mangue	Mango
Marrons	Chestnuts
Melon	Melon
Myrtilles	Bilberries
Noisette	Hazelnut
Noix	Nuts
Orange	Orange
Pamplemousse	Grapefruit
Pêche (blanche)	(White) peach
Pistache	Pistachio
Poire	Pear
Pomme	Apple
Prune	Plum
Pruneau	Prune
Raisins	Grapes

Fruit: related terms

Beignets	Fritters
Compote de . . .	Stewed . . .
Coulis	Sauce
Flambé	Set aflame in alcohol
Frappé	Iced

Desserts (desserts or entremets) and pastries (pâtisserie)

Barquette	Small boat-shaped flan
Bavarois	Refers to the mould, could be mousse or custard
Bombe	A moulded ice cream dessert
Brioche	Sweet, high yeast breakfast roll
Charlotte	Custard & fruit in lining of almond fingers
Coupe	A serving of ice cream
Crème Chantilly	Vanilla-flavoured & sweetened whipped cream
Crème fraîche	Sour cream
Crème pâtissière	Thick eggy pastry-filling
Crêpe	Pancake
Crêpe suzette	Thin pancake with orange juice & liqueur
Fromage blanc	Cream cheese
Galette	Buckwheat pancake
Génoise	Rich sponge cake
Glace	Ice cream
Île flottante/ œufs à la neige	Soft meringues floating on custard
Macarons	Macaroons
Madeleine	Small sponge cake
Marrons Mont Blanc	Chestnut purée & cream on a rum-soaked sponge cake
Mousse au chocolat	Chocolate mousse
Palmiers	Caramelized puff pastries

Parfait	Frozen mousse, sometimes ice cream
Petit suisse	A smooth mixture of cream & curds
Petits fours	Bite-sized cakes/pastries
Poires Belle Hélène	Pears & ice cream in chocolate sauce
Sablé	Shortbread biscuit
Savarin	A filled, ring-shaped cake
Tarte	Tart
Tartelette	Small tart
Truffes	Truffles, chocolate or liqueur variety
Yaourt, yogourt	Yoghurt

Cheese (fromage)

There are over 400 types of French cheese, most of them named after their place of origin. *Chèvre* is goat's cheese and *brebis* is cheese made from sheep's milk. *Le plateau de fromages* is the cheeseboard, and bread – but not butter – is served with it.

French and architectural terms: a glossary

These are either terms you'll come across in this book, or come up against on signs, maps, etc, while travelling around.

Abbaye abbey

Ambulatory covered passage around the outer edge of a choir of a church

Apse semicircular termination at the east end of a church

Arrondissement district of the city

Assemblée Nationale the French parliament

Auberge de Jeunesse (AJ) youth hostel

Baroque High Renaissance period of art and architecture, distinguished by extreme ornateness

Beaux-Arts fine arts

Car bus

Carolingian dynasty (and art, sculpture, etc) founded by Charlemagne, late eighth to early tenth centuries

CFDT Socialist trade union

Carrefour intersection

CGT Communist trade union

Chasse, Chasse Gardée hunting grounds

Château mansion, country house, castle

Château Fort castle

Chemin path

Chevet end wall of a church

CIDJ (Centre d'Informations Jeunesse) youth information centre

Classical architectural style incorporating Greek and Roman elements – pillars, domes, colonnades, etc – at its height in France in the seventeenth century and revived in the nineteenth century as **Neoclassical**

Clerestory upper storey of a church, incorporating the windows

Codene French CND

Consigne luggage consignment

Cours combination of main square and main street

Couvent convent, monastery

Défense de . . . It is forbidden to . . .

Dégustation tasting (wine or food)

Département county – more or less

Eglise church

En Panne out of order

Entrée entrance

Fermeture closing period

Flamboyant florid form of Gothic

FN (Front National) far-right party led by Jean-Marie Le Pen

FO Catholic trade union

Fresco wall painting – durable through application to wet plaster

Gallo-Romain period of Roman occupation of Gaul (first to fourth centuries AD)

Gare station; – **Routière** bus station; – **SNCF** train station

Gobelins famous tapestry manufacturers, based in Paris; its most renowned period was in the reign of Louis XIV (seventeenth century)

Grande Randonnée (GR) long-distance footpath

Halles covered market

HLM public housing development

Hôtel a hotel, but also an aristocratic townhouse or mansion

Hôtel de ville town hall

Jours fériés public holidays

Mairie town hall

Marché market

Merovingian dynasty (and art, etc) ruling France and parts of Germany from the sixth to mid-eighth centuries

Narthex entrance hall of church

Nave main body of a church

PCF Communist Party of France

Place square

Porte gateway or door

PS Socialist party

Poste post office

Quartier district of a town

Renaissance art/architectural style developed in fifteenth-century Italy and imported to France in the early sixteenth century by François 1er

Retable altarpiece

Rez-de-chaussée (RC) ground floor

RN (Route Nationale) main road

Romanesque early medieval architecture distinguished by squat, rounded forms and naive sculpture

RPR Gaullist party

SI (Syndicat d'Initiative) tourist information office; also known as OT, OTSI and Maison du Tourisme

SNCF (Société Nationale des Chemins de Fer) French railways

Soldes sales

Sortie exit

Stucco plaster used to embellish ceilings, etc

Tabac bar or shop selling stamps, cigarettes, télécartes, etc

Tour tower

Transept cross arms of a church

Triforium narrow, middle storey of a church

Tympanum sculpted panel above a church door

UDF centre-right party

UMP new umbrella party grouping parties of the right and centre-right

Vauban seventeenth-century military architect – his fortresses still stand all over France

Villa a mews or a series of small residential streets, built as a unity

Voussoir sculpted rings in an arch over church door

Zone Bleue restricted parking zone

Zone Piétonne pedestrian zone

Travel store

Kenya
Marrakesh D
Morocco
South Africa, Lesotho & Swaziland
Syria
Tanzania
Tunisia
West Africa
Zanzibar

Travel Specials
First-Time Africa
First-Time Around the World
First-Time Asia
First-Time Europe
First-Time Latin America
Travel Health
Travel Online
Travel Survival
Walks in London & SE England
Women Travel
World Party

Maps
Algarve
Amsterdam
Andalucia & Costa del Sol
Argentina
Athens
Australia
Barcelona
Berlin
Boston & Cambridge
Brittany
Brussels
California
Chicago
Chile
Corsica
Costa Rica & Panama
Crete
Croatia
Cuba
Cyprus
Czech Republic
Dominican Republic
Dubai & UAE
Dublin
Egypt
Florence & Siena
Florida
France
Frankfurt
Germany
Greece
Guatemala & Belize
Iceland
India
Ireland
Italy
Kenya & Northern Tanzania
Lisbon
London
Los Angeles
Madrid
Malaysia
Mallorca
Marrakesh
Mexico
Miami & Key West
Morocco
New England
New York City
New Zealand
Northern Spain
Paris
Peru
Portugal
Prague
Pyrenees & Andorra
Rome
San Francisco
Sicily
South Africa
South India
Spain & Portugal
Sri Lanka
Tenerife
Thailand
Toronto
Trinidad & Tobago
Tunisia
Turkey
Tuscany
Venice
Vietnam, Laos & Cambodia
Washington DC
Yucatán Peninsula

Dictionary Phrasebooks
Croatian
Czech
Dutch
Egyptian Arabic
French
German
Greek
Hindi & Urdu
Italian
Japanese
Latin American Spanish
Mandarin Chinese
Mexican Spanish
Polish
Portuguese
Russian
Spanish
Swahili
Thai
Turkish
Vietnamese

Computers
Blogging
eBay
iPhone
iPods, iTunes & music online
The Internet
Macs & OS X
MySpace
PCs and Windows
PlayStation Portable
Website Directory

Film & TV
American Independent Film
British Cult Comedy
Chick Flicks
Comedy Movies
Cult Movies
Film
Film Musicals
Film Noir
Gangster Movies
Horror Movies
Kids' Movies
Sci-Fi Movies
Westerns

Lifestyle
Babies
Ethical Living
Pregnancy & Birth
Running

Music Guides
The Beatles
Blues
Bob Dylan
Book of Playlists
Classical Music
Elvis
Frank Sinatra
Heavy Metal
Hip-Hop
Jazz
Led Zeppelin
Opera
Pink Floyd
Punk
Reggae
Rock
The Rolling Stones
Soul and R&B
Velvet Underground
World Music (2 vols)

Popular Culture
Books for Teenagers
Children's Books, 5-11
Conspiracy Theories
Crime Fiction
Cult Fiction
The Da Vinci Code
His Dark Materials
Lord of the Rings
Shakespeare
Superheroes
The Templars
Unexplained Phenomena

Science
The Brain
Climate Change
The Earth
Genes & Cloning
The Universe
Weather

Small print and
Index

A Rough Guide to Rough Guides

Published in 1982, the first Rough Guide – to Greece – was a student scheme that became a publishing phenomenon. Mark Ellingham, a recent graduate in English from Bristol University, had been travelling in Greece the previous summer and couldn't find the right guidebook. With a small group of friends he wrote his own guide, combining a highly contemporary, journalistic style with a thoroughly practical approach to travellers' needs.

The immediate success of the book spawned a series that rapidly covered dozens of destinations. And, in addition to impecunious backpackers, Rough Guides soon acquired a much broader and older readership that relished the guides' wit and inquisitiveness as much as their enthusiastic, critical approach and value-for-money ethos.

These days, Rough Guides include recommendations from shoestring to luxury and cover more than 200 destinations around the globe, including almost every country in the Americas and Europe, more than half of Africa and most of Asia and Australasia. Our ever-growing team of authors and photographers is spread all over the world, particularly in Europe, the USA and Australia.

In the early 1990s, Rough Guides branched out of travel, with the publication of Rough Guides to World Music, Classical Music and the Internet. All three have become benchmark titles in their fields, spearheading the publication of a wide range of books under the Rough Guide name.

Including the travel series, Rough Guides now number more than 350 titles, covering: phrasebooks, waterproof maps, music guides from Opera to Heavy Metal, reference works as diverse as Conspiracy Theories and Shakespeare, and popular culture books from iPods to Poker. Rough Guides also produce a series of more than 120 World Music CDs in partnership with World Music Network.

Visit www.roughguides.com to see our latest publications.

Rough Guide travel images are available for commercial licensing at www.roughguidespictures.com

Rough Guide credits

Text editor: Melissa Graham
Layout: Ankur Guha
Cartography: Amod Singh
Picture editor: Mark Thomas
Production: Vicky Baldwin
Proofreader: Jann McCann
Cover design: Chloë Roberts
Editorial: **London** Kate Berens, Claire Saunders, Ruth Blackmore, Alison Murchie, Karoline Densley, Andy Turner, Keith Drew, Edward Aves, Nikki Birrell, Alice Park, Sarah Eno, Lucy White, Jo Kirby, James Smart, Natasha Foges, Roisín Cameron, Emma Traynor, Emma Gibbs, Kathryn Lane, Joe Staines, Duncan Clark, Peter Buckley, Matthew Milton, Tracy Hopkins, Ruth Tidball; **New York** Andrew Rosenberg, Steven Horak, AnneLise Sorensen, Amy Hegarty, April Isaacs, Ella Steim, Anna Owens, Joseph Petta, Sean Mahoney; **Delhi** Madhavi Singh, Karen D'Souza
Design & Pictures: **London** Scott Stickland, Dan May, Diana Jarvis, Jj Luck, Chloë Roberts, Nicole Newman, Sarah Cummins; **Delhi** Umesh Aggarwal, Ajay Verma, Jessica Subramanian
Pradeep Thapliyal, Sachin Tanwar, Anita Singh
Production: Rebecca Short
Cartography: **London** Maxine Repath, Ed Wright, Katie Lloyd-Jones; **Delhi** Jai Prakash Mishra, Rajesh Chhibber, Ashutosh Bharti, Rajesh Mishra, Animesh Pathak, Jasbir Sandhu, Karobi Gogoi, Alakananda Bhattacharya, Swati Handoo
Online: Narender Kumar, Rakesh Kumar, Amit Kumar, Amit Verma, Rahul Kumar, Ganesh Sharma, Debojit Borah
Marketing & Publicity: **London** Liz Statham, Niki Hanmer, Louise Maher, Jess Carter, Vanessa Godden, Vivienne Watton, Anna Paynton, Rachel Sprackett; **New York** Geoff Colquitt, Megan Kennedy, Katy Ball
Manager India: Punita Singh
Series Editor: Mark Ellingham
Reference Director: Andrew Lockett
Publishing Coordinator: Helen Phillips
Publishing Director: Martin Dunford
Commercial Manager: Gino Magnotta
Managing Director: John Duhigg

Publishing information

This eleventh edition published January 2008 by
Rough Guides Ltd,
80 Strand, London WC2R 0RL
345 Hudson St, 4th Floor,
New York, NY 10014, USA
14 Local Shopping Centre, Panchsheel Park,
New Delhi 110017, India
Distributed by the Penguin Group
Penguin Books Ltd,
80 Strand, London WC2R 0RL
Penguin Group (USA)
375 Hudson Street, NY 10014, USA
Penguin Group (Australia)
250 Camberwell Road, Camberwell,
Victoria 3124, Australia
Penguin Books Canada Ltd,
10 Alcorn Avenue, Toronto, Ontario,
Canada M4V 1E4
Penguin Group (NZ)
67 Apollo Drive, Mairangi Bay, Auckland 1310,
New Zealand

Cover concept by Peter Dyer.

Typeset in Bembo and Helvetica to an original design by Henry Iles.

Printed and bound in China

512pp includes index

A catalogue record for this book is available from the British Library

ISBN: 978-1-84353-992-6

1 3 5 7 9 8 6 4 2

Help us update

We've gone to a lot of effort to ensure that the eleventh edition of **The Rough Guide to Paris** is accurate and up to date. However, things change – places get "discovered", opening hours are notoriously fickle, restaurants and rooms raise prices or lower standards. If you feel we've got it wrong or left something out, we'd like to know, and if you can remember the address, the price, the time, the phone number, so much the better.

We'll credit all contributions, and send a copy of the next edition (or any other Rough Guide if you prefer) for the best letters. Everyone who writes to us and isn't already a subscriber will receive a copy of our full-color thrice-yearly newsletter. Please mark letters: **"Rough Guide Paris Update"** and send to: Rough Guides, 80 Strand, London WC2R 0RL, or Rough Guides, 345 Hudson St, 4th Floor, New York, NY 10014. Or send an email to **mail@roughguides.com**

Have your questions answered and tell others about your trip at
www.roughguides.atinfopop.com

Acknowledgements

The authors would like to thank Melissa Graham, our editor; Mark Thomas, who handled all the pictures; Ankur Guha, who designed and set the text; Amod Singh, who dealt with the cartography; and everyone at Rough Guides. Our thanks also to Maryse Courberand, at the Cité des Sciences et de l'Industrie; Anne Dechenaud, at Saint James Paris; Claire Fine, at Disneyland UK; Natalie Goulet, at the Maison de la France; Fanny Hastoy, at Lodgis; Marie-Claude Hattet, on the rue Mouffetard; and Adrien Kao at Astotel; Violaine Solari, at the Versailles tourist board. James would like to say a special thank you to Amy Jordan, for all her work in Paris; and Ginny Power, Kristen Jestin and Anna Jestin, for their splendid Disney reviews. Ruth Blackmore would like to say "un grand merci" to Sarah Dallas, Fenella Fairbairn and Dylan Reisenberger.

Readers' letters

Thanks to all the readers who have taken the time to write in with comments and suggestions (and apologies if we've inadvertently omitted or misspelt anyone's name):

Mrs Phil Barker, W.J. Bell, Les Berger, Eleanor Bishop, Brendan & Marc, Neville Browne, Margot Clarke, Mark Foot, G.D.K. Fraser, Amanda Garrett, Pauline Gaunt, Peter Gerrard, Kerry Graham, Jenny Green, Roger Gregory, Leo Lacey, David J. Lane, Theresa Lloyd, Martin, Sheridan MacInnes, Richard Mills, Slavomir Oslovsky and Marcela Vincencikova, Nik Petrovic, E. Phillips, Peter Rog, Eric & Sally Rowland, Simon and Christine Rowntree, James Seidler, Veronica Simpson, Jan Smith, Anthony Steele, Peter Thompson, David Tucker, Pam Walker, Andrew Watts, Jeff Wells.

Photo credits

All photos © Rough Guides except the following:

Title page
Pont Alexandre © Ian Cumming/Axiom

Introduction
Street sign © Ingrid Rasmussen/Axiom
Métro sign © Mark Thomas
Bridge over the River Seine © Steve J Benbow/Axiom

Things not to miss
01 The Eiffel Tower © Steve J Benbow/Axiom
04 Notre Dame © Charles Kogod/Getty Images
06 Musée du Quai Branly © Nik Hanna/Alamy
09 The Marais © Michel Setboun/Corbis
16 Chartres Cathedral © James McConnachie
18 Brasserie Balzar © James McConnachie

Colour insert: From wine bars to three stars
Plat du Jour mosaic © Ingrid Rasmussen/Axiom
Menu board © Anthony Webb/Axiom

Colour insert: Paris architecture
View over rooftops © Michel Setboun/Getty images
Haussmann apartment buildings © James McConnachie
The Eiffel Tower rising behind buildings © John Lawrence/Getty
The Louvre Pyramid © Cosmo Condina/Getty Images
Musée du quai Branly © James McConnachie

Black and white pictures
p.84 Jardin du Luxembourg © James McConnachie
p.102 The Pompidou Centre © Mark Thomas
p.112 Café Les Philosophes © James McConnachie
p.135 Rue Mouffetard market © James McConnachie
p.198 Sacré-Coeur © James McConnachie
p.217 Bercy Village © Hemis/Alamy
p.222 Canal St-Martin © Hideo Kurihara/Alamy
p.248 Parc de Bagatelle © TB Photo/Alamy
p.262 St-Denis market © James McConnachie
p.276 Chartres Cathedral © James McConnachie
p.287 Disneyland Paris © Robert Harding/Alamy
p.331 Brasserie Balzar © James McConnachie
p.336 Gaya restaurant © James McConnachie
p.347 Pause Café © James McConnachie
p.386 Galeries Lafayettes © Coverspot/Alamy
p.419 Skating outside the Hôtel de Ville © Magali Delaport/Axiom
p.451 Coronation of the Emperor and Empress © Jacques Louis David/Getty Images

Index

Map entries are in colour.

A

B

INDEX

D

E

F

INDEX

K

L

M

INDEX

INDEX

Q

R

INDEX

INDEX

S

T

U

V

W

Y

Z

INDEX

Map symbols

maps are listed in the full index using coloured text

- Autoroute
- Main road
- Minor road
- Pedestrianized road
- Steps
- Unpaved road
- Tunnel
- Railway
- TGV
- Funicular railway
- Footpath
- Wall
- River
- Gate
- Airport
- Ⓜ Metro station
- Ⓡ RER station
- Ⓣ Tram stop
- Place of interest
- Information office
- Post office
- Parking
- Toilets
- Accommodation
- Restaurant
- Statue
- Synagogue
- Church
- Building
- Stadium
- Park
- Cemetery

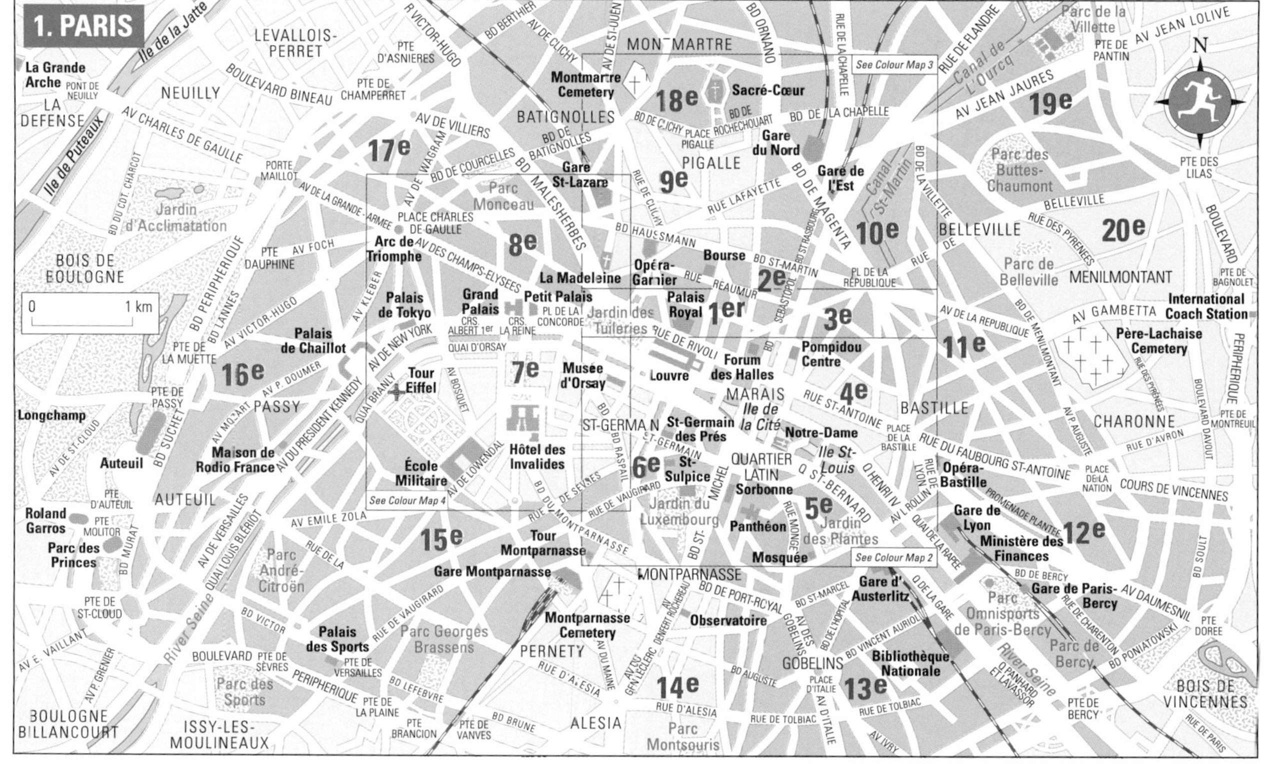
1. PARIS
N
0
1 km
La Grande Arche
PONT DE NEUILLY
LA DEFENSE
Ile de la Jatte
Ile de Puteaux
LEVALLOIS-PERRET
NEUILLY
BOULEVARD BINEAU
PTE D'ASNIERES
PTE DE CHAMPERRET
R VICTOR-HUGO
BD BERTHIER
AV DE CLICHY
AV DE ST-OUEN
MONTMARTRE
BD ORNANO
RUE DE LA CHAPELLE
RUE DE FLANDRE
Parc de la Villette
PTE DE PANTIN
AV JEAN LOLIVE
See Colour Map 3
Montmartre Cemetery
18e
Sacré-Cœur
Canal de L'Ourcq
AV JEAN JAURES
19e
AV CHARLES DE GAULLE
AV DE VILLIERS
BATIGNOLLES
BD DE CLICHY
PLACE PIGALLE
BD DE ROCHECHOUART
BD DE LA CHAPELLE
Gare du Nord
17e
BD DE COURCELLES
BD DE BATIGNOLLES
Gare St-Lazare
9e
PIGALLE
Gare de l'Est
Canal St-Martin
BD DE LA VILLETTE
Parc des Buttes-Chaumont
PTE DES LILAS
BD DU COT. CHARCOT
Jardin d'Acclimatation
PORTE MAILLOT
AV DE WAGRAM
AV DE LA GRANDE-ARMEE
Parc Monceau
BD MALESHERBES
RUE DE CLICHY
RUE LAFAYETTE
BD DE MAGENTA
10e
BELLEVILLE
RUE DES PYRENEES
20e
BOULEVARD
BOIS DE BOULOGNE
PTE DAUPHINE
AV FOCH
PLACE CHARLES DE GAULLE
Arc de Triomphe
AV DES CHAMPS-ELYSEES
8e
BD HAUSSMANN
Opéra-Garnier
Bourse
BD ST-MARTIN
BD DE STRASBOURG
PL DE LA REPUBLIQUE
Parc de Belleville
MENILMONTANT
PTE DE BAGNOLET
BD PERIPHERIQUE
BD LANNES
AV VICTOR-HUGO
AV KLEBER
La Madeleine
RUE REAUMUR
2e
Palais de Tokyo
Grand Palais
Petit Palais
PL DE LA CONCORDE
Jardin des Tuileries
Palais Royal
1er
SEBASTOPOL
3e
AV GAMBETTA
International Coach Station
CRS. ALBERT 1er
CRS. LA REINE
AV DE LA REPUBLIQUE
Palais de Chaillot
AV DE NEW YORK
QUAI D'ORSAY
RUE DE RIVOLI
Pompidou Centre
11e
Père-Lachaise Cemetery
PTE DE LA MUETTE
16e
AV P. DOUMER
Tour Eiffel
AV BOSQUET
7e
Musée d'Orsay
Louvre
Forum des Halles
BD DE MENILMONTANT
PERIPHERIQUE
PTE DE PASSY
PASSY
QUAI BRANLY
MARAIS
4e
RUE ST-ANTOINE
BASTILLE
CHARONNE
PTE DE MONTREUIL
Longchamp
AV DE ST-CLOUD
BD SUCHET
AV MOZART
AV DU PRESIDENT KENNEDY
ST-GERMAIN
St-Germain des Prés
Ile de la Cité
Notre-Dame
PLACE DE LA BASTILLE
AV P. AUGUSTE
RUE D'AVRON
BOULEVARD DAVOUT
Auteuil
Maison de Rodio France
Hôtel des Invalides
BD RASPAIL
6e
St-Sulpice
QUARTIER LATIN
Ile St-Louis
RUE DU FAUBOURG ST-ANTOINE
École Militaire
AV DE LOWENDAL
BD DE SEVRES
Sorbonne
Q ST-BERNARD
Q HENRI IV
Opéra-Bastille
PLACE DE LA NATION
COURS DE VINCENNES
PTE D'AUTEUIL
AUTEUIL
See Colour Map 4
RUE DE VAUGIRARD
BD ST-MICHEL
Jardin du Luxembourg
5e
Jardin des Plantes
RUE DE LYON
AV L ROLLIN
PROMENADE PLANTEE
Roland Garros
PTE MOLITOR
AV DE VERSAILLES
AV EMILE ZOLA
15e
BD DU MONTPARNASSE
Panthéon
RUE MONGE
Gare de Lyon
QUAI DE LA RAPEE
Ministère des Finances
12e
BD SOULT
Parc des Princes
BD MURAT
QUAI LOUIS BLERIOT
Parc André-Citroën
RUE DE LA
Tour Montparnasse
Mosquée
See Colour Map 2
Gare Montparnasse
MONTPARNASSE
BD DE PORT-ROYAL
BD ST-MARCEL
Gare d'Austerlitz
Q DE LA GARE
BD DE BERCY
Gare de Paris-Bercy
AV DAUMESNIL
PTE DE ST-CLOUD
River Seine
BD VICTOR
Palais des Sports
Parc Georges Brassens
Montparnasse Cemetery
Observatoire
AV DES GOBELINS
BD DE L'HOPITAL
BD VINCENT AURIOL
Parc Omnisports de Paris-Bercy
RUE DE CHARENTON
Parc de Bercy
BD PONIATOWSKI
PTE DOREE
AV E. VAILLANT
AV P. GRENIER
BOULEVARD
PTE DE SEVRES
PTE DE VERSAILLES
PERIPHERIQUE
Parc des Sports
PTE DE LA PLAINE
BD LEFEBVRE
PERNETY
AV DU MAINE
RUE D'ALESIA
AV DU GEN LECLERC
AV DENFERT ROCHEREAU
14e
BD AUGUSTE
GOBELINS
PLACE D'ITALIE
13e
Bibliothèque Nationale
Q PANHARD ET LAVASSOR
PTE DE BERCY
BOIS DE VINCENNES
BOULOGNE BILLANCOURT
ISSY-LES-MOULINEAUX
PTE BRANCION
PTE DE VANVES
BD BRUNE
ALESIA
Parc Montsouris
RUE DE TOLBIAC
AV D'ITALIE
AV IVRY
RUE DE PARIS

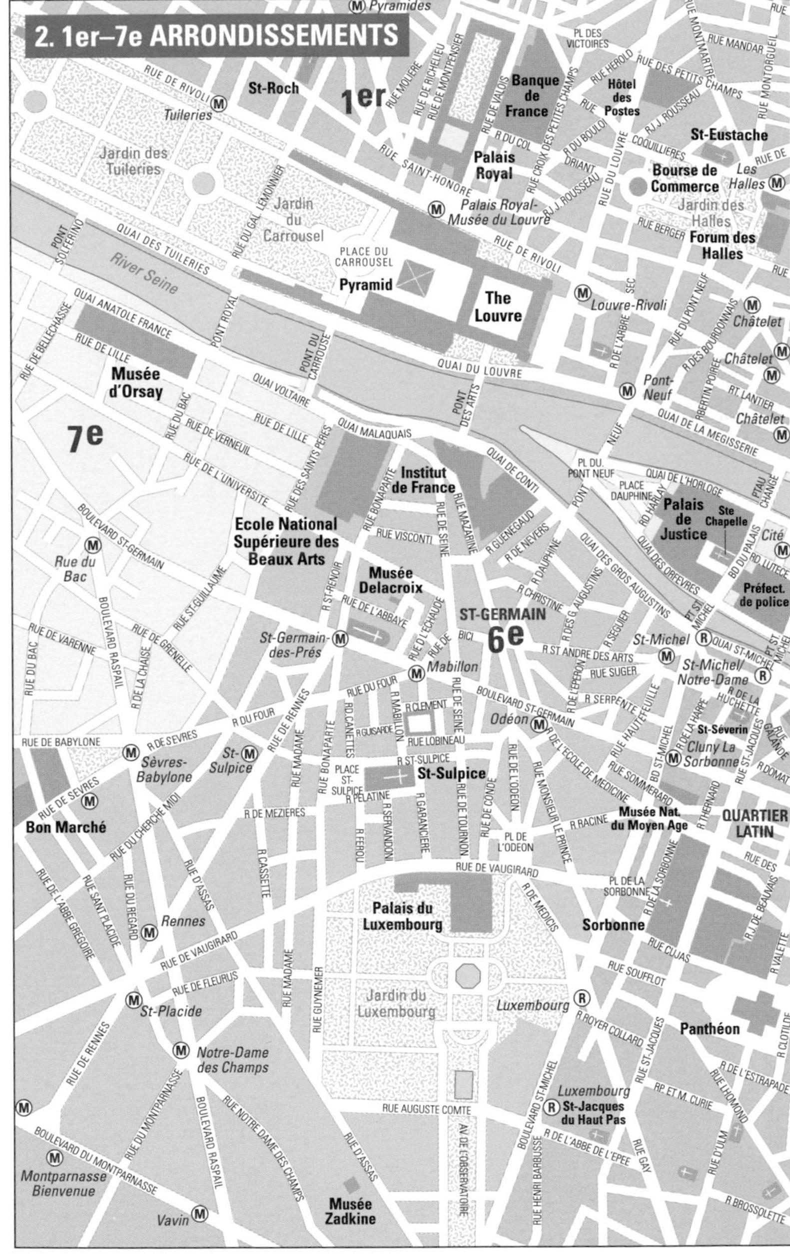
2. 1er–7e ARRONDISSEMENTS
1er
6e
7e
ST-GERMAIN
QUARTIER LATIN
Pyramides
Tuileries
St-Roch
Jardin des Tuileries
Jardin du Carrousel
PLACE DU CARROUSEL
Pyramid
The Louvre
Palais Royal
Palais Royal-Musée du Louvre
Banque de France
PL DES VICTOIRES
Hôtel des Postes
St-Eustache
Bourse de Commerce
Les Halles
Jardin des Halles
Forum des Halles
Louvre-Rivoli
Châtelet
Pont-Neuf
River Seine
Musée d'Orsay
Institut de France
Ecole National Supérieure des Beaux Arts
Musée Delacroix
PL DU. PONT NEUF
PLACE DAUPHINE
Palais de Justice
Ste Chapelle
Cité
Préfect. de police
Rue du Bac
St-Germain-des-Prés
Mabillon
St-Michel
St-Michel/Notre-Dame
St-Séverin
Cluny La Sorbonne
Odéon
Sèvres-Babylone
St-Sulpice
PLACE ST-SULPICE
Bon Marché
Musée Nat. du Moyen Age
PL DE L'ODEON
PL DE LA SORBONNE
Palais du Luxembourg
Sorbonne
Rennes
St-Placide
Jardin du Luxembourg
Luxembourg
Panthéon
Notre-Dame des Champs
St-Jacques du Haut Pas
Montparnasse Bienvenue
Vavin
Musée Zadkine
RUE DE RIVOLI
RUE SAINT-HONORE
QUAI DES TUILERIES
QUAI ANATOLE FRANCE
QUAI VOLTAIRE
QUAI MALAQUAIS
QUAI DE CONTI
QUAI DU LOUVRE
QUAI DE LA MEGISSERIE
QUAI DES GRDS AUGUSTINS
QUAI DES ORFEVRES
QUAI DE L'HORLOGE
QUAI ST-MICHEL
PONT SOLFERINO
PONT ROYAL
PONT DU CARROUSEL
PONT DES ARTS
PONT NEUF
RUE DE LILLE
RUE DE VERNEUIL
RUE DE L'UNIVERSITE
BOULEVARD ST-GERMAIN
RUE DE VARENNE
RUE DE GRENELLE
RUE DE BABYLONE
RUE DE SEVRES
BOULEVARD RASPAIL
RUE DES SAINTS PERES
RUE BONAPARTE
RUE DE SEINE
RUE MAZARINE
RUE DU FOUR
RUE DE RENNES
RUE DE VAUGIRARD
RUE D'ASSAS
RUE MADAME
RUE GUYNEMER
RUE DE FLEURUS
RUE AUGUSTE COMTE
AV DE L'OBSERVATOIRE
BOULEVARD ST-MICHEL
BOULEVARD DU MONTPARNASSE
RUE NOTRE DAME DES CHAMPS
RUE DE TOURNON
RUE DE L'ODEON
RUE MONSIEUR LE PRINCE
RUE DE L'ECOLE DE MEDICINE
RUE SOUFFLOT
RUE ST-JACQUES
RUE CUJAS
RUE D'ULM
RUE GAY LUSSAC
RUE HENRI BARBUSSE
RUE DU LOUVRE
RUE DU PONT NEUF
RUE MONTMARTRE
RUE MONTORGUEIL

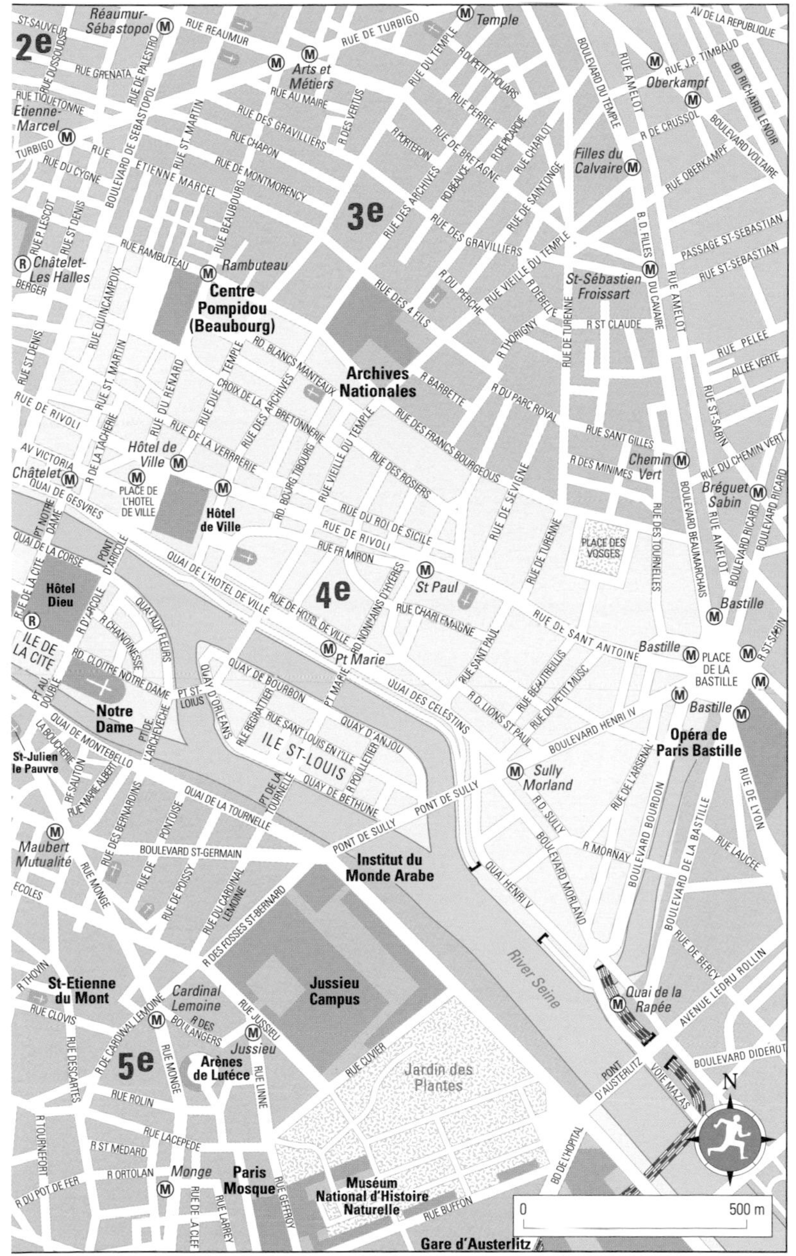
2e
3e
4e
5e
Réaumur-Sébastopol
Temple
Arts et Métiers
Oberkampf
Etienne-Marcel
Filles du Calvaire
Châtelet-Les Halles
Rambuteau
Centre Pompidou (Beaubourg)
St-Sébastien Froissart
Archives Nationales
Hôtel de Ville
Châtelet
Chemin Vert
Bréguet Sabin
Place des Vosges
St Paul
Hôtel Dieu
Bastille
Place de la Bastille
Ile de la Cité
Pt Marie
Notre Dame
Ile St-Louis
Opéra de Paris Bastille
St-Julien le Pauvre
Sully Morland
Maubert Mutualité
Institut du Monde Arabe
River Seine
St-Etienne du Mont
Cardinal Lemoine
Jussieu Campus
Quai de la Rapée
Jussieu
Arènes de Lutéce
Jardin des Plantes
Monge
Paris Mosque
Muséum National d'Histoire Naturelle
Gare d'Austerlitz
0
500 m
N

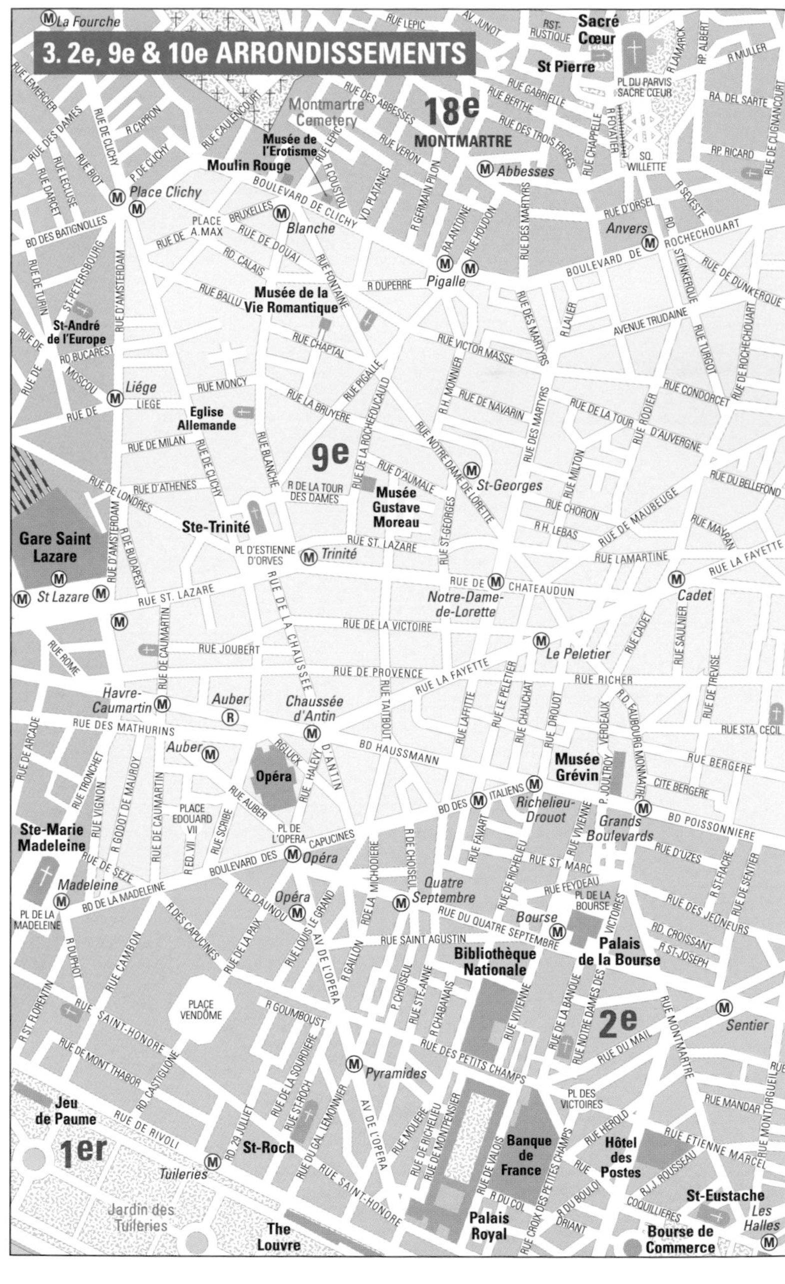

3. 2e, 9e & 10e ARRONDISSEMENTS
La Fourche
Sacré Cœur
St Pierre
18e
MONTMARTRE
Montmartre Cemetery
Musée de l'Erotisme
Moulin Rouge
Abbesses
Place Clichy
Blanche
Anvers
Pigalle
Musée de la Vie Romantique
St-André de l'Europe
Liège
Eglise Allemande
9e
St-Georges
Musée Gustave Moreau
Ste-Trinité
Gare Saint Lazare
St Lazare
Trinité
Notre-Dame-de-Lorette
Cadet
Le Peletier
Havre-Caumartin
Auber
Chaussée d'Antin
Opéra
Musée Grévin
Richelieu-Drouot
Grands Boulevards
Ste-Marie Madeleine
Madeleine
Quatre Septembre
Bourse
Bibliothèque Nationale
Palais de la Bourse
2e
Sentier
Place Vendôme
Pyramides
Jeu de Paume
1er
Tuileries
Jardin des Tuileries
St-Roch
The Louvre
Banque de France
Palais Royal
Hôtel des Postes
St-Eustache
Les Halles
Bourse de Commerce
BOULEVARD DE CLICHY
BOULEVARD DE ROCHECHOUART
RUE DE DUNKERQUE
AVENUE TRUDAINE
RUE DES MARTYRS
RUE VICTOR MASSE
RUE DE LA TOUR D'AUVERGNE
RUE NOTRE DAME DE LORETTE
RUE DE MAUBEUGE
RUE LAMARTINE
RUE LA FAYETTE
RUE DE CHATEAUDUN
RUE ST. LAZARE
RUE DE LA VICTOIRE
RUE DE PROVENCE
RUE DE LA CHAUSSEE D'ANTIN
RUE DES MATHURINS
BD HAUSSMANN
BD DES ITALIENS
BD POISSONNIERE
BOULEVARD DES CAPUCINES
BD DE LA MADELEINE
RUE DU QUATRE SEPTEMBRE
RUE SAINT AUGUSTIN
AV DE L'OPERA
RUE DE LA PAIX
RUE SAINT-HONORE
RUE DE RIVOLI
RUE DES PETITS CHAMPS
RUE MONTMARTRE
RUE ETIENNE MARCEL
RUE RICHER
RUE BERGERE
RUE DE CLICHY
RUE D'AMSTERDAM
RUE DE CAUMARTIN
RUE DE RICHELIEU
RUE VIVIENNE
RUE DU MAIL

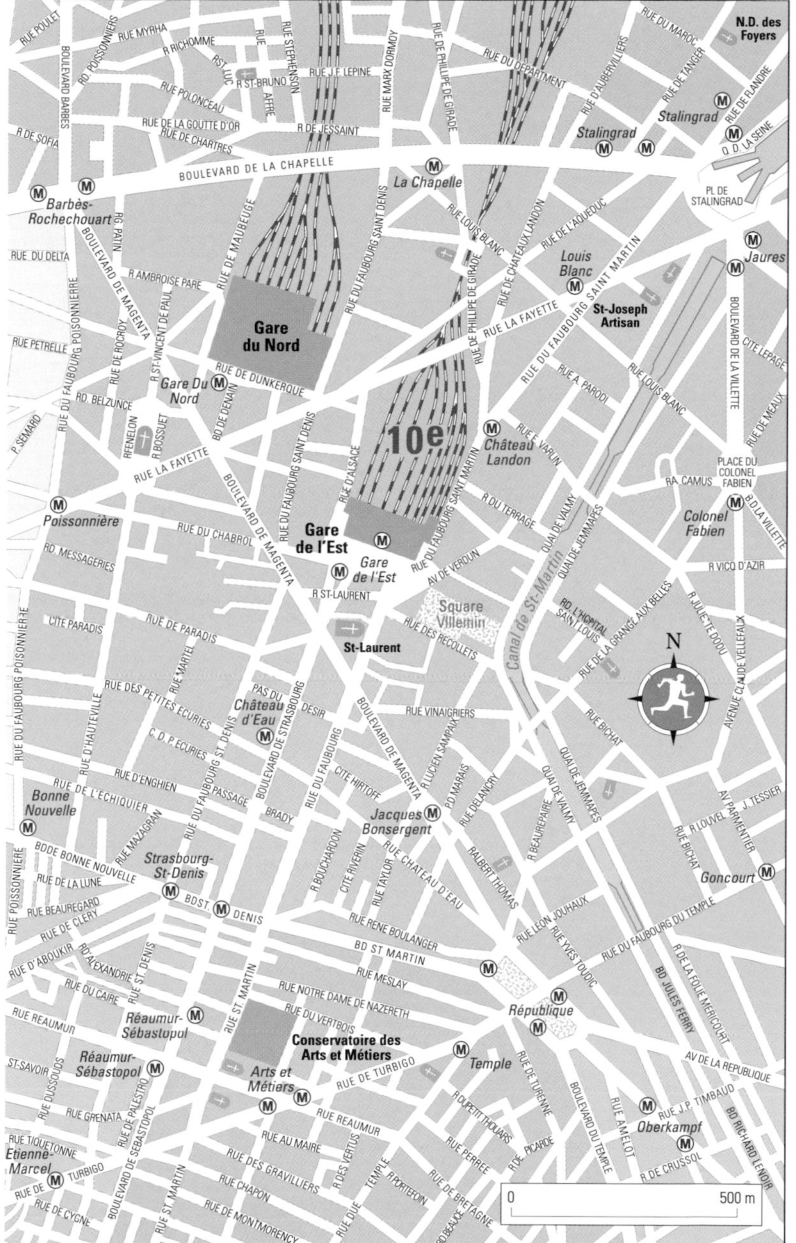
N.D. des Foyers
Stalingrad
Stalingrad
La Chapelle
Barbès-Rochechouart
Louis Blanc
Jaures
St-Joseph Artisan
Gare du Nord
Gare Du Nord
10e
Château Landon
Poissonnière
Gare de l'Est
Gare de l'Est
Square Villemin
St-Laurent
Canal de St-Martin
PL DE STALINGRAD
PLACE DU COLONEL FABIEN
Colonel Fabien
Château d'Eau
Bonne Nouvelle
Jacques Bonsergent
Strasbourg-St-Denis
Goncourt
République
Réaumur-Sébastopol
Réaumur-Sébastopol
Conservatoire des Arts et Métiers
Arts et Métiers
Temple
Oberkampf
Etienne-Marcel
BOULEVARD DE LA CHAPELLE
BOULEVARD DE MAGENTA
BOULEVARD DE STRASBOURG
RUE LA FAYETTE
RUE DU FAUBOURG SAINT DENIS
RUE DU FAUBOURG SAINT MARTIN
QUAI DE VALMY
QUAI DE JEMMAPES
BOULEVARD DE LA VILLETTE
RUE DU FAUBOURG DU TEMPLE
BD ST MARTIN
BOULEVARD DE SEBASTOPOL
RUE DE TURBIGO
RUE REAUMUR
AV DE LA REPUBLIQUE
BOULEVARD DU TEMPLE
BD RICHARD LENOIR
BD JULES FERRY
AVENUE CLAUDE VELLEFAUX
RUE DU FAUBOURG POISSONNIERE
RUE DE PARADIS
RUE DU CHABROL
0
500 m

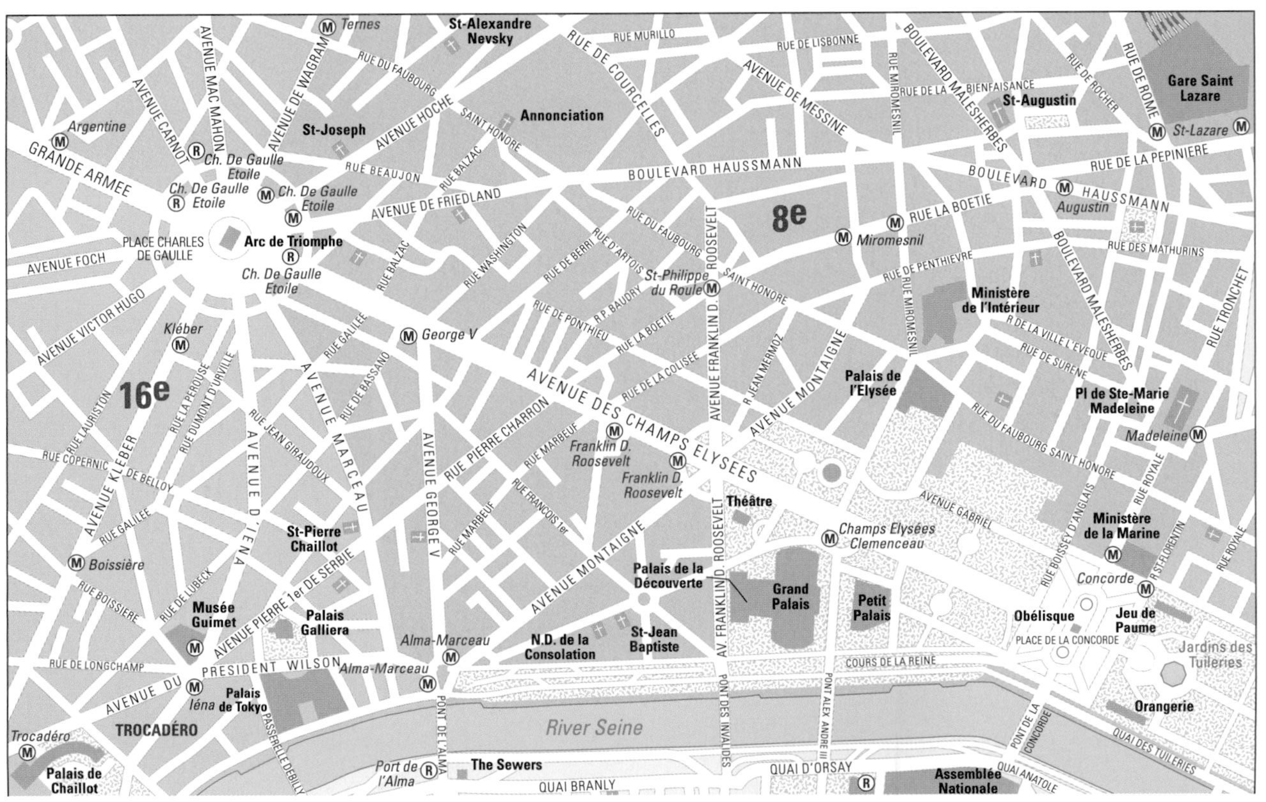

Ternes
St-Alexandre Nevsky
Rue Murillo
Rue de Lisbonne
Boulevard Malesherbes
Rue de la Bienfaisance
St-Augustin
Rue de Rocher
Rue de Rome
Gare Saint Lazare
St-Lazare
Avenue Mac Mahon
Avenue de Wagram
Rue du Faubourg Saint Honoré
Rue de Courcelles
Avenue de Messine
Rue Miromesnil
Avenue Carnot
Argentine
St-Joseph
Avenue Hoche
Annonciation
Grande Armee
Ch. De Gaulle Etoile
Rue Beaujon
Rue Balzac
Boulevard Haussmann
Rue de la Pepiniere
Augustin
Avenue de Friedland
8e
Rue La Boetie
Miromesnil
Rue des Mathurins
Place Charles de Gaulle
Arc de Triomphe
Avenue Foch
Rue Washington
Rue de Berri
Rue d'Artois
St-Philippe du Roule
Avenue Franklin D. Roosevelt
Rue de Penthievre
Ministère de l'Intérieur
Rue Tronchet
Avenue Victor Hugo
Kléber
George V
Rue Galilee
Rue de Ponthieu
R.P. Baudry
R. de la Ville l'Eveque
Rue de Surene
16e
Rue Lauriston
Rue la Perouse
Rue Dumont d'Urville
Avenue d'Iena
Rue Jean Giraudoux
Avenue Marceau
Rue de Bassano
Avenue George V
Avenue des Champs Elysees
Rue Pierre Charron
Rue de la Colisee
R. Jean Mermoz
Avenue Montaigne
Palais de l'Elysée
Pl de Ste-Marie Madeleine
Madeleine
Rue Copernic
De Belloy
Avenue Kleber
Rue Marbeuf
Franklin D. Roosevelt
Théâtre
Avenue Gabriel
Rue du Faubourg Saint Honoré
Rue Royale
Rue Galilee
St-Pierre Chaillot
Rue François 1er
Champs Elysées Clemenceau
Ministère de la Marine
Boissière
Rue Boissiere
Rue de Lubeck
Musée Guimet
Avenue Pierre 1er de Serbie
Palais Galliera
Palais de la Découverte
Grand Palais
Petit Palais
Rue Boissy d'Anglais
Concorde
R. St Florentin
Obélisque
Jeu de Paume
Place de la Concorde
Jardins des Tuileries
Rue de Longchamp
Avenue du President Wilson
Alma-Marceau
N.D. de la Consolation
St-Jean Baptiste
Av. Franklin D. Roosevelt
Cours de la Reine
Iéna
Palais de Tokyo
Trocadéro
TROCADÉRO
River Seine
Pont des Invalides
Pont Alex Andre III
Pont de la Concorde
Orangerie
Quai des Tuileries
Palais de Chaillot
Passerelle Debilly
Pont de l'Alma
Port de l'Alma
The Sewers
Quai Branly
Quai d'Orsay
Assemblée Nationale
Quai Anatole

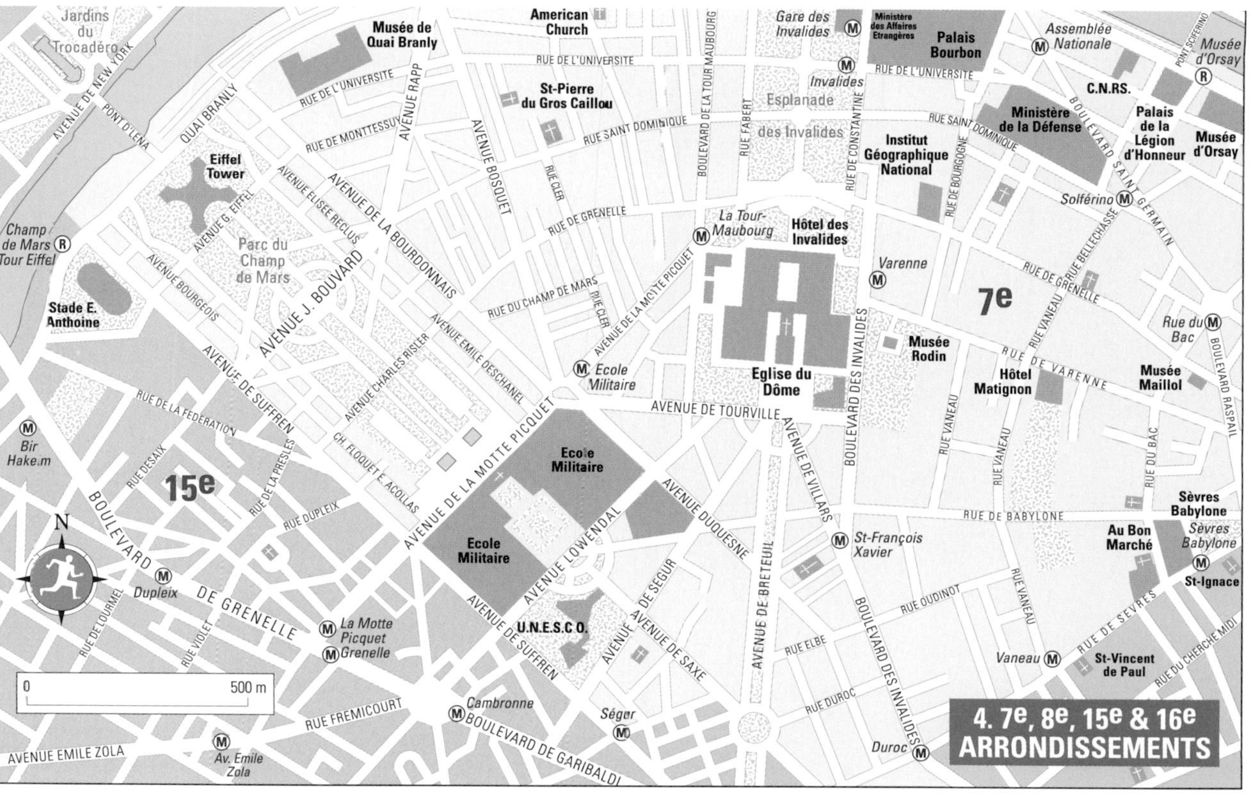
4. 7e, 8e, 15e & 16e ARRONDISSEMENTS
7e
15e
Jardins du Trocadéro
Musée de Quai Branly
American Church
Gare des Invalides
Ministère des Affaires Etrangères
Palais Bourbon
Assemblée Nationale
Musée d'Orsay
Pont Solférino
C.N.RS.
Ministère de la Défense
Palais de la Légion d'Honneur
Musée d'Orsay
St-Pierre du Gros Caillou
Invalides
Esplanade des Invalides
Institut Géographique National
Solférino
Eiffel Tower
Parc du Champ de Mars
Champ de Mars Tour Eiffel
Stade E. Anthoine
La Tour-Maubourg
Hôtel des Invalides
Varenne
Eglise du Dôme
Musée Rodin
Hôtel Matignon
Musée Maillol
Rue du Bac
Ecole Militaire
Bir Hakeim
Dupleix
La Motte Picquet Grenelle
U.N.E.S.C.O.
Cambronne
Ségur
Av. Emile Zola
St-François Xavier
Sèvres Babylone
Au Bon Marché
St-Ignace
Vaneau
St-Vincent de Paul
Duroc
N
0
500 m
Avenue de New York
Pont d'Iena
Quai Branly
Rue de l'Université
Rue de Monttessuy
Avenue Rapp
Avenue Bosquet
Rue Cler
Rue Saint Dominique
Rue de Grenelle
Boulevard de la Tour Maubourg
Rue Fabert
Rue de Constantine
Rue de Bourgogne
Boulevard Saint Germain
Rue Bellechasse
Avenue G. Eiffel
Avenue Elisée Reclus
Avenue de la Bourdonnais
Avenue J. Bouvard
Avenue Bourgeois
Rue du Champ de Mars
Avenue de la Motte Picquet
Avenue Emile Deschanel
Avenue Charles Risler
Avenue de Suffren
Rue de la Fédération
Ch. Floquet E. Acollas
Rue Desaix
Rue de la Presles
Rue Dupleix
Boulevard de Grenelle
Rue de Lourmel
Rue Violet
Avenue de Tourville
Boulevard des Invalides
Avenue de Villars
Avenue Duquesne
Avenue Lowendal
Avenue de Segur
Avenue de Saxe
Avenue de Breteuil
Rue Vaneau
Rue de Varenne
Rue du Bac
Boulevard Raspail
Rue de Babylone
Rue Oudinot
Rue de Sèvres
Rue du Cherche Midi
Rue Elbe
Rue Duroc
Rue Fremicourt
Boulevard de Garibaldi
Avenue Emile Zola

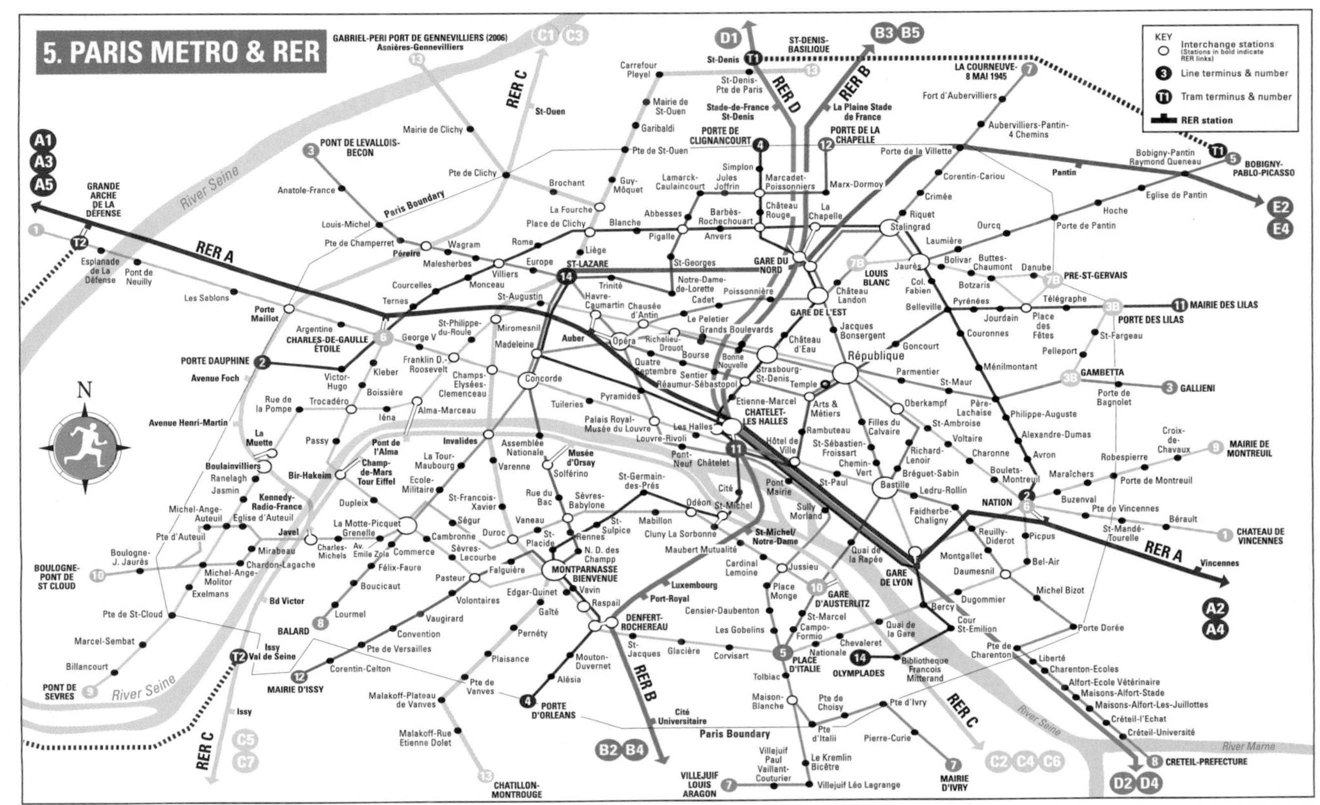

5. PARIS METRO & RER
KEY
Interchange stations (Stations in bold indicate RER links)
Line terminus & number
Tram terminus & number
RER station
GABRIEL-PERI PORT DE GENNEVILLIERS (2006)
Asnières-Gennevilliers
RER A
RER B
RER C
RER D
River Seine
River Marne
Paris Boundary
N
GRANDE ARCHE DE LA DÉFENSE
Esplanade de La Défense
Pont de Neuilly
Les Sablons
Porte Maillot
Argentine
CHARLES-DE-GAULLE ÉTOILE
PORTE DAUPHINE
Avenue Foch
Avenue Henri-Martin
PONT DE LEVALLOIS-BECON
Anatole-France
Louis-Michel
Pte de Champerret
Péreire
Wagram
Malesherbes
Villiers
Monceau
Courcelles
Ternes
Pte de Clichy
Mairie de Clichy
St-Ouen
Brochant
La Fourche
Place de Clichy
Guy-Môquet
Pte de St-Ouen
Garibaldi
Mairie de St-Ouen
Carrefour Pleyel
St-Denis
St-Denis-Pte de Paris
Stade-de-France St-Denis
ST-DENIS-BASILIQUE
La Plaine Stade de France
PORTE DE CLIGNANCOURT
PORTE DE LA CHAPELLE
Simplon
Marcadet-Poissonniers
Marx-Dormoy
Lamarck-Caulaincourt
Jules Joffrin
Château Rouge
La Chapelle
Abbesses
Barbès-Rochechouart
Blanche
Pigalle
Anvers
Rome
Liège
Europe
ST-LAZARE
Trinité
St-Georges
Notre-Dame-de-Lorette
GARE DU NORD
Poissonnière
Cadet
Havre-Caumartin
Chaussée d'Antin
Le Peletier
St-Augustin
Miromesnil
St-Philippe-du-Roule
George V
Kleber
Victor-Hugo
Franklin D. Roosevelt
Champs-Elysées-Clemenceau
Madeleine
Auber
Opéra
Richelieu-Drouot
Grands Boulevards
Bonne Nouvelle
Quatre Septembre
Bourse
Sentier
Réaumur-Sébastopol
Strasbourg-St-Denis
Château d'Eau
GARE DE L'EST
Château Landon
LOUIS BLANC
Stalingrad
Jaurès
Riquet
Crimée
Corentin-Cariou
Porte de la Villette
Fort d'Aubervilliers
LA COURNEUVE-8 MAI 1945
Aubervilliers-Pantin-4 Chemins
Pantin
Bobigny-Pantin Raymond Queneau
BOBIGNY-PABLO-PICASSO
Eglise de Pantin
Hoche
Porte de Pantin
Ourcq
Laumière
Bolivar
Buttes-Chaumont
Danube
PRE-ST-GERVAIS
Botzaris
Col. Fabien
Belleville
Pyrénées
Jourdain
Place des Fêtes
Télégraphe
MAIRIE DES LILAS
PORTE DES LILAS
St-Fargeau
Pelleport
GAMBETTA
GALLIENI
Porte de Bagnolet
Couronnes
Ménilmontant
Goncourt
Jacques Bonsergent
République
Parmentier
St-Maur
Temple
Arts & Métiers
Oberkampf
Père-Lachaise
Philippe-Auguste
Alexandre-Dumas
St-Ambroise
Voltaire
Charonne
Avron
Filles du Calvaire
Richard-Lenoir
Bréguet-Sabin
Boulets-Montreuil
Maraîchers
Robespierre
Croix-de-Chavaux
MAIRIE DE MONTREUIL
Porte de Montreuil
Buzenval
NATION
Pte de Vincennes
Bérault
St-Mandé-Tourelle
CHATEAU DE VINCENNES
Vincennes
Concorde
Tuileries
Pyramides
Palais Royal-Musée du Louvre
Louvre-Rivoli
Les Halles
Etienne-Marcel
CHATELET-LES HALLES
Rambuteau
Hôtel de Ville
St-Sébastien-Froissart
Chemin-Vert
St-Paul
Bastille
Ledru-Rollin
Faidherbe-Chaligny
Reuilly-Diderot
Picpus
Montgallet
Bel-Air
Daumesnil
Michel Bizot
Porte Dorée
Dugommier
Bercy
Cour St-Emilion
Pte de Charenton
Liberté
Charenton-Ecoles
Alfort-Ecole Vétérinaire
Maisons-Alfort-Stade
Maisons-Alfort-Les-Juillottes
Créteil-l'Echat
Créteil-Université
CRETEIL-PREFECTURE
GARE DE LYON
Quai de la Rapée
Pont Marie
Sully Morland
Pont-Neuf
Châtelet
Cité
St-Michel
Odéon
St-Germain-des-Prés
Mabillon
Cluny La Sorbonne
St-Michel/Notre-Dame
Maubert Mutualité
Cardinal Lemoine
Jussieu
Place Monge
GARE D'AUSTERLITZ
St-Marcel
Campo-Formio
Quai de la Gare
Chevaleret
Nationale
Bibliotheque Francois Mitterand
OLYMPLADES
PLACE D'ITALIE
Tolbiac
Maison-Blanche
Pte de Choisy
Pte d'Ivry
Pte d'Italii
Pierre-Curie
Le Kremlin Bicêtre
Villejuif Léo Lagrange
Villejuif Paul Vaillant-Couturier
VILLEJUIF LOUIS ARAGON
MAIRIE D'IVRY
Les Gobelins
Censier-Daubenton
Corvisart
Glacière
St-Jacques
Luxembourg
Port-Royal
DENFERT-ROCHEREAU
Cité Universitaire
Mouton-Duvernet
Alésia
PORTE D'ORLEANS
Raspail
Vavin
Edgar-Quinet
Gaîté
Pernéty
Plaisance
Pte de Vanves
Malakoff-Plateau de Vanves
Malakoff-Rue Etienne Dolet
CHATILLON-MONTROUGE
MONTPARNASSE BIENVENUE
N. D. des Champp
Rennes
St-Sulpice
Sèvres-Babylone
Rue du Bac
St-Placide
Vaneau
Duroc
Falguière
Pasteur
Volontaires
Vaugirard
Convention
Pte de Versailles
Corentin-Celton
MAIRIE D'ISSY
Musée d'Orsay
Solférino
Assemblée Nationale
Varenne
Invalides
St-Francois-Xavier
Ségur
Cambronne
Sèvres-Lecourbe
La Tour-Maubourg
Ecole-Militaire
La Motte-Picquet Grenelle
Commerce
Av. Emile Zola
Charles-Michels
Félix-Faure
Boucicaut
Lourmel
BALARD
Dupleix
Bir-Hakeim
Champ-de-Mars Tour Eiffel
Pont de l'Alma
Alma-Marceau
Iéna
Boissière
Trocadéro
Rue de la Pompe
Passy
La Muette
Boulainvilliers
Ranelagh
Jasmin
Kennedy-Radio-France
Javel
Eglise d'Auteuil
Michel-Ange-Auteuil
Mirabeau
Chardon-Lagache
Michel-Ange-Molitor
Exelmans
Pte d'Auteuil
Boulogne-J. Jaurès
BOULOGNE-PONT DE ST CLOUD
Pte de St-Cloud
Marcel-Sembat
Billancourt
PONT DE SEVRES
Bd Victor
Issy Val de Seine
Issy